$47.05

MW00986707

Governments and Politics in Russia and the Post-Soviet Region

Vicki L. Hesli

University of Iowa

Houghton Mifflin Company   *Boston   New York*

This book is dedicated to my sons.

Publisher: Charles Hartford
Senior Sponsoring Editor: Traci Mueller
Senior Development Editor: Jeff Greene
Editorial Assistant: Kristen Craib
Senior Project Editor: Kathryn Dinovo
Senior Manufacturing Buyer: Renee Ostrowski
Executive Marketing Manager: Nicola Poser
Marketing Associate: Kathleen Mellon

Cover image: Peter Christopher/Masterfile

Printed in the U.S.A.

Library of Congress Control Number: 2003109902

ISBN 13: 978-0-618-34736-0
ISBN 10: 0-618-34736-4

123456789-MP-10 09 08 07 06

CONTENTS

Preface xi

PART I Introduction

CHAPTER 1
Post-Soviet States in Comparative Perspective 1

The Comparative Method 4
Theories of Democratization 7
The Historical–Cultural Approach 9
Organization of the Book 10

Key Terms 11
Critical Thinking Questions 11
Suggested Reading 12
Websites of Interest 12

PART II The Soviet System

CHAPTER 2
The Ideological Foundations of Russian Socialism 13

Marxism 14
   The Revolutionary Careers of Marx and Engels 15
   Basic Principles of Marxism 15
Origins of the Russian Socialist Movement 19
Leninism 20
Stalinism 26
The Relationship Between Leninism and Stalinism 28
The Philosophical Leanings of Khrushchev and Brezhnev 31
Communism in the World System 34
The Ideological Functions of Communism 36

Key Terms 37
Critical Thinking Questions 37
Suggested Reading 38
Websites of Interest 38

CHAPTER 3

The Legacy of the Past 39

Inheritances from Tsarism 44
The 1905 Russian Revolution and Beyond 46
The 1917 Revolutions 48
The Establishment of the Soviet Government 50
Democratic Failures 51
The Stalin Era 54
   The Great Patriotic War 58
The Khrushchev Era 60
The Brezhnev Era 61
Gorbachev, Glasnost, and Perestroika 63
Boris Yeltsin and the Fall of the USSR 66
Post-Soviet Russia 69

Key Terms 72
Critical Thinking Questions 73
Suggested Reading 73
Websites of Interest 73

PART III   Politics and Government in the Russian Federation

CHAPTER 4

Russia as a Multinational State: Federal Structures and Ethnic Cleavages 74

Ethnic Heterogeneity in Russia 74
The History of Russia's National and Ethnic Cleavages 75
Using Theories of Nationalism to Explain the Breakup of the
   Soviet Union 81
A Comparative Perspective of the Basic Territorial Administration
   Systems 87
Russian Federalism 88
Case Studies About Major Non-Russian Nationality Groups 92
   Yakuts 93
   Tatars 95

Chechens 97
Conclusion 105

Key Terms 106
Critical Thinking Questions 106
Suggested Reading 106
Websites of Interest 107

CHAPTER 5

Russian Political Culture   108

Russian Nationalism 108
A History of Russian and Soviet Political Culture 112
Political Culture and Democratic Ideas 115
Political Culture Themes in Russia 117
   Anti-Semitism—A Controversial Theme in Russian Political Culture 119

Key Terms 122
Critical Thinking Questions 122
Suggested Reading 122
Website of Interest 122

CHAPTER 6

Russia's Governing Institutions in Comparative Context   123

Government Structures and Institutions in the Soviet Era 123
The Structure of Legislative Institutions in the Russian Federation 127
The Role and Function of Russia's Legislature 129
Members of Parliament in Comparative Perspective 131
The Emergence of Russia's Presidential System 137
**Parliamentary and Presidential Systems in Comparative
    Perspective 140**
The Authority of Russia's Presidency 140
Russia's Two Presidents: Yeltsin and Putin 142
   Boris Yeltsin 142
   Vladimir Putin 144
The Dual Executive: Russia's Prime Minister 146
The Judicial Branch 148
   The Court System in the Russian Federation 150
   The Constitutional Court 150
   The Supreme Court 151
   The Superior Court of Arbitration 151

Key Terms 152
Critical Thinking Questions 152
Suggested Reading 152
Websites of Interest 153

CHAPTER 7

Political Participation and Public Opinion in Russia   154

Different Forms of Political Participation 154
   Voting 154
   Conventional–Legal Participation 160
Political Opposition in Russia 163
Electoral Systems in Comparative Perspective 171
Elections to Russia's National Parliament 172
Elections to Russia's National Presidency 178
Regional Elections 180
Conclusion 181

Key Terms 182
Critical Thinking Questions 182
Suggested Reading 183
Websites of Interest 183

CHAPTER 8

Political Parties in Russia from a Comparative Perspective   184

The Soviet Union as a One-Party System 184
A Comparative Perspective of Party Systems 188
   Major Goals of Political Parties 189
   Party Ideologies in Europe 191
The Emergence of Political Parties in Russia 191
Russia's Major Parties 192
   Communist Party 195
   Yabloko 195
   Liberal Democratic Party of Russia 196
   Fatherland–All Russia Coalition 197
   Union of Right Forces 197
   Unity 198
   United Russia 198
   Motherland 199
The Electoral Performance of Russia's Political Parties 199

Political Parties and Russia's Transition to Democracy 202
Key Terms 206
Critical Thinking Questions 206
Suggested Reading 206
Websites of Interest 207

CHAPTER 9

Russia's Associational Groups in Comparative Perspective 208

Insights from the Literature on Established Democracies 208
Organized Interests in the Soviet Era 210
The Emergence of Public Associations in the Gorbachev Era 211
Labor Organizations 212
The Oligarchs 213
    The Role of the Media 218
Security and Military Services 219
    Corruption and the Armed Forces 222
Women's Groups 223
Conclusion 227
Key Terms 230
Critical Thinking Questions 230
Suggested Reading 230
Websites of Interest 231

CHAPTER 10

Public Policy Issues in Russia and the Former USSR 232

Economic Planning in the Soviet Union 233
Economic Policy in the Gorbachev, Yeltsin, and Putin Eras 236
    The Outcomes of Market Reform 239
    The Agricultural Economy 242
The Model: Presidential Policymaking 243
Foreign Policy 244
    Soviet Foreign Policy (1918–1990) 244
    Russia's Foreign Policy Since 1991 248
    The Russian–CIS Relationship 249
    Russia's Relationship with the United States 251
    Russia–NATO Relations 252
Military Reform 254
    Arms Exports 255

Russia's Health Issues 256
Crime and Corruption 260
Conclusion 263

Key Terms 263
Critical Thinking Questions 263
Suggested Reading 264
Websites of Interest 264

PART IV Country Studies

CHAPTER 11

Lithuania 265

History of Incorporation into and Independence from the
    USSR 265
The Dynamics of a Successful Independence Movement 270
The Nature of Society and Political Culture 272
Political Parties and Political Participation 273
The Main Constitutional Structures and Government Processes 275
    Lithuania's Presidency 275
    Legislative Institutions 280
    Legislative Elections 282
    The Prime Minister 291
    Local Government 291
    The Judicial Branch 292
Political Participation 293
The Main Public Policy Questions 294
    Economic Development 294
    European Union Participation 299
    Foreign Affairs and the Military 300
    Demographic Issues 301
    Health-Care Access 302
    Violence 302
Conclusion and Overview 303

Key Terms 305
Critical Thinking Questions 306
Suggested Reading 306
Websites of Interest 307

CHAPTER 12

Ukraine 308

The Political History of Ukraine 309
Political Culture and Regional Differences 312
Government Institutions and Structures 313
    The President 314
    Mass Media 322
    The Legislative Branch 323
    Results of the 1994 Parliamentary Elections 323
    Results of the 1998 Parliamentary Elections 325
    Results of the 2002 Parliamentary Elections 326
Voting Behavior in Ukraine 329
The Political Economy of Democratic Transition 332
Foreign Policy and National Security 335
    Ukraine and Russia 335
    Ukraine and Europe 336
    Ukraine and the United States 338
    Ukraine's Military 341
Prospects for the Future 341

Key Terms 342
Critical Thinking Questions 342
Suggested Reading 343
Websites of Interest 343

CHAPTER 13

The Republic of Georgia 344

Historical Overview 344
Political Institutions and Processes 351
    The Presidency and Presidential Elections 351
    The Parliament, Parliamentary Elections, and Political Parties 354
    The Judicial System 363
The Nature of Society and Political Culture 364
    Separatism Within South Ossetia 366
    Abkhazia as a Sovereign Region 367
    The Challenge from Adjara 370
Economic Policy 371

Foreign Policy and International Relations 374
    Relations with Russia 374
    Relations with the United States 375
    Relations with Europe 376
Conclusion 376

Key Terms 378
Critical Thinking Questions 378
Suggested Reading 378
Websites of Interest 378

CHAPTER 14

Uzbekistan 379

Historical Overview 379
Political Institutions and Processes 385
    Uzbekistan's National Parliament—The Oliy Majlis (the Supreme Assembly) 386
    Presidential Rule and Executive Authority 388
    Cabinet of Ministers 389
    Local (Regional) Government 389
    Judicial Authority 390
The Nature of Society, Political Culture, and Political Opposition 391
Political Parties and Parliamentary Elections 395
The Main Public Policy Issues 401
    The Economy 401
    Foreign Policy 404
Conclusion 409

Key Terms 411
Critical Thinking Questions 411
Suggested Reading 411
Websites of Interest 411

Epilogue: Making Sense of Political Change 413

Glossary 417

Endnotes 428

References 439

Index 447

PREFACE

THIS TEXTBOOK IS WRITTEN for students who are interested in learning about the politics of Russia and the former Soviet Union within a broad, comparative context. The book is different from other texts on the market in that most post-Soviet political science texts focus only on Russia. In addition to several detailed chapters about political institutions and processes in Russia, this book includes country studies of Ukraine, Georgia, Lithuania, and Uzbekistan, which allows for representation and discussion of each of the major geographical and cultural regions of the former USSR. The goal of this text is to provide factual material and scholarly analysis of the governments and politics in these states through comparison with the governments and politics found in other countries. These five post-Soviet countries have established new political institutions, and the functioning of these institutions can be best understood by comparing them to similar institutions and structures found in other transitioning countries and in the established democracies of Europe and North America. The range and diversity of political forms found throughout the region, however, defies description and full understanding within a single book. Thus, the focus is primarily on Russian politics, with brief coverage of the other four selected countries as part of the investigation and evaluation of the political processes that are developing throughout the region.

ORGANIZATION

The introductory chapter briefly reviews the frameworks for analyses that are used in the rest of the text. These include the comparative method, theories of democratization, and the historical-cultural approach. Because all of these countries have proclaimed the goal of establishing consolidated democracies, an analytical framework based on the study of democratic transitions supplements the historical-cultural approach. Some examples of questions posed within an historical-cultural framework are: How have Russia's heterogeneous population and the conflicts that have existed for centuries among the various ethnic groups in the region affected the ability of the Yeltsin and Putin regimes to establish a new basis for political stability? In what ways have the historical patterns of political autocracy and administrative centralization in Tsarist Russia and the Soviet Union provided a congenial climate for the emergence and maintenance of continued hierarchical rule in post-Soviet society? The advantage of the historical-cultural approach is that it recognizes the important mixture of traditional and modern factors in every institution, procedure, and behavior.

To provide the necessary historical background for the subsequent chapters, Part II of the book focuses on the Soviet era. Chapter 2 provides a synopsis of the basic notions of Marxist philosophy upon which the Soviet state was built. Included are a review of the origins of the Russian socialist movement and outlines of the basic principles of ideology found in Leninism and Stalinism. Chapter 3 is an historical overview of the establishment of the Russian Empire, the Soviet era, the transformations of the system under Mikhail Gorbachev, and the fall of the USSR.

Chapters 4 through 10, which comprise Part III of the book, cover the basic topics found in standard comparative politics courses and textbooks. Chapter 4 evaluates the federal structures and the ethnic cleavages within the Russian multinational state, while Chapter 5 outlines the main features of Russian political culture. This chapter introduces the notion that the successful operation of democracy depends on the existence of supportive preferences among the people about government behavior.

Chapter 6 turns to the main structures of government in Russia, most notably the presidency and the parliament. The different forms that each of these structures may take are discussed, along with the advantages and disadvantages of these forms. The chapter acknowledges the extraordinary powers in the Russian presidency and looks at the two men who have held the position: Boris Yeltsin and Vladimir Putin.

Chapter 7 moves from a look at leaders to a look at citizens and discusses different forms of political participation with particular emphasis on elections and how these work in Russia. The hallmark of any democracy is a competitive political system in which every citizen can take part in regular free and fair elections. Ideally, elections should also produce stable governments, where a single party is in charge or where a workable coalition of two or more parties directs decision making. As we will see, elections often fall short of these ideals.

Chapter 8, on political parties, begins with a review of the dominant role of the Communist Party in the Soviet Union and concludes with a critique of Russia's multiparty system today. This chapter also discusses what functions political parties are supposed to provide within democratic systems and which among the different party system types may best perform these functions. Chapter 9 looks at Russia's major associational groups, such as labor unions and women's organizations, and describes their role and influence within the political system. Chapter 10, the last chapter focused on the Russian Federation, outlines the main public issues within both domestic and foreign policy realms. Notable here is an extensive discussion of privatization and the problems associated with making the transformation from a command to a market economy.

Part IV of the book is devoted to the country studies. The presentation for each country follows a similar outline. Each chapter begins with a brief political history and ends with a discussion of the country's prospects for political stability, democratic freedoms, and individual security. Overviews of the structure and functions of the political institutions and processes within the country furnish the central core of each chapter.

Lithuania (Chapter 11) was selected for study to represent the Baltic region of the former USSR. Along with Estonia and Latvia it has moved the furthest toward integration with the European community. Lithuania also represents the shortest legacy of communist control, as the region was incorporated into the Soviet Union during World War II.

Ukraine (Chapter 12) is included as an emerging major European power, second in size geographically only to Russia. In addition to Ukraine's strength in its own right—containing nearly 50 million persons and abundant resources —the country is also important to the United States for national security reasons. Georgia (Chapter 13) represents the Transcaucasian region of the former Soviet Union. In the aftermath of the breakup of the Soviet Union, Georgia struggled with a civil war, and more recently the "Rose Revolution" led to the ouster of long-time leader Edward Shevardnadze. Chapter 14 examines the central Asian republic of Uzbekistan. Countries from this region have followed rather different paths during the post-Soviet period, a result of their special histories and cultures. The epilogue discusses more generally the challenges facing newly independent states and their prospects for democracy.

STRUCTURE

The overall goal of the text is to create critical thinkers by nurturing an interest in the process of political change in post-Communist states. This textbook is designed to teach analytical skills, including the discovery of generalizations and evaluation and interpretation of empirical data, in order to improve our understanding of human behavior, political institutions, and social systems. Several methods are employed to reach these goals. Critical thinking questions appear at the end of each chapter; these may be used as stimulation for classroom discussions or as study guides for written tests. Key terms are also listed and the definitions of these terms can be found in a glossary located at the back of the text. Each chapter includes references to additional readings and to relevant online materials. Tables, charts, photos, and maps are included throughout.

This book integrates my research findings into the instructional narrative. I have traveled to all the countries described in this book, and my own first-hand observations have critically informed my analysis and have altered the ways in which I think about political change and development. These insights will become apparent as students delve more deeply into the pages of this text. I believe that an active research agenda serves to enrich immeasurably both undergraduate and graduate education. As principal investigator or co-principal investigator on projects funded by the United States Department of State and the U.S. National Science Foundation, I have had the opportunity to conduct field research in several countries of the former USSR. My goal now is to expand, revise, and deepen our understanding of post-Soviet states by providing the information offered in this book. No other books of which I am aware that are currently on the market take a similar approach. However, several standard textbooks in comparative politics apply methods that I have emulated here. An example of such a book, with a strong conceptual focus supplemented with valuable case studies, is by Mark Kesselman and his colleagues titled *European Politics in Transition*, published by Houghton Mifflin.

ACKNOWLEDGMENTS

In writing this book, I received valuable assistance. My first "thank you" goes to Katherine Meisenheimer, sponsoring editor for political science at Houghton Mifflin. She encouraged this project and gave me the confidence that I needed to bring the idea to completion. In addition, Houghton Mifflin provided two helpful development editors, Terri Wise and Jeff Greene, without whose assistance this manuscript would not have made it to fruition. Seven excellent reviewers helped to shape the manuscript in its formative stages: Stephen Crowley, Oberlin College; Henry E. Hale, Indiana University; Charles E. Ziegler, University of Louisville; Christopher Marsh, Baylor University; Meredith Heiser-Duron, Stanford University; John P. Willerton, University of Arizona; and Bryon Moraski, University of Florida.

Within my own institution, the University of Iowa, I received secretarial and administrative support from Karen Stewart, Wendy Durant, and Carole Eldeen. Chapters about specific countries were written with the help of scholars from those countries. Andriy Gorbachyk, Pavel Ignatiev, and Nickolay Kapitonenko provided valuable feedback on the chapter on Ukraine. Rasa Alisauskiene provided data for the chapter on Lithuania. Merab Pachulia and Katie Kiknadze provided analyses for the chapter on Georgia. Jumanazar Sultanov helped to write and Sevara Sharapova provided research assistance for the chapter on Uzbekistan.

V. L. H.

CHAPTER 1

Post-Soviet States in Comparative Perspective

DURING THE ERA OF THE COLD WAR, the Union of Soviet Socialist Republics (USSR) battled with the United States of America for ideological, military, and economic domination within the world system. After the two countries teetered on the edge of nuclear war during the Cuban Missile Crisis of 1962, this rivalry evolved into ideological and economic competitiveness and surrogate wars in Asia and Africa. The leaders of the United States and the USSR signed treaties to limit stockpiles of lethal nuclear weapons, yet the United States continued to see the Soviet Union as its primary national security threat for four decades, from the late 1940s to the late 1980s. It is difficult now to imagine an era during which U.S. authorities threw Communist sympathizers in jail and leaders in the Soviet Union were constantly on guard against spies from the West.

In the aftermath of the September 11, 2001, attacks on New York City and Washington, D.C., a new battle gripped the contemporary world. States that were once part of the Soviet Union became partners in the U.S.-led "antiterrorist coalition." The United States conducted joint military exercises with Ukraine and Georgia and made ample use of supply bases in Uzbekistan and Tajikistan. How can we understand such a transformation? The best way to answer this question is to study the post-Soviet region from a broad historical and comparative perspective.

An historical overview helps identify the factors that account for the nature of the transitions that have occurred in the political systems of the Russian Federation and other post-Soviet states. A comparative perspective highlights the contrasting forms of **government** that are evolving within the region. In addition to an in-depth treatment of **politics** and government in the Russian Federation, this textbook includes case studies about Lithuania, Georgia, Ukraine, and Uzbekistan. For each country, we evaluate the progress that has been made toward the goals of creating effective governing institutions and realizing free and open democratic societies.

The countries we explore were all part of the Soviet Union prior to 1991. As such, the countries share the communist legacy. The degree to which people were socialized into the ideology of communism varies depending on the length of time that a country was part of the Soviet Union. Each country studied here has a history of inclusion in the Russian Empire and the Soviet Union, but the length of this incorporation varies significantly from country to country. When they were part of the Soviet Union, the countries had the same political system, tightly integrated economies, and unified foreign policies.

Although the focus of this book is primarily on Russian politics, other countries that represent the major geographical and cultural regions of the former USSR are included. Russia and Ukraine represent the Slavic core of the former Soviet Union. Georgia represents the **Transcaucasian region**, Lithuania corresponds to the **Baltic region**, and Uzbekistan characterizes the **Central Asian republics** of the former Soviet Union. The countries range in population size from nearly 145 million in the Russian Federation to a little more than 3.5 million in Lithuania and 4.9 million in Georgia (see Table 1.1). The range of religions and languages represented by these countries is just as broad. The majority religion in Russia, Ukraine, and Georgia is Orthodoxy, while most people in Lithuania are Catholic and in Uzbekistan most are Muslim.

Even though all former USSR societies have struggled with economic hardship during the post-Soviet transition, Lithuania's people are not so poor as the people of Uzbekistan. Lithuania's gross national income (GNI) per capita is $4,500, Russia's GNI per capita is $2,610, Ukraine's is $970, Georgia's is $770, and Uzbekistan's is $420 (for 2003). To put these numbers into perspective, note that China's GNI per capita is $1,100, while the United States's GNI is $37,610.

We might expect that these countries are following quite varied political paths since the breakup of the Soviet Union given their diversity, yet forces of convergence are also at work. When countries face similar challenges, they often adopt parallel policies and programs. Policy diffusion and policy learning lead to a sometimes unquestioned attempt to copy programs that other countries have tried and successfully use. Globalization, in and of itself, operates as a force of convergence. One similarity in institutional structure that has evolved in most post-Soviet countries is strong presidentialism. Do powerful **presidential systems** arise because a strong authority figure can implement initially hurtful policies that can bring significant benefits to society in the end? An answer to this question and to others like it will emerge from the historical background and the comparative analyses presented in the chapters that follow.

The structure of the country comparisons in this book is similar to that found in textbooks about European politics. Each chapter about a country begins with a brief political history and ends with a discussion of the country's prospects for political stability and democratic reform. When discussing the politics and government of each country, we explore the following topics:

TABLE 1.1   The Russian Federation in Comparative Perspective

	Russian Federation	Ukraine	Uzbekistan	Georgia	Lithuania
Total area (sq km)	17,075,200	603,700	447,400	69,700	65,200
Population	144,526,278	47,425,336*	26,851,195*	4,677,401*	3,596,617*
Size of majority ethnic group	Russian 82%	Ukrainian 78%	Uzbek 80%, (1996 est.)	Georgian 84%	Lithuanian 83% (2001 census)
Second largest ethnic group	Tatar 4%	Russian 17%	Russian 5%	Azeri 6%	Polish 7%
Third largest ethnic group	Ukrainian 3%	Belarusian 1%	Tajik 5%	Armenian 6%	Russian 6%
Major religions	Russian Orthodox 78%, Muslim 5%	Ukrainian Orthodox 54% (Moscow and Kiev Patriarchate), Catholic 8% (Uniate)	Muslim 88% (mostly Sunnis), Orthodox 9%	Orthodox Christian 84%, Muslim 10%	Roman Catholic 79%, Orthodox 3%
Languages	Russian 93%	Ukrainian 50%, Russian 48%	Uzbek 74%, Russian 14%, Tajik 4%	Georgian 71% (official), Russian 9%, Armenian 7%	Lithuanian 85% (official), Russian 10%, Polish 2%

* July 2005 estimate.
Figures are from *The World Factbook*, published by the CIA, and from public opinion surveys.
See http://www.cia.gov/cia/publications/factbook/index.html.

- The constitutional structures and main institutions of government, including the presidency, the parliament, and the court system
- The nature of the society and the political culture, including ethnic conflict and regional divisions
- The political participation of the people and the country's political parties, including the main political organizations' ideologies
- The primary public policy questions, associated with economic performance and foreign policy, including relationships with neighboring countries

The countries selected for study represent a broad spectrum of diversity in post-Soviet transitions. Lithuania, along with the other two Baltic countries of Estonia and Latvia, has joined the European Union; it also has the shortest legacy of Communist control. The Soviet Union incorporated this region in the aftermath of gains made by the **Red Army** during World War II.

Ukraine, as a potentially significant European power, is second in size geographically to Russia. Because both Ukraine and Russia are Slavic, are primarily Orthodox, and have a shared history that dates back to the ninth century, one might expect similarities in their post-Communist trajectories. Indeed, in many ways, Ukraine's post-Soviet evolution mirrored that of Russia; however, Ukraine's transition diverged radically from Russia's because of the Orange Revolution of December 2004. The possibility of Ukraine's entry into the European Union is now realistically on the horizon.

Georgia provides a critical contrast to both Ukraine and Lithuania because of its experience with civil war and violent ethnic conflict. An armed rebellion forcefully removed Georgia's first president from power in January 1992 and Edward Shevardnadze, who had served as USSR foreign minister under Mikhail Gorbachev, returned to Georgia to form a government. Shevardnadze, however, was not able to gain control over corruption and lawlessness, or over the secessionist province of Abkhazia, and was forced to resign in 2003.

Central Asian countries as a whole have followed still different paths during the post-Soviet period. Uzbeks comprise the most populous ethnic group in the region. Although Uzbekistan has an authoritarian political system, it became a strategic partner with the United States in the post–September 11 period. U.S. forces made extensive use of military bases in the country.

For each of these five post-Soviet countries (including Russia), we will compare the new institutions that have been established with others in the region and with similar institutions and structures found around the world. A formal institutional analysis, however, is insufficient for explaining political processes and outcomes if not supplemented by historical and cultural details. In this book, we use an analytical approach that combines the comparative method with theories of democratization and an historical–cultural perspective.

THE COMPARATIVE METHOD

Comparative political inquiry offers much of value. In-depth studies of other countries help with overcoming **ethnocentrism** and building a more balanced view of the world, thereby avoiding the prejudice that can arise when we think that the U.S. system of government is the best possible system or the only sensible way to establish a proper social order. Comparative political inquiry reminds us that enormous diversity and complexity exist within human societies and cultures.

The comparative approach to the study of government and politics has two components. The first includes a description of the structure and the history of the formal institutions of government—the presidency, the legislature, the council of ministers (or cabinet), the bureaucracy, the courts, and the security structures such as the military. The second component of the comparative approach involves evaluating the operation of the institutions in the specific context of a particular country. Contextual characteristics include historical lega-cies, natural resources, economic structure, population characteristics, and geo-graphic position. Each of these influences the operation of the governing institutions and the nature of political debate, conflict, and discussion within a society.

Systematic comparative analysis also requires an awareness of additional forces that affect the political processes within each country. Among these are the citizens' and government leaders' behavior patterns and belief systems that directly influence political outcomes and the overall efficiency and productiv-ity of the system. We also need to evaluate the extraconstitutional and informal relationships within countries' systems that affect conflict resolution and the actual realization of public policy. Comparative analyses take into account the regional and international organizations to which a country belongs because these too influence policy direction and policy options. Thus, we are better able to appreciate that Russia and the other post-Soviet states cannot escape from the pressures emanating from the international environment.

For some purposes, it will be useful to compare the operation of post-Soviet governing institutions with similar institutions found in established democracies—for example, those located in Western Europe. We may discover that the political experiences and processes occurring in Russia and other post-Soviet states have elements in common with other industrialized coun-tries. Thus, studying Russia in the context of other European countries and industrial democracies provides external standards by which to judge the political systems of Russia and surrounding countries more objectively. In other words, we improve our comprehension of Russia by comparing it to other countries.

Nonetheless, we must avoid an institutional approach that relies solely on consolidated democracies as standards for comparison. Certain institutions, such as political parties, may operate very differently in Russia than in the more established democracies. That is, Russia's political party system should be com-pared with party systems found in other countries that are in the process of transition from an authoritarian to a more democratic system of government. Competitive political parties are new entities in all new democracies, so study-ing them within a comparative framework that includes other countries in the process of a democratic transition is likely to yield the most useful insights.

In making decisions about comparative cases for study, scholars often cate-gorize the countries of the world into similar groupings. The assumption is that generalizations can best be made about the operation of politics within these general groupings rather than across them. One such categorization schema is to organize countries according to basic regime type, either democratic or authoritarian. Democratic systems strive toward citizen participation in deci-sion making, full representation of diverse interests, and accountable and responsible government. Authoritarian systems (or **dictatorships**) contrast with democracy in that they limit the extent of control that citizens have over their rulers. Totalitarian systems are extreme forms of **authoritarianism** that seek to control and manipulate people for the purpose of reconstructing society according to a design envisioned by the rulers. An example of a totalitarian system is the Soviet Union when it was ruled by Joseph Stalin.

Authoritarian systems may involve rule by a single person (for example, a king or religious leader), by a dominant political party, or by the military. Kings or emperors who receive their mandate to rule through inherited rights lead monarchies. Religious leaders, who often wield extreme power, stand at the head of a theocracy. Examples of dominant-party states include Mexico under the rule of the Institutional Revolutionary Party (IRP) and Japan under the Liberal Democratic Party (LDP). Such countries do hold regular elections, but the ruling party strictly regulates the ability of any opposition organization or candidate to challenge its power. The third type of authoritarianism is rule by military officers. Generally, this represents a transitional stage, when the military seizes control because of political and economic problems but ultimately relinquishes authority to civilian leaders.

This leads to another more general categorization that is frequently made between transitional regimes and consolidated systems. Transitional states are moving from one form of government to another. In consolidated states, the ruling institutions, which could be authoritarian or democratic, are well established and generally accepted.

In the past, the study of political systems was often divided into the First World (industrialized democracies), the Second World (communist systems), and the Third World (developing countries). The Soviet Union, China, Eastern Europe, and other states in Africa and Central America were all considered "communist systems." They shared a similar ideology, rigid and hierarchically structured governing institutions, and close ties with the Soviet Union.

With the demise of the Soviet Union, it made less sense to categorize countries into First World, Second World, and Third World states. Currently, comparative politics textbooks tend to take a geographic focus, that is, Western Europe, African countries, Latin American countries, South Asia, or the Middle East. Countries also can be grouped according to their level of popular support (legitimate versus tyrannical systems) or their level of involvement in the international system (integrated versus isolated). When grouping countries based on their economies, a distinction is often made between rich and poor countries. Countries can also be grouped according to the size of their economy (gross domestic product—GDP), the structure of their economy (percent employed in agriculture), and the degree of government regulation of the economy. When grouping countries according to social and cultural variables, we might consider population size, prevalence of social welfare or educational programs, and/or dominant religion (Christian versus Muslim).

Categorizing countries and focusing on only one particular group of countries allows for the discovery of patterns of politics that are similar within a particular type of system. Studying a group of countries that are similar according to defined dimensions allows for the development of generalizations about political relationships within the group. One of the most common approaches for the study of post-Communist countries is to evaluate them as part of a group that contains all countries in the process of democratic transition.

THEORIES OF DEMOCRATIZATION

Thus, in addition to an application of the comparative method, we use theories about democratization to inform our understanding of the politics and governments of Russia and other post-Soviet societies. Although many commentators argue that democracy did not exist in the Soviet Union, others note that Soviet leaders such as Lenin and Khrushchev believed they were establishing a more humane and just form of democracy than was evident in the West's bourgeois, capitalist systems. Thus, we need to carefully define what we mean by democracy. **Democracy** is a form of government selected by the citizens through free and fair elections. All major theorists acknowledge that holding competitive elections is a necessary step in the implementation and consolidation of democracy. Elections not only foster the **legitimacy** of the new democratic institutions, they are also the essence of the democratic process itself.

More is required for the existence of a democracy, however, beyond the holding of regular competitive elections. For a democracy to become institutionalized, consolidated, and legitimate, it must realize key goals in several areas, including civil society and the rule of law. Much of the literature on democratization focuses on the idea that institutional design plays a pivotal role in the establishment of a new order (Di Palma 1990; Przeworski 1995; Linz and Stepan 1997; Remington 1997).

Certain "legacies of the past," however, may undermine a successful transition to liberal democracy (Jowitt 1992). Such legacies include economic backwardness, a centrally planned economy, unfinished **nation**-building, a political culture of intolerance, a weak state with illiberal traditions, and a weak civil society (Crawford and Lijphart 1997). Structural theorists consider economic development, a supportive political culture, and state–civil society relations as preconditions for democratization and consolidation (Reisinger 1997; Plasser, Ulram, and Waldrauch 1998). According to the neo-institutional tradition, legacies matter (as constraining factors), but they are not overriding in determining the outcome of a democratic project. From this perspective, consolidation primarily entails "institutionalizing competitive politics" (Lijphart and Waisman 1996, 3).

The practice of holding regular elections in most post-Soviet countries seems to indicate that, at least at the level of its electoral institutions, democracy in the region is working toward consolidation. The problem is the criticism raised regarding the procedural fairness of the elections. Allegations of fraud, misuse of campaign funds, and partisanship of state and private media

Vladimir Putin, President of the Russian Federation.
Alexander Zemlianichenko / AFP / Getty Images

surround the electoral campaigns. An example is the disproportionate share of news coverage across all the major Russian television channels that Vladimir Putin receives in periods preceding presidential elections.

Russia's experience with democracy has been both convulsive and checkered from the beginning. Violent conflict occurred between the executive and legislative branches of Russia's government in the early 1990s. More recently, a political party closely aligned with the president achieved electoral success and gained control of the Russian legislature through questionable practices. Russian President Putin's efforts to rein in the **oligarchs** and the regional governors may be considered repressive rather than a legitimate means for reducing corruption and achieving national integration.

Therefore, we must raise cautionary flags with regard to Russia's post-Soviet transition. The sweeping constitutional authority granted the presidency under

Boris Yeltsin, together with Vladimir Putin's success at concentrating even more power into the position of president, raises issues of democratic accountability. The consolidation of democracy in Russia, as in any system in transition, is a complex process involving multiple dimensions and multiple tasks. Democracy is an ideal to which many countries aspire but often never fully realize. By studying Russia and the other countries described in this book from the perspective of the process of democratization, we have specific criteria to use to evaluate the structures and the functions of the various institutions of government.

THE HISTORICAL–CULTURAL APPROACH

The discussion about democratization referred to "legacies of the past" and their potential impact on the democratization process. This reference to legacies is part of a broader historical–cultural approach that looks at ways in which current government institutions and policies are influenced by prior practices, experiences, and ideas. Russia today cannot escape the legacy of the Soviet Union, just as the Soviet Union could not escape the legacy of the Russian Empire under the tsars.

An advantage of the historical–cultural approach is that it recognizes the mixture of historical and contemporary factors in the structure and function of any government. Study is not limited to a snapshot of political events since the breakup of the Soviet Union or only to the last few years. Rather we seek to identify historical patterns and experiences that continue to influence the formation, evolution, and operation of political systems. Within this framework, we consider the following:

- To what extent does the political culture of Russia affect that country's receptiveness to Western, liberal notions of democracy?
- How have historical patterns of political autocracy and administrative centralization provided a congenial environment for the emergence of strong presidential, possibly authoritarian, systems in these countries?
- To what extent has the development of other post-Soviet countries (besides Russia) been hindered by a legacy of colonialism associated with the Soviet Empire and the Russian Empire before that?

A useful analytical framework for answering the third question is dependency theory. *Dependency theory* contends that imperial rule by Russia established patterns of dependency that disproportionately benefited Russia as the Soviet Union's core state and as the dominate power in the region. Even though a country such as Uzbekistan now has formal independence from the Soviet Union, Uzbekistan's continued dependence on Russia in its trade relations may, in part, leave it in a condition of de facto colonialism.

A potential disadvantage of such an analytical framework is that it may put too much emphasis on the past and may assume that little has changed. In this book, however, we merge the historical–cultural approach with an explicitly comparative design. While acknowledging the importance of historical legacies, we also emphasize the commonalities and the practices that Russia shares with countries like Germany and the United States. We value the long-term perspective, while comparing Russia's government institutions directly with those found in Western democracies.

ORGANIZATION OF THE BOOK

Chapter 2 provides a synopsis of Soviet philosophy and ideology. This includes an introduction to the intellectual inheritance of socialism and a discussion of the basic principles of Marxism, Leninism, and Stalinism. We evaluate the relationship between Leninism and Stalinism and touch briefly on the philosophical leanings of other Soviet leaders.

Chapter 3 provides a political history of the Tsarist, Soviet, and post-Soviet periods. Key historical turning points in the development of the Soviet state are identified. The basic operation of government during the Soviet period is described. We also review the transformation of the Soviet Union during the rule of Mikhail Gorbachev and discuss the forces that led to the breakup of the USSR.

The foci of Chapter 4 are the national and ethnic cleavages that provide the foundation for political conflict within the multiethnic Russian Federation. The analysis in this chapter addresses the question of how the heterogeneous nature of the population of the Soviet Union, together with the conflicts that have existed for centuries among various ethnic groups, have affected the ability of the current Russian government to establish a new basis for political stability. In this chapter, we make a distinction between Russians and other nationalities, such as the Chechens and Tatars, who share the territory of the Russian Federation.

Chapter 5 takes a more general look at the political culture in Russian society today. Political culture refers to the orientations that people have toward involvement in the political process. A major section of the chapter examines the rise of Russian nationalism and the imprint of this ideology on the policies and orientations of the government. We also analyze the existence of certain beliefs or values that scholars have identified as being required for democracy.

Chapter 6 is about Russia's government institutions. The goal here is to describe as accurately as possible the formal institutions—the presidency, the legislature, and the judicial system—and to appraise how well they are working. An explicitly comparative approach guides the discussion of Russia's governing institutions, putting them in the context of presidential and parliamentary systems more generally.

Chapter 7 presents a quantitative and analytical study of the participatory role of Russian citizens; we identify which types of people are most involved in the political process. Included in this chapter is an overview of what current research tells us about voting behavior and public opinion in post-Soviet states. In addition, we examine other forms of political participation, such as contacting public officials or engaging in violent antigovernment activities.

Chapter 8 is devoted to Russia's main political parties and Chapter 9 looks at interest groups. The focus is on how political parties and other groups organize to influence or to control government decision making. We discuss the operation of labor organizations, the oligarchs, and women's organizations in detail.

Chapter 10 reviews major areas of public policy within the Russian Federation. We evaluate both the achievements and the negative aspects of market reform and privatization. Attention is also given to Russia's foreign policy and international relations. In addition, we discuss health-care policy because this is a serious concern in a country with a population that is declining in both size and heartiness.

A list of key terms and critical thinking questions appear at the end of each chapter. A glossary with definitions is located at the end of the book. The critical thinking questions provide a structure for chapter review and a direction for further study. Several useful references and interesting websites are also provided for more in-depth reading about the materials covered in each chapter.

Key Terms

Authoritarianism
Baltic region
Central Asian republics
Democracy
Dictatorship
Ethnocentrism
Government

Legitimacy
Nation
Oligarchs
Politics
Presidential systems
Red Army
Transcaucasian region

Critical Thinking Questions

1. How did the relationship between the United States and Russia change from the Cold War period to the period of the International Anti-Terrorist Coalition?

2. What is the value of adopting an historical–cultural approach for studying post-Soviet countries?

3. What are the advantages of studying political systems from a comparative perspective?

4. What are the characteristics of a democratic political system? How can we recognize a democracy when we see one?

Suggested Reading

McFaul, Michael, et al. *Between Dictatorship and Democracy.* Washington, D.C.: Brookings Institution Press, 2004.

Sakwa, Richard. *The Rise and Fall of the Soviet Union: 1917–1991 (Sources in History).* Oxford, U.K.: Routledge, 1999.

Websites of Interest

Historical map showing the growth of the Russian Empire: http://www.lib.utexas.edu/maps/historical/shepherd/russian_growth_1300_1796.jpg

A country report about the Soviet Union published by the U.S. Library of Congress, Federal Research Division: http://lcweb2.loc.gov/frd/cs/sutoc.html

Documents based on a CIA analysis of the Soviet Union: http://www.cia.gov/csi/books/princeton/

CHAPTER 2

The Ideological Foundations of Russian Socialism

OCIALISM IS AN IDEOLOGY that advocates social change for the purpose of achieving greater equality. **Communism** is more radical in advancing societal transformation through the elimination of private property. Communist ideology provided the foundation for the 1917 Bolshevik Revolution and the establishment of the Soviet Union. Communist doctrine, as accepted by the Soviet Union, was based on basic assumptions from the writings of Karl Marx and Friedrich Engels. According to their ideas, capitalist society has two classes, a small privileged class of owners and a huge majority class of workers who are exploited by the dominant minority. The theory of Marxism states that as a capitalist society matures, the conflict between the classes becomes irreconcilable and the inevitable result is a "social revolution." The revolution replaces private ownership with collectivist ownership; it also abolishes the division of society into classes and liberates all oppressed workers by putting an end to the exploitation of labor.

This was the **ideology** of the Bolsheviks when they seized power in 1917. Communist political philosophy had been developing long before Marx and Engels made their contributions during the nineteenth century. The concept of communal life, in which sharing and community ownership are valued over individualism and the acquisition of private property, and where the needs of all members are equally and adequately met, is expressed in the earliest institutions and writings of Western civilization. Plato was one of the first to focus on answering the question of how a state (government) can be best ordered for the benefit of the people.

Modern socialist theory took shape in Europe amidst the political and economic turmoil of the eighteenth and nineteenth centuries. One of the most influential philosophers of the time was a Frenchman named Jean-Jacques Rousseau (1712–1778). In *Discourse on the Origins of Inequality* (1755), Rousseau argued that aggrandizement of private property led not only to tyranny over the unpropertied, but also to alienation, victimization, and other forms of social injustice. By abolishing private ownership of the means of production and by forbidding the exploitation of labor by a minority of property owners, liberation could be achieved and people could decide for themselves what would be best for society.

Attempting to implement the ideas of Rousseau, François Noel Babeuf (1760–1797) founded a group known as the Conspiracy of the Equals. Sylvain Marechal, a contemporary of Babeuf's, wrote the first revolutionary socialist document, the *Manifesto of Equals* (1796), which declared:

> No more individual ownership of the land. . . . We are demanding, we
> desire, communal enjoyment of the fruits of the earth. . . . We declare
> ourselves unable any longer to tolerate a situation in which the great
> majority of men toil and sweat at the service and at the pleasure of a tiny
> minority.[1]

Another Frenchman, Count Henri de Saint-Simon (1760–1825), called for the redistribution of rewards from the privileged to the unprivileged members of society. He also emphasized the need for solidarity among the "productive" classes, whom he referred to as *les industriels*.

Equally important to the development of modern **socialism** were critiques of economics and politics being offered by English writers such as Adam Smith and William Godwin. A particularly significant contribution came from David Ricardo in his *The Iron Law of Wages* (1817), which predicted the increasing impoverishment of workers because of the way in which their labor was valued (or devalued). Toward the end of the nineteenth century, the various theories put forth by the Enlightenment thinkers began to come together as a cohesive force to form a conceptual framework for socialism.

MARXISM

Marxism as a political philosophy evolved not only from the works of earlier socialist writers but also developed specifically as an intellectual reaction to the industrial revolution. Industrialization, as it occurred in Western Europe, involved deriving energy from coal, the advent of steam power and railroads, and the extraction of raw materials from worldwide empires. The appearance of the industrial worker was itself a new phenomenon. The hard life, long hours, and horrible conditions that became characteristic of factory workers led to a level of human suffering that reasonable people began to question. A widely held sense of exploitation of the workers by the owners of the factories (the capitalist class) developed.

The Revolutionary Careers of Marx and Engels

Political philosophers often think of communism as designating those theories and movements that are in accord with the teachings of Karl Marx (1818–1883) and Friedrich Engels (1820–1895). Neither man was from a working-class background; Marx was the son of a middle-class lawyer and Engels was the son of a textile manufacturer. Marx entered the University of Bonn's Faculty of Law in 1835 and transferred to the University of Berlin's Faculty of Law in 1836, where he received his Ph.D. in 1841. In 1844, Marx was accused by the Prussian government of high treason for his articles published in opposition newspapers and was to be arrested should he return to Prussia.* In 1845, Marx was banished from Paris by the French government under pressure from Prussia. Marx took his first trip to England (with Engels) in 1845 and returned again in 1847 for the meeting of the Communist League in London.

The Communist League, formed in 1836 by German radicals living in Paris, asked Marx and Engels, who were both members, to draw up its platform. In the platform, published in 1848 and titled the *Communist Manifesto*, Marx and Engels urged the workers of the world to unite to achieve "scientific socialism"— communism. Marx and Engels advocated the abolition of capitalism and all private profit and were willing to take the extreme stance of achieving this by means of a violent revolution, if necessary.

Marx and Engels published several lasting theoretical works, including *A Contribution to the Critique of Political Economy* (1859), *Theories of Surplus Value* (1863), and *Capital* (Volumes 1–3, 1867–1894).† Both men were active in the International Working Men's Association (frequently called the First International), an alliance of trade union groups that was founded in London in 1864.‡ After Marx's death in 1883, Engels took part in the founding of the Second International (also known as the Socialist International) in 1889 in Paris. The Second International represented national-level socialist parties and movements from all over Europe, the United States, Canada, and Japan.

Basic Principles of Marxism

Although it was their gut-wrenching reactions to the squalor of the factories and the slums that caused people to question the existing order of things, Marxism as a philosophy was based on a set of logical premises and rational arguments. One of the foundational principles of Marxism, historical materialism, is borrowed from the German philosopher Georg Wilhelm Friedrich

*Prussia is a former kingdom of north-central Europe including present-day northern Germany and Poland. Prussia was instrumental in the unification of Germany, and in 1871 its king was declared Emperor William I of Germany.
†The Russian language edition of *Capital* was published in 1872 and the first Russian language edition of the *Communist Manifesto* became available in 1869 (translated by Bakunin).
‡Internal feuding led to the association's dissolution in 1876.

Hegel. According to historical materialism, historical development is deter-mined by laws of human relationships that are in turn determined fundamen-tally by the ways in which men and women obtain their livelihood. A basic component of historical materialism therefore is the idea of **economic deter-minism**, which can be explained using two terms—**the base and the super-structure**.

The base is the economic structure of the society; it represents the combi-nation of production relations at a certain stage of development. With the onset of the industrial revolution, production relations were mainly centered on manufacturing, extraction (mining), and commerce. The superstructure is the particular form of social consciousness that corresponds to and is deter-mined by the base; it includes legal, political, and cultural institutions devel-oped on and reflecting the economic base. Thus, the major institutions within a society, existing in any given historical stage, such as systems of gov-ernment and systems of education, parallel the economic base of the society. This means that principles of right, liberty, and justice do not exist in the abstract but support the economic system (the base).

According to the idea of economic determinism, the people who own the means of production—including resources such as land, raw materials, tools and machines, labor, and money—dominate not only the economic system but also the social and political systems. Political ideologies or philosophies advo-cated by rulers simply serve as rationalizations of the existing order. The own-ers of resources and productive forces employ every available means to keep themselves in power at the expense of the less fortunate people.

The economic determinism argument leads to another key concept of Marxism, the idea of **class struggle**. Classes emerge as a result of a division of labor and as a result of private ownership of the means of production. The term *class* refers to a group of people within society who share the same social and economic conditions. Considering nineteenth-century society, Marx and Engels perceived a class struggle raging between the **bourgeoisie** (the ruling class under capitalism), who controlled the means of production, and the **proletariat** (the wage laborers).

Marx and Engels argued that human society and history are characterized by a constant struggle between the classes. In all societies, only a small minority of people own or control the resources for production, including both raw materials and the technology for production. This minority is the ruling class; and because it controls the means of production, the ruling class also has polit-ical power. Law, religion, and philosophy are weapons used by the ruling class to justify their privileged status.* The state therefore is nothing more than an instrument of the ruling class, which uses its economic power to exploit work-ers by appropriating their labor unfairly. As a result, workers, as wage laborers, become alienated from the products of their labor.

---

*Thus, atheism is an essential element of scientific socialism. According to Karl Marx, "religious sentiment is itself a social product" (Tucker 1972, 109).

Exploitation and alienation are explained by the concept of **surplus value**. Although the value of a commodity reflects the labor that went into it, market prices reflect more than labor costs. Thus, profit represents theft from, or exploitation of, the worker. Exploitation occurs when profits (or surplus value) are greater than the amount of money expended for labor (wages) and raw materials.*

Marx and Engels argued that the struggle between the classes was the force for social change, causing revolutions and leading history from one period to the next; such a theory of history is known as the **law of dialectics**. Based on a method of logic used by Georg Wilhelm Friedrich Hegel and adapted by Marx, *dialectics* is the theory that a thesis generates its opposite (antithesis), leading to a reconciliation of opposites (synthesis). The dialectic is progressive because humanity's development occurs from contradiction and conflict; therefore every phenomenon (or **historical stage**) contains contradictory parts. As the parts conflict, transformations in the phenomenon gradually occur until the changes are large enough to create an essentially new phenomenon (new stage). Thus, according to the law of dialectics, the history of society is the history of class struggle. Movement from one stage to the next is the result of a dialectical conflict between classes representing two sides of the social division of labor—owners and nonowners of the means of production.

Capitalism, as the historical stage that follows feudalism, is progressive at first because it eliminates feudal relations. The bourgeoisie in its early stages is also good because it promotes transformation, change, and economic development. But eventually the contradictions within capitalism undermine its very existence.† Consequently, capitalism is doomed as a result of the conflict between the bourgeoisie and the proletariat. The proletariat is destined to overthrow capitalism and establish socialism, which will eventually evolve into communism.

The final stage of history is communism, which is preceded by a period of socialist transformation. Socialist leaders use state power only temporarily, until private property is abolished and the division of labor becomes unnecessary. During this brief transitional period, industry is owned by the commonwealth; that is, industry is nationalized. The population must endorse a temporary absolute rule by the workers in order to seize the property of the bourgeois minority and to stifle any attempts by remnants of the bourgeoisie to sabotage the new government. Unlike previous periods, the working class would not seek to install a new system of domination and exploitation; its goal would be a system of cooperation in which the vast majority, the proletariat, rules for the benefit of all.

---

*Marx and Engels acknowledge that some of the "proceeds from labor" must be invested in replacement and expansion of the means of production, insurance funds, and general costs of administration (Tucker 1972, 385–86).

†In Marx's later work, notably *Capital*, colonialism is seen as a fundamental element in the primary accumulation of capital within Europe.

Once capitalism is overthrown (when the exploiters are eliminated), relations between classes should become friendly and nonantagonistic. According to Marx and Engels, "with the abolition of class distinctions, all social and political inequality rising from them would disappear of itself" (Tucker 1972, 392). Eventually, society would evolve into a full communist state. As the worker-directed state emerged, more cohesive and prosperous classes would cease to exist and the division and dehumanization of labor found in earlier forms of society would end.

Communism would produce a new kind of person. Labor that had once been performed because of economic necessity would give way to truly voluntary activity. Ultimately men and women would realize true fulfillment from their labor and would work voluntarily. Under communism, the proceeds from labor would be distributed among all the members of the cooperative society. In the words of Marx: "From each according to his ability, to each according to his needs!" (Tucker 1972, 388).

In interpreting their theory of class struggle, Marx and Engels held that the conflict between the bourgeoisie and the increasingly impoverished proletariat was long overdue in the class-based societies of Europe. They foresaw a revolution in which the proletariat would displace the bourgeoisie as the ruling class. According to Marx, this revolution would be violent because the bourgeoisie would not give up power by electoral means.

In an address to the Central Committee of the Communist League, Marx and Engels vocalized the necessity of militia preparation: "The arming of the whole proletariat with rifles, muskets, cannon and munitions must be put through at once" (Tucker 1972, 369). A political revolution was essential, in Marx's view, because the state is the coercive instrument of capitalist society. Thus, Marx and Engels concluded their *Communist Manifesto* with the following call:

> The immediate aims of the Communists are the same as that of all the other proletarian parties: formation of the proletariat into a class, overthrow the bourgeois supremacy, and conquest of political power by the proletariat.
>
> The theory of the Communists may be summed up in the single sentence: Abolition of private property.
>
> United action, of the leading civilized countries at least, is one of the first conditions for the emancipation of the proletariat. . . . In short, Communists everywhere support every revolutionary movement against the existing social and political order of things.
>
> WORKING MEN OF ALL COUNTRIES, UNITE! (Tucker 1972, 346–62)

Marxism increased in popularity during the late nineteenth century, particularly in countries whose significant urban population was impoverished and whose intellectuals were excluded from participation in government. By the early twentieth century, followers of Marx and Engels (Marxists) held a range of stances on the issues of capitalism and class subjugation. More militant Marxists admonished leftist parties to generate class conflict and thereby accelerate the death of capitalism and hasten the start of the workers' revolution. More moderate Marxists rejected the revolutionary perspective and held rather that public control of the economy could be achieved by nonviolent ways—for example, by electing Marxists to government positions. They sought to improve the capitalist system with various socialist reforms. These Marxist **"revisionists"** believed that the debut of a welfare state would encourage social equality and give security to ordinary citizens. Few of these Marxists, whether militant or revisionist, expected that the first workers' revolution would occur in Russia because it lacked the preconditions they considered essential, namely a mature industrial economy.

ORIGINS OF THE RUSSIAN SOCIALIST MOVEMENT

During the eighteenth century, Russia was relatively isolated from the intellectual revolutions sweeping Europe. Coercive force and scare tactics used by Tsarist police kept intellectuals and revolutionary activists quiet. Radical ideas, however, began to feed revolutionary fervor in Russia during the nineteenth century. Russian intellectual Mikhail Bakunin (1814–1876), for example, called for the violent destruction of government. **Anarchists** saw government as an instrument of oppression and as an impediment to human development. They believed that society would be better off without the repressive and destructive institutions of the state.

Another radical political position prominent between 1850 and 1880 in Russia was expressed by the ***Narodniki*** (Going to the People) movement. Being both traditional and socialist, it looked to the simplicity of peasant life as a guide to a more collectivized human existence. Alexander Herzen (1812–1870), a leader of the Narodniki movement, was persuaded by the ideas of Marx and Engels, but he did not agree with the requirement that the proletariat class instigate the revolution. It was Herzen's views that stirred impatient students in Russian academia to form the movement called Going to the People (1873–1874). Young college students went into the Russian countryside to spread their message of social reform and economic change. Not too surprisingly, the illiterate and poor peasantry received the message of the students neither positively nor enthusiastically.

In spite of their lack of success, the activities of the Narodniki were nonetheless met with government repression (imprisonment and exile), and, as a result, the movement became more radicalized. The movement split into two groups—People's Will (*Narodina Volya*) and Black Repartition (*Chernyi Peredel*). People's Will advocated a tightly disciplined party of professional revolutionaries; its members assassinated the tsar of Russia, Alexander II, in 1881. Black Repartition, in contrast, opposed terrorism and advocated propaganda and agitation as the means to achieve change.

Marxism became an influential philosophy in Russia when a leader of Black Repartition, Georgi V. Plekhanov (1856–1918), abandoned the Narodniki ideology and concurred with the original doctrine of Marx and Engels, which said that capitalism was a necessary step between feudalism and socialism.* Plekhanov argued that peasants were basically conservative, not revolutionary, and that the industrial proletariat was the coming revolutionary force.†

In 1883, Plekhanov founded the first Russian Marxist group, Emancipation of Labor, but had to flee the country to avoid arrest. In 1898, this organization became the Russian Social Democratic Labor Party (RSDLP or Workers' Party), holding its First Party Congress in Minsk.‡ The statement of goals (the party program) that was adopted in 1903 at the Second Party Congress of the RSDLP was similar to the program of the French Workers Party adopted in 1882 and to the German Social Democratic Party program adopted in 1891. The 1903 RSDLP program advocated the inauguration of a democratic regime with a parliament, elected by direct universal suffrage. It acknowledged the right to strike and equal rights for men and women. The 1903 program promised nations the right to govern themselves, an eight-hour workday and a day of rest each week, and a set of social laws that would improve the working conditions for city workers and peasants. A crucial difference between the RSDLP program and that of the French and German workers' parties was that the Russian program called for the seizure of political power by the proletariat. This more revolutionary position caught the attention of many young people; one of them would leave a lasting legacy—Vladimir Lenin.

LENINISM

Vladimir Ilyich Ulyanov (1870–1924), better known as Lenin, studied law until he was expelled from Kazan University for revolutionary activities. He relentlessly propagandized the teachings of Karl Marx among the workers until he was exiled to Siberia in 1895. When Lenin was released from exile, he joined

---

*Leon Trotsky (1879–1940), another revolutionary of the time, rejected Plekhanov's argument that Russia must pass through the capitalist stage. Trotsky advanced the notion of "permanent revolution" whereby workers could seize control of the state and use the institutions of the state to continue the revolution. Therefore, revolution became a permanent feature until the full socialist state was achieved.

†In the preface to the 1882 Russian edition of the *Communist Manifesto*, Marx and Engels modified their original stance by acknowledging the unique situation in Russia where "more than half the land is owned in common by peasants" (Tucker 1972, 334). They asserted that a Russian revolution could be successful if complemented by a "proletarian revolution in the West."

‡This Congress ended shortly after it convened when most of the delegates were arrested. The Socialist Revolutionary Party, founded in 1902, revived the Narodnik traditions and focused its activities on the peasantry.

Plekhanov in Switzerland. After the tsar of Russia abdicated in March 1917, Lenin returned to Russia, led the Bolshevik overthrow of the provisional government, and ruled the Soviet Union until his death in 1924.

Leninism developed as a result of Lenin's efforts to apply the nineteenth-century doctrines of Marx and Engels to Russian conditions. So, rather than being highly theoretical like Marx and Engels, Lenin offered practical solutions to deal with the very specific problems of having a successful revolution. According to him, an agrarian proletariat, under the leadership of industrial workers, could make a real contribution to the revolutionary movement in Russia. For this reason, Lenin believed that Russia was ready for a revolution led by both peasants and workers in alliance, and that revolution would result in the overthrow of the imperial regime and the establishment of a socialist economy and state.

Lenin also believed that the working class, on its own, could only be expected to develop trade union consciousness, and that revolutionary consciousness would need to be brought to the workers by an organization of professionals. In 1902, Lenin published *What Is to Be Done?* in which he argued that the working masses should be led by an elite party of professional revolutionaries organized in a disciplined, military style. Lenin was committed to the idea that revolutionary struggle could be successful only if guided by a political party composed of a limited number of dedicated and trained communists. The party organization was to serve as a vanguard for the working class.

The implications of Lenin's vision for the Russian Marxists became evident at the Second Congress of the Russian Social Democratic Labor Party held in 1903. At that congress, Lenin argued for a tightly organized party, limited in number, with its members actively engaged in organizational work. In opposition to his position, other members of the RSDLP argued that the party should be more loosely structured and should extend membership to anyone who accepted its program. This division of opinion led to the emergence of two factions within the RSDLP: the **Bolsheviks** (from the Russian word for *majority*) led by Lenin and the **Mensheviks** (from the Russian word for *minority*). Although a formal split in the party did not take place until 1912, Lenin would spend much of the next few years attacking the Mensheviks and defining his vision of the modern revolutionary party.

Communism as a modern ideology of action is oft seen as emerging from the split of the RSDLP into the Bolsheviks and the Mensheviks. Lenin advocated immediate and violent revolution to bring about the downfall of capitalism and the establishment of an international socialist state. While revolutions were said to be the result of objective conditions in society, Lenin believed that the process of social change could be accelerated by means of revolutionary action. He believed it was possible for socialist revolutions to occur in underdeveloped countries if the Communists worked hard to instill a proper class consciousness in the workers.

Russian revolutionary leader Vladimir Ilyich Lenin feared that the Russian peasants and workers would be unable to sustain a Marxist revolution in 1917. He believed the people needed the leadership of a small party of professional revolutionaries who would then control the new, classless society.

Hulton Archive / Getty Images

This call to seize power, rather than settling for reforms within the framework of capitalism, represented a particular Russian version of Marxism—*Leninism.* While Lenin was alive, the ideology of Soviet communism flowed chiefly from his writings and speeches. No other socialist leader in Europe could claim the same legitimacy as Lenin because no other socialist party had been successful in overthrowing capitalism within its own country.

In addition to altering Marx's ideas about the revolutionary potential of the workers, Lenin modified the notion of **dictatorship of the proletariat**. The source of this idea was the French socialist Louis Auguste Blanqui, although it is Marx who is often credited with this term. According to Marx, "between capitalist and communist society lies the period of the revolutionary transformation of one to the other. . . . There corresponds to this also a political transition period in which the state can be nothing but the revolutionary dictatorship of the proletariat" (Tucker 1972, 395). Lenin equated the dictatorship of the proletariat with rule by the Communist Party. The state could not be expected to "wither away"; rather, the socialist state needed to be strengthened against internal and external enemies.

It was during the period between March and November 1917 that Lenin further developed the notion that the state was simply an instrument of domination by the propertied classes. He maintained that, once the proletariat took power, the party (not the people) would determine when the state would wither away; that is, when the bureaucracy, the police, and the army could be replaced by direct rule by the people. As history ultimately revealed, the Soviet state never did wither away; rather it grew in power and scope to the point where the professional bureaucracy, the secret police, and the army together became a highly developed apparatus of coercion.

Another principle that can be attributed to Lenin's writings is the idea of *partiinost* or party mindedness. This means that disciplines, such as philosophy and the social sciences, should give support to the party and its cause. During the Soviet era, writings in the social sciences were required to correspond to the party's perception of reality; otherwise, such writings were denounced as idealist or subjective.

The theory of imperialism was another major extension of Leninism. Unlike Marx and Engels, Lenin lived to witness World War I. He argued that the war resulted from the conflict of imperial powers over the spoils of colonialism. Because World War I was an imperialist one, he rejected Russia's participation in it. The popularity of the Bolsheviks in 1917 was enhanced by the fact that Lenin opposed the Tsarist war effort.

According to Lenin, imperialism was the highest stage of capitalism. Colonies provided raw materials and abundant, cheap labor supplies. Once all colonial territories were annexed, the only way to get new territory was through war. Lenin also believed that wars were inevitable so long as capitalism existed. He stuck to his theory of imperialism and the prediction that this "supreme stage of capitalism" would generate an "era of the universal socialist revolution."[2] The theory of imperialism was carried forward to the program ratified by the Twenty-Second Communist Party Congress in 1961.

World War I served to divide the international socialist movement into the more radical elements that rejected participation in the war because it represented a fight among capitalist imperialists and the more moderate socialist parties that cooperated with their governments in an effort to win the war. The more radical elements that advocated a worldwide revolution found a natural leader in Lenin, while the moderate elements began to operate as socialist political parties within parliamentary systems of government. Two radical movements, one in Germany and one in Hungary, made revolutionary bids to seize power in the immediate aftermath of World War I, but both were unsuccessful.

The break between the moderates and the radical revolutionaries was complete when the radicals withdrew from the Second International to form the Third International in 1919. This Russian-dominated organization came to be known as the **Comintern**. Those political parties that accepted the leadership of the Comintern were officially named Communist parties (the Bolshevik Party changed its name to the Communist Party in 1918). The goal of the Comintern was to coordinate the action of all Communist parties for the purpose of uniting all workers in support of a worldwide revolution. Communist parties around the world were encouraged by the Bolsheviks to win control of labor unions and foment labor unrest with the ultimate goal of weakening and overthrowing the capitalist system. Thus, Lenin's ideas not only dominated the development of the early Soviet state but also the evolution of Communist Party organizations in other societies.

Following the lead of Lenin and the Bolsheviks, all Communist parties that were members of the Comintern were required to organize hierarchically, based on cells of active members who were completely subject to party rule. That rule was based on **democratic centralism**, a doctrine whereby decisions were made democratically as a result of open discussion. Once a decision was made, however, it was expected to be enforced by the central mechanism of the party and no dissent was allowed.

To summarize, Lenin advocated a party composed of professional revolutionaries, a violent seizure of power, and revolutionary action to accelerate historical change. The activist and elitist notion of the "proletariat's vanguard," together with the view that the peasants would play an active part in the revolution, constituted fundamental modifications of the original ideas of Marx and Engels. Lenin's revolutionary rhetoric is best appreciated by reading his own words (see Box 2.1).

Lenin's own writings rejected the theory of the withering away of the state and rather declared that the dictatorship of the proletariat signified "unlimited power depending on violence and not on law." He accepted the use of terror and its growing application throughout society even while the program of the party continued to promise democracy and freedom. In this vein, Lenin is credited with the notion of tactical flexibility. Since circumstances change, he recognized the need, when necessary, to postpone the achievement of goals, so tactical retreats were regarded as proper. In 1921, for example, Lenin decided to retreat to small-scale capitalism (to adopt the **New Economic Policy** [NEP]) in order to revive the economy in the aftermath of World War I and the Civil War period. Retreats were acceptable so long as the basic purpose of socialist transformation remained the ultimate goal. Thus, Soviet ideology as it emerged under Lenin represented the union of Leninist "tactics" with the "theory" of the Russian Social Democratic Labor Party. The idea of a special version of Marxism known as Leninism did not emerge until after Lenin's death in 1924. Lenin claimed that his ideas were Marxist, and it was left to Stalin to adopt the expression *Marxism-Leninism*.

BOX 2.1 ILLUSTRATIVE QUOTATIONS FROM LENIN

The liberation of the oppressed class is impossible not only without a violent revolution, but also without the destruction of the apparatus of [existing] state power, which was created by the ruling class.

The doctrine of class struggle . . . leads inevitably to the recognition of the political rule of the proletariat. . . . The proletariat needs state power, the centralized organization of force, the organization of violence, both for the purpose of crushing the resistance of the exploiters and for the purpose of guiding the great mass of the population.

Progress marches onward, [that is,] towards Communism, through the dictatorship of the proletariat. . . . The dictatorship of the proletariat produces a series of restrictions on liberty in the case of the oppressors, the exploiters, the capitalists. We must crush them in order to free humanity from wage-slavery; their resistance must be broken by force. . . .

Democracy for the vast majority of the people, and suppression by force, [that is,] exclusion from democracy, of the exploiters and the oppressors of the people—this is the modification of democracy during the transition from capitalism to Communism.

Source: From V. I. Lenin, *State and Revolution* (New York: International Publishers, 1932), pp. 9, 23, and 73.

The fundamental economic interests of the proletariat can be satisfied only by a political revolution that will replace the dictatorship of the bourgeoisie by the dictatorship of the proletariat.

. . . [W]orkers . . . are capable of displaying enormous energy and self sacrifice in strikes and in street . . . but the struggle against the *political* police requires special qualities; it requires *professional* revolutionaries.

If we begin with the solid foundation of a strong organization of revolutionaries, we can ensure the stability of the movement as a whole. . . .

I assert . . . that no movement can be durable without a stable organization of leaders to maintain continuity . . . that in a country with an autocratic government, the more we *restrict* the membership of this organization to persons who are engaged in revolutionary activities as a profession and who have been professionally trained in the art of combating the political police, the more difficult will it be to catch the organization, and the *wider* will be the circle of men and women of the working class or of other classes of society able to join the movement and perform active work in it.

Source: From V. I. Lenin, "What Is to Be Done?" In *Collected Works,* vol. 5 (Moscow: Foreign Languages Publishing House, 1961), pp. 347-530.

STALINISM

Joseph Stalin, who commanded the Soviet Union and world communism from the late 1920s until his death in 1953, made contributions to communist ideology through such publications as *Principles of Leninism* (1926) and *Questions on Leninism* (1926). The ideology of Marxism-Leninism became one of the many tools used by Stalin to maintain absolute power. As a self-proclaimed disciple of Lenin, Stalin worked as a revolutionary activist in the Caucasus Region until 1911, when he went to St. Petersburg to become one of the first editors of *Pravda*. Eventually this newspaper became the official mouthpiece of the Communist Party of the USSR. Stalin was arrested five times between 1902 and 1913. When arrested in 1913, Stalin was exiled to Siberia, where he remained until an amnesty was granted after the tsar abdicated the throne in March 1917.

Stalin's first theoretical work, *Marxism and the National Questions*, was written prior to the 1917 revolution. In this work, he entered a raging debate about whether working men and women of the world would maintain their separate national identities and loyalties as the transition was made to an internationally based socialist system. Following the arguments in Stalin's work and with the

Communist leader Joseph Stalin forged the Soviet Union into a major twentieth-century power. His ruthless political purges removed all internal opposition and by the mid-1930s, his leadership was undisputed.

© Bettmann / Corbis

establishment of the USSR by the Union Treaty of 1924, non-Russian nationality groups within the Soviet Union were allowed to maintain their distinct languages and culture; each nationality group had its own administrative structures, but its production was expected to contribute to the building of the socialist state.

When an international proletarian revolution did not materialize in the aftermath of World War I, Stalin associated himself with the notion of "socialism in one country." He adopted the idea in 1924 during his struggle for power with Leon Trotsky after the death of Lenin. Stalin argued (borrowing from Nikolai Bukharin) that the building of socialism could be accomplished in the Soviet Union without communist revolutions occurring in Western Europe. Stalin did not deny the desirability of communist victories in other countries, but he made the case that it was logical to concentrate on building socialism in the Soviet Union first.

This contrasted directly with Trotsky's argument that it was not possible to build socialism in Russia unless the workers of the West revolted. In other words, according to Trotsky, socialism in Russia required a continued or worldwide revolution because a single, socialist revolution in one country could not survive alone. Marx and Engels had anticipated that revolution would come first in countries characterized by the most advanced states of capitalism, such as Germany. Lenin had modified this notion in 1916, when he justified the launching of a revolution in comparatively backward Russia with the argument that a revolution there would trigger revolutions in more advanced countries, which would in turn assist the Russian revolution.

With the decision to focus on building "socialism in one country," Joseph Stalin's primary goal was to build a true communist system within the Soviet Union. Because the emphasis on the revolutionary transformation of a single country departed so radically from Marxist internationalism and from the theory of "permanent revolution," which stressed the necessity of a world revolution, Leon Trotsky founded a Fourth International to rival the Comintern after he was expelled from the Soviet Union in 1929. Trotsky, however, was unsuccessful in his defiance of Stalin and was assassinated while in exile.

An important component of Stalinism that follows from socialism in one country is the doctrine of **capitalist encirclement**. The encirclement of the Soviet Union by hostile capitalist countries justified a program of forced development of heavy industry (along with the collectivization of agriculture) in order to build socialism. The withering away of the Soviet state was indefinitely delayed given the condition of capitalist encirclement. Stalin cautioned that as socialism grew stronger, the class struggle would intensify as the enemy became more and more desperate (see Box 2.2).

Stalin also revised Marx's original orientation toward the superstructure, declaring that it does not merely reflect the base in a passive, neutral manner but rather can be used as an exceedingly active force to help reshape the base. The superstructure was not dependent on the base but transcended historical epochs, serving various ruling classes.

BOX 2.2 ILLUSTRATIVE QUOTATIONS FROM STALIN

The Russian Marxists have long had their theory of the nation. According to this theory, a nation is a historically constituted, stable community of people, formed on the basis of the common possession of four principal characteristics, namely: a common language, a common territory, a common economic life, and a common psychological make-up manifested in common specific features of national culture.

It would be incorrect to think that after the defeat of world imperialism national differences will be abolished and national languages will die away immediately, at one stroke, by decree from above, so to speak. . . .

Only . . . when the world socialist system of economy becomes sufficiently consolidated and socialism becomes part and parcel of the life of the peoples . . . national differences and languages will begin to die away and make room for a world language, common to all nations.

Such, in my opinion, is the approximate picture of the future of nations, a picture of the development of the nations along the path to their merging in the future.

Source: From J. V. Stalin, "The National Question and Leninism." In *Works,* vol. 1 (Moscow: Foreign Languages Publishing House, 1954), pp. 348, 362, and 364.

Capitalist encirclement means that here is one country, the Soviet Union, which has established the socialist order on its own territory and besides this there are many countries, bourgeois countries, which continue to carry on a capitalist mode of life and which surround the Soviet Union, waiting for an opportunity to attack it, break it, or at any rate to undermine its power and weaken it.

It should be remembered and never forgotten that as long as capitalist encirclement exists there will be wreckers, diversionists, spies, terrorists, sent behind the frontiers of the Soviet Union by the intelligence services of foreign states.

Source: From J. V. Stalin, "Report by Joseph Stalin, General Secretary, to the Plenary Session of the Central Committee of the Communist Party of the Soviet Union," March 3, 1937. In *Mastering Bolshevism* (New York: Workers Library Publishers, 1937), pp. 11 and 26.

Stalin recognized the need to be flexible given changing circumstances. He was even more willing than Lenin to modify doctrine to fit changing conditions. During World War II, for example, the United States and the USSR faced a common enemy, Germany, and in an effort to appease its allies, the USSR dissolved the Comintern in 1943.

THE RELATIONSHIP BETWEEN LENINISM AND STALINISM

It was under Stalin that the practice of communism in the USSR came to be equated with **totalitarianism**, where the state dominated every aspect of life.

Soviet citizens were limited in their ability to travel outside the USSR and they were restricted from receiving uncensored information about life outside the borders of their country. The Communist Party and its related organizational and administrative branches penetrated most aspects of life, from the workplace to the neighborhood. Those who dared to speak out against the regime were imprisoned or repressed through loss of jobs or denial of access to valued goods such as educational opportunities. Stalin's purges of the 1930s, whereby any person suspected of opposition was arrested and millions were executed, created an even more negative impression of communism throughout the Western world. Communism had already been classified as treasonous in the West, as it called for the overthrow of established governments; now it was also seen as brutal, repressive, and inhumane.

A question has been raised among scholars as to whether the totalitarian system that emerged under Stalin was an inevitable result of the 1917 Revolution and of the patterns of behavior that were established under Lenin as the leader of the Bolsheviks, or whether Stalin should be held personally responsible for the emergence of totalitarianism in the Soviet Union. Two contradictory answers have been offered to this question; the first represents the "continuity" argument. According to this argument, Leninism and Stalinism should be judged equally harshly. Representative of this position is what Leszek Kolakowski wrote: "Many observers, including the present author, believe that the Soviet system as it developed under Stalin was a continuation of Leninism, and that the state founded on Lenin's political and ideological principles could only have maintained itself in Stalinist form" (Kolakowski 1978, 2). The second answer represents the "discontinuity" argument, which judges Leninism less harshly than Stalinism.

Under the continuity argument, Lenin's distrust of the revolutionary potential of the proletariat and his Bolshevik elitism are said to have led directly to the dictatorship of Stalin. This thesis states that Marxism, which argued that "the emancipation of the working class is the task of the working class itself," had already been altered by Lenin, who believed that the proletariat needed the leadership of professional revolutionaries in order to emancipate them. The discontinuity argument, in contrast, points out that Lenin had written that "the proletarian state will begin to wither away immediately after its victory" (Lenin 1916/1932, 25). Thus, Lenin would have been opposed to the extension of state power carried out under Stalin after the revolution.

According to the continuity argument, Lenin fashioned the organizational principle of democratic centralism, which prohibited factionalism and opposition once a decision had been made, thus laying the groundwork for Stalin's later ruthless elimination of essentially all opposition. Conversely, the discontinuity argument stated that genuine democracy did exist within the Bolshevik Party when led by Lenin. Under Lenin, party decision making did include consultation and, although he usually got his way, this occurred because of his ability to persuade and guide rather than because of Lenin's complete control. Stalin, in contrast, replaced the rule of the Communist Party with his own personal rule. Only party members personally loyal to Stalin survived the 1936–1939 purges. The terror that engulfed the Soviet Union under Stalin during the 1930s, according to the continuity argument, had its roots in the repression of the Civil War period. The main instruments of terror—the secret police, labor camps, and show trials—were in place before Lenin's death.

At the Tenth Party Congress, which introduced the New Economic Policy, Lenin proposed a ban on factions, destroying the remaining democracy within the party and increasing the climate of repression. Factional opposition was manifested by the Left Communists at the beginning of 1918, then the Democratic Centralists in 1919 and the Workers' Opposition in 1920–1921.* The continuity thesis points out that these oppositional tendencies were defeated one by one and finally eliminated in 1921 while Lenin was still at the helm. This means that the democratic foundations of the proletarian revolution in Russia were lost early on, during the period between 1918 and 1921, not late in the 1920s when Stalin was struggling for control of the party in the aftermath of Lenin's death. ·

According to the discontinuity thesis, the actual existence of the Workers' Opposition in 1921 provides evidence that the system of democratic centralism was characterized by internal debate under Lenin. The ban on factions was seen as a temporary measure adopted in the midst of Civil War and in anticipation of the unpopularity of NEP. Lenin's consent to the banning of factions was qualified, for he spoke against an amendment to ban elections according to political platforms. Factions only disappeared under Stalin when the old Bolsheviks were executed and terror was launched on a wide scale.[3] The discontinuity thesis states that the numbers purged during Stalin's terror were so much greater than under Lenin that the two are beyond comparison.

The final question raised in the continuity–discontinuity debate has to do with whether Lenin actually endorsed and supported Stalin as his chosen successor to lead the Soviet Union. The continuity thesis points to the fact that Stalin was appointed to the position of general secretary of the Communist Party in 1922 while Lenin was still healthy and the undisputed leader of the Bolsheviks. The discontinuity thesis, in contrast, argues that at the time of Stalin's appointment, the position of general secretary did not have much power. Stalin transformed the position himself and used it to appoint his own loyal followers to positions of leadership within the Communist Party. The

---

*The Workers' Opposition denounced the increasing bureaucratization of the state and of the party, as well as the growing separation of the party from the workers. The Workers' Opposition demanded that management of production and of the economy be entrusted to "workers' collectives" in the factories. Lenin, however, determined that the management of production should be in the hands of individual administrators, bourgeois "specialists," or workers selected for their "character and capacity" under the control of the party (Alexandra Kollontai, "The Workers Opposition." In *Pravda* January 25, 1921—see http://www. marxists.org/archive/kollontai/works/1921/workers-opposition/index.htm).

discontinuity thesis also points to *The Testament* written by Lenin just before his death, which severely criticized Stalin and his leadership style. The Twelfth Congress of the Communist Party was scheduled for April 1923 at which Lenin intended to remove Stalin as general secretary; however, Lenin had a stroke in March, so his ability to influence the course of events had come to an end.

Other arguments that serve to remove blame for the development of totalitarianism in the Soviet Union from Lenin are the legacy of Tsarism, which provided an authoritarian governing tradition from which Stalinism arguably emerged, and the disastrous social conditions that prevailed following the revolution, which required strong leadership. The 1917 Revolution took place in a backward country that found itself isolated from the rest of Europe. Much of the infrastructure of Russia had been shattered by World War I and by the Civil War that followed. From 1917 through the Civil War period, Russian workers experienced extreme deprivation while supplying the manpower to defeat the White armies. Thus, even though there were links between Leninism and Stalinism, the discontinuity thesis states that Lenin cannot be held accountable for the emergence of Stalinism. Although Lenin's own dictatorial tendencies point toward Stalin's rule, other conditions and factors contributed significantly to the cult of personality that emerged under Stalin.

THE PHILOSOPHICAL LEANINGS OF KHRUSHCHEV AND BREZHNEV

By the time that Stalin died in March 1953, the main contours of Soviet ideology were firmly in place. The doctrine of communism, based on foundational principles of Marxism and adapted and interpreted by Lenin and Stalin, was steadfastly held, mostly unquestioned, and remained the "creed" of the Soviet Union until the leading and guiding role of the Communist Party itself was officially challenged during the Gorbachev era. Although the most rigid and totalitarian characteristics of communism were relaxed under Soviet leaders Khrushchev and Brezhnev, the basic tenants of the ideology were changed little until the late 1980s.

Stalin's successor as leader of the USSR was Nikita Khrushchev, who had joined the Communist Party in 1918, fought in the Civil War, and rose rapidly through the ranks to become general secretary of the Communist Party of the Soviet Union (CPSU) in 1953. From the perspective of developing Soviet ideology, Khrushchev is most famous for his speech at the Twentieth Congress of the Communist Party held in 1956, where he denounced the methods of Stalin and called for a return to the principles of Lenin. With this speech, Khrushchev launched a full-scale campaign against the **cult of personality**—a code phrase for criticizing the excesses and brutality of Stalin's rule. By disavowing the cult of personality, Khrushchev was saying that the leader of the Communist Party need not be worshipped and need not act as a tyrant. After 1956, the Soviet Union entered a period of de-Stalinization during which Stalin's ruthless tactics and his totalitarian system were repudiated.

Khrushchev also declared the end of capitalist encirclement of the Soviet Union. The end of encirclement was the result of the rise of the world socialist system and the enhanced position of the Soviet Union as a great power. As a reflection of the Soviet Union's new international stature, Khrushchev advanced a doctrine of **peaceful coexistence** with Western nations. Such coexistence was to be based on the avoidance of nuclear war while continuing the uncompromising ideological and economic competition between communist and capitalist states.

Peaceful coexistence rejected war as a means of solving controversial issues among countries with differing social systems, but it did not mean a reconciliation of the socialist and bourgeois ideologies. On the contrary, it implied an intensification of the struggle of the working class of all the communist parties for the triumph of socialist ideas.[4] As Khrushchev explained at the Twenty-First Party Congress in 1959, the economic front was "the main field in which the peaceful competition of socialism and capitalism is taking place."[5] Strengthening of the domestic economy was intended to give the Soviet Union "a decisive advantage in the international alignment of forces."[6]

Why did the leadership of the CPSU opt for a policy of peaceful coexistence? The Soviet leadership realized that a nuclear or general war would end in the destruction of both camps. Khrushchev argued that because the balance of world forces had shifted more favorably toward the socialist camp, a modification of Lenin's thesis was in order. The noninevitability of war was directly related to the growing strength of the socialist camp under the leadership of the Soviet Union. By the time of the 1959 Twenty-First Party Congress, Khrushchev boasted that "[c]apitalist encirclement of our country no longer exists."[7]

Peaceful coexistence did not mean the renunciation of the use of all force and violence. The Soviet Union still maintained its vast nuclear arsenal. The leadership also continued to support "just wars of national liberation." Khrushchev saw it as the duty of the Soviet Union "to support the sacred struggle of the oppressed peoples and their just anti-imperialist wars of liberation."[8] Wars of liberation would be waged either to destroy the remnants of colonialism, to establish communist regimes, or to assist regimes more vulnerable to communist influences.

Khrushchev's position on peaceful coexistence can be summarized by these three points: (1) the world is divided into two eternally antagonistic systems that are bound to try to dominate one another; (2) communism will prevail in the end; and (3) in this struggle, all methods are permissible except those that involve a risk of general nuclear war.[9]

The ideology of the Soviet Union was also influenced by the decision made in 1956 to invade Hungary. Khrushchev's Twentieth Party Congress speech opened the door to a critical evaluation not only of Stalin but also of the entire Soviet model of development. Criticism of the Soviet Union emerged most vocally in Poland and Hungary. As protests grew, demonstrators demanded the replacement of Hungary's prime minister. When demonstrators in Magyarovar, Hungary, demanded that a red star—a symbol of the Soviet occupation—be removed from police headquarters, the police responded with gunfire, killing eighty people. The crowd then went to a nearby army barracks to get weapons and took over the police headquarters. The Hungarian uprising was defeated by the intervention of Soviet tanks in November 1956. Brezhnev, as Khrushchev's successor, reaffirmed the unwillingness of the Soviet Union to tolerate any challenge to its leadership of the international Communist movement by also invading Czechoslovakia in 1968.

Leonid Brezhnev, born in 1906, joined the Komsomol (the Communist Youth Organization) in 1923 and the Communist Party (CPSU) in 1931. During World War II, Brezhnev served as a political commissar and after the war became head of the Communist Party organization in the Soviet republic of Moldavia. When Stalin died, Khrushchev sent Brezhnev to another republic, Kazakhstan. After Brezhnev and other members of the Politburo ousted Khrushchev, Brezhnev ultimately became general secretary of the CPSU and chairman of the Supreme Soviet.

In terms of ideological contributions, Brezhnev is most well known for the **Brezhnev Doctrine** and for **détente**. The Brezhnev Doctrine emerged as the rationale for the 1968 Soviet invasion of Czechoslovakia. Brezhnev declared that when a threat to the cause of socialism arises (in any communist country), that threat can be considered to be a danger of general concern to all socialist countries. Thus, Brezhnev asserted that Soviet forces could cross the border into any country to bolster a threatened socialist regime. Czechoslovakia was perceived to be a constituent part of the Soviet realm, and therefore a threat to the sociopolitical system of an Eastern European satellite country brought forth the same response as an attack on the Soviet Union itself.

Communist political parties in countries such as France, Spain, and Italy, however, began to seriously question the leading and guiding role of the Soviet Union. The Italian Communist Party, for example, had supported the repression of the Hungarian uprising in 1956, but it condemned the 1968 Soviet invasion of Czechoslovakia. Many communist parties in Western Europe abandoned deference to the Soviet Union under the banner of **Euro-Communism**. A statement by Frenchman Jean Ellenstein represents the Euro-Communist ideology:

> Contrary to the Leninist conception of revolution, revolution in the West European countries, and especially in France, can only be peaceful, democratic, legal and gradual. . . . It will consist of a series of reforms which will modify economic conditions, social relations and transform people's consciousness—a cultural revolution, French-style.[10]

Partly in reaction to the very negative response of the West to the 1968 invasion of Czechoslovakia, Brezhnev came to support the concept of détente, which referred to a relaxation of tensions between the Soviet Union and Western countries. The Nuclear Nonproliferation Treaty went into effect in 1970, and the United States and the Soviet Union began the Strategic Arms Limitation Talks in 1971. At a Moscow summit meeting of May 1972, Brezhnev and President Richard M. Nixon signed the Anti-Ballistic Missile Treaty. Another important result of détente was the signing of the 1975 Helsinki Accords, which bound the signatories to respect basic principles of human rights. But even during détente, significant unease remained between the United States and the Soviet Union.

As the Brezhnev era came to a close, evidence emerged that Soviet leaders' perceptions of their role in the world system had changed dramatically. In 1980, a wave of strikes swept over Poland; yet, in this instance, Brezhnev and the Soviet leadership decided not to invade. Thus, ideological commitments gave way to the realities of the time and the Brezhnev Doctrine expired as a main tenet of Moscow's foreign policy.

Still, a formalized adherence to ideological principles remained central to the Soviet system. The centrality of communism was continually reaffirmed by the attention given to the ideology in the speeches of Soviet leaders, by the emphasis put on ideological training within the Communist Party and throughout society, and by the time devoted to elaborating the nuances of any changes in this ideology. Marxist-Leninist ideology underwent modifications as successive Soviet leaders manipulated it for their own purposes, but the basic core ideas remained relatively constant.

COMMUNISM IN THE WORLD SYSTEM

At the height of their power, from the mid-1970s through the early 1980s, communist systems were located in all sectors of the globe. Communism enveloped the largest country in the world geographically, the USSR, and also the country with the largest population, the People's Republic of China, together with the Republic of Cuba, the Socialist Republic of Vietnam, the People's Democratic Republic of Laos, the People's Republic of Kampuchea, and the Mongolian People's Republic. Communism covered most of Eastern Europe, including Albania, Yugoslavia, Bulgaria, Romania, Poland, East Germany (the German Democratic Republic), Hungary, and Czechoslovakia. These were the states that officially professed a commitment to Marxist policies and had close relations with the Soviet Union. During the 1980s, the policies of several other countries, even though unstable, also were guided to various degrees by Marxism and by the powerful influence of the Soviet Union. These included Afghanistan, Angola, Congo, Mozambique, Ethiopia, Madagascar, and the People's Democratic Republic of Yemen. Liberation forces, which had received support from the Soviet Union, briefly ruled another group of countries, including Sandinista-dominated Nicaragua and Grenada until U.S. military forces invaded in 1983.

Adding all these "communist" countries together, they accounted for about one-third of the world's population and about 40 percent of the world's industrial production. With regard to origin, Communist parties came to power in these countries through three different methods.[11] The first method by which Communist parties came to power was primarily through independent internal revolutionary movements. This category contains the USSR, China, Albania, Yugoslavia, Cuba, and Vietnam. Ho Chi Minh of Vietnam and Fidel Castro of Cuba, as leaders of revolutionary movements, were both intent on ending the exploitation of their countries by imperialist powers, and they were able to over-throw the existing rulers without the direct involvement of Soviet military forces. Likewise, Mao Zedong of China led a huge and powerful army that defeated Chiang Kai-shek with extremely limited support and assistance from the Soviet Union. In the case of Yugoslavia, Tito led both the Communist Party and an 800,000-strong partisan army. Indeed, because of Tito's "independence" from the Stalinist line, the Cominform expelled the Yugoslav Communist Party in 1948.

As a second method, invading forces imposed communist governments in occupied countries. This category includes the Eastern European countries of Romania, Poland, and East Germany, plus Mongolia and North Korea. With this second group, Soviet forces installed a coalition government in the occupied country and later transformed the government into one dominated by a Communist Party. Most of these impositions of communist rule occurred at the end of World War II.

The third category represents a mixture of the previous two patterns, where Communist parties came to power as a result of both the use of outside force and an internal movement. Bulgaria, Hungary, and Czechoslovakia, for exam-ple, had internal revolutionary movements, but it is unlikely that they would have been able to seize the reins of power had not the countries been occupied by Soviet forces at the end of World War II. The Communist parties that took over in Laos and Cambodia in 1975 did so with Vietnamese assistance.

As these cases demonstrate, communist takeovers tended to occur in the wake of either an international or a civil war. The wars created the instability that provided the conditions for revolutionary change.* In all cases, involve-ment in a war, corruption and inefficiency within government, or economic decline weakened the regimes that preceded the takeovers. As the governments lost the confidence of the people, the revolutionary ideology of Marxism held a powerful appeal. Even with a weakened government, however, to overthrow an

---

*A Marxist government was elected in the 1970s in Chile, but this government of Salvador Allende was overthrown by military leaders with the covert assistance of the United States.

established system of rule required extremely capable leadership and people who were willing to employ the means necessary to seize power. Tightly organized and highly disciplined revolutionary organizations were created and used force to take control of the governments. The use of force and the suppression of opposition in turn became a characteristic of most all governments led by a Communist Party. In this context, we also must note that Communist parties competed successfully within electoral democracies such as Italy, France, and Spain. The ideology of communism appealed not only to the leaders of the Soviet Union, but also to those in different parts of world and in countries with different levels of economic development.

THE IDEOLOGICAL FUNCTIONS OF COMMUNISM

Although the core ideas remained constant, the functions of ideology within the Soviet system and its satellite countries changed over a seventy-year period. Communism as it was first employed under Lenin was an ideology of revolution that called for the overthrow of the Tsarist system. Under Khrushchev, communism served as blueprint for constructing a new Soviet society. Under Brezhnev, communism became an ideology of conservatism—a philosophy that legitimated the status quo. In all eras, it served as a tool for persuasion and as a means for justifying the Soviet system and the policy decisions made by the leadership. Emphasis on the *scientific* nature of Marxism lent credence to the idea that socialism would inevitably triumph over capitalism.

Communist ideology served other purposes as well within the Soviet system: It provided a set of concepts for understanding and interpreting the world and a discourse of communication between the elites and the great masses of people. Communist ideology also provided the justification for the sacrifices that the citizens were to make to strengthen and build the Soviet Union. It rationalized and legitimated pronouncements by the Communist Party arguing that Soviet society was the best possible one.

The ideology was important in the socialization process. Like some religions, communist ideology taught people to accept their position and their status in society by promising a better life ahead. It kept alive memories of a glorious past and promised liberation in the future. It encouraged discipline, self-sacrifice, and conformity—all of which were important for training and educating future civil servants.

The ideological principles of Marxism-Leninism had significant implications for the political system. They created a justification for the refusal to share power, for the repression of all other political parties, for forced collectivization and industrialization, and for the support of revolutionary war. Belief in the ideology was reinforced by the success of the Soviet Union in achieving rapid industrialization, developing nuclear weapons, taking a lead in space exploration, and challenging the United States within the international system. The victory of the Soviet Union during World War II also provided proof of the correctness of the communist ideology among those who decided to accept it. It is in the context of this ideological heritage that the history of Russia and the Soviet Union, as presented in the next chapter, can best be understood.

Key Terms

Anarchists
The base and superstructure
Bolsheviks
Bourgeoisie
Brezhnev Doctrine
Capitalist encirclement
Class struggle
Comintern
Communism
Cult of personality
Democratic centralism
Détente
Dictatorship of the proletariat
Economic determinism
Euro-Communism

Historical stage
Ideology
Law of dialectics
Marxism
Mensheviks
Narodniki
New Economic Policy (NEP)
Partiinost
Peaceful coexistence
Proletariat
Revisionists
Socialism
The State
Surplus value
Totalitarianism

Critical Thinking Questions

1. What were some of the basic principles of Marxism as put forward by Karl Marx and Friedrich Engels?

2. What basic premises about human nature underlay Marx and Engels's philosophy? Do you think that communism as envisioned by Marx and Engels could work?

3. Given that Russia did not have the classic characteristics that Marxists predicted would lead to a socialist revolution, which special conditions (according to Lenin) would allow the revolution to succeed in Russia?

4. What were the two factions into which the Russian Social Democratic Labor Party split in 1903? What were the philosophical differences that led to the split?

5. What contributions were made by Lenin to Marxist philosophy? What accounts for the adjustments that Lenin made to Marxism? How true do you believe Lenin was to the core ideas of Marx and Engels?

6. How did Khrushchev's orientation toward the political world differ from Stalin's?

7. What are some of the positive aspects of socialist philosophy that may provide a useful approach for thinking about and organizing society and politics?

Suggested Reading

Luxemburg, Rosa, and Bertram D. Wolfe. *The Russian Revolution, and Leninism or Marxism?* (Ann Arbor Paperbacks for the Study of Communism and Marxism). Westport, Conn.: Greenwood Press reprint, 1981.

Pipes, Richard. *Communism: A History (Modern Library Chronicles)*. New York: Modern Library, 2001.

Robinson, Neil. *Ideology and the Collapse of the Soviet System: A Critical History of Soviet Ideological Discourse (Studies of Communism in Transition)*. Cheltenham, U.K.: Edward Elgar Publishing, 1995.

Tucker, Robert, ed. *The Marx-Engels Reader*. New York: W. W. Norton, 1972.

White, Stephen. *Communism and Its Collapse (Making of the Contemporary World)*. New York: Routledge, 2001.

Websites of Interest

Encyclopedia of Marxism:
   http://history1900s.about.com/gi/dynamic/offsite.htm?
   site=http%3A%2F%2Fwww. marxists.org%2Fglossary%2Findex.htm

The Manifesto of the Communist Party by Karl Marx and Friedrich Engels:
   http://history1900s.about.com/gi/dynamic/offsite.htm?site=http%3A%2F%2F
   www. anu.edu.au%2Fpolsci%2Fmarx%2Fclassics%2Fmanifesto.html

Marxists Internet Archive:
   http://history1900s.about.com/gi/dynamic/offsite.htm?
   site=http%3A%2F%2Fwww. marxists.org%2F

Socialism: Internet Modern History Sourcebook:
   http://www. fordham.edu/halsall/mod/modsbook33.html

CHAPTER 3

The Legacy of the Past

THE RUSSIAN EMPIRE evolved from a territory located in East-Central Europe. Beginning in the ninth century, this territory of Eastern Slavic* people had its center of administration in Kiev (now the capital of Ukraine). Located on the Dnieper River, which served as part of a major trade route from the Baltic Sea to the Black Sea, Kiev grew by the eleventh century to be the largest city in Eastern Europe. Princes within **Kievan Rus** fought among themselves, and by the second half of the twelfth century, political power had shifted to principalities farther to the northeast, including the principalities of Vladimir-Suzdal' and Novgorod. Kievan Rus was conquered between 1223 and 1242 by an empire of Mongols and Tatars (Turks) shaped by Genghis Khan. During this period of subjugation to the Tatars, the Eastern Slavic people became isolated from developments in Europe but were nonetheless able to retain their Orthodox Christian traditions.†

Although under Mongol rule, the Principality of Moscow flourished and began to expand beginning around 1340. **Muscovy** princes were assigned the role of tax collectors for the Tatars and eventually grew in strength to the point where they were able to challenge the rule of the Tatars. In 1380, Muscovite Prince Dmitry Donskoy refused to pay the taxes as demanded by the Tatars. Thereafter the Muscovite state expanded rapidly in territorial size, in wealth, and in military power. Ivan III (the Great) conquered Novgorod in 1478 and Tver in 1485. By 1533, all the previous Kievan Rus territory, except the regions

*Slavic refers to people who speak a Slavonic language. The most numerous ethnic and linguistic group in Europe, Slavic people live primarily in East and Central Europe and can be divided into East Slavs (Russians, Ukrainians, and Byelorussians), West Slavs (Poles, Czechs, Sorbs, and Slovaks), and South Slavs (Bulgarians, Croats, Serbs, Bosniaks, Macedonians, and Slovenians).
†In 989, Prince Vladimir of Kievan Rus converted to Orthodox Christianity, thus recognizing the supremacy of the Patriarch of Constantinople.

that were part of the Grand Duchy of Lithuania, was subject to rule by the grand princes of Muscovy.* In 1552, Ivan IV (the Terrible) ended the formal subordination of the Russian princes to the Tatars when he took control of Kazan, one of the major regional centers of the Tatar empire. By 1554, Russian rule was extended to where the Volga River enters the Caspian Sea.

Ivan the Terrible's efforts to reduce the power of the nobility and his decades-long wars against Poland, Lithuania, Sweden, and Denmark led to a period of decline—the Time of Troubles (1598–1613). Several factions of nobility, called the Boyars, competed for the throne. The Muscovite state was so weakened during this period that a Polish army penetrated deep into the region. A new dynasty was established in 1613 when Mikhail Romanov was crowned tsar. Through peace treaties with Sweden (1617) and Poland (1634) stability was achieved.

By the middle of the seventeenth century, Romanov tsars had captured the territory of Siberia (across the Ural Mountains to the Pacific Ocean), which was rich in gold and furs. During the second half of the seventeenth century, the tsars began efforts to expand their rule westward. Eastern Ukraine (east of the Dnieper River) was incorporated in 1654 and Kiev in 1667. Exposure to the West increased as international trade grew and more foreigners came to Muscovy.

Under Peter the Great (1689–1725), Muscovy became more Western-oriented and emerged as a major European power. In 1709, the armies of Peter defeated those of Sweden's King Charles XII. In celebration, Peter assumed the title of emperor as well as tsar, and Muscovy officially became the Russian Empire in 1721. Peter the Great also expanded Russian control southward into the Caucasus region. He founded St. Petersburg in 1703 and made it the new capital of the Russian Empire, replacing Moscow.†

Peter the Great is often credited with an effort to modernize Russia and bring in Western ideas. He built a Russian navy, reorganized the army according to European models, and brought Western discoveries and methods of administration to Russia. Peter increased the revenues of the state treasury through heavy taxation, required Western-style education for all male nobles, and developed metallurgical and textile industries.

Russia allied with Austria against the Ottoman Empire in 1726. In 1762, however, Peter III, a grandson of Peter the Great, allied with Prussia's Emperor Frederick the Great. Peter III's wife Catherine, who was of German ancestry, ousted her husband, had him murdered, and became Empress of Russia. The Russian Empire expanded significantly under the reign of Catherine the Great (Catherine II). In 1783, she annexed Crimea; thereafter, Imperial Russia built a naval base at Sevastopol and founded a new port at Odessa (both on the Black

---

*Ivan III was the first Muscovite ruler to use the titles of tsar and "Ruler of All Rus." *Tsar* is an alternate spelling of *czar*, meaning emperor. In 1589, the Metropolitan of Moscow assumed the title of Patriarch of All the Russians.

†St. Petersburg has also been called Petrograd and Leningrad at different points in its history. St. Petersburg was the capital of the Russian Empire from 1713 to 1917. Moscow became the capital of the Soviet government in 1918.

Sea). Catherine II participated in the three successive partitions of Poland (1772, 1793, and 1795), thereby adding Lithuania, the rest of Latvia, Belarus, and a large part of Western Ukraine to the Russian Empire. Under Catherine the Great, Russia grew even stronger militarily, politically, and diplomatically. Russia's elite class became culturally more like the elites of Central and West European countries.

Catherine II died in 1796 and her son Paul succeeded her. During his reign, the Russian American Company, a semigovernmental firm of the tsars, gained control of the Pacific coastal areas south of Alaska in North America. In 1812, the company established Fort Ross just seventy miles north of San Francisco. With continued settlement of California by U.S. citizens, the Russians abandoned Fort Ross in 1841. The Russians decided to sell Alaska and the Aleutian Islands to the United States in 1867 for $7.2 million when the territory became an economic liability.

In 1801, Paul was assassinated and a new tsar, Alexander I, a grandson of Catherine the Great, came to the throne. Alexander became Napoleon's ally and was able to acquire Finland from Sweden in 1809 and Bessarabia from Turkey in 1812. Napoleon, however, turned against Russia and invaded in June 1812; he actually occupied Moscow but was forced to retreat when his army was endangered by cold and hunger. After Russia and its allies defeated Napoleon, Alexander was heralded as a liberator, and he participated in the redrawing of the map of Europe at the Congress of Vienna in 1815, thereby acquiring more of Poland. During the first half of the nineteenth century, Russia absorbed into its empire the Moldavians, Georgians, and Armenians and incorporated substantial Muslim territories in the Caucasus region, including Azerbaijan.

Russia's defeat in the Crimean War of 1853–1856, however, demonstrated the challenges of defending such a far-flung empire. British and French forces landed in Crimea with the goal of winning control of the Russian naval base at Sevastopol. Soldiers from throughout the Russian Empire were brought to Crimea to defend the base, but after a year of fighting, Sevastopol was conquered. Having lost control of its major Black Sea port, Russia's imperial ambitions began to be questioned. Still, during the 1860s, Russia conquered much of Central Asia. Parts of Afghanistan were annexed in 1889 and 1895. The Russians also pushed into the Far East and seized areas in northeastern China.

The Russo-Japanese War of 1904–1905 halted Russia's territorial advancement. Russia was forced to abandon significant territory in the east—notably southern Sakhalin and the Kuril Islands—after its defeat by the Japanese. When Russia pulled out of World War I after the Revolution of 1917, the Russian Empire shrank further with the loss of Poland, Finland, Estonia, Latvia, Lithuania, and Bessarabia. During World War II, however, the Soviet Union retook the Baltic States, Bessarabia, and other territories, including Kaliningrad. This resulted in a significant surge in both the amount of territory controlled and the size of the Soviet state's population. (See Box 3.1 for a list of significant dates in the growth of the Russian Empire.)

A question raised among historians is what motivated this relentless territorial expansion on the part of Russia's tsars. Although it is often explained in terms of a desire for access to the world's oceans (to acquire ports), the reasons for the drive to expand just as likely include the search for resources (furs, gold, and other sources of wealth), the search for security (the desire to neutralize enemies), and the desire to convert those perceived as "barbarians" to Christianity. Arguably weak neighbors who were unable to defend themselves invited aggression. The open plains and lack of natural frontiers also facilitated the expansion. Finally, this territorial acquisition can be attributed to individual ambitions. Ivan III, Ivan IV, Peter I, and Catherine II sought to increase their personal power and prestige through territorial expansion, while governor generals in the empire's peripheral regions pursued military victories for the purpose of achieving decorations and recognition.

BOX 3.1: THE RISE AND FALL OF THE RUSSIAN EMPIRE IN THE CONTEXT OF WORLD HISTORY

1237–1242	Kievan Rus is conquered by Mongols (Tatars).
1462–1505	Ivan (III) the Great rules Muscovy (Russia).
1492	Columbus becomes the first European to encounter the Caribbean Islands.
1547–1584	Ivan (IV) the Terrible rules Muscovy.
1552	Ivan the Terrible captures Kazan and ends subjugation to the Tatars.
1613	Mikhail Romanov becomes tsar, beginning the Romanov dynasty in Muscovy.
1620	Pilgrims, after a three-month voyage on the *Mayflower*, land at Plymouth Rock.
1689	In England, the Bill of Rights is accepted by William and Mary, ensuring political supremacy of parliament.
1689–1725	Peter (I) the Great rules Russia.
1762–1796	Catherine (II) the Great rules Russia.
1776	The U.S. Declaration of Independence is written.
1789–1794	The French Revolution abolishes the monarchy and establishes the First French Republic.
1801–1825	Alexander I rules Russia.
1803	The United States negotiates Louisiana Purchase from France for $15 million, thereby doubling its domain.
1825	Decembrist Revolt against Tsarism.
1825–1855	Nicholas I rules Russia.

1836	The Mexicans attack the Alamo; Texas gains independence from Mexico.
1848	The *Communist Manifesto* is published by Karl Marx and Friedrich Engels.
1853–1856	The Crimean War.
1855–1881	Alexander II rules Russia.
1861	The U.S. Civil War begins. Alexander II's Act of Emancipation frees the Russian serfs.
1864	The International (the first international organization of socialist workers) is established by Marx and others.
1864–1885	Russian tsars conquer Muslim areas of Central Asia.
1867	Russia sells Alaska to the United States.
1870	Vladimir Ilyich Ulyanov (Lenin) is born.
1881	Alexander II of Russia is killed by a terrorist bomb.
1881–1894	Alexander III rules Russia.
1882	The Triple Alliance between Germany, Austria-Hungary, and Italy is signed. Plekhanov publishes the first pamphlet introducing Marxist socialism to Russia.
1894–1917	Nicholas II rules Russia.
1904–1905	The Russo-Japanese War.
1905	On Bloody Sunday, Russian workers carrying a petition to Nicholas II are cut down by the tsar's troops. Organizations of workers (soviets) are established in Russia. Nicholas II signs the October Manifesto, which promises reform.
1906	First Russian Duma meets.
1907	A second Russian Duma is elected and dissolved; a third Duma is elected.
1911	The Manchu dynasty in China is overthrown.
1914	World War I begins; Germany declares war against Russia.

The 1917 Russian Revolution

February 25	A general strike occurs in Petrograd.
February 26	The Duma is dissolved by Russian Tsar Nicholas II.
March 2	Nicholas II abdicates the throne in favor of Grand Duke Mikhail; a Provisional Government is formed by deputies of the Duma.
March 3	Grand Duke Mikhail abdicates and transfers power to the Provisional Government under Prince Lvov.
March 6	The Provisional Government declares amnesty for political prisoners.
April 3	Lenin, Zinoviev, and other Bolsheviks arrive from Switzerland.
April 4	Lenin delivers his April Theses outlining his policy of proletarian revolution.
May 4	Trotsky arrives from America, seconding the policies of Lenin.

(*Continued*)

BOX 3.1: THE RISE AND FALL OF THE RUSSIAN EMPIRE IN THE CONTEXT OF WORLD HISTORY—Cont'd

1917

June 3	First All-Russian Congress of Soviets meets.
July 3–5	The "July Days" uprising against the Provisional Government is followed by an arrest of Bolsheviks in Petrograd. Prince Lvov resigns; Kerensky becomes premier.
November	The October Revolution in Russia (October 25–November 7).
1918	Russian revolutionaries execute the former tsar and his family. The Russian Civil War begins between Reds (Bolsheviks) and Whites (anti-Bolsheviks). Allied troops (U.S., British, and French) land on Russian soil in March but leave in 1919.
1919	Third International (Comintern) establishes Soviet control over international Communist movements.

Note: Russian dates are given according to the old (Julian) calendar. Add 13 days to find the date according to the (Gregorian) calendar that is now international. From Leon Trotsky's "The History of the Russian Revolution"—http://www.marxists.org/archive/trotsky/works/1930-hrr/u.htm

INHERITANCES FROM TSARISM

A major legacy associated with Russia's territorial expansion between the fifteenth and the nineteenth centuries was an almost continuous series of wars. The expansion led to the incorporation of an increasing number of non-Russians into the empire. The wars also contributed to severe poverty among the people. Foreign war, actual or threatened, was a major force in Russian national development. The country was organized to prepare for and to sustain war efforts.

Another legacy associated with **Tsarism** was the tradition of the unlimited authority of the ruler. The tsars did not have restrictions on their supremacy as did the monarchs of Europe. One reason why Russian tsars were absolute rulers was because the Russian Orthodox Church was weak and unable to act as a counterweight to their authority. European churches, in contrast, had independent rights and could act as checks on the monarchs. Unlike in Europe, no national representative assembly operated in Russia between 1649 and 1905.

After the death of Alexander I in 1825 and with the ascension to the throne of his brother, Nicholas I, a group of officers refused to swear allegiance to Nicholas, demanding instead a constitution. Nicholas easily suppressed the revolt, which led to increased repression in Russian society. The government exercised censorship and other controls over education, publishing, and all associational activities. The ideas that the people possessed rights against the tsar and that his authority should be limited by a constitution were set aside in the aftermath of the 1825 Decembrist Revolt. In 1833, the guiding principles of "autocracy, Orthodoxy, and nationality" were adopted, and everyone was expected to accept the unlimited authority of the tsar, to abide by the traditions of the Orthodox Church, and to show loyalty to the Russian nation.

The tradition of unrestrained **autocracy** hindered cultural growth in Russia. National strength and the wealth needed to finance the arts were exhausted by continual wars. Russia's relative isolation from the common heritage of Western Europe, the Renaissance, the Reformation, and the French Revolution, created a distinct culture and history. During the nineteenth century, however, Russia experienced its own cultural renaissance, including achievements in literature, art, science, and philosophy. Many of the most famous Russian writers emerged during this period: Aleksandr Pushkin, Nikolay Gogol, Ivan Turgenev, Fyodor Dostoevsky, and Leo Tolstoy—to name just a few. A number of them, however, were imprisoned or exiled under Tsarism.*

Despite cultural achievements, Russia lagged behind the rest of Europe during the nineteenth century in terms of industrial development, agricultural production, adequate banking systems, and technological advances. Its economic development was no match for the transformation the industrial revolution was causing in Western European countries. When Russia did experience a surge in industrial growth during the 1890s, it was driven primarily by the state; government ministries took the initiative in the reorganization of the textile, coal, steel, and petroleum industries.

Agriculture, however, remained in awful straits. Peasants, the majority of the Russian population, were desperately poor. Landlords had complete power over their serfs and could sell or trade them as they chose. The **Emancipation of the Serfs** in 1861 did not lead to peasant ownership of agricultural land. Instead, peasant communes (*mir*) or villages were allocated areas of land collectively and were jointly responsible for redemption payments and taxes. The land designated as communal was only a portion of the former estates, as the nobles retained control over their own separate portions.

When serfdom was abolished in 1861, it was not as a result of pressure from a peasant insurrection but rather by means of an order from the tsar. Afterwards, the standard of living of most peasants actually declined. Because the population of peasants increased dramatically during the latter part of the nineteenth century, individual allotments of land shrank in size. Millions of landless serfs moved to urban areas. When the harvest was poor, famines occurred. Peasant rebellions were brutally suppressed.

---

*The author suggests that the reader consider examining the works of these great writers because each served as a social and/or political critic of his time; see, for example, Nikolay Gogol's *Dead Souls* (1842), Fyodor Dostoevsky's *Crime and Punishment* (1866), and Leo Tolstoy's *Anna Karenina* (1877).

The industrial workers' situation was equally horrible, with long hours, low wages, and dreadful conditions. Housing was inadequate with no plumbing or electricity and disease was rampant. The bourgeoisie also was weak because the state or foreign investors owned most industries.

Alexander II, who had instituted the Emancipation of the Serfs in 1861, also attempted other reforms. Local leaders in counties and in towns were granted greater control over schools, medical affairs, and roads. As a result of judicial reforms in 1864, court procedures were improved and courts were made more efficient. The reforms, however, were not adequate to make the lives of workers and peasants bearable and created more frustration, demands for further change, and ultimately radicalization. Workers, although small in number in comparison with the peasantry, became a more potent political force because they were concentrated in the large cities.

At the same time, the nobility demanded more of a share of governing power. The most significant push for change came from the **intelligentsia**—the new social class that emerged as the sons and daughters of clergy, merchants, nobles, and civil servants received university educations. Leaders of the intelligentsia published newspapers and magazines, which called for both social and political change.

A powerful wave of oppositional activity arose during the early 1870s; notable was a call for elected, representative governments at both local and national levels. The demand for a constitution for Russia was once again expressed. Often, reform movement participants were arrested and/or their publications were censored. These repressive actions by the government contributed to a radicalization of the movement so that, by the middle of the 1870s, revolutionaries began to use terrorism and attempted to kill members of the government.

The culmination of the opposition was the assassination of Tsar Alexander II in the spring of 1881. Alexander III, who took over after his father's death, sought to strengthen government control in all areas where popular dissatisfaction might manifest itself. One of the revolutionaries executed by the government under Alexander III was Alexander Ulyanov, Vladimir Lenin's older brother. Lenin himself was arrested and imprisoned in 1895, then sent into Siberian exile until 1900.

THE 1905 RUSSIAN REVOLUTION AND BEYOND

Nicholas II, the son of Alexander III, ascended to the throne in 1894 after the death of his father. The defeat of the Russian government in the 1904 war with Japan contributed to an unprecedented rise in political opposition. The political activity of the intellectuals took the form of lectures on politics, the organization of societies, and, in some cases, riots on the part of students. Workers, in efforts to improve intolerable working conditions and to increase wages, used strikes as a recourse. The discontent among the peasants found expression in agrarian riots. Disorder spread to the army and soldiers began to revolt in opposition to officers. The period also was characterized by a series of assassinations of government officials.

The mounting discontent culminated in January 22, 1905, when thousands of Russian workers came together in St. Petersburg to appeal directly to the tsar for reforms. Government troops opened fire, killing and wounding hundreds. The day came to be known as Bloody Sunday and is considered to be a turning point in the history of political opposition in Russia. The Bolsheviks and Mensheviks set aside their differences and combined efforts to support workers in their strikes and protests. Organizational activities led to the formation of worker councils called **soviets**. The Soviet of Workers' Deputies, established in St. Petersburg, coordinated the revolutionary activity.

In October 1905, faced with a general strike throughout Russia, Nicholas II conceded constitutional reforms, including universal suffrage, freedom of speech, and the creation of an elected legislative assembly called the **Duma**. The tsar, however, retained full power to initiate legislation, control government, and conduct foreign affairs. The confluence of rebellions, strikes, riots, and mutinies, together with the concessions made by the tsar in his **October Manifesto**, constituted the Russian Revolution of 1905.

Although socialist parties rejected the October Manifesto and strikes went on, the majority of the people did not support the actions of the revolutionaries. The soviets were disbanded and riots were suppressed by force. In keeping with the October Manifesto's commitment, the first elections to the Duma were held in 1906. When the Duma met from May to July 1906, it demanded that the government be held responsible to a democratically elected parliament. The tsar refused to accept this and dissolved the Duma. New elections were held to the Second Duma in 1907, but that Duma was even more radical than the first and was also dissolved by the tsar within just a few months. Before elections were held again, laws were changed to give large landowners preference, so the Third Duma that was elected in late 1907 had a different membership. The majority of the deputies now belonged to parties of the right (conservative parties) and this Duma sat without interruption from 1907 to 1912. Although political terrorism continued (and was ruthlessly suppressed), the Third Duma did manage to institute some reforms; the legal status of peasants was equalized to that of other citizens and the educational system was significantly expanded. The Fourth Duma, elected in 1912, also was dominated by conservatives, but even these deputies evolved over time into oppositional forces.

During this time period, Russia experienced a rapid growth in population, especially in urban areas. Although expansion in cities and in industry was phenomenal, the majority of Russia's population remained occupied by agriculture. According to the Agrarian Reform of 1906, instituted by Peter Stolypin,*

---

*Stolypin became Minister of Internal Affairs in the spring of 1906. He combined this position with Russian Premier (Prime Minister) from July 23, 1906, until his assassination in September 1911.

landholdings in Russia were reorganized such that peasant communes were allowed to dissolve themselves. The goal of the reform was to establish law and order in the countryside by making peasants true owners of land, with the hope that if they owned property, they would respect nobles' estates.

The rapid expansion of the working class also was accompanied by legislation aimed at improving the conditions for the workers. The length of the workday was limited, wages were increased, and accident and health insurance were introduced. Restrictions on labor unions and on labor organizations continued and the tsar's secret police (Okhrana) infiltrated and disrupted independent political organizations. This contributed to the development of illegal revolutionary movements.

THE 1917 REVOLUTIONS

As compared with the late nineteenth century, the population was experiencing improved conditions at the beginning of the twentieth century. It is possible that if World War I had not intervened, progress and reform might have allowed for a peaceful transition to a constitutional regime. But Russia became involved in the devastating war. The ultimate collapse of Tsarism can be tied directly to Russia's involvement in World War I.

The people rose to the conflict with an upsurge of patriotism, but Russia's army was unprepared for the war against Germany; it lacked the capacity to produce modern weapons and to transport troops and supplies to the front. In 1915, 2 million Russian people were killed or wounded, while 1.3 million were taken prisoner. Two million more were killed or wounded and another 350,000 were taken prisoner during 1916. By 1917, Russia had lost a total of 12 million—either killed, wounded, or captured.[1]

Domestically, the government was not strong enough to withstand the strains of war. The deteriorating economic situation and rumors of inefficiency and corruption at the highest levels deepened already-existing public distrust of the regime. The economic strains (skyrocketing inflation and food and fuel shortages) were most heavily felt by the working class and peasants. Protests erupted in St. Petersburg against living conditions and shortages of food. Thousands of workers went on strike and many engaged in confrontations with the police in the streets. Troops were brought in but were unable to quell the disturbances that engulfed the city; a number of the soldiers even joined the insurgency. On February 28, 1917, troops in St. Petersburg loyal to the tsar surrendered. Under pressure from his advisers, Nicholas II abdicated the throne on March 15, 1917.*

In response, members of the Fourth Duma established a temporary government, known as the Provisional Government, which declared an end to Tsarist

---

*Between 1613 and 1917, Russia had been ruled by the Romanov dynasty; Nicholas II, the last Romanov ruler, became tsar in 1894.

oppression and promised democratic elections for a Constituent Assembly. The Constituent Assembly was to decide the future structure and policies of Russia's government. The abdication of the tsar led to the return of thousands of revolutionaries from prisons or from exile abroad; many soon arrived in St. Petersburg or Moscow, where they spread their radical messages among the masses. They found a receptive audience in the dissatisfied and distressed workers and soldiers.

In April 1917, Lenin returned to St. Petersburg from exile in Finland. Immediately, he met with both Bolsheviks and Mensheviks and presented his famous April Thesis. In the very first paragraph, Lenin called for an immediate withdrawal from the war, which he labeled a "predatory imperialist war." He denounced the Provisional Government and called for the transfer of all authority to the Soviet of Workers' Deputies. In his theses, Lenin also called for the nationalization of land (to be put under the control of local soviets) and the creation of a single national bank to be controlled by the deputies. Indeed, between March and late October 1917, two institutions shared political authority in Russia: the Provisional Government and the Petrograd Soviet of Workers' Deputies (led by Leon Trotsky). Lenin rallied the increasing numbers of bitter and disillusioned young workers and soldiers with the slogan "Bread, Land and Peace!"

As the Provisional Government grew increasingly weaker, the army's discipline broke down and soldiers began to desert en masse. Militant workers

Street demonstration on Nevsky Prospekt in Petrograd, July 4, 1917.
akg-images

joined the existing Soviets and formed factory committees to assert their authority at a growing number of workplaces. In elections held in September 1917, the Bolsheviks won majorities in the Soviets in Petrograd, Moscow, and many other cities. In parts of rural Russia, peasants seized estates from land-lords and divided the land among themselves.

Alexander Kerensky, the head of the Provisional Government, tried to work out a political solution to the crisis, but the authority of the Provisional Government was dissolving as German forces moved closer to St. Petersburg. On October 24, the Bolshevik Central Committee adopted Lenin's urgent pro-posal that the party begin organizing to seize power.

Lenin had to work hard to convince the Bolsheviks to seize power from the Provisional Government. In fact, Grigorii Zinoviev and Lev Kamenev registered strong opposition to Lenin's plan. Through relentless persuasion Lenin ulti-mately got his way. No date was set for the seizure of power, however, and it was only when Kerensky ordered that the Military Revolutionary Committee of the Petrograd Soviet be dissolved that Trotsky reacted and took over the govern-ment. On the night of November 7, a coordinated group of armed, revolution-ary soldiers, sailors, and other activists stormed the Winter Palace, where the cabinet of the Provisional Government was meeting. Bolsheviks arrested mem-bers of the government, seized government offices, and assumed control of the Russian state; the Provisional Government had been overthrown.

THE ESTABLISHMENT OF THE SOVIET GOVERNMENT

The rule of the Bolsheviks was institutionalized the next day when the Second All-Russian Congress of Soviets endorsed the seizure of power. The Mensheviks and many Socialist Revolutionaries walked out in protest, while Leftist Socialist Revolutionaries (Left SRs) stayed with the Bolsheviks. The Congress of Soviets cre-ated a cabinet called the **Sovnarkom** (the Council of People's Commissars) com-posed entirely of Bolsheviks, although Left SRs were later granted some of the ministerial positions. The first business of the congress was to pass a decree on peace and a decree on land. The peace decree promised an immediate armistice, and the land decree validated the peasants' seizure and redistribution of land.

Building on their revolutionary ideals, the goal of the Bolsheviks was to establish a democratic and benevolent society characterized by material abun-dance, equality, and brotherhood. The Sovnarkom abolished all civil ranks and social class privileges, and established policies to advance equal rights for women. The right to self-determination of all oppressed nationalities was affirmed. The Bolshevik-led government also took steps to create government control of all banks, institute workers' control of industry, and provide progres-sive health care, education, and housing to all as a matter of entitlement. In January 1918, the separation of church and state was decreed, ending the priv-ileges of the Russian Orthodox Church and establishing freedom of worship for believers of all denominations. (The process of reducing church authority already had been started under the Provisional Government.) Freedom of the press and freedom to assemble were welcomed in political life.

The decisions of the Congress of Soviets on peace and land evoked widespread support for the Bolsheviks. The policies were decisive in assuring their victory in other cities. Although the new government faced limited armed opposition from Kerensky and Generals Alexi Kaledin and Lavr Kornilov, workers and soldiers in Moscow and Petrograd supported the Bolsheviks. The Bolsheviks, who decided to allow the elections for the Constituent Assembly that had been promised by the Provisional Government, won the most votes in the large cities, but in the countryside, the Socialist Revolutionaries won.* When the Constituent Assembly convened on January 5, 1918, the largest number of the deputies were SRs, with the Bolsheviks having the second-largest group of deputies. When the assembly refused to immediately recognize the new Soviet government, Lenin signed a decree dissolving the Constituent Assembly. The doors were bolted and the delegates were prevented from returning for the second day of the session. Lenin argued that power should be in the hands of the Soviets—the governing units designated by the Second All-Russian Congress of Soviets, which were increasingly coming under Bolshevik control.

DEMOCRATIC FAILURES

The ideal of a workers' democratic state that the Bolsheviks attempted to build was overwhelmed by the harsh realities of the times. Lenin, Trotsky, and other leaders of the October Revolution had anticipated an international wave of revolutions, but attempts at socialist uprisings outside Russia were not successful. The Bolsheviks continued to advocate the violent overthrow of capitalist governments and sent agents to Germany, Hungary, and other countries in an effort to foment revolution. These activities, plus the decision to renege on Russia's debts, led to a hostile reaction from the capitalist world. The Soviet Union was isolated as other "workers' revolutions" attempted in Europe failed.

The plan to pull Russia out of World War I also proved more difficult than anticipated. Trotsky had hoped that working-class uprisings in Germany and Austria would soon take the ground out from under Russia's wartime enemies. He therefore played for time, hoping that Russia would not need to withdraw from the war and accept the terms imposed by Imperial Germany. Rather than being undermined, however, the Germans launched a successful military offensive and the terms for peace with Russia became even harsher. Germany demanded that Russia give up the Baltic States (Lithuania, Latvia, and Estonia), Finland, Poland, and West Ukraine. When the Treaty of Brest-Litovsk was signed on March 3, 1918, the Left SRs, who opposed the peace settlement, angrily resigned their

*Lenin had wanted to postpone the elections, but he was outvoted.

government posts. With the Bolsheviks now in complete control of the Council of People's Commissars, the Left SRs openly challenged the Bolsheviks through armed violence. Opponents of the regime fiercely resisted the Bolsheviks and in 1918 they organized assassination attempts against Lenin and members of his government. The Bolsheviks responded by arresting and executing their enemies.

In December 1917, the Cheka (the Russian secret police organization) was created. It replaced the Petrograd Military Revolutionary Committee and was designed to defend the revolution against counterrevolution. The death penalty, initially abolished by the Soviet regime, was reestablished. In addition, restrictions were placed on freedom of the press, and other civil liberties were drastically reduced.

The various groups in Russia who shared the goal of ousting the Bolsheviks organized formations of soldiers, which together were called the White Army. Outside nations imposed a devastating economic blockade on Russia to strangle the Soviet government; they also gave substantial material support to the White armies in an effort to help overthrow the Soviet regime. British and French military forces landed at Murmansk, the Japanese landed at Vladivostok, and the United States also sent troops. Less well organized and without widespread domestic support, however, the various White Army groups were eventually defeated by the Communist Red Army, though the Civil War lasted from 1918 to the fall of 1920.

The period between 1918 and 1921 is called the period of **War Communism**. During this time, the Communists carried out a shift in economic policy that was to have lasting consequences. Threats of economic sabotage by capitalist factory owners hostile to the regime led the government to take over more and more of the economy—much more rapidly than originally intended. The measures adopted were meant to be temporary, but the experiences of those years shaped future conceptions of political authority. Because the ordinary workers who had taken charge of factories were inexperienced as managers, difficulties occurred almost immediately. Strict labor discipline was imposed, workers' control of factories was revoked, and the authority of the manager over the workers was reasserted. Thousands of Tsarist managers were retained in their posts due to the shortage of skilled Bolshevik cadres. Former Tsarist officers also were recruited to provide a leadership corps for the army. The peasants were allowed to retain land, but grain was forcefully confiscated to feed the army and the urban workers. As a result, the peasantry became hostile to the Communists, but they did not join the counterrevolutionary forces, fearing that a victory by the Whites would result in a return of the monarchy.

In the aftermath of World War I, the 1917 Revolution, and the Civil War period, agricultural and industrial production plummeted. Russia was isolated and blockaded. Dissent and disillusionment were evident everywhere. The once vibrant working-class movement, which had spearheaded the revolution, evaporated. Conditions in Russia at this time were unbearable. As the Red Army was demobilized, soldiers returned home to find no work. Millions faced

A starving family of five in the Volga region of Russia, 1921.

Photo by Slava Katamidze Collection / Hulton Archive / Getty Images

starvation and peasant uprisings were frequent and brutally repressed. While claiming to defend the interests of the workers and the peasants, the new government increasingly found itself quelling peasant rebellions and workers' strikes. Opposition parties were banned, allowed to operate again, and banned again at various points. By 1922, the Russian Communist Party (the Bolsheviks) was the only political organization permitted to function legally.

How was it possible that a small group of revolutionaries could overthrow an existing government and take control of the Russian Empire? Several factors contributed to the Bolshevik victory and their ability to hold onto power. When the Bolsheviks seized power, they did so with the support of Russia's workers. As early as February and July 1917, workers in Petrograd were seizing control of their workplaces, were gaining control of the soviets, and were setting up factory committees. Thus, the success of the Bolsheviks can be attributed to conditions within Russia that led to a revolt among workers who wanted to rid themselves of their managers and tsar, as well as to the activities of the Bolshevik Party.

At the time of the 1917 Revolution, the radicalism of the Bolshevik program had broad mass appeal, especially the call for the seizure of land. Bolshevik support also was strengthened by their willingness to withdraw from World War I unilaterally. Because the Russification policies of the tsars had oppressed the non-Russian nationality groups that made up the empire, the Bolsheviks won support from these groups by promising national self-determination.

The Bolsheviks were able to step into a power vacuum because they were well organized and determined to seize power and to hold it. Critically important was the fact that the party was led by dedicated, brilliant men who had military talents and were extremely self-disciplined. The Bolsheviks were willing to use force to achieve their objectives and were ruthless in dealing with enemies. An important component of the Bolsheviks' ability to maintain power was the fact that they controlled major cities and had the advantage of interior lines of communication.

Once the Bolsheviks eliminated the organized opposition to their rule, the various factions within the Communist Party began to argue over the future course of the revolution. The Bolsheviks were still very insecure, convinced that they were operating on the verge of an attack from capitalist countries. Lenin asserted that even discussion within the party needed to be limited so that the country could get on with the task of socialist reconstruction. The Tenth Communist Party Congress in 1921 adopted a resolution on party unity that prohibited factionalism within the party and gave the Central Committee power to expel factionalists. This resolution eliminated the last possible check on the leadership.

The Tenth Communist Party Congress was also important because it inaugurated the New Economic Policy (NEP), marking the end of the period of War Communism. The goals were to stimulate economic growth and to revive the agricultural sector. The Bolsheviks stopped requisitioning the grain of the peasants and allowed them to sell it on the free market. Consumer and retail trade industries were turned over to private control; only heavy industry, banking, and foreign trade remained in the hands of central planners. Higher salaries were offered to those experts who were needed as managers and technicians. Former Tsarist civil servants were reinstated to positions within the bureaucracy, former businessmen were allowed to reestablish themselves, and **kulaks** (farmers who had risen to relative prosperity) emerged as important contributors to the economy.

Although the NEP represented a betrayal of the Bolsheviks' original program of radical social and economic transformation, it did result in impressive growth. Industrial production reached pre–World War I levels by 1926 and agricultural production improved, although more slowly. Lenin, however, did not live to see the results of these policies; he fell ill and died on January 21, 1924.

THE STALIN ERA

After Lenin's death, an enormous struggle developed among his associates over who was to become the next leader of the Soviet Union. The ultimate winner was Joseph Stalin, who after the October Revolution of 1917 had entered the government, the Sovnarkom, as the People's Commissar for Nationalities and had emerged as a leader within the new regime. Stalin (1879–1953) had been expelled from seminary school in 1899 because of his revolutionary activity. He organized a large workers' demonstration in 1902, was hunted down by the imperial police, and was sentenced to exile in the Russian region of Siberia. He escaped but was arrested again. When the Russian Social Democratic Labor Party (RSDLP) split into two factions, Stalin was drawn to the more militant Bolsheviks. As an extraordinarily tough and cunning man, he raised revenue for the Bolsheviks through a variety of means, including bank robberies.

Stalin was one of many who regained freedom after the abdication of the tsar in 1917. In early October 1917, before the overthrow of the Provisional Government, Stalin, a member of the Bolshevik Central Committee since 1912, was elected to the party's highest decision-making body—the Political Bureau of the Central Committee of the Bolshevik Party.

In April 1922, Lenin elevated Stalin to the leadership of the Central Committee; Stalin was named general secretary of the Communist Party. Lenin held the leading position of Chairman of the Council of People's Commissars and was a member of the **Politburo**. The banning of factions in April 1921 had the effect of increasing the authority of the Central Committee and the Politburo. This meant that enormous power came to be concentrated in the hands of General Secretary Joseph Stalin.

Shortly before his death, Lenin expressed doubt about Stalin's abilities as a leader. At the Twelfth Congress of the Communist Party, scheduled for April 1923, Lenin wanted to speak against Stalin as general secretary, but he was physically unable to do so. After Lenin's death, Stalin outmaneuvered his political opponents and by 1929 became the singular leader of the Union of Soviet Socialist Republics (USSR).

Many thought that Leon Trotsky, as head of the Soviet Military Revolutionary Committee and the Red Army and as Commissar of Foreign Affairs and War, would be Lenin's successor. Stalin, however, joined with Grigorii Zinoviev, head of the Petrograd (later renamed Leningrad, then St. Petersburg) party organization and head of the Comintern, and with Lev Kamenev (head of the Moscow party organization) in a successful effort to marginalize Trotsky. Trotsky headed up the **Left Opposition**, which criticized the Comintern for the failure of proletarian uprisings in other countries after World War I. In December 1925, Zinoviev broke with Stalin over the policies supporting the kulaks, wage-cutting, and accelerated output targets for factory workers. In early 1926, Kamenev also broke with Stalin, joined the Left Opposition, and supported Trotsky's call for rapid industrialization. In turn, Stalin temporarily aligned himself with other party leaders who advocated a more moderate program of industrialization.

Although Zinoviev, Kamenev, and Trotsky were united in opposition to Stalin in 1926 and 1927, this joint effort to curb his increasing power came too late. By this time Stalin had made good use of his position as general secretary of the Communist Party, filling important posts within party organs with his own loyal followers. By September 1927, Stalin was able to defeat those who challenged his authority and many Oppositionists were expelled from the party and sent into exile.

The fact that Stalin's competitors for the Soviet Union's top leadership spot were first outmaneuvered and later arrested, exiled, and/or shot represents not only his cold-blooded nature but also a fundamental weakness of communist systems: They lack institutionalized procedures for an orderly transfer of power. Without a legally constituted mechanism for the transfer of power, leaders of the Soviet Union (with the exception of Khrushchev and Gorbachev) stayed in office until their death. Although violence was used extensively only by Stalin in his struggle for power, the Stalin, Khrushchev, and Gorbachev successions were each marked by uncertainty and intrigue until a transition could be made to a new leadership group.

In his struggle for the supreme leadership position in the Soviet Union, Stalin vacillated between support for continuing the moderate New Economic Policy program, which had been adopted in 1921, and support for a more concerted effort at industrialization. In 1929, Stalin rejected the NEP policy, which had encouraged limited private enterprises as a postwar economic stimulus, and adopted a program of rapid industrialization with amazingly ambitious targeted growth rates.

Between 1929 and 1934, Stalin presided over a broad attack on "backwardness" in the Soviet Union.* The process had four components, first of which was the program of rapid, breakneck industrialization. Stalin's government put primary emphasis on creating the infrastructure for heavy industry and military power. Certain sectors of the economy were given absolute priority in the allocation of resources: iron and steel works, dam construction, machine building, and the engineering industry. The hardships were tremendous as consumer comforts were denied (many goods simply were not produced at all) and agricultural development was ignored.

The second component of the attack on backwardness occurred in the rural sector, where small private holdings were forcefully replaced by large-scale collectivized agriculture. Small traditional farms were reorganized into huge agricultural collectives, and all peasants were required to join them. Land and animals became the property of the collective and the peasants became laborers who were subject to the orders of the state. The damage associated with this forced **collectivization** program was far-reaching. Many farmers destroyed their machinery and animals rather than turn them over to the state. The kulaks were wiped out, agricultural production fell, and famine became widespread. In Ukraine, the process of collectivization was particularly violent. Of the 7.5 million people who starved to death during 1932 and 1933 as a result of forced collectivization and grain requisition, it is estimated that 5 million of these deaths occurred in Ukraine (Kort 2001, 196).

---

*This period in Russia's history corresponds with the Wall Street crash of October 1929 and the Great Depression of the 1930s in the West. Hitler came to power in Germany in January 1933.

A third component of Stalin's assault was a program of social transformation. Thousands of churches and monasteries were closed. A massive extension of education, vocational training in particular, and public health programs were undertaken in an effort to infuse a semiliterate peasantry with the skills, discipline, and stamina required for the industrialization effort. All these changes created turbulence and social disorder. Millions of peasants were on the move. Labor discipline was on the verge of breakdown and a black market flourished.

Along with this transformation of society came increased government controls. The state's bureaucracy expanded and further penetrated society. This expansion of the role of the state occurred most forcefully after 1932, partly as a reaction to the disorganization of the earlier period. State, party, and police operations grew rapidly. Many restrictions were instituted to keep workers from moving from job to job, and severe punishments were put into effect for infractions of labor discipline. The imposition of such extreme programs led more and more to the use of force. Because failure in any area could be blamed on the "class enemy," few felt secure and suspicion and distrust were widespread throughout the country.

The extension of state control was accompanied by a return to more traditional values in the family and in social relations and a curtailment of experimentation in literature and the arts. Education, historiography, the arts, and literature were censored by the party and the state. Under the banner of "socialist realism" artists were expected to produce works that exemplified patriotic themes and extolled heroic workers.

Russia under Stalin was a totalitarian society. The development of the Communist Party apparatus and its expansion into all parts of Soviet society provided the institutional mechanism by which the Communist dictatorship uprooted and destroyed every organized form of resistance to its demands. Stalin instilled loyalty through the manipulation of his charismatic authority and through the uninhibited application of terror, thereby keeping the essence of control in his own hands. During the years of collectivization and industrialization, Stalin was increasingly deified. His portrait and statue appeared everywhere. This "cult of personality" reached its height in the late 1940s and early 1950s.

Using the instruments of totalitarianism, Stalin realized his goal of dramatic increases in industrial production but at great cost to the Soviet people. The Soviet Union ranked fourth in the world in coal production, third in steel production, and was the largest producer of tractors in the world. But life for workers was difficult, with long hours and staggering production targets.

Natural climaxes of Stalinist totalitarian rule were the **Great Purges** and the terror of the 1930s. A massive purge of the Communist Party membership began with selective arrests in 1934 and 1935. By 1936 the Soviet secret police were arresting and executing party members by the thousands. Zinoviev and Kamenev were shot following public trials based on confessions extracted using torture.* Many of the top commanders of the Soviet armed forces were shot. According to an official Soviet history, between May 1937 and September 1938 victims of the purges included "nearly half the regimental commanders, nearly all brigade commanders, all commanders of army corps and military districts, members of military councils, heads of political directorates, the majority of political commissars and many military instructors."[2]

Of the 139 members and candidate members of the CPSU Central Committee elected in 1934, 98 were arrested and executed, most in 1937–1938. Of the 1,966 delegates to the Seventeenth Congress of the Communist Party held in January 1934, 1,108 were eventually arrested. By 1939, 60 percent of those who had been party members in 1933 had been driven out, imprisoned, or shot (Suny 1998, 265). The Great Purges wiped out most of those who had actively participated in the revolution and in the Civil War. These were people whose loyalties were primarily to the party rather than to Stalin personally. Winding down at the end of 1938, the purges left Stalin with a new generation of officials loyal to him alone.

During the period of the Great Purges, terror extended throughout Soviet society. Millions of people were taken into custody and shot or sent to concentration camps. Those arrested were accused of "antistate" or "counterrevolutionary" activity. Once the terror had been set into motion, it took on a momentum of its own marked by mass paranoia. Capital punishment was extended down to the age of twelve and the secret police established quotas for the denunciation and arrest of citizens. Only a very small number of people who were arrested and sent to prison survived the labor camps. Such terror results when an absolute dictator demands sudden, radical social change and the people are either unable or unwilling to act or transform in the required manner.

The Great Patriotic War

The decimation of the military ranks left the country more vulnerable to an attack by Germany. Hoping to protect the Soviet Union against invasion, Stalin agreed in August 1939 to a Non-Aggression Treaty with Adolf Hitler. The "Secret Protocols" of the German-Soviet nonaggression pact carved up East-Central Europe into German and Soviet spheres of influence in exchange for Hitler's promised nonaggression against any Soviet territory. Despite warnings, Stalin was caught by surprise in June 1941 when Germany broke the agreement and invaded the Soviet Union.

The Soviet people and their territory suffered terribly during the **Great Patriotic War** (World War II). Although estimates vary, the Soviet Union lost between 7 and 8 million soldiers and about 19 million civilians. This compares with 405,000 soldiers lost by the United States and 375,000 by Great Britain. Of the 13.6 million Germans killed, wounded, missing, or taken prisoner during World War II, 10 million of them met their fate on the Eastern Front (Suny 1998,

---

*Trotsky was assassinated in Mexico in August 1940 by one of Stalin's agents.

331). The Soviet Union suffered casualties unmatched by any country in any other twentieth-century war. Twenty-five percent of the Soviet population was killed or injured during the war. These casualties were primarily males, and the resulting population imbalance is characteristic of Russia and Ukraine even today. Families had to survive without fathers and brothers. Because the Soviet Union was so barren of men, many women who came of age during World War II went through their lives without husbands.

The Second Front (Western Front) against Germany was not launched until the Normandy landing on June 6, 1944. Thus, for three years the Soviet Union suffered unbearably in the war against Germany. The tide turned in favor of the Soviet Union following the German defeat at the Battle of Stalingrad (now Volgograd) in January 1943. The Nazis were forced out of Soviet territory battle by brutal battle, and the costs of victory were enormous. With Germany's retreat, Stalin moved Soviet forces into Eastern Europe.

As it became clear that the Soviet Union, the United States, and the United Kingdom would ultimately defeat Hitler's armies, a series of summit meetings were held between November 1943 and August 1945, during which Stalin, Churchill, and Roosevelt "carved up the world" between the Soviet Union and the West.

Because the Soviet Union had defeated Germany, many now viewed the Communist Party, and Stalin as its living expression, as the embodiment of national survival. The war had led to a sense of national unity and the people took pride in the fact that the Soviet Union had surpassed not only Germany but also France and Britain in military power. Governments modeled after the Soviet Union were installed in Albania, Poland, Czechoslovakia, Hungary, Bulgaria, Romania, and East Germany.* With the victory of Mao Zedong in China, Communists also ruled the world's most populous state.

Soon the Soviet Union would challenge even the United States as it became a superpower. Stalin, who was determined to catch up to the United States in the development of the atomic bomb, channeled a significant amount of money and manpower into the project. The USSR exploded its first atomic (fission) bomb in 1949, followed by a hydrogen (fusion) bomb in 1953. Increasing tensions between the United States and the Soviet Union in the aftermath of World War II led to a period of threats and counterthreats; the creation of two competing military alliances—the North Atlantic Treaty Organization (NATO) and the Warsaw Pact; fear of mass destruction associated with nuclear war; indirect military confrontation through surrogates, such as Vietnam and Ethiopia; and relentless competition for ideological and economic influence in the world arena. This Cold War era is described in detail in the foreign policy section of Chapter 10.

---

*Germany was partitioned into East and West Germany in 1949 with U.S., French, and British zones in West Germany becoming the Federal Republic of Germany and the Soviet zone in East Germany becoming the German Democratic Republic.

THE KHRUSHCHEV ERA

The Soviet Union entered a new stage when Stalin died on March 5, 1953. Immediately after his death, George Malenkov, Chairman of the Council of Ministers (Prime Minister); Lavrentii Beria, head of the Soviet Secret Police (the KGB); and Foreign Minister Vyacheslav Molotov established a collective leadership. Nikita Khrushchev (1894–1971) joined the inner circle of rulers when he was given the post of General Secretary of the Communist Party in mid-March 1953. In December 1953, Beria was executed along with some of his followers, allegedly for failing to prevent a violent anti-Soviet uprising that occurred in East Germany in the summer of 1953. Malenkov remained the senior powerholder for about two years, but Khrushchev was successful in ousting Malenkov from the position of prime minister in February 1955 and replaced him with Nikolay Bulganin. Khrushchev placed more and more of his supporters in prominent positions in both the party and the state apparatus. In 1957, Khrushchev's opponents were dropped from the Politburo and replaced by his supporters, among them Leonid Brezhnev. In March 1958, Khrushchev took over the position of Chairman of the Council of Ministers.

As Stalin had done before, Khrushchev, after a lengthy struggle for power, took over the leadership of both the party and the state's apparatus. In contrast, however, Khrushchev did not have his political opponents killed as Stalin had after winning control. For example, Malenkov and Molotov, once defeated as part of the Anti-Party Group, were given assignments in the remote regions of Central Asia and Mongolia.

As general secretary of the CPSU, Khrushchev gave his famous Secret Speech at the Twentieth Party Congress of the Communist Party in 1956. He criticized Stalin for his purge of party members, the executions of Soviet citizens, and various other injustices.* Millions of people were released from prison camps in 1956 and 1957. Nonetheless, the population of the Soviet Union remained tightly controlled. Evidence of the limits of reform is Khrushchev's decision to suppress the Hungarian uprising of 1956 through military force.

Khrushchev did attempt to improve the Soviet system during his tenure; most important was his effort to raise the standard of living for the people. He stressed agriculture and consumer goods, and during the 1950s, Khrushchev initiated the Virgin Lands Campaign, which brought vast new tracts of land under cultivation for farming. He decentralized government ministerial control over enterprises by establishing regional Economic Councils (*sovnarkhozy*) and introduced educational reforms.

By the end of the 1950s, Russia had developed a formidable military and

---

*The changes in communist doctrine and the renunciation of Stalinism precipitated a division between the Soviet Union and China's Communist Party under Mao Zedong. Mao remained loyal to the more militant brand of communism and was still uncomfortable with any rapprochement toward the West.

industrial capacity. The working class was skilled and disciplined. The Soviet Union also had large, well-educated classes of bureaucrats, technicians, and professional people. Living standards did improve during the Khrushchev period; on average, economic growth rates in the Soviet Union surpassed those reported for the United States. Khrushchev provided significant support for the Soviet space program, resulting in Russia being the first to send a man (Yuri Gagarin) to orbit the earth in 1961. He also built up the Soviet Union's nuclear weapons arsenal.

By 1964, however, Khrushchev had alienated many of his contemporaries in the party and the government. A plan to divide the party into industrial and agricultural sections had been announced in 1962. Another reorganization scheme, simultaneous with bad harvests in 1963 and compounded by foreign policy failures during the Berlin Crisis of 1961 and the Cuban Missile Crisis of 1962, undercut Khrushchev's authority. His opponents within the party were able to remove Khrushchev from power in October 1964.

THE BREZHNEV ERA

The key actor in ousting Khrushchev was Leonid Brezhnev (1906–1982), who became General Secretary of the Communist Party in 1964. For several years Brezhnev shared power with Prime Minister Aleksey Kosygin and with Nikolay Podgorny, who was head of state. In 1977, Brezhnev took over chairmanship of the Presidium of the Supreme Soviet from Podgorny and thus became head of state as well as head of the Communist Party.

In contrast to the dramatic shifts in policy introduced by his predecessors, Brezhnev displayed a more cautious approach to leadership. He promoted stability within the ruling elite (with little turnover in office) and gave significant policymaking powers (autonomy) to the bureaucracy and to the leaders of the Communist Party organizations in the regions (union republics). Rejecting the populism of Khrushchev, Brezhnev believed that technical progress and scientific management would create sustained economic growth in the Soviet Union. This approach initially led to positive results in the economy as well as to progress in improving relations with the West.

Serious problems in the Soviet developmental model, however, emerged during the Brezhnev era. **Dissident activity** grew as the people became disgruntled with the economic conditions and limited freedoms. Famous dissidents, such as Andrei Sakharov and Alexander Solzhenitsyn, protested Soviet policies of repression and human rights abuses, but such people were forced into exile. Others, such as Viacheslav Chornovil, were arrested and exiled for alleged Ukrainian nationalism. Muslims were also a problem for the Soviet government, as Islamic and ethnic identities were closely connected.

In spite of the challenges, Soviet society remained remarkably unchanged in terms of institutions and structures during Brezhnev's tenure as general secretary of the Communist Party from 1964 to 1982—eighteen years. How can this stability be explained? First and foremost was the role of the secret police organization of the Soviet Union (the KGB, the Committee of State Security) in actively repressing dissident individuals and groups. Although the KGB employed terror to a lesser degree under Brezhnev than it had under Stalin, the threat of arrest or deportation was enough to keep the dissident population small in number. Second, the Communist Party remained in total control of the nation's political, military, and economic institutions. Its members, through the **nomenklatura** system, held the lion's share of the leading positions throughout the government, the economy, and the society. Soviet authorities also maintained strict censorship rules and tightly controlled what information was given to the citizens about conditions and events in the rest of the world. The stability of the Brezhnev era can also be explained by the attitudes of the Soviet people; they had become used to what was happening in their country. As long as conditions remained bearable, most citizens were unwilling to risk the consequences of expressing dissatisfaction with the system (Diller 1993, 95).

Yet the foundation on which the system was built was increasingly characterized by a broad set of unresolved problems, which ultimately culminated in the breakdown of the government's entire structure. Four major problems characterized the Soviet Union at the end of Brezhnev era: widespread alcoholism and absenteeism from work, a declining economy, lopsided foreign economic relations, and an aging leadership circle.

Excessive drinking created attendant problems of health (most notably fatal alcohol poisoning), domestic fights, accidents, absenteeism, low labor productivity, and crime. Per capita consumption of alcoholic beverages increased measurably in the late Brezhnev era.* Although the Soviet Union did not register the highest rates of overall alcohol consumption in the world (for example, France had and still has higher rates), the people of the Soviet Union (and Russia today) drink primarily hard liquor, usually vodka, which is linked to the most severe health problems.

The second threat to the welfare of the people and to the legitimacy of the Soviet system was the decline of its economy. This decline can be explained in part by low labor productivity (partially a result of inadequate incentives) but, more significantly, by shortcomings in the economic planning system (the poor allocation of resources), environmental degradation, and the inefficiencies associated with the wasteful extraction and use of natural resources. The agricultural sector suffered from long-term problems such as underinvestment in infrastructure (storage facilities and roads) and machinery, waste, soil erosion, and few incentives. A period of poor harvests in the early 1970s led to massive purchases of grain from the United States. The increasing complexity and differentiation within the economy created enormous challenges for the central

---

*For a thorough treatment of alcohol consumption and abuse in the Soviet Union and Russia, see the paper by Vladimir G. Treml at http://papers.ssrn.com/sol3/delivery.cfm/9704182.pdf?abstractid=2293.

planners. Illegal economic activity, often referred to as the "second economy," was widespread, along with stealing from the state and various forms of bribery.

With regard to foreign economic relations, the Soviet Union was like a Third World country in the sense that it sold raw materials abroad to pay for the importation of manufactured goods and high technology. The economy was particularly vulnerable to declines in oil prices. Huge oil exports during the 1970s and 1980s helped to keep the Soviet economy afloat, but when oil prices dropped in 1986, the imbalances were painfully manifest. By the mid-1980s, the USSR and its satellite countries were trapped in a quagmire of economic and social decline, which was reflected in a weakening of its influence throughout the world.

The Soviet Union also faced a severe leadership problem at the end of the Brezhnev era. Communist Party and government officials rarely retired or were replaced. Rather they stayed in their positions until they died or became seriously ill. By the early 1980s, most of the top leaders were in their seventies, were unwilling to consider meaningful change, and maintained a hands-off policy toward the regions and republics. The stagnation within the leadership created stagnation in institutions and policies.

Brezhnev, after many years of poor health, died in November 1982 at the age of seventy-five. Yuri Andropov (1914–1984) succeeded Leonid Brezhnev as general secretary of the CPSU, serving from November 1982 until his death in 1984. Andropov had been appointed to the Politburo in 1973 and chaired the KGB from 1967 to 1982. Although his service as general secretary was short, he initiated programs to revive the Soviet economy through campaigns against corruption and alcoholism. Andropov also retired many older government and party officials and promoted younger men, including Mikhail Gorbachev, to positions of authority.

When Andropov died, Konstantin Chernenko, a member of Brezhnev's entourage for thirty-five years, was selected as Andropov's successor. Relations between the United States and the Soviet Union were at a low point as a result of the Soviet military presence in Afghanistan and a NATO* decision to deploy cruise and Pershing II missiles in Europe in response to the Soviet deployment of SS-20 missiles. Chernenko's tenure was also short; he died in March 1985 at the age of seventy-three. The very next day, March 11, 1985, the Central Committee appointed fifty-four-year-old Gorbachev, the youngest member of the Politburo, as general secretary.

GORBACHEV, GLASNOST, AND PERESTROIKA

Born in 1931, Mikhail Gorbachev was the last General Secretary of the Communist Party of the Soviet Union. He became a member of the Central Committee of the CPSU in 1971 and joined the CPSU Secretariat as agriculture secretary in 1978. In

*For more information on NATO, see Chapter 10, p. 245.

1980, Gorbachev became a full member of the Politburo as the protégé of Yuri Andropov. Gorbachev served as general secretary of CPSU for six years, instituting reforms in the Soviet system that ultimately led to its dissolution in 1991.

When Gorbachev became CPSU general secretary in 1985, he attempted to liberalize and stimulate the Soviet system by continuing Andropov's policy of retiring aged comrades of Brezhnev and Chernenko. He also deepened his predecessor's efforts to combat alcoholism, improve labor discipline, and scale back Soviet military and economic assistance programs abroad. When Gorbachev became dissatisfied with the meager results of these early reform attempts, he initiated more radical ones.

Major components of Gorbachev's reform effort included **glasnost** (openness or candor), **perestroika** (restructuring), *demokratizatsiia* (democratization), and *novoe myshlenie* (new thinking in foreign affairs). Under glasnost, censorship was dramatically reduced, dissidents were released from prison, and religious free-dom was officially endorsed. Andrei Sakharov, the Nobel Peace Prize–winning dissident of the Brezhnev era, was freed from internal exile in December 1986. New associations, independent of state control, began to emerge.

The new openness led to frank public debates about weaknesses in the Soviet system. During the late 1970s and early 1980s, evidence had been mounting that the Soviet economy was not only in serious trouble but also that previous and existing efforts to fix the problems were ineffective. Reports that would have been censored under prior leaders about the wastefulness and irrationality of the Soviet economy found outlets in the press. Specialists began to recognize that major new initiatives were needed to address the country's manifold problems.

Perestroika represented an effort to restructure the nation's economic sys-tem. A Law on Individual Labor Activity (May 1987) legalized the provision of services such as medical care and house repair. A Law on State Enterprises (June 1987) allowed enterprises to conclude their own contracts. A Law on Cooperatives (May 1988) legalized private ownership of small businesses and the hiring of workers. The scope of each of the laws was restricted, however. Many activities were still controlled, and public support, given years of propa-ganda against the concepts of profit and private enterprise, was far from enthu-siastic. Gorbachev never did achieve a complete restructuring of the Soviet economy. His main accomplishment was to legalize individual entrepreneur-ship and small cooperative businesses. Throughout the Gorbachev era, the state sector remained dominant and resistant to serious modifications.

Resistance to the perestroika initiatives surfaced early on among "hard-liners" in the Communist Party leadership. Partly in an effort to overcome this resistance, Gorbachev introduced the *demokratizatsiia* reforms in 1987. He announced that it was time to inaugurate secret ballots and competitive elec-tions for leadership positions. Previously, citizens were only able to vote yes or no to a single candidate put forward by the Communist Party, ballots were not secret, and "no" voters could face repercussions. In 1988, a decision was made to establish a new 2,250-member USSR Congress of People's Deputies. Elections to the new congress, held in March 1989, heralded the defeat of many old party bosses by more reformist candidates. From within the membership of the USSR Congress, a new USSR Supreme Soviet was also elected. Contrary to the rubberstamp role played by this institution in the past, real debate, discussion, and disagreement were exercised by members of this new parliament. In addition, the USSR Congress, of People's Deputies created a new position of President of the USSR. In March 1990, Gorbachev was elected to this position by the membership of the congress.

Nonetheless, opposition from conservative elements in the Communist Party continued to place limits on the extent of reform. At the same time, more radical forces pressured the regime for even more and greater change. In part because of the emergence of organized opposition from the newly elected Supreme Soviet deputies, and also because of resistance to his reforms among entrenched members of the Communist Party, Gorbachev's difficulties multiplied after the 1989 elections. On one flank, he was increasingly estranged from conservative leaders within the CPSU establishment; on the other side, his ability to lead the reform movement was slipping from his hands as more radical leaders, such as Boris Yeltsin, came to the fore.

Not only opposition but also violent conflict erupted in the non-Russian republics of the USSR. An omen of serious trouble occurred in December 1986 when the people in the union republic of Kazakhstan rioted. Even more dangerous was deadly fighting in 1988 between the Armenia and Azerbaijan republics over control of an autonomous territory called Nagorno-Karabakh. Then too, the people of the Baltic republics of Lithuania, Estonia, and Latvia demanded dramatic increases in political autonomy.

In early 1990, each union republic in the Soviet Union elected its own representative legislature (Supreme Soviet). By mid-1991, most of these legislatures, such as the Supreme Soviet of Ukraine and the Supreme Soviet of Georgia, had declared **sovereignty,** meaning that laws passed by the republic-level Supreme Soviet were to take precedence over laws emanating from the USSR Supreme Soviet. The Supreme Soviets of the most assertive republics, such as Lithuania, declared outright independence from the Soviet Union. Violence erupted in the capital cities of Lithuania and Latvia in January 1991 when Soviet forces attempted to restore control.

In addition, far-reaching changes were occurring in the international position of the Soviet Union. Gorbachev's "new thinking" in the realm of foreign policy ultimately led to an entirely different relationship with the West. He met with sitting U.S. presidents (Ronald Reagan and George H. W. Bush) and signed the START I and Intermediate Nuclear Forces (INF) treaties. Gorbachev unilaterally withdrew Soviet troops from Afghanistan and Eastern Europe and scaled back aid to communist regimes around the world. With the dismantling of the Berlin Wall in 1989, Soviet support for the communist governments of Eastern and Central Europe officially came to an end.

BORIS YELTSIN AND THE FALL OF THE USSR

Yeltsin's rise to the presidency of the Russian Federation started when he was named First Secretary of the Communist Party in the Sverdlovsk Oblast in November 1976 (under CPSU General Secretary Leonid Brezhnev). After Mikhail Gorbachev became the new general secretary of the CPSU in 1985, Yeltsin was one of the first provincial officials to be brought to Moscow as part of Gorbachev's drive to revitalize the Soviet system. Yeltsin was given the important post of First Secretary of the Moscow Communist Party organization.

The turning point in Yeltsin's career came when he publicly expressed his frustration with the gradual pace of perestroika. Taking the floor at a CPSU Central Committee meeting in October 1987, Yeltsin lambasted Gorbachev, Egor Ligachev, and other party leaders for being content with "half measures." For this affront, he was not only dismissed from his position as head of the Moscow party machine but also from the Politburo in February 1988. Yeltsin's dramatic confrontation of Gorbachev made him a natural pole of attraction for the people's anger at the failings of Soviet communism and the questionable progress of Gorbachev's reforms. When Gorbachev overhauled the Soviet electoral system and allowed competition among candidates for political office, Yeltsin tapped into the mass grievances and waged a populist campaign in March 1989 to represent Moscow in the USSR Congress of People's Deputies.

In March 1990, voters in the Russian Soviet Federated Socialist Republic (RSFSR) elected their own Russian Congress of People's Deputies and this congress selected a Russian Supreme Soviet from among their membership. This Supreme Soviet became the parliament of the RSFSR, which represented a separate institution of legislative and representative authority distinct from the USSR Supreme Soviet.

Yeltsin was elected a deputy to the RSFSR Congress of People's Deputies and was subsequently elected chairman of that body in May 1990, giving him constitutional authority as head of the government of the Russian Soviet Federated Socialist Republic (the largest of the fifteen USSR union republics). In July 1990, he announced that membership in the Communist Party was incompatible with his position as the head of the Russian republic and resigned from the party. Yeltsin argued loudly for acceleration of economic and social reforms, accusing Gorbachev and more orthodox elements within the party of obstructing them.

The office of president for the RSFSR was first instituted as a result of a March 1991 referendum. In June 1991, the first multicandidate presidential race in Russia's history was held. Boris Yeltsin won with 57.4 percent of the popular vote in an election contested by six candidates.* These dates are listed in Box 3.2.

---

*Ruslan Khasbulatov was elected chairman of the Russian Congress and the Russian Supreme Soviet in 1991 after Yeltsin became president of Russia.

BOX 3.2: THE BREAKUP OF THE SOVIET UNION

June– October 1988	The formation of popular fronts (oppositional movements) within the republics of the Soviet Union.
March 1989	Multicandidate elections to the new USSR Congress of People's Deputies are held.
June 1989	The USSR Supreme Soviet is selected from within the membership of the USSR Congress of People's Deputies.
December 1989– March 1990	Elections are held to republic-level Supreme Soviets.
March 1990	The newly elected Lithuanian Supreme Soviet declares independence; Estonia declares independence through a transition period.
March 1990	Gorbachev is elected first president of the USSR (indirectly by the USSR Congress of People's Deputies).
May 1990	Yeltsin is elected chairman of the RSFSR (after independence the RSFSR is called the Russian Federation) Congress of People's Deputies.
June 1990	The RSFSR Congress of People's Deputies votes for sovereignty.
July 1990	The Supreme Soviets of Ukraine and Belarus declare sovereignty.
February 1991	Lithuania holds a referendum on independence.
March 1991	Gorbachev sponsors an all-union referendum on preserving the Soviet Union.
June 1991	Yeltsin is elected president of the RSFSR by direct popular vote.
August 19, 1991	Conservative members of Gorbachev's government attempt to take control of the Soviet Union (August Coup Attempt); Yeltsin defies the coup leaders and takes control.
December 1991	The formal end of the USSR.

In contrast to Gorbachev, who never faced election by direct popular vote to his position either as General Secretary of the Communist Party in 1985 or as president of the Soviet Union in 1990, Yeltsin was first elected by Moscow voters to the USSR Congress of People's Deputies in 1989 and then to the Russian Congress of People's Deputies in 1990. In 1991, he was elected by voters through-out the RSFSR to the position of Russian president. Yeltsin used his position as President of Russia to defy Gorbachev's leadership as general secretary of the CPSU and as President of the USSR.

When hard-liners in the government became upset by the crisislike down-turn in the Soviet economy and the prospect of the breakup of the Soviet Empire, they attempted a coup against Gorbachev on August 19, 1991. The coup plotters arrested Gorbachev at his dacha in the Crimea, and tanks were sent into the streets to take control of Moscow. Yeltsin rallied resistance around the parliament building of the RSFSR and helped guarantee the plotters' defeat. Gorbachev was rescued, and the attempted coup was foiled.

The coup failed because of strategic mistakes made by the plotters, such as not arresting Boris Yeltsin before he could mount a resistance; they also acted without making certain that the army and KGB troops would follow their orders. Rather than fire on their own people, army units joined Yeltsin's resistance. In addition, the coup plotters were opposed by the leaders of most republics and by major players from abroad, such as the United States, which refused to recognize the new government. An even more important reason for the failure of the August 1991 coup was that the perestroika, glasnost, and *demokratizatsiia* reforms had already taken hold in Russia and other parts of the Soviet Union. The people were determined to stand up against the possibility of a return to a dictatorship.

In the aftermath of the coup attempt, Gorbachev was never able to recover his authority, for those who had attempted to oust him were members of his own government. In contrast, Yeltsin enhanced his standing among the people with his unyielding resistance to the hard-line members of Gorbachev's government. Yeltsin successfully pressured Gorbachev to dissolve the Communist Party, then declared all party property within the RSFSR to be Russian state property. Gorbachev agreed to dissolve the USSR Congress of People's Deputies and to establish a transitional State Council made up of leaders of the union republics. One of the first acts of the State Council was to recognize the independence of the Baltic States of Lithuania, Latvia, and Estonia.

In Ukraine, the most populous of the Soviet republics after Russia, Leonid Kravchuk was elected president on December 1, 1991, on a pro-independence platform. On December 8, Yeltsin decided—with the agreement of Kravchuk and Stanislau Shushkevich, the leader of Belarus—to end the USSR. After a summit meeting in Minsk, the three presidents simply announced that the USSR had ceased to function and that they would establish a voluntary Commonwealth of Independent States (CIS) in its place. After the commonwealth expanded in mid-December to include the Central Asian republics, Gorbachev resigned as Soviet president on December 25, 1991, and the USSR ceased to exist.

The legacy left by Gorbachev was a set of countries (the former union republics) divided politically between hard-liners and reformers. Hard-liners continued to work toward maintenance of state control and ownership, while reformers (called democrats) pushed for reduced state planning and some form of economic marketization. Hard-liners wanted a restoration of the Soviet Union, while democrats wanted increased independence for each republic. Each newly independent country also faced the difficult task of determining a new constitutional division of authority between their own lawfully elected president and parliament, and between the central government and the regions. Ethnic conflict, and the potential of ethnic conflict, divided people in many regions of the former Soviet Union.

Gorbachev also left a legacy of support for individual initiative and genuine democracy. He demonstrated true courage and determination when he loosened the control exercised by the Communist Party, gave the people a real role in decision making, and initiated lasting change. In Gorbachev's resignation speech, he summed up his accomplishments by noting that the "totalitarian system that long ago deprived the country of an opportunity to succeed and prosper has been eliminated" (Kort 2001, 382).

POST-SOVIET RUSSIA

The basic institutions and policies of the Russian Federation are described in detail in Chapters 6, 8, and 10. To conclude this chapter, we note that the Russian Federation emerged as one of fifteen newly independent countries in January 1992. All the new countries were former republics of the USSR. Even after the breakup of the Soviet Union, Russia is still the largest country geographically in the world and encompasses about three-fourths of the territory of the former Soviet Union. The population of Russia represents about half the number of people who lived in the former Soviet Union.

All of the former USSR republics, including Russia, Ukraine, and Uzbekistan, faced the daunting tasks of forming new nation-states, reviving their economies, reorganizing their political systems, and developing foreign policies. The republic-level presidents and the Soviet-era legislatures (elected in 1990–1991) remained in place after the December 1991 dissolution of the Soviet Union. Constitutions had to be adopted to clarify the jurisdictional powers of these two governing institutions. Drops in production, inflation, and dramatic increases in unemployment remained persistent problems throughout the transition period.

In Russia, Yeltsin initiated reform by executive orders, bypassing the lawmaking authority of the Russian Congress of People's Deputies and the Supreme Soviet. The result was a bitter conflict with Yeltsin's successor as chairman of the Russian parliament, Ruslan Khasbulatov. Khasbulatov called for a slower approach to economic reform and protections for Russia's key industries.

The confrontation deepened when the two branches of government were unable to agree on the basic framework for a new constitution to replace the much-amended Russian one that had been carried over from the Soviet era. Leaders in the Russian parliament also disagreed with the strongly pro-Western orientation of Yeltsin's foreign minister, Andrei Kozyrev. After the Russian parliament attempted to impeach Yeltsin, he took matters into his own hands in September 1993. Yeltsin dissolved the Russian Congress of People's Deputies and the Supreme Soviet and called for new elections. Khasbulatov and his allies refused to step down, holing up with hundreds of armed supporters in the parliament building. Riots ensued in central Moscow, and on October 4, Yeltsin used army troops to shell and occupy the building. According to official reports, about 140 people were killed and 550 were wounded (Kort 2001, 388; Treadgold and Ellison 2000, 437).

In the aftermath of this crisis, Yeltsin banned the political parties associated with the opposition leaders. By decree, Yeltsin scheduled elections for a new parliament—to be called a Federal Assembly—for December 1993. A new constitution of the Russian Federation, which significantly increased presidential powers, was ratified simultaneously with the parliamentary elections.

Although internal problems were of overwhelming concern during his tenure as president, Yeltsin faced a number of urgent foreign policy issues as well. The Commonwealth of Independent States turned out to be a relatively weak organization, and relations among the former republics tended to develop on the basis of bilateral agreements. Disputes over pricing of Russian energy exports and the division of the USSR's Black Sea naval fleet clouded Yeltsin's dealings with the second-largest successor state, Ukraine. In 1997, the two countries finally arrived at a treaty providing for the division of the fleet and a Russian lease on the Sevastopol naval base. In Transcaucasia, Central Asia, and Moldova, where ethnic conflicts erupted, Yeltsin signed agreements that provided for Russian mediation and the temporary stationing of Russian troops. Of major concern to the Russian government was the well-being of the 24 million ethnic Russians who were left living in the other newly independent states in the aftermath of the dismantling of the Soviet Union.

Yeltsin held several summits with U.S. presidents and courted aid and backing in international organizations such as the International Monetary Fund. He also cultivated relations with the leaders of Germany, France, and the United Kingdom. NATO's war against Yugoslavia in the spring and summer of 1999, however, strained relations with the United States and led Yeltsin to freeze all Russian contacts with NATO. In Asia, Yeltsin promoted trade and cooperation with China.

During the 1990s, the Russian government was plagued by an internally based armed insurrection originating in Chechnya, a mostly Muslim republic in the North Caucasus, whose government had been trying to secede from Russia since 1991. In December 1994, Yeltsin ordered the army to intervene and assert Moscow's control. The military assault caused enormous damage, virtually destroying the capital city of Chechnya. Despite months of savage fighting, Russian forces were unable to subdue the Chechen fighters. The death toll was so high among Russian troops that they were withdrawn in 1996.

Given the unpopular war in Chechnya and his lack of majority support in parliament, the presidential elections in 1996 represented a major challenge for Boris Yeltsin, yet he was determined to secure a second presidential term. In the 1996 election, citizens faced an important choice between very different visions for Russia's economic, social, and political future, as represented by the Communist Party candidate and the incumbent Yeltsin. Despite the hardship of the previous five years, the majority of the voters decided to continue the reform path of Boris Yeltsin.

Yeltsin battled serious problems during his second term of office (1996–1999), including problems with his own physical health; he was hospitalized and away from work frequently. The viability of the Russian economy rested insecurely on foreign earnings from energy exports. Organized crime controlled a significant sector of Russia's economy. Bribery, thefts by government officials, and other forms of corruption discredited the rulers in the eyes of the people. Through its ties with the oligarchs, the government maintained control over the news presented on the most frequently viewed television stations.

In late summer 1999, hostilities in Chechnya and the neighboring republic of Dagestan precipitated a second Russian military response. With economic problems continuing to plague the government, and the situation in Chechnya still unresolved, Yeltsin named Vladimir Putin prime minister in August 1999. Yeltsin made it clear that Putin was his chosen successor. (Yeltsin was prohibited by the constitution from running for a third term as president of the Russian Federation.)

Putin had served as a KGB agent in East Germany, where he specialized in economic intelligence. When he returned in 1989, he went to work for the mayor of St. Petersburg (then called Leningrad) to promote foreign investment and business in the city. In 1996, Putin moved to Moscow, where he joined the inner circle of central government officials and was appointed head of the Federal Security Service in 1998. Putin's popularity as prime minister was confirmed in the December 1999 parliamentary elections; political parties that he had endorsed or was associated with did very well.

While the December 1993 and 1995 Russian State Duma elections had resulted in legislatures that operated as obstacles to the reform agenda advanced by President Yeltsin, the December 1999 elections produced a new configuration of parties distinct from that found in the preceding Duma. That election marked the shifting of power in the Duma away from the communist-nationalist bloc toward a more centrist, pro-reform orientation. Although the Communist Party remained the largest single party in the State Duma after the 1999 parliamentary elections, its share of the seats shrank considerably compared with the 1995 Duma.

In the aftermath of the December 1999 parliamentary elections, Boris Yeltsin resigned from his position as president of the Russian Federation. Vladimir Putin, as prime minister, assumed the position of acting president. When presidential elections were held in March 2000, Putin won in the first round.

In assessing the positive and negative achievements of the Yeltsin era, we conclude that reform was much less impressive than it could have been. The robbery of the state and the people by a small group of insider Russian politicians and businesspeople during the privatization process can hardly be condoned as representing a positive contribution to the long-term development of the Russian economy. Yeltsin must also be held accountable for the poor investment climate in Russia during the 1990s that kept sorely needed foreign funds from ever being invested in the country. Overall, the decade was one of severe economic decline. Social indicators revealed not only increased poverty and economic inequality in Russia but also increased crime, alcoholism, substance abuse, and numerous forms of disease.

We must be careful, however, in placing blame for Russia's woes on Boris Yeltsin. The task of reforming the Soviet economy could not have been more demanding and complex. As mentioned earlier in this chapter, serious problems with the productivity and the efficiency of the economy were already painfully apparent during the Brezhnev era. Also, no successful model exists for how to transform a monopoly-based, state-owned economy into a competitive, privately owned one. In addition, the twin tasks of economic and political reform, attempted simultaneously in Russia, made the whole process even more daunting. Throughout his entire reign, Yeltsin faced significant opposition to his reform efforts, both from the Communist Party and from entrenched economic interests.

Although civil liberties were expanded and solidified during the Yeltsin era, the democratic process remained constrained. The regularly held parliamentary and presidential elections of Yeltsin's tenure were in and of themselves extremely positive for democratic consolidation; however, criticism must be leveled regarding the procedural fairness of these elections. Allegations of fraud, misuse of campaign funds, and partisanship of state and private media in covering the electoral campaigns were widespread.

Despite differences over the role of NATO and other foreign policy positions, Yeltsin did manage to continue a dialogue with the West. He also managed to avoid further dissolution of the Russian state by negotiating bilateral agreements with republics such as Tatarstan and Sakha. The use of brute force to quell the Chechen insurgency, however, remains a black mark on Yeltsin's overall record.

The retirement of Yeltsin and the ascension of Putin to the presidency changed the nature of the political system of the Russian Federation. Putin's vitality and health stand in sharp contrast to Yeltsin's fading condition. Putin has made a sincere and concerted effort to reduce the power and influence of the oligarchs. He also has worked untiringly with Western powers, particularly in supporting, with a few reservations, the U.S.-led international antiterrorist coalition. Putin's efforts to rein in the power of regional governors bodes well for the national integration of the Russian state. A cautionary note should be raised in this regard, however. Putin's success at concentrating even more power into the position of the president raises questions of democratic accountability within Russia's political institutions. Issues of foreign and domestic policy and democratic accountability will be evaluated in greater detail in Chapters 7 and 10.

Key Terms

Autocracy
Collectivization
Demokratizatsiia (democratization)
Dissident activity
Duma
Emancipation of the Serfs
Federal Assembly
Glasnost
Great Patriotic War
Great Purges
Intelligentsia
Kievan Rus
Kulaks

Left Opposition
Muscovy
Nomenklatura
Novoe myshlenie (new thinking)
October Manifesto
Perestroika
Politburo
Sovereignty
Soviets
Sovnarkom
Tsarism
War Communism

Critical Thinking Questions

1. From the fifteenth century to the nineteenth century, the territory controlled by the Russian Empire continued to expand. What motivated this relentless territorial expansion on the part of the tsars?

2. What were some of the causes of the collapse of Tsarism? What are some of the major legacies of Tsarism? How did these inherited characteristics of the Russian Empire affect the development of the Soviet state?

3. What problems were specifically related to Russia's involvement in World War I?

4. Which factors contributed to the emergence of totalitarianism under Stalin? What is totalitarianism? How did it manifest itself in Russia?

5. Despite the emergence of dissidents during the Brezhnev era, the system was remarkably stable. How can the stability in society and in politics during the Brezhnev era be explained?

6. What were some of the objectives pursued under the umbrella terms *glasnost* and *perestroika*? To what degree were these objectives achieved?

7. What were some of the major accomplishments of the Soviet system overall (from Lenin to Gorbachev) in terms of social and economic policies?

8. Which factors contributed to the dissolution of the Soviet Union in 1991? Could it have been avoided? If so, how?

9. Discuss the successes and the failures of the Boris Yeltsin presidency. Did he leave a positive legacy for Vladimir Putin?

Suggested Reading

Kort, Michael. *The Soviet Colossus: History and Aftermath,* 5th ed. Armonk, N.Y.: M. E. Sharpe, 2001.

Suny, Ronald Grigory. *The Soviet Experiment: Russia, the USSR, and the Successor States.* New York: Oxford University Press, 1998.

Treadgold, Donald W., and Herbert J. Ellison. *Twentieth-Century Russia,* 9th ed. Boulder: Westview Press, 2000.

Websites of Interest

Chronology of Russian history:
  http://www.departments.bucknell.edu/russian/chrono3.html

The Eastern Front: A World War One Summary:
  http://www.richthofen.com/ww1sum2/

Reform, Coup, and Collapse: The End of the Soviet State by Archie Brown:
  http://www.bbc.co.uk/history/war/coldwar/soviet_end_01.shtml

Russia, Library of Congress, Federal Research Division Country Studies/Area Handbook Series:
  http://countrystudies.us/russia/

For photos, see http://news.bbc.co.uk/hi/english/static/in_depth/europe/2001/collapse_of_ussr/photofile/default.stm

CHAPTER 4

Russia as a Multinational State: Federal Structures and Ethnic Cleavages

MOST STATES IN THE WORLD SYSTEM have heterogeneous populations in terms of religious beliefs and language use. The Russian Federation (Russia) is heterogeneous because it is home to more than a hundred different ethnic groups. The nature of Russia's multicultural state is the focus of this chapter, which begins with a description of the process by which the state was formed. Key concepts, such as ethnicity and national identity, are presented. A set of theories that may be used to explain the failure of the effort to build an overarching Soviet identity are reviewed. The administrative structure of federalism is discussed because it is a mechanism that allows a degree of autonomy to different ethnic groups living within a **multinational state**. After the historical introduction and the theoretical discussion, we examine three of the ethnic groups (Yakuts, Tatars, and Chechens) more closely, paying attention to their different cultures, histories, and major concerns.

ETHNIC HETEROGENEITY IN RUSSIA

Ethnic Russians make up 80 percent of the population of the Russia Federation (RF) and the rest of the population is divided among other nationality groups. The largest of the non-Russian groups each have a population of more than 1 million. The percentage of the total population of the RF represented by each of these groups is: Tatars, 3.8 percent; Ukrainians, 2 percent; Chuvash, 1 percent; Bashkirs, 1 percent; Chechens, 0.9 percent; and Armenians, 0.8 percent.[1]

Russians, as the major ethnic group, constitute a greater percentage of the population of Russia than do Caucasians (whites) in the U.S., who comprise 77.1 percent of the population. As can be seen in Table 4.1 (see pp. 76–77), China (the largest country in Asia) and Germany (the largest country in Europe) are more ethnically homogeneous than is Russia, with major ethnic groups constituting 91.9 percent and 91.5 percent of their populations, respectively. Brazil (the largest country in South America) and Nigeria (the largest country in Africa), in contrast, are much more ethnically heterogeneous. Thus, when looking across all continents at those countries that have the largest populations, Russia, even though composed of people speaking many different languages and following different cultures, is very much dominated by ethnic Russians.

In the former Soviet Union, most of the large non-Russian nationality groups each had their own designated ethnic territory. Ukrainians, for example, lived primarily within the Ukrainian Soviet Socialist Republic (Ukrainian SSR), one of the administrative units located within the overarching federal structure of the Union of Soviet Socialist Republics (USSR). With the breakup of the USSR in 1991, Russia, Ukraine, and the other SSRs are now independent countries. But numerous other ethnic territories, which were also administratively part of the USSR, did not become independent states with the breakup of the Soviet Union, and the people of these territories now reside within the borders of one of the fifteen newly independent states of the former USSR. Noteworthy is the fact that some of the USSR's smaller nationality groups, such as the Latvians and Estonians, now have their own independent countries, while relatively large nationality groups, such as the Tatars, remain part of the Russian Federation.

As a new independent state, Russia would not accept claims for independence by different ethnic groups within its own borders. Maintaining **territorial integrity** is a major issue for all the union republics of the former USSR. The challenges of maintaining the integrity of Russia's territory in the face of armed resistance from Chechnya and of building a new national identity have confounded the process of cementing a democratic political culture. Thus, the discussion here about ethnic groups in the Russian Federation leads to the question of whether building a democratic society in a country where citizens are raising arms against one another is even possible.

THE HISTORY OF RUSSIA'S NATIONAL AND ETHNIC CLEAVAGES

The federal structure of Russia today includes administrative units called **oblasts,** which are not associated with any particular ethnic group, and ethnic republics, which are named after the ethnic group that historically occupied the region. Although each republic is named for the indigenous nationality group, colonization over the centuries has resulted in the presence of a significant number of Russians in most of the ethnically defined regions.

The diversity of Russia's population, and the much greater diversity of the former Soviet Union, are the legacy of the expansion of the Russian Empire that

TABLE 4.1 Ethnic Composition of the Russian Federation in Comparative Perspective

	Russian Federation	United States	China	Brazil	Nigeria	Germany
Total area (sq km)	17,075,200	9,629,091	9,596,960	8,511,965	923,768	357,021
Population (July 2003 est.)	144,526,278	290,342,554	1,286,975,468	182,032,604	133,881,703	82,398,326
Size of majority ethnic group	Russian—80%	White—77.1%* (2000)	Han Chinese—91.9%	White (Portuguese, German, Italian, Spanish, Polish)—55%	Hausa and Fulani—29%**	German—91.5%,
Second largest ethnic group	Tatar—3.8%	Black—12.9%	Other nationalities—8.1%	Mixed white and black—38%	Yoruba—21%	Turkish—2.4%
Third largest ethnic group	Ukrainian—2%	Asian—4.2%		Black—6%	Igbo (Ibo)—18%	Other—6.1%

Major religions	Russian Orthodox, Muslim	Protestant—56%, Roman Catholic—28%, Jewish—2% (1989)	Officially atheist but includes Daoist (Taoist), Buddhist, Muslim—1-2%, Christian—3-4% (2002 est.)	Roman Catholic (nominal)—80%	Muslim—50%, Christian—40%, indigenous beliefs—10%	Protestant—34%, Roman Catholic—34%, Muslim—3.7%
Languages	Russian, other	English, Spanish (spoken by a sizable minority)	Mandarin, Yue (Cantonese), Wu (Shanghai-ese), Minbei (Fuzhou)	Portuguese (official), Spanish, English, French	English (official), Hausa, Yoruba, Igbo (Ibo), Fulani	German

Figures are from *The World Factbook* published by the CIA—see http://www.cia.gov/cia/publications/factbook/index.html.

* A separate listing for Hispanic is not included because the U.S. Census Bureau considers Hispanic to mean a person of Latin American descent.

** Nigeria, which is Africa's most populous country, is composed of more than 250 ethnic groups.

occurred during the sixteenth through the twentieth centuries. Russia became a multinational empire as the state increased in size—as new territories inhabited by different nations were incorporated into the empire. The policies of the Soviet and the Tsarist governments in dealing with these different groups created a set of memories and patterns of behavior that partially determine the current relationships between Moscow and the different ethnic groups living in the Russian Federation.

As the reader will recall, by the middle of the seventeenth century, Muscovite princes had captured the territory of Siberia. During the eighteenth and nineteenth centuries, tsars (for example, Peter the Great, Catherine the Great, and Alexander I) expanded Russian control into the Baltic States; Eastern Europe (Belarus, parts of Poland, and Western Ukraine); the territory between the Black and the Caspian Seas, including what is now Georgia and Armenia; and substantial Muslim territories in Central Asia. These lands were forcefully incorporated into the Russian Empire as a result of the military might of the tsars' armies. Over the course of history, the conquered people made periodic attempts to break free of Russian rule. Confrontations occurred when conditions were particularly intolerable, such as during times of famine, or when leaders willing to challenge the Tsarist and Soviet governments emerged.

Tsarism was intolerant of most non-Russian cultures, and thus any efforts to defend those divergent cultures in the face of the tsars' **Russification** policies were met with repression. After the middle of the nineteenth century, Russian imperial rule became increasingly irritated with demands for greater **autonomy** and independence that emanated from conquered people, the Armenians and the Ukrainians, for example. Many non-Russian nationality groups within the empire were targeted by the Tsarist state for discrimination. Social problems were blamed on Jewish conspiracies, while the underdevelopment of Muslim groups was blamed on deficiencies in their language or culture. Separatist demands, based on anti-Russian nationalism, came increasingly from the urban areas of the Russian Empire.

Russian Marxists wanted to distance themselves from the intolerance of the Russian tsars. The Russian Social Democratic Labor Party (RSDLP) adopted a policy on the "national question" at its Second Congress in 1903. This policy, personally drafted by Lenin, included the following key promises should the RSDLP come to power.

- People of non-Russian nations would have the right to receive an education in their own language, "a right to be secured by the setting up of the necessary schools at the expense of the State."
- Every citizen would have the right to express himself or herself at meetings in his or her own language, meaning that native languages would have "equal status" with the "State Language" (Russian) in all local, public, and state institutions.

■ Every nation comprising the State would have the "right of **self-determination** [in this context, self-determination implied the right to secession and the formation of independent states]."[2]

The clause promising self-determination in the program of the RSDLP was a necessity given rising nationalism throughout Europe and Asia; its purpose was to win the trust of non-Russians and to facilitate their merger into a larger state. Lenin believed that the process of historical development would ultimately lead to a merging of nations, and therefore the adoption of a policy allowing for self-determination was a matter of expediency for moving toward the overarching goal of socialist unity. Thus, although he acknowledged the right to secede, Lenin discounted the significance of national differences in the full course of history. As a genuine Marxist, he believed that the overthrow of capitalist exploitation would be a panacea, and that workers of different nations would ultimately have no reason to differentiate themselves from one another. Indeed, at the time of the 1917 Revolution, the Bolshevik Party's membership included many non-Russians, given the repression of minorities under Tsar Nicholas II and given Lenin's promise of self-determination.

In the immediate aftermath of the Bolshevik Revolution, Marxist organizations that had emerged among non-Russians within the empire moderated their demands in the hope of aiding a truly international socialist revolution. But the economic collapse and state disintegration that followed the October 1917 Revolution in Russia contributed to armed opposition to the Bolsheviks, foreign intervention, and the rise of a more resolute nationalism among non-Russians. A new level of national consciousness arose during the Civil War period as groups with distinct religious and ethnic cultures fought to retain their independence in the face of the occupying forces of the increasingly **Russo-centric** Red Army.

The Bolsheviks, like the tsars before them, used military force to control non-Russian territories. When they proclaimed the formation of the Federal Union of Soviet Socialist Republics of Transcaucasia in March 1922, the Bolsheviks did so in spite of vocal opposition from the Central Committee of the Communist Party of Georgia. Once the Bolsheviks conquered territories, such as Eastern Ukraine and Belarus, "treaties" were signed between the Russian Soviet Federated Socialist Republic (RSFSR) and the governments of these territories (December 1920 and January 1921, respectively). (The Belarusian Soviet Socialist Republic had been proclaimed on January 1, 1919.) According to the treaties, the government of the RSFSR took control of the main ministries (commissariats) of these governments (Pipes 1991, 46).

Nationalist resistance to Soviet rule in Ukraine occurred principally because of the failure of Moscow to adhere to the terms of the treaty of December 1920. According to the treaty, Moscow's directives were to be approved by the Ukrainian Sovnarkom (Ukrainian Council of People's Commissars) before being implemented on Ukrainian soil. Not only did the Russian commissars not bother to adequately consult them, but they also neglected to give Ukrainians promised representation on the commissariats taken over by the RSFSR.

In the Central Asian regions, the incorporation began with relatively benign agreements (signed in 1921 and 1922) that granted the RSFSR economic privileges in the People's Republics of Bukhara, Khorezm, and the Far East. The Bolsheviks gradually increased their authority in these regions and ultimately abolished all three People's Republics, and their territories were either directly incorporated into the RSFSR or were distributed among five new republics— Uzbekistan, Turkmenistan, Tajikistan, Kazakhstan, and Kyrgyzstan.

This forceful process of incorporation occurred despite determined opposition and resistance. For example, Enver Pasha, a leader of the **Basmachi Rebellion**, sent an ultimatum to the government of the RSFSR in May 1922 demanding the immediate withdrawal of all Russian troops from Turkistan. Although Enver Pasha was able to build an army of several thousand men, Red Army troops killed him in August 1922 (Pipes 1991, 50).

The fierce resistance that the Bolsheviks encountered during the Basmachi revolt did cause them to rethink their policy of military suppression. To bring order to Central Asia, Lenin realized that some concessions would need to be made to the non-Russian people. Religious lands (*vakuf*) were returned, religious schools (*medresse* and *mektebe*) were reopened, and religious courts (*shariat*) were brought back (Pipes 1991, 51). The New Economic Policy (NEP) of 1921 also permitted the return of some private trade and put an end to forced requisitions of cotton and food. The Bolsheviks' willingness to make concessions, augmented by coercion, accounts for the ability of the Soviet state to crush the defiance of the Muslims of Central Asia.

The resistance of the indigenous party apparatus in Ukraine and Georgia also caused the Communist Party Central Committee of the RSFSR to review its policies. In August 1922, when Stalin proposed that Ukraine, Belarus, Georgia, Azerbaijan, and Armenia be incorporated as autonomous republics within the RSFSR, the Central Committees of Ukraine and Georgia vehemently protested. (In fact, the entire Central Committee of the Georgian Communist Party resigned in protest in October 1922, but a new central committee was appointed to replace the old Georgian Marxists.) On this question, Lenin disagreed with Stalin and called for an arrangement whereby all republics, including the RSFSR, would be reconstituted as a new federation. Lenin declared that the desire to incorporate places such as Ukraine and Georgia directly into the RSFSR constituted "Great Russian Chauvinism" (Pipes 1991, 63). As an alternative to Stalin's proposal, and reflecting Lenin's preferences more than Stalin's, a Union of Soviet Socialist Republics was established in December 1922. The right of secession of union republics remained in the agreement, but this right could only be effected by the central government. On January 31, 1924, the Second All-Union Congress of Soviets ratified the constitution of the USSR.

As it evolved over the years, the Soviet system of federalism came to be based on fifteen union republics (that is, Soviet Socialist Republics, SSRs). The

Russian Soviet Federated Socialist Republic (RSFSR) had a somewhat different status administratively than the other fourteen SSRs because it included 76 percent of the total area of the USSR. Three of the union republics—Russia, Ukraine, and Belorus—were based on Slavic nationality groups, with an Orthodox religious tradition. The Ukrainians were the second largest nationality group in the USSR. Three other union republics were the Baltic republics; Lithuania is overwhelmingly Catholic, while Latvia and Estonia are primarily Lutheran. An additional three republics comprised Caucasus people; Georgia and Armenia are mostly Christian, and Azerbaijan is predominantly Muslim. Five SSRs—Turkmenistan, Kazakhstan, Uzbekistan, Tajikistan, and Kyrgyzstan—were based in Central Asia; all of them populated largely by Muslims.

These fifteen Soviet Socialist Republics had the highest administrative status and the most (although limited) autonomous decision-making authority. Below the level of the SSR, and territorially located within an SSR, were oblasts (provinces or states) and also Autonomous Soviet Socialist Republics (ASSRs). ASSRs, like SSRs, were each associated with the territory of a non-Russian ethnic group. Sixteen ASSRs were located within the RFSFR (including the Tatar ASSR, the Yakut ASSR, and the Chechen-Ingush ASSR). The Abkhaz ASSR and the Adjar ASSR were located within the Soviet Socialist Republic of Georgia. The Nakhichevan ASSR was inside Azerbaijan and the Karakalpak ASSR was inside Uzbekistan. In addition, the Soviet federated structure included Autonomous Oblasts (AO), such as the Jewish AO in the RSFSR and the Nagorno-Karabakh AO in Armenia, and Autonomous Okrugs (AOK), such as the territorially vast Taymyr AOK and Evenk AOK inside the RSFSR.

When the last census of the Soviet Union was conducted in 1989, Russians lived throughout the territory of the USSR and constituted roughly half (50.8 percent) of its population. The percentage of the population that was Russian had declined to this point steadily after World War II because the rate of population growth was significantly lower among ethnic Russians than among Central Asians and Caucasus people (see Map 4.1 and Figure 4.1).

USING THEORIES OF NATIONALISM TO EXPLAIN THE BREAKUP OF THE SOVIET UNION

Having looked at how the Soviet Union was created, it becomes easier to understand how it came apart. The disintegration of the Soviet Union has been explained by a variety of factors including, but not limited to, the economic downturn of the 1980s, the democratizing reforms of Mikhail Gorbachev, the weakened control of the Communist Party, the overextension of the Soviet Empire, the strains associated with the Cold War nuclear arms race, and the delegitimization of Soviet institutions because glasnost removed censorship and people learned truths about the failings of the system. In addition to these

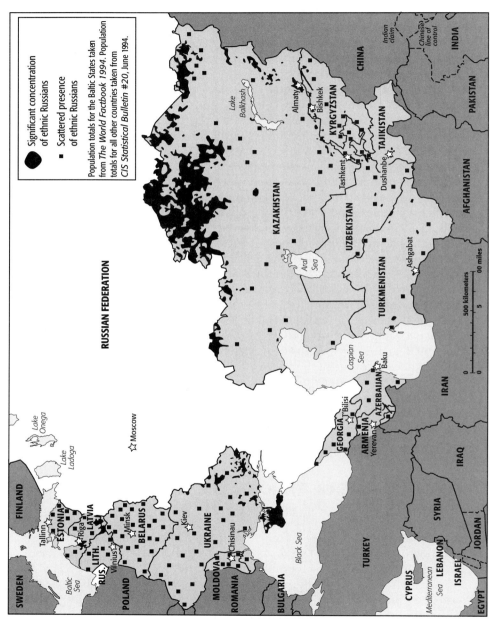

MAP 4.1 Ethnic Russians in the Newly Dependent States

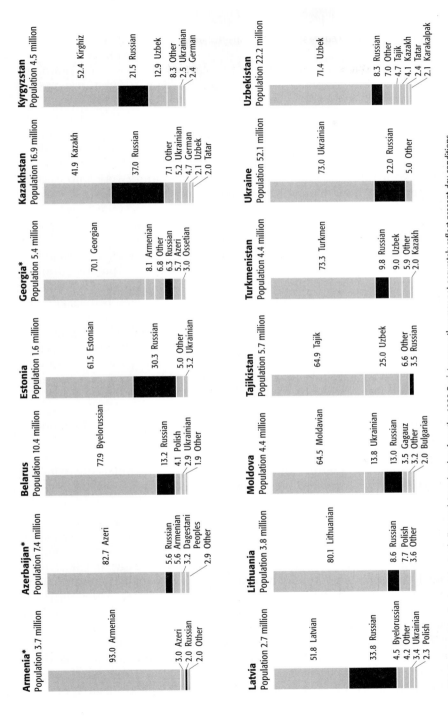

*Ethnic percentages for Armenia, Azerbaijan, and Georgia taken from the 1989 Soviet census; they may not accurately reflect present-day conditions.

FIGURE 4.1 Percentages of Ethnic Russians in the Newly Independent States

forces, the rise of anti-Russian nationalism among the people living in the Baltic republics and in Armenia, Georgia, and Ukraine contributed to the breakup of the Soviet Empire. The preceding descriptive historical overview of the forced incorporation of so many people into the Russian Empire and into the Soviet Union explains why many non-Russians became so vociferous in their demands for independence in the late 1980s.

By the 1980s, non-Russian nationality groups, such as the Armenians, the Georgians, and the Estonians, were well educated, professionally skilled, and highly political. The structure of the Soviet Union, with each of these nationality groups having its own territory, its own Communist Party organization, and its own institutions of government, provided a framework within which they could assert their demands for independence from Soviet rule. Thus, the same institutions that had been used by Lenin, Stalin, and their successors to assert control over the non-Russian nationalities became resources in the hands of non-Russian political leaders in the late 1980s; they saw the weakening of the Soviet state as their chance to regain the independence and autonomy that had been lost when they were forcefully incorporated into the Russian Empire.

The Estonian people, the Lithuanian people, the Georgian people, and others were all mobilized into political action by homegrown leaders, who gave speeches that accused Soviet leaders of suppressing the cultures (notably the languages and religions) of non-Russian groups. Glasnost provided the freedom for local leaders to publicize such views. Native leaders pointed out to their audiences that they, as non-Russians, had suffered injustices under communism. The local leaders also blamed the Soviet system for poor living conditions, economic exploitation, and environmental ruin. After the competitive elections of 1990 in Lithuania, Latvia, Estonia, Georgia, and Armenia, local nationalist leaders took control of the SSR legislatures and quickly adopted declarations of independence and sovereignty. (The Soviet system was also resisted by Russians who felt that their culture and traditions had been undermined by the Bolsheviks and by communist policies and practices.)

Independence-oriented leaders who took over in Ukraine put the final nail in the coffin of the Soviet Union. Although Boris Yeltsin, as president of the RSFSR, was amenable to restructuring the union in the aftermath of the failed August 1991 coup against Mikhail Gorbachev in Moscow, Ukrainian leaders were unwilling to negotiate a new power-sharing arrangement with the RSFSR. Rather, Ukrainians used the opportunity of a weakened Soviet state to distance themselves from their Russian brothers, demanding full independence from the USSR.

The role that nationalism and ethnic cleavages played in the breakup of the former Soviet Union can best be studied from a theoretical perspective. To consider theories further, we begin with a few definitions. An ethnic group or **ethnicity** refers to a group of people within a larger society that are considered as distinct from others because of common traits or culture within the group. Language, religion, a common sense of ancestry, a shared history, or some other characteristic can be used to define an ethnic group. *Ethnic identity* refers to the feeling of belonging to such a group. A *nationality group* is an ethnicity that desires to be respected as an independent political community. *Independence* means full self-government, while *autonomy* involves self-determination for a nationality group within a larger state. *Nationalism* is an ideology that requires that an ethnic group's territorial boundaries coincide with political boundaries. Nationalism calls on an ethnic group, or nationality, to strive for sovereign statehood, and it promotes the interests of a particular national group or culture over those of other groups or cultures.

The first theory to consider is the Marxist theory of nationalities, which was incorporated into the official ideology of the Soviet state. From this perspective, nationalist identities are seen as characteristic of the capitalist stage of historical development, and with further progress toward socialism, these will become obsolete. Marxism treats ethnic conflict as a diversion from the real problem of class struggle between the bourgeoisie and the proletariat. National identities are illusions of cleavage that prevent the working class from uniting across national borders against the ills of capitalism. As a corollary, nationalism's continued existence is dependent on the continuation of capitalism. Marxism views cultural and religious symbolism as a tool that the ruling class uses to perpetuate the submissiveness of the workers.

According to the Austrian Marxist Otto Bauer (1907), a nation can be distinguished by its national character, which includes shared historical experiences, residence in a common territory, and a common language. Advanced education, industrialization, and migration to cities each contributes to an "awakening" of historical nations and to increased rivalry among newly mobile populations. Bauer's solution to the problems of nations in the capitalist stage was to grant limited autonomy to national communities.

A related but different theoretical perspective posits that the process of modernization alters society in ways that can lead to changes in the nature of ethnic identities. According to this perspective, nationalism can be seen as an integral part and even a product of the modernization process. The link between modernization and manifestations of nationalism is based on defining modernization as expanding industrial and service sectors, widening markets, increasing secularism and literacy, and rapid urbanization. Each of these processes brings about increased interaction among diverse peoples. Modernization generally creates unequal development and opportunities across groups, which tends to breed ethnic-based and regional hostilities. Simultaneously, processes of urbanization and education equip national elites and ordinary people with the resources they need to challenge a central state.

A third perspective is the cultural–pluralist one. This perspective argues that ethnic conflict arises repeatedly when groups with distinct value systems and contrasting social structures attempt to coexist in a single society. Ethnic groups, by their very nature, form closed, sociocultural units; yet when different ethnic groups share a single territory, they must interact intermittently in common markets and in an overarching political system. Through this interaction, one group generally comes to dominate all others. The dominant group then attempts to force the assimilation of the subordinate groups into the dominant culture. Power inequality, accompanied by forced assimilation, breeds resistance on the part of the subordinate groups and ultimately leads to conflict between dominant and subordinate groups.

An historical example of forced assimilation is the attempted Russification of non-Russian people. The long-term Soviet goal was assimilation into a more unified culture that was clearly dominated by the Russians. The non-Russians were threatened by Russian language requirements and religious repression and fought to save their separate cultures and ethnic identities.

A fourth perspective that also has value for understanding ethnic cleavages in the Soviet and post-Soviet context is called the relative group worth theoretical perspective. According to it, ethnic groups are understood as extended kinship clusters; thus, ethnic groups fulfill functions similar to those filled by family ties and obligations (Horowitz 1985). Ethnicity provides a sense of familiarity, community, and emotional support for the members of a group. When government policies, such as the policy of Russification, threaten group status, ethnic ties become a natural base for political organization. Movements of national separatism therefore tend to emphasize those characteristics, such as language, that make a group distinctive. According to Smith, the fundamental goals of a separatist movement are the realization of citizen self-government, the establishment of a territorial home, and the maintenance of a distinct ethnic history (1976, 3). Control of state structures conveys the ultimate in group power and prestige.

A fifth theory sees nations as imagined political communities (Anderson 1991). Nations are constructed through processes such as drawing maps, making a population census, and creating museums. The idea behind the argument of imagined communities is that many people in the world did not historically identify themselves as being part of any nationality group, but state policies and programs categorize them as such. In the Soviet Union, for example, administrative regions for nationality groups were created, thus reinforcing and in some cases even creating the sense of group identity.

None of these theories argues that groups are inevitably separated by permanent cultural boundaries. Ethnicity, although prevalent and powerful, is by no means invariant. For different groups in different situational contexts, national identities can be more or less salient in comparison to other forms of group identity. At specific times, even within any ethnic category, great variation exists across individuals with regard to their levels of nationalist passion. Nonetheless, states must deal with the challenges of different cultures, unequal in economic resources and opportunity, living within their borders. All the preceding theoretical approaches support the idea of using a federated state structure if different nationality groups must share the same overarching political system.

A COMPARATIVE PERSPECTIVE OF THE BASIC TERRITORIAL ADMINISTRATION SYSTEMS

In terms of territorial administration, governments may be unitary, federal, or confederal, depending on the relative distribution of authority between the central government (often referred to as the national government or the federal government) and the lower-level governments such as states or provinces. In a unitary system, the central government directly controls regional and local affairs; the country may have administrative districts, but these do not have autonomous decision-making authority.

In contrast, in a confederation, power resides with constituent units. Few true confederations exist in the world today. (Switzerland, officially the Swiss Confederation, is a rare example of a confederal system that still exists.) The best examples of the confederal form of government come from history; for instance, the Confederation of German States, which existed between 1815 and 1866, consisted of 39 states (35 monarchies and 4 free cities). That confederation was little more than a loose union for mutual defense. Another historical example is the Articles of Confederation ratified in 1781 and superseded by the Constitution of the United States in 1789; Article 3 characterized the confederation as a "league of friendship" constituted for common defense.

Federal (federations) or confederal (confederations) systems are distinguished from one another on the basis of the degree of autonomy (independent jurisdictional authority) characteristic of the regional or local governments. In a federal system, states or provinces recognize the sovereignty of the central government while retaining certain residual powers. The distribution (division) of powers (jurisdictions of authority) between the central government and its constituent administrative units is specified in the country's constitution. Substantial power over matters affecting the people as a whole, such as external affairs, commerce, coinage, and the maintenance of military forces, are usually granted to the central government. One of the major characteristics of a federal form of government is the ability of the constituent units to raise their own revenues through taxation. Without revenue sources independent from the central government, regions would be unable to maintain independent decision-making authority.

The Russian Federation of today and the Soviet Union before it are examples of federal systems of government. In both systems, however, the fiscal independence of the regions has been limited. For instance, Putin increased the salaries of all civil servants by a sizable 89 percent in December 2001. That decision applied to the entire Russian Federation. An ongoing goal of the Putin administration is to increase its control over the assets of the resource-rich regions. The stakes are particularly high in regions with sizable natural resource deposits such as Siberia and parts of the Far East.

RUSSIAN FEDERALISM

The Russian Federation (RF) today, with a territorial size that is approximately 1.8 times larger than the United States (see Table 4.1), is separated into 89 different federal administrative regions.* In terms of territory, Russia is the largest country in the world today. The RF consists of 2 federal cities (Moscow and St. Petersburg), 49 oblasts (for example, Novgorod), and 6 krais (for example, Stavropol). Russia's 49 oblasts are in some respects comparable to the 50 states in the United States. An additional 32 of Russia's 89 constituent entities are arranged on the principle of national territories, defined by ethnoterritorial characteristics; these include 21 republics (for example, Tatarstan), 1 autonomous oblast (the Jewish Autonomous Oblast of Birobidzhan), and 10 autonomous **okrugs** (for example, Evenk). Of the 21 republics, 7 are in the North Caucasus region, 6 are located in the middle Volga and Urals region, and 5 are in Siberia, while the others cannot be grouped together. The **titular nationality** represents a majority in just 7 of these ethnoterritorial entities. (See Map 4.2.)

For the most part, the ethnically based political units have the same boundaries as they did under the Soviet government. With the demise of the Soviet Union, the Autonomous Soviet Socialist Republics located within the RSFSR declared their intention to govern themselves. Recognition of the rights of minorities within their own administrative units by the new Russian state was a strategic necessity in Moscow's effort to hold Russia together. If violence was to be avoided, the minority populations needed to have guarantees that their interests would be protected in various areas such as language and school curriculum, the distribution of resources, and the opening of employment opportunities in the private and public sectors. Thus, Russia today is an example of a federal state with a multitude of ethnic groups living in traditional homelands. In addition, Russia has federal administrative units that are not based on the ethnoterritorial principle: the oblasts, cities, and krais.

Under President Yeltsin (1991–1999), Russia was a loosely structured federal system. Many regions acted virtually as independent states because Moscow was unable to fully exert its control throughout the territory. When Vladimir Putin became president of Russia, he began to deal with the problem of limited centralized control: the lack of uniformity in laws, particularism at the regional level, and the existence of relatively autonomous regional regimes. Putin has pushed consistently for legislation that would reduce the regions' abilities to act unilaterally. He has strengthened central authority and has reined in the powers of regional governors and republic presidents. Putin's reforms include the creation of seven federal districts (okrugs) each with a presidential envoy, the restructuring of the **Federation Council** (the upper house of the Russian parliament), and the adoption of laws enabling the removal of elected heads and the dissolution of legislative assemblies in Russia's eighty-nine constituent

*The Soviet Union was nearly 2.5 times larger than the United States.

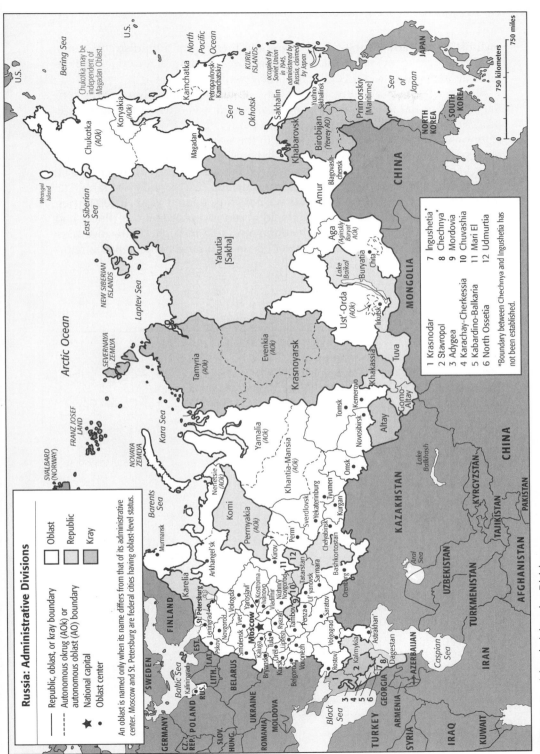

Russia: Administrative Divisions

— Republic, oblast, or kray boundary
- - - Autonomous okrug (AOk) or autonomous oblast (AO) boundary
★ National capital
• Oblast center

An oblast is named only when its name differs from that of its administrative center. Moscow and St. Petersburg are federal cities having oblast-level status.

☐ Oblast
☐ Republic
☐ Kray

1 Krasnodar
2 Stavropol
3 Adygea
4 Karachay-Cherkessia
5 Kabardino-Balkaria
6 North Ossetia
7 Ingushetia*
8 Chechnya*
9 Mordovia
10 Chuvashia
11 Mari El
12 Udmurtia

*Boundary between Chechnya and Ingushetia has not been established.

MAP 4.2 Russia's Administrative Divisions

regions. In addition, he has encouraged the merging of administrative units and has sought to increase Moscow's control over the natural resources and the revenue-generating sectors of the regional economies.

Shortly after becoming Russia's president, Putin appointed his own presidential envoys to the federal districts, each of whom was ordered to oversee the process of bringing all laws throughout the country into line with the federal constitution and laws. By transferring power to the seven presidential envoys, Putin reduced the power of regional governors and presidents. The federal districts have since become an institutionalized layer in the Russian Federation structure. The names of each of these districts and their population size are shown in Table 4.2.

Putin's power over the regions was further consolidated in April 2002 when the Russian Constitutional Court upheld a controversial law that Putin had signed two years before, which granted the president the right to fire governors and also gave the State Duma (the lower house of Russia's national parliament)

TABLE 4.2   Russia's Federal Districts (Okrugs)

Federal Okrug	Number of Territorial Administrative Units Within the District	Population Figures (Oct. 2002)	Capital City
Severo-Zapadnyj Federal'nyj Okrug (Northwestern)	11	13,974,466	St. Petersburg
Južnyj Federal'nyj Okrug (Northern Caucasus or Southern)	13	22,907,141	Rostov-na-Donu
Dal'nevostocnij Federal'nyj Okrug (Far Eastern)	10	6,692,865	Chabarovsk
Sibirskij Federal'nyj Okrug (Siberian)	16	20,062,938	Novosibirsk
Ural'skij Federal'nyj Okrug (Ural)	6	12,373,926	Jekaterinburg
Central'nyj Federal'nyj Okrug (Central)	18	38,000,651	Moscow
Privolžskij Federal'nyj Okrug (Volga)	15	31,154,744	Niznij Novgorod
Total	**89**	**145,166,731**	Moscow

For information on all the administrative units within the federal districts, see http://www.citypopulation.de/Russia.html.

the right to disband regional legislatures.* Later in 2002, the State Duma passed legislation that gave local officials specific duties and holds them responsible for carrying them out. If they fail, local officials face the prospect of external management of their municipalities. A mayor can be fired if he or she issues an act that violates the law (that is, if a court finds that it is illegal and the transgression is not fixed within two months), abuses human rights, threatens the overall unity of Russia's legal system or market, or improperly uses money transferred from the federal or regional level (again, at a court's determination). If a local legislature adopts a law that violates the country's legal norms, the governor of the region can disband the legislature. Thus, governors were given new authority to pressure mayors, including mayors of regional capitals who have long been their political opponents.[3]

The federal center likewise has "external oversight" of governors. In three instances—a natural disaster, indebtedness amounting to more than 30 percent of a region's own revenue, and improper use of money transferred from the federal government—federal authorities can temporarily take away power from regional institutions. As one among several possible examples, in May 2004 the Saratov oblast prosecutor filed charges against Governor Dmitri Ayatskov for abuse of his office and for exceeding the authority of his position. As another example, the Ivanovo oblast prosecutor announced in March 2003 an investigation of Vladimir Tikhonov, its governor, with regard to real-estate transactions.[4]

President Putin also has consistently supported a reduction in the number of Russian regions from eighty-nine to a more manageable figure. He signed a law in December 2002, the purpose of which was to facilitate voluntary regional consolidation between regions with contiguous borders. This process would require a constitutional amendment because the Russian constitution lists all of Russia's administrative regions by name.

In addition, the Putin administration is requiring that republic-level constitutions and regional laws be in line with the Russian Federation Constitution and with federal laws. One of the responsibilities of **procurators** in the federal okrugs is to bring regional legislation into conformity with federal laws.[†] In June 2003, however, the parliaments of Bashkortostan and Tatarstan challenged these practices and asked the Russian Constitutional Court to decide whether Russia's courts of general jurisdiction had the right to determine whether regional constitutions were in line with federal norms. In July 2003, the Russian Constitutional Court ruled that only it can declare passages of regional constitutions and charters in violation of federal law.[‡] It ruled that the courts of general jurisdiction can only overturn parts of regional constitutions that have

---

*The full force of these reforms took effect in January 2006.

[†]A procurator's responsibilities are like a prosecutor's in the United States, but much wider because they instigate investigations and respond to complaints of corruption, rights abuses, and abuses of power.

[‡]Russian courts are neither free of political pressure nor are they experienced at constitutional interpretation.

already been declared unconstitutional in the basic laws of other regions. In all other cases, the Constitutional Court has to make the decision.[5]

Other reforms in Russia's federal system have served to rein in the powers of governors; these include the removal of governors from the Federation Council, the introduction of a federal right to remove governors from office if a court determines that they have violated federal legislation, provisions restricting the number of terms governors can serve, the annulment of bilateral power-sharing treaties between the federal and regional governments, and the possible transfer of natural resource ownership and management to the federal level. Overall, the final distribution of authority between the federal center in Moscow and the governments of Russia's regions remains contested. The reforms consolidate the control of governors over the local governments within their regions; however, at the same time, the federal government has increased its own powers over both regional and local levels. While many of the reform provisions genuinely do aim to improve local governance, efficiency, and service delivery, they also make local governments more financially and institutionally dependent on central and regional authorities.

The next section presents specific case studies of Russia's regions. Each case provides a different example of the ongoing contests between the center and the regions of the Russian Federation.

CASE STUDIES ABOUT MAJOR NON-RUSSIAN NATIONALITY GROUPS

The three nationality groups—Yakuts, Tatars, and Chechens—selected for in-depth analysis represent very different cultures and relationships with Moscow. Yakuts live primarily in the Sakha Republic, which is geographically the largest of Russia's republics. Tatarstan is the largest republic in the Russian Federation in terms of population. Sakha is a diamond producer while Tatarstan is an oil producer. Both have seen their natural resources exploited by the Soviet state and the Russian Empire before it. Over the centuries, each has experienced an influx of Russians. In contrast, Chechnya has relatively few Russians within its territorial boundaries, and its economy has not provided riches for the Russians. The Chechens and the Tatars are two of the seven largest nationality groups living within the RF. In studying Yakuts, Chechens, and Tatars, we touch on the diverse geography of the Russian Federation. An overview of these divergent peoples and places helps to provide a sense of the range of challenges faced by the Putin administration in responding to the heterogeneity of the federation.

The two ethnic republics that have been particularly assertive in demanding greater sovereignty are Chechnya and Tatarstan. After years of negotiation, Tatarstan signed a bilateral power-sharing agreement with Moscow in February

1994 that granted it a high degree of economic autonomy. The leadership of Tatarstan continues to try to maintain this autonomy while Moscow works to rein in Tatarstan's sovereignty. This contest over jurisdictional authority occurs primarily through legal battles. Chechnya and Moscow, in contrast, have not resolved their differences through nonviolent means. Many factors account for the differences, two of which are the relative ethnic heterogeneity of Tatarstan and the fact that Tatarstan is completely surrounded by Russian territory. In contrast, Chechnya is located on the international border with Georgia, increasing both the opportunity and incentive for Chechnya's independence drive. The Tatars and Chechens are discussed in further detail later; before turning to them, the Yakuts are considered.

Yakuts

The Yakuts have an ethnic homeland located within the Siberian region of the Russian Federation. After the collapse of the Soviet Union, the Yakut Autonomous Soviet Socialist Republic was renamed the Republic of Sakha (Yakutia). In 1989, the Yakut ASSR was home to a population made up of roughly 365,000 Yakuts, 14,000 Evenks, 9,000 Evens, 1,000 Jews, 77,000 Ukrainians, and 550,000 Russians. Among the 1 million people living in Yakutia, the Yakuts (Turkic-speaking Sakhas) constitute about 34 percent of the republic's population. The Yakuts and the Buryats are the most numerous native ethnic groups of Siberia. Evens and Evenks are also indigenous to the region. Over time, the proportion of Yakuts gradually declined in favor of Russians, who now constitute the largest ethnic group residing in the Sakha Republic.

The land size of Yakutia is huge, almost twice the size of Alaska; the largest of all the regions in Russia, it occupies one-fifth of Russia's total territory. Yakutia is one of the coldest inhabited regions on earth with more than 40 percent of the republic's territory inside the Arctic Circle. Most of Yakutia's territory is covered by forests rich in game animals. The region, which also has an abundance of minerals and is famous for furs, gold, and diamonds, was used by both the tsars and Soviet officials as a place of exile and labor camps.

Penetration of this region began in 1632 when Russian explorers built a fort at Yakutsk, now the capital of the republic. The main purpose of the fort was to control the Lena River—the main transport artery of the entire region—and the rich fur, gold, and logging territories in its vicinity. Few Russians moved into the area even during the gold rush of the 1850s and despite the lucrative trade in furs. Everything changed after 1934 as a result of the collectivization and industrialization programs of Stalin. Collectivization destroyed traditional tribal rule and much of the indigenous economy, as Sakha nomads were forcefully settled on state farms. Large numbers of Russians and Ukrainians were sent to the region as part of the labor camp prison system or were attracted by the higher wages offered for working in the mining industry. Native inhabitants were gradually outnumbered by immigrant workers. The proportion of

Yakuts in the overall population of the republic dropped from 90 percent in 1920 to 43 percent in 1970, to 36.6 percent in 1979, to 33.4 percent in 1989. Russians settled in the cities and also controlled the mining industries, which created a social cleavage between Russian cities and mining industry on the one hand and the Sakha countryside and agriculture on the other.[6]

With the start of glasnost under Gorbachev came a revival of native culture, including a resurgence of interest in the Yakut–Sakha native language and a renewed pride in national traditions and historical events (Lempert 2002, 54). Sakha national consciousness is also closely linked with the ecological situation in the republic. The large-scale exploitation of raw materials severely disrupted the natural environment of the region.

The Yakut Supreme Soviet adopted a Declaration of Sovereignty in September 1990 and officially declared its territory a republic in 1991, asserting control over the territory's diamonds, timber, and other resources. On April 27, 1992, Yakutia was granted the status of autonomous republic. Yakutia signed the Federation Treaty, but only after receiving much more autonomy than it had under the Soviet Union. As a republic within the Russian Federation, Yakutia elected its first president, Mikhail Nikolayev, in December 1991. Nikolayev was reelected in December 1996. As of 2004, the president of Sakha was Vyacheslav A. Shtyrov. The republic also has a legislature, but it is weak vis-à-vis the president.

During the Yeltsin years, the republic was able to develop a strong, export-oriented economy. Still, the Republic of Sakha faces problems of limited control over its own mineral wealth, difficulties associated with ecological destruction, food shortages, a high cost of living, and an ethnic dilemma because such a large portion of the republic's inhabitants are ethnic Russians. Diamond and coal mining are the main industries; Sakha is the second largest producer and exporter of diamonds in the world. Sakha also mines a significant part of Russia's gold and has considerable oil and gas resources. A main priority of Yakutia's government is the development of oil and gas industries.

In spite of the mineral deposits, Yakutia is one of the administrative units in the Russian Federation that receives significant fund transfers from the federal government.[7] In 2002, seventy-one regions received direct financial support from the Federal Fund for the Financial Support of the Regions. The largest recipients of this support were Dagestan and Sakha.

Given the richness of the mineral resources in Sakha, it is understandable that local officials would demand to keep a degree of control over the wealth. The situation is complicated by the fact that Russians still dominate many of the power positions in the republic's administrative apparatus and major industries. The fact that Sakhas are a minority in their own republic is deeply resented by the titular inhabitants. There is a sense among the indigenous Yakut population that Russians keep for themselves taxes collected in the republic and that the Russians continue to control foreign investments and trade. The Yakuts feel that the Russians do not adequately consult the indigenous local people on questions about economic development.

Despite their protests, ethnic Yakuts appear to have limited leverage over the federal government given that the Republic of Sakha is geographically located inside the Russian Federation and that the majority of its population is Russian. The republic will remain within the Russian Federation, and therefore the best it can do is attempt to counter the powerful influence of Moscow by strengthening its relations with other republics that also want to preserve their autonomy. Tatarstan and Bashkortostan, for example, which are two other republics within the Russian Federation whose titular nationality speaks a Turkic language, have attempted to preserve their autonomy in relation to Moscow. Their geographic, economic, and demographic situation is, however, different from that of the Republic of Sakha.

Tatars

The Tatars are the largest—more than 5.5 million—non-Russian ethnic group living in the Russian Federation. Many Tatars live within the territory of the Republic of Tatarstan; others are spread throughout different parts of the federation. The population of the Republic of Tatarstan numbers some 3.7 million people. According to the 1989 census, Tatars were 48.5 percent of Tatarstan's population, while Russians were 43.3 percent of its population. Tatarstan is located in the Volga Federal Okrug.

Even after the territory of what is now Tatarstan was incorporated into the Russian Empire, the area remained an important center of Muslim religion and culture. The Tatar Autonomous Soviet Socialist Republic was founded in 1920. In August 1990, the Supreme Soviet of the Tatar ASSR (located within the territory of the RSFSR) passed a declaration of sovereignty. The Tatar leadership asserted that the region had been exploited by Moscow and that greater local autonomy and control over resources would serve to check these "colonialist" tendencies. In March 1992, the residents of Tatarstan participated in a referendum and voted in favor of establishing a sovereign state by a margin of 61 to 37 percent.[8] With the resource of popular support in hand, the leadership of Tatarstan successfully sidestepped the signing of the Russian Federation Treaty in March 1992, and chose rather to negotiate bilaterally with Moscow regarding various issues such as autonomy, control over natural resources, and economic arrangements. According to the constitution adopted in November 1992, the Republic of Tatarstan is a sovereign state, a subject of the international law and associated with the Russian Federation on the basis of a bilateral treaty. For nearly ten years after the dissolution of the Soviet Union, the State Council of Tatarstan passed legislation with little regard for the Russian constitution or federal law.

A cornerstone of Tatar identity is their Islamic faith. Most Tatars and Bashkirs are Sunni Muslims, although some have converted to Orthodoxy. Conflicts that have arisen between the Tatar government and the Russian government are frequently over issues associated with the fact that Russian laws are geared toward an Orthodox Christian society. As an example, Sunday is accepted as a day of rest under Christianity, which makes it necessary for Muslims to gain special permission to attend Friday religious celebrations. Related religious problems involve service in the Russian Federation Army—all males are obligated to serve for two years in the army when they turn eighteen. Human rights violations have allegedly occurred in the Russian army when Tatar recruits are abused because of their religion or are given no alternative to pork or foods cooked in pork grease. Also, recruits are not given time to say daily prayers as required by their faith and Islamic services are banned even though Orthodox chapels and priests are accepted. Many Tatars have deserted the Russian Federation Army rather than be sent to Chechnya to fight.

In May 2003, Muslim women in Russia's Republic of Tatarstan won a court battle that many saw as an important step in recognizing the equality of religions in the Russian Federation. Ten Muslim women from Tatarstan asked the Russian Supreme Court to overturn a Tatarstan Interior Ministry ban on wearing headscarves in photographs for their domestic passports and other official documents. The women argued that the ban on headscarves violated their constitutional right to freedom of conscience.* The court ruled that "citizens whose religious convictions do not permit them to appear before strangers without head attire may present a passport photograph with head attire."[9] From a comparative perspective, it is important to note that Russia's laws, as revised after the ruling, are now more tolerant of such religious practices than are the laws of the United States or France. In many countries, applicants for passports must submit photos with the face, one ear, the neck, and hair visible. In France, Interior Minister Nicolas Sarkozy provoked the anger of the French Muslim community in 2003 when he stated that photographs for the compulsory French identity card must be taken bareheaded.[10]

In addition to adherence to Islam, Tatars' identity is tied to an attachment to their own language. The Republic of Tatarstan has two official languages: the Tatar language (Turkic group of Altaic language family) and Russian (Slavic group of Indo-European language family). The republic has adopted legislation to support the preservation, study, and growth of the languages of the people of Tatarstan. In 1999, Tatarstan passed a law that adopted the Latin alphabet for the Tatar language as opposed to the Cyrillic alphabet used by the Russians. (Since 1938 the Tatar written language had been based on the Cyrillic script.) In 2002, however, amendments to the federal Law on Languages required that all languages of the Russian Federation be written using the Cyrillic alphabet. Given that republic laws must be in line with federal legislation, this represented a direct blow to Tatarstan.

In addition to the religious and cultural differences between the Russian-dominated federal state and the Tatar-dominated republican government, differences arise between the two governments over jurisdictions of lawmaking authority and the disposition of natural resources. Tatarstan is rich in oil and

*Union of Tatarstan Muslim Women Chairwoman Almira Adiatulina said that the Koran forbids Muslim women from appearing in front of strange men with their heads bared.

gas, and it has a well-developed industrial base in areas such as machine, truck, aircraft, and chemical industries.

On several occasions, Tatarstan President Mintimer Sharipovich Shaimiev, who was first elected in June 1991 and reelected in March 1996, registered his disapproval of President Putin's efforts to diminish the autonomy of Russia's regions. In spite of his protests, and under pressure from Moscow, Shaimiev agreed to bring his republic's legislation in line with federal norms. The presidential envoy to the Volga Federal District (former Prime Minister Sergei Kiriyenko) established a bilateral conciliatory commission whose job it was to modify Tatarstan legislation that conflicted with the Russian constitution or with federal laws. Tatarstan's legislature, the State Council, was then required to consider the amendments to its laws as determined by the commission.

In some cases, the Tatarstan State Council was willing to amend republican laws that contradicted federal legislation but, in other cases, the council felt its own laws were more forward thinking than federal law, so it was reluctant to make amendments.[11] During the period from 2000 to 2003, the Kremlin forced Tatarstan to rewrite dozens of republican laws, particularly legislation affecting budgetary processes and allowing the republic to distribute federal tax income gathered on its territory. A July 2003 ruling by the Russian Constitutional Court determined that only the Russian Constitutional Court could determine whether regional constitutions violate federal norms. Tatarstan, however, has refused to drop the references to regional sovereignty and republican citizenship in its constitution. The Russian–Tatarstan power-sharing treaty of February 1994 was also allowed to stand, even though it contradicts both the federal and republican constitutions in several places.

Despite the continuing legal battle, the important point is that this competition for power, authority, and jurisdiction is taking place through political, legal, and legislative means. Representative of the working relationship that has developed between Moscow and Tatarstan was Putin's formal nomination in March 2005 of Shaimiev to continue as Tatarstan's president after his third five-year term was due to end in March 2006. Putin submitted the nomination to Tatarstan's legislature for approval. If the Tatar parliament had failed to approve Shaimiev for president, Putin had the authority to dismiss the State Council.

Chechens

The Chechens are the only people within the Russian Federation still fighting for independent statehood through violent confrontation; the continuing warfare in Chechnya is the most brutal in the region of the former Soviet Union. Chechnya is located on the international border with Georgia in the Northern Caucasus federal district. Fighting in the region has been endemic since late 1991. Chechnya's independence movement is complicated by unsettled border issues, smuggling, illegal arms sales, refugee flows, corruption, and armed mercenaries from contiguous conflicts. Russia is absolutely committed to maintaining its territorial integrity and will not allow Chechnya to become an independent country. The region is strategically important to the Russian Federation because of the oil pipelines that run through it and because of its proximity to further oil wealth.

The Chechen Republic is one of the most ethnically homogeneous of those in the Russian Federation. Chechens have long been the majority within Chechnya. Recent census numbers indicate Chechnya's current population is approximately 1.088 million, despite an estimated death toll of 100,000 to 140,000 that resulted from the 1994–1996 war.[12] As the Chechen independence movement gained strength and tensions mounted, Russians began leaving the area and the exodus continued throughout the war. It can be assumed that few Russian civilians remain living in Chechnya; however, no recent data are available.

When the Russian Empire expanded into the Caucasus region, the Chechens, most of whom are Sunni Muslim, violently resisted Russian forces but were eventually defeated. With much bloodshed, the Russians established power in Chechnya by 1865. Approximately 1 million Chechens left the region for destinations throughout the Middle East, thereby creating a significant diaspora in Jordan, as well as in Turkey. It was during this period that ethnic Russians began moving into the area.

Although free of Russian control between 1917 and 1922, the resistance of the Chechens was again defeated, this time by harsh measures employed by the Bolshevik Red Army. The Chechen-Ingush ASSR was proclaimed in 1923. During World War II, Stalin accused the Caucasus ethnic groups of collaborating with the Germans, and mass deportations to Central Asia followed. In 1944, the entire Chechen population was herded into cattle cars and transported to either Siberia or Central Asia (Williams 2000, 102). Stalin attempted to remove any trace of Islam as well by closing mosques and religious colleges. It was not until 1978 that Soviet authorities again allowed the operation of mosques within the region (Damrel 1999, 2).

After the death of Stalin, the Chechen people were allowed to return to the Chechen-Ingush ASSR. But, when they did return in 1957, their homes and lands had been taken over by others. The result of Stalin's actions was serious ethnic turmoil between regional groups.

As the Soviet Union began unraveling in 1990 and independence movements throughout it gained strength, Chechnya also stood up against the Soviet empire. The Chechen-Ingush ASSR was divided into Chechnya and Ingushetya, with the largest portion going to the Chechens. On October 27, 1991, General Dzhokher Dudayev was elected president of Chechnya and independence from Russia was formally declared. Russian troops were sent to Chechnya in the aftermath of the declaration (in late 1991), but when confronted by armed Chechens at the airport landing strip, the troops withdrew. For the next several months, leaders in Moscow and Grozny, Chechnya's capital city, conducted negotiations but no settlement was reached.

In December 1993, Dudayev, as president of Chechnya, boycotted the Russian parliamentary election and referendum on the new federal constitution. He also dismissed the Chechen parliament and began direct presidential rule. Opposition forces within Chechnya, some with Russian support, engaged forces loyal to Dudayev, in civil war. When Moscow's November 1994 cease-fire demands were disregarded, Russian troops entered the combat and began a military offensive toward Grozny. The ensuing war destroyed urban areas and resulted in civilian and combatant casualties estimated at more than 100,000. In 1996, Chechen forces launched a major counteroffensive, and Russian forces were pushed out of Grozny. Under the Khasavyurt agreement, the Russian leadership agreed to withdraw its troops from Chechnya and accept Chechen self-government, leaving the question of formal independence to be decided within five years.

No peace came to Chechnya however. After Dudayev was killed in 1996 in a Russian rocket attack, Chechens elected Aslan Maskhadov as the new president in 1997. Maskhadov was a military man who had served in the Soviet army before becoming chief of staff of the Chechen army in 1992. It was under his leadership that Chechen forces won battles against the Russian forces during the 1994–1996 Chechen war. Even though democratically elected (running against the more radical Shamil Basayev), Maskhadov was unable to control the multitude of forces operating within Chechnya. As president, he swore to reinforce the independence of the Chechen state. Russia's aim of destabilizing the Maskhadov government created an almost impossible situation for effective government.

In August 1999, Chechen rebel forces invaded the neighboring Republic of Dagestan to help Islamic fundamentalists seeking to create a separate nation.* When hundreds of people died from bombs that ripped through apartment buildings in Moscow and other Russian cities in September 1999, the explosions were blamed on Chechen terrorists. Russian troops carried out air strikes against rebel forces in Dagestan, and then nearly 100,000 Russian troops were redeployed in Chechnya. When the Russian government, under the direction of Prime Minister Putin, dispatched its forces to Chechnya in September 1999, official statements described the action as an antiterrorist operation with the goal of restoring law and order in the territory. Using intense air attacks and artillery bombardment, Russia claimed control of Grozny in 2000.[13]

The second war resembled the first in the bombardment of urban areas, the number of deaths, and the constant flow of refugees. Worldwide condemnation of human rights violations in Chechnya ostracized Russia in international circles. Yet, following the attacks of September 11, 2001, on New York and Washington, D.C., world powers essentially gave Russia the green light to pursue terrorists within Chechnya.

---

*Between 1998 and 2002, Dagestan received more federal grants, transfers, and subsidies per person than any other Russian region. This money came to the region primarily because the federal government wanted to ensure that Dagestan, situated right next to Chechnya, remained stable.

The Russians refused to accept the authority of President Maskhadov and appointed Akhmed-hadji Kadyrov as the Chechen administration head in June 2000. Maskhadov, as the legitimately elected president of the Chechen Republic, opposed the Russian-approved administration.* Also in opposition to Moscow's actions were Maskhadov's two major rivals, military commanders Shamil Basayev and Samir Khattab. Khattab was killed, but Basayev remained a significant force in the region. Basayev had been appointed Chechen prime minister in 1997 but resigned after serving for only six months.[14]

The Russian government attempted institutional reform in the hope of establishing political stability. Under Moscow's direction, a new constitution, replacing the 1991 Chechen constitution, was approved in a referendum in Chechnya in March 2003. According to official figures, well over 90 percent of the voters, with an 80 percent turnout, approved the new constitution along with new laws on electing a president and parliament. Such results were recorded despite Maskhadov's call to the Chechen people to boycott the referendum and demand a fully independent state.

The first article of the new Chechen constitution recognized Chechnya's sovereignty even though the Russian Constitutional Court declared in June 2000 that Russian regions could not describe themselves as "sovereign." Articles 29 and 30 of the new Chechen constitution also introduced the concept of being a "citizen of the Chechen Republic." This clause contradicts the law on citizenship that Putin signed in 2002, a law that does not provide for any other form of citizenship than Russian.[15] Putin's Chechen policy thus acknowledged that if fighting was to end, Chechnya must be treated as a special case, necessitating rules different from those for the other regions. Institutional reform and the adoption of new constitutions, however, are having a limited impact in a region in the midst of an armed insurgency against central authorities.

As of September 2003, operational command of the antiterrorism operation in the North Caucasus was transferred from the Federal Security Service (FSB) to the Interior Ministry. The FSB had taken over operations in Chechnya from the Russian Defense Ministry in January 2001.[16] Three years after the beginning of the 1999 antiterrorist operation, casualties in Chechnya remained high; Russian officials reported nearly 20,000 dead or wounded. Many more Chechen fighters are estimated to have been killed in the same period. No accurate numbers are available for civilian casualties, but they are likely to be higher than official figures indicate. Suicide bombings against representatives of the pro-Russian Chechen administration are augmenting classical guerrilla operations against the Russian military.†

*Deputies to the Chechen parliament (elected in July 1997) voted in September 2003 to remove Aslan Maskhadov from the post of Chechen president. Acting Chechen parliament speaker, Isa Temirov, said Maskhadov violated the Chechen constitution by introducing Shari'a law and had plunged Chechnya into war.
†Terrorism is a two-way street. Two Russian secret service employees were charged with carrying out the February 2004 assassination of former acting Chechen president Zelimkhan Yandarbiev in Qatar.

Several reasons can be offered for the intractable nature of this conflict. The first has to do with problems associated with Christian rule of a Muslim region. The Islamic religion has been the key cultural element in the differentiation of Chechens from Orthodox Russians. Although religion is a part of daily life in the region, Islam was not linked to the Chechen independence movement in its early years. The original demand for independence from Russia was supplemented in 1997 with a plan to introduce Islamic law. Chechen leaders have publicly supported the creation of a "state based on Islamic values and laws" to function as a base for further Islamic actions within the region (Bodansky 2000, 10). Moscow in turn has been following a containment policy toward radical Islam in the region. According to Russian sources, some support for Chechen militants has come from fundamentalist Sunni elements in the Middle East. The goal of Russia is to prevent the establishment of an enclave in support of extremist and terrorist orientations within or on its borders.

Another reason for the intractable nature of the conflict in Chechnya has to do with economic payoffs associated with the continuation of the war. Illegal smuggling, arms sales, and counterfeiting have found fertile ground in this region. The lack of Russian control over the oil pipeline that runs from the port of Baku on the Caspian Sea allowed oil to be siphoned off and sold to generate cash. Although oil reserves on Chechen territory are relatively small, the oil pipelines in the area are of strategic importance not only to Russia but also to Ukraine and Azerbaijan.

It is partly for this reason that the Russian government has offered financial inducements as a way of luring Chechen guerrillas away from combat. In June 2003, the Russian State Duma passed an amnesty bill that the Russian leadership hoped would reduce popular support for the Chechen resistance. A rehabilitation program (a job or a chance to go to school) was offered for those Chechen fighters who would take advantage of the amnesty and lay down their arms. The amnesty, which expired in September of the same year, did not extend to Chechen President Aslan Maskhadov and several other prominent field commanders, for example, Shamil Basayev.[17]

A third reason for the intractable nature of the conflict is the perceived necessity on the part of the Moscow leadership for a decisive victory in Chechnya. The Russian military suffered a defeat in the first Chechen war (1994–1996), so they desperately want a victory in the ongoing hostilities to restore their reputation. The Russians also believe that their previous attempts at negotiation were undermined by Chechen leaders; therefore, they are skeptical of any negotiated pacts.

With the adoption of the new Chechen constitution, the Moscow-approved administration in Chechnya, headed by Akhmed-hadji Kadyrov, organized an October 2003 election for a new president. Kadyrov was widely regarded as the clear favorite, not because of his popularity but because he controlled enough administrative and financial resources to neutralize his opponents. Although he was not a direct puppet of the Putin administration, most observers felt he had the backing of the Kremlin and that, by a combination of intimidation and falsification, Kadyrov would secure a convincing victory. Indeed, when the results of the October presidential election were announced, Akhmed-hadji Kadyrov was declared to have defeated six other candidates with more than 80 percent of the votes. Voter turnout was reported to be more than 80 percent; such a high turnout rate, however, is extremely unlikely given the questionable legitimacy of the election in the eyes of many Chechens. The election was also marred by the fact that the three most popular opposition candidates were either barred from the ballot or quit under pressure.[18] The elections were criticized by the U.S. State Department for not meeting "international standards for fair and free elections."[19]

Even though the legitimacy of the elections was questioned, Kadyrov began operating as president of Chechnya because he was officially recognized as such by Moscow.* The relationship between Moscow and Kadyrov, however, was an uneasy one. In October 2003, Kadyrov publicly stated that hostilities would already have ended had the Russian military not fueled the ranks of the Chechen resistance by their brutal behavior toward the civilian population.[20] In March 2004, he alleged that a large portion of the funds earmarked by the federal budget for Chechnya were being stolen by various federal ministries and agencies. In addition, Kadyrov asserted that Chechnya should be given exclusive control over oil production on its territory and the use of the profits from oil sales. He said that the Chechen administration needed the oil proceeds to rebuild the economy and to fund health care and education.[21]

A major focus of Kadyrov's government was the continued campaign to quell the armed resistance. In addition, the fighting among Chechen leaders and against Russian forces created a major refugee problem; and living conditions in refugee camps in surrounding areas, such as in Ingushetia and in the Pankisi Gorge region of Georgia, are extremely difficult. Chechnya also lacks adequate housing should refugees want to return and security issues are substantial. According to the UN High Commissioner for Refugees, among all countries of the world, Russia has the highest number of citizens seeking political asylum abroad; most are former residents of Chechnya.

Moscow had hoped that Chechnya's presidential election, and the constitutional referendum that preceded it, would initiate a political process for the stabilization and reconstruction of Chechnya; however, this was not to be. In May 2004, Chechen President Akhmed-hadji Kadyrov was killed by a bomb blast at the main stadium in Grozny. It should be noted that Kadyrov had joined the Chechen rebellion in 1991 and had fought in the 1994–1996 war against

---

*Meanwhile the Chechen president elected in 1997, Aslan Maskhadov, made a bid to the European parliament for the establishment of an interim UN administration in Chechnya.

A devastated street in Grozny, the Chechen capital.

© Said Tsarnayev / Reuters / Corbis

Russian forces, proclaiming that the Chechen independence fight was a jihad (holy war). In 1996, Kadyrov took part in peace talks with Moscow that ended in the Russian withdrawal from Chechnya. He broke with other Chechen rebel commanders after the excursion into Dagestan in August 1999. Just prior to his assassination, he had been pressuring Russia to once again withdraw its forces from Chechnya.

Aslan Maskhadov, the Chechen president who was elected in 1997, condemned the assassination of Kadyrov as an inexcusable act of terrorism and offered three possible scenarios that could explain it: (1) Kadyrov might have been killed by those who had installed him there in the first place, namely the Russian government and the FSB; (2) the **mujahideen** may have executed the sentence (contract) on Kadyrov's life that had existed since he started cooperating with the Russians; (3) the killing might have been retribution in a blood feud.[22] Maskhadov's speculation provides a reasonable range of explanations for Kadyrov's death given that at the time of writing no one had yet been brought to trial.

In late May 2004, Aslan Maskhadov ordered all field commanders subordinate to him to abide strictly by the Geneva Conventions and to avoid using weapons against Chechen citizens unless their own lives were in danger.[23]

Yet, Army General Nikolai Kovalev, head of the Duma Veterans Affairs Committee and a former director of the FSB, reported that after the assassination of Chechen leader Akhmed-hadji Kadyrov the situation in Chechnya sharply deteriorated and continued to worsen.[24] (Chechen field commander Shamil Basayev claimed that his fighters were responsible for the bomb explosion that killed Kadyrov.) President Vladimir Putin signed a decree that authorized sending additional Interior Ministry units to Chechnya.

When asked whether the Chechen resistance would field a candidate in the August 2004 elections for a successor to Kadyrov, Maskhadov said:

> That is simply not possible. Whoever runs in this election—a fighter or otherwise—becomes a traitor to his people. He becomes the enemy of the people. He will have to stand next to the Russians and destroy his own people. How can those who vowed to rid their people of the Russian oppression participate in an election organized by the Russians in accordance with the Russian Constitution, turning against their own people?[25]

When the election to replace the slain president was held in August 2004, the man who was serving as Chechen interior minister, Major General Alu Alkhanov, was widely regarded as the Kremlin's preferred choice. According to official figures, Alkhanov received 74 percent of the vote with an estimated turnout of 85 percent. Other candidates complained of widespread violations during the election.

Although a positive development occurred in the aftermath of the election—Russian authorities agreed to Alkhanov's request that all revenues from the extraction and sale of Chechen oil be channeled into the republic's budget to help finance reconstruction, a concession that Akhmed-hadji Kadyrov had lobbied for without success—some observers have questioned whether the new institutional arrangements imposed by the 2003 constitutional referendum are workable within Chechnya's traditional social structure. In the presidential system that Chechnya has, most power ends up in the hands of a single leader, who is expected to favor his own personal interests and associates.[26] In addition, although officially given autonomy by Moscow, the Kremlin has been unwilling to relinquish control of Chechnya. By (allegedly) manipulating the outcomes of the referendum on the constitution and elections of Chechnya's presidents, the Kremlin undermines the legitimacy of new institutions in the republic. In a sense, Moscow has yet to allow Chechens the chance to "get it right" themselves, given the continued interference. The Chechens, arguably, should have such a chance, as most people now realize the necessity of some form of integration with Russia and recognize the problems associated with trying to set up an Islamic state.

A major factor that has worked against a peaceful resolution of the Chechen conflict is that since the hostage-taking at a Moscow theater in late October 2002, Russian officials have ruled out holding talks with those they label "bandits and terrorists," including Maskhadov. Although most attacks against Russian personnel or the Russian-associated administration in Chechnya have been blamed on fighters loyal to Maskhadov or to Shamil Basayev, Basayev himself absolved Maskhadov of any role in the October 2002 Moscow theater incident.[27] Maskhadov repeatedly rejected Basayev's tactics. Basayev also claimed responsibility for a suicide truck-bombing in December 2002 that virtually demolished the government building in Grozny and killed more than seventy people.[28]

The violence continues. In September 2004, international headlines carried reports of a hostage-taking crisis in a southern Russian school in Beslan, North Ossetia, which borders Chechnya. The result was the death of at least 335 of the hostages, mostly children. Although Maskhadov condemned the terrorism at the school, Russian authorities offered a $10 million reward for the capture of both Maskhadov and Basayev. On March 8, 2005, special forces attached to the Russian FSB killed Aslan Maskhadov, a disturbing development because he had been legitimately elected as the leader of the Chechen people. Although he insisted that Chechnya must be independent, he was willing to negotiate a close relationship with Russia. Even though Maskhadov had called for peace talks with Russia, Moscow had branded him a terrorist.

In late May 2004, a grenade launcher was used to bombard the State Council building in Grozny.[29] In July 2004, assassins shot the head of the Chechen chapter of United Russia in her own home. The same month, a radio-controlled land mine in Grozny exploded as acting Chechen leader Sergei Abramov's motorcade drove past, but it failed to kill him. Other incidents of death are too numerous to list.

CONCLUSION

To conclude this chapter on Russia's federated structures and ethnic minorities, we note that during 1990 and 1991, as the Soviet Union was disintegrating, all the ethnic republics adopted declarations of sovereignty. Since then, all these regions, except Chechnya, have negotiated power-sharing deals with Moscow. The federal reforms of the Putin administration have secured Moscow's control over the territory of the Russian Federation. Secession is simply not an option, not only because the Russian military will not allow it, but also because only in the Northern Caucasus are the titular nationalities a majority of the population in any ethnic republic. Many ethnic republics do not touch an international border but rather are surrounded by Russian territory. Most important, support for separation from the Russian Federation among the people in these regions is weak. The people instead want to have assurances that their distinct cultures, languages, and religions will be appreciated and preserved, that their environment and resources will be protected, and that their right to select their own indigenous leaders to run local affairs will be respected.

Because Russia is multiethnic, the Russian government will continue to be challenged by the demands of the various ethnic groups. The way in which the government meets these challenges will be significant not only for democratic government but also for the power and the capability of the state as a cohesive entity.

Key Terms

Autonomy
Basmachi Rebellion
Ethnicity
Federation Council
Mujahideen
Multinational state
Oblasts

Okrugs
Procurators
Russification (Russified)
Russo-centric
Self-determination
Territorial integrity
Titular nationality

Critical Thinking Questions

1. According to Table 4.1, how is Russia different from the United States, Germany, and Brazil in terms of population characteristics? How might such differences affect how government functions in each of these countries?

2. What role did Ukraine play in the breakup of the USSR? Why was the independence movement in Ukraine so much more damaging to the integrity of the Soviet State than the independence movements in the Baltic States?

3. Among the different theories about nationalism/ethnicity presented in this chapter, which seems most reasonable to you? What would the theory predict as the end result of the conflict in Chechnya?

4. What has Putin done to preserve the territorial integrity of the Russian Federation? To what extent do you think his efforts have been successful?

5. Why have the Republic of Sakha's and Tatarstan's relationships with Moscow evolved so differently from Chechnya's relationship with Moscow? Which factors account for the difference?

6. Why has the war in Chechnya dragged on for so long?

7. What reasons can be given to argue that secession is an unlikely prospect for Russia's republics?

Suggested Reading

Bremmer, Ian, and Ray Taras, eds. *Nations and Politics in the Soviet Successor States.* Cambridge, U.K.: Cambridge University Press, 1993.

Reddaway, Peter, and Robert Orttung. *The Dynamics of Russian Politics: Putin's Reform of Federal-Regional Relations,* vol. 2. Lanham, Md.: Rowman and Littlefield, 2004.

Pipes, Richard. *The Russian Revolution.* New York: Vintage, 1991.

Smith, Graham, ed. *The Nationalities Question in Post-Soviet States,* 2nd ed. New York: Longman, 1996.

Websites of Interest

The Constitution of the Russian Federation:
http://www.constitution.ru/en/10003000-01.htm

Homepage of the president of the Republic of Tatarstan:
http://www.tatar.ru/president/index_e.htm

Official website of the Republic of Tatarstan:
http://www.tatar.ru/?DNSID=d1f0d0680bc4ca747b5417334d23274b

Sakha republic website:
http://www.sakha.ru/Eversion/HTMLs/default.htm

EthnoLinguistic groups in the Caucasus region:
http://www.lib.utexas.edu/maps/commonwealth/ethnocaucasus.jpg

News about Chechnya:
http://www.chechenpress.info/english/

CHAPTER 5

Russian Political Culture

USSIAN NATIONALISM constitutes a core component of Russia's political culture and provides a foundation for state-building; it is a key component of Soviet and Russian national identities. The realization of citizenship is based on what it means to be *Russian* and who is considered to be Russian. This chapter highlights nationalism and other characteristics of Soviet political culture, and includes a discussion of democratic values and the degree to which these do or do not exist in Russian society today.

Russia's political culture is important because it provides the context within which political ideas and institutions develop. Although political culture is not deterministic, it does predispose individuals and groups to think and act in certain ways, and it tends to be relatively stable over time. The process of cultural change usually is prolonged and rather subtle, though some regimes do attempt to engineer changes in societal attitudes and orientations more quickly. The Bolshevik Revolution, for example, was a deliberate effort to change the political system and the ways that people thought and acted politically. The extent to which the Bolsheviks were successful in accomplishing their revolutionary agenda can only be evaluated by taking a long-term perspective that considers the main historical themes in Russia's political culture. To this end, we begin with a study of Russian nationalism.

RUSSIAN NATIONALISM

The Russian Federation (Russia) emerged from the Soviet Union as both a new and an old state. Russia is new because its international borders cover a territory 76 percent smaller than the former Soviet Union. Russia also has new national goals. The legacy of communism and the goal of building a socialist society have been repudiated and replaced by a national ideology of democratization and market reform. The Russian state is old in the sense that many characteristics of the Soviet government's culture and institutions remained intact after 1991. Old national goals, such as the desire to retain and enhance power and prestige on the world stage, were inherited from the Soviet Union.

Nationalism is an enduring and evolving characteristic of Russian society. During the perestroika era, Russian nationalism emerged as a significant political force, primarily as a reaction to the rejection of Russian dominance by the non-Russian groups within the USSR. Russian nationalism contributed to the dissolution of the USSR as much as anti-Russian nationalism did. For some, the fear of loss of status and prestige, plus widespread experiences with severe economic decline, has culminated in the idea that Russians are faced with a constant "us or them" battle for survival as a culture and a people. The most rigid, ideological ultranationalists are driven to support all things Russian, while questioning and condemning non-Russians and foreigners.

Mainstream Russian nationalism encompasses a variety of components, broadly including taking pride in Russian identity, history, culture, and religion. National identity is tied to speaking the Russian language and worshiping in Russian Orthodox churches. Russian identity was enhanced during the Soviet period by giving credit to Russians for winning World War II and by emphasizing the sacrifices that Russians made when they subsidized building the Union (Hirszowicz 1991). The exaltation of patriotism associated with World War II had a negative side—Russian chauvinism and suspicion, which ultimately led to the oppression of non-Russian nationality groups. Stalin transferred entire nationality groups, those whom he identified as being "disloyal" (Chechens, Volga Germans, Crimean Tatars, and others), to Central Asia and Siberia during World War II. Similar transfers of hundreds of thousands of people from the Baltic republics occurred during 1948 and 1949. In addition, mass deportations from the western parts of Ukraine and from Belarus and Bessarabia took place in the aftermath of World War II. The various groups were condemned for their deviant views, while Russians were glorified for their contributions to building the Russian Empire and the Soviet Union.

Russian nationalism, when it merged with Stalinism during the period following World War II, manifested dangerous chauvinistic trends. When Leningrad Communist Party Secretary Andrei Zhdanov was killed in 1949, his alleged murderers were accused of disloyalty to Stalin. The sense of xenophobia and anti-Semitism associated with this event came to be known as *zhdanovshchina,* and it included a program of cultural and intellectual repression.

The more recent history of Russian nationalism dates to the formation of the All-Russian Society for the Preservation of Historical and Cultural Monuments (VOOPIK) in 1966. VOOPIK grew rapidly, and the membership exceeded 14 million by 1982 (Spechler 1990, 282–83). Pamyat, a more overtly dogmatic organization, originated under Brezhnev. With the introduction of glasnost it became a forum for expressing popular ideas, such as Stalinism, anti-imperialism,

Russian Orthodox Church Patriarch Alexi III in the Kremlin, May 2000.
Misha Japaridze / AP–Wide World Photos

anti-Semitism, and anti-Westernism, in addition to those related to Russian cultural preservation.

Grievances put forward by Russian nationalists during the late 1980s included the following three: (1) Russians had borne the burden of developing the country while minority nationalities had reaped the benefits; (2) Russians were unfairly blamed for the evils of the system; and (3) Russian minority groups in other republics were being discriminated against with new laws on citizenship, language, and voting. Russian nationalists were critical of the Soviet system for having "sacrificed the Russian nation in its drive for economic and military power and societal reconstruction" (Spechler 1990, 292; see also Hammer 1989, 198 and Moro 1988, 2).

These issues were particularly salient to a people who saw a decline in their share of the total USSR population from 52.4 percent in 1979 to 50.8 percent in

1989. Russians felt a sense of demographic threat because it was predicted that other nationality groups would soon outnumber Russians within the Soviet Union. Standards of living in Russia were also lower than in many other republics (Sakwa 1990, 252–53). Nationalists sought to preserve and enhance the economic, political, and military power of the Russian nation vis-à-vis other republics and the rest of the world.

The establishment of a separate Communist Party for the Russian Soviet Federated Socialist Republic (RSFSR) in June 1990 and the July 1990 declaration of sovereignty by the Supreme Soviet of the RSFSR, with its assertion of veto power over All-Union laws, documented the desire of the Russian people to reassert their preeminence and control. Boris Yeltsin, chairman of the Supreme Soviet of the RSFSR and later president of Russia, openly articulated this position. Russian nationalism also came to the fore when it provided the base for resistance to the August 1991 coup attempt. When Yeltsin asserted his authority as RSFSR president, he challenged the legitimacy of the Soviet Union. In September 1991, the RSFSR Supreme Soviet decreed that St. Petersburg should resume its original name (dropping the name Leningrad). Symbolically, this move evoked the memory of Peter the Great and simultaneously downgraded Lenin and the Bolshevik Revolution.

With the dissolution of the USSR, new questions of nationalism began to surface. According to Sakwa (2002, 260), two types of Russian nationalists emerged: those who were state-builders and those who were revivalists. The state-builders wanted to strengthen Russia as a multinational state and wanted to build a modern sense of civic identity. The revivalists, on the other hand, believed that Russia should be based in the traditions of the Russian people and the culture and moral values of the Orthodox Church.

Given the multinational character of the Russian state, it is a challenge to define a single, overarching national identity. If one is a citizen of the Russian Federation (RF), that person is a "Russian," just as a citizen of the United States is an "American." The category *American* includes African Americans, Asian Americans, Latino Americans, Native Americans, and many others. By analogy, the category *Russian* includes Tatars, Chechens, and many others.* Generally, the dominant nationality group within a state dictates the identity of its citizens, even though some groups resist such an all-inclusive characterization. Members of the minority nationality groups desire to preserve and enhance their separate identities. The we–they dichotomy is an essential aspect of nationalist movements that seek to achieve group cohesion and solidarity by highlighting commonalities within the national group while simultaneously emphasizing the distinctiveness of the group in comparison with others.

*We need to be careful with this analogy because the United Sates is a country composed primarily of immigrants, whereas Russia is composed primarily of indigenous peoples.

A HISTORY OF RUSSIAN AND SOVIET POLITICAL CULTURE

Moving beyond Russian nationalism and evaluating Russian political culture more generally, it is reasonable to ask about the degree to which this evolving culture is supportive of democratic values. *Political culture* refers to the orientations, beliefs, values, attitudes, and assumptions that people have toward the political system in which they live. An understanding of a country's political culture helps us to appreciate how citizens relate to the politics of their country and their involvement in the political process; it also helps explain why certain types of political systems exist in a state.

Russia's political culture is related to and shaped by past experiences. However, it is difficult to go back in history to accurately determine what the political orientations of the people who lived in Russia during the Soviet and Tsarist eras were. Starting during the 1960s, Soviet social scientists conducted surveys of citizens and workers living in the Soviet Union, but the goal of such surveys was primarily to collect information that would help improve economic productivity. Surveys that asked explicitly about how the people felt about their government and political leaders were not conducted in the Soviet Union until the late 1980s. Thus, when attempting to characterize Russian political culture as it existed decades ago, even centuries ago, we are making inferences based primarily on the literature of the periods and on reports of political debates preserved in official publications or in old newspapers. We hasten to point out that no single culture existed throughout the Russian Empire or the Soviet Union. Not only were there significant differences in worldviews across nationality groupings, but there were also differences between towns and the countryside and between the nobility and the peasants. The RF likewise does not have one, single homogeneous political culture. When discussing political culture here, only some of the more dominant themes are being identified, knowing that important subcultures exist within Russian society.

Given these cautions, it is still reasonable to describe the political culture of Russia prior to the Bolshevik Revolution as one that was based on the absolute authority of the tsar. Divine authority was vested in that person and no formal institutional limits existed on a tsar's power. Even the nobility, when they attempted to challenge the tsar, were exiled or executed. Thus, an important political culture theme that emerges from the Tsarist period is one of unlimited and basically unquestioned authority of a single, powerful ruler. Along with this came a highly centralized bureaucratic structure and an economy that relied primarily on state funding and direction. Important decisions were made in Moscow and implemented through a bureaucracy staffed by people who gained their positions through heredity. Supporting attitudes and behavior, together with a peasant-based mass culture, were major legacies of Tsarism.

Russia was mostly a peasant society at the time when the Bolsheviks took power. Eighty-five percent of Russia's population was peasant and the agricultural system was decades behind that of Western Europe (Suny 1998, xvi). Lenin, as the leader of the Bolshevik Party, was well aware of the limitations of the country he and his party controlled. The challenges that had to be overcome in building a socialist political culture included not only underdeveloped industrialization but also Russia's vast size and undereducated population. For Lenin, constructing communism meant changing Russian culture to a "proletarian culture" (Tucker 1987, 45). Lenin knew that the Russian population had to be educated in terms of literacy, technical skills, and ideology; his plan was to build socialism through the education of the masses. Lenin argued, "To build communism . . . involved a lengthy learning process; it meant first of all, 'learning communism'" (Tucker 1987, 45). As Lenin put it, "The generation of those who are now fifteen will see a communist society, and [they] will . . . build this society. This generation should know that the entire purpose of their lives is to build a communist society" (Tucker 1987, 45). The official political culture under Lenin can be summarized this way: "[B]eing a Soviet citizen was to be a member of a goal-oriented all-Russian collective of builders of socialism and communism" (Tucker 1987, 46).

Such an official culture continued under Stalin with a more ruthless approach. The main difference was that because Russia was a backward peasant land, Lenin accepted that the process of building a socialist economy and society would be a generation-long effort (Tucker 1987, 63). Stalin also was aware of the magnitude of this process but was convinced that the transformation could occur more quickly. The Stalinist industrial revolution from above, a perfect example of Stalin's impatience, is best characterized by its very slogan: "Fulfill the Five-Year Plan in Four" (Tucker 1987, 75). Under Stalin, being a Soviet citizen no longer meant believing that you were building a socialist state in order to someday live in a communist one; it meant believing that the goal of socialism had been reached, with a communist state in sight (Tucker 1987, 117).

Although the ideology of the state changed under the Bolsheviks to one of communism, political culture reflected a degree of continuity between the Tsarist and the Soviet systems. The absolutism of the all-powerful tsar was reimposed as totalitarianism under Stalin. Political institutions were weak in the Soviet Union under Stalin just as they were under Tsarism. The Soviet Union was governed by a person, not by laws or by assemblies. Stalin's emphasis on forced industrialization was also reminiscent of the war-footing characteristic of Imperial Russia. The emphasis on security, the threat of war, and the actual participation in a series of wars justified a militarized and tightly controlled society. The importance of conformity was a major theme of this era as well.

Khrushchev tried to distance himself from Stalin's legacy. This was clearly demonstrated with his Secret Speech at the Twentieth Party Congress on February 25, 1956, in which he denounced the crimes of Stalin. Although the speech was welcomed in the West, reactions among those people within the Soviet Union who had sacrificed so much, even the lives of loved ones, and who believed that they had created a better state under Stalin's rule were much more uncertain. In fact, a legacy from the Khrushchev era is unquestionably the discomfort associated with radical change or restructuring of the existing order. Khrushchev's attack on Stalin left many citizens shocked and disoriented (Tucker 1987, 123). The disorientation that characterized the era accounts in part for the decision of Khrushchev's associates in the Communist Party to remove him from his position as general secretary.

Stabilization became the central tenet of the Brezhnev era, which also witnessed a distinct break in society between the people in the party nomenklatura, the privileged class, and the ordinary Soviet citizen. A legacy of Brezhnev's time was the advantages enjoyed by party and government officials. The nomenklatura political culture not only tolerated elitism among party members but also supported a view that the masses were not capable of caring for themselves—that they needed the leading and guiding light of the party. This elitist political culture was characterized by a degree of pluralism as different institutional and professional groups, such as the armed forces and economic managers, developed their own subcultures.

At the masses' level, one of the major characteristics of the Soviet Union's political culture was **collectivism**—a sense of collective responsibility for the group. Collectivism provides a belief foundation for the idea that the state should be responsible for the well-being of its citizens. Collectivism contrasts to individualism, which is the view that government should play only a limited role in the lives of citizens. Collectivism was the political culture legacy of the Soviet state. An implied social contract—that the state would take care of those who did not rock the boat—developed.

Although the average Soviet citizen was relatively poor compared to those living in other industrialized countries, the people did enjoy a sense of security. Almost everyone was employed, and it was very difficult to get fired from a job once hired. Plus, medical care and education were readily available to all Soviet citizens.

But the state failed to uphold the ideals of socialism—that every citizen is equal—and repressed free speech, press, and assembly. This led some Soviet citizens to become disillusioned with the official myth of Soviet communism (Tucker 1987, 134). From this disillusionment came the search for alternate forms of expression. The people who were brave enough to express their dissatisfaction with the regime came to be known in the West as dissidents. Some dissidents turned to old religious beliefs, others to different forms of nationalism, and still others called for radical reform and modernization of the Soviet system. No matter what the form of the beliefs, the dissemination of alternative views led to the creation of parallel Russian cultures distinct from the official one exemplified in propaganda efforts (Tucker 1987, 134).

When Gorbachev came to power in 1985, it was clear that he was a reformer determined to bring a more open society to the people of the USSR (Suny 1998, 451). Gorbachev's reforms eventually led to a questioning and an ultimate discrediting of the ideology of communism. He encouraged people to stop thinking of themselves as subjects and more as citizens. Gorbachev challenged the value of security over reform and encouraged risk-taking over conformity. Indeed, Gorbachev had revolutionary transformation goals for the political culture of the Soviet system. Revolutionary changes in people's political attitudes and orientations, however, are not easy to engineer, as noted on the first page of this chapter.

During Gorbachev's period of rule, the legacies of Russian history and the forces of Western marketization and liberalization came into contact with one another. Russia was confronted with the question of whether the country should preserve its own culture and traditions or whether the country should adopt and incorporate Western notions of society and culture. During the nineteenth century, this debate involved a juxtaposition of the Westernizers' position and the Slavophiles' position. Slavophiles stressed that the greatness of Russia rested on the collective nature of Russian society and Orthodox traditions. Westernizers argued that for Russia to be strong and competitive, it had to adopt not only Western technology but also its institutions and practices.

A related consideration was whether borrowing institutions and policies that worked in the West would work in Russia. A common argument is that Western market principles based on individualism and a laissez-faire doctrine may not work in a society like Russia, which has traditions of collectivism and dependency on the state. A similar argument is made about the appropriateness of liberal democracy in a state with an autocratic tradition, where the people really value and desire strong leadership.

POLITICAL CULTURE AND DEMOCRATIC IDEAS

The official political culture of Russia today endorses the principle of democracy. Yet scholars have argued that the survival of democracy as a system of government within a society requires not only democratic institutions but also a certain set of beliefs among the leaders and the people. Those who study Russia often question whether it is possible for the country to overcome its authoritarian past.

Linz and Stepan (1997) identify five major arenas of a consolidated democracy:

1. Civil society, with freedom of association and communication;
2. Political society, with free and inclusive electoral contests;
3. Rule of law, with constitutionalism;
4. State apparatus, including rational, legal bureaucratic norms;
5. Economic society, with an institutionalized market.

These authors argue that Russia's transition is particularly difficult because of the surge of nationalist politics and the privileging of independence over democratization, collective rights over individual rights, and economic restructuring over state restructuring. Analysts raise doubts about whether the leaders and the citizens of post-Soviet Russia are ready to accept and participate in democratic government. The necessity of the participation of the people is a basic principle of democracy. In addition, average citizens should be able to question state authority without fear of reprisals from the government.

At the level of leadership, the principle of a political leader's need to compromise is considered essential to functional democracy. The idea that electoral competition is good for a political system represents not only an acceptance of different views as being legitimate but also the idea that power can and should be shared. The belief that the government should protect minority rights reflects the idea that democracy is for everyone not just one major group of people.

A few other important factors deemed necessary for well-functioning democratic institutions are political efficacy, trust of the government, and interpersonal trust in society. *Political efficacy* refers to the degree to which people feel that they can have an impact on the political decisions that affect them. *Political trust* is a measure of the degree to which people trust the people and institutions that represent them in the government. *Interpersonal trust* is the extent to which people feel that they can trust those around them. Trust is essential for democracy because people must delegate decision-making authority to representatives and to leaders. *Democratic values* include political tolerance, willingness to compromise, support for dissent, rights consciousness, support for an independent media, support of competitive elections, and support for personal liberties.

Political scientists have sought to study the existence and the depth of democratic values in Russian society. Surveys conducted in Russia during the 1990s examined the level of support among the Russian people for the preceding list of democratic values. The studies showed that both elite and mass members of Russian society support democratic values in principle. Principles, such as individuals' right to organize opposition, party competition, protection of minority rights, and the need for participation of the people, are all supported by the citizens and elites of Russia (Miller, Hesli, and Reisinger 1997, 177). Certain types of people, however, have stronger leanings toward these values than others. The type of person most likely to be supportive of democratic values is an urban resident, male, young, educated, less religious, wealthier, and more politically active than his comparative counterpart (Reisinger, Miller, Hesli, and Maher 1994, 201, 217).

Although results from other surveys present mixed pictures, most observers agree that Russian political culture encompasses an acceptance of the main principles of democracy. The depth and the spread of these values are, however, difficult to determine and the actual operation of the political system in Russia is by no means fully democratic. When studying democratic values, we should remember that these are an ideal, or a shared goal, to which many political systems aspire but none has yet achieved.

POLITICAL CULTURE THEMES IN RUSSIA

Support for democratic values and nationalism are only two aspects of political culture in Russia. Other major themes should also be considered. One such theme is nostalgia and a desire (by some) for the stability and order of the old Soviet system. Public opinion data provide evidence of this orientation. Interviews of 1,800 individuals, based on a representative sample of the population of the Russian Federation, were conducted in 1997* by the author with her colleagues, Arthur Miller and William Reisinger. The survey revealed that during the Yeltsin era well over half of respondents preferred the Soviet system as it was before perestroika over the present system or a Western-style democracy (see Table 5.1). Forty-four percent of respondents agreed with the statement that "Stalin is not adequately admired for the building of socialism" (see Table 5.2).

Another continuing theme in Russian political culture is the personalization of political leadership. The focus on individual leaders, and on their personal leadership qualities, strongly characterizes the attitudes of Russian citizens. When the respondents to our 1997 survey were asked to agree or disagree with the statement that "Participation of the people is not necessary if decision making is left in the hands of a few trusted, competent leaders," 50 percent agreed (see Table 5.3). Even more significant, a full 85 percent of respondents, representing the lion's share of people in Russia, agreed that "Russia needs strong leadership more than it needs democracy" (see Table 5.4). Older people, people living in rural areas, and people with lower levels of education are significantly more likely than younger people, urban residents, and the better educated to prefer the Soviet system over the present system or a Western-style democracy, to feel that Stalin is not adequately admired, and to feel that Russia needs strong leadership more than it needs democracy.

The Levada Center in Moscow (formerly VCIOM) regularly conducts public opinion polls on the attitudes of people toward the president and toward other

TABLE 5.1   Public Opinion in Russia: Nostalgia for the Soviet System

Which political system, in your opinion, would be best for Russia?

	Valid Percent
1 The Soviet system, as it was before perestroika	59.1
2 The political system that exists today	13.9
3 A Western-style democracy	26.9
Total	**100.0**

*The research was funded by the National Science Association.

TABLE 5.2 Public Opinion in Russia: Nostalgia for Stalin

These days Stalin is not adequately admired for the building of socialism.

	Valid Percent
1 Fully agree	16.4
2 Partially agree	28.1
3 Hard to say	24.0
4 Partially disagree	19.6
5 Fully disagree	11.9
Total	**100.0**

institutions of government. In one of the questions, respondents throughout the country were asked: "On the whole do you approve or disapprove of Vladimir Putin's performance as president?" Putin's highest rating was registered in December 2003 when 82 percent responded "approve." In February and March 2005, however, Putin's approval rating was lower, at 66 percent.

A consistently important goal of rulers, both in the present and in the past, is to maintain Russia's status and prestige on the international scene. Related to this are attitudes among the Russian people toward America, where we see Russian patriotism being mixed with an anti-American theme. Another major theme in Russia's political culture is territorial integrity, which has been a leading factor in defining Russia as a state. To preserve the territorial integrity of the new Russian state, "Yeltsin made large concessions in a series of bilateral treaties to particular republics (most notably Tatarstan) and, on the other hand, gave his

TABLE 5.3 Public Opinion in Russia: Democratic Values (I)

Participation of the people is not necessary if decision making is left in the hands of a few trusted, competent leaders.

	Valid Percent
1 Fully agree	16.0
2 Partially agree	33.8
3 Hard to say	17.7
4 Partially disagree	22.7
5 Fully disagree	9.8
Total	**100.0**

TABLE 5.4 Public Opinion in Russia: Democratic Values (II)

Right now, Russia needs strong leadership more than it needs democracy.

	Valid Percent
1 Fully agree	53.7
2 Partially agree	31.3
3 Hard to say	7.5
4 Partially disagree	6.5
5 Fully disagree	1.0
Total	100.0

---

blessing to two fierce military onslaughts (in 1994–1996 and again from 1999) on Chechnya" (Brown 2001, 346). Maintaining control over all territories in the Russian Federation has been particularly important to the Putin administration.

Russia's political culture also continues to be characterized by a sense that the government can and should be held responsible for taking care of the people. In responding to a public opinion survey question about whether the central government of the Russian Federation should guarantee everyone work or whether every person should look after himself or herself, more than 50 percent chose the option that the government should guarantee work for all (see Table 5.5). Those who were the most likely to say that the government should guarantee work were older, less educated, and more likely to live in rural areas than those who selected the option that every person should look out for himself or herself.

Another theme is Orthodoxy. Not only can it be distinguished from other major religions of the world (Muslim, Hindu, Confucianism), but Orthodoxy also represents a particular worldview that carries forward the collectivist spirit of the past. The prevailing structure of the society also carries forward the lack of strong, autonomous institutions that can challenge the authority of the state. Even though independent organizations now exist, such as political parties, enterprises, associations, and private educational institutions, many observers note that post-Soviet Russia still lacks a vibrant **civil society**.

Anti-Semitism—A Controversial Theme in Russian Political Culture

This chapter concludes with a discussion of anti-Semitism, an extremely controversial component of Russia's political culture. Extensive literature exists on the specific relationship between Russians and one particular non-Russian

---

TABLE 5.5 Public Opinion in Russia: Government Responsibility to Care for the People

Some people say the central government of the Russian Federation should guarantee everyone work and a high standard of living; others argue that every person should look after himself or herself. On this card is a scale from 1 to 7, where 1 signifies that the government guarantees everyone work and 7 signifies that every person should look after himself or herself. You may select any number from 1 to 7. Which number corresponds to your views?

	Valid Percent
1 Government should guarantee work for all	51.3
2	11.1
3	9.3
4	17.0
5	4.4
6	2.4
7 Every person should look out for self	4.5
Total	100.0

---

nationality group of the former USSR—the Jewish people. The following paragraphs summarize some of the studies.

Because life has been difficult for many people since the fall of the Soviet Union, blame for the suffering is sometimes placed on Jews (Chuprov and Zubok 1999, 104). Jews first became a significant portion of the population within the Russian Empire during the eighteenth century with the partitioning of Poland. Even though they were repressed throughout the nineteenth century, the Jewish population numbered 5.5 million by the 1880s. Although Jewish people were prevalent as merchants, landowners, and intellectuals in the Tsarist state, the government considered Jewish inhabitants undesirable. Because the Tsarist government was suspicious of Jewish economic exploitation and revolutionary activity, it allowed three major waves of **pogroms** against the Jews between 1881 and 1921.

In 1905 and 1917, Jewish intellectuals played a major role in the revolutions that overthrew Tsarism. Leon Trotsky, for example, was Jewish by nationality.* After the Bolsheviks took power in 1917, anti-Semitism was officially rejected. This more tolerant position did not last long, however. When Joseph Stalin started purges in the 1930s, Jews were targeted and heavily persecuted until

---

*Trotsky was a leading Marxist who served in the Politburo of the Communist Party and held the titles of Commissar of Foreign Affairs and Commissar of War in Lenin's government. See Chapters 2 and 3 for more about him.

Stalin's death in 1953 (Blustain 1997, 5). Anti-Jewish tenets were useful because Zionist elements could be blamed for economic, political, or social failures in communist, Third World, and Middle Eastern regimes. The Soviet state's anti-Jewish ideology was evidenced by Stalinist pogroms and negative Jewish images found in Russian literature and the popular press and perpetuated in history books (Ettinger, 1985). Stalin segregated the Jewish people by creating the Jewish Autonomous Oblast in a desolate area in a far eastern corner of the RSFSR along the Chinese border.

After Stalin's death, repression was not as extensive, but Jews still faced discrimination. Some were able to reach prominent positions in the sciences and the arts but strict quotas placed limits on how many of them could enter universities and institutes of higher learning throughout the Soviet Union. Jews were almost completely excluded from security, foreign service, and high-level military jobs (Walters 1985). Less-favored non-Russian nationality groups suffered ethnic discrimination in employment, education, and housing opportunities, and in interactions with bureaucrats into the 1980s (Hirszowicz 1991, Ettinger 1985, Gitelman 1991).

Jews voiced their unhappiness with the USSR and demanded the right to emigrate.* This dissident movement reached its peak during the 1970s when the Soviet government agreed to liberalize Jewish emigration (Blustain 1997, 5–6). During the perestroika period, the Jewish people of the Soviet Union benefited from legislation that lifted bans on religious activities, allowed the import of religious texts and objects, and extended freedom to various religious practitioners. A Law on Freedom of Conscience and Religion was adopted in September 1990. After 1991, foreign investment funded Jewish language and religious programs throughout Russia. Jewish writers were rediscovered, translated, and published (Blustain 1997, 6).

Despite the changes that began during the Gorbachev period, some authors argue that possibilities for ethnic violence and anti-Jewish prejudice continued in the newly established states of the former Soviet Union (Brym and Degtyarev 1993, 11). Braham and Sachs asserted that "anti-Semitism has been increasing in both word and deed" (1999, 28). Politicians and deputies in parliament continue to make statements blaming Jews for Russia's problems. The most well-known person, who built a political career by tapping into this sense of threat by promising to restore Russia's imperial role was Vladimir Zhirinovskii, leader of the Liberal Democratic Party of Russia (LDPR). Legal restrictions on religious freedom still exist even though Judaism is one of four officially recognized religions in the Russian Federation. Jewish emigration rose dramatically during the late 1980s, reaching a high point in late 1990. According to an American

---

*The United States still has trade restrictions on Russia associated with Soviet-era treatment of the Jewish population. The Jackson-Vanik amendment, passed by the U.S. Congress in 1974, linked trade with the Soviet Union and other Eastern bloc countries to their allowing the free emigration of Jews and other religious minorities.

Jewish Committee report, the total number of Jews on the territory of the former Soviet Union declined from 1.5 million* in 1989 to 440,000 in 2000.

Although they still face troubles in Russia, President Vladimir Putin has been careful to recognize the cultural and religious rights of Jews and other minorities. In September 2000, Putin made a point of attending the opening of a Jewish Community Center in Moscow, where he said the "upsurge experienced by the Russian Jewish community is an integral part of the general revival of folk traditions and spiritual values in Russia." Putin also noted that "Russia's spiritual revival is unthinkable without understanding that Russian culture is a combination of traditions of all the people who have lived in Russia for centuries."[1] Putin's public speeches are part of an ongoing effort to construct Russia's national identity and political culture. He realizes the importance of a national ideology in building a strong state. In January 2002, Putin asked Russian historians to outline the most important events in the history of ancient Rus and to answer questions such as: "How, based on the historical forms of Russian statehood, can one formulate the modern Russian national idea?"[2] In 2003, he participated in the Independence Day (June 12) celebration in Moscow's Red Square. There, Putin declared that Russia has the right to play a role on the world stage "appropriate to its rich history, the creative potential of its people, and its enormous size."[3]

Key Terms

Civil society
Collectivism
Pogrom

Critical Thinking Questions

1. What is Russian nationalism? What are its foundations and major themes?
2. How can Russian political culture be characterized? Is it conducive to democracy?

Suggested Reading

Barghoorn, Frederick C. *Soviet Russian Nationalism.* New York: Oxford University Press, 1956.

Dunlop, John B. *The Faces of Contemporary Russian Nationalism.* Princeton, N.J.: Princeton University Press, 1983.

Website of Interest

Political culture in Russia:
http://www.carnegie.ru/en/pubs/procontra/66521.htm

---

*Other estimates state that only a little more than 530,000 Jews lived in Russia at the time of the 1989 census (see RFE/RL Newsline, vol. 4, no. 178, Part I, September 14, 2000).

CHAPTER 6

Russia's Governing Institutions in Comparative Context

THIS CHAPTER IS DEVOTED TO Russia's governing institutions. The official structures and functions of the main institutions of government in the Soviet era are described, together with a brief overview of the institutional changes that Mikhail Gorbachev initiated. Next, the legislative, executive, and judicial institutions in Russia today are discussed. Included is a review of the structure, functions, roles, and membership of Russia's parliament along with a description of the emergence and main features of the Russian presidency. Biographical information on Russia's two presidents, Boris Yeltsin and Vladimir Putin, is also included. The final section touches briefly on Russia's judicial institutions—courts, judges, and Procuracy. Russia's institutions of internal and external security (the police, the security services, and the military) are described in Chapters 9 and 10.

GOVERNMENT STRUCTURES AND INSTITUTIONS IN THE SOVIET ERA

The Soviet Union had four constitutions, which were ratified in 1918, 1924, 1936, and 1977. The first constitution of 1918 was just for the Russian Federation (RF). The second constitution in 1924 was for the newly constituted Soviet Union. The 1936 constitution is referred to as "Stalin's Constitution"; that constitution introduced universal suffrage and a directly elected Supreme Soviet. The 1977 constitution, "Brezhnev's Constitution," was similar in many ways to the 1936 constitution although it made the leading and guiding role of the Communist Party in Soviet society more prominent. The 1977 constitution officially designated the Communist Party as the core of all public and state institutions and organizations. Each of the Soviet constitutions listed the rights of the people, but these rights could only be exercised if they contributed to the construction of a socialist society.

The 1977 constitution declared that the two-chamber Supreme Soviet of the USSR was the highest organ of state authority (Figure 6.1). The Supreme Soviet, which consisted of delegates from throughout the country, met too rarely and its sessions were too short for it to be a real decision-making body; rather it served as a forum for the regime to announce major programs. As described by Merle Fainsod, the role of the Supreme Soviet was "strictly ornamental. . . . [The] proceedings of the Supreme Soviet convey[ed] the impression of a well-rehearsed theatrical spectacle from which almost all elements of conflict [were] eliminated. . . . All important decisions [came] ready-made from the Party leadership" (1967, 384).

Elections to membership in the Supreme Soviet were not competitive. The ballot for each seat listed the name of only one person, selected by the Communist Party of the Soviet Union (CPSU). The choice available to citizens

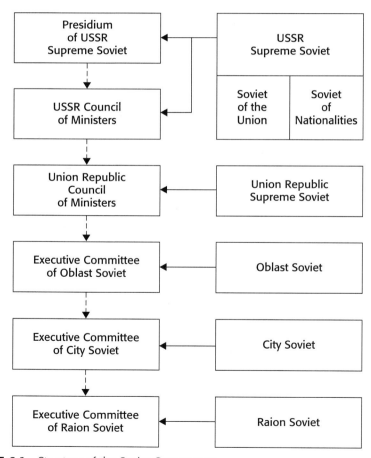

FIGURE 6.1   Structure of the Soviet Government

was to vote for the candidate, to vote against the candidate, or to abstain. Most candidates won their elections to the Supreme Soviet of the USSR with 99 to 100 percent of the vote. That is, the leaders of the Communist Party handpicked the membership of the Supreme Soviet so that the loyalty of these members was assured and the membership nicely represented a cross section of the Soviet population. In addition to seats given to exemplary workers and collective farmers, the membership of the Supreme Soviet included CPSU regional first secretaries, generals, scientists, and prominent writers and artists. Given that the most important people in the Soviet Union were members of the Supreme Soviet, the institution did provide an important legitimating function for the political system.

The membership of the Supreme Soviet confirmed the membership of the Presidium, the top of the government hierarchy in the Soviet system. The Presidium had the power to issue decrees that had the force of law; to convene sessions of the Supreme Soviet; to appoint and dismiss cabinet ministers, on recommendation of the Council of Ministers and with subsequent approval by the Supreme Soviet; to annul decisions of the Council of Ministers, if the decisions did not conform to law; and to proclaim martial law. Headed by its chair and composed of vice chairs from each union republic, the Presidium functioned as a collegial presidency.

The constitution vested executive and administrative authority in the Council of Ministers, which included those officials who ran the various ministries of government, such as agriculture, culture, finance, foreign affairs, health, trade, and defense. Ministers were confirmed by the Supreme Soviet, but in practice, leaders of the CPSU both appointed and relieved members of the Council of Ministers. The Council of Ministers was quite a large body that included the premier, deputy premiers, and more than fifty ministers; heads of other agencies, such as the KGB and GOSPLAN; and union republic premiers. A smaller body, the Presidium of the Council of Ministers, had about ten members, and its primary responsibility was the overall coordination of the economy.

At the head of the Council of Ministers was the premier (sometimes referred to as the prime minister). While Vladimir Lenin was premier, that position was the most powerful one in the political system; after Lenin's death, the position became subordinate to the General Secretary of the Communist Party. In 1941, Stalin assumed the office of premier while continuing to be General Secretary of the Communist Party. After Stalin's death, two different people held these offices until 1958, when Khrushchev was both premier and general secretary. Starting in 1964, two different people again held the two offices. The long-time premier under General Secretary Leonid Brezhnev was Alexis Kosygin, premier from 1964 to 1980.

Each union republic, such as the Ukrainian Soviet Socialist Republic (SSR) and the Lithuanian SSR, had its own Supreme Soviet, Presidium, and Council of Ministers, which were directly subordinate to the USSR Supreme Soviet and Council of Ministries. The corresponding union republic committee of the Communist Party kept a watchful eye over the republic-level governing institutions.

The Soviet government had two different kinds of ministries: Union-republic ministries and All-Union ministries. The All-Union ministries were concerned primarily with heavy industry and foreign trade; they operated strictly on a centralized basis, and Moscow managed them directly. The Union-republic ministries dealt with other matters such as finance, health, police, and the like. The Union-republic ministries were subject to **dual accountability**; the ministries at the republic level were accountable to the corresponding ministry in Moscow and to the republic's Communist Party organization and Council of Ministers.

Mikhail Gorbachev initiated significant alterations to these institutions. Under his direction, the Central Committee of the CPSU introduced a program of democratization at its January 1987 meeting. Following the Central Committee's guidelines, the Supreme Soviet adopted amendments in 1988 to the constitution that made the following changes to the structure of the government:

- Established a USSR Congress of People's Deputies
- Established procedures for multicandidate elections
- Increased the power of the Supreme Soviet and its chair, with the goal of making it a functioning legislature
- Limited tenure to two five-year terms for elected officials
- Initiated judicial reform
- Established a committee for constitutional oversight

Governments at the Union-republic level were encouraged to adopt similar democratizing reforms.

According to the constitutional amendments, a 2,250-member USSR Congress of People's Deputies was elected in March 1989. Using the single-member district (SMD) system, Soviet citizens elected 1,500 of the deputies by voting in districts throughout the country. Official organizations, such as the Communist Party and the Academy of Sciences, elected the other 750 deputies from among their members. In previous Soviet elections, the Communist Party had nominated only a single candidate for each seat to be filled. In the 1989 SMD elections, the ballots listed the names of several candidates. This, therefore, was the first multicandidate election for Soviet governing institutions.

In May 1989, the Congress of People's Deputies elected from within its own membership a parliament of a more manageable size, the USSR Supreme Soviet. Membership in this 542-person parliament was to rotate with a fifth of its members to be replaced by other Congress deputies each year. The new Supreme Soviet kept the bicameral structure of its predecessor, with one house called the Council of the Union and the other called the Council of Nationalities.

For the first time in history, the Supreme Soviet actually became involved in the policymaking process. During sessions held in the spring and the autumn, lasting three to four months, Supreme Soviet deputies argued all types of political issues in publicly televised debates. Deputies criticized party and government officials, even though most were themselves Communist Party members.

The USSR Supreme Soviet Presidium was headed by a chairperson who was elected by the Congress of People's Deputies from within its own ranks. In March 1990, new amendments to the constitution created an executive presidency. The position of president of the USSR had broad powers, including the authority to propose legislation, to negotiate treaties, to veto laws passed by the Supreme Soviet, and to declare a state of emergency. The president was the commander-in-chief of the Soviet armed forces and head of state. Another important change in the constitution approved in 1990 eliminated the article that gave special status to the Communist Party as the vanguard of the people. This constitutional change allowed for the registration of competing political organizations.

Mikhail Gorbachev served as the first and only president of the Soviet Union. (See Box 6.1.) He was elected to the position of president of the USSR in March 1990 not by direct popular election, but rather by the deputies of the USSR Congress of People's Deputies. The Congress elected Gorbachev president with 95.6 percent of the membership voting in his favor. The next presidential election, planned for 1994, was to be a direct popular one; however, the Soviet Union dissolved before that election ever happened.

THE STRUCTURE OF LEGISLATIVE INSTITUTIONS IN THE RUSSIAN FEDERATION

After the August 1991 aborted coup, the locus of authority shifted from the USSR president and USSR Supreme Soviet to the Russian presidency and institutions of government. Even with the establishment of an interim State Council for the USSR in the aftermath of the August coup attempt, the Soviet government was collapsing and power moved to the Russian parliament and the presidency.* Through the end of 1991, throughout 1992, and into the fall of 1993, the Russian parliament battled the Russian president over constitutional issues such as the division of authority between the executive and legislative branches of government, the degree of devolution of power from the central government to constituent territories, and the speed and nature of economic reform in Russia.

During 1992 and into 1993, confrontations between Russia's executive and legislative branches escalated. Unable to agree on a new constitution for the Russian Federation or on a state budget, the Russian Congress of People's

*The State Council was composed of leaders of the ten remaining union republics; Moldavia, Georgia, and the Baltic republics refused to participate.

BOX 6.1 CPSU GENERAL SECRETARY MIKHAIL GORBACHEV

A native Russian, Mikhail Gorbachev was born in 1931 in the Stavropol region, where he worked on local collective farms during his youth. After earning a law degree at Moscow University in 1955, Gorbachev returned to Stavropol, where he earned a promotion to First Secretary of the Communist Party in the region. In 1978, he was brought to Moscow to become Secretary for Agriculture in the Central Committee of the CPSU. In 1979, he became a candidate member of the Politburo and became a full member in 1980. When Yuri Andropov died in 1985, Mikhail Gorbachev took over the supreme leadership position as General Secretary of the Communist Party. General Secretary Gorbachev initiated "new thinking" in the foreign policy realm, democratization in the political sphere, and a restructuring of the economy—perestroika. In 1988 as Communist Party general secretary, Gorbachev took over the position of chair of the Soviet government with the forced retirement of Andrei Gromyko. Gorbachev was president of the USSR from March 1990 through December 1991.

Deputies attempted to impeach Boris Yeltsin in March 1993 but fell short of the required votes. In response to the obstructionist stance taken by the parliament, Yeltsin unilaterally dissolved it in late September 1993; he also scheduled an election for a new parliament. The election took place in December 1993 simultaneously with a referendum on the approval of Yeltsin's preferred version of a new constitution. Official reports of the voting indicated approval of Russia's new constitution. Articles 94 through 104 of the 1993 Constitution of the Russian Federation established a bicameral legislature called the Federal Assembly (see Figure 6.2). The two chambers of the Federal Assembly are the State Duma and the Federation Council. The lower house of the Federal Assembly, the Duma, has 450 members. (For information on the electoral rules used to select these members, see Chapter 7.)

The Federation Council is the upper house of the Russian parliament (the Federal Assembly). In contrast to the State Duma, members of the Council do not stand for election. Prior to January 2002, the governor and the speaker of each regional legislature automatically each held a seat in the Federation Council.* According to laws passed in July 2000 and implemented as of January 2002, governors and the regional chairs no longer serve on the Federation Council. Governors now appoint one of their region's two representatives to the upper house and this appointee must be approved by the regional legislature, which also selects the second representative. In December 2001, the Federation Council elected Sergei Mironov as chair. Mironov, head of the Russian Party of

*In Russia's republics, the executive position is called president rather than governor.

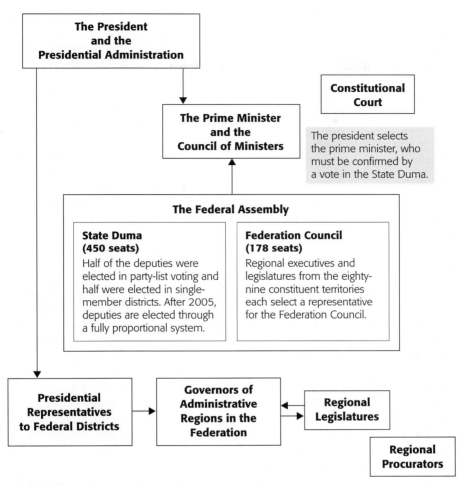

FIGURE 6.2 Structure of Russia's Government

Life, was President Putin's choice. As chair (speaker) of the Federation Council, Mironov is third in line in Russia's constitutional hierarchy, after the prime minister and the president.

THE ROLE AND FUNCTION OF RUSSIA'S LEGISLATURE

In the Russian system, most lawmaking takes place within the Federal Assembly, even though the president has the power to issue decrees that have the force of law. Members of the assembly, the president, or members of government can submit bills to the State Duma, except for a few categories of bills that are under the jurisdiction of the Federation Council. If a law receives majority support in the State Duma, the Duma forwards the legislation to the Federation Council for consideration. For certain categories of bills, voting in the Federation Council can be bypassed. If such legislation receives strong support in the State Duma, it can be sent directly to the president for approval.

If the upper house rejects a law, it goes to a commission, composed of members of both houses, which tries to create compromise legislation. If the Duma rejects the commission's compromise, it can override the Federation Council by a two-thirds vote. If the Federation Council and the Duma pass the law, they send the bill to the president for his signature; if he signs a bill, it becomes law. If he rejects a bill, it may go back to the Duma for rewriting, or the Duma and the Federation Council can try to override the president's veto. This would be a very rare occurrence because it takes a two-thirds vote by both chambers to overcome rejection of a law by the president.

The State Duma is a legitimate, lawmaking institution. After the 1999 election, a coalition of centrist forces formed within the Duma, which included Unity, Fatherland–All Russia, People's Deputy, and Russian Regions groups. This coalition was able to pass legislation that supported the president's policy agenda. After the 2003 parliamentary election, a pro-Putin majority coalesced around United Russia. Thus, the realization of a pro-Putin majority and the reduction of factionalism in the Duma have made legislative activity significantly more efficient under Putin than under Yeltsin.

In addition to lawmaking, the Duma approves the president's nominee for prime minister; may conduct votes of no confidence in the government; and appoints and removes the chair of the state bank, state auditors, and the chair of the office for human rights. At the head of the Duma is the speaker (chair), and the leadership organization within the Duma is the Council of the Duma. The Council of the Duma, composed of the speaker and one representative from each of the registered deputy groups (factions) in the parliament, coordinates the work of the parliament. (For a faction within the State Duma to be viable, it must have at least thirty-five members. Deputies elected from districts can choose to join an existing political party faction within the parliament, or they can form a new deputy group.)

The leadership of the Duma has shown remarkable stability. Gennadii Seleznev served as State Duma speaker through two full terms from 1995 through December 2003. Before him, Russia's first Duma speaker, Ivan Rybkyn, served through the entire 1993 term (until December 1995). In December 2003, after that month's parliamentary elections, the Duma elected former Interior Minister Boris Gryzlov (head of the United Russia party) as speaker.

The role of the Federation Council, in contrast to that of the State Duma, tends to be more limited. Votes taken tend to be unanimous. As explained by Danielle Lussier (2003), "members [of the Federation Council] are under the constant risk of being recalled by their regional executive or legislative branch sponsors and thus cannot freely engage in the give-and-take often required of politics." Arguably, the Federation Council has become a rubberstamp institution, approving presidential initiatives in a pro forma manner.

Although the Federation Council tends to comply with President Putin's wishes, its formal constitutional authority is substantial. The Council has the power to approve presidential decrees on martial law, states of emergency, and sending Russian troops abroad. It has the constitutional authority to impeach the president, although the process of impeachment is difficult. The Federation Council also approves the appointment of Constitutional and Supreme Court judges and the General Prosecutor.

MEMBERS OF PARLIAMENT IN COMPARATIVE PERSPECTIVE

In looking at the career backgrounds and sociodemographic characteristics of the members of Russia's Federal Assembly, remember that, in other parliaments around the world, deputies tend on average to be different from the rest of society. Parliaments tend to be composed primarily of well-educated, middle-aged men. Women comprise slightly more than half of the population in every country, yet women on average comprise only 15.9 percent of the membership of national parliaments. Table 6.1 lists the countries where the percentage of women in parliaments is at least 9 percent of the total members.* Russia ranks eighty-eighth on the list as of April 2005, with just 9.8 percent of seats in the State Duma and 3.4 percent of the Federation Council seats held by women. For comparative purposes, note that the United States ranks sixty-first on the list, with 15.2 percent of representatives in the U.S. House of Representatives being women. The European countries of Sweden, Denmark, Finland, the Netherlands, and Norway together hold five of the top six rankings, each with more than 36 percent of lower- or single-house parliamentary seats held by women. The world average proportion of women in the lower or single house of parliament is 16.1 percent.

Almost half of the members of the Federation Council are permanent residents of Moscow. Of the 91 new representatives that joined the Federation Council by November 2001, 34 percent came from business, 23 percent were regional legislators, and 19 percent were former federal officials.[1] This is quite different from the United States, where law is the most common professional background (Hague, Harrop, and Breslin 1998, 196–97). In many cases, representatives to the Federation Council are appointed in consultation with the Kremlin because regional elites do not want to "upset the Kremlin" or "compromise potential lobbying possibilities."[2]

*Data collected by the Inter-Parliamentary Union.

TABLE 6.1 Women in National-Level Government Branches (Seats Held as a Percentage of Total Seats as of April 30, 2005)

Rank	Country	Lower or Single House		Upper House or Senate	
		Election Dates	Percent Women	Election Dates	Percent Women
1	Rwanda	09 2003	48.8	09 2003	34.6
2	Sweden	09 2002	45.3	—	—
3	Norway	09 2001	38.2	—	—
4	Finland	03 2003	37.5	—	—
5	Denmark	02 2005	36.9	—	—
6	Netherlands	01 2003	36.7	06 2003	29.3
7	Cuba	01 2003	36.0	—	—
"	Spain	03 2004	36.0	03 2004	23.2
8	Costa Rica	02 2002	35.1	—	—
9	Mozambique	12 2004	34.8	—	—
10	Belgium	05 2003	34.7	05 2003	38.0
11	Austria	11 2002	33.9	N.A.	27.4
12	Argentina	10 2001	33.7	10 2001	33.3
13	South Africa (1)	04 2004	32.8	04 2004	33.3
"	Germany	09 2002	32.8	N.A.	18.8
14	Andorra	04 2005	32.1	—	—
15	Iraq	01 2005	31.6	—	—
16	Guyana	03 2001	30.8	—	—
17	Iceland	05 2003	30.2	—	—
"	Belarus	10 2004	29.4	11 2004	31.6
18	Seychelles	12 2002	29.4	—	—
19	New Zealand	07 2002	28.3	—	—
20	Viet Nam	05 2002	27.3	—	—
21	Namibia	11 2004	26.9	11 2004	26.9
22	Grenada	11 2003	26.7	11 2003	38.5
23	Bulgaria	06 2001	26.3	—	—
24	Timor-Leste (2)	08 2001	25.3	—	—
25	Switzerland	10 2003	25.0	10 2003	23.9
26	Australia (3)	10 2004	24.7	10 2004	35.5
27	Mexico	07 2003	24.2	07 2000	21.9

TABLE 6.1 Women in National-Level Government Branches (Seats Held as a Percentage of Total Seats as of April 30, 2005)—Cont'd

Rank	Country	Lower or Single House		Upper House or Senate	
		Election Dates	Percent Women	Election Dates	Percent Women
28	Liechtenstein	03 2005	24.0	—	—
29	Uganda	06 2001	23.9	—	—
30	Luxembourg	06 2004	23.3	—	—
31	Lao People's Democratic Rep.	02 2002	22.9	—	—
32	Tunisia	10 2004	22.8	—	—
33	Saint Vincent and the Grenadines	03 2001	22.7	—	—
"	Eritrea	02 1994	22.0	—	—
34	Lithuania	10 2004	22.0	—	—
35	Croatia	11 2003	21.7	—	—
36	United Republic of Tanzania	10 2000	21.4	—	—
"	Pakistan	10 2002	21.3	03 2003	18.0
37	Portugal	02 2005	21.3	—	—
38	Canada	06 2004	21.1	N.A.	37.1
39	Latvia	10 2002	21.0	—	—
40	Monaco	02 2003	20.8	—	—
41	Nicaragua	11 2001	20.7	—	—
"	China	02 2003	20.2	—	—
42	Poland	09 2001	20.2	09 2001	23.0
43	Dem. People's Republic of Korea	08 2003	20.1	—	—
44	Bahamas	05 2002	20.0	05 2002	43.8
45	Suriname	05 2000	19.6	—	—
"	Dominica	01 2000	19.4	—	—
46	Trinidad and Tobago	10 2002	19.4	10 2002	32.3
47	Guinea	06 2002	19.3	—	—
"	Bolivia	06 2002	19.2	06 2002	11.1
"	The F.Y.R. of Macedonia	09 2002	19.2	—	—
48	Senegal	04 2001	19.2	—	—
49	Estonia	03 2003	18.8	—	—
50	Burundi	06 1993	18.4	01 2002	18.9
51	Peru	04 2001	18.3	—	—

(*Continued*)

TABLE 6.1 Women in National-Level Government Branches (Seats Held as a Percentage of Total Seats as of April 30, 2005)—Cont'd

Rank	Country	Lower or Single House		Upper House or Senate	
		Election Dates	Percent Women	Election Dates	Percent Women
52	United Kingdom	06 2001	18.1	N.A.	17.8
53	Equatorial Guinea	04 2004	18.0	—	—
"	Tajikistan	12 2004	17.5	01 2005	15.0
54	Uzbekistan	02 2005	17.5	03 2005	23.5
55	Dominican Republic	05 2002	17.3	05 2002	6.3
56	Czech Republic	06 2002	17.0	10 2004	12.3
"	Bosnia and Herzegovina	10 2002	16.7	N.A.	0.0
"	Panama	05 2004	16.7	—	—
"	San Marino	06 2001	16.7	—	—
57	Slovakia	09 2002	16.7	—	—
58	Cyprus	05 2001	16.1	—	—
"	Ecuador	10 2002	16.0	—	—
"	Singapore	11 2001	16.0	—	—
59	Turkmenistan	12 2004	16.0	—	—
60	Philippines	05 2004	15.3	05 2004	16.7
61	United States of America	11 2004	15.2	11 2004	14.0
"	Angola	09 1992	15.0	—	—
62	Israel	01 2003	15.0	—	—
63	Sierra Leone	05 2002	14.5	—	—
64	Greece	03 2004	14.0	—	—
"	Guinea-Bissau	03 2004	14.0	—	—
65	Malawi	04 2004	13.6	—	—
66	Barbados	05 2003	13.3	05 2003	23.8
"	Ireland	05 2002	13.3	07 2002	16.7
67	Gambia	01 2002	13.2	—	—
68	Republic of Korea	04 2004	13.0	—	—
69	Zambia	12 2001	12.7	—	—
70	Chile	12 2001	12.5	12 2001	4.2
71	Niger	11 2004	12.4	—	—
72	France	06 2002	12.2	09 2004	16.9

TABLE 6.1 Women in National-Level Government Branches (Seats Held as a Percentage of Total Seats as of April 30, 2005)—Cont'd

Rank	Country	Lower or Single House		Upper House or Senate	
		Election Dates	Percent Women	Election Dates	Percent Women
"	Slovenia	10 2004	12.2	—	—
73	Colombia	03 2002	12.1	03 2002	8.8
74	Maldives	01 2005	12.0	—	—
"	Dem. Republic of the Congo	08 2003	12.0	08 2003	2.5
"	Syrian Arab Republic	03 2003	12.0	—	—
75	Burkina Faso	05 2002	11.7	—	—
"	Jamaica	10 2002	11.7	10 2002	19.0
"	Lesotho	05 2002	11.7	N.A.	36.4
76	Italy	05 2001	11.5	05 2001	8.1
77	Indonesia	04 2004	11.3	—	—
78	Romania	11 2004	11.2	11 2004	9.5
79	Botswana	10 2004	11.1	—	—
"	Cape Verde	01 2001	11.1	—	—
"	Saint Lucia	12 2001	11.1	12.2001	36.4
"	Uruguay	10 2004	11.1	10 2004	9.7
80	Ghana	12 2004	10.9	—	—
81	Djibouti	01 2003	10.8	—	—
"	Morocco	09 2002	10.8	10 2003	1.1
"	Swaziland	10 2003	10.8	10 2003	30.0
82	El Salvador	03 2003	10.7	—	—
"	Zimbabwe	03 2005	10.7	—	—
83	Thailand	02 2005	10.6	03 2000	10.5
84	Antigua and Barbuda	03 2004	10.5	03 2004	17.6
"	Azerbaijan	11 2000	10.5	—	—
85	Kazakhstan	09 2004	10.4	09 2004	7.7
86	Mali	07 2002	10.2	—	—
87	Paraguay	04 2003	10.0	04 2003	8.9
88	Cambodia	07 2003	9.8	03 1999	13.1
"	**Russian Federation**	12 2003	**9.8**	N.A.	**3.4**
89	Sudan	12 2000	9.7	—	—

(Continued)

TABLE 6.1 Women in National-Level Government Branches (Seats Held as a Percentage of Total Seats as of April 30, 2005)—Cont'd

Rank	Country	Lower or Single House		Upper House or Senate	
		Election Dates	Percent Women	Election Dates	Percent Women
"	Venezuela	07 2000	9.7	—	—
90	Georgia	03 2004	9.4	—	—
91	Gabon	12 2001	9.2	02 2003	15.4
"	Malta	04 2003	9.2	—	—
92	Hungary	04 2002	9.1	—	—
"	Malaysia	03 2004	9.1	03 2004	25.7
"	Sao Tome and Principe	03 2002	9.1	—	—

Note: Figures correspond to the number of seats currently filled in a legistative branch or a parliament. Countries not listed have less than 9 percent of seats held by women in the lower or single house of the national government.

1. South Africa: The figures on the distribution of seats do not include the 36 special rotating delegates appointed on an ad hoc basis; the percentages given are therefore calculated on the basis of the 54 permanent seats.

2. Timor-Leste: The purpose of elections held on August 30, 2001, was to elect members of the Constituent Assembly. This body became the National Parliament on May 20, 2002—the date on which the country became independent, without any new elections.

3. Australia: The figures for the senate reflect its composition up to July 1, 2005.

Source: Data obtained from the Inter-Parliamentary Union website at http://www.ipu.org/wmn-e/classif.htm.

An unfortunate characteristic of membership in Russia's State Duma is that it can be a dangerous job. On April 18, 2003, State Duma deputy and cochair of the Liberal Russia Party, Sergei Yushenkov, was shot dead outside his Moscow home; he was the ninth deputy to die a violent death since 1994. Moscow police chief Vladimir Pronin told journalists at the scene of the killing that Yushenkov was "the victim of a professional killer" and that the slaying was "most likely linked with his activity as a [Duma] deputy."[3] Yushenkov had served as the Duma Defense Committee chairman (1993) and as a member of the Duma Security Committee (1999).

In most parliaments, reelection rates are high. The success rate of **incumbents** in winning reelection is more than 85 percent in Taiwan, Denmark, Germany, Japan, New Zealand, and the United States. It is around 60 percent in France, Great Britain, and Israel (Hague, Harrop, and Breslin 1998, 198). In general, the frequency of reelection can be explained by referring to the fact that incumbents have greater visibility and greater access to resources than most challengers do.

Turnover in Russia's parliamentary elections has been higher; for example, in the 1995 parliamentary elections, only 35 percent of the deputies elected had been members of the 1993 Duma. In 1999, the share of incumbents who won SMD races for the State Duma was 35.8 percent (Golosov 2002, 26). For the Duma elected in 2003, 46 percent of all deputies had been members of the 1999–2003 Duma.[4]

THE EMERGENCE OF RUSSIA'S PRESIDENTIAL SYSTEM

The position of president of Russia was created by the Congress of People's Deputies of the Russian Soviet Federated Socialist Republic prior to the demise of the Soviet Union. In creating this new chief executive position, the RSFSR Congress of People's Deputies held a referendum in April 1991 that asked the people whether a popularly elected presidency should be instituted for Russia. The proposal received strong support and an election for the position was held on June 12, 1991. In this first contested presidential race in Russia's history, Boris Yeltsin garnered nearly 60 percent of the valid vote to defeat his nearest competitors, Nikolai Ryzhkov and Vladimir Zhirinovsky, with 18 percent and 8 percent of the votes, respectively. Yeltsin had resigned his membership in the Communist Party a little over a year earlier.

After completing a five-year term, Yeltsin entered the 1996 presidential election as the incumbent. In that election campaign, the leader of the Communist Party, Gennadii Zyuganov, emerged as a formidable opponent to President Yeltsin. The elections were forced into a **second round runoff** when Zyuganov challenged Yeltsin in the first round with 32 percent to Yeltsin's 35 percent of the vote. According to Russia's electoral rules, the top two vote-getters in the first round of voting—that is, Yeltsin and Zyuganov—move on to a second round if no candidate receives 50 percent in the first round. Yeltsin emerged victorious in the second round in July 1996 after forming an alliance with General Alexander Lebed, the third-highest vote-getter from the first round. Prior to the second round of voting, Yeltsin invited Lebed to join the Security Council in the presidential administration. This alliance, however, did not last long; just months after Yeltsin won the presidential election, Lebed was dismissed from his Security Council position.

Elections for the president of the Russian Federation were due to be held again in the summer of 2000, but right after the December 1999 parliamentary elections, Boris Yeltsin resigned from his position as president. According to the Russian Constitution, new elections had to be held within three months, so the Yeltsin resignation pushed presidential elections forward to March 2000.

After Yeltsin's resignation, Prime Minister Vladimir Putin, whom Yeltsin had appointed in August 1999, assumed the position of acting president while remaining prime minister. As acting president, Putin was the clear favorite in the 2000 presidential elections. The prospects of other candidates, which had appeared to be significant before December 1999, quickly faded and the election campaign narrowed to a two-man race between Putin and Communist Party leader Gennadii Zyuganov. Among Putin's supporters in the presidential election period were Unity and several other parties close to the Kremlin (Fatherland and the Union of Right Forces), as well as a large number of regional governors.

The March 2000 presidential election registered a turnout of 68.74 percent, with 1.88 percent of the votes being cast "Against all" candidates. The results of the election were hardly surprising (see Table 6.2): Putin, as acting president and prime minister, won the race in the first round with 52.9 percent of the votes. Note that the Communist Party candidate, Zyuganov, received 29 percent (nearly one-third) of the votes cast. People voted for Zyuganov because they were uncomfortable with Boris Yeltsin's pro-market reforms and his Western-oriented policies. They believed that Yeltsin's agenda would continue under Putin.

After four years in office, Vladimir Putin's position was much stronger. When elections for the presidency of Russia took place again in March 2004, 64 percent of all registered voters participated. Incumbent President Putin emerged triumphant with a landslide victory (see Table 6.3).

It should be noted that Putin competed in the election without a party affiliation. The Communist Party candidate received less than 14 percent of the vote, a smaller portion than had been received by the Communist Party candidate in the 2000 and 1996 presidential elections. This smaller percentage may actually demonstrate continued support for the ideals and platform of the Communist Party, considering the significant advantages enjoyed by President Putin as an acknowledged popular incumbent. Nikolai Kharitonov, although nominated by the Communist Party of the Russian Federation, was actually a member of the Agrarian Party, a Communist Party ally. The party put him forward as its candidate after Communist Party leader Gennadii Zyuganov

TABLE 6. 2 Russian Federation Presidential Election Results (March 2000)

Candidate	Percentage of Votes
Vladimir Putin (Acting President)	52.94%
Gennadii Zyuganov (Communist Party leader)	29.17%
Grigorii Yavlinsky (Yabloko Party leader)	5.79%
Aman Tuleev (Kemerovo region governor)	2.95%
Vladimir Zhirinovsky (Liberal Democratic Party of Russia leader)	2.70%
Other candidates	4.55%
Against all	1.88%

Note: Results listed here are for only the top five candidates.

Sources: Data is from the *RFE/RL Russian Election Report*, 7 April 2000, and the Central Electoral Commission at http://www.fci.ru/prez2000.

TABLE 6.3 Russian Federation Presidential Election Results (March 2004)

Candidate	Party Affiliation	Percentage of Total Votes
Vladimir Putin	Independent	71.3%
Nikolai Kharitonov	Communist Party of the Russian Federation (CPRF)	13.7%
Sergei Glazyev	Independent	4.1%
Irina Mutsuovna Khakamada	Independent	3.8%
Oleg Malyshkin	Liberal Democratic Party of Russia (LDPR)	2.0%
Sergei Mironov	Party of Russia's Rebirth–Party of Life	0.8%
Against all candidates	—	3.5%

The results shown here are from the Russian Central Electoral Commission.

Note: For a candidate to be included on the ballot, he or she was required to collect two million signatures (up from one million in 1996 and 2000), of which no more than 7 percent could be from one of the eighty-nine regions of the RF. However, political parties winning party-list seats in the most recent Duma election were exempt from the requirement to collect signatures (Article 36.2). To be approved for a place on the ballot, candidates had to submit to further checks, including statements of income and property. By February 2004, seven candidates were approved for a place on the ballot; one candidate, Ivan Rybkin, withdrew leaving just six candidates.

declined to stand for a third time. Zyuganov and Grigorii Yavlinsky of the Yabloko Party did not enter the 2004 race because they asserted that the electoral process would not be fair.

Another candidate, Sergei Glazyev, was nominated by a nonpartisan voter group because just weeks prior to the 2004 election, the Rodina (Motherland) Party voted to drop him from its membership, even though he was the party's cofounder. Glazyev was a minister for foreign trade under Yeltsin and a Communist Party member of the State Duma; but the party did not support his presidential candidacy, so he had set up the Motherland Party. He campaigned as a critic of economic reforms and argued that the Yeltsin and Putin regimes had undermined social justice.

International election observers criticized the conduct of the 2004 presidential election. Representing the Organization for Security and Cooperation in Europe and the Parliamentary Assembly of the Council of Europe, observers cited abuses of government resources, bias in the state media, and instances of ballot stuffing on election day: "The election process overall did not adequately reflect principles necessary for a healthy democratic election process," said Julian Peel Yates, head of the observer mission.[5]

This is not to deny the genuine popularity of Vladimir Putin, who would likely have won the elections if they had been free and fair. The media, however, particularly television, was extremely biased toward Putin and gave him largely uncritical coverage while limiting coverage of his challengers. Also, it was alleged that directors of state enterprises and institutions put pressure on their employees to vote for Putin. Official figures from Chechnya showed Putin receiving more than 92 percent of the vote, which is difficult to believe.

PARLIAMENTARY AND PRESIDENTIAL SYSTEMS IN COMPARATIVE PERSPECTIVE

Scholars regularly classify governments into parliamentary and presidential systems. In **presidential systems**, the president is directly elected by the total electorate (the exception here is the United States, which uses an electoral college). The president is not part of the legislature, and the legislature cannot remove the president from office except through a legal process of impeachment. Usually the president and the legislature serve for fixed terms.

In contrast to a presidential system, in a **parliamentary system**, the executive (the prime minister and his or her cabinet) emerges from the membership of the parliament. The United Kingdom is the classic example of a parliamentary system of government: "After an election, the party which wins a majority of seats in the House of Commons forms the government; the leader of the winning party becomes prime minister and selects twenty or so parliamentary colleagues to form the cabinet" (Hague, Harrop, and Breslin 1998, 206). In parliamentary systems, the prime minister is leader of the party with the majority of seats in the legislature. The prime minister (premier or chancellor) and the cabinet (government ministers) are drawn from the membership of the parliament and can be dismissed from office through a no-confidence vote by parliament. There is no limit on how long the prime minister stays in office, provided elections are held and his or her party wins enough seats.

The top leader in a parliamentary system is the prime minister. In a presidential system, the top leader is the president. A third system exists, called the **dual executive**, where a president and a prime minister share power. The dual executive system is a mixture of the parliamentary and presidential forms with divided powers between an elected president and a prime minister. The classic example of this system is France. In general, the prime minister is responsible for day-to-day domestic government (including relations with parliament) but the president retains an oversight role, responsibility for foreign affairs, and usually can assume emergency powers.

THE AUTHORITY OF RUSSIA'S PRESIDENCY

The Russian political system has a strong executive presidency. Since the adoption of the 1993 constitution, the person who holds the position of president of the Russian Federation has extensive powers and constitutional prerogatives.

Former USSR President Gorbachev complained that Russia's 1993 constitution gave Boris Yeltsin more power than even the tsar had exercised before the revolution (Hague, Harrop, and Breslin 1998, 214).

Two of the variants of a strong presidential system are the **unlimited presidential executive** and **superpresidentialism**. In these systems, the president has so many powers that the legislature functions primarily as a formal approval mechanism—as a rubberstamp institution—for presidential initiatives. Such systems may take on dictatorial or authoritarian characteristics. The Russian system under President Vladimir Putin has exhibited such tendencies.

Articles 80 through 92 of the Russian constitution give the president control over the armed forces (as commander-in-chief), over foreign policy, and over the military doctrine of the federation. The president also determines basic guidelines for domestic policy. The president has the power to dissolve the State Duma (under restricted conditions), call a referendum, and issue decrees and directives. The president can submit draft laws to the Federal Assembly and veto legislation, although both houses of the assembly can override a veto with a two-thirds majority vote. The constitution gives the president the authority to settle differences between federal bodies and regional and local governments, to suspend decisions by regions if they are in variance with the federal constitution, and to declare states of emergency.

The president is empowered to select the prime minister (to be approved by the parliament); to appoint cabinet members (with the advice of the prime minister), the chairman of the state bank, and presidential representatives to the regions; and to nominate judges. The president can impose his choice for prime minister on the Duma; if the Duma rejects his nominee three times, the Duma can be dissolved and new elections scheduled. The president has the power to dismiss his chosen prime minister and cabinet ministers.

Despite these considerable powers, some legal and political limitations on presidential prerogatives do exist. For example, the Federation Council does "confirm" presidential decrees on the introduction of martial law or states of emergency and on the use of armed forces abroad. The Duma, for its part, can make a no-confidence vote against the government, which can be both inconvenient and embarrassing to a president. In addition, the president is restricted to some extent by public opinion. Although most Russians acknowledge the president's right to make major decisions about what direction the country should take, unpopular policies could definitely engender a reaction; such was the case when popular pressure was critical in bringing about the withdrawal of troops from Chechnya in 1996.

The most important ministries of state authority—the Federal Security Service, the Defense Ministry, the Foreign Ministry, and the Interior Ministry— answer directly to the president. The heads of these ministries have been extremely powerful men, including Defense Minister Sergei Ivanov, Foreign Minister Sergei Lavrov, Interior Minister Rashid Nurgaliev, and Federal Security Service (FSB) Director Nikolai Patrushev. The president also leads the Security

Council, which consists of the heads of the most powerful ministries and other security-related agencies, such as Emergency Situations Minister Sergei Shoigu, the prime minister, and the chairmen of the Duma and the Federation Council.

The president exercises his power through the staff of the presidential administration (see Figure 6.2). Units within the administration oversee the work of regional governments and federal ministries. A central component of the presidential administrative apparatus is the group of seven presidential representatives (envoys) to Russia's federal districts. First appointed in May 2000, these envoys are responsible for supervising the implementation of federal laws at the regional level, monitoring federal budgetary transfers to regions, assisting with regional socioeconomic development plans, checking on whether regional laws are in line with the constitution and with federal legislation, and overseeing the actions of the governors. The high status of presidential envoys is indicated by the appointment of Sergei Kiriyenko as the envoy to Volga Federal District; Kiriyenko had served as Russia's prime minister in 1998.

In September 2000, Russian President Vladimir Putin, by decree, created a State Council. Putin announced that the State Council would be an executive body that would include all eighty-nine governors and heads of the republics. The full State Council meets four times a year to discuss important strategic issues. The Presidium of the State Council includes the envoys to each of the seven federal districts.

Legislation passed since 1993 has enhanced presidential powers. In July 2000, for example, the president received the right to remove regional governors if they break federal law or come under investigation. In institutional terms, the Russian superpresidency dominates the legislative organs (the Federal Assembly) and the constituent administrative units of the federation.

RUSSIA'S TWO PRESIDENTS: YELTSIN AND PUTIN

Given that the presidency is relatively new, Russia's first two presidents have played a significant part in determining the nature of the position. When a person occupies an office, especially a new office, he or she thereby shapes that office.

Boris Yeltsin

Russia's first president, Boris Nikolayevich Yeltsin, was born in 1931. He graduated from the Urals Polytechnic Institute in 1955 and worked in construction engineering from 1955 to 1968. Although Yeltsin joined the Communist Party of the Soviet Union in 1961, his family had a history of persecution under the Soviet regime. Yeltsin's grandfather was declared a kulak and his home and land were confiscated. His father was convicted of anti-Soviet agitation in 1934 and spent three years in a forced labor camp.[6]

Yeltsin became first secretary of the Sverdlovsk Region Central Committee of the CPSU in 1976 and soon established a reputation as an energetic reformer. In 1985, Yeltsin was appointed first secretary of the Moscow City Communist Party Committee. This also elevated him to the status of alternate member of the Politburo of the CPSU. Boris Yeltsin was head of the Communist Party organization in Moscow, the largest city in the Soviet Union. This was an extremely powerful position and Yeltsin used his power to arrest corrupt officials, to criticize the state-run media, to advocate for the elimination of special privileges for party officials, and to encourage the establishment of small-scale private businesses. Yeltsin himself demonstrated austerity by riding city buses rather than being chauffeured around in fancy cars.

Yeltsin's unqualified commitment to a rapid pace of reform ultimately led him into conflict with the more conservative members of the CPSU (see Chapter 3). In February 1988, he was removed from his membership in the Politburo. Despite this setback, Boris Yeltsin's popularity as a reformer led to his election to the USSR Congress of People's Deputies in 1989. He received a seat in the Supreme Soviet of the USSR and became a co-leader of the Inter-Regional Group of Deputies, which promoted human rights and democratic reforms. In 1990, he was elected to membership in the Russian Soviet Federated Socialist Republic Congress of People's Deputies and, subsequently, in May 1990 was elected by its membership to the post of speaker (chair) of the RSFSR Supreme Soviet. Under Yeltsin's leadership, the RSFSR Congress of People's Deputies adopted a Declaration of Sovereignty in June 1990. On June 12, 1991, Yeltsin became the first popularly elected president of Russia.

USSR President Gorbachev, Russian President Yeltsin, and the heads of several other Soviet republics were scheduled to sign a new Union Treaty on August 20, 1991. But on August 18, USSR Vice President Gennadi Yanayev, along with other coup plotters, announced the takeover of Gorbachev's presidential power. Boris Yeltsin condemned the August 1991 coup attempt and called for popular resistance. Ultimately, the coup's leaders were arrested, most were accused of treason, and three committed suicide. As head of the Russian government, Yeltsin banned the activities of the Communist Party in the Russian Federation and confiscated party property. When the Soviet Union ceased to exist in December 1991, Yeltsin stayed on as president of the largest part—the Russian Federation—of the former USSR.

Yeltsin's popularity as Russian president waned, however, in the aftermath of the demise of the Soviet Union as people suffered the hardships associated with the economic transformation of the system. Yeltsin was also subject to criticism domestically and internationally for the "undemocratic" means he employed to dissolve the Russian Supreme Soviet and the Congress of People's Deputies in September 1993. Only after troops loyal to Yeltsin shelled the Russian parliamentary building did the parliamentary leadership surrender.

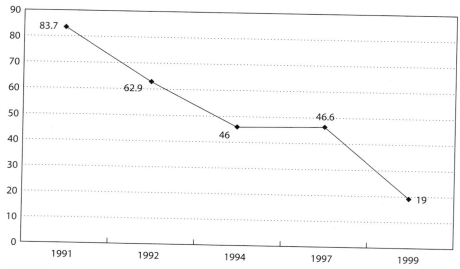

FIGURE 6.3 Yeltsin's Positive, Neutral, and Negative Ratings Over Time

Also devastating to Yeltsin's popularity was the unsuccessful and troubling war in Chechnya that dragged on from 1994 to 1996. The eastward expansion of NATO, despite Russia's objections, also caused apprehension and disillusionment among the people. In addition, Yeltsin's health problems raised issues about his capacity to serve a second term as president. He was so ill in late 1996 and early 1997 with heart problems and pneumonia that opposition forces in parliament once again called for his impeachment. Yeltsin made a recovery, however, and was able to win reelection in 1996 and ruled Russia until his resignation in December 1999.

Changes in Yeltsin's popularity ratings over time are apparent from public opinion polls conducted between 1991 and 1999. In 1991, 83.7 percent of the people gave him positive ratings, but between 1995 and 1999 people, on average, evaluated Yeltsin negatively.* The changes in the percent that evaluated him positively over time are shown in Figure 6.3. The trend during the decade of the 1990s definitely shows declining support for Yeltsin.

Vladimir Putin

Vladimir Vladimirovich Putin, elected in 2000 as Russia's second president, had a different family history and a very different career path from that of Boris Yeltsin. Putin was born in Leningrad (now St. Petersburg) in 1952.† His father

*The public opinion polls were funded by the National Science Foundation and conducted by the author with Arthur Miller, William Reisinger and Elena Bashkirova.
†More information about Putin can be found at http://www.cbc.ca/news/indepth/background/putin.html.

was a war veteran who defended St. Petersburg from the Germans during World War II. Putin won the sambo championships of St. Petersburg and became Master of Sports in sambo (1973) and in judo (1975).*

Putin graduated from Leningrad State University (Faculty of Law) in 1975 and joined the Soviet state security service's (KGB) foreign intelligence unit. Between 1985 and 1990, Putin worked in East Germany (the former German Democratic Republic). He resigned from the USSR state security service on August 20, 1991.

As an ally of St. Petersburg's mayor, Putin became head of the International Committee of the Mayor's Office in June 1991. His tasks in this capacity were to attract foreign investment to the city and to oversee the creation and opening of joint ventures. In 1994–1996, Putin combined his job as the head of the International Committee with a new post of first deputy mayor of St. Petersburg, monitoring the activities of law-enforcement agencies and working closely with the city's legislative assembly.

In August 1996, Putin was transferred to Moscow to work under President Boris Yeltsin as deputy property manager. In July 1998, he was appointed director of the Russian Federal Security Service (FSB) and in March 1999, Putin became secretary of the Russian Security Council while keeping his FSB director post. He was appointed prime minister of the Russian Federation in August 1999 and became acting president on December 31, 1999, following the resignation of Yeltsin. After Putin won the election on March 26, 2000, he was inaugurated as Russia's second president on May 7, 2000.

Robert Daniels (2000) has argued convincingly that Putin's extraordinary authority comes not only from the constitution and from enabling legislation but also from his close ties with the secret police. His career background in the security service (KGB) provides him with personal networks and additional resources for exerting his power. In addition, certain oligarchs that helped to finance his presidential campaign remained powerful allies until Putin undertook a campaign to limit their influence in 2003. Putin's extraordinary authority also derives from his leadership and political skills. He is incisive, realistic, analytically acute, and a powerful speaker. His strong personality has been demonstrated both in his "taming" of the legislature and in his ability to rein in the powerful regional governors. Daniels (2000) also argues that the authoritarian and nationalistic tendencies in Russia's political culture enable Putin to act with relatively limited public accountability requirements.

At the start of his second term, President Putin continued to receive strong approval ratings according to public opinion polls conducted among Russian citizens. The All-Russia Center for the Study of Public Opinion (VCIOM) has

---

Sambo is a Russian acronym for Self-Defense Without Weapons; it refers to a form of sport wrestling that was developed in the Soviet Union. It was also used in the Soviet military as a way to prepare and train soldiers for hand-to-hand combat without weapons.

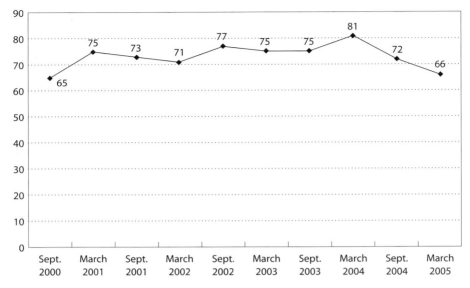

FIGURE 6.4 Approval Rating of Putin's Performance

Source: Nationwide VCIOM (now the Levada Center) surveys 1998–2004, found at http://www.Russiavotes.org.

consistently asked respondents to answer the following question: "On the whole do you approve or disapprove of the performance of Vladimir Putin?" The percentage of respondents who answered affirmatively in polls conducted in the months of March and September for every year since 2000 are shown in Figure 6.4.

THE DUAL EXECUTIVE: RUSSIA'S PRIME MINISTER

The constitution calls the president "head of state" but not chief executive; the chief executive is the prime minister. If the president dies or is incapacitated, the prime minister becomes acting president for a three-month period until new elections can be held. The president names the prime minister, but the State Duma must vote to confirm this nomination. If the Duma rejects the president's nominee for prime minister three times or votes no confidence in the government twice within three months on its own initiative (or once if the government itself requests the confidence vote), the president can dissolve the Duma and call for new parliamentary elections.

The president can appoint and remove deputy prime ministers and other ministers without parliamentary approval. In Russia, the party affiliations of those who fill the top ministerial positions do not necessarily reflect the factional strength of the parties in the parliament. Most ministers are career administrators rather than party representatives.

The prime minister, as head of the Council of Ministers, directs the government through ministries and state agencies. The Council of Ministers is responsible for the formulation and implementation of economic and social policy, including credit and monetary policy, culture, science, education, health, social security, and ecology.[7]

As a dual executive system, Russia's government is constitutionally accountable to the parliament. The Duma held no-confidence votes periodically throughout the 1990s and 2000s. In June 2003, for example, the government of Prime Minister Mikhail Kasyanov survived a no-confidence vote. The motion, put forward and supported by the Communist and Yabloko factions, needed 226 votes to pass but garnered only 172. In arguing for the no-confidence vote, Yabloko leader Grigorii Yavlinsky asserted that the Russian political system lacks "an independent judiciary, an independent legislature, and independent media organs. He described the political system as one in which business interests are integrally combined with those of the bureaucracy."[8] Communist Party leader Gennadii Zyuganov expressed serious concern about export of natural resources and about the country's demographic crisis, citing Russia's low life expectancy and high suicide rate.[9] Although the government of Kasyanov survived the no-confidence vote, the incident highlighted the constitutional oversight prerogatives of the Duma. Russia did get a new prime minister when Putin replaced Kasyanov with Mikhail Fradkov in March 2004.

Despite the importance of prime ministers in Russia's dual executive system, the tremendous power vested in the president has caused scholars to question if such a system contributes to or hampers the building of democracy in Russia. Political scientists such as Lijphart (1994), Sartori (1994), and Linz (1990, 1997) have argued that strong presidential powers are associated with low democratic performance throughout the post-Communist world. Shugart and Carey (1992) define three broad categories of fundamental deficiencies in presidential systems. First is temporal rigidity: With a fixed term in office, presidential systems have limited mechanisms for removing an unpopular president. The second deficiency is the winner-take-all characteristic of presidentialism: Minority views and minority parties have less opportunity for representation than would be the case in a cabinet coalition government. Third is dual democratic legitimacy: With both branches legitimately and separately elected, incentives for cooperation are limited.

Still, proponents of presidentialism argue that the system provides greater effectiveness than a parliamentary system and therefore promotes political stability. Presidential systems can, under certain circumstances, operate more efficiently than parliamentary systems and may be better at articulating national goals rather than local constituency interests. Matthew Shugart (2000) argues forcefully in favor of presidentialism under conditions of weak parties.

In this context, we must note that Russian presidentialism functions differently under Putin than it did under Yeltsin. Both the Russian president (elected in 1991) and the Russian Congress of People's Deputies (elected in 1990) remained in place after the dissolution of the Soviet Union in December 1991. Members of the Congress of People's Deputies were openly critical of President Boris Yeltsin's economic reform initiatives right from the start. Even after the constitutional crisis of 1993, which pitted the Soviet-era Russian legislature against the pro-market and anti-Soviet executive represented by President Yeltsin, groups opposed to reform—pro-Communist and nationalist forces—maintained their majorities in the December 1993 and 1995 State Duma elections. The resulting legislatures were frequently in conflict with the executive branch and operated as obstacles to the reform agenda that President Yeltsin advanced.

The office of the president and relations between the president and parliament changed considerably when Vladimir Putin took over as acting president in December 1999. His popularity gave him distinct advantages in shaping the office. Putin's ability to work with Unity and other pro-presidential factions in the Duma after the 1999 election, and his solid majority support from United Russia in the Duma after the 2003 election, allowed him to build and maintain a much more productive relationship with the legislative branch than had been characteristic of the Yeltsin era. Thus, the presidential office has assumed a different profile under President Putin.

The relationship between the president and the prime minister has also been more stable during Putin's terms in office. The last few years of Yeltsin's rule were characterized by frequent turnover in the position of prime minister. Prime Minister Victor Chernomyrdin had the longest tenure in office, from December 1992 until March 1998, when Yeltsin dismissed the entire government (see Table 6.4). Putin did dismiss Prime Minister Mikhail Kasyanov just weeks before the 2004 presidential election. Kasyanov's replacement, Mikhail Fradkov, had been serving as the Russian Federation's representative at the European Commission. Fradkov speaks English and Spanish and had previously worked in India, Geneva, and Brussels. In 1997 and 1998, Fradkov was minister of Foreign Economic Relations and he headed the Trade Ministry in 1999 and 2000. He had served as director of the Federal Tax Police Service before taking the Brussels post.

THE JUDICIAL BRANCH

Just as with the presidency and the legislature, judicial institutions operating in the Soviet Union were carried over to the Russian Federation with the demise of the USSR. All courts in the Soviet Union were constitutionally subject to the authority of the USSR Supreme Soviet. Judges for the different courts were selected at the various levels by the Soviet at the same level. As of 1949, voters began to directly elect judges to the lowest-level courts; however, the Communist Party tightly controlled these elections, just as it controlled the selection of deputies to the local soviets. Most judges (approximately 95 percent) were members of the Communist Party or the Komsomol (Reshetar 1989, 257).

TABLE 6.4   Russia's Political Leaders (1990–October 2004)

Year	President	Prime Minister	Foreign Minister	Chair (Speaker) of the State Duma
1991	Boris Yeltsin (June 1991)*	Ivan Silayev (1990) Boris Yeltsin (November 1991)		
1992		Yegir Gaidar (acting June 1992) Viktor Chernomyrdym (December 1992)		
1994			Andrei Kozyrev	Ivan Rybkyn
1996	Yeltsin, reelected		Yevgenii Primakov† (January 1996)	Gennadii Seleznev
1998		Sergei Kiriyenko (March–April 1998) Yevgennii Primakov (September 1998)	Igor Sergeevich Ivanov (October 1998)	
1999	Vladimir Putin (acting as of December 1999)	Sergei Stepashin (May 1999) Vladimir Putin (August 1999)		
2000	Vladimir Putin (elected March 2000)	Mikhail Kasyanov	Igor Ivanov	
2003				Boris Gryzlov (December 2003)
2004	Putin, reelected	Mikhail Fradkov (March 2004)	Sergei Lavrov	

Note: Russia's four defense ministers during this same period were Pavel Gravchev, Sergei Radionov, Igor Sergeev, and Sergey Ivanov.

*Date of election or appointment of leaders is shown in parentheses following their names.

†Primakov was formerly head of the Foreign Intelligence Service (December 1991 to January 1996).

In the Soviet judicial system, a lengthy preliminary investigation was conducted before trial. The report on the investigation was sent to the court for use during the trial. Usually this report argued the guilt of the accused, and generally judges went along with the report. For this reason, the system was criticized in the West for lacking the "presumption of innocence."

A very important official within this system was the procurator, who investigated the case and presented evidence of guilt. The judge's role was reduced primarily to determining a sentence. The Procuracy as an institution was responsible for the legality and validity of all court actions and all judicial rulings. In addition, the Procuracy supervised detention facilities and checked on the execution of sentences. The USSR Procurator-General, who was elected by the Supreme Soviet, named procurators for the lower levels of the court system. Procurators were subject to influence by the higher Communist Party organs.

The Court System in the Russian Federation

Since 1991, the Procuracy has retained its dual responsibility for the administration of judicial oversight and for criminal investigations. The Procuracy remains a centralized agency with branches in all subnational jurisdictions. With the approval of the State Duma, the president appoints the chief of the agency, the Prosecutor-General. Vladimir Ustinov held the position as of mid-2005.

According to the 1993 constitution, the political system of the Russian Federation has a greater degree of **separation of powers** than the previous Soviet system. In addition to the executive and legislative branches of government, Russia has a judicial branch, supporting police, and an internal security apparatus. The constitution declared that state power in the Russian Federation was to be exercised based on a division into legislative, executive, and judicial authority and that all these branches should be independent.

A continuing problem associated with Russia's court system, however, is the relative lack of independence of the judges. Financial support for the courts comes from the Ministry of Justice, but salaries for judges are very low, and they depend on local authorities for housing in the jurisdiction where they sit. According to Russia's 1993 constitution, sitting justices do have immunity from prosecution and can only be removed through lawful procedures; nonetheless, the judiciary remains subject to the influence of security agencies and politicians.

Legal reform in post-Soviet Russia has been a top-down process, often based heavily on recommendations of foreign advisers. New civil codes have been adopted in post-independence Russia, as well as new codes on criminal procedures. Still, most Russians go to great lengths to avoid the court system, which remains flawed in terms of delays in the process and in the ability to get judicial decisions enforced. A large case backlog, trial delays, and lengthy pretrial detention continue to be problems.[10]

The Constitutional Court

At the top of the hierarchy of the judicial system in Russia are the Constitutional Court, the Supreme Court, and the Superior Court of Arbitration.* Judges for

---

*The information about these three courts is compiled from details provided by the Ministry of Justice of the Russian Federation—see http://www.supcourt.ru/.

these three courts are appointed by the president and confirmed by the Federation Council. In addition, the system includes military courts.

The Constitutional Court of the Russian Federation was first established in July 1991. As the confrontation between Boris Yeltsin and the Russian Supreme Soviet under the leadership of Ruslan Khasbulatov escalated in 1992 and 1993, the chair of the Constitutional Court, Valerii Zorkin, increasingly aligned himself with Khasbulatov. Thus, when Yeltsin dissolved Russia's parliament in 1993, he also suspended the operation of the Constitutional Court. It was not until March 1995 that the Federation Council confirmed all of Yeltsin's nominees to a new court. Since then, the Constitutional Court has been functional.

The Constitutional Court considers cases relating to compliance with the Constitution of the Russian Federation; federal laws; acts of the president and the government of Russia; constitutions of republics; and charters and other normative acts of the subjects of the federation. The primary role of the court therefore is to make sure that all laws and decrees conform to the constitution. The Constitutional Court also resolves jurisdictional disputes between federal or local organs of power. Both government agencies and citizens can submit cases for consideration. Republics and other subjects of the Russian Federation also have lower-level constitutional courts.

The Supreme Court

The Supreme Court of the Russian Federation is the supreme judicial body for civil, criminal, administrative, and other cases under the jurisdiction of courts of general jurisdiction, including military courts. The Supreme Court provides judicial supervision of the activities of lower-level courts and clarifies issues of court proceedings. The Supreme Court also has the right of legislative initiative.

The Supreme Court of the Russian Federation consists of three chambers: the Judicial Chamber on Civil Cases, the Judicial Chamber on Criminal Cases, and the Military Chamber. The court acts as a court of first instance for cases of special importance or special public interest when it accepts them for consideration. In most cases, however, the Supreme Court reviews cases brought to it from lower-level courts.

At the foundation of the system of general jurisdiction courts of the Russian Federation are the **raion** courts. The law attributes to the jurisdiction of raion courts all civil cases, an overwhelming majority of criminal cases, and cases relating to administrative offenses. Courts of general jurisdiction of the krai, oblast, city, or autonomous oblast and autonomous districts act as higher-instance courts for raion courts.

The Superior Court of Arbitration

The Superior Court of Arbitration, headed by a board of one chairperson and four deputy chairpersons, is the highest court for the resolution of economic disputes. Courts of arbitration also exist at lower jurisdictional levels. The courts hear disputes related to tax issues and respond to lawsuits between enterprises and between firms and the government.

Key Terms

Dual accountability	Second round runoff
Dual executive	Separation of powers
Incumbent	Superpresidentialism
Parliamentary system	Unlimited presidential executive
Raion	

Critical Thinking Questions

1. Presidential, parliamentary, and dual executive systems are three forms democracies can take. Discuss some of the advantages and disadvantages of each.

2. What constitutional changes did Gorbachev put into place in 1988 and 1990? How did these changes affect the representation of women in the Supreme Soviet? How did they influence the transition to democracy?

3. What is the purpose of the Federal Council, and how are its members selected?

4. What role do legislatures generally play? How is this different or the same in the case of Russia?

5. Does a separation of powers arrangement exist in Russia?

6. What is meant by the term *superpresidency*? How have Yeltsin and Putin shaped the power of the Russian presidency?

7. What kind of problems plagued the Yeltsin presidency and how have the Putin years differed?

8. How are the Soviet and Russian judicial systems different? How is the current court system similar/dissimilar to that in other countries? What issues remain of concern in Russian judicial politics?

Suggested Reading

Barany, Zoltan, and Robert G. Moser. *Russian Politics: Challenges in Democratization*. New York: Cambridge University Press, 2001.

Boilard, Steve D. *Russia at the Twenty-First Century: Politics and Social Change in the Post-Soviet Era*. Orlando: Harcourt Brace College Publishers, 1998.

Hough, Jerry, and Merle Fainsod. *How the Soviet Union Is Governed*. Cambridge, Mass.: Harvard University Press, 1979.

Reshetar, John S., Jr. *The Soviet Polity*. New York: Harper and Row, 1989.

Sakwa, Richard. *Russian Politics and Society*. New York: Routledge, 2002.

Websites of Interest

Inter-Parliamentary Union homepage is a good resource for parliamentary data from around the world:
http://www.ipu.org

Official websites of the president of the Russian Federation:
http://www. kremlin.ru/eng and http://president.kremlin.ru/eng/

Websites for the Russian State Duma and Federation Council (some English pages are available, but most are in Russian):
http://www.duma.gov.ru and www.council.gov.ru

Links for everything from Russian politics to culture:
http://www.therussiasite.org

Two sites for Russian newspapers available in English:
http://www.themoscowtimes.com and www.sptimes.ru

CHAPTER 7

Political Participation and Public Opinion in Russia

T HIS CHAPTER FOCUSES ON the role citizens play in Russia's political system. What current research says about voting behavior is reviewed first. The electoral laws that govern Russia's parliamentary, presidential, and regional elections are also described. A discussion of other forms of political participation, such as contacting public officials, demonstrating, and supporting opposition parties, follows. Public opinion data on key questions of public policy is also included.

DIFFERENT FORMS OF POLITICAL PARTICIPATION

Political participation is the behavioral expression of political interests, and it includes a variety of activities undertaken by citizens to make demands or requests of political authorities. Voting for elected officials is the most common form of citizen participation. **Conventional–legal participation,** which goes beyond just voting and requires a higher level of effort, includes contacting public officials, signing a petition, or participating in lawful demonstrations or strikes. **Violent participation** involves challenging authority through potentially illegal actions such as occupying public buildings or participating in violent actions. Given that punishments inflicted on those who engage in violence against a state are usually severe, discontent must be extreme for people to turn to illegal actions.

Voting

Voting is a mechanism by which present leaders are replaced with new ones. In addition, by participating in the electoral process, citizens legitimate the existing system. Establishing electoral institutions and holding competitive elections are major and necessary steps in the implementation and consolidation of democracy.

The officially recorded turnout in Russia's 1999 parliamentary elections was 62 percent, meaning that 62 percent of those eligible to vote did indeed vote on election day in December. For the 2003 parliamentary elections, only 56 percent of the eligible electorate voted. Official turnout for the Russian 2000 presidential election was 69 percent of all registered voters. For the 2004 presidential election, turnout was 64 percent. Even with the declines over time, voter turnout in Russia's elections is higher than that found in the United States, where participation in the national election in 2000 was 51 percent.

When political scientists study voting behavior, they attempt to answer the following questions:

1. Who votes and who does not vote: What are the characteristics of the people who do participate in elections as compared to the characteristics of those who do not go to the polls on election day?

2. Once at the polls, what factors influence the voting decision: How do citizens decide which candidates or political parties will receive their votes?

Political scientists use survey research to determine which types of people are the most likely to vote in elections. The author of this text, in collaboration with colleagues in Russia, conducted a survey (a public opinion poll) immediately after the 2000 presidential election.* The research involved selecting a representative sample of people from throughout the Russian Federation and then interviewing them. The field workers who conducted the interviews asked each person whether he or she had voted in the 2000 presidential election and in the 1999 parliamentary elections. In addition to asking about electoral participation, interviewers recorded each person's age, education, occupation, and position on important issues. Table 7.1 shows which personal characteristics best explain the decision to vote in the 1999 parliamentary elections and Table 7.2 shows which factors best explain participation in the 2000 presidential election.

As shown in Tables 7.1 and 7.2, the factors considered as potential predictors of voting can be divided into four groups: personal characteristics, identity effects, economic motivators, and political values. Beginning with personal characteristics, research from other countries has established socioeconomic status as the characteristic most strongly related to political action. Findings

*Elena Bashkirova, the president of public opinion polling firm ROMIR, supervised the research in Russia.

TABLE 7.1 Predicting Who Decided to Vote in Russia's 1999 Parliamentary Elections (logistic regression)

Predictor Variables	Estimated Coefficients	Standard Error of the Coefficient	Wald Statistic	Significance of the Coefficient
Male	−0.057	0.119	0.228	0.633
Age (older)	0.037	0.004	84.993	0.000
Education (higher)	0.126	0.032	15.553	0.000
Unemployed	−0.549	0.187	8.654	0.003
Residence (urban rather than rural)	−0.156	0.032	24.186	0.000
Russian nationality	−0.176	0.168	1.095	0.295
Professes a religion	0.246	0.153	2.572	0.109
Ideological extreme	0.201	0.073	7.521	0.006
Negative economic assessment[a]	−0.008	0.035	0.058	0.810
Efficacy[b]	0.146	0.051	8.193	0.004
Interested in politics[c]	0.371	0.083	20.134	0.000
Political knowledge[d]	0.045	0.013	12.465	0.000
Constant	−2.600	0.436	35.540	0.000

Number of cases in the analysis: 1,823
Number of missing cases: 177

Goodness-of-fit statistics
▪ Percent correctly predicted: 73.8%[e]
▪ −2 Log likelihood: 1,918.479
▪ Cox & Snell R square: 0.151
▪ Nagelkerke R square: 0.215

[a]This was a negative retrospective assessment of both the national economy and respondents' financial situation. We tested this by asking the following questions:

1. Thinking about the economy in the country as a whole, how would you say the nation's economy has changed over the past year? (Much better, Somewhat better, Same, Somewhat worse, Much worse)

2. Now please tell how the financial situation of your family has changed in comparison with the one you had a year ago? (Much better, Somewhat better, Same, Somewhat worse, Much worse).

Answers to the two questions were highly correlated, so we created an additive scale that combines answers to these two economic assessment items.

[b]Agreement or disagreement with this statement: "People like me don't have any say about what the government does."

[c]Respondents report that they have been very interested in the election campaigns.

[d]Respondent follows news on TV and in newspapers and also discusses politics with friends.

[e]Of those surveyed, 70.1 percent reported having voted in the 1999 parliamentary elections.

TABLE 7.2 Predicting Who Decided to Vote in Russia's 2000 Presidential Election (logistic regression)

Predictor Variables	Estimated Coefficients	Standard Error of the Coefficient	Wald Statistic	Significance of the Coefficient
Male	0.092	0.143	0.417	0.519
Age (older)	0.038	0.005	61.920	0.000
Education (higher)	0.047	0.038	1.498	0.221
Unemployed	−0.501	0.208	5.803	0.016
Residence (urban rather than rural)	−0.152	0.038	16.058	0.000
Russian nationality	0.057	0.197	0.085	0.771
Professes a religion	0.159	0.178	0.799	0.372
Ideological extreme	0.292	0.097	9.040	0.003
Negative economic assessment	−0.037	0.042	0.789	0.375
Efficacy	0.315	0.067	22.272	0.000
Interested in politics	0.287	0.096	8.882	0.003
Political knowledge	0.064	0.015	17.707	0.000
Constant	−1.814	0.508	12.733	0.000

Number of cases in the analysis: 1,828

Number of missing cases: 172

Goodness-of-fit statistics
- Percent correctly predicted: 82.8%
- −2 Log likelihood: 1,436.516
- Cox & Snell R square: 0.128
- Nagelkerke R square: 0.212

from Western democracies show that higher-status individuals (in terms of income, occupation, and education) are more likely to have the time, money, and knowledge to become involved politically (Verba and Nie 1972, 1978; Parry, Moyser, and Day 1992; Rosenstone 1982; Shields and Goidel 1997). Besides socioeconomic status, scholars have also presented evidence that gender and age predict political participation (Inglehart 1981; Strate et al. 1989). In Western European democracies, men tend to be more active politically than women.* With regard to age, research shows that in Western democracies older people are more likely to vote.

To check whether our study of voting in the 1999 and 2000 elections in Russia confirms previous results, we look to the information in Tables 7.1 and 7.2. Each row of each table is devoted to one factor and each row provides statistical information on the relationship between that factor and the likelihood of voting. Row 1 of the tables reports the estimated coefficient for the predicted relationship between gender (male or female) and voting. Because the coefficient is not significant, we conclude that men are *not* more likely to vote than women are. In other words, males and females were equally likely to vote in Russia's 1999 parliamentary and 2000 presidential elections.

Age, however, does motivate turnout in Russia (see row 2 of Tables 7.1 and 7.2). We conclude that older people are significantly and dramatically more likely to vote in both parliamentary and presidential elections in Russia than are younger people. With regard to education (row 3), those with a higher level of education are more likely than less-educated people to turn out for parliamentary elections, but in presidential elections in Russia, education makes no difference in the decision of whether to vote.

Occupational status is highly correlated with educational attainment, so it is not included in the tables. Income also is not included among the list of predictors in Tables 7.1 and 7.2 because we did not have information on the incomes for all the people in the survey. A separate analysis, however, reveals that those with higher monthly incomes are more likely to vote in parliamentary elections than those with lower incomes. For presidential elections, monthly income is unrelated to participation. In both parliamentary and presidential elections, unemployed people are less likely to vote than are employed people (notice the negative sign in row 4, "Unemployed," of Tables 7.1 and 7.2). Thus, analysis of the 2000 survey data confirms that Russian voting behavior is similar to that found in Western European democracies in that people with higher education and income are generally more likely to vote. Noteworthy as well is that urban dwellers are significantly less likely to vote in both parliamentary and presidential elections than are those who live in more rural areas (row 5).

Identity-based forces, such as national identity and religious identity, make up the second group of potential predictors. Shared cultural traits permit, though do not necessarily create, sufficient social solidarity to turn individuals into active participants. Looking at Tables 7.1 and 7.2 again, notice that membership in the main nationality group (whether a person is an ethnic Russian or not) or whether he or she belongs to a particular religious group is unrelated

---

*Differences in political resources, such as education, income, and employment patterns, explain a large part of this phenomenon, however.

to voter participation. Thus, identity factors do not influence voting participation in Russia.

Economic motivations are the third potential predictor of political participation. Some scholars hold that economic adversity ignites people's dissatisfaction with the government and increases their propensity to vote as they aim to change government policies (Lipset 1981, 192; Schlozman and Verba 1979; Kernell 1977). Others argue that because economic difficulties make people focus on concerns other than politics, economic problems suppress turnout (Brody and Sniderman 1977; Wolfinger and Rosenstone 1980). In Russia, however, we find that economic assessments are unrelated to a decision to participate in either parliamentary or presidential elections.

An individual's political values represent the final set of influences with regard to participation (Verba, Schlozman, and Brady 1995). Michael Lewis-Beck and Brad Lockerbie (1989) found that being located politically at the ideological left or right extreme is especially important in increasing the likelihood of voting in Western Europe. This was also true in Russia's 1999 and 2000 elections. The survey included a question about left–right ideological self-placement. In creating an "ideological extreme" measure, those people who placed themselves at the endpoints (either left or right) of the ideology scale were given the highest scores, while people who placed themselves in the middle, or did not place themselves on the scale, received the lowest score. As can be seen in row 8 of Tables 7.1 and 7.2, those who do place themselves at a left or right ideological extreme were significantly more likely to vote in both parliamentary and presidential elections than those who do not have a strong ideological leaning.

Another group of political attitudes includes beliefs about citizens' role in political action. Efficacy, political interest, and political knowledge are all significantly related to voting in the Russian Federation. In both the 2000 presidential and the 1999 parliamentary elections, those with stronger feelings of political efficacy; those with a greater interest in the political campaign; and those who frequently watch news programs, read newspapers, and/or speak about politics to friends were significantly more likely to vote than those who lacked efficacy, were less interested in politics, or had limited exposure to political information.

To summarize, we first note that the majority of Russia's citizens do vote in both presidential and parliamentary elections. The people who are the most likely *not* to vote are young, have less education, are unemployed, and live in an urban area. The likelihood of voting increases dramatically when a person feels efficacious, shows interest in the campaign, and exposes himself or herself to news and political discussions. An earlier analysis of voting during the 1995 parliamentary election and the 1996 presidential election similarly demonstrated that older people, those living in rural areas, those with higher socio-economic status, and those with higher levels of religiosity were the more frequent voters (see Hesli et al. 1999).

Conventional–Legal Participation

In trying to describe the full range of possible ways to participate in a political system, beyond voting, Myron Weiner defines *political participation* as "any voluntary action, successful or unsuccessful, organized or unorganized, episodic or continuous, employing legitimate or illegitimate methods, intended to influence the choice of public policies, the administration of public affairs, or the choice of political leaders at any level of government, local or national" (1971, 164). Other authors have categorized political participation in different ways: active versus inactive, overt versus covert, autonomous versus compliant, episodic versus continuous, voluntary versus involuntary, and conventional versus unconventional (Kim 1980; Milbrath 1965; Dalton 1998).

The focus of this section is on conventional–legal participation, which encompasses most forms of political activity in addition to voting. To study conventional participation in Russia, we once again turn to survey research. In a poll conducted throughout Russia in 1997, people were asked whether they had personally undertaken any of a series of six different activities for influencing political authorities.* Table 7.3 provides a list of the activities and the corresponding percentage of people who had participated in the activity in the year before the survey. The overall message shown in the table is that very few people engage in any form of political activity beyond voting. Of those who do, the most common activity is to advise someone else to vote for a particular candidate or party.

To study who participates and who does not, a measure of level of political activism among the Russian populace was created. For each person surveyed, we counted how many of the six activities listed he or she had done in the previous year; most people had not undertaken any. Twenty-four percent had done just one of the activities, 7 percent had done two, and 3 percent had done three of the activities.

In Table 7.4, the measure of level of political activism is regressed on the same set of predictors that explained the voting participation shown in Tables 7.1 and 7.2. The significance levels for the *t*-tests, as reported in column 5, indicate which factors are related to political activism. In contrast to what was found with regard to voting, age is unrelated to nonvoting forms of conventional–legal political participation. Education, however, is an important contributing factor to political activism; higher levels of education statistically correlate with higher levels of participation. Likewise, being at an ideological extreme, either left or right, is strongly associated with higher levels of political activism. The third significant factor that emerges from the data in Table 7.4 is political knowledge. The more an individual reads newspapers and watches TV

*The National Science Foundation funded this survey, which was organized by Arthur Miller, William Reisinger, and Vicki Hesli.

TABLE 7.3 Frequency of Nonvoting Forms of Conventional–Legal Political Participation

Political Activity	Percentage Who Did the Activity Within the Past Year
Advised someone to vote for a certain party or person	22.0
Signed a petition (collective letter)[a]	14.0
Participated in a rally or demonstration[b]	6.7[c]
Contacted a Deputy or other public official	5.9
Contacted a newspaper, magazine, or television station	4.6
Took part in the activities of a political party[d]	1.4

Source: The data in the table are from the author's survey. The data in the table's footnotes are from the 2000–2002 World Values Surveys and from the 1999 European Values Survey, as reported in Almond et al. (2004, 80).

[a] Corresponding figures for the percentage of the people who signed a petition in other countries are: United States (81 percent), Britain (81 percent), France (68 percent), Germany (52 percent), Mexico (19 percent).

[b] Corresponding figures for the percentage of the people who participated in a lawful protest demonstration in other countries are: United States (21 percent), Britain (13 percent), France (39 percent), Germany (28 percent), Mexico (4 percent).

[c] The 2000-2002 World Values Surveys list this figure at 24 percent, as reported in Almond et al. (2004, 80).

[d] Corresponding figures for the percentage of the people who participated in political party activities in other countries are: United States (18 percent), Britain (3 percent), France (2 percent), Germany (3 percent), Mexico (5 percent).

news programs, the more likely he or she is to get involved in nonvoting forms of conventional–legal participation.

The data on conventional political participation shows that employment status (unemployed) and negative economic assessments are unrelated to higher levels of political activism. We also tested whether the family's total monthly income was associated with higher levels of political activism and found that this is not the case. These findings contradict earlier research on Russia that suggested a link between the likelihood of protest and economic dissatisfaction (McAllister and White 1998). Instead, the information in Tables 7.1, 7.2, and 7.4 conform better to a "resource" model explanation for political participation (Tilly 1975; Lipsky 1968). According to such a model, protest and other conventional–legal forms of participation should be higher among better-educated and politically sophisticated people who have the skills and resources to engage in these demanding forms of activity (Dalton 1998).

TABLE 7.4 Predicting the Level of Political Activism[a]: Who Participates in Nonvoting Forms of Conventional–Legal Activity (OLS regression)

Predictor Variables	Unstandardized Estimated Coefficients	Standard Error of the Coefficient	Standardized Coefficients	Significance of the Coefficient
Male	−0.015	0.045	−0.008	0.746
Age (older)	0.000	0.001	0.000	0.996
Education (higher)	0.076	0.011	0.194	0.000
Unemployed	−0.102	0.076	−0.032	0.183
Residence (urban rather than rural)	−0.033	0.017	−0.046	0.058
Russian nationality	0.105	0.056	0.044	0.060
Professes a religion	−0.068	0.044	−0.037	0.128
Ideological extreme	0.112	0.023	0.114	0.000
Negative economic assessment	0.010	0.014	0.017	0.486
Efficacy	0.015	0.025	0.014	0.550
Political knowledge[b]	0.051	0.015	0.084	0.001
Constant	−0.195	0.176	—	0.268

Number of cases in the analysis: 1,702

Number of missing cases: 108

Percent of Variance Explained
- R square: 0.
- Adjusted R square: 0.066

Source: This data based on a 1997 survey of the population of the Russian Federation co-directed by Arthur Miller, William Reisinger, and Vicki Hesli; funded by the National Science Foundation.

[a]The level of political activism was measured by counting how many of the activities listed in Table 7.3 the respondents had done in the previous year.

[b]Political knowledge was measured through the use of two questions: "How many different newspapers do you read each day?" and "How often over the past week did you watch a news program on television (any channel)?"

POLITICAL OPPOSITION IN RUSSIA

Thus far, we have discussed political participation in Russia from the perspective of individual acts of voting or conventional–legal activism. This section covers something different—the concept of organized opposition. **Political opposition** is defined as an organization or a person that does not share the basic positions (for example, values, policies, or strategies) of those who currently control decision-making power. In addition, the opposition challenges the current power-holders and has a desire to become the primary decision maker for the state.

In post-Soviet Russia, the most influential oppositional force that has competed for political influence through conventional–legal channels is the Communist Party of the Russian Federation (CPRF). Gennadii Zyuganov, head of the Communist Party, received 29 percent (nearly one-third) of the votes in the 2000 presidential election. The CPRF represented a real alternative to the policies and to the general worldview pursued by the Putin administration.

Given that the Communist Party has been the most significant legally recognized oppositional force operating in Russia, we need to identify who supports it. A useful way to look at this question is to compare who voted for Vladimir Putin with who voted for Zyuganov in the 2000 election. Logistic regression is used to identify which factors are significantly associated with a higher probability of voting for Zyuganov in contrast to Putin in that presidential election. According to Table 7.5, the most important determinants of a vote for Zyuganov are ideology and negative economic assessments (rows 8 and 9). Support for the CPRF candidate corresponds to ideological distance from the center. Communist Party supporters also tend to view their personal finances and the national economy more negatively than do supporters of Putin.

Efficacy is lower among Zyuganov supporters in comparison with Putin supporters. Given that inefficacy is associated with **alienation,** which can lead to opposition, it is not surprising that opposition supporters have relatively lower levels of efficacy than government supporters. The two demographic features that differentiate Zyuganov supporters from Putin supporters are age and level of education. Those who voted for the Communist Party candidate tended to be older and less educated than those who voted for Putin.

Noteworthy as well are the factors that are *not* significant, as shown in Table 7.5. Men are no more likely to vote for the Communist Party candidate than are women. Likewise, the Communist Party vote comes equally from rural and urban areas, from Russians and non-Russians, from employed and unemployed, and from those with high and low levels of political interest and knowledge. According to this scientific survey, therefore, the factors that really drive Communist Party support are ideology and perceptions of a poor economy and insufficient personal finances. (In a study of differential voting support for Yeltsin in contrast to Zyuganov during the 1996 presidential election, a vote for Zyuganov was unrelated to gender, age, socioeconomic status, or rural

TABLE 7.5 Predicting Who Decided to Vote for the Main Oppositional Candidate—Zyuganov, Head of the Communist Party, Instead of Putin, Representing the Incumbent Administration—in Russia's 2000 Presidential Election[a] (logistic regression)

Predictor Variables	Estimated Coefficients	Standard Error of the Coefficient	Wald Statistic	Significance of the Coefficient
Male	−0.166	0.142	1.369	0.242
Age (older)	0.017	0.005	13.481	0.000
Education (higher)	−0.078	0.037	4.512	0.034
Unemployed	−0.149	0.270	0.306	0.580
Residence (urban rather than rural)	−0.045	0.038	1.441	0.230
Russian nationality	−0.002	0.195	0.000	0.992
Professes a religion	−0.219	0.199	1.210	0.271
Ideological extreme	0.544	0.075	51.970	0.000
Negative economic assessment	0.256	0.039	42.269	0.000
Efficacy	−0.148	0.059	6.330	0.012
Interested in politics	−0.013	0.103	0.017	0.897
Political knowledge[b]	0.019	0.015	1.484	0.223
Constant	−2.833	0.537	27.871	0.000

Number of cases in the analysis: 1,200

Number of missing cases: 0

Goodness-of-fit statistics
- Percent correctly predicted: 72.4%
- −2 Log likelihood: 1,347.331
- Cox & Snell R square: 0.125
- Nagelkerke R square: 0.175

[a]Among those who voted for either Putin or Zyuganov, 32% of those surveyed reported a vote for Zyuganov.
[b]Respondent follows news on TV and in newspapers and also discusses politics with friends.

residence; however, it was statistically associated with negative economic assessments and lower levels of religiosity [Hesli et al. 1999].)

In the same public opinion poll reported in Table 7.5, people were also asked to report their preferred positions on the most controversial issues that divide the Putin regime from the communist opposition. According to an "issue-voting" model, the positions taken by presidential candidates on key issues should demonstrably affect the electoral fortunes of the candidates in their contest for the people's votes. Table 7.6 includes four issue-position questions along with the already known factors that are important for explaining a vote for Zyuganov rather than for Putin during the 2000 presidential election. Starting with row 6 of the table, notice that perceptions of Russia's position in the world system do influence presidential vote choice. (See the footnotes to Table 7.6 for the full wording of the survey questions.) Those who voted for the Communist Party candidate are more likely to think that Russia's position has grown weaker than those who voted for Putin. Figure 7.1 demonstrates this relationship graphically. Although most of those who voted for Putin and Zyuganov view Russia's world position negatively, negativity is significantly more prevalent among Zyuganov supporters.

The second issue included in the public opinion poll was a question about respondents' opinions on whether Russia should be integrated with the

TABLE 7.6 Main Issue Positions of Those Who Voted for the Main Oppositional Candidate in Russia's 2000 Presidential Election

Predictor Variables	Estimated Coefficients	Standard Error of the Coefficient	Wald Statistic	Significance of the Coefficient
Age (older)	0.011	0.005	4.400	0.036
Education (higher)	−0.008	0.040	0.043	0.836
Ideological extreme	0.522	0.083	39.408	0.000
Negative economic assessment	0.202	0.045	20.096	0.000
Efficacy	−0.128	0.065	3.863	0.049
Russia's world position has grown stronger[a]	−0.308	0.114	7.307	0.007
Russia and Europe should go in different directions[b]	0.189	0.059	10.245	0.001
Support for return to a planned economy[c]	0.564	0.079	51.104	0.000
Support for individualism[d]	−0.141	0.044	10.470	0.001
Constant	−4.292	0.649	43.720	0.000

(*Continued*)

TABLE 7.6 Main Issue Positions of Those Who Voted for the Main Oppositional Candidate in Russia's 2000 Presidential Election—Cont'd

Number of cases in the analysis: 1,069

Number of missing cases: 131

Goodness-of fit-statistics

- Overall percent correctly predicted: 75.7%
- −2 Log likelihood: 1,085.527
- Cox & Snell R square: 0.225
- Nagelkerke R square: 0.312

[a]Answer to the following question: "During the past year, would you say that Russia's position in the world has grown WEAKER, STAYED ABOUT THE SAME, or has it grown STRONGER?"

[b]Answer to the question: "People have different views on the question how the relations between Russia and Europe should be conducted. Using the variants of the answers given on this card, tell how, in your opinion, the relations between Russia and Europe should be constructed?"

1. Russia should become integrated with European Community
2. Russia should increase ties with Europe, but only gradually
3. Relations should stay the same
4. Russia should limit its ties with Europe
5. Russia and Europe should go in different directions completely

[c]Answer to the question: "Please tell in what direction, in your opinion, the economy of Russia should develop?"

1. Move more quickly toward a free, market economy
2. Move more gradually toward a free, market economy
3. Have a market economy with some state regulation
4. Increase centralized control and return some enterprises to the state ownership
5. Return to planned economy of the Soviet period

[d]Answer to the following question: "Some people feel the government in Moscow should see to it that every person has a job and a good standard of living. Others think the government should just let each person get ahead on his/her own. And, of course, some other people have opinions somewhere in between. Using the scale on the card, tell please where you would place your own opinion?"

1.............................2.............................3.............................4.............................5.............................6.............................7

Government should see to a job and good standard of living

Government should let each person get ahead on own

European Community or whether Russia and Europe should go in different directions completely. The issue of how closely Russia should be associated with Europe is tied to questions of security alliances, economic aid packages, cultural distinctiveness, territorial integrity, and maintenance of independence for action in the international arena. The debate among Russians is

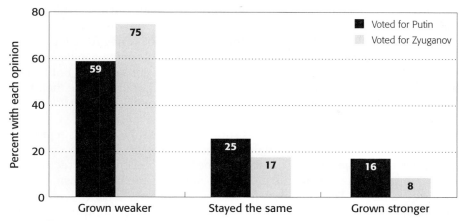

FIGURE 7.1 Differences in Opinion Between Putin and Zyuganov Supporters with Regard to Russia's Position in the World

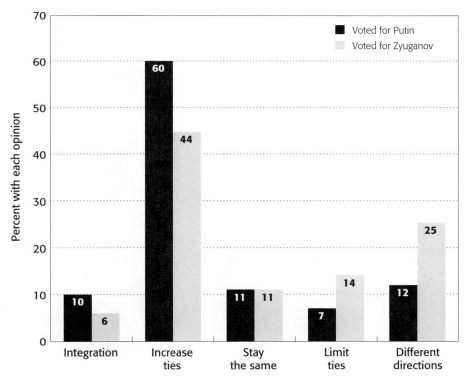

FIGURE 7.2 Differences in Opinion Between Putin and Zyuganov Supporters with Regard to the Future of Relations Between Russia and Europe

whether the benefits of greater cooperation with Europe outweigh the potential costs.

The results in Table 7.6 show that the probability of voting for Zyuganov is higher among those who believe that Russia and Europe should go in different directions. Figure 7.2 shows that the most common response among both Putin and Zyuganov supporters is that Russia and Europe should increase their ties. Putin supporters, however, take this position more frequently than Zyuganov supporters.

The two issues discussed so far, as shown in Figures 7.1 and 7.2, represent foreign policy concerns. The following paragraphs discuss some domestic issues. First is the question of what would be the best economic structure for Russia; the survey's respondents selected an answer from those shown in footnote *c* of Table 7.6. The responses to the question were dramatically different for Zyuganov and Putin supporters. Indeed, a person's position on this one issue is the best single predictor of whether that person will vote for Zyuganov or Putin (see coefficients in row 8 of Table 7.6). As shown in Figure 7.3, 32 percent of those who voted for Zyuganov prefer a return to the planned economy characteristic of the Soviet period. Another 39 percent of Zyuganov supporters want more centralized control and the return of some enterprises to state ownership. Putting these two figures together (32 percent plus 39 percent) means that the vast majority of Zyuganov supporters wanted to *reverse* the direction of economic reform. In contrast, Putin supporters were significantly more likely to approve of continued moves toward a free market economy.

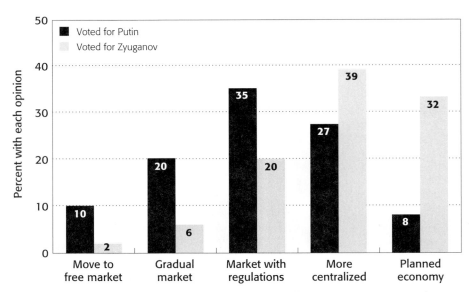

FIGURE 7.3 Differences in Opinion Between Putin and Zyuganov Supporters with Regard to What Would Be the Best Structure for the Russian Economy

The last issue question included in Table 7.6 is also a significant predictor of a vote for the Communist Party candidate Zyuganov in the 2000 presidential election. The question asked whether the respondent thinks that the government in Moscow should see to it that every person has a job and a good standard of living or whether the government should just let each person get ahead on his or her own. The probability of voting for Zyuganov was lower among those who believe that the government should just let everyone get along on their own. Among Zyuganov supporters, 55 percent wanted the government in Moscow to be responsible for people's well-being (see Figure 7.4), while only 37 percent of Putin supporters selected this option.

The data summarized in the tables and figures demonstrate a wide range of public opinion in Russia on major questions of policy and a significant degree of difference between those who voted for Putin and those who voted for the Communist Party candidate during the 2000 presidential election. Thus, the role of the Communist Party in offering the electorate an alternative set of policy options to those implemented by the governments of Yeltsin and Putin is good for Russia from the perspective of democratic theory. Although definitions of democracy differ, by almost any definition, within a democracy there

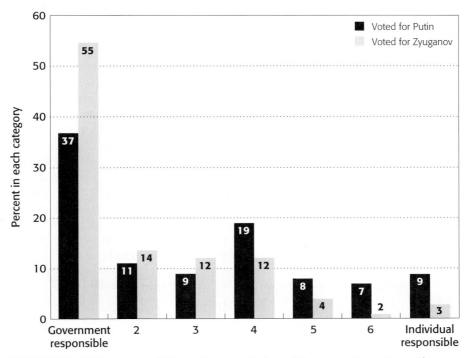

FIGURE 7.4 Differences in Opinion Between Putin and Zyuganov Supporters with Regard to Government or Individual Responsibility for People's Well-being

should be competition among candidates who offer the electorate different sets of policy goals.

The Communist Party, even though frustrated with many of Putin's policies, has remained a conventional–legal opposition that competes against the government through electoral and legislative channels. At an official congress (meeting) of the Communist Party of the Russian Federation held in January 2002, party leader Gennadii Zyuganov sharply criticized President Putin's policies as a "betrayal of Russia's interests." The congress then proceeded to adopt a resolution that the CPRF is in "irreconcilable opposition" to the Russian president. Putin, as the one who holds power in Russia in the early 2000s, is almost patrimonial toward the communists: Putin acknowledged the Congress of the Communist Party and called the CPRF "a creative and constructive political association that has united a considerable part of society."[1] Putin takes a much different position toward oppositional groups in Chechnya; he labels them "terrorists." He not only refuses to negotiate with the Chechen opposition but also put a price on the heads of the leaders.

Democratic governance requires that those currently in power be willing to share power and to hold elections that allow for free and fair contests for offices. But when the political opposition feels excluded, repressed, threatened, or insecure, the level of conflict in a society can increase. Suicide bombings represent the epitome of alienation and frustration with existing political channels. Branding those who perpetrate acts of violence against a state as terrorists does little to solve the underlying problems.

An August 2000 bomb blast in a pedestrian underpass near Moscow's Pushkin Square killed 13 people. A suicide bomb attack killed 15 people at an open-air rock festival in Moscow in July 2003.[2] Putin's government labeled all such bombings the work of terrorists, often identified as appearing to be from the Caucasus region. In August 2003, a suicide bomber killed 50 people at a military hospital in North Ossetia in Southern Russia. In the aftermath of a December 9, 2003, bombing near Moscow's National Hotel, which left 6 dead and caused an estimated $500,000 in damage, President Putin called for new efforts to halt terrorists, but the Federal Security Service (FSB) has not been able to stop the activities of the groups responsible.[3] The December Moscow blast came just four days after a suicide bomber had killed 36 people on a commuter train in Southern Russia. In February 2004, another 30 people died in a blast on a train in Moscow. In June 2004, 92 people were killed in Ingushetia, which borders Chechnya. In August 2004, two Russian airplanes were blown up, killing 89; and a suicide bomber killed another 9 people in Moscow.

Such incidents represent the most violent political action. Chechen separatists are the major oppositional force in Russia today operating outside the conventional–legal channels. Their tactics contrast with those of the Communist Party, which challenges the Putin regime through the electoral process and other legal means.

A democracy should be able to guarantee an open, free, and secure arena for political competition. Democratic government allows for pluralism, expression of diverse viewpoints, articulation of concerns, and mobilization in support of group interests. However, good government does not imply weak government. Governments need to have the capacity to collect taxes to fund transportation and communication infrastructures, social welfare programs, and a military for territorial defense. Governments not only need to be able to ensure law and order so that citizens are secure and safe from violence, but they also need to respond when citizens demand changes in current practices and policies.

ELECTORAL SYSTEMS IN COMPARATIVE PERSPECTIVE

As discussed above, the most common form of political participation is voting. The hallmark of a democracy is an **electoral system** (voting system) in which every citizen can take part in regular free and fair elections. Ideally, elections should produce stable governments in which a single party is in charge or two or more parties agree to a workable coalition. In an effort to achieve both effective government and representation of diverse interests, different countries have experimented with a variety of electoral systems. These systems can be grouped in four categories: plurality, majority, proportional representation (PR), and combination or mixed.

The **plurality system** also is known as the "winner-take-all" or "first-past-the-post" system. Under the plurality system, which the United States and Great Britain both use, the country is divided into districts of roughly equal population size, and each district is contested by candidates representing different parties (or by unaffiliated independent candidates). A district corresponds to a seat in the legislature, and the candidate who gets the most votes in the district wins the legislative seat.

A **majority system**, also based on district voting, requires that a candidate win a certain minimum percentage of the vote (for example, 50 percent) to be elected. If no candidate wins the minimum percent of votes, a second round of voting is held with only the top two vote-getters from the first round competing. The advantage of the **single-member district (SMD) electoral system**, whether plurality or majority, is that it connects a deputy to a district, giving him or her the incentive to look out for and respond to the interests of the people in his or her constituency.

In a **proportional representation (PR) electoral system**, political parties win seats in proportion to the number of votes they receive. There are many forms, but the most basic is the **party-list electoral system**. In this system, the whole country can operate as a single electoral district or the country can be divided into a few large districts. The political parties on the ballot offer a list of candidates, and the number of seats in the legislature won depends on the overall proportion of the vote that the party receives. Examples of countries with a PR system are the Netherlands and Israel. In many countries, a party must receive some minimum percentage, or a **threshold** (say 4 percent) of the votes to receive any seats at all. Under this system, a relatively small party can theoretically receive representation, whereas in single-member district voting, it is very difficult for smaller parties to win legislative seats.

Combination (mixed) electoral systems use SMD and PR together. The German system is the most frequently studied example of such a system in which each voter has two votes: one vote for a district representative and one vote for a party. During the 1990s, the Russian Federation, Ukraine, and several other post-Soviet countries adopted a variant of Germany's **mixed electoral system** for their parliamentary elections.

ELECTIONS TO RUSSIA'S NATIONAL PARLIAMENT

Prior to 1993, elections in Russia and the Soviet Union used the single-member district system exclusively: The country was divided into electoral districts and the number of districts equaled the number of seats that needed to be filled in the parliament. Between 1993 and 2003, Russia used a mixed system for electing the membership of the Duma—the lower house of the Federal Assembly. Half of the seats were filled by the winners of electoral districts, while the other 225 seats were filled by candidates listed on party lists. Thus, voters in single-seat constituencies (single-member districts—SMDs) elected 225 members directly; the other 225 members of the Duma were determined by proportional representation (PR) based on votes for party lists. Voters had two ballots: one to choose a candidate competing to represent their electoral district and the other to choose a political party or an electoral organization that was running a list of candidates (party-list voting). Seats awarded according to the party-list portion of the ballot went only to those parties that received at least 5 percent of the vote.

In the SMD elections, a district ballot often contained the names of several candidates. If those candidates received a relatively equal share of the votes, a person could win a seat in the Duma with less than half of the votes from the district. The winning candidate was simply the one who received the most votes. Candidates were not required to have a party designation in the SMD elections. Candidates and parties obtained access to the ballot either by satisfying a signature requirement or by paying a financial deposit. (For detailed information about how a party got on the PR ballot and how candidates got onto the district ballot, see Clark [2002].[4]) Candidates nominated by political parties or independent candidates could contest these plurality races. In addition, each ballot offered the option of voting "Against all."

In the 1995 Duma elections, the PR part of the ballot listed 43 electoral associations and blocs—generally referred to as political parties. With so many parties listed on the ballot, almost half of the nationwide vote went to parties that failed to clear the 5 percent threshold, effectively doubling the number of seats awarded to those parties that did receive at least 5 percent of the votes. With fewer parties on the ballot in the 1999 and 2003 elections as compared with the 1995 election, this **disproportionality** declined. In the 1999 elections, 26 political parties ran lists of candidates on the nationwide ballot and 6 parties passed the 5 percent threshold. Between them, the parties received about 81 percent of the nationwide PR vote. They divided the 225 PR seats among themselves according to the proportion of the vote each received. In 2003, the PR ballot listed 23 parties and electoral blocs and 4 parties garnered enough votes to pass the 5 percent threshold for PR seat allocation in the State Duma (see Table 7.7). Together, the parties that did pass the threshold received 71 percent of the nation's votes and divided the PR seats among themselves.

The 1999 election came closest to achieving true proportional representation. The list of the Communist Party received 24.3 percent of the nationwide vote. The communists received 67, or 30 percent, of the 225 PR seats in the 1999 State Duma. In 1995, in contrast, communists received a smaller percentage of the PR vote (22.7 percent) but obtained more of the PR seats (42 percent). The Unity movement came in second in 1999 with 23.3 percent of the votes and received 28 percent of the PR seats.

For those seats in the Duma won by candidates competing in SMDs, the role of political parties is less important to the electoral results. In the 1999 elections, 2,318 candidates participated across 225 single-member districts (Clark 2002, 102). This means that the ballots, on average, listed ten candidates per district. With so many candidates the average winner in 1999 received only 34.3 percent of the votes cast in his or her respective district (Clark 2002, 105). (Golosov reports that 2,227 candidates competed in the 1999 SMD races [2002, 26].)

The most successful candidates in the SDM races were the people who already held positions of authority in regional administrations or governments. Indeed, holding a position within the state power apparatus was more important as a determinant of a successful, winning campaign than was identification with a political party in the 1999 SMD races (Golosov 2002, 29, 32). Also, according to Clark, independent candidates did better overall than party candidates in the races: "party candidates performed quite poorly in the district contests" (2002, 105).

More than half (1,147) of the SMD candidates in 1999 ran as independents without an official political party nomination. With the seating of the 1999 Duma, most of the newly elected independent deputies formed or joined parliamentary factions. Three independent-based Duma factions emerged—the People's Deputy Group, which aligned itself with the Unity bloc; the Agro-Industrialists, which was close to and controlled by the Communist Party; and the Russian Regions.

In the 2003 elections, United Russia performed the best in the SMD races. This electoral bloc, composed of Unity and Fatherland–All Russia, won nearly half of the 225 district races. The next largest group of winning candidates in the 2003 SMD races was the independents. The Communist Party did significantly worse than it had in the past. In 1995, the CPRF won 54 single-member

TABLE 7.7   Results of the December 7, 2003, Elections to the State Duma of the Russian Federation

Parties	Percentage of Votes Cast for Each Federal List of Candidates	Number of PR Seats Awarded	Number of SMD Seats	Total Number of Seats
United Russia (also called Unified Russia)—Bloc of Unity (Medved) and Fatherland-All Russia (OVR)	37.6	120	102	222
Communist Party of the Russian Federation (CPRF)	12.6	40	12	52
Liberal Democratic Party of Russia (LDPR)	11.5	36		36
Motherland National-Patriotic Union (Rodina)	9.0	29	8	37
Yabloko	4.3		4	4
Union of Right Forces (SPS)	4.0		3	3
Agrarian Party of Russia	3.6		2	2
Russian Party of Pensioners and Party of Social Justice	3.0			
People's Party of the Russian Federation (NPRF)[a]	1.2		17	17
Other parties[b]	8.6		6	6
Independents			68	68
Against all	4.7			
Total seats	100 (225)		222[c]	447

Turnout: 55.75 percent of registered voters cast ballots.

Source: Results are from the Central Election Commission of the Russian Federation at http://gd2003.cikrf.ru/way/1402493.

[a]The People's Party was created for the 2003 election. The top three names on its list of candidates were party leader Gennadii Raikov; Colonel General Gennadii Troshev, a former commander of Russian forces in Chechnya; and Nikolai Derzhavin, an aide to Moscow Patriarch Aleksii II. Raikov described the party as "a socially oriented party, located close to the center-left." People's Party delegates joined the United Russia parliamentary faction with the sitting of the new Duma in December 2003.

[b]The Central Election Commission used a lottery to determine the order in which the 23 other parties participating in parliamentary elections would be listed on the federal ballot.

[c]The elections were not valid in three districts.

district elections, and in 1999, it won 47 of these elections. In 2003, the CPRF won only 12 SMD elections.

The December 7, 2003, elections to the State Duma represented the first national election to take place under the presidency of Vladimir Putin. During the period just prior to these elections, public opinion polls showed that many Russian citizens believed that voting would make no difference in their lives. Indeed, voter participation decreased significantly from a 62 percent turnout in December 1999 to a 56 percent turnout in December 2003.

Numerous accusations were made that the 2003 Duma election was not conducted in a fully democratic manner. The day after the election, the International Election Observation Mission (IEOM), which had 500 international observers from 42 countries monitoring the voting, published the following statement in reaction to the elections: "The Central Election Commission deserves credit for its professional organization of these elections. However, the pre-election process was characterized by extensive use of the state apparatus and media favoritism to benefit the largest pro-presidential party."[5]

According to the official results of the 2003 parliamentary elections, the four parties that passed the 5 percent threshold needed to win seats through the PR portion of the ballot were United Russia, the Communist Party, the Liberal Democratic Party of Russia (LDPR), and Motherland National-Patriotic Union (Rodina). United Russia, created by a merger* of Unity and Fatherland–All Russia, was openly supported by President Putin. The common theme of United Russia's campaign commercials was "Together with the President." Advertisements lacked specific policy proposals,[6] but the federal list of United Russia candidates contained some of Russia's most powerful politicians, including the mayor of Moscow, Yuri Luzhkov.

The electoral results showed that United Russia won nearly 38 percent of the party-list vote in a field of 23 parties/blocs. United Russia received 120 of the 225 Duma seats allocated by the PR system, as shown in Table 7.7. The victory of United Russia in the nationwide party-list voting was supplemented by a triumph in the single-member district races as well. The success of United Russia candidates in the SMD races can be attributed to regional governors who supported these Kremlin-backed candidates with their substantial local resources:

> To assure that United Russia candidates won as many seats as possible in the country's 225 single-member districts, the party formed a close alliance with Russia's most powerful governors. . . . In fact, in almost all regions, the governors were the dominant players, using their resources to make sure that the voters approved their choice to represent them in the State Duma.[7]

In 2003, the CPRF polled only 12.6 percent of the party-list vote, down from 24.3 percent in 1999. After 2003, the Communist Party had to accept a much

---

*For more on this merger, see Chapter 8.

weaker position in serving as the "opposition" to President Putin. According to public opinion polls, support for the Communist Party had held steady at its traditional levels through to the summer of 2003. An August 2003 poll conducted by VCIOM reported that 28 percent of respondents would support the Communist Party, while 23 percent said that they would back United Russia.[8]

Why then did the Communist Party win just under 13 percent of the vote in December 2003? One explanation is Putin's personal popularity and the people's desire to vote for parties associated with the president. Another explanation is the control exercised by the Kremlin over the messages emanating from the state-controlled media. Most of the messages were singularly critical of the Communist Party and overwhelmingly supportive of United Russia. In addition, a new electoral bloc—the Motherland National-Patriotic Union (Rodina)—competed successfully during the 2003 election, pulling votes away from the Communist Party.

When registered in September 2003, Rodina was made up of leftist and nationalist organizations and leaders.* Anatolii Chubais, one of the leaders of the Union of Rightist Forces (SPS), charged that the Kremlin created the Motherland organization to siphon votes from the communists.[9] In contrast to the limited and negative media coverage given to the Communist Party, Rodina benefited from significant positive coverage on state-controlled national television during the weeks prior to the election. The Agrarian Party, likewise, helped to split leftist support in 2003 by appealing to rural voters. That party secured almost 4 percent of the vote, taking votes away from Communist Party candidates; however, it did not win enough (less than the 5 percent threshold) votes to receive seats from the PR section of the ballot.

In the 2003 election, Yabloko and SPS also failed to secure 5 percent of the party-list vote required to receive a share of the 225 Duma seats allocated through the PR system. Yabloko-sponsored candidates won four SMD contests and the SPS won three. The 2003 election was the first time that Yabloko had been shut out of PR representation in the Duma. SPS coleaders Boris Nemtsov, Irina Khakamada, and Anatolii Chubais all tendered their resignations on December 7, 2003, in the wake of the party's poor showing.[10]

As mentioned previously, independents often join parliamentary factions in the aftermath of elections to gain office facilities and committee assignments. Some party-affiliated members elected from districts may change affiliations if their parties do not win enough party-list votes to form a parliamentary faction. Other deputies switch for more opportunistic reasons, such as to join the group that they see as having the greatest access to political resources. As Table 7.8

---

*Party leaders also competed in SMD races: Motherland National-Patriotic Union (Rodina) coleader and State Duma Foreign Affairs Committee chair Dmitri Rogozin polled 79 percent of the vote in his Voronezh Oblast district, while People's Party head Raikov won his district in Tyumen Oblast with almost 48 percent of the vote. Motherland coleader and former Communist Party deputy Sergei Glazyev won an SMD mandate in the Moscow Oblast.

TABLE 7.8 State Duma Party Alignment, as of December 29, 2003

Factions	Number of Seats
United Russia (led by Boris Gryzlov)	300
Communist Party of the Russian Federation (led by Gennadii Zyuganov)	52
Liberal Democratic Party of Russia (led by Igor Lebedev)	36
Motherland National-Patriotic Union (Rodina) (led by Sergei Glazyev)	36
Independents	23
Total seats	447

Source: From "Parties in Play," December 2003, at http://www.russiavotes.org/.

shows, the size of United Russia's faction within parliament grew to 300 by the December 29 opening of the 2003 Duma.

The 2003 results revealed a significant change in Russia's electoral alignments. For the first time since independence in 1991, pro-Kremlin political parties controlled a full majority of the seats in Russia's lower house. The Communist Party was severely weakened and the liberal democratic force of Yabloko was left without an influential voice in parliament. The results represented a successful drive by President Putin to consolidate his power. With control of the Duma in 2003, Putin won a mandate for pushing his vision of Russia's future. That Duma, though filled with a large number of Kremlin "yes men," was not fully compliant. Although Putin's government dominated policymaking, Duma deputies from both the Communist Party and Rodina forced a discussion of some more controversial issues (for example, the privatization process and pension benefit reform).

Proportional representation systems aim to increase accurate *representation*, while majority/plurality systems aim to increase *effectiveness* and clarity of responsibility (Powell 1989). The goal of Russia's 1993–2003 electoral system, employing both a PR ballot and an SMD ballot, was to achieve a balance between the two objectives of representation and responsibility. Given the results of the 1999 and 2003 elections, and the work that was accomplished in the following legislative sessions, one could argue that Russia's electoral system was beginning to render those potential benefits. The work of electoral reform in Russia continues, however.

In 2002, the Duma introduced new laws for electing the members and the president. Putin ultimately signed the laws in December 2002 and January 2003, respectively.[11] The main change was the increased role assigned to political parties in the electoral process. Starting in July 2003, only national political parties could nominate candidates in federal and regional elections. The law allowed for the formation of electoral blocs, but these blocs could have no more than three members and at least one member had to be a political party.

Individual citizens could nominate themselves for office, but groups of voters no longer had this right. Nonpolitical organizations could still nominate candidates in local elections.

Starting after the 2003 Duma elections, parties receive financing from the state budget proportional to the number of votes they receive. Additionally, the candidates nominated by these parties do not have to gather signatures or provide a deposit to join the ballot. This process of electoral change culminated in May 2005 with President Putin's signature on a new law for elections to the State Duma that established a pure proportional representation system, banned electoral blocs, and established the threshold for party-list representation at 7 percent of the vote.

ELECTIONS TO RUSSIA'S NATIONAL PRESIDENCY

Elections for Russia's president are regularly held in the year following parliamentary elections. The Russian Constitution requires the holding of presidential elections every four years and the constitution limits presidents to two terms in office. Because Boris Yeltsin won the elections for Russia's presidency in 1991 and 1996, the constitution prohibited him from seeking reelection in 2000. When Yeltsin resigned early on December 31, 1999, Prime Minister Vladimir Putin became acting president pending a new presidential election. The constitution mandated that elections be held within three months of Yeltsin's resignation; thus, elections scheduled for June 2000 were held three months early, in March 2000.

Also on December 31, 1999, Yeltsin signed a "Federal Law on the Election of the President of the Russian Federation." Under this law, the presidential election campaign officially started on January 6, 2000, and candidates had to submit their registration documents by February 13. The law also required that each candidate collect 500,000 signatures. All candidates were obligated to declare the size and the source of all their income. Eleven candidates met all the requirements to be listed on the ballot; three of them—Zyuganov, Yavlinsky, and Zhirinovsky—had participated in the 1996 presidential election.* To win in the first round of voting, a candidate was required to receive 50 percent of the votes cast with at least 50 percent of eligible voters participating. If no candidate received enough votes, an April 16, 2000, runoff was to be held between the two top vote-getters from the first round. For the runoff, the winner would be the candidate who received a simple majority.

As acting president, Vladimir Putin won the 2000 presidential election in the first round of voting with 52.94 percent of the vote. He had successfully appealed to a prevailing desire among the people of Russia for a strong leader.

*Yevgenii Primakov (OVR leader and former prime minister) pulled out of the presidential race in early February 2000.

The Russian populace's orientation is amply demonstrated by public opinion poll answers—respondents were asked to agree or disagree—to the following statement: "Right now, Russia needs strong leadership more than it needs democracy." As shown in Figure 7.5, 54 percent of the adults in the Russian Federation fully agreed with this statement and another 31 percent partially agreed. Those who voted for Putin perceived him as a strong leader because of his conduct of the war in Chechnya, because of his experience in the KGB and as prime minister, and because of his athletic achievements. In addition, Putin was able to enlist the backing of powerful regional leaders (governors) and influential oligarchs, who saw Putin's leadership as being much less threatening to their interests than a regime led by the Communist Party candidate would be.

The Central Election Committee provided funds for the campaign activities of all duly registered candidates; however, candidates failing to win at least 3 percent of the vote were required to repay the money to the Central Election Committee. A January 2003 presidential electoral law provided additional free airtime and newspaper space to parties and blocs that nominated presidential candidates beyond the free time and space given to all candidates. Under these rules, incumbent President Vladimir Putin won reelection in the March 2004 presidential elections with more than 70 percent of the vote (see Table 6.3 in Chapter 6).

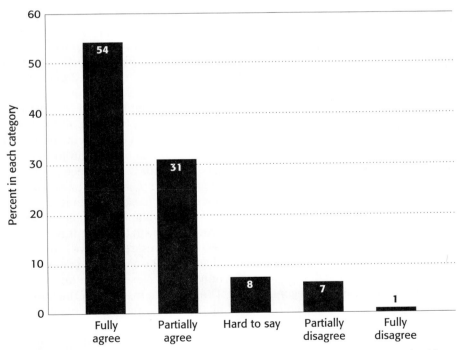

FIGURE 7.5 Public Opinion with Regard to Whether Russia Needs Strong Leadership More Now Than It Needs Democracy

REGIONAL ELECTIONS

The Russian Federation consists of eighty-nine regions (primarily oblasts or provinces and republics), and each has its own chief executive and elected legislative assembly. According to a May 2002 law, elections to regional legislatures were required to follow the State Duma election procedures, which mandated that half of the deputies be elected from party lists. Most regions had not previously used party-list voting to select members of their legislatures. The election of regional executives followed a system similar to one used to elect the Russian president. If a candidate for a region's governorship received more than 50 percent of the vote in the first round of voting, he or she was the winner. If no candidate won 50 percent of the vote, a second-round, runoff election was held.

The Kremlin kept a very close eye on regional elections. In eleven of fifteen regional races for the chief executive held in 2002, the Kremlin succeeded in placing its favored candidate for governor into office.[12] The conduct of these elections was controversial and often marked by demonstrably unequal access to the media and last-minute disqualification of unwanted contenders. In December 2003, the incumbent mayor of Moscow, Yuri Luzhkov, won a third term with 75 percent of the vote. Three other incumbent governors won with more than 75 percent of the vote: Moscow Oblast Governor Boris Gromov, Yaroslav Oblast Governor Anatolii Lisitsyn, and Tambov Oblast Governor Oleg Betin. Nonetheless, in some regions, elections for the executive post involved significant competition. The incumbent president of Bashkortostan, Mutaza Rakhimov, had to compete in a second-round runoff race in 2003 because he won only 46 percent of the vote in the republic during the first round.

In July 2002, the Constitutional Court upheld amendments to the law for organizing legislative and executive branches in the regions that allowed governors to seek third terms. This was widely interpreted as a concession to powerful regional elites from the administration of Vladimir Putin in the run-up period to the 2003–2004 electoral cycle.[13] Elections held in December 2004 and January 2005 resulted primarily in victories by incumbents or candidates supported by Putin's government, but once again these outcomes were not under the complete control of the Kremlin. One popular incumbent, Governor Viktor Ishaev of Khabarovsk Krai, won a third term with 85 percent of the vote even though he had come into conflict with the president's envoy to the Far East Federal District. In another region, Ulyanovsk, the candidate supported by Unified Russia emerged victorious, but only after a close competitor was disqualified just before the second round. The negative reaction of the voters to this disqualification was demonstrated by the "Against all" percentage, which was unusually high at 25 percent.[14] After January 2005, elections for the executive of Russia's main regions (governors and presidents) ended altogether.

Beginning in 2005, the president of the RF nominates regional executive-branch heads and regional legislatures approve the nominations. This means that direct elections of regional executive-branch heads have been replaced with a system under which regional legislatures confirm candidates nominated by the president. Incumbent republic presidents and oblast governors must request reconfirmation by Russia's national president. In September 2004, Putin announced the change by arguing that the war on terrorism necessitated "securing the unity of state power and the logical development of federalism."[15]

Those regional executives with close relationships with the president applauded the new system. In September 2004, St. Petersburg Governor Valentina Matvienko said that under direct elections "a random person can come to power and there is no mechanism to recall him," adding that voters are easily swayed by populist rhetoric. Yaroslav Governor Anatolii Lisitsyn said that direct elections mean that governors can be "pushed around" by voters.[16]

During the period between January and May 2005, twenty regions were up for reconsideration and Putin reappointed seventeen incumbents. One could argue that he was supporting the choices made in earlier elections by the voters, and that Putin only denied nomination to those incumbents who were exercising dictatorial rule within their regions. On the other side of the debate are those who say that the democratic process at the local level has stalled. The system effectively abolishes term limits. In the Republic of Tatarstan, President Mintimer Shaimiev was given a fourth term in March 2005. One critic of the system, Nikolai Petrov, alleged that governors pay for Putin's endorsement, either with cash or by placing Kremlin-selected officials in key positions within their regions.[17] Independent State Duma Deputy Vladimir Ryzhkov argued that governors would be weaker with the loss of their popular mandates.[18]

CONCLUSION

The 2003 parliamentary elections, the 2004 presidential election, and regional elections and appointments represent movement through a series of epic challenges associated with the process of state-building in the world's territorially largest country. An important question is whether the outcomes of these elections and appointments served to improve the effectiveness and performance of Russia's political institutions. As scholars and students, we might feel uneasy given the considerable criticism of the procedural fairness of Russia's elections, the allegations of fraud, and the biased coverage of the campaigns in state and private media. United Russia, for example, received a disproportionate share of news coverage across all the major Russian TV channels during the period leading up to the 2003 parliamentary election. This raises concerns about the ability of the public to access uncontrolled and unmanipulated information. When incumbent authorities restrict media access of opposition organizations and politicians, democratic free choice is constrained.

One also might be concerned about the relationships between regional governors and federal elected officials. The lack of a clearly articulated political platform by the 2003 election winner—United Russia—is disconcerting as well. The refusal of United Russia to participate in any televised preelection debates also limited serious discussion about policy across the political parties. Each of the preceding raises questions about citizen representation and the accountability of government.

Citizen participation serves other purposes, in addition to those of ensuring representation and holding a government accountable, however. Conventional–legal participation legitimizes the polity and provides structure to a national political community. One can reasonably argue that the stronger and the more stable the Putin regime remains, the better the prospects are for institutional development in the Russian setting.

Key Terms

Alienation
Conventional–legal participation
Disproportionality
Electoral system
Ideology
Majority system
Mixed electoral system
Party-list electoral system
Plurality system
Political efficacy

Political opposition
Political participation
Proportional representation (PR) electoral system
Single-member district (SMD) electoral system
Threshold
Violent participation
Voting

Critical Thinking Questions

1. Why is voting important? What functions does it serve in a democracy?

2. Which sociodemographic characteristics do those more likely to vote in the Russian Federation share? How is this similar or dissimilar to what we know from studies of voting participation in other countries?

3. What characteristics and policy positions do those most likely to support a candidate nominated by the Communist Party share?

4. What other forms of political participation are available to citizens, other than voting? How does participation in nonvoting activities in the Russian Federation compare to the United States and other Western democracies?

5. What are the four categories of electoral systems? Provide examples of each. What are the advantages and disadvantages of each?

6. How are deputies elected to Russia's State Duma?

7. How democratic are the Russian elections: How do the concepts "free" and "fair" apply to the 2003 parliamentary elections?

Suggested Reading

Brader, Ted, and Joshua A. Tucker. "The Emergence of Mass Partisanship in Russia, 1993-1996." *American Journal of Political Science*, 45 (1) (2001): 69–83.

Gibson, James L. "Social Networks, Civil Society, and the Prospects for Consolidating Russia's Democratic Transition." *American Journal of Political Science*, 45 (1) (2001): 52–68.

White, Stephen, Richard Rose, and Ian McAllister. *How Russia Votes*. Chatham, N.J.: Chatham House Publishers, 1997.

Whitefield, Stephen, and Geoffrey Evans. "Support for Democracy and Political Opposition in Russia, 1993-1995." *Post-Soviet Affairs*, 12 (1996): 18–42.

Websites of Interest

Inter-Parliamentary Union homepage—a good resource for parliamentary data from around the world (links to Parline Database):
http://www.ipu.org

Website contains information on elections around the world, as well as links to other useful sites:
http://www.electionworld.org

A site containing links to political parties, organizations, governments, and media around the world:
http://www.politicalresources.net

CHAPTER 8

Political Parties in Russia from a Comparative Perspective

P OLITICAL PARTIES IN RUSSIA are quite different from political parties in established European democracies. In part, this is a result of the histori-cal role of the Communist Party in Soviet society, the correspondingly recent establishment of competing parties, and the institutional disincentives of the Russian political system. This chapter examines political parties in the context of Russia's historical evolution, as well as through the use of a compar-ative framework. To get a broader perspective for the study of Russia's political parties, the major types of party systems in the world and the functions gener-ally served by political parties, are reviewed.

A *political party* is defined as an organized group of people with particular views and goals concerning government policies who attempt to win and keep control of government. Well-functioning political parties provide the electorate with systematic choices among packages of policy programs and groups of can-didates. Parties also may help to integrate citizens into the political community by mobilizing them for political participation. Parties may help aggregate demands and organize the lawmaking process in a legislature (King 1974, 303).

In many countries, however, television now plays a more significant role in political socialization and community integration than do political parties. Sometimes, parties appear to be incapable of mobilizing the population, as indi-cated by declining levels of voting in elections. Political parties are often highly dependent on state financial assistance or operate as appendages of the state.

THE SOVIET UNION AS A ONE-PARTY SYSTEM

The history of Russian society provides yet another portrayal of the role of political parties. To understand the Soviet period, when only one political party—the Communist Party—was allowed to function, we turn briefly to the end of the nineteenth century when a number of political parties opposed to Tsarism emerged and were harshly repressed. For example, the founding meeting of the Russian Social Democratic Labor Party was dispersed by police in 1898. The party held its Second Congress outside the country, splitting into two factions—the Bolsheviks and the Mensheviks. Other political parties operating in Russia at the time included the Socialist Revolutionary Party (SR), formed in 1900–1902. The SRs supported socialist ideas but rejected Marx's teachings on agriculture and the peasants. The Liberals, in contrast to the Social Revolutionaries and the Social Democrats, wanted a constitution and a parliamentary regime similar to those found in the West. Two of the other parties, formed in 1905, were the Constitutional Democrats (Kadets) and the Octobrists, with the latter being more inclined toward compromise with the tsar.

When elections were held for the First Duma in 1906, the contesting political parties were the Mensheviks, the SRs, the Kadets, and the Octobrists. The Bolsheviks boycotted the first Duma election and the Kadets emerged as the prevailing force. After this Duma was dissolved by the tsar and elections were scheduled for a Second Duma, the Bolsheviks decided to compete. As a result, the Second Duma was dominated by Social Democrats (twelve of them Bolsheviks). The Second Duma was dissolved in 1907 in response to the urging of the tsar's prime minister, Peter Stolypin. After the SRs organized the assassinations of a number of government officials, and the Bolsheviks undertook a series of robberies, Stolypin's government cracked down and most socialist party leaders were arrested or sent into exile.

The electoral rules were changed prior to the voting for the Third Duma, and this time the Octobrists emerged as the largest party, followed by the Kadets and the Progressists—a new party with a strong industrial component (Treadgold and Ellison 2000, 78–79). Within the Third Duma, the Octobrists formed an alliance with a new Nationalist Party and were able to legislate some reforms. When elections were held to the Fourth Duma in the fall of 1912, the Octobrists again emerged as the strongest party but with a smaller majority than in the Third Duma.

When Tsar Nicholas II abdicated, a provisional government was formed by representatives of the major parties in the Fourth Duma. Prime Minister Georgii Lvov and Foreign Minister Paul Miliukov were Kadets. The leader of the Octobrists became the minister of war. The minister of trade and industry was a Progressist. Alexander Kerensky, who became minister of justice, was an SR.

As described in Chapter 3, the Provisional Government was overthrown in late 1917 by the Bolsheviks, who violently repressed all other political parties and any organized opposition to their rule. By the early 1920s, the Bolsheviks, who had renamed themselves the Communist Party, were the only legal political party in the Soviet Union.* Thus, even though Russia had a multiparty system between 1905 and 1917, during the seventy-four-year Soviet era (1917–1991), people experienced only a one-party system based on the dominant and dominating role of the Communist Party.

The Communist Party of the Soviet Union (CPSU) was organized hierarchically like a pyramid (see Figure 8.1). At the apex of the pyramid was the leader of the Secretariat, the Communist Party's general secretary. The **Secretariat of the Communist Party** carried on the day-to-day administrative work of the party and was very large, employing more than 100,000 individuals by the 1980s. The **General Secretary of the Communist Party** was responsible for the execution of overall party policy, while other secretaries were in charge of administering departments such as agriculture, defense, science, and education.

The **Politburo** was the primary policymaking body within the CPSU. The size of the Politburo varied over time, but consisted of approximately twenty candidate (nonvoting) and full members. The general secretary presided over meetings of the Politburo. Khrushchev and Brezhnev both reported that Politburo decisions were made by consensus after discussion. When leaders did disagree on policy directions, the conflict and negotiation between opposing views tended to occur informally outside of actual Politburo meetings.

Decisions made by the Politburo were sent to the **Central Committee** for formal adoption and then were made public. Central Committee meetings were held about once every six months and were frequently timed to correspond to meetings of the Supreme Soviet—the parliament of the Soviet era. The most powerful officials in the country were members of the Central Committee, including the heads of departments within the Secretariat, republic and regional party leaders, government administrators, military leaders, scientists, and leading intellectuals. Important speeches were given at Central Committee meetings and binding decrees were issued in its name; sometimes decrees were issued jointly with the Council of Ministers—the Cabinet of the Soviet government.

Formally, the **All-Union Party Congress** was the supreme organ of the CPSU. As many as 5,000 delegates attended Party Congress meetings, which were held once every five years; however, no congresses took place between 1939 and 1952. When they were held, congresses performed the function of mobilizing party members to support major aspects of Soviet policy. New state policy visions or directions were announced at congresses, frequently coinciding with the introduction of a new five-year plan. At the Twentieth Party Congress in 1956, for example, Khrushchev introduced his "de-Stalinization" program.

---

*In 1918, the original name of the party, the Russian Social Democratic Workers Party (Bolsheviks), was changed to the Russian Communist Party. In 1924, the word *Russian* was changed to All-Union. In 1952, the name was changed again, to the Communist Party of the Soviet Union.

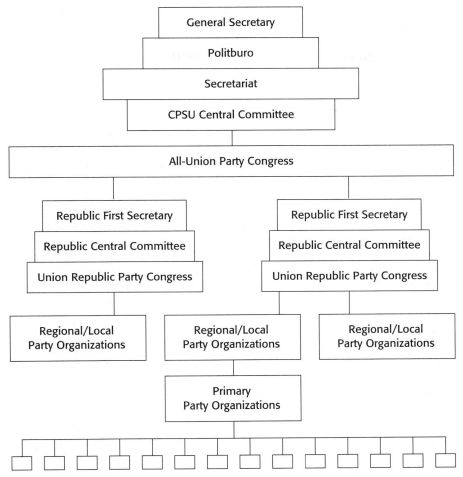

FIGURE 8.1 The Organizational Structure of the Communist Party of the Soviet Union (CPSU)

The foundation of the CPSU was the **primary party organization** (PPO). These organizations were located throughout the country at places of work (factories, universities, and collective farms) and in residential areas (large housing complexes). More than 400,000 primary organizations were functioning in the Soviet Union during the 1980s. The largest of the PPOs had more than 1,000 members and the smallest ones were composed of just three party members. It was at this level that an individual joined the party, and this is where many of the basic functions, such as political education (agitation), mobilization, organization, and oversight, were carried out. The CPSU had nearly 19 million members during the mid-1980s.

Above the PPOs were the local (district or city), regional (oblast, krai) and republic-level organizations. The party organizations of the union republics, such as those of Ukraine, Lithuania, and so forth, were major decision-making bodies and frequently had a fair degree of autonomous authority. It was the delegates from these organizations, and from lower-level organizations, that would gather in Moscow to attend meetings of the All-Union Party Congress.

The responsibilities of Communist Party members were considerable. They were expected to uphold the leadership role of the party in Soviet society and to identify and rectify any ideological or political shortcomings among fellow workers, classmates, and neighbors. Party members were expected to be alert to any problems in enterprises within their jurisdiction and to report to higher authorities about the fulfillment of state plans. The principle of **democratic centralism** required members of lower-level party organizations to accept the decisions of higher-level organizations as binding, and party members were to ensure the implementation of these directives.

One of the mechanisms by which the party exercised its control throughout society was called **nomenklatura**. This term refers to a list of the most important positions in the government, the economy, the military, the media, and the sciences, all of which required party approval whenever a personnel change was made. Thus, appointments to all key positions were controlled by the Communist Party.

The party was able to prevent the emergence of any competing political organizations that could challenge its monopoly control over the direction of state policy. This power monopoly held sway until a February 1990 Central Committee plenum endorsed a proposal to remove Article 6 from the Soviet Constitution. Article 6 explicitly identified the Communist Party as the "leading and guiding force of Soviet society and the nucleus of its political system," guaranteeing the party sole control over domestic and foreign policy. The removal of this article from the constitution meant that other parties were allowed to compete for and to seek political power. Thus, 1990 marked the beginning of the transition from a one-party to a multiparty political system in Russia.

A COMPARATIVE PERSPECTIVE OF PARTY SYSTEMS

Party systems can be classified into three categories: single-party, two-party, and multiparty. The Communist Party of the Soviet Union before the Gorbachev era is a perfect example of the **single-party system**. Leaders in single-party systems maintain political power by building a powerful party organization that controls both the legislative and executive branches of government. The reach of the party extends to the general public through propaganda and repression. Propaganda involves spreading (disseminating) information that advocates support for party doctrine through discussion or through the media. Repression is achieved through the work of security organizations that spy on and monitor the citizens of the country. Maurice Duverger (1963), who provided the first thorough assessment and categorization of political parties, labels such systems "dictatorship(s) based on a party" (255). Governments use a single-party system to "inculcate common attitudes of national unity, support for the government, and ideological agreement" (Almond, Powell, and Mundt 1996, 47).

The second type is the **two-party system.** Although more than two political parties can exist in countries having this party system, usually only two of them take dominant roles in the government. An example is the United States, which has a two-party system dominated by the Republican Party and the Democratic Party; however, smaller parties, such as the Socialist Party and the Reform Party, do exist.

Two-party systems are generally found in electoral systems based on **single-member districts** (SMD). The plurality type of electoral system hinders the development of a multiparty system because a third party needs either an extremely powerful national organization or an extremely secure regional base of support to break into the traditional support base of the two major parties. It is the voters' belief that votes for the third party would essentially be wasted that keeps a third party from ever gaining the support necessary to become another dominant party.

The **multiparty system** encompasses all countries in which at least three different parties have recently won control of the government—rotating control of government from one election to the next—or have shared control of a government through a coalition. Because several parties with a significant degree of support among the population contest national elections (therefore dividing the total vote among several parties), a single party is rarely able to win a majority of seats in a parliament. In such situations, effective government depends on forming stable coalitions among the parties that do receive significant portions of the vote.

Although electoral systems based on proportional representation (PR) contribute to the maintenance of multiparty systems, another influential factor is the division of opinion within an established party, which can cause a split among the party's membership and the creation of two new parties. If factions within a political party become aggravated and members can no longer find common ground, the tendency is for the party to split, giving way to the emergence of new parties. This is exactly what occurred when the Russian Social Democratic Labor Party split into the Bolsheviks and the Mensheviks at the beginning of the twentieth century.

Major Goals of Political Parties

Regardless of the type of party system, most political parties have the same goal—to control the political decisions and the public policies of the country within which they operate. Such control can be exercised either directly or indirectly (Duverger 1963, 354–94). A political party has *direct* power when either the constitution or the laws governing elections specifically mandate certain rights, such as control over the nomination of candidates for political office, to political parties. The nomination process consists of a party appointing the candidates who will represent it in the election. Simply associating a candidate's name with a party will get the votes of both those knowing nothing about the candidate and those who consistently vote along party lines. In Russia, the PR party-list ballot for the State Duma requires that all candidates be affiliated with a party because the actual vote is for each party's list of candidates rather than for any individual.

In addition to their role in the nomination process, another way in which political parties exercise direct power is through financial support. Electoral campaigns, especially those run in populated regions, are very expensive. For this reason, candidates often seek political party affiliation in order to receive extra financial backing.

After members of a party are elected and take control of the executive or legislative branches of government, party officials can have a direct impact on the formulation of policy. If the party that holds a majority of the seats in the legislature is also the party of the executive, then it has primary control over policy. This situation characterized Russia after the 2003 election: The pro-presidential party, United Russia, controlled the majority of the seats in the State Duma and served as a dependable ally to President Vladimir Putin, voting in support of his legislative initiatives in the Duma.

Divided government, in contrast, occurs when the president and the majority in the legislature (parliament) are not affiliated with the same political party. This was the situation faced by Russia's first president, Boris Yeltsin, throughout the 1990s. The Communist Party had enough votes to block Yeltsin's legislative agenda.

Parties can also wield *indirect* clout in a political system through their ability to influence people's attitudes and preferences. Parties use propaganda to promote not only their candidates but also their political agendas and philosophies. For political parties to influence public opinion, they must be well organized and well administered. Well-functioning parties present citizens with principled choices on important issues and provide continuity and structure to the political landscape. For a political party to contribute to government's effectiveness, it must itself be well organized and clearly articulate programs and goals. To foster government accountability, the party must be able to hold its members accountable; that is, government leaders who have been elected with the backing of a political party must vote in accordance with the stated program of that party. If, on the contrary, political parties are beset by internal fragmentation and are poorly organized, this can lead to unstable regimes.

Party Ideologies in Europe

Political parties promote platforms and policy priorities that reflect their basic differences in ideological orientation. In Western European countries, the differences among political parties are frequently represented graphically by placement on a **left–right ideological continuum**. Those parties near the left end of the continuum tend to show greater support for state welfare programs; their party platforms usually call for reducing unemployment and eliminating poverty. Parties on the right of the continuum are considered to be "conservative" in the sense that retaining the status quo is more important than undertaking any radical redistribution programs. For example, when communist parties exist in European multiparty systems, they are located on the left of the ideological spectrum. Social Democratic parties are also located on the left, but they are not as far left on the spectrum as communist parties. European liberal parties, which are more toward the center of a left–right continuum, support limited government and free markets and oppose church influences in politics and education (Curtis 1997, 17). Right-of-center are Christian Democratic parties. Further to the right are conservative parties, which often emphasize patriotism and seek to uphold religious beliefs. By placing limits on government spending, conservative parties reject the funding of any radical changes in the domestic structure.

THE EMERGENCE OF POLITICAL PARTIES IN RUSSIA

Western European political parties, which fit rather neatly into the left–right continuum, formed more than a century ago around cleavages between worker and employer interests and cleavages between rural and urban dwellers (Lipset and Rokkan 1967). In contrast, Russia's political parties emerged in a much later era. The range of socioeconomic interests was very different at the end of the twentieth century than it was during the late nineteenth century, when many European parties were in their formative stages. In addition, the role of political parties was changing in Europe at the same time that new parties were emerging in the geographical space of the former Soviet Union. Traditional political party alignments were less clear and unstable.

Because political parties in Russia developed in a different time and place than did Western European parties, they have quite a different character. Popular front organizations, rather than political parties, were the most common form of political associational activity in Russia during the late 1980s and very early 1990s. Popular front organizations were encouraged by Gorbachev because they were originally formed as movements in support of perestroika. Overtly political oppositional organizations were banned until the Soviet Constitution was amended in 1990. Thus, popular front movements played a critical role in keeping pressure on the regime to continue its democratizing reforms, but political parties did not operate as major agents of change during the transition process (Lewis 2000, 20).

In addition, the relative absence of a civil society in the Soviet Union and in early post-Soviet Russia provided only a weak base for institutional development and the establishment of effective political organizations. Related to this is the legacy of the Soviet Union's totalitarian state structures, which provided only limited experience with the concepts of political compromise and competition. This legacy holds back the process of political party development (Lewis 2000, 22–23). Russian political parties have much weaker links with well-defined social groups and tend to be highly media- and candidate-focused. With the exception of the Communist Party of the Russian Federation (CPRF), political parties in Russia tend to be centered on a few well-known politicians; and competition among the parties reflects competition among political rivals rather than among clearly articulated packages of policy goals.

RUSSIA'S MAJOR PARTIES

Although Russia has scores of political parties, only a minority of all the registered parties have stayed in existence long enough to compete in every election since 1993. An even smaller set of parties has won seats in Duma elections. Russia has an inordinate number of parties; new parties tend to appear shortly before an election and then fade away after electoral defeat. Those parties that did win seats in the 1999 and 2003 parliamentary elections can be classified according to two criteria. The first is longevity—whether the party had competed in the 1993 and 1995 Duma elections. The second criterion divides parties between "insiders" and "outsiders." Using these two criteria, Russia's main parties are categorized in Table 8.1.

Insider parties are those formed by former members of Yeltsin's or Putin's government. **Insider parties** emerged not so much from ideological or programmatic differences with the incumbent government, but rather were created by political elites to compete for public support. Two of the insider parties—Fatherland–All Russia (OVR) and the Union of Right Forces (SPS)—created for the 1999 election were led by former prime ministers (Yevgenii Primakov and Yegor Gaidar) who had been dismissed by President Yeltsin.

Unity, which emerged as the "party of power" in 1999, was formed by Emergency Situations Minister Sergei Shoigu just months prior to the December election. For the 2003 parliamentary elections, Unity joined an electoral bloc with Fatherland and with The Whole Russia, led by Republic of Tatarstan President Mintimer Shaimiev, to create a new party of power—United Russia.

Outsider parties have challenged insider parties in election after election, but they have not been successful in gaining control of the Russian govern-

TABLE 8.1 Major Russian Federation Political Parties That Competed in the 1999 and 2003 Parliamentary Elections

Government Orientation	Party Longevity		
	Old Parties (Competed in 1993 or 1995 elections)	Parties Created for 1999 Elections	New Parties (Created for 2003 election)
Insider Parties Led by 1999–2003 Government Team		Unity (Yedinstvo) Founded: September 1999 Leaders: Sergei Shoigu, Alexander Karelin, Boris Gryzlov	United Russia (or Unified Russia) Founded: December 2001 Leaders: Boris Gryzlov, Sergei Shoigu, Yurii Luzhkov, Mintimer Shaimiev
Led by Former Insiders	Our Home Is Russia (NDR) Founded: May 1995 Leaders: Viktor Chernomyrdin and Vladimir Ryzhkov	Fatherland–All Russia (OVR) Founded: August 1999 Leaders: Yevgeny Primakov, Yuri Luzhkov, Vladimir Yakovlev Union of Right Forces (SPS) Founded: August 1999 Leaders: Boris Nemtsov, Sergei Kiriyenko, Yegor Gaidar[a]	
Parties Led by Outsiders	The Communist Party of the Russian Federation (CPRF) Founded: February 1993 Leader: Gennadii Zyuganov Yabloko Founded: October 1993 Leader: Grigorii Yavlinski Liberal Democratic Party of Russia–Zhirinovskii Bloc (LDPR) Founded: March 1990 Leader: Vladimir Zhirinovskii		Motherland National-Patriotic Union (Rodina) Founded: September 2003 Leaders: Sergei Glazyev, Dmitrii Rogozin People's Party of the Russian Federation[b] Leader: Gennadii Raikov

[a] Gaidar was head of Russia's Democratic Choice, which competed in the 1995 parliamentary election.

[b] This party fits somewhat uncomfortably here because members elected in SMDs under this name in December 2003 quickly joined the United Russia faction in the 2003 parliament.

ment. These parties are oppositional in the sense that they have their own preferred positions on public policy that contrast with those being implemented by the Yeltsin and Putin administrations. The Liberal Democratic Party of Russia (LDPR) and the CPRF are the outsider parties that form the most prominent core of political opposition to the parties of power.

Although the categories in Table 8.1 are useful, it is not always easy to define Russian political parties in terms of whether they are newly created or old (having been in existence throughout the 1990s). The Union of Right Forces (SPS) was technically a new bloc created in 1999, yet the bulk of its members and leaders came from the party named Russia's [Democratic] Choice, which competed in the 1993 and 1995 elections. In addition, parties may present themselves as outsider parties during electoral campaigns, but after elections they may enter coalitions with insider parties in order to pass legislation. For example, during its preelection campaigning, the LDPR presented itself as an alternative to the choices and decisions made by the government; however, according to roll-call analyses conducted in the early 2000s, the LDPR frequently voted for legislation proposed by the Putin administration. Nevertheless, the LDPR should be classified as an outsider party because its leaders have never had the power to define the direction of post-Soviet Russian politics.

Newly created parties performed better on the whole than established (old) parties in the 1999 and 2003 elections. The lack of stability and continuity in Russia's party system is offered as evidence that the system remains weak and underdeveloped. Wealthy leaders create parties and finance them because these vehicles are required to legitimate their competition for political power. Yet, three older parties led by outsiders have demonstrated a degree of consistency and stability in their organization and platforms over time. The Communist Party of the Russian Federation, in particular, exhibits an established organizational structure and ideological coherence. Nonetheless, outsider parties have not been able to prevail over the new parties for two reasons: (1) the programmatic appeals of outsider parties do not have majority mass support, and (2) the insiders have such enormous resources at their disposal that it may be nearly impossible to successfully challenge their control.

Because there is no perfect way to categorize the Russian political party system, other authors have used various schemes, such as placing the parties on a left–right continuum, a pro-reform versus an anti-reform dimension, or a pro-region versus a pro-center dimension. Russia does have parties that are clearly leftist (for example, the Communist Party). Russia also has the LDPR, which is generally labeled as rightist because of its ultranationalist orientation. The Liberal Democratic Party of Russia, however, also could be considered leftist because of its emphasis on social welfare. Thus, the left–right continuum is not particularly useful for categorizing Russian political parties.

Thomas Remington (2002, 107) divides Russian parties into two categories: those that push a particular ideological outlook and those that avoid taking a clear policy stance, instead making vague appeals for support of the status quo.

Most often the latter types of political parties serve primarily as vehicles for individual office seeking and office holding. Of those that do have an ideological orientation, three main strains are apparent: democratic, communist, and nationalist. As described next, communist parties support a state-dominated political and economic system, while democratic parties support a capitalist economy and a pro-Western foreign policy. Nationalist parties are anti-West in their foreign policy orientation. Such ideological groupings, however, are only one possible way among many to classify Russian political parties. The pages that follow review the platforms of Russia's main parties, starting with the old ones (see Table 8.1) that are still operating.

Communist Party

The program of the Communist Party of the Russian Federation during the 1999 and 2003 election campaigns was consistent with the programs it had for the 1993 and 1995 parliamentary elections, although somewhat more moderate. The program advocated a more temperate drive toward economic reform than had been characteristic of the Yeltsin–Putin "terrible regime." The official goals of the CPRF include the propagation of socialism: to build a society with social justice, a collective character, and equality. The Communist Party also supports the restoration of the Soviet Union on a "voluntary basis" and the establishment of a strong Russian nation.

Although the Communist Party of the Soviet Union was banned in the aftermath of the August 1991 coup, the Russian Constitutional Court reversed Yeltsin's ban and the Communist Party of the Russian Federation was officially registered in 1993. The CPRF directly inherited the structures of the Communist Party of the Soviet Union (CPSU). Although the share of the Duma seats controlled by the Communist Party shrank considerably after the 1999 parliamentary elections (compared with the seats won in the 1995 election), the party was still the largest single party in the State Duma. In the 2003 elections, however, the vote share won by the communists dropped further to 13 percent of the PR vote. As a result, the Communist Party's membership in the Duma shrank to a much smaller **faction**.

Yabloko

Although completely different in ideological orientation, the Yabloko Russian Democratic Party is similar to the CPRF in the sense that it participated in the 1999 and 2003 Duma elections as one of just a few parties that had also contended in the first Duma elections in 1993 and the second Duma elections of 1995. Yabloko's leader throughout the years was Grigorii Yavlinsky, the author of the "500 Days Program"—a plan of economic reform for the Soviet Union—and deputy prime minister of Russia in 1990. The party's name means *apple* and was derived from the initials of its three founders: Yavlinsky, Yuri Boldyrev, and Vladimir Lukin. In its manifesto released on December 10, 2001, the party issued several goals, including the establishment of a democratic regime with rule of law, an effective market economy system, a civil society, and a European framework of a postindustrial strategy.[1] In the lead-up to the 2003 parliamentary elections, Yabloko openly criticized the war in Chechnya and sided with the Communist Party in a no-confidence vote against Putin's prime minister, Mikhail Kasyanov, in June 2003. In December 2003, Yabloko was unable to win the 5 percent threshold of the party-list vote required to receive a share of the 225 Duma seats allocated through the PR system.

Liberal Democratic Party of Russia

Vladimir Zhirinovsky's Liberal Democratic Party of Russia is a competitor that survived through Russia's first (1993) and second (1995) post-Soviet parliamentary elections. It also won seats through PR party-list voting in both 1999 and 2003. The political platform of the LDPR, although known for a nationalist orientation that calls for reincorporating former union republics into Russia, makes significant promises in the area of social welfare.

Vladimir Zhirinovsky clashing with another lawmaker inside the Russian State Duma, March 2005.

Vladimir Fedorenko / RIA–Novosty / AP–Wide World Photos

These three parties—the Communist Party, Yabloko, and Zhirinovskii's organization—are the only ones that competed relatively successfully in all parliamentary elections between 1993 and 2003. The newer political forces that emerged prior to the December 1999 or 2003 elections are described below.

Fatherland–All Russia Coalition

According to public opinion polls from the summer of 1999, Fatherland—formed in December 1998 and led by Moscow Mayor Yuri Luzhkov—was the second most popular political party, after the Communist Party. All Russia, founded in April 1999, brought together governors (heads of oblasts within the Russian Federation), presidents (heads of the autonomous RF republics), members of the State Duma, and directors of large enterprises. The coalition, Fatherland–All Russia (OVR for *Otechestvo-Vsya Rossiya*), was formed prior to the 1999 elections as a strategy to ensure parliamentary representation for both parties. Fatherland–All Russia supported market reforms, but also called on the state to control and regulate the market. The party list for the OVR in the 1999 election was headed by Yevgenii Primakov, former foreign minister and former prime minister. Primakov was prime minister from September 1998 until dismissed by Yeltsin in May 1999.

Union of Right Forces

The Union of Right Forces (SPS for *Soyuz Pravykh Sil*) was formed in August 1999 as a center-right, pro-market coalition composed of New Force, led by former Prime Minister Sergei Kiriyenko; Young Russia, led by former Deputy Prime Minister Boris Nemtsov; Russia's Democratic Choice, led by former Prime Minister Yegor Gaider; and Voice of Russia, led by Saratov Governor Konstantin Titov. The coalition sought to enhance the representation of the country's developing middle class, entrepreneurs, managers of small businesses, and private farmers. Their election campaign focused on calls for the protection of private property, on the idea of a professional army, and on anti-corruption efforts. In 2003, the SPS party list was headed by Nemtsov and included former government insiders Anatolii Chubais, who was in charge of the 1990s privatizations, and Yegor Gaidar, the architect of the early economic reforms.

In 2003, the SPS failed to secure 5 percent of the party-list vote, which was required to receive a share of the 225 Duma seats allocated through the PR system. The two relatively liberal (democratic) parties, Yabloko and SPS, together may have been able to pass the 5 percent threshold for PR representation in the Duma had negotiations between the parties' two leaders to form an electoral bloc been successful. Such a merger, however, would not have guaranteed an electoral win. One Yabloko faction deputy suggested that few voters would have voted for a party that united Yabloko with SPS: "There are those who cannot forgive Gaidar for losing all their savings and cannot forgive the leaders of SPS for their support of the Chechen war."[2]

Unity

The most successful party newly created for the 1999 parliamentary elections was the organization called Unity (*Yedinstvo*, also known as *Medved*—Russian for bear). Unity was formed as a party of power, and from its very inception enjoyed the support of both President Boris Yeltsin and Prime Minister Vladimir Putin. Although not formally a member of the party, the latter attended its founding congress in October 1999 and explicitly endorsed the party before the elections. Even though Unity was formed just months before the December elections, once it became clear that Putin was emerging as the likely successor to Yeltsin, astute politicians switched their support from the Fatherland–All Russia bloc to Unity. Led by Emergency Situations Minister Sergei Shoigu, Unity took a populist strategy as a way of challenging the OVR bloc led by Moscow Mayor Yuri Luzhkov and former Prime Minister Yevgenii Primakov. The main message coming from Unity's leaders was a call to make Moscow more accountable to the people.

In 1999, all the major electoral blocs competed to win the support of regional governors and presidents. Because these officials had the power to influence voters in their respective regions, support by the regional leaders was an important asset for the electoral contenders. Thus, virtually all the major political parties and all serious candidates courted and were in turn courted by regional elites.

After winning second place in the 1999 elections, Unity emerged as one of the strongest forces in the Duma. The fact that no single faction had a majority in the Duma between 1999 and 2003 conferred on the centrist forces (especially Unity) a position of leverage in coalition-building. Unity initially aligned with the Communist Party to select the speaker for the 1999 Duma and to allocate committee chairmanships; however, it subsequently realigned with other factions in voting on substantive policy issues.

United Russia

In December 2001, Unity joined with Fatherland to create United Russia (*Yedinaya Rossiya*). When President Putin addressed the inaugural meeting that created United Russia he welcomed the formation of the new party but avoided associating himself directly with the organization. In September 2003, however, Putin openly endorsed United Russia for the December 2003 parliamentary elections.[3]

When originally formed, the bloc was headed by a triumvirate of Moscow Mayor Yuri Luzhkov, Tatarstan President Mintimer Shaimiev, and Minister of

Emergency Situations Sergei Shoigu. Operational leadership was transferred to Interior Minister Boris Gryzlov in November 2002. Because Russian ministers are not legally allowed to be members of political parties, Gryzlov served as leader (chairman of the United Russia party's Supreme Council—the body that determines the party's overall political strategy) without officially being a member of United Russia. Before his March 2001 appointment as interior minister, Gryzlov had served as leader of the Unity faction in the Duma.

The 2003 official platform of United Russia stated: "We must together make Russia a strong, united country." According to the manifesto adopted on March 29, 2003, United Russia proclaimed the following goals: external and internal security for the country; economic competitiveness and freedom; policies to fight poverty; social defense of the needy; and support for education, public health, culture, and ethics.[4] United Russia favored a strong executive branch as a guarantee of political stability and constitutional order and openly supported the policies of President Vladimir Putin.

Motherland

In 2003, the challenge to the traditional supporters of the Communist Party came from a new player on the Russian political scene—the Motherland National-Patriotic Union (Rodina). Rodina, formed in August 2003 and registered in September 2003, offered voters a nationalist-leftist alternative to the Communist Party. Headed by Duma deputies Sergei Glazyev* and Dmitrii Rogozin, Rodina was composed of twenty-nine left-patriotic parties and organizations. Included among the constituent parties was the Party of Russian Regions, led by Glazyev and Rogozin; the Socialist Unified Party of Russia; and the Party of National Rebirth (also known as the People's Will Party), headed by Sergei Baburin.

Motherland's political platform criticized the injustices of the country's system of exploiting Russia's natural resources. Rodina ran a campaign that called for social justice and a redistribution of the wealth "stolen" from the people by a handful of billionaires during the privatization process. The proposed vehicle for this redistribution would be a huge tax on those corporations that controlled Russia's vast natural resources.[5]

THE ELECTORAL PERFORMANCE OF RUSSIA'S POLITICAL PARTIES

When the first post-Soviet parliament was elected in December 1993, pro-Communist parties and nationalist parties together gained more than 40

---

*Glazyev was elected to the Duma in 1999 from the Communist Party list. He competed in the March 2004 presidential election in opposition to incumbent President Putin. In early April 2004, the membership of the Motherland Party dismissed Glazyev as head of its Duma faction.

percent of the seats in the State Duma, while pro-reform (that is, pro-Yeltsin) parties won 35 percent of the seats. Vladimir Zhirinovsky's Liberal Democratic Party of Russia did relatively well on the basis of proportional representation on party lists, while heads of administration and former members of local soviets (many associated with the Communist Party) did well in the single-member constituencies.

For the 1995 election campaign, the political field was amazingly fragmented and disordered with forty-three political organizations listed on the ballot. When the votes were counted, four parties crossed the 5 percent threshold and received representation through the party-list portion of the ballot: the Communist Party, Our Home Is Russia, the LDPR, and Yabloko. The pro-reform vote and the centrist vote were split among so many parties that half of all votes cast went to parties that failed to win any seats through PR allocation—the vote total for each was less than the 5 percent needed to pass the threshold. The communists had the best showing among all the parties in both the SMD elections and the proportional vote share and ended up being the largest faction in parliament. Thus, in the State Duma elections of both 1993 and 1995, groups opposed to the reform agenda advanced by President Yeltsin performed better than the pro-market/pro-West reform parties.

In preparation for the 1999 elections, the Central Electoral Commission approved the qualifications of twenty-six parties for the ballot. When all the votes were counted, the results showed that six parties had managed to win at least 5 percent of the party-list ballot and therefore passed the threshold for proportional representation in the Duma. The best performers in the PR race were the Communist Party and Unity, with 24.3 and 23.3 percent of the vote, respectively. The Fatherland–All Russia coalition got 13.3 percent of the vote, while the Union of Right Forces, the Zhirinovsky bloc, and Yabloko managed to get 8.5 percent, 6.0 percent, and 5.9 percent, respectively (see Table 8.2).

Each of the new parties that passed the 5 percent threshold in the 1999 elections was associated with one of Russia's former or then-current prime ministers: Vladimir Putin (Unity), Evgenii Primakov (Fatherland–All Russia), and Sergei Kiriyenko (Union of Right Forces). The older parties—the Communist Party, Yabloko, and Zhirinovsky's LDPR—each saw its share of the Duma seats reduced in the aftermath of the December 1999 voting. Yabloko's losses were due mainly to the strength of the newly created SPS, which competed with Yabloko for the "democratic" vote.

The Communist Party and OVR were the only parties with a significant number of candidates winning single-member district (SMD) seats in the 1999 election. The largest category of SMD candidates were independents (those who competed in the elections without a party label), and they won half of the 225 directly elected single-member seats in 1999. With the sitting of the Duma, most of the independent candidates formed or joined parliamentary factions; the three major ones formed by independent deputies were the People's Deputy Group, which aligned itself with the Unity bloc; the Agro-Industrialists, which was close to and controlled by the Communist Party; and Russian Regions.

TABLE 8.2   Russian Federation State Duma December 19, 1999, Election Results*

Parties	Percentage of PR List Votes (Number of seats)	Single-Member District Seats	Total Seats
Communist Party of the Russian Federation (CPRF)	24.3% (67) 1995: *22.7% (95)*	47 1995: *51*	114 1995: *149*
Unity (Yedinstvo)	23.3% (64)	9	73
Fatherland-All Russia (OVR)	13.3% (37)	29	66
Union of Right Forces (SPS)	8.5% (24)	5	29
Yabloko	5.9% (16) 1995: *7% (31)*	5 1995: *15*	21 1995: *46*
Zhirinovskii Bloc of LDPR	6.0% (17) 1995: *11.4% (50)*	0 1995: *1*	17 1995: *51*
Our Home Is Russia (NDR)	1.2% 1995: *10.3% (45)*	8 1995: *20*	8 1995: *65*
Other parties		8	8
Independents		112	112
Total seats	**225**	**223**	**448**

*The overall turnout was 60.1 percent of the population. Election results for 1995 are in italics.

Source: Election results are from Russia's Central Election Commission, as reported by Radio Free Europe/Radio Liberty, Inc., at http://www.rferl.org/elections/russia99results/index.html; see also Clark (2002, 103).

After the 1999 election, some Duma members changed their party affiliations. During the period from 1999 through the summer of 2003, CPRF, Yabloko, and the LDPR lost members, while factional groupings created by independents (Russian Regions and Agro-Industrialists) gained members. During much of the 1999–2003 Duma era, major initiatives by Putin were backed by a coalition of Unity and OVR, plus Russian Regions and People's Deputy. The LDPR and SPS deputies at times also voted with the government. As discussed above, Unity and Fatherland merged in 2001 and registered as a single party—United Russia (*Yedinaya Rossiya*)—for the 2003 election. Moscow Mayor Yurii Luzhkov's Fatherland party, the All-Russia movement, and the Unity party all held congresses in February 2002 at which delegates agreed to dissolve their respective political organizations in favor of forming the new party called United Russia.[6]

When election day arrived on December 7, 2003, the pro-Kremlin United Russia party polled 38 percent of the PR vote (see Table 7.7). It benefited from its close association with President Putin and from the support it received from regional leaders. Several scholars have noted that part of United Russia's success in the 2003 Duma elections can be attributed to an unofficial agreement between leaders in the Kremlin and regional executives under which Moscow allegedly allowed governors to win second and third terms in exchange for their support of the pro-Kremlin United Russia party in the parliamentary election. For example, nearly 80 percent of voters in Mordovia supported United Russia, whose governor, Nikolai Merkushkin, was on United Russia's Supreme Council.[7]

In addition, the electoral fortunes of United Russia were helped by abundant, positive media coverage. The message sent to the electorate by the media in the 2003 parliamentary campaign was that Unity and former rival Fatherland–All Russia had joined forces for the election to support President Putin's 2004 presidential campaign. Beginning in July 2003, the party began campaigning under the slogan "Side by Side with the President."

The Communist Party of the Russian Federation polled just under 13 percent of the PR vote in December 2003 (see Table 7.7), down significantly from December 1999. Although its platform remained consistent with previous years, the decision of party leader Gennadii Zyuganov to include wealthy businessmen on the party list may have served to alienate some of his veteran supporters. More important, the CPRF suffered from division within its ranks and from constant negative coverage in the government-controlled media in the period leading up to the 2003 election.

In addition, many older and economically disenfranchised voters switched their support from the Communist Party to the new party, Motherland (Rodina), in the 2003 election. This bloc came in fourth in December with 9 percent of the PR vote. Motherland accused the oligarchs of robbing the country and demanded that proceeds from the sale of Russia's mineral wealth be redistributed as social welfare benefits. Such a political platform placed this political party squarely on the left of a traditional ideological continuum.

The Liberal Democratic Party of Russia secured third place in the 2003 party-list voting. This relatively strong showing by one of Russia's older parties can be attributed to the continued popular appeal of its leader, Vladimir Zhirinovsky, who had been extremely successful in attracting the votes of the "protest electorate."[8] Thus, LDPR and Motherland, two nationalist parties that had also called for a renewed emphasis on social welfare, did well in the 2003 election. In contrast, Yabloko and SPS, the liberal parties, did not even break the 5 percent threshold for representation through party-list voting.

POLITICAL PARTIES AND RUSSIA'S TRANSITION TO DEMOCRACY

After the December 2003 election, United Russia immediately became the single largest party ever in the Duma. Boris Gryzlov was elected speaker at the first Duma plenary session on December 29, 2003. (Gryzlov had resigned from his position as Minister of Internal Affairs the previous week.) The Duma also formally registered the four factions that had received 5 percent or more of the total votes cast on December 7, 2003: United Russia, the CPRF, the LDPR, and Rodina. United Russia's faction in the Duma subsequently grew to 306 deputies, making it a constitutional majority, which meant that it had enough votes to initiate amendments to the constitution. United Russia's two-thirds majority in the new Duma also gave it the power to take control of all the key committees. Representatives of the United Russia party held all committee head and deputy head positions in the 2003 Duma, and it set the legislative agenda by deciding which bills were to be debated.[9]

The 2003 parliamentary election therefore ensured a new structure for Russia's party system, which could be called a "one-and-a-half party" system. This means that the party of power, United Russia, had more influence than all other parties combined. Previously, the Communist Party had been able to block initiatives coming from the president's office, but after 1999, this was no longer the case. Putin was able to build coalitions of parties in the Duma that would vote affirmatively for his policy priorities. By 2001, the power of the Communist Party in the Duma had been curtailed. In April 2002, the CPRF lost control over its committee chairmanships, as OVR gained control of three additional committees, the SPS two, and Yabloko and Russian Regions each received one. The CPRF pronounced itself a party of "strict opposition" to Putin's government. The Duma speaker was still Gennadii Seleznev, a member of the Communist Party faction.

In terms of more productive executive–legislative relations, the government's plans for reform, and increased institutional effectiveness, the majority control of the Duma by United Russia was a positive development. The strength of the United Russia faction in the Duma, together with its lack of ideological rigidity, provided President Putin with a powerful legislative ally that almost without fail supported his policy initiatives. A problem, however, was that the elections that produced a legislative majority in Putin's favor had been judged by international observers to be less than fair. The Organization for Security and Cooperation in Europe (OSCE) said that the use of the state apparatus and the media to promote the program of United Russia "created an unfair environment for the other parties and candidates." Bruce George, head of the OSCE's parliamentary assembly, said: "The major criticism was the media. Every outlet was attacking all the opposition parties. There was also an abuse of administrative resources. All governments make use of their incumbency, but there is a line past which you should not go." He said that the Kremlin had "orchestrated the machinery of government towards the goal of protecting it and its party." In the months before the 2003 election, opposition parties found their funding cut off and, in some cases, leaders were arrested. The three major TV channels (First, Rossiya and NTV) "devoted between 60 percent and 70 percent of their election campaign news to broadly positive coverage of the Kremlin or United Russia."[10]

Concerns about the undue influence of governors over voters in their regions also continued to be heard. Preelection agreements negotiated between local authorities and national political elites were an important component of the maneuvering that took place prior to the 1999 and 2003 parliamentary elections and the 2000 and 2004 presidential elections. Thus, a significant portion of the vote in national elections appears to have been determined through the will and the influence of the regional governors. This means that, in several regions of Russia, governors were able to control the outcome of local elections and thereby greatly influence the national elections.

In such an environment, it is not too surprising that the concept of **party identification** has limited applicability. Political parties in post-Communist systems generally have loose electoral constituencies and party leaders play a more dominant role than party members in electoral outcomes (Kopecky 1995). In describing early Russian parliamentary elections, Richard Sakwa stated that "electors were faced with a choice not so much between parties and distinct programs as between lists of stars" (1995, 207). More recent research, however, determined that a little more than 40 percent of the Russian electorate in 1999 could be described as partisans in the sense that they identified themselves with a recognized political party (Colton 2003). Consistent partisans in Russia tended to be the most numerous among the supporters of the CPRF, Yabloko, and the LDPR.

Nonetheless, parties are among the least-trusted political institutions in Russia. Party-building is difficult given the cynicism that remains a legacy of the Leninist system and historical dominance of the Communist Party of the Soviet Union. If political parties are not trusted by the people, it is very difficult for them to influence public opinion or structure electoral choice. The phenomenon of disillusionment with political parties, however, is not limited to people in the Russian Federation. Survey evidence throughout the 1990s indicates a weakening of citizens' ties to political parties in Germany (Scarrow 2002). An even more intense rejection of parties was found in Italy (Ginsborg 1996). Throughout advanced industrial democracies, evidence shows weakening party links with society, electoral instability, and membership decline (Dalton and Wattenberg 2000).

The underlying question is whether political parties are necessary for a well-functioning political system. One aspect of the role of parties is their ability to channel and funnel the interests and the demands of voters, which may depend more on the way parties function within the parliament than on their linkages with voters. Political parties may have limited membership and limited loyalty among the electorate, but they may be strong in other respects, such as recruiting new leaders, setting priorities, or acting as decision makers. If political parties do play a role in shaping public policy, and if different parties are responsive to the needs of particular sectors of the electorate when defining policy priorities, then the interests of diverse social groups receive representation.

Unfortunately, Russian political parties remain highly personalistic entities. They are controlled by political notables and are organizationally weak. The names and leaders of many parties change often and their social roots are slight.

Political parties in Russia do not play a central role in shaping public policy. This function is dominated by the executive branch. Steven Fish (2003) identifies superpresidentialism as the primary obstacle to party development. **Superpresidentialism** is characterized by the extraordinary power of the president vis-à-vis other potential sites of power within and outside government. The disproportionate power of the presidential office, the scheduling of parliamentary elections shortly prior to presidential elections, and a nomination process not fully controlled by parties are all factors that have been judged to be detrimental to the strengthening of political parties in Russia (Shvetsova 2003).

A major impediment to the institutionalization of political parties is that presidential elections are contested without the participation of parties. Both Yeltsin and Putin entered and won presidential contests without a party nomination. Arguably, Yeltsin's lack of an official affiliation with a party undermined the prospects for party-building in Russia. The limited reach of national parties and the corresponding strength of distinctively regional parties that marked the Russian political scene during the late 1990s have since been overshadowed by the victory of United Russia, which represented a win for Russia's central authority. Thus, Putin's willingness to confront regional demands for autonomy, as well as to associate with United Russia, bodes well for political party development in Russia.

The turbulent conditions prior to 2000 also explain the slow development of genuine party organizations (Hanson 2003). With the political and economic environment so uncertain, it was not "rational" for leaders in Russia to invest time and effort to build party organizations. With Putin's ascension to the presidency, however, and given Russia's relative economic stability since 1998, long-term political strategizing has become more feasible for politicians. Thus, institutions, including political parties, are becoming more stable as both the state and the economy become stronger.

After Putin came to power, the Duma passed legislation with the specific goal of strengthening the party system. A law on political parties that became effective in July 2003 forbids the establishment of regional parties and requires that all parties function at the national level. The Justice Ministry now requires that a party register branches in at least forty-five regions of the Russian Federation in order to be listed on the ballot for the national parliamentary elections. In addition, to qualify for the party-list ballot, Russian law requires political parties and electoral blocs to collect at least 200,000 signatures, with no more than 14,000 coming from any one of Russia's eighty-nine regions. The rules for electing members of the Duma were changed in 2005 so that all seats are to be filled according to a party-list (PR) system.

In assessing their development, remember that Russian political parties have had less than two decades in which to mature. Party systems in Western European democracies took much longer than this to crystallize. Political parties do remain central to democratic systems even though their role has become more marginal and they share communication and articulation functions with other "actors," such as the mass media and interest groups (Webb 2002). To ensure accountability to the electorate, political parties need to be able to play a role in governance, to serve as a counterweight to individual charismatic authority and the pursuit of narrowly defined political programs.

Key Terms

All-Union Party Congress
Central Committee
Democratic centralism
Faction
General Secretary of the Communist
    Party
Insider parties
Left–right ideological continuum
Multiparty system
Nomenklatura

Outsider parties
Party identification
Politburo
Primary party organization (PPO)
Secretariat of the Communist Party
Single-member district (SMD)
Single-party system
Superpresidentialism
Two-party system

Critical Thinking Questions

1. Why are well-functioning political parties important for well-functioning demo-cratic government?

2. What were the main organizational components of the Communist Party of the Soviet Union? What role did each of the components play?

3. What was the significance of the decision in 1990 to remove Article 6 from the Soviet Constitution?

4. Discuss the pros and cons of single-party, two-party, and multiparty political systems. Which type of system do you think is the most conducive to effective government?

5. Briefly describe the political orientations of the main political parties that won seats in the State Duma in the 1999 and 2003 elections. Discuss why parties with such policy orientations would appeal to Russian voters.

6. Discuss reasons why party development has been delayed in Russia. Which fac-tors would need to change for political parties to be more effective and stable?

Suggested Reading

Hesli, Vicki L., and William M. Reisinger, eds. *The 1999-2000 Elections in Russia: Their Impact and Legacy.* New York: Cambridge University Press, 2003.

March, Luke. *The Communist Party in Post-Soviet Russia.* Manchester, U.K.: Manchester University Press, 2002.

Moser, Robert G. *Unexpected Outcomes: Electoral Systems, Political Parties, and Representation in Russia (Pitt Series in Russian and East European Studies).* Pittsburgh: University of Pittsburgh Press, 2001.

Pammett, Jon H., and Joan DeBardeleben. "Citizen Orientations to Political Parties in Russia." *Party Politics*, 6 (July 2000): 373–84.

Remington, Thomas. "Putin, the Duma and Political Parties." In *Putin's Russia, Past Imperfect, Future Uncertain,* edited by Dale R. Herspring. Lanham, Md.: Rowman & Littlefield, 2003.

Rose, Richard, and Neil Munro. *Elections Without Order: Russia's Challenge to Vladimir Putin.* New York: Cambridge University Press, 2002.

Websites of Interest

United Russia website:
   http://www.edinros.ru/
Motherland National-Patriotic Union website:
   http://rodina-nps.ru
Communist Party of the Russian Federation website:
   http://www.kprf.ru/

CHAPTER 9

Russia's Associational Groups in Comparative Perspective

T HIS CHAPTER FOCUSES ON ORGANIZATIONS, institutions, and groups within Russian society that undertake actions to influence or pressure the government to create change in policy. We also look at groups that do not push for change but instead attempt to preserve an existing policy against forces advocating reform. First, to put the discussion into a comparative framework, an overview is provided of what studies have shown about the roles and the functions of interest groups in Western industrial democracies. The concept of an interest group as developed in the West, however, has limited applicability for post-Soviet states. To understand the different nature of associational groups in Russia, we conduct four case studies about major groups in Russian society.

INSIGHTS FROM THE LITERATURE ON ESTABLISHED DEMOCRACIES

Interest groups, otherwise known as **pressure groups,** are organizations that represent specific sectors of the community and strive to influence the political process in ways favorable to that sector. The British Medical Association, the Swedish Association of Employers, and the National Association of Manufacturers in the United States are examples of sectional interest groups (Coxall 1986, 128; Hancock 1998, 469). Members form these organizations for the purpose of protecting the economic situation and promoting the financial interests of their group vis-à-vis the government and potential competitors. In contrast, promotional interest groups form to advocate public policy changes (Coxall 1986, 16). Such groups include Greenpeace, the Royal Academy of Arts in Britain, and the National Rifle Association in the United States.

In general, the well-educated and more affluent sectors of a community provide the majority of interest group members (Curtis 1997, 253; Walker 1991, 53).

Interest groups with affluent memberships have more resources to use for building better organizations, funding campaigns, and communicating group interests. As gaps in education and income broaden within a society, the interests promoted by the most influential groups are likely to be less and less representative of the interests of the majority of the population.

In Western industrialized democracies, interest groups use varied means to gain access to and to influence government officials. One of the most common channels of influence is the use of personal connections. This involves making contacts to persuade members of parliament to pass favorable legislation; requesting favors; or asking for priority consideration to gain government contracts through family, friends, neighbors, school ties, and colleagues. Interest groups also employ the mass media to help them mobilize support throughout the country, to gain attention for their concerns, and to increase resources through monetary donations (Almond and Powell 1996, 77). Interest groups provide information to legislators and contribute to their political campaigns. Pressure groups may also focus their attention directly on government bureaucracies when the issue at hand is of narrow concern and falls strictly within the jurisdiction of a bureaucratic department. In France and the United Kingdom, for example, representatives of large corporations and professional organizations often sit on advisory boards that provide bureaucrats with the expert information needed to make decisions (Curtis 1997, 66; Hancock 1998, 184–85).

Attempts to influence public policy decisions may include protests, marches, demonstrations, and strikes.* Protest rallies bring media attention to interest groups and may help rally popular support (Hancock 1998, 182). When legitimate channels of influence are not working, interest groups may act more aggressively (even violently) or use illegal, coercive, or covert channels. Groups are more likely to use violence, even terrorism, or unlawful channels, such as bribery or payoffs, when the government is perceived to be corrupt or illegitimate. Terrorism involves excessive violence and loss of lives. Groups use this tactic mainly when they believe that they have exhausted all "legitimate" channels of influence. Terrorists attempt to promote regime changes or change the balance of power in the political world (Almond and Powell 1996, 79–80).

The access channels that a group uses often reflect the broader system to which the interest organization belongs (Almond and Powell 1996, 73–79). In a pluralistic interest group system, autonomous interest groups are well organized and financed. The United States is an example of a pluralistic interest group system because it has a variety of professional associations, business groups, and labor unions that frequently employ a professional staff to lobby elected officials to further group goals.

In a democratic interest group system, the process of coordination among different organizations, such as labor unions and business sector associations,

*In some countries, protest activities are severely restricted and official permission must be secured or such acts are unlawful.

is institutionalized. Interest groups have an official role in policymaking activities. Leaders of interest groups work directly with political parties and government administrative departments. Germany is an example of this type of system.

In a controlled interest group system, the ruling political party penetrates all levels of society and does not allow autonomous associations to function. Under this system, the government (or ruling party) creates state-sponsored associations and uses them to gain control over the people and to make it look as if the people have participated in the decisions made by the leadership. As described in the next section, the former Soviet Union provides an example of this type of system.

ORGANIZED INTERESTS IN THE SOVIET ERA

In the former Soviet Union, different sectoral and institutional groups, such as the military–industrial complex and the scientific establishment, communicated their concerns to Communist Party officials, but all Soviet organizations were required to articulate their interests in the way dictated by party leadership. In fact, any deviation from this format of articulation was considered anti-Soviet. Those found guilty of promoting ideas that challenged the core principles of the Soviet system were harassed and often arrested.[1]

The right of the Communist Party to oversee all societal organizations was fixed in the USSR Constitution (1977 version), Article 6, which explicitly identified the Communist Party of the Soviet Union (CPSU) as "the leading and guiding force in Soviet society and the nucleus of the political system: of all state organizations and public organizations." Auxiliary organizations served as transmission belts whose primary purpose was to ensure support and compliance with the policies of the Communist Party. Key officials in the organizations were subject to party approval through the nomenklatura system and a provision in Article 61 of the Statutes of the Communist Party of the Soviet Union (1986) obligated party members in these organizations to "carry out Party policy . . . and . . . verify the fulfillment of Party and state decisions."

The largest among the public organizations that operated during the Soviet era were the Komsomol (the All-Union Leninist Communist Youth League) and the labor (trade) unions. Trade unions, which included among their membership the majority of the Soviet labor force, had hierarchical structures like the rest of the Soviet system, with the All-Union Central Council of Trade Unions (ACCTU) at the top of the pyramid. Soviet trade unions did not have the right to strike or compel the government to reconsider wages or hours of work. At the level of the factory, however, trade union committees often participated actively in making job assignments, establishing work quotas, and determining bonus systems. Soviet trade unions sponsored a variety of facilities and activities and helped to promote production quantity and quality. They also administered social insurance funds and worker benefits.

The Komsomol (VLKSM) was a party-sponsored mass organization for young people ages fourteen through twenty-eight. The membership included both students and employed people. Members would "volunteer" their labor for special projects, such as aiding collective farms at harvest time, and students needed an established record of participation in the Komsomol to attain entrance to the best universities.

During the Soviet era, state-sponsored organizations also represented agricultural workers, scientists, and other professionals. Likewise, in the arts and literature, the primary professional organizations were not interest groups or pressure groups but rather administrative arms of the Soviet government. Because the Communist Party tightly controlled these organizations, Western scholars who studied the Soviet Union sometimes assumed that there were no competing interests in the country struggling to influence policy. It is, however, unreasonable to assume a homogeneity of viewpoints in any society and equally unreasonable to assume that people will not try to convince others of the correctness of their own views. It is true that the overarching organization and ideology of the Communist Party, together with the party's monopoly control of government structures, did limit certain kinds of expression of "divergent" interests. Nevertheless, debate did occur. In fact, the membership of the Central Committee of the CPSU purposefully included representatives of the major institutional interests in Soviet society. Within the state bureaucracy, as well, agencies, regional leaders, and various factions struggled with one another over the direction of policy and for control of key appointments.

THE EMERGENCE OF PUBLIC ASSOCIATIONS IN THE GORBACHEV ERA

In contrast to the controlled interest group system of the Soviet era, in a pluralistic or democratic interest group system different organizations, movements, and associations exist that are not themselves a part of the governing structure. Russia had to establish a **civil society**—a system of societal organizations that have a high level of autonomy from the state—to move away from the legacy of the Soviet system of control. When a civil society is fully developed, the state does not have the capacity to interfere or manipulate other societal groups such as churches and professional organizations, or even the courts. To make the transition to a civil society or to a pluralistic system, citizens had to take the initiative to build, from the ground up, organizations whose purpose was to represent their interests to the government.

It was not until Gorbachev's initiation of glasnost that competing interests and dissenting views were allowed open expression in public forums in the

Soviet Union. A 1990 law provided a legal basis for the formation of "public associations." Even before this, in 1988 and 1989, the system witnessed an upsurge in informal organizations and independent citizen activity. Since the breakup of the Soviet Union in 1991, professional organizations, unions, veterans groups, youth organizations, sports clubs, women's associations, and interest groups of all kinds have further developed. Such groups no longer function as transmission belts for directives from the Communist Party, although the government does continue to maintain close ties with many professional and economic-sector associations and organizations.

The rest of this chapter is devoted to the presentation of brief case studies about four types of interest groups in operation in Russia today: labor organizations, oligarchs, the military and the security service structures, and women's groups.

LABOR ORGANIZATIONS

As described earlier, trade unions in the Soviet Union were an extension of the government bureaucracy and auxiliary agencies of the Communist Party rather than autonomous organizations. The main trade union in the USSR was the All-Union Central Council of Trade Unions (ACCTU). Although this organization was limited in its ability to campaign on behalf of workers' concerns, its massive membership numbers succeeded in solidifying the perception that the Communist Party was looking out for the working people of the Soviet Union.

The ACCTU has since split into multiple labor organizations, with the Federation of Independent Trade Unions of Russia (*Federatsiya nezavisimykh profsoyuzov Rossii*, FNPR) being the largest. The FNPR is itself composed of numerous unions—many of them quite small—grouped by type of occupation. In 1995 and early 1996, the FNPR cooperated with top businesspeople in an umbrella party called Trade Unions and Industrialists of Russia. It also played a central role in organizing large-scale rallies to protest chronic late wage payments by enterprises all over the Russian Federation (RF). In the coal industry, the Independent Miners' Union (*Nezavisimyy profsoyuz gornyakov*, NPG) and the Independent Trade Union of Workers in the Coal-Mining Industry (*Nezavisimyy profsoyuz rabochikh ugol'noy promyshlennosti*, NPRUP) organized large-scale strikes.[2] In May 2004, more than 150 miners in the Republic of Khakasia went on a hunger strike, seeking back wages. The same month, 380 miners and retired miners in Rostov Oblast blocked local railroad lines to demand payment of wages and pensions.[3]

In general, labor organizations in Russia have not been very effective in pressuring the state to respond to workers' needs. Unions continue to face numerous obstacles to independent organization, such as limited resources and the legacy of cooperation with the state rather than advocacy for worker demands. In studying the FNPR, Thomas Remington (2002, 164–65) listed the following three reasons for its ineffectiveness. The reasons apply equally well to other trade unions in Russian society.

1. Because workers depend on the enterprises where they work for a variety of social benefits, the fear of unemployment and the loss of benefits limit their willingness to challenge enterprise managers through union activity.

2. Many workers remain registered at an enterprise as their place of employment in order to receive social benefits, although they actually work in the private economy for higher wages. Thus, increasing wages and improving working conditions at the enterprise are secondary to access to the social benefits that workers have through enterprises.

3. Unions have diminished power because, at some enterprises, workers can choose to affiliate with any of a number of competing labor unions and federations; thus, no single, unified voice speaks for the workers.

In contrast to labor unions, the pro-business organizations that have emerged in Russia operate more like powerful lobbies in the Western sense. For example, the Russian Union of Industrialists and Entrepreneurs, the Association of Russian Banks, and the Union of Petroleum Industrialists directly lobby government officials and provide funding to members of the legislature. Indeed, members of the Duma are often on the boards of directors of Russia's industrial conglomerates. To understand the nature of the influence of these commercial interests, we need to look at the **oligarchs.**

THE OLIGARCHS

During Russia's transition to a market economy, a new group known as the oligarchs made fortunes by taking advantage of the privatization of enterprises that previously had been fully owned and operated by the state. During privatization, well-positioned individuals within the nomenklatura purchased oil production and distribution facilities, TV broadcast stations, and other major enterprises at extremely low prices. After gaining control of enterprises, oligarchs lobbied government officials to obtain tax exemption statuses. Through bribes, some businesses got away without paying taxes; others did not even register with the tax service.[4] Thus, privatization of Russia's economy occurred in a way that made some people incredibly wealthy. Rather than reinvesting their fortunes in the economy, many oligarchs put money into foreign bank accounts, contributing to the "flight" of capital from Russia, which amounted to billions of dollars.

In the early to mid-1990s, several of the oligarchs had close relationships with President Yeltsin and with his Deputy Prime Minister Anatolii Chubais, who headed the State Property Committee responsible for privatization (Treisman 2002). The oligarchs were so powerful that when Prime Minister Kiriyenko tried to collect taxes from the oligarchs and reduce subsidies to enterprises owned by them in 1998, he lasted in office just five months, and subsidies, noncompetitive contracts, and tax breaks continued to be given to the companies owned by a small number of extremely wealthy businesspeople.

One tremendously powerful oligarch was Vladimir Gusinsky, who made his fortune through the Media-Most banking group and came to control Russia's independent TV channel, NTV; the Ekho Moskvy radio station; and several print media, including the *Segodnya* and *Sem Dnei* newspapers and *Itogi* magazine. Another famous oligarch was Boris Berezovskii, who accumulated his wealth from holdings ranging from media outlets to Aeroflot (Russia's main airline). Berezovskii gained control of the oil company Sibneft (privatized in 1995) and later bought stakes in Lukoil (then Russia's largest oil company), the TV channel ORT, and the former state-run *Izvestia* newspaper. In 1996, Berezovskii and Gusinsky helped finance Yeltsin's reelection campaign.[5] By 1997, *Forbes* magazine named Berezovskii the richest man in Russia, with an estimated wealth of $3 billion. At the height of his influence, Yeltsin appointed Berezovskii to lead the Commonwealth of Independent States. With his control over shares of ORT television and the newspaper *Nezavisimaia Gazeta*, Berezovskii was also able to influence the 2000 presidential election in ways that helped to put Vladimir Putin into power.[6]

After Putin became president, however, he set out to limit the extensive powers of the oligarchs. In essence, he made a deal with the oligarchs in November 2001: If they would stay out of oppositional politics, he would provide them regular access to the Kremlin through the Civic Forum. The forum was an umbrella organization for civic groups through which they could express their concerns. Those oligarchs that deviated from the pro-government line faced prosecution for tax evasion and other economic crimes, thereby forcing them to turn over their companies to government-associated interests. Berezovskii,

The Kremlin.
Photo by Grant Fisher, April 2004. Used with permission.

Gusinsky, and several other oligarchs fled abroad rather than face government prosecution.

Great Britain granted Berezovskii political asylum in September 2004; the London Magistrates Court was convinced by his argument that the Russian government was persecuting him for criticizing Moscow's policies in Chechnya and was suppressing the independent mass media. Moscow, however, continued to call for the extradition of Berezovskii, wanted in Russia on charges of fraud and money laundering.[7] In fact, the prosecutor's office in Moscow Oblast issued an additional international arrest warrant in late September 2004, charging Berezovskii with large-scale fraud involving abuse of office and exceeding his official powers.[8]

Another one of Russia's oligarchs, Mikhail Khodorkovskii, did not flee the country and ended up in jail. Khodorkovskii began amassing his great wealth when he created one of the USSR's first private banks, Menatap. During the privatization process, Khodorkovskii bought into the oil industry. As chairman and top shareholder of the Yukos oil company, Khodorkovskii eclipsed Berezovskii as Russia's richest man (number 26 on the *Forbes* 2003 list of the world's wealthiest people) with a personal fortune estimated at $8 billion.[9] When evidence emerged that Khodorkovskii was backing political parties in opposition to Putin, a pattern of intimidation began.[10] The chair of the holding company (Group Menatap) that controlled Yukos, Platon Lebedev, who was number 427 on the *Forbes* list, with $1 billion, was jailed in July 2003 on charges of defrauding the state out of more than $280 million in a 1994 fertilizer plant privatization deal.[11]

In October 2003, Mikhail Khodorkovskii was arrested on multiple charges including fraud and tax evasion. His arrest prevented a merger of Yukos with Sibneft that would have created Russia's largest oil company and the world's fourth largest oil firm. The giant company could have produced 2.2 million barrels of oil per day, only slightly less than ExxonMobil's 2.5 million and Royal Dutch/Shell's 2.4 million, and could have accounted for nearly 30 percent of Russia's oil production.[12] Russian authorities, however, halted the trading of Yukos shares after the arrest of Khodorkovskii.

Even though international human rights organizations criticized the Russian government for its imprisonment of Khodorkovskii, the Russian public was generally supportive of Putin's campaign against the oligarchs. Public opinion polls have shown a significant degree of hostility among the Russian population toward those who have benefited, in some cases illegally, from the post-Soviet economic reforms, notably the privatization of state-owned industries. In July 2003, the Russian polling agency, ROMIR, released the results of a survey that found that 77 percent of respondents had a negative view of the role that the oligarchs were playing in Russian society. Average Russians believe that the privatization of state industries was highly unjust and that the oligarchs have benefited unfairly and to the misfortune of ordinary people. Figure 9.1 shows the results of the ROMIR survey monitoring study of Russian people's attitude

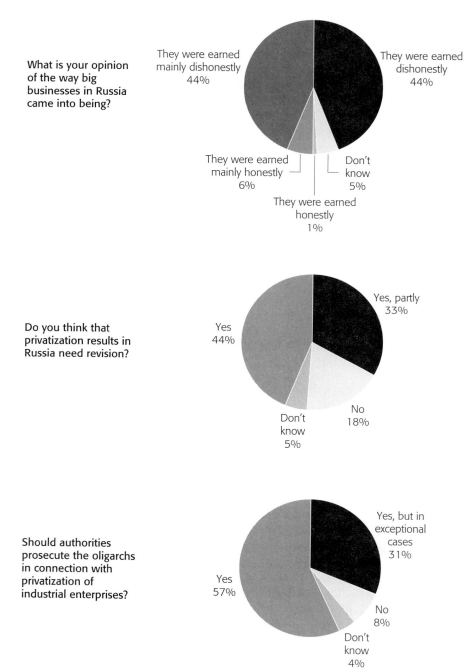

What is your opinion of the way big businesses in Russia came into being?

They were earned mainly dishonestly 44%

They were earned dishonestly 44%

They were earned mainly honestly 6%

Don't know 5%

They were earned honestly 1%

Do you think that privatization results in Russia need revision?

Yes 44%

Yes, partly 33%

No 18%

Don't know 5%

Should authorities prosecute the oligarchs in connection with privatization of industrial enterprises?

Yes 57%

Yes, but in exceptional cases 31%

No 8%

Don't know 4%

FIGURE 9.1 Russian Public Opinion About the Oligarchs and the Legality of the Privatization Process

toward big business and the possibility of revising privatization results. (The 1,500 people questioned were age eighteen and older.)

The issue of illicitly won fortunes was in the forefront of the 2003 parliamentary election campaign. Federal Security Service (FSB) Director Nikolai Patrushev announced in July that the FSB would oversee all issues of industrial privatization, especially when defense facilities were involved.[13] Shortly after the elections, in January 2004, President Putin appointed then Prime Minister Mikhail Kasyanov as chair of a new Council for the Struggle Against Corruption. Such investigations into alleged improper business dealings and into unfair profit from the privatization of previously state-owned companies were extremely threatening to Russia's major business interests. Not only businesspeople but also regional politicians expressed alarm at the prospect of further investigations into the legality of the fortunes of the oligarchs. Members of the Russian Union of Industrialists and Entrepreneurs (RUIE) approved a letter to Putin urging him not to do anything that would disturb the country's political stability. The executive secretary of the RUIE, Igor Yurgens, cautioned that any further reexamination of Russia's privatization process could have an extremely negative impact on the country's investment climate.

Although the RUIE was originally opposed to the market reforms of the early Yeltsin era because of the expected economic upheaval associated with interruptions in supply and trade, members ultimately worked with the government to design the privatization process. The RUIE continues to be an influential force with its membership including both the conglomerates headed by the oligarchs and the state-owned or partly state-owned industrial firms.

The RUIE provides an important contrast to the Federation of Independent Trade Unions of Russia discussed in the previous section. Although both emerged from Soviet-era organizations, the RUIE has been much more successful than the FNPR in adapting itself to the post-Communist environment. One reason is the paucity of resources available to the FNRP compared with the RUIE. As discussed in the first pages of this chapter, interest groups with affluent members are more capable of pressuring government officials. In the case of the oligarchs, their resources were virtually unlimited.

The arrest of Khodorkovskii and the assault on other oligarchs that had been critical of the government's policies raise important points about the process of interest articulation in Russia. The tactics employed by the oligarchs and the means by which they gained their incredible wealth were highly unethical in most cases. Yet, as long as these owners and operators provided support to the "Yeltsin Family" and later to Putin's "Leningrad Group," they were given relatively free rein in their business dealings. Once they challenged the president and moved into political opposition, however, they were subject to intimidation and arrest.

Putin's attack on the oligarchs was one way to reclaim the wealth of the Russian nation that had been stolen during privatization under Boris Yeltsin. However, state confiscation of privatized enterprises through an anticorruption campaign based on allegations of embezzlement, tax evasion, and fraud may not be the best way to renationalize major industries. Reducing the excessive influence of the oligarchs on government officials, however, is a positive development. The problem is that the crackdown also represents a tendency toward authoritarianism and a reduction in the ability of independent or autonomous groups to bring pressure on the government.

The Role of the Media

A more complete discussion of the oligarchs requires returning to a point made earlier in this chapter: Interest groups frequently employ the mass media to help mobilize support for their cause. During the Soviet era, the content of stories published in newspapers and broadcast on television was subject to strict censorship by the Communist Party. Under Mikhail Gorbachev, the media sensationally covered previously banned subjects, such as information on food shortages or accidents at nuclear power plants. In June 1990, a new Law on the Press and Other Media guaranteed press and media freedom.

With privatization under Yeltsin, major media outlets came under the control of the oligarchs. The fact that independent media outlets were concentrated in the hands of a few oligarchs is another indication of the significant influence that they had on Russian politics. Although the independent NTV channel provided daring and critical coverage of the first Chechen War (1994–1996), it worked with the government to avoid a Communist Party victory during the 1996 presidential election campaign. Under Vladimir Putin, the government reasserted its control over the independent channels. When Vladimir Gusinsky began to use his media empire to oppose the second war in Chechnya, he was accused of money laundering and fraud and fled Russia in 2000. Gazprom, by this time government-controlled, took over Gusinsky's media holdings in 2001. Most of the TV networks and newspapers previously owned by the oligarchs have since come under Russian government control.

The government now owns controlling shares in Public Russian Television (ORT) and fully owns Russian Television and Radio (RTR); and both broadcast pro-Kremlin materials. Tamara Gavrilova, who studied at the Leningrad State University law school with President Putin, was made NTV's first deputy general director.[14] The Russian government also runs the major radio stations and the national news agencies—Information-Telegraph Agency of Russia–Telegraph Agency of the Soviet Union (ITAR-TASS) and RIA-Novosti (*Rossiiskoe informatsionnoe agentstov-Novosti*). Laws passed by the Duma and decrees from the presidential administration regulate the degree to which foreign media are allowed to penetrate the Russian market. With regard to print media, the primary newspapers and weekly magazines are products of government organs or are owned by large business enterprises (McCormick 2004, 217). Two of the most well-known oligarchs that did own independent newspapers and weekly magazines, Vladimir Gusinsky and Boris Berezovskii, fled the country rather than be jailed under criminal charges.

SECURITY AND MILITARY SERVICES

Just as the trade unions and oligarchs represent very different types of groups, Russia's security forces represent another form of pressure group. Although the security forces are part of the institutional structure of the Russian state, they also operate like an associational group in pressuring the legislative and executive branches of government. The security apparatus is able to sway government decisions through its command of the coercive forces of the state.

In addition, President Putin served for a short period as head of the Russian Federal Security Service (FSB), as did former Prime Minister Sergei Stepashin. Putin's career experiences with the Committee for State Security (KGB) arguably make him a natural ally of Russia's security establishment. Some commentators have criticized Putin for relying too heavily on the security services (*siloviki*—security apparatchiks) and on his friends and allies from his days of working in the administration of St. Petersburg.

From the beginning, the Soviet regime employed security services composed of three branches—police, intelligence agencies, and the military—to suppress internal enemies and to guard against external threats. The Committee for State Security formed the core of the state's intelligence apparatus. Named the KGB in 1954, the organization had its origins in the Cheka (the Extraordinary Commission for the Struggle Against Counter-Revolution, Sabotage, and Breach of Duty by Officials), which was established in December 1917. The Cheka was transformed into the People's Commissariat for Internal Affairs (NKVD) in 1934 and into the Ministry of Internal Affairs in 1946. A separate Commissariat of State Security (NKGB) was established in 1943, whose task was focused primarily on uncovering Nazi collaborators. Under Stalin, the NKVD was the country's largest employer, with millions of people working in forced labor camps, on construction projects, and in mining operations (Reshetar 1989, 159).

Ordinary police functions, such as combating crime and maintaining public order, fell under the jurisdiction of the Ministry of Internal Affairs. After the death of Stalin, under the leadership of Lavrentii Beria, a unified Interior Ministry was established; subsequently, it was divided with the establishment of the KGB in 1954. The Soviet secret police had vast powers and employed personnel numbering in the hundreds of thousands. The KGB was responsible for intelligence-gathering, espionage, surveillance, investigations of activities deemed harmful to the regime, and protection of top leaders. Under Stalin, the KGB operated as a machine of political terror. During the Brezhnev era, however, particularly under the directorship of Yuri Andropov from 1967 to 1982, the KGB turned away from its strict reliance on terror and modernized and improved its image. Nonetheless, the KGB continued to have a relatively free hand in the use of extra-legal methods through the end of the Soviet era (Medish 1991, 142–43). Andropov's accession to the position of General

Secretary of the CPSU and Vladimir Putin's later rise from head of Russia's FSB to president of the country provide unmistakable evidence of the close relationship between the center of decision-making power in the Soviet and Russian political systems and the security services.

The Federal Security Service is the primary successor organization to the KGB in the Russian Federation. The main tasks of the FSB are to uphold federal laws, to conduct intelligence and counterintelligence operations in foreign countries and domestically, and to operate and maintain special armed detachments and special units.* The rapid growth in crime within Russia provided a rationale for strengthening the FSB; yet, these services, like those of the Ministry of Internal Affairs (MVD), must fight for limited government funds.

President Putin initiated a major reorganization of the country's security agencies in March 2003. He disbanded the Federal Agency of Governmental Communications and Information (FAPSI) and the Federal Border Guard Service (FSP), incorporating both of the agencies into the FSB. In addition, Putin abolished the Federal Tax Police Service (FSNP) and transferred its functions to the Interior Ministry; he also established the State Committee on Drug Trafficking.[15] As of the summer of 2005, the FSB director was Nikolai Patrushev.

Just as the FSB is the successor organization to the KGB, the Interior Ministry of the Russian Federation is the successor to the USSR Ministry of Internal Affairs.† The Russian Ministry of Internal Affairs commands Russia's extensive police structures and has its own troops and specialized forces, which are separate from the police and from the military units of the Ministry of Defense. The Interior Ministry was primarily responsible for supplying troops for the 1994–1996 Chechen war. Their mandate is not to fight crime, but rather to protect the state against subversive elements, including terrorist organizations, and to protect the people from violence and instability associated with internal conflicts. Government funds provide the resources the police and Interior Ministry forces need to do their jobs. When the MVD lacks funds, repercussions occur in terms of its effectiveness in fighting crime.

The third branch of the security services is the military. The main component of the Soviet military establishment was the Ministry of Defense. Initially, after the 1917 Revolution, Lenin favored the establishment of a nonprofessional people's army and the abolition of standing armies, but the need to protect the Bolshevik regime from internal and external enemies necessitated the establishment of the Red Army (Reshetar 1989, 164).

The Communist Party played a crucial role in the operation and function of the Soviet Armed Forces—the army, the strategic rocket forces, the air defense

---

*The Foreign Intelligence Service (SVR) is a separate organization whose charge is to gather information in foreign countries that relates to Russia's national security. Yevgenii Primakov served as director of the SVR from 1991 until his appointment as prime minister in 1996.
†The Ministry of Justice and the court system are described in Chapter 6.

forces, the air force, and the navy (Medish 1991, 149–50). Throughout the Soviet era, the CPSU leadership used a variety of controls to maintain its dominance over the military. Nearly all officers were members of the Communist Party and officers enjoyed privileged status in Soviet society. Political indoctrination was a core component of military training. In addition, the minister of defense generally served on the CPSU Politburo.

During the Gorbachev era, the Soviet army had mixed reactions to the process of reform. Some military leaders were supportive of the changes because they felt that the Red Army was falling behind the United Sates in terms of technological innovation; they hoped that Gorbachev's economic reforms would ultimately contribute to modernization of the military. Others, however, were extremely uncomfortable with the withdrawal of Soviet troops from Eastern Europe and the scaling back of the Soviet military presence in the Southern Hemisphere. Some elements of the military supported the August 1991 coup attempt against Mikhail Gorbachev.

With the demise of the Soviet Union, the Red Army ceased to exist. Boris Yeltsin, as president of the newly independent Russian Federation, established the Russian Armed Forces through presidential decree in May 1992. The military, like the trade unions, is characterized by considerable continuity with the Soviet past. Frequent discussions occur at the highest levels of government involving military reform and military budgets. Russian military leaders want to secure and enhance their power, resources, and prerogatives. The political views and voting patterns of Russia's servicemen (and women) are also important to politicians because military personnel constitute a significant sector of the electorate.

President Putin has steadfastly supported the military, although he has also expressed criticism when problems or failings in the performance of the armed forces become public. He has resolutely attempted to maintain and project Russia's military power on the world stage. Nonetheless, the military must compete in the budget allocation process with other powerful interests and claims. Although the army remains an institution with significant political influence, it represents a frustrated and partially demoralized interest group within Russian society. The conditions that armed service members must endure are wretched in comparison to the advantages U.S. service personnel have.

In the mid-1980s, the Soviet government devoted nearly one-quarter of the country's gross domestic product to supporting the armed forces. During the 1990s, the Russian government cut the defense budget and reduced the overall size of the military. As acting president in January 2000, Putin announced a 50 percent rise in defense spending and, indeed, the military received more support under his tenure.

Minister of Defense Sergei Ivanov, a close associate of President Putin, was counted "among Russia's most influential politicians."[16] One reason Ivanov held such power is the authority given to him by the president. The minister of defense is appointed by the president and can make decisions without approval from the prime minister or other members of the government. With Ivanov's persuasion, Putin closed the Cam Rahn naval base, Russia's only military presence in Southeast Asia. Ivanov was also responsible for shutting down the Russian radio-technical monitoring center in Lourdes, Cuba. This action went directly against the recommendations of the Foreign Intelligence Service.[17]

Another example of the military's influence on Russian politics is the continuing presence of security forces in Chechnya. Ivanov and his predecessor as minister of defense, Igor Sergeev, were both behind the decision in 1999 to redeploy Russia's security forces in Chechnya.* In a September 2004 interview with NTV, Defense Minister Ivanov said that pressure on Russia's security forces remains significant given the ongoing war against terrorism. Thus, wars in Chechnya, as well as the international war on terrorism, provide the major rationale for increasing both the size of and the budgets for Russian military and security forces.

Corruption and the Armed Forces

Just as we devoted a section to a discussion of the role of the media when the influence of the oligarchs on Russian society was described, we need to devote space to a discussion of corruption when evaluating the security services as an institutional pressure group in Russian society. **Corruption** in the military constitutes a separate, coercive channel, in addition to the institutional and personalistic channels, through which the military influences the government. Frustration, cynicism, and basic suffering have caused some members of the military to become involved in criminal acts, including murder and the illegal sale of military property, such as weapons and ammunition (Barinov 2001; Herspring 1995, 163, 171).

Military personnel in Chechnya have been accused of stealing oil and selling it elsewhere (Bransten 2001). They have also sold weapons and ammunition to Chechen fighters. One of the main field commanders of the Chechen resistance forces, Shamil Basayev, admitted in a 1999 interview that the main source of weapons and supplies for the Chechen side was the Russian army. In July 2004, Military Intelligence Colonel Viktor Imaledino admitted that "some banks working as a front for the Interior Ministry were involved in the trade of weapons and the transferring of funds to Chechnya."[18] What is disconcerting about these revelations is the realization that as long as Russian military officials are able to make large profits from the war in Chechnya, they have a stake

---

*In 1995, during the Yeltsin era, generals who opposed the use of military forces in Chechnya were actually removed from the Ministry of Defense; at that time, Pavel Grachev was Russia's defense minister.

in prolonging the conflict. Chechnya itself has been able to partially finance and supply its military operations through smuggling and organized crime (Lieven 2000, 146). Chechnya has allegedly turned its economy in the direction of illegal trade and organized crime and has been referred to as a "free criminal zone" (Tishkov 1997, 183).

Problems of corruption in the military go beyond those associated with the Chechen wars. In 2001, Duma staffer Anton Surikov accused the Russian military of being engaged in drug trafficking in Tajikistan. According to Surikov, military officials transport drugs from Afghanistan to Russia, where the military sells drugs to criminal groups, making large profits for themselves (Azamova 2001; Cockburn 2001). Corruption in the military is also encouraged by the Russian method of fund allocation whereby the military doles out lump sums based on general categories, such as personnel or operations. This system of allocation enables commanders to siphon off funds relatively easily.

Dmitry Kholodov, a journalist reporting on corruption in the Russian military, was murdered in October 1994.[19] The leading air-defense company's acting director, Igor Klimov, was killed in June 2003. Duma Deputy Vitkor Ilyukhin (of the Communist Party) asserted that Klimov's slaying provides evidence of the penetration of criminal elements into the defense sector.[20] Later, the executive branch openly acknowledged corruption problems within the military and within the security services. In July 2004, President Putin dismissed a group of top military and security officials, in part because of the lack of progress in bringing stability to the North Caucasus region, but also in an attempt to end corrupt practices.[21] Nonetheless, Russia still faces problems of crime and corruption in the security services. (Chapter 10 discusses the problem of crime and corruption in Russian society more generally.)

WOMEN'S GROUPS

Women's organizations are an example of a different type of associational group operating in Russia today. Although attempting to represent the interests of half of the population of the country, women's groups have had relatively limited influence in the political arena. Women, in general, suffered even more hardships than their male counterparts did during the tumultuous economic restructuring of the Gorbachev and Yeltsin eras. The lack of positive changes for women during the 1990s through to the early 2000s can be explained by several factors including, but not limited to, the persistent image of women as belonging to the domestic sphere, the association of feminism with negative aspects of the Communist system, and the lack of grassroots support for organizations that serve as advocates for women's interests.

Throughout the Soviet era, most women worked full-time outside the home. Millions of men were killed in World Wars I and II, and women moved into non-traditional jobs to fill the gap. Economic necessity also dictated high labor force participation by women in the Soviet Union because wages were so low that one breadwinner was unable to support a family. Women's labor force participation was not matched, however, by an easing of the burden of household duties. Political pronouncements claimed that the Soviet Union had achieved the liberation of women by providing opportunities for advanced education and employment outside the home, but scholars denounced the myth of emancipation through full labor force participation as the double burden of work and domestic responsibilities.

In the Soviet Union, sex-role stratification pervaded the workplace, patriarchal relations dominated the home, and positions of political power remained almost exclusively in male hands (Glickman 1984). Women were excluded from the top levels of decision making in the Communist Party, although a quota system did provide for female representation in soviets (government councils) and lower-level party organs. With the demise of the quota system during the Gorbachev era, female representation in the Central Committee of the Communist Party and in the USSR Supreme Soviet declined. The percentage of women in the Supreme Soviet dropped from 33 percent of deputies being women in 1984 to only 16 percent after the relatively competitive elections of 1989 (Nechemias 1994, 4).

In addition to the decline in political representation, women suffered the burdens of the economic transition far more severely than did men. Data from the early 1990s reveal that unemployment and poverty figures rose more rapidly among women than among men (Buckley 1992; Browning 1989; Lissyutkina 1993; Voronina 1994; Racanska 1996). In 1993 in Russia, women accounted for 73 percent of the unemployed.[22] Similar trends continued through the late 1990s.[23] The professions that registered the most dramatic unemployment figures were teachers, researchers, and specialists with higher education.

In response to their relative loss of political representation and to their declining economic security, a group of women's organizations came together to form an electoral bloc called Women of Russia. The lead organization within the bloc was the Committee of Soviet Women, which had previously been associated with the communist regime. Renamed the Union of Women of Russia and led by Alevtina Fedulova, this organization had broken away from state authorities in 1991. The Union of Women of Russia joined with the Association of Business Women of Russia and the Union of Women in the Navy to compete in the parliamentary elections held in December 1993 (Slater 1994, 27).

Party leaders had purposefully formed the Women of Russia bloc because other parties lacked an interest in women's issues. The program of the bloc emphasized social welfare, education, human rights, and law and order; it was against violence and pornography (Racioppi and See 1995, 833). After her election, Duma Deputy Yekaterina Lakhova promised "to work seriously in parliament in order to overcome the traditional idea of women's low political activeness and to fight to increase women's social status—right now it is intolerably low."[24]

Female candidates won 13.5 percent of the seats in the 1993 election of the Russian State Duma—61 women were elected to the 450-seat Duma. This result was considered evidence of the success of the mobilization efforts of Women of Russia—Women of Russia had won 21 seats through the proportional representation (PR) list.* In comparison, women held 6 percent and 10.8 percent of seats, respectively, in the U.S. Senate and the U.S. House of Representatives during mid-1993. In the 1995 elections to the Russian State Duma, however, the Women of Russia party was unable to gain 5 percent of the nationwide vote total and, as a result, was not awarded any seats through the PR seat assignment system. The forty-six women who were elected to the 1995 Duma (representing just 10.2 percent of its membership) gained their seats through single-member district victories or by being on the party list of one of the other parties. Other established parties included women in their lists of candidates, and women gained seats in the parliament when the party did well in the PR voting. Thus, voters might vote for an established party with women on the party's list rather than vote for an explicitly women's party as a more certain way to ensure at least some female representation in parliament.

Prior to the 1999 elections, the faction led by Alevtina Fedulova reestablished itself as the Union of Women of Russia, while another faction, led by Yekaterina Lakhova, went on to establish the All-Russian Socio-Political Movement of Women. Lakhova's organization was part of the Fatherland–All Russia alliance during the Duma campaign. In the 1999 elections, Women of Russia (as it was listed on the ballot) received 2.04 percent of the party-list votes, down from 4.6 percent in 1995 and 8.1 percent in 1993.

In the period before the 2000 presidential election, Putin was endorsed by both Fedulova's and Lakhova's organizations. Ella Pamfilova, the first woman registered as a candidate for the Russian presidency, did not receive the endorsement of these women's parties because, according to Fedulova, "Pamfilova, unlike Putin, could not cardinally change the situation in the country for the better."

Thus, the decade of the 1990s saw a decline in the strength of organizations representing women's interests. How can this be explained? One problem was the lack of financial resources. Women of Russia was not as well endowed as other political organizations in terms of campaign contributions. Another problem was the factionalism that has plagued women's organizations. A legacy of distrust of any organization once associated with the state apparatus, such as the former Women's Committee, and a lack of consensus have prevented women's groups from working together during election campaigns.

A belief that women were playing the role of "yes-women" in the previous two Dumas and voters' preferences for more active candidates also contributed to the loss of seats by women in the late 1990s compared with the early 1990s

---

*At that time, elections were also held for the upper house, the Federal Council, where women won 5 percent of the seats.

(Buckley 1992). The Women of Russia political party did pursue women's issues in their legislative agenda during 1994 and 1995, but some judged their efforts as inadequate (Yevgenyev 1994, 11–12). According to a hard-line communist newspaper, most of the members of Women of Russia used their deputies' mandates merely to ensure that they had a job after the collapse of the Soviet-era organizations for which they had previously worked (Orttung 1995). Women of Russia also came under fire for not taking a more vociferous stand against the government's decision to send troops into Chechnya.

In addition, Women of Russia's appeals and promises were arguably too similar to those of the Communist Party; thus, many women voted for the communists. The Communist Party of the Russian Federation earned a significant portion of women's votes in the three parliamentary elections that occurred in the 1990s.* The communists win many of the votes of those who support gender equality and social welfare. Historically they have offered quota representation for women, which the "democratic" and "nationalist" parties have not done. During the Soviet period, the Supreme Soviet always had a substantial representation of women, because this was the way that the party structured the nomination process. Thus, the Communist Party has a "good" reputation of requiring that women receive representation in legislative bodies.

Women's organizations are also challenged by strong cultural orientations that see little, if any, place for women in politics. Any reference to feminism or emancipation in political platforms may take on negative connotations because these terms are associated with the dual obligations that women had during the Soviet era (Pavlychko 1992). In addition, the influence of Western views of feminism on the Russian women's movement makes it easier for Russians to dismiss feminism as an alien philosophy, not applicable to the real-life issues in their country (Richter 2002).

Pavlychko (1992) has also suggested that women candidates lose elections in part because they are generally depicted as emotional rather than rational beings. This pervasive stereotyping has arguably limited Russian women's thinking about their own possibilities and prospects. In addition, society's ills continue to be blamed to some degree on working women who are unable to spend enough time with their children, and the theme that women should return to their traditional roles contributes to the attitude that they do not belong in politics.

Evidence suggests that women themselves would rather leave running the country to men. In a 1997 poll of Russians, 55 percent of women agreed that if given the choice, most women would prefer to stay home and care for their children rather than work outside the home; 63 percent of men agreed with the statement.† In addition, 26 percent of women and 32 percent of men agreed

*Younger women, however, were less inclined to vote for the Communist Party as compared to older women.
†This poll was funded by the National Science Foundation and was organized by Arthur Miller, William Reisinger, and Vicki Hesli.

that women should leave running the country to men. A fair number, 27 percent of women and 33 percent of men, felt that a woman's place is in the home rather than playing an equal role in the administration of industry and the state (see Table 9.1). These statistics are representative of the internalized nature of the **patriarchal system**. A major obstacle to increased support for women's political organizations is the large number of Russian women who believe that they do not have a place in political leadership.

The value of the traditional family and traditional gender roles was propagandized through public school curricula in the 1980s as a way of dealing with rising divorce rates, abandoned children, and decreasing birth rates (Rosenberg 1989). The popular press, TV and print advertisements, and the rhetoric of politicians also carry overt messages that separate spheres of activity should exist for men and women and that women should return to family care and leave state business to men (Racioppi and See 1995, 826–27). Moreover, Russian scientific and sociological traditions reinforce the notion that the "societal" male role and the "domestic" female role are predetermined and conditioned by biology (Attwood 1991, 1996).

This ideology of commitment to the patriarchal family is, in a sense, similar to that found in the United States after World War II. During the war, women joined the work force to fill vacancies left by men who were off fighting the war. When women were needed in the factories, they filled the jobs, but when the men returned to the jobs, women were expected to return to the home. The ideology of *domestic* roles for women dictates that when jobs are in short supply, such as during periods of economic hardship, women should abandon their jobs in favor of men. In Russia, where the introduction of market mechanisms, privatization, and democratic procedures threw society into chaos, a renewed emphasis on family values and rhetoric calling for women's return to the home followed.

CONCLUSION

The preceding descriptions of labor organizations (trade unions), oligarchs, security services, the military, and women's groups in Russia show how mixed and varied they are. The oligarchs had vast influence in the government as a result of both their substantial monetary assets and their insider connections through the Soviet nomenklatura system. The use of bullying tactics by those who have the means to do so is prevalent and hardly unique to Russia. The military is able to use coercive influence and in some cases proceeds from illegal dealings to sway policymakers. The FSB and other power ministry elites currently have the upper hand in Moscow over other rival factions or interest organizations in part because of their close personal connections with President Putin. Labor organizations have followed in the footsteps of their predecessors, leaving the working men and women of Russia with little

TABLE 9.1 Percentage Frequency Distributions for Opinions About Women's Place in Russian Society

Response Categories	1. If women had a choice, most would stay home		3. Women should leave running country to men		Response Categories	2. Debate about women's role in society	
	Women Only	Men Only	Women Only	Men Only		Women Only	Men Only
1. Fully agree	28.8[a]	30.8	7.1	11.6	1. Men and women should have equal roles	30.6	29.4
2. Partially agree	26.3	32.3	18.6	20.5	2	18.9	14.2
3. Hard to say (not presented in interview)	8.7	12.0	11.3	11.8	3	23.7	23.3
4. Partially disagree	25.9	18.1	39.2	38.2	4	14.6	16.6
5. Fully disagree	10.2	6.9	23.8	17.9	5. Women's place is in the home	12.2	16.4
Mean score	2.6[b]	2.4	3.5[b]	3.3	Mean score	2.6[c]	2.7
Number of valid responses	1,067.0	724.0	1,056.0	727.0	Number of respondents	1,058.0	724.0

Note: The 1 percent who did not answer the first question represents only 16 respondents who were treated as missing in the analysis. The 1.5 percent who did not answer the second and third questions represents 25 and 26 respondents, respectively, out of a total of 1,809.
[a] All numbers are given in percentages unless they indicate the number of responses or a score.
[b] The t-test for the difference between the mean score for women and the mean score for men is significant with the probability of Type 1 error at less than 0.001.
[c] For a t-test of the difference between means, the probability of Type 1 error is less than 0.05.

independent "voice." Women's groups, although representing such a large part of society, have limited power for the myriad of reasons reviewed. Women do, however, tend to be activists in promotional interest groups in Russia, such as environmental and educational organizations.

For political activism to become widespread in any country, the idea of volunteering one's time in support of a cause must be supported by a belief that the effort will make a difference. The heritage of the Soviet Union is one in which political participation was a duty and it is difficult to move from state-sponsored mobilized enthusiasm for party directives to focused pressure on the government for change. During the periods of glasnost and perestroika, however, informal groups and organizations did emerge, and today Russian society has a large variety of associations and nongovernmental organizations. The degree of pluralism that characterizes the Russian political system represents a dramatic change from the Soviet system of the past. Russia can now best be categorized as a limited pluralistic interest group system in contrast to the Soviet Union, which was a controlled system.

In addition to the case studies presented in this chapter, another example of pluralistic interest group activity can be found in the area of environmental concerns. Starting as early as the late 1980s, Russia witnessed a proliferation of local and regional ecological and environmental cleanup groups. For example, the Epitsentr organization in St. Petersburg focused on controlling pollution in the city's water supply, stopping the construction of a controversial dam in the Gulf of Finland, and preserving St. Petersburg's historic buildings and cultural monuments. As another example, students at Moscow State University formed the Socio-Ecological Union that helped to direct public attention to massive environmental degradation throughout Russia.[25] Other examples of pluralistic group action can be found in the arts and in the operation of charity organizations.

Another important area of associational activity is in the sphere of human rights. The most visible human rights groups operating in Russia are branches of major international organizations—for example, Human Rights Watch and Amnesty International. Some homegrown organizations do exist, such as the Glasnost Defense Foundation, the Andrei Sakharov Foundation, "Memorial," the Helsinki Group, and "Mothers of Soldiers," but their progress has been limited, particularly in addressing violations of international human rights and humanitarian law in Chechnya.

The analysis in this chapter indicates that the ability to pressure and influence the Russian policymaking process is primarily limited to those few who control wealth or coercive power. Russians are creating new groups, but most of them have limited if any access to the political elites—to the decision makers. This is why the notion of a limited pluralist system works well in describing Russia today. Unequal access to political authority is a direct result of the fact that some groups have visibly more resources than others. As discussed earlier in this chapter, interest groups with affluent memberships have resources that can be used to better communicate groups' interests. Interest groups in Russia are in this sense similar to interest groups worldwide—the capability of an interest group to articulate interests is directly related to membership demographics—and inequality of access and influence is characteristic of most modern political systems. With the lack of strong grassroots organizations, the ordinary person in Russia has a relatively limited opportunity to influence government policy except during elections; and, even here, the choice is more between competing personalities than between clear, programmatic policy packages.

Key Terms

Civil society

Corruption

Interest groups and pressure groups

Oligarchs

Patriarchal system

Critical Thinking Questions

1. How is the membership of interest groups related to socioeconomic inequality in a society? Do you think that interest groups contribute to more or less inequality in a society?

2. Discuss the different channels that interest groups use to gain access to and influence of government officials. Give examples of a few different interest groups and discuss how and why the channels of influence used may be different.

3. What are some of the obstacles faced by trade unions in Russian society today that limit their effective representation and advocacy for workers?

4. Why has Vladimir Putin attempted to limit the power and influence of the oligarchs? How successful has he been?

5. As an interest group, which major policy areas would the military like to influence? In attempting to pressure the government, what channels of influence does the military use?

6. Why is corruption in Russia's military such a major problem?

7. Why have women fared less well than men in Russia's post-Soviet transition?

8. How can the continuing decline of organizations representing women's interests be explained?

Suggested Reading

Atkinson, Dorothy, Alexander Dallin, and Gail Warshofsky Lapidus, eds. *Women in Russia.* Palo Alto: Stanford University Press, 1977.

Appel, Hillary. "Voucher Privatization in Russia: Structural Consequences and Mass Response in the Second Period of Reform." *Europe-Asia Studies* (Taylor & Francis Ltd) 49(8) (1997).

Boycko, Maxim, Vishny Shleifer, and Sachs Fischer. *Privatizing Russia* (Brookings Institution Papers on Economic Activity, 1993) (2).

Griffiths, Franklyn, and H. Gordon Skilling, eds. *Interest Groups in Soviet Politics.* Princeton, N.J.: Princeton University Press, 1971.

Hoffman, David E. *The Oligarchs: Wealth and Power in the New Russia.* New York: Public Affairs, 2002.

Lapidus, Gail W. *Women in Soviet Society: Equality, Development, and Social Change.* Berkeley: University of California Press, 1978.

Lapidus, Gail W. "Gender and Restructuring: The Impact of Perestroika and Its Aftermath on Soviet Women." In *Democratic Reform and the Position of Women in Transitional Economies,* edited by V. M. Moghadam. Oxford: Clarendon Press, 1973.

Malyakin, Ilya. "Voluntary Organizations in Russia: Three Obstacle Courses." *Prism,* 5(8) (April 23, 1999). http://www.jamestown.org/publications_details.php?volume_id=6&issue_id=358&article_id=3652.

Sutela, Pekka. "Insider Privatization in Russia: Speculations on Systemic Change." *Europe-Asia Studies* 36(3) (1994): 425.

Websites of Interest

World Press Freedom Review of Russia:
http://www.freemedia.at/wpfr/Europe/russia.htm

"Russia's Oligarchs—A Spent Political Force?" World Markets Research Centre:
http://www.worldmarketsanalysis.com/wma_sample_pages/site_pages/WMCASamp SpecReport.htm

Russia's Federal Security Service:
http://www.fas.org/irp/world/russia/fsb/

Women's Organizations in Russia:
http://www.distel.ca/womlist/countries/russia.html

Human Rights Watch in Russia and Chechnya:
http://hrw.org/doc/?t=europe&c= russia

CHAPTER 10

Public Policy Issues in Russia and the Former USSR

T
HIS CHAPTER REVIEWS the process of policymaking and the main issues of public policy in the Russian Federation. In analyzing public policy in Russia, we look at three broad areas: economic policy, foreign policy, and social policy. The primary policy challenge faced by the Yeltsin and Putin regimes has been the reform of the old Soviet administrative and economic planning structure, which appears to resist change. To understand why, we start with a review of planning and administration in the Soviet Union. After considering Soviet and Russian efforts to build a strong economy, we discuss foreign policy and relationships with former Soviet states, the United States, and Europe. The last sections of this chapter explore the problem of the declining health and size of Russia's population and the challenge of crime and corruption in government and society.

In thinking more generally about public policy decision making, two models are considered: the rational and the incremental. The first, the **rational model,** views policy as emerging from a "systematic search for the most efficient means of achieving defined goals" (Simon 1983). According to this model, policymakers "rank all their values, formulate clear options, calculate all the results of choosing each option and select the alternative which achieves [the] most values" (Hague, Harrop, and Breslin 1998, 256). The central planning agencies of the Soviet Union provide an example of an attempt at rational decisionmaking.

The second, the **incremental model,** sees policy as "resulting from a compromise between actors who have ill-defined or even contradictory goals" (Hague, Harrop, and Breslin 1998, 255). This model, developed by Charles Lindblom (1959), assumes that policy is continually remade in a series of minor adjustments, rather than as a result of a single, comprehensive plan. Decisions result from the interaction and exchange of information among the affected interest groups and decision makers. Ideally, from these discussions, a consensus emerges about how to best proceed. The incremental model provides a reasonable description of decision making in most political systems and of policymaking in Russia in the post-Soviet era.

ECONOMIC PLANNING IN THE SOVIET UNION

Prior to the Bolsheviks' seizure of power, Russia was predominantly an agricultural country and was among the top five countries in the world in terms of overall economic production (Medish 1991, 161). After the 1917 Revolution, the Bolsheviks created a **command economy** to mobilize resources for the Civil War. Industries were nationalized, factory and farm output was requisitioned for the war, goods were confiscated, and a system of rationing was imposed. The Civil War and War Communism together led to mass starvation and economic chaos.

In an effort to reestablish productivity, Lenin instituted the New Economic Policy (NEP), which allowed for the restoration of small-scale capitalism. The state, however, retained its control over heavy industry, banking, communications, transportation, and foreign trade. The State Planning Commission (**Gosplan**), established in 1921, was charged with obtaining an accurate view of the economy and setting production goals based on observed trends.

In 1932, the Council of Ministers took legal control over the economy and established a system based almost entirely on state ownership and centralized decision making. Gosplan became responsible for preparing both long-term and short-term economic plans. Communist Party congresses and meetings of the USSR Supreme Soviet provided arenas for the announcement of new five-year plans. Thus, each *plan* set the **policy discourse**—the way in which the issues were framed, defined, and discussed. It was under the First Five-Year Plan that the collectivization of agriculture began in 1929. Also part of that plan was the rapid industrialization drive, dictated by Joseph Stalin and continued until World War II.

Each five-year plan was broken down into annual, quarterly, and even monthly plans by government ministries and agencies. The plans were then distributed to the appropriate enterprises and industries. Each factory or enterprise was told what to produce and expend. For example, if a factory produced tires, directives from Moscow to the factory would establish what kinds of tires to produce, according to what schedule, how many to produce, and where to send finished tires. In addition, the plan allocated a specific quota of raw materials and energy supplies to each factory. Central planners also dictated the maximum number of workers a factory could employ and limited the amount that could be spent on wages.

Soviet planners often emphasized producing greater quantities of a product rather than improving the quality of the product or increasing variety and consumer satisfaction. Sometimes managers would circumvent the plans. They might falsify production statistics to show that a plan had been met when it had not, or they might conceal full production so that extra products could be sold for a profit. Illegal transfers of funds and materials were made from one enterprise to another, in some cases, because it was the only way to meet plan objectives; in other cases, illegal transfers were done for illicit gain.

Because planners did not always have accurate information about local conditions and needs, some important planning decisions made at the center were out of sync with local circumstances. A fundamental difficulty arose with the inability of the system to effectively and efficiently allocate resources as the economy grew more and more complex. The underlying problem was the huge planning burden placed on the central authorities given the lack of market mechanisms.

Nikita Khrushchev made a concerted effort to reform the Soviet economy in the late 1950s and the early 1960s. He attempted to eliminate the overly centralized economic ministries and to replace them with economic councils dispersed throughout the country. This attempt at decentralization was never fully implemented, and the entire reorganization effort he initiated was dropped after Khrushchev was ousted from power.

By the Leonid Brezhnev era, the state had monopoly control over all factories, land, and natural resources. Yet, the system did contain elements of personal and private property. Households had personal possessions and people had deposits in savings banks. Certain professions, including lawyers and doctors, were permitted some private practices. The vast majority of the adult population, however, was employed by the state. State ownership included all large industrial enterprises; banking, transportation, and communication systems; most trade and public services; and a large segment of agriculture. The selective use of market mechanisms, profits, and investments on capital were allowed, but detailed planning, the centralized allocation of resources, and top-down determination of investment priorities remained the principle tenets of the system.

By the mid-1980s, the Soviet Union was producing some 20 percent of the world's industrial output, but the quality of consumer goods and housing was comparable to underdeveloped countries of the world (Medish 1991, 160). Investments went disproportionately to heavy industry and to the military complex. Housing needs were inadequately met by building low-quality apartments. Scarcity of consumer goods and foodstuffs was endemic to the system.

A "second economy" developed in part as a result of the inadequacies in the official command economy. The failure of planners to provide for the needs of the population and the insufficient wages offered by the state as the sole official employer led people to seek additional earnings and goods through semilegal or illegal economic activities. Such activities could be the simple provision of services, such as plumbing and sewing, paid for with cash or with a trade of goods. Highly profitable clandestine manufacturing, theft of state property, and the use of bribes and side payments for the purpose of procurement also became characteristic of the system. The existence of this second economy was tolerated to some degree by the authorities, unless abuses were too blatant, because it helped to meet the needs of the people; however, it undermined the legitimacy of the system and diminished the revenues available to the state.

The Soviet economy was officially known as a *socialist economy*, not as communism, which remained a distant goal. The following lists show the essential features—characteristics and problems—of a socialist system and a market system.

Characteristics of a Socialist System
- Centrally planned command pattern of resource allocation
- Growth through investment in heavy industry
- State ownership of the means of production, natural resources, and land
- Job security

Characteristics of a Market System
- Competition for resources
- Volunteerism with regard to transactions
- Growth through a profit incentive
- Individuals' right of private ownership
- Absence of hierarchical relationships
- Personal responsibility for one's well-being

Problems of a Socialist System
- Stagnant labor productivity
- Massive waste
- Inability to compete on world markets
- Chronic shortages and scarcity of consumer goods

Problems of a Market System
- Ethical issues
- Everything valued in monetary terms
- Inequality between rich and poor
- Exploitation

The Soviet Union, with the most planned economy the world had ever seen, sought a rational way to organize the economy that would overcome the negative aspects of capitalism. John Kenneth Galbraith (1971) argued that because market economies operate in an incremental way, they are more adaptable. Because prices more accurately reflect supply and demand, the market interaction of consumers and producers yields more sensitive production plans than is possible in a command economy.

ECONOMIC POLICY IN THE GORBACHEV, YELTSIN, AND PUTIN ERAS

Despite the efforts of Soviet planners, the momentum of economic growth began to slow in the 1970s. High oil prices, caused by the Middle East oil shock of 1973, helped the Soviet Union improve its economic situation temporarily through increased exports of oil to Western Europe. By the mid-1980s, the Soviet system of centralized planning and state ownership of the means of production was no longer generating the revenue and wealth that the Soviet government and people wanted. It was for this reason that Mikhail Gorbachev initiated perestroika, with the goal of restructuring and revitalizing the economic system. Efficiency was to be enhanced by legalizing and promoting individual initiative and private economic activity.

Gorbachev first laid out his plans to experiment with market reforms at a June 1987 Communist Party of the Soviet Union (CPSU) meeting devoted to the economy. The operation of small private enterprises with limited hired help became legal, although they still faced many restrictions and taxes were high. Some prices were allowed to better reflect production costs. The reforms also attempted to reduce the detail associated with centralized planning by providing a degree of autonomy to the managers of larger enterprises. In principle, an unproductive or inefficient company could go bankrupt.

In July 1991, the USSR Supreme Soviet passed a law on the denationalization of industry; it outlined a long-term process for the transfer of state industries to private ownership. Many republics, including the Russian Federation (RF), adopted their own **privatization** laws. After the December 1991 breakup of the Soviet Union, Boris Yeltsin, as president of the Russian Federation, attempted to further and deepen economic reform by following the advice of acting Prime Minister Yegor Gaidar and the head of the State Property Committee, Anatolii Chubais.* Policymakers, including Gaidar and Chubais, were optimistic that Russia could make the leap to a market economy within a few years.

The economic reform plans adopted in the early Yeltsin era were similar to Stalin's breakneck industrialization program of the 1930s. In both instances, a decision was made by the top leadership as to what would be best, in the long run, for the Russian people. The people were called on to sacrifice and endure short-term hardships for the purpose of reaching an ultimate, societal goal. During the Stalin era, the goal had been to build socialism. During the Yeltsin era, the goal was to build capitalism.

In late 1991, limitations on wages were lifted and restrictions on foreign economic activities and individual labor were eased. In early 1992, Yeltsin's

---

*Gaidar was minister of finance and the economy from November 1991 to April 1992; first deputy prime minister and then acting prime minister from June to December 1992. Chubais later became the head of state-owned mega-utility Unified Energy Systems (EES).

government adopted a program of **shock therapy**—a process that involved the rapid liberalization of prices and the opening up of markets to foreign competition. About 90 percent of retail prices and 80 percent of wholesale prices were freed from administrative controls.* Restrictions on trading eased and little shopping stalls (*kiosks*) appeared along the streets.

The negative outcomes of this shock therapy were hyperinflation—prices soared, increasing much more rapidly than wages—and a drop in manufacturing production. As the ruble fell in value, people were forced to spend their savings and many found themselves living in poverty. Millions of government employees went unpaid and factories stopped producing when they were unable to purchase needed materials.

After gaining membership in the International Monetary Fund (IMF) and the World Bank in 1992, Russia received assistance that helped to stabilize the currency and finance imports. Simultaneously, however, the international debt of Russia rose considerably because of heavy borrowing from those financial organizations. Economic hardship and the turn to the West for assistance provided ample ammunition for the opposition's criticism of economic reform. Communists and nationalists in the Russian parliament challenged Gaidar's policies. Victor Chernomyrdin, who served as prime minister until 1998, replaced Gaidar in December 1992. Under Chernomyrdin, the state resumed state subsidies for enterprises and stepped away from radical market reforms. Limits on profits associated with some consumer goods and services were announced in an attempt to keep prices down.

In addition to **price liberalization,** Yeltsin's government began the process of privatizing the Russian economy. Among the many reasons for privatization, two stand out. First, government subsidies to inefficient enterprises dominated the Russian budget (McFaul 1995, 228). In 1992, before the reform program began, total subsidies accounted for 21.6 percent of the Russian gross domestic product (GDP) (Boycko et al. 1993, 173). With privatization, the assumption was that if a company did not make a profit, the company would either downsize or go bankrupt (McFaul 1995, 229). The second reason for reform was that under the command system, industrial enterprises had no incentive to find ways of increasing production, so output was falling at a dangerous rate.

After evaluating a variety of different options as to how to best transfer state-owned factories and enterprises into private hands, Yeltsin's team of advisers decided to conduct the privatization of state enterprises in two phases. The first phase—the issuing of privatization vouchers—began in August 1992. According to a plan devised by Chubais and approved by Yeltsin, all Russia's

---

*Most prices in Russia today are free from government control. The major exceptions are utility prices, which are regulated by the governments of most countries; railways; local public transportation systems; and communal services. Price ceilings are also set for a group of companies that dominate Russian industry.

citizens received 10,000-ruble vouchers, which could be used to buy shares in state-owned enterprises. According to RTV's program *VESTI (rtr-vesti.ru)*, about 25 million Russians put their vouchers into investment funds and about 40 million invested them directly in an enterprise, often investing in the place where they worked. The remainder of the people sold their vouchers for cash.

The first phase of privatization (1992–1994) was followed by a second phase, launched in July 1994. According to a presidential decree, remaining shares in state holdings could be sold for cash at competitive auctions, with part of the proceeds to go to the companies as capital for their restructuring; the rest was to go to the government. By 1995, the number of private enterprises in Russia exceeded the number of state enterprises. Most enterprises in the Russian Federation no longer belonged to the state; however, significant delays occurred in the privatization of firms dealing with natural resources and defense because of the hesitation by the government to relinquish control of the backbone of the economy of the old Soviet Union (Boycko et al. 1993, 149).

The experience of Russia in its effort to dismantle and replace the Soviet economy demonstrated that it was more difficult and costly in human terms than policy planners ever imagined. No standard exists by which we can evaluate and analyze Russia's progress in building a market economy because the task undertaken was unprecedented and gigantic. Not only did the system of property ownership and management need to change, but new financial and regulatory institutions also needed to be built. All this had to occur simultaneously with the adoption of a new constitution and the building of new government structures.

In the immediate term, privatization did not reduce state subsidies or create competitive markets. The "shares-for-loans" deals created the tremendously wealthy oligarchs in the society. Some of the biggest and most profitable Russian enterprises became the property of a small group of very rich people with close connections to the government. Graft and corruption increased. Privatization, in this sense, did not serve to rid Russia's economy of old, Soviet-style inefficiencies, and the state budget received only a fraction of the real value of the privatized enterprises.

A December 2001 study by Peter Boone and Denis Rodionov of the Moscow-based investment bank UBS Warburg found that 85 percent of the sixty-four largest privatized companies in Russia were controlled by a mere eight shareholder groups. Two state-owned banks, Sberbank and Vneshtorgbank, dominated the banking sector. Nonetheless, in collaboration with international financial organizations and Western countries, the Russian state did establish some of the institutional underpinnings of a capitalist economy, including a stock exchange, a central reserve bank, and a civil law code. To trim its budget deficit, the government slashed military spending and social assistance. It also continued to sell its stakes in energy, machine building, and construction companies. Longer-term plans called for the privatization of government holdings in civil aviation, the petrochemical industry, and the agriculture sector.[1]

With regard to small businesses, the number grew rapidly in the early 1990s, but in the mid- to late-1990s and through 2002, the development of small businesses in Russia stagnated. Plagued with high taxes, petty bureaucratic interference, unchecked corruption, racketeering, scarcity of loan funds, and limited consumer demand, small businesses remained severely challenged. They account for a much smaller part of Russia's economy than they do in other countries such as France and the United States (Millar 2002).

The Outcomes of Market Reform

The people of Russia suffered tremendous hardship during the economic restructuring of the Gorbachev and Yeltsin eras. Data from the early 1990s reveal that unemployment and poverty figures rose rapidly. Russia's decline in GDP during the 1990s exceeded the decline that the United States experienced during the Great Depression (Millar 2002, 19).

Despite the long decline in GDP through to 1996, annual growth in gross domestic product was positive in 1997 (see Table 10.1). The worldwide currency crisis, which disrupted Asian markets in the fall, reversed positive outcomes for 1997 and ultimately led to loan defaults and currency devaluations in Russia in August 1998. Not only did Russia have a huge budget deficit financed by the sale of short-term securities at high interest rates, it was also behind in collecting taxes* and receivables from industries. The August 1998 financial crisis occurred when the IMF refused to extend additional financing to the Russian government.

The 1999 indicators had positive rather than negative signs attached to them. Russia's 1998 default and devaluation, more realistic government budgeting, and a rise in world oil prices contributed to strong economic growth in 1999 and subsequent years. In the two years preceding August 2003, the number of people living in extreme poverty declined by 50 percent.[2] Despite the growing number of billionaire oligarchs,[†] inequality in Russian society was no more significantly skewed than it was in U.S. society. In 2002, the richest 10 percent of Russia's population controlled 32 percent of all cash income. In the United States in 1997, the top 10 percent received 31 percent of income.

In 2003, Russia's macroeconomic growth indicators were actually stronger than in other industrialized countries (see Table 10.2). The growth in Russia's exports accounts for a large part of this positive trend, but trade relations have a downside. More than half (54 percent) of Russia's total exports are fuel exports.

---

*Prime Minister Mikhail Kasyanov announced in October 2003 that Russia's level of collected taxes stood at 96 percent, compared with 1996, when it was only 60 percent.[3]
†When *Forbes* drew up its 2003 list of the world's billionaires, Russia had added ten new ones for a total of seventeen. Four out of five wealthy Russians live in Moscow, which partially explains why the city is the most expensive one in Europe and the second most expensive city in the world after Tokyo. Moscow also was named the most dangerous capital in Europe by Mercer Human Resource Consulting.[4]

TABLE 10.1 Russia's GDP Growth and Inflation Rates Over Time

Year	Average Annual GDP Growth (in percentages)	Change in Consumer Prices (inflation, GDP deflator) (in percentages)
1991	−5.0	138
1992	−14.5	1,353
1993	−8.7	875
1994	−12.6	307
1995	−4.2	197
1996	−3.5	48
1997	0.9	15
1998	−4.6	28
1999	3.2	72
2000	9.0	38
2001	5.0	16
2002	4.3	16
2003	7.3	14

Source: Data from the *World Development Indicators* database.

This lack of diversification and primary reliance on oil and gas exports means that Russia's economy is very much at the mercy of the worldwide price of oil, which tends to fluctuate widely. Russia also was weighed down with the expense of subsidizing energy supplies for countries that were once part of the Soviet Union and financing expensive military operations in Georgia, Armenia, and Tajikistan.

A disinclination of Russians to invest in Russia is reflected in the continued outflow of capital from the country. Nonetheless, foreign trade figures have been positive in more recent years, mainly because of high international oil prices. Exports exceeded imports to create a trade surplus of almost $60 billion (in U.S. dollars) in 2003.[5] The major markets for Russian exports in 2002 were Germany, Italy, the Netherlands, and China. The major suppliers of Russia's imports in the same year were Germany, Belarus, Ukraine, and the United States.

Despite recent positive trends in foreign investment and foreign trade, the challenges to full competitiveness in the international arena remain daunting. According to the Heritage Foundation's Index of World Economic Freedom, Russia ranks number 114 among 156 countries. The 2002 World Economic Forum's Growth Competitiveness Index ranked Russia number 64 out of

TABLE 10.2 2003 Economic Indicators for Select Countries

Economic Indicators[a]	Russia	Brazil	Canada	China	Germany	India	Japan	Nigeria	United Kingdom	United States
Exports of goods and services (% of GDP)	31.73	–	–	33	–	14.86	–	35.76	–	–
GDP (US$, in billions)	433	492	834	1,410	2,400	599	4,330	502	1,790	10,900
GDP growth (annual %)	7.3	-0.2	1.8	9.1	0	8	2.7	10.61	2.2	2.9
GNI per capita, Atlas method (US$)	2,610	2,710	23,930	1,100	25,250	530	34,510	320	28,350	37,610
Imports of goods and services (% of GDP)	20.84	–	–	32	–	16.91	–	40.4	–	–
Inflation, GDP deflator (annual %)	14.45	12.77	2.44	2.07	0.89	3.19	-2.46	17.13	3.1	1.85
Population growth (annual %)	-0.45	1.2	0.85	0.7	0.07	1.49	0.05	2.12	0.09	0.92
Population, total (in millions)	143	177	31.6	1,290	82.6	1,060	127	136	59.3	291
Life expectancy at birth, total (years)	65.85	68.55	79.22	70.66	77.73	63.18	81.12	45.34	77.49	78.02
Military expenditures (in millions of US$)	–	10,439	9,801	60,000	35,063	14,018	42,488	470	42,836	370,700
Military expenditures (% of GDP)	2.64[b]	2.1	1.1	4.3	1.5	2.4	1.0	.90	2.4	3.3 (Feb 2004)

Source: Figures for the first eight rows are from the World Bank; figures for the last two rows are from the CIA's *World Factbook*—"Rank Order-Military expenditures-dollar figures" at http://www.odci.gov/cia/publications/factbook/rankorder/2067rank.txt. See also "Russian Federation: Statistical Appendix" available from the International Monetary Fund (IMF) at http://www.imf.org/external/pubs/cat/longres.cfm?sk=16575.0. Military expenditure figures (as percent of GDP) for Russia are from the Center for Defense Information (1779 Massachusetts Ave., NW, Washington, DC 20036-2109) at http://www.cdi.org/russia/251-12.cfm.

[a]Up-to-date and current macroeconomic indicators can be found on the website of the Central Bank of the Russian Federation at http://www.cbr.ru/eng/statistics/credit_statistics/print.asp?file=macro_03_e.htm.

[b]The actual figure for Russia may be closer to 3.5 percent of the GDP.

80 countries.[6] These rankings reflect a set of regulatory factors, a burdensome licensing regime, and an overall government policy that has yet to be fully liberalized and rationalized in a way that will facilitate rather than hinder Russia's successful participation in the world economy.

Foreigners may establish companies that are fully foreign-owned in most sectors of the economy, but Russia's registration process can be burdensome. In "strategic" sectors of the economy such as gas, oil, banking, insurance, media, diamonds, and aviation, foreign ownership is limited to specific percentages. Foreigners cannot buy agricultural land in Russia, although they can lease land for forty-nine years and purchase nonagricultural land and property.

The decline in investments during the 1990s means that fixed capital stock in Russian industry is aging. Educational expenditures also fell precipitously over the decade, and this weakened the human resource potential of the country. Another obstacle that Russia faces in its efforts at economic reform is the geographical location of production facilities, which are often located in remote regions away from the largest cities. Russia faces the problem of finding skilled workers in the more remote areas. Another problem has to do with transportation and distribution of materials and goods to and from these remote locations.

Corruption, in and of itself, remains a serious obstacle in Russia's goal to reach its full economic potential. According to a report issued by the European Bank for Reconstruction and Development, in the Commonwealth of Independent States as a whole, officials extract some 5.7 percent of the annual revenues in the form of bribes from companies operating there. By adding to the cost of doing business, bribery keeps many firms from making a profit. Also the demand for bribes discourages investors both within the country and from abroad.

Questions remain about the legitimacy of Russian billionaires' fortunes. The oligarchs are vulnerable to the possibility of prosecution, although presidential administration head Aleksandr Voloshin provided assurances in September 2003 that no overarching review or reconsideration of the privatization process would occur.[7] According to a July 2003 survey by the ROMIR polling agency, 77 percent of Russians believe that the results of the country's privatization process should be fully or partially revised. Just 18 percent of respondents were categorically opposed to such a step, and 77 percent of respondents said that the oligarchs have played a negative role in Russian history.[8]

The Agricultural Economy

An extremely challenging component of Russia's economy is the agricultural sector. During the Brezhnev era, the Soviet Union negotiated the purchase of massive amounts of grain from the United States to meet its own shortfall in domestic needs. Just as it was during the Soviet era, agriculture has been neglected in the reform process in post-Soviet Russia. Farming is inefficient and technologically backward. Limited investments and losses in the work force, together with soil and water pollution, have all undermined agricultural productivity. Farm equipment is worn out, roads are extremely poor, and housing is very rustic. Another problem is the climate, marked by a short growing season and the uncertainty of rainfall.

The three types of farms in Russia are (1) large state and collective farms, (2) independent farms, and (3) small household plots. Most farms are large, on average covering around 15,000 acres, with the same essential structure as they had in the Soviet era as state and collective farms (most becoming joint stock companies). Smaller, independent farms average about 140 acres in size; many do not operate efficiently and together produced only about 4 percent of total agricultural output in 2001. Independent farmers are workers from former state and collective farms who have obtained land from their parent farm, and they remain dependent on those farms for certain supplies and machinery.[9]

Small household plots of land (family vegetable gardens) produced 52 percent of the gross agricultural output in 2001. "According to Russian official statistics, these plots comprise only about 7 percent of the country's total farmland, and yet produce about half of all agricultural output, in particular livestock products, potatoes, and vegetables. These figures understate the actual amount of land that plot-holders manage to use in their operations. They use land within [the former collective and state farms] to graze their livestock and grow crops."[10]

THE MODEL: PRESIDENTIAL POLICYMAKING

In reviewing the privatization of state-owned property that occurred in Russia during the 1990s and early 2000s, it is useful to think in terms of five analytical stages of the policy process as outlined by Hague, Harrop, and Breslin (1998, 262):

- Initiation—the decision to make a decision in a particular area; also called agenda-setting
- Formulation—the detailed development of a policy into concrete proposals
- Implementation—putting the policy into practice
- Evaluation—appraising the effects and success of the policy
- Decision—continuation, revision, or termination

Each of the five stages is amply represented in the overview of economic reform and privatization in the preceding sections of this chapter. Although decisions to initiate a new program may emerge from the Kremlin, deep-rooted interests may stall implementation as they retain significant power to sabotage or sidestep central directives. The lack of constructive debate over policy (given the weakness of competing political parties and the compliance of the legislative branch) means that the policy reflects the input of only a limited number of viewpoints.

Today the center of decision making in Russia is the presidency, and the primary organization that oversees the implementation of policy is the presidential administration. Although the prime minister has responsibility for economic management, the president sets the course of policy and monitors progress along that course. During Putin's first years in office, stabilization and consolidation were the watchwords of the day. In his second term, Putin became more resolute in initiating reforms. With his resource of popular support, demonstrated during elections and in public opinion surveys, Putin had a mandate to initiate a new round of reform. He also had the advantage of majority support in parliament, which facilitates the adoption of legislation needed for reorganization and change.

As Putin became more secure in his control of the state apparatus, the armed forces, and the security organizations, he was able to use these to bring regional bosses (governors) and big businesses (oligarchs) back under the political authority of the central administration. Putin, nonetheless, has had to be sensitive to the fact that Russian society is tired of "shocks," "revolutionary change," and "crisis." Oligarchic empires, for example, were centers of resistance to political and economic reform; building small businesses, fostering entrepreneurs, and creating a civil society are not necessarily in their interests. When Putin was reelected in 2004, he had the power to risk more radical steps, including an attempt to rein in the oligarchs.

FOREIGN POLICY

Soviet Foreign Policy (1918–1990)

Russian foreign policy today is defined and constrained by the legacy of Cold War competition between the United States and the Soviet Union. The Communist government of the USSR from the very beginning supported the overthrow of capitalist governments. For this purpose, the Bolsheviks established the Comintern in 1919 with the aim of promoting workers' revolutions throughout the world. An alteration in the policy of the Comintern occurred in July 1934 when it permitted French communist and socialist parties to form a "united front" for the purpose of opposing the rising strength of the Nazis in Germany and the fascists in Italy, Spain, and Portugal. The Soviet Union joined the League of Nations in 1934 and promoted a concept of collective security against the increasing threats from Germany and Japan.

The United States, for its part, was hostile toward the new Bolshevik government from its very first days in power and spearheaded military interventions in Russia during and immediately after World War I. In 1933, however, the United States granted diplomatic recognition to the Soviet Union. A major setback occurred when the Soviet Union, lacking progress in its security negotiations with Britain and France, concluded a nonaggression treaty (the Molotov-Ribbentrop treaty) with Nazi Germany in 1939. Despite the treaty, Germany attacked the Soviet Union in June 1941. The World War II alliance between Britain, the United States, and the Soviet Union brought about the defeat of the German–Japanese–Italian Axis in 1945.

In the Yalta agreement of March 1945, U.S. President Roosevelt, USSR General Secretary Stalin, and British Prime Minister Churchill agreed to assist European people to form interim governments as they were liberated from German occupation. Stalin used this agreement (plus the Soviet Union's overwhelming troop presence in the region) to establish friendly communist governments (under Soviet domination) in East Germany, Poland, Czechoslovakia, Hungary, Romania, Bulgaria, Yugoslavia, and Albania.

In the aftermath of World War II, Stalin was intent on building a buffer zone of friendly states between the Soviet Union and Germany and potentially unfriendly "capitalist" states. Soviet military force suppressed revolts in East Germany in 1953 and in Hungary in 1956. During the period after the end of World War II, a series of confrontations between Moscow and Western Europe and the United States triggered the Cold War. Churchill labeled the divide between communist and capitalist systems in Eastern and Western Europe as the Iron Curtain. A major component of the Cold War was containment—the United States' commitment to counter any Russian expansive tendencies. Under the Truman Doctrine, adopted in 1947, the United States assigned itself a new global role: to provide economic and military support to "friendly" governments while at the same time attempting to isolate, or contain, the Soviet Union. The United States planned to help in the reconstruction of Europe only to the extent that recipient countries aligned themselves with the West and cut relations with the USSR.

Moscow perceived the Truman Doctrine and the policy of containment, which surrounded the Soviet Union with U.S. military bases, as a new form of capitalist encirclement. In 1948, Stalin reacted by blockading access to Berlin, which was overcome by U.S. and British airlifts over Soviet-occupied East Germany. The Berlin Blockade stimulated the 1949 creation of the North Atlantic Treaty Organization (NATO). Hostility escalated further with the establishment of a communist government in the People's Republic of China in 1949 and the North Korean invasion of South Korea in 1950.

When Germany joined NATO in 1955, the Soviets created the **Warsaw Pact**, a mutual defense alliance (including all East European satellites except Yugoslavia and Albania), as a balance-of-power response to NATO; however, the general tone of Soviet foreign policy after Stalin's death in March 1953 was peaceful coexistence with the West. Moves, such as the Korean War Truce of 1953, were taken to reduce tensions. The policy of peaceful coexistence reflected an understanding of the mutual destruction that the use of nuclear weapons could cause.

Yet, the Cuban Missile Crisis of 1962 demonstrated that the Cold War was not over.* After Khrushchev began shipping Soviet intermediate-range nuclear missiles for installation in Cuba, U.S. President John F. Kennedy demanded that the missiles be removed and instituted a naval blockade around Cuba. A successful installation of Soviet nuclear missiles in Cuba would have brought U.S. cities within target range. The Soviets did withdraw their missiles but, in the aftermath, intensified their development of long-range missiles; within ten years they had redressed the balance of power with larger and more destructive weapons.

The Cold War also grew deeper with the escalation of the Vietnam War under U.S. President Lyndon Johnson in 1965 because the Soviets were a major supplier of arms to the North Vietnamese. Under U.S. President Richard M. Nixon, who was elected in 1968, fighting spread to Laos and Cambodia in 1971 and the United States conducted large-scale bombing raids against North Vietnam. Overall, however, Soviet support for their Vietnam allies was restrained and supplemented by efforts to improve relations with the West.

Relations between the USSR and China were also strained during this period. Mao Zedong's condemnation of Soviet foreign policy as "revisionist" and his competition for influence in the developing world challenged Soviet leaders. The Sino–Soviet relationship reached a new low in 1969 when fighting broke out along a disputed boundary between the two countries. After U.S. troops withdrew from Vietnam in 1975, fighting between Cambodia (Kampuchea) and Vietnam took on the character of a proxy war between China and the USSR for influence in Indochina.

During the Brezhnev era, communist-oriented governments also took power in Angola, Ethiopia, Mozambique, and Nicaragua. Cuban troops and Soviet advisers were involved in nine African countries: Angola, Congo, Mozambique, Tanzania, Somalia, Ethiopia, Guinea, Guinea-Bissau, and Equatorial Guinea. In the Middle East, the Soviet Union supported the Palestinians' claim to an independent state.

Concurrent with Soviet involvement in these lower-level proxy wars of national liberation was a "relaxation of tensions" at the highest levels of diplomacy that came to be known in the West as détente. Under Willy Brandt, Germany's *Ostpolitik* paved the way in the early 1970s for treaties between Germany and the Soviet Union and with East European countries. U.S. President Nixon and USSR General Secretary Brezhnev signed the first Strategic Arms Limitation Treaty (SALT) at a summit meeting in 1972.† The United States and the Soviet Union signed the Anti-Ballistic Missile (ABM) Treaty, which limited each country's defensive missile systems, and the Threshold Test Ban Treaty, which limited underground nuclear tests.

*Although Fidel Castro had received no support from the Soviet Union before he came to power in Cuba in January 1959, he did, after his successful national liberation struggle, join the Soviet bloc and change the name of his own party to the Communist Party.
†The agreement limited the number of intercontinental ballistic missiles (ICBMs) and sea-launched ballistic missiles (SLBMs) that each country was allowed to have. The purpose was to deter an attack by leaving both sides vulnerable to mutual assured destruction in case of nuclear war.

Richard M. Nixon and Leonid Brezhnev met on June 19, 1973, during the Soviet leader's visit to the United States.

© Bettmann / Corbis

U.S. President Jimmy Carter negotiated SALT II, which expanded the coverage of the limited missiles to those carried by bombers and to missiles with multiple warheads (MIRVs). Carter, however, took a critical stance on human rights violations within the Soviet Union, and this damaged relations between the two countries. The situation worsened further when Brezhnev sent Soviet troops into Afghanistan in December 1979. The resulting war turned into a Soviet version of the Vietnam War for the United States, claiming the lives of tens of thousands of soldiers and eroding the legitimacy of the government. The Soviet intervention in Afghanistan, perceived by the United States to be an act of aggression, led to a U.S. embargo of grain sales to the Soviet Union and a boycott of the 1980 Olympics in Moscow. The United States also provided weaponry and training to forces in Afghanistan who were fighting against the Soviets. Thus, the early 1980s saw a revival of Cold War suspicions and behaviors.

When Gorbachev became General Secretary of the CPSU in 1985, he became head of one of the world's two superpowers, presiding over a vast empire of socialist nations. He was, however, very aware of the precarious balance of power based on nuclear arsenals. In addition, protecting and subsidizing other socialist regimes and supporting wars of liberation were huge burdens on the Soviet government's budget. The financial strain, the international backlash associated with the Afghan war, and the loss of so many young lives led to a reconsideration of Soviet foreign policy under Gorbachev.

Gorbachev asserted that success in domestic reform required New Thinking in the foreign policy realm. New Thinking emphasized "collective security" and a "shared destiny" between the two superpowers and called for a "demilitarization" of international relations. Gorbachev and U.S. President Ronald Reagan signed the Intermediate Nuclear Forces (INF) agreement in December 1987 to eliminate medium-range and certain shorter-range missiles in Europe. In May 1990, Gorbachev and U.S. President George H. W. Bush initialed a treaty to end production and reduce stockpiles of chemical weapons.

Gorbachev's adjustments in other areas of foreign policy were equally striking. In 1988, he withdrew Soviet troops from Afghanistan. He reduced the number of conventional forces stationed in Eastern Europe and along the China–USSR border. In 1989, he allowed the dismantling of the Berlin Wall, agreed to the full withdrawal of Soviet troops from East and Central Europe, and resumed normal relations with China. That same year, at a meeting with Pope John Paul II in Rome, Gorbachev promised that the Soviet Union would allow full religious freedom, which was codified in a new Law on Religion in 1990. Restrictions on Jewish emigration were relaxed. After August 1990, the USSR generally supported the U.S.-led effort to use economic and military pressure to force Iraq to give up its annexation of Kuwait. When considering all these developments together, it is reasonable to credit Gorbachev with bringing the Cold War to an end. In recognition, he was awarded the Nobel Peace Prize in 1990.

Russia's Foreign Policy Since 1991

Although the Russian president has paramount authority to determine the direction of foreign policy, he also must respond to pressures and interests emanating form the military, political parties, and public opinion. Russia's post-Soviet leaders have followed in Gorbachev's footsteps in the sense that they have largely abandoned the global ambitions that characterized the Stalin, Khrushchev, and Brezhnev regimes. The overall foreign policy goals of Putin (and Yeltsin before him) are to enhance security, defensive capability, and international trade relations and to maintain Russia's status and influence in the world arena. Within this broad framework, foreign policy has swayed from a conciliatory and cooperative orientation toward the West under Foreign Minister Andrei Kozyrev to a more combative and assertive orientation under Yevgenii Primakov. More recently, under Foreign Ministers Igor Ivanov and Sergei Lavrov, Russia's foreign policy has been flexible and pragmatic.

President Putin has pursued multipolarity in his foreign policy. The goal of **multipolarity**, as originally envisioned by former Prime Minister Yevgenii Primakov, is to counterbalance the exceptional international power of the

United States by fostering relations between Russia and many other countries.* Multipolarity recognizes the existence of multiple power centers around the world; and multilateral cooperation emphasizes the important role to be played by the United Nations Security Council, regional organizations, and bilateral ties among countries.[11]

Multipolarity is the concept that leaders use to define Russia's bilateral relationship with the People's Republic of China. During a visit by President Putin to China in late 2004, the two countries not only reaffirmed adherence to a multipolar world order and mutual respect of sovereign rights, but also set goals to triple bilateral trade and to expand joint nuclear and space programs.[12] One of the most visible examples of regional Sino–Russian cooperation is the existence of the Shanghai Group, which consists of Russia, China, and post-Soviet countries of Central Asia. The group cooperates in the fight against terrorism and human and drug trafficking.

In maintaining multipolarity in foreign policy, Russia has also tried to work with Saudi Arabia to stabilize world oil markets. Saudi Arabia and Russia are the world's two largest exporters of crude oil. Saudi Arabia is a key member in the Organization of Petroleum Exporting Countries (OPEC), which has attempted to keep oil prices high by limiting production. Russia does not limit production but rather attempts to profit from high worldwide energy prices. Russian–Saudi relations are challenged by the ongoing separatist violence in Muslim Chechnya, where Russian security forces suspect that Chechen rebels receive financial support from Middle East sympathizers.

The Russian–CIS Relationship

In addition to the pursuit of multipolarity, a high priority of Russia's foreign policy is to maintain influence and control in the territory of the former USSR. Russia regards the entire region of the former Soviet Union as the **Near Abroad**, and sees its own economic and military security as inextricably linked with the region. Russia's leaders have claimed a "special responsibility" to maintain peace and stability in the region, in part because the Kremlin feels responsible for protecting the interests of the approximately twenty-five million Russians who live in the countries that were once part of the Soviet Union.

The Commonwealth of Independent States (CIS), comprising the former republics of the Soviet Union except for the Baltic States, was established at the time of the demise of the Soviet Union, but its organization is weak. Although CIS member states do not always implement agreements, the structure does provide one among many frameworks through which Russia attempts to coordinate

---

*While fostering multiple international relationships, Russia has simultaneously continued to scale back on costly overseas commitments. For example, in October 2001, Russia announced that it was giving up its electronic espionage center in Lourdes, Cuba, and its Cam Ranh Bay naval base in Vietnam.

economic and military policy in the region. Russia is the moving force behind the establishment of a CIS Free Trade Zone (CIS FTZ). Russian leaders want to have the authority to speak on behalf of the whole CIS and to represent it in relations with the World Trade Organization (WTO) rather than having each CIS state undertake negotiations directly. In addition, Russia wants CIS states to coordinate their arms export policies[13] and is trying to establish improved military cooperation among CIS states. In 1992, Russia, Armenia, Belarus, Kazakhstan, Kyrgyzstan, and Tajikistan created the CIS Collective Security Organization (CIS CSO) to combat terrorism, drug trafficking, and threats to the security of member states. The threat of terrorism is a central issue in Russia's overall foreign policy priorities. In an effort to combat terrorism, Russia has attempted to preserve stability and promote security along the Central Asian corridor. Russia has been using multilateral organizations, such as the CIS CSO, and bilateral agreements with individual states, to strengthen the international borders of Tajikistan, Kyrgyzstan, and Kazakhstan. The arrival of U.S. forces in Central Asia in the aftermath of September 11, 2001, actually helped solve one of Russia's major problems by neutralizing some of the threats to its security.

The Transcaucus region is equally important to Moscow. In 1997, Russia signed a bilateral military treaty with Armenia that provides for mutual assistance in the event of a military threat to either one. Russia supplies weapons and forces to patrol Armenia's borders with Iran and Turkey. Armenian President Robert Kocherian described Russia's military bases in his country as a "strong stabilizing factor" in its relations with Turkey.

Azerbaijan and Georgia are not members of the CIS CSO but are members of two other CIS military and security structures—the Air Defense Agreement and Anti-Terrorism Centre. Since July 1994, the CIS has sponsored a contingent of some 3,000 Russian peacekeeping troops in Georgia's Abkhaz conflict zone and a smaller Russian contingent serves in the Republic of South Ossetia.[14] Georgia has been frustrated in its relations with Moscow because it has not always perceived the peacekeepers as being fully neutral. Russia, for its part, accuses Georgia of not being vigilant enough in tracking down Chechen militants and international terrorists on its territory (in the Pankisi Gorge) and criticizes Georgia for its failure to prevent fighters from crossing the border into Russian territory. Georgia insists that Russia must vacate the military bases that it still operates on Georgian territory. Moscow claims that it needs more time to build new barracks in Russia where service members can live when they are withdrawn from Georgia.

Russia also has peacekeeping forces deployed in the Transdniester region of Moldova and maintains special interests in Ukraine and Belarus. Ukraine's president ascended to the head of the CIS Council of Heads of State in January 2003.* That same year, Ukraine's foreign minister became head of the CIS

---

*Kuchma's role as *head* of the CIS was legally dubious since Ukraine is merely a "participant" in the CIS, not a full member. Membership in the CIS requires charter ratification, which the Ukrainian parliament has never done.

Council of Foreign Ministers. Such moves send a strong message to Russians and Ukrainians alike that Russia expects the two countries to work in close coordination. Russia leases a naval base in Sevastopol on the Crimean peninsula from Ukraine; it is the home port for Russia's Black Sea Fleet.

The emphasis that Russia has put on strengthening its relationship with CIS states does not mean that Russia is able to control Ukraine or any other former republic through its efforts. For example, although Moscow requested that member states refrain from involvement in the 2003 U.S.-led military operation against Iraq, Ukraine sent a contingent of military personnel in support of the U.S. intervention.

Russia's Relationship with the United States

In addition to fostering relations with CIS states, Russia's presidents value a good relationship with the West. Putin has made a concerted effort to incorporate Russia into Western structures, while simultaneously preserving the sovereignty and national interests of the Russian Federation. The challenge is that Russia's presidents must play a balancing act between staying friendly with Washington and being responsive to the people at home who are suspicious of U.S. intentions and interests. Conservative and nationalist elements in Russian politics are upset by what they see as a desire by the United States to dominate international politics, so they have been critical of both Yeltsin's and Putin's friendliness toward the West. Even those segments within Russia who are predisposed to be positive toward the United States have been frustrated and dismayed by the amount of aid flowing into Russia from the West.

In the aftermath of the events of September 11, 2001, Putin supported the U.S.-led military operation in Afghanistan and affirmed Russia's desire to cooperate fully with the United States in fighting terrorism. Russia's immediate support of the antiterrorist coalition and its willingness to accept a U.S. military presence in Central Asia appeared to be a significant pro-Western foreign policy shift. However, fighting international terrorism had already been a top priority of the Kremlin. Indeed, Russia's military doctrine,* as published in 2000, had already identified "international terrorism" as one of the primary threats to the integrity of the state.

Russian forces directly assisted the U.S.-led coalition in its military operations in Afghanistan by airlifting supplies, providing support to security staff, and deploying military engineering units to help restore transportation facilities. Russia also provided weapons, tanks, armored personnel carriers, and

---

*Other major categories of threat to Russia were identified as "the struggle for spheres of influence in the former Soviet republics, U.S. and NATO assertiveness, advanced weapons systems, large conventional armies, organized criminal groups gaining access to weapons of mass destruction, and extremists and religious threats to the integrity of the Russian Federation."[15]

trucks to the anti-Taliban Northern Alliance and set up centers for humanitarian aid within Afghanistan. In addition, Russia acquiesced to U.S. use of Krygyzstan and Uzbekistan airbases.

In contrast to Russian support of the U.S.-led military action in Afghanistan, Russian leaders did *not* support the U.S.-led action in Iraq, which began in 2003. In a TV address, President Putin objected to what he referred to as "fist law" imposed by stronger states on weaker states. Foreign Minister Igor Ivanov argued that military action against the regime of Iraqi President Saddam Hussein would have negative consequences throughout the region. Ivanov also stated that any U.S. military action in Iraq without the United Nations's authorization would be a violation of the UN Charter.[16]

Although Russia and the United States differ significantly over Iraq, the two countries have managed to preserve the fundamentals of their bilateral relations. In the midst of disagreements over U.S. military actions, in May 2003 Russian Duma deputies ratified the Strategic Offensive Reductions Treaty, which the U.S. Senate had approved in March 2003. Diplomatic wrangling between the two countries is standard and represents business as usual. As an example: Secretary of State Colin Powell declared in December 2004 that the United States would not ratify the amended Treaty on Conventional Forces in Europe (CFE) until Moscow withdraws its troops from Moldova and reaches an agreement with the Georgian authorities on the length of Russia's presence in that country.[17]

Russia–NATO Relations

Closely related to the status of relations with the United States is Russia's relationship with the North Atlantic Treaty Organization. NATO was originally formed in 1949 as a defensive military alliance to repel a military attack by the Soviet Union against one of its member states. The counteralliance, the Warsaw Pact created by the Soviet Union in 1955, was dismantled during the Gorbachev era. NATO, in contrast, not only continues to exist but also has expanded its membership.

The original signers of the North Atlantic Treaty in 1949, and therefore the original members of NATO, were Belgium, Canada, Denmark, France, Iceland, Italy, Luxembourg, the Netherlands, Norway, Portugal, the United Kingdom, and the United States. In 1999, the NATO alliance was expanded to include three former Warsaw Pact countries: Hungary, Poland, and the Czech Republic. This expansion was adamantly opposed by Russian leaders who could see no reason for the alliance to add new members. Indeed, they saw NATO expansion as a violation of an understanding that Mikhail Gorbachev had made with U.S. President George H. W. Bush. Under that agreement, the United States was not to take strategic or geopolitical advantage of Russia's decisions to withdraw forces from Eastern Europe, accept German reunification, and dismantle the Warsaw Pact. Russian leaders argued that NATO expansion would undermine the legitimacy of those people in Russia who have been friendly to the West and therefore damage moves toward a Western-style democracy in Russia.

When NATO forces bombed Kosovo in Yugoslavia in 1999, relations between Russia and the alliance became extremely tense. The NATO-sponsored air strikes entailed intervention in a state that was not a member of the organization and were done without UN consent. Russia lobbied hard to avoid and then to end NATO air strikes in Yugoslavia. NATO's military action in Yugoslavia amplified Russia's perception of the alliance as a threat to its own security. As a result, Russia increased its military expenditures and reaffirmed its commitment to keeping nuclear deterrence forces at maximum combat readiness and to developing air defense troops.

In the aftermath of the September 11, 2001, attacks on the World Trade Center in New York and the Pentagon in Washington, Russia's leaders continued to view the NATO alliance as an outmoded and unnecessary relic of the Cold War, but the importance of maintaining close bilateral ties with the United States overshadowed Russia's objections to NATO. Since September 2001, Russia's military has cooperated closely with U.S. and NATO forces in order to counter terrorist threats. A NATO–Russia Permanent Joint Council was established in December 2001. Improved cooperation between NATO and Russia is also a reflection of the more pragmatic leadership of Vladimir Putin, who became Russia's president after NATO's military action in Yugoslavia but before the September 11 attacks in the United States.

Concurrent with the increased cooperation between Russian and NATO forces, seven additional former communist Eastern European countries (Estonia, Latvia, Lithuania, Slovenia, Slovakia, Bulgaria, and Romania) joined NATO in 2004. As a result, four CIS countries—Russia, Ukraine, Belarus, and Moldova—directly border the newly enlarged NATO. Although opposition to NATO's enlargement remains widespread, Defense Minister Sergei Ivanov declared in November 2002 that Russia was "absolutely calm" about NATO's plan to expand to include seven former Soviet bloc countries—so long as Russia is consulted and allowed to directly participate in security decisions in Europe.

Russia is not seeking NATO membership for itself; it would be unacceptable to the Russian military for its forces to be placed under a U.S. Supreme Commander. Putin asserted, "Russia is a self-sufficient state, capable of securing its own defense."[18] Russia's official military doctrine declares that as long as NATO remains a military entity with an "offensive military doctrine," Russia will consider the limited use of its nuclear strategic deterrence forces as an "element of national military strategy." The main goal of such a strategy is "preventing any form of power pressure and aggression against Russia and her allies." At the same time, according to the doctrine, Russia strives to further develop constructive political and economic relations with the countries of NATO and the European Union.[19]

Nuclear weapons—their construction, storage, and use—remain a point of debate between Russia and the United States. In June 2002, Russia withdrew from the START II strategic arms treaty. That withdrawal was interpreted as a response to the U.S. decision to withdraw from the 1972 Anti-Ballistic Missile Treaty (ABM Treaty) earlier in June. In October 2003, Defense Minster Sergei Ivanov said the role of nuclear weapons remains crucial to the country's defense.[20] In explaining Russia's military doctrine, Ivanov stated the following:

- Russia could carry out a preemptive military strike if there was a distinct, clear, and inevitable military threat to the country.
- Moscow might opt for such a measure if threatened with reduced access to regions of the world where it has crucial economic or financial interests.
- Russia might use its military might within the CIS if a complex, unstable situation developed or if there was a direct threat to its citizens or ethnic Russians.
- Military force would be used only if all other means, including the application of international sanctions, were exhausted.[21]

MILITARY REFORM

In his annual state-of-the-nation address to a joint session of the Russian parliament in May 2003, President Putin listed the modernization of the armed forces as one of the country's top three priorities, together with doubling the GDP and overcoming widespread poverty. He said that, by 2007, Russia's paratroops, marines, and infantry forces would be entirely made up of volunteers serving on a contract basis. According to Defense Minister Ivanov, by 2007, the military will have established a rapid-reaction force based on volunteers. By 2008, the term of conscription is to be reduced to one year.[22]

In July 2003, the cabinet of the Russian government approved a military reform proposal put forward by the Ministry of Defense. The plan was somewhat less ambitious than the targets outlined by Putin in May 2003. According to the plan, military salaries will increase by 2007, about half of the military will comprise contract personnel, and the conscripts' term of service will be cut to one year.[23] Effective in 2004, civilian service is available as an alternative to compulsory military service; however, the term is twice as long as ordinary military duty. Labor Minister Aleksandr Pochinok announced that most young men who opt for alternative service will be given heavy manual labor, including working for polar expeditions or doing sanitation work at hospitals.[24]

According to data released by the General Staff, Russia faces a severe shortage of officers because of low salaries, inadequate social conditions, lack of status, and the poor condition of military equipment.[25] For example, the Russian air force has received very few new airplanes and helicopters. Stanislav Kucher said that in 2002 the Russian Army had purchased only two new airplanes and just 600 new Kalashnikov automatic rifles.[26]

In October 2003, President Vladimir Putin told Defense Ministry officials that the military budget faces no more radical cuts. "Since 1992 the armed forces have been cut by more than half," he said. "This is enough."[27] (See Table 10.2, p. 241, for information about Russia's military expenditures in comparison to those of other countries.) Putin said that Russia will develop its strategic missile forces and redeploy mothballed UR-100 NU strategic nuclear missiles (classified by NATO as the SS-19). He went on to say that the country has a significant supply of the Soviet-era ICBMs and that "their capabilities to defeat any missile-defense system are unmatched."[28]

Officials at the Moscow Center for the Study of the Problems of Disarmament, however, have reported that Russia's nuclear force is aging. In November 2001, Russia had 3,444 ICBMs—2,024 on submarines and 626 on bombers. Those on submarines have a predicted useful life that will last until 2010, while those on bombers are expected to last until 2020. Other land-based nuclear weapons are beyond their projected life spans as of mid-2005.[29]

Arms Exports

Despite the aging of Russia's military arsenal, arms exports are a major source of revenue for the government. Although its share of the world's arms market shrank in the aftermath of the collapse of the Soviet Union, Russia has since regained much of that market share. In April 1996, the Russian State Corporation for Export and Import of Armaments (Rosoboronexport or *Rosvooruzheniye*) reported fifty-one countries as current customers, with the largest sales involving China, India, Syria, and the United Arab Emirates. Together with Algeria, Cuba, Kuwait, Malaysia, Turkey, and Vietnam, those countries accounted for 75 percent of Russia's arms sales in early 1996. Arms exports were being produced at more than 500 enterprises in Russia and more than 1,200 enterprises in ten other CIS nations had production-sharing agreements with Russia.[30]

Between 1998 and 1999, Russia increased its share of the world's arms trade from 4.4 percent to 6.6 percent. With this share, Russia held fourth place behind the United States, the United Kingdom, and France. Figures from the U.S. Congressional Research Service for 2000 reveal that Russia exported $7.7 billion worth of arms in 2000, trailing only the United States, which exported $18.6 billion during the same period.[31] In 2002, Russia surpassed the United States and became the world's leading weapons dealer, selling arms abroad worth $5.9 billion according to an annual study by the Stockholm International Peace Research Institute (SIPRI).[32] According to the SIPRI, Russia was 2002's most prolific exporter of armaments with 36 percent of all global deliveries. Russian factories supplied advanced fighter planes, tanks, warships, and other equipment to many countries, including India, China, Iran, Greece, Syria, and Algeria. Russia dominates Africa's arms market, supplying everything from

Kalashnikov rifles to MiG fighters. China and India are the biggest customers for Russian military hardware and are the world's largest arms importers.[33]

In 2004, Russia again exported weapons and military equipment with a total value of more than $5 billion through Rosoboronexport. Russia delivers its military products to more than sixty countries. The priority countries for Russian military exports remain China and India. Russia has also experienced considerable success in promoting its arms and military equipment in Latin American countries, as well as continuing sales to Middle Eastern, Southeast Asian (including Malaysia and Indonesia), and African states.[34] Such contracts are important to the state's coffers; as of November 2000, all existing and new defense sector companies are required to reserve 51 percent of their shares for the state.[35]

RUSSIA'S HEALTH ISSUES

Just as the economy and military strength of a country affect the overall capability of the system, so do social issues, particularly the health of its population. A healthy workforce contributes to economic productivity as well as to military strength. A major challenge of Russian social policy is to improve the health of the citizens. This section reviews the decline of Russia's population and discusses the problem of alcohol abuse in detail.

Under the Soviet Union, medical care was provided to the population as part of the overall central plan. The availability of universal access to free health care was a hallmark of the Soviet system. Through the Ministry of Public Health, the Soviet Union had a greater number of hospital beds for the size of its population than any other nation in the world. The Ministry of Public Health's obsession with predetermined quotas, however, constrained possibilities for quality, personalized care. Under the Soviet system, physicians had little status and pay rates were low. Doctors were not allowed to form associations and were thus isolated from one another and from communication to improve health-care services. In Russia, the legacy of the Soviet system remains.

Contrary to trends characteristic of most industrialized states, life expectancy in Russia dropped during the early 1990s. Between 1990 and 1994, life expectancy declined from 63.8 years to 57.7 years for males and from 74.4 to 71.2 for women. During that same period, the infant mortality rate increased. In 2005, the estimated life expectancy at birth in Russia for both sexes combined was 67 years (61 years for males and 74 years for females) compared to the estimated average life span in the United States of 78 years (75 years for males and 81 years for females). Life expectancy in France and Germany was 80 and 79 years, respectively.

Demographic and health-care experts confirm that the following are the chief factors behind the poor life expectancy figures for Russia:[36]

- Alcohol abuse
- Psychological stress caused by economic uncertainty
- Widespread smoking
- Poor personal safety practices
- Unhealthy diet, including nutritional deficiencies and shortages of vitamins
- General lack of exercise
- Poor working and environmental conditions as a result of air, water and soil pollution
- Deterioration of the health-care system
- Poor food safety regulation enforcement

Official statistics give the two leading causes of death in Russia as heart disease—accounting for about 60 percent of all deaths—and accidents, followed by cancer, drug abuse, and suicide.[37] AIDS is also a growing threat to Russia's population. AIDS is spreading more rapidly in the former USSR than in other parts of the world.

During the first half of 2003, Russia's population dropped by nearly half a million, to 144.5 million. Its population is declining because the birth rate is not high enough to make up for the losses associated with migration and the higher death rate. The Russian State Statistics Committee released figures showing that by 2016 Russia's population may decline to 134 million people.[38] As one mechanism to combat Russia's demographic problems, President Putin promised to provide support and assistance to any ethnic Russians living in the former republics should they decide to re-immigrate to Russia. The long-term solution, however, requires an improvement in the health of Russia's population and an increase in the birth rate.

A major factor in the high death rate is alcohol consumption. Alcohol contributes directly to death in cases of alcohol poisoning and suicide; and it indirectly contributes to other leading causes of death such as heart disease. In 1985, Gorbachev tried to reduce the level of alcohol consumption in Russia. Measures were implemented to increase penalties for drunkenness, raise the drinking age from 18 to 21, reduce liquor store hours, increase the price of alcoholic beverages, and reduce the amount of alcoholic products manufactured. Rather than reducing the amount of alcohol consumed, Gorbachev's campaign caused an increase in the production of *samogon* (home-brewed liquor); home brewing became a large-scale industry that provided alcohol to Russians while depriving the state of tax revenue. The alcohol reform began to have a negative effect on the economy. People would leave work early to get to liquor stores before they closed, and evidence emerged of organized crime activity developing in the production and distribution of alcoholic products. In short, the campaign was a failure.

A 1995 study found that regular drunkenness affected between 25 and 60 percent of Russian blue-collar workers and 21 percent of white-collar workers, with the highest incidence found in rural areas. Alcoholism and drunkenness have deep historical roots in Russia and part of the problem is cultural. At business meetings and at social gatherings with friends, custom nearly demands a system of toasting. Men are obligated to empty their glass with every toast, and a polite host speedily refills the glasses. On holidays and for birthdays and weddings, many consume vodka straight and quickly, plus Russians drink vodka more frequently than wine, beer, or mixed drinks.

Alcohol use is related to crime, violence, public disorder, and loss of labor productivity. Also related to alcohol consumption is suicide. The suicide rate began increasing in 1988 and had doubled by 1994. The highest suicide rate is found among 45- to 54-year-old men. Men are six times more likely to commit suicide than women.[39] Almost 57,000 people committed suicide in Russia in 2000 and 57,200 did so in 2001.[40] Alcohol plays a crucial role in suicide—60 percent of victims were found to have alcohol in their bloodstreams and 40 percent of those were legally drunk.[41]

A 2004 report by the United Nations says that Russia's demographic crisis is being exacerbated by an extraordinarily high death rate among male teens. The UNICEF report blames alcoholism, stress, a culture that places little value on human rights, and widespread disregard for basic safety rules for the dismal statistics. According to the report, 1 in 30 males aged 15 to 19 dies each year of accidents, poisoning, suicide, or violence. Russia has the highest rate of teen suicides annually, about 45 per 100,000 teens, and teen homicides, which occurred at a rate about twenty times greater than in Western European countries.[42]

Tobacco use is also a serious and growing public health problem. Smoking prevalence rates in the country are 63 percent for men and 14 percent for women. Youth smoking rates are equally alarming. The 1999 Global Youth Tobacco Survey found that 33.5 percent of Russian schoolchildren aged 13 to 16 were regular smokers and 22.4 percent of those youth had started smoking before age 11. The smoking problem is exacerbated by aggressive, persistent Western-style tobacco advertising.[43] When import restrictions on tobacco products ended in the early 1990s, the U.S. tobacco companies moved quickly into the Russian market. It took until the mid-1990s for the Russian government to respond with policies designed to regulate tobacco companies and tobacco use. In January 1996, cigarette advertising in Russia's print media was prohibited. Designated smoking areas in workplaces and public areas have been established, but, generally, Russians smoke whenever and wherever they want.

Smoking and alcohol consumption are lifestyle choices that contribute to poor health. Russian health-care policy also contributes to the negative health trends because it has failed to adapt to the changing health-care problems. Most physicians receive very low salaries. The Russian system remains acute-care-oriented rather than preventive-care-oriented, which emphasizes health maintenance.

The preponderance of effort in health reforms has focused on creating a private sector (delivery and insurance), restructuring the payment scheme, and decentralizing health-care administration and ownership of facilities. Russia has decentralized the health-care sector and assigned expenditures to subnational authorities, including those for paramedics, medications, primary health clinics, secondary and tertiary hospitals (that is, psychiatric, veterans, and special service hospitals), and diagnostic centers (Bird and Wallich 1993, 108). One problem with this was that responsibility was decentralized without the corresponding money to properly execute programs.

In 1993, the legislature created a system of mandatory health insurance, which was intended to cover all residents of the Russian Federation. The system has not been fully established, however, because of inadequate financing, corruption, resistance, and inefficiency. While locally imposed taxes are expected to fill the resource gap, locally controlled tax structures and mechanisms are decidedly underdeveloped.

An indicator of the low priority that health care has in Russia is the amount allocated by the government to this policy sector. In the former Soviet Union in the 1960s and 1970s, approximately 6 percent of the GNP was designated for health care. The Russian government designated only 1 percent of its budget for health care in 1994, the same percentage as the poorest African countries. The government portion of its GNP allocated to health care is still well under that of Western European countries (ranging from 4.1 percent in Portugal to 7.6 percent in Norway). In terms of care delivery, the declining budget means buildings and facilities continue to be substandard, shortages plague systems, and hygiene and sanitary infrastructures are lacking. Shortages in essential medical supplies and drugs complicates the situation and increases the incidence and severity of illnesses. In rural areas, health-care clinics often operate without hot (or even running) water and/or a heating system.

Many people avoid contact with doctors, clinics, and hospitals even though most basic health services remain free in Russia and other former republics. Although services are officially free, medical professionals may expect small gifts of money or foodstuffs from patients. Medicines are expensive and often in short supply. Thus, an additional component of the high mortality rate in Russia is the decision of patients not to seek care, to seek care only when diseases are in advanced stages, or to refuse hospital admittance or suggested treatments. As B. R. Cassileth et al. (1995, 1570) stated:

> The cycle persists—public wariness of the physicians; patients' delays in seeking health care; scarce availability of modern facilities, technology and public health; inadequate clinical knowledge and care; and a profession that draws those willing to work into low-salaried, poorly esteemed jobs.

According to responses given in interviews conducted in Russia in 1995 by the public opinion polling organization VCIOM, Russians are very aware of the declining size and degeneration of the population. The most frequently identified contributor was the poor living conditions of the majority of the people (43.1 percent selected this). The second most frequently cited reason for the grave state of the Russian population was widespread alcohol and drug abuse (38.2 percent selected this). The third reason was the devastation of the environment (36.6 percent selected this), and the fourth reason was the poor state of the health-care system (34.6 percent selected this).[44]

CRIME AND CORRUPTION

Crime and corruption in Russia represent a second major social policy challenge. Although the Soviet state did not publish crime statistics, the Soviet system was quite successful in suppressing crime rates. Violent crimes, such as murder, assault, and armed robbery, occurred much less frequently than in the United States. The Soviet Union had a larger police presence, strict gun controls, and a relatively low incidence of drug abuse. In contrast, petty economic crime permeated the Soviet system. Theft of state property by employees was common. Bribery and covert payments for goods and services were universal, mainly because of the paucity of them on the open market. The two most frequent reasons why a person ended up in jail during the late 1980s were property crimes and hooliganism. Article 206 of the 1987 RFSFR Criminal Code described *hooliganism* as "intentional actions rudely violating public order and expressing a clear disrespect toward society."

Death penalties were imposed during the Soviet era for the more serious cases of economic crime. The most frequent forms of punishment, however, were correctional tasks and deprivation of freedom. When assigned to correctional tasks, a person could serve his or her sentence while working a regular job and while being closely supervised.

Since embarking on its transition to a market economy, the country has experienced an explosion in criminal activity, including the violence of organized gangs, contract killings, and kidnappings. Even as Russia has experienced an increase in crime, it should be noted that the United States has even higher crime rates in certain categories. A comparison of 2001–2002 U.S. and Russian crime figures is shown in Table 10.3. By focusing on the volume of crime per 100,000 inhabitants, we see that murder is more frequent in Russia compared to the United States. A 2003 report, issued jointly by the Russian Health Ministry and the World Health Organization, states that Russia has three times more murders and suicides each year than the Western European average. For 2002, Russia stands in third place globally after South Africa and Colombia in terms of its murder rate.[45]

TABLE 10.3 Russian Federation and United States Crime Statistics

Offenses	Number of Cases Known to Police		Volume of Crime Per 100,000 Inhabitants		Percentage of Offenders Who Are Female		Percentage of Offenders Who Are Juveniles	
	Russia	U.S.	Russia	U.S.	Russia	U.S.	Russia	U.S.
Murder	32,285	15,980	22.43	5.61	11.7	12.5	8.3	10.2
Rape	8,117	90,491	5.64	31.77	1.3	1.2	17.5	16.8
Serious assault	58,469	907,219	40.62	318.55	12.0	20.1	9.3	13.6
Theft (all kinds)	1,141,134	10,835,316	792.71	3,804.58	8.7	29.2	21.0	29.7
Robbery and violent theft	214,319	422,921	148.88	148.50	7.0	10.1	22.6	23.6
Theft of motor cars	47,448	1,226,457	32.96	430.64		16.4		32.7
Fraud	69,348		48.17		39.4		2.6	
Drug offenses	189,576		131.69					

Source: Data are from Interpol/International Crime Statistics at http://www.interpol.int/Public/Statistics/ICS/downloadList.asp.

Note: Figures are based on national crime statistics. For Russia, the figures are from 2002 statistics, based on 143,954,391 inhabitants; for the United States, the figures are from 2001 statistics, based on 284,796,887 inhabitants. Figures on fraud and drug offenses were not available for the United States.

In contrast, rape, serious assault, and theft of all kinds are more frequent in the United States than in Russia. According to 2000 data, Russia ranked as follows:

- Nineteenth in the world in the number of car thefts (the United States is first)
- First in the world for number of embezzlements (the United States is third)
- Seventh in the world for number of frauds (the United States is second)
- Second in the world for number of murders (the United States is sixth)
- Tenth in the world for number of rapes (the United States is first)
- Fifth in the world for number of robberies (the United States is second)

The figures given here represent convictions and may be better indicators of the prevalence of law enforcement and people's willingness to report crimes than of the actual prevalence of the crimes themselves.[46]

Accurate data on drug use in Russia is hard to find. Unquestionably, Russia has seen an increase in drug use since the demise of the Soviet Union, although evidence of a substantial drug problem among Soviet soldiers serving in Afghanistan had emerged in the 1980s.* Drug use appears to be the most frequent among young people with above-average family incomes, but a large number of homemakers and workers also use drugs. As in other countries, the use of illegal narcotics is linked to crime. Young adults and juveniles are primarily the ones who commit registered crimes in Russia, as well as in other parts of the world, and males are the most apt to perpetrate violent crimes.

Organized crime (the mafia) also exists in Russia. The term *mafia* covers a broad range of people and diverse organizations. It includes local "thugs," who demand and receive protection money from businesses, and sophisticated money-launderers employed in the country's top banks. The diversity of post-Soviet organized crime is one of its hallmarks (Shelley 2003, 108). Crime groups may specialize in drugs or arms trafficking, but most are involved in several activities, including legitimate holdings and investments. Organized crime activity in Russia is marked by significant political involvement, and corruption in the judiciary remains a serious problem.

Weak law-enforcement agencies, the disorientations of the transition, and legacies of distrust from the Soviet era all make it difficult to stem the tide of organized and individual crimes. The crime figures presented in Table 10.3 do not accurately reflect the extent of the problem of crime in Russian society because they do not measure corruption in government, theft of government property, and various aspects of organized crime that siphon off the resources of the state. The people who are actually prosecuted for crimes generally come from the lowest economic and social levels of Russian society, while the more privileged members of society, who also commit crimes, often

---

*The United Nations Office for Drug Control and Crime Prevention has given Russia millions of dollars to help to reduce drug trafficking in the Central Asian region.

enjoy immunity, are able to manipulate the system, or bribe themselves out of arrest and prosecution. The pervasiveness of organized crime and violent crime, such as contract killings, means that crime is not only a social problem but also a problem that constrains Russia's economic and political development and potential.

CONCLUSION

In addition to the policy challenges of economic reform, foreign relations, health issues, and crime and corruption, Russia is confronted with other problems, including environmental degradation. Space constraints limit our ability to cover more policy areas here, but it should be noted that the Soviet legacy affects these other areas as well. Old problems are combined with new challenges associated with the breakup of the USSR, new defense issues, and expanding globalization. Now that Putin has brought a degree of stability to Russia, the prospects for addressing both old and new policy challenges have improved. As success is achieved, it is reflected in new levels of economic and social development as well as increased national security.

Key Terms

Command economy
Gosplan
Incremental model
Multipolarity
Near Abroad
Policy discourse

Price liberalization
Privatization
Rational model
Shock therapy
Warsaw Pact

Critical Thinking Questions

1. Compare and contrast the rational and incremental models. Which model is better? Which model is seen more often?
2. Why did the Soviet Union change decision models? Did it help with economic and social problems?
3. What are the main factors affecting Russian economic reform? How has each one impacted Russia's recovery?
4. What were the causes of the Cold War? Why did it last so long?
5. What effect does the CIS have on Russian foreign and economic policies?
6. What would be the ramifications of CIS countries joining NATO? Of Russia joining?
7. What are the main contributing factors to the poor health of Russia's population? What steps could improve the situation?

Suggested Reading

Brown, Archie, and Michael Kaser, eds. *Soviet Policy for the 1980s*. Bloomington: Indiana University Press, 1982.

Cutler, Robert M. "The Formation of Soviet Foreign Policy: Organizational and Cognitive Perspectives," *World Politics* 34(3) (1982): 418–36.

Hough, Jerry F. *The Logic of Economic Reform in Russia*. Washington, D.C.: Brookings Institution Press, 2001.

Petro, Nicoai N., and Alvin Z. Rubinstein. *Russian Foreign Policy: From Empire to Nation-State*. New York: Longman, 1997.

Wegren, Stephen K, ed. *Russia's Policy Challenges: Security and Stability and Development*. Armonk, N.Y.: M. E. Sharpe, 2003.

Zimmerman, William. *The Russian People and Foreign Policy: Russian Elite and Mass Perspectives, 1993–2000*. Princeton, N.J.: Princeton University Press, 2002.

Websites of Interest

Cold War International History Project:
http://wwics.si.edu/index.cfm?topic_id=1409&fuseaction=topics.home

The Crisis of Russian Health Care and Attempts at Reform:
http://www.rand.org/publications/CF/CF124/CF124.chap5.html

Adult Mortality in Russia:
http://www.lshtm.ac.uk/ecohost/projects/mortality-russia.htm

CHAPTER 11

Lithuania

G EOGRAPHICALLY, Lithuania sits along the eastern shore of the Baltic Sea and shares borders with Russia, Belarus, Poland, and Latvia (see map on the inside cover). The capital city is Vilnius. The land area measures 65,200 square kilometers, which is slightly larger than the U.S. state of West Virginia, and its estimated population is 3,596,617.* This population size is very close to that of Connecticut or Oklahoma.

Lithuania is the largest and most populous of the Baltic States. Within the Soviet Union, the **Baltic republics** of Lithuania, Estonia, and Latvia were the most vociferous in their demands for independence during the Gorbachev era. Although free from Russian control between 1918 and 1939, the Soviet Union forcefully incorporated these republics in 1940. After defying Soviet authority through a series of demonstrations, Lithuania declared independence from the Soviet Union in March 1990. This declaration was not recognized by Moscow until September 1991, when all three Baltic republics regained their political independence. The Baltic States joined the European Union in 2004.

HISTORY OF INCORPORATION INTO AND INDEPENDENCE FROM THE USSR

The Grand Duchy of Lithuania, established in the thirteenth century, expanded southward and eastward during the fourteenth century. By the sixteenth century, the Commonwealth of Lithuania and Poland (established by the Union of Lubin in 1569) comprised one of Europe's larger empires. The sixteenth century witnessed rapid agricultural and cultural development but also a series of wars,

*July 2005 estimate by the U.S. Central Intelligence Agency.

which ultimately led to the defeat of the Commonwealth. Russia, Prussia, and Austria partitioned the Commonwealth in 1772, 1792, and 1795. In the third partition, in 1795, the Lithuanian–Polish state disappeared from the map of Europe; the Russian Empire annexed the Grand Duchy of Lithuania.

Lithuanian uprisings against Russian rule, which occurred in 1830, 1831, and 1863, were suppressed and followed by increased repression of Lithuania's language and culture. The attempted Russification of Lithuanian culture included the closure of Vilnius University in 1832, an 1864 ban on the printing of Lithuanian books using Latin characters, and the suppression of the Roman Catholic Church. Despite repression in the nineteenth century, Vilnius became a leading center for Jewish culture.

Modern Lithuanian nationalism arose during the nineteenth century as a reaction against both Polish and Russian domination. After World War I and with the collapse of the Russian Empire, Lithuania claimed independence on February 16, 1918. Lithuanians fought to secure this independence against Russians, Germans, and Poles. In July 1920, Vladimir Lenin signed a peace treaty with Lithuania that renounced Russia's claims to territory and recognized the Lithuanian state. At the end of 1920, however, Poland annexed Vilnius and the surrounding region, which it held until World War II.

The constitution adopted in 1922 declared Lithuania a parliamentary republic. In 1926, however, Antanas Smetona overthrew the democratic government and established a dictatorship. According to the secret protocol to the 1939 **Soviet–German Non-Aggression Pact** (also called the Molotov-Ribbentrop Pact), Lithuania came under the Soviet sphere of influence. Troops entered Lithuania in June 1940 and in August the USSR officially incorporated the country. Vilnius, then occupied by Soviet forces, was returned to Lithuania. Within months, the main sectors of the economy were nationalized. In mid-June 1941, Soviet authorities deported, imprisoned, or killed thousands upon thousands of Lithuanians. Shortly thereafter, German forces invaded. From late June 1941 to 1944, the Germans occupied Lithuania. The occupiers repressed the Lithuanian people and sent many to forced labor camps in Germany. The Nazis massacred an estimated 200,000 to 240,000 of Lithuania's Jews.

In the summer of 1944, the Red Army reclaimed the territory from Germany and the Soviet Union annexed Lithuania. Opposition to Soviet rule after 1944 led to mass deportations and the killing of hundreds of thousands of Lithuanians. (For information on the number of casualties, see Vardys [1990].) Armed resistance to foreign occupation and to **Sovietization** lasted into the 1950s. **Dissident activity**, which rejected Russian domination and control, was present in Lithuania throughout the post–World War II period.

Soviet rule in Lithuania displayed the standard features of authoritarianism. The Communist Party held the monopoly of power, the management of the economy was centralized, and agriculture was collectivized. After initial declines in production, industry and agriculture grew rapidly, in part because equipment, raw materials, and fuel were allocated to the republic by central planners in

Moscow. Urbanization increased from 39 percent in 1959 to 68 percent in 1989. All three Baltic republics experienced a rise in economic well-being during the 1960s, but the impressive growth in productivity ended in the 1970s. The period also witnessed immigration of Slavic workers and managers. Meanwhile, membership in the Communist Party grew. Those who were looking for career advancement realized that party membership provided increased opportunities within the economic, political, and even cultural life of the country.

Religion was brutally repressed and efforts to defend the Catholic Church provided a foundation for a resistance movement that has never disappeared. Lithuanian Catholic priests helped support long-standing anti-Soviet dissidence. Underground publications (called **samizdat**) criticized Soviet policies, such as controls over seminaries and textbooks, and provided an independent source of information for the population on a variety of topics. The Lithuanian intelligentsia, especially writers and artists, continued to demand greater freedom of creative expression and protection of the Lithuanian language and traditions.

By the 1980s, a coming together of grievances and changes associated with Soviet rule led to a spectacular mobilization of the Lithuanian people in support of independence from the Soviet Union. Lithuania, along with Estonia, was the most determined proponent of independence among the republics in the Soviet Union. Prevalent in the minds of Lithuanians was the memory of the forced annexation into the Soviet Union in 1940.

Mikhail Gorbachev launched his perestroika initiative soon after becoming General Secretary of the Communist Party in March 1985. In July 1986, the Communist Party of the Soviet Union (CPSU) and the Supreme Soviet of the USSR adopted a decree that decentralized authority by increasing the responsibility of the fifteen union republic governments.[1] A year later, in July 1987, Councils of Ministers within the republics received near total authority to plan economic and social development and to allocate investments.

Gorbachev, hoping to revive and rejuvenate the Soviet system, called on the citizens of the Soviet Union to mobilize in support of his perestroika initiative. In response, people living in the Baltic republics organized **popular fronts**. The Lithuanian Movement for Perestroika (**Sajudis**) held its founding congress in October 1988. The movement supported Gorbachev's policies, but at the same time promoted national issues such as the restoration of Lithuanian as an "official" language. Demands included disclosure of "secrets" associated with Stalin's rule and protection of the environment. The movement elected Vytautas Landsbergis, a professor of musicology who was not a member of the Communist Party, as its chair. Also in October 1988, a reformer, Algirdas Brazauskas, became First Secretary of the Lithuanian Communist Party, replacing Lithuania's old guard communist leadership.*

---

*As was the case in many republics of the Soviet Union, the first secretary of the republic-level Communist Party was always a native Lithuanian, but the second secretary (since 1956) was a native Russian.

As part of Mikhail Gorbachev's democratization reforms, elections were held in March 1989 to the **USSR Congress of People's Deputies**. The Lithuanian delegates elected to this congress were primarily members of Sajudis and others were also pro-independence in orientation. Inspired by Sajudis, the Lithuanian Supreme Soviet declared sovereignty in May 1989 by passing constitutional amendments that asserted the supremacy of Lithuanian laws over Soviet legislation. In addition, the Supreme Soviet annulled the 1940 decisions that made Lithuania part of the USSR and legalized a multiparty system.

Conservative CPSU leaders in Moscow, led by Yegor Ligachev, reacted strongly against these changes and publicly criticized those party officials who had stirred up, or who had been responsive to, nationalist feelings in the Baltic republics. Nonetheless, the central government proceeded with reforms, granting the republics a large degree of economic independence. When the USSR government offered leaders more authority and autonomy in managing their affairs, the Lithuanian response was to demand, without ambivalence, full independence. In December 1989, the Brazauskas-led Lithuania Communist Party declared itself formally independent of the CPSU. An even more critical step occurred in February 1990 when elections were held for a new Lithuanian Supreme Soviet. The elected representatives to this republic-level Supreme Soviet demonstrated their courage when they declared outright independence on March 11, 1990. In addition, these representatives elected from among their membership the chairman of Sajudis, Vytautas Landsbergis, as the new Lithuanian president (see Box 11.1). In the months following this declaration, more than five million signatures were gathered from all over the world demanding the recognition of Lithuania's independence from the USSR.*

The USSR Communist Party leadership used economic, political, and military pressure to keep Lithuania within the union. After proclaiming that the Lithuanian declaration of independence violated the Soviet Constitution and was therefore illegal, Gorbachev imposed an economic embargo on Lithuania. He appealed to the Lithuanians to remain part of the Soviet Union and help him implement his reform program (Goldman 1994, 51). In January 1991, Soviet forces seized a central publishing house and TV broadcast tower in Lithuania's capital city, killing seventeen civilians and injuring hundreds. The event served to solidify Lithuanian opposition to Soviet rule. In a referendum held in February 1991, 90 percent of the participants voted in favor of an independent, democratic Lithuania.

It was not until after the failed August attempt to overthrow Mikhail Gorbachev that the revamped Soviet government conceded the independence of Lithuania, Estonia, and Latvia on September 6, 1991. Lithuania, Estonia, and Latvia were released from the Soviet Union on the basis of a decree issued by the State Council and were quickly recognized as independent countries within

*This petition was acknowledged in March 1993 in the *Guinness Book of World Records* as the world's largest petition.

BOX 11.1 LITHUANIA'S INDEPENDENCE MOVEMENT

June–October 1988	Formation of popular fronts
November 1988	Estonian Supreme Soviet declaration of sovereignty (the right to veto All-Union laws)
March 1989	Elections to the new Congress of People's Deputies (multicandidate elections) held
May 1989	Lithuanian Supreme Soviet adopts sovereignty laws
June 1989	Latvian Supreme Soviet passes sovereignty resolution
December 1989	Lithuanian branch of the Communist Party withdraws from the CPSU; Estonia follows in March 1990 and Latvia in April 1990
December 1989–March 1990	Elections held to republic-level Supreme Soviets
March 11, 1990	Lithuanian Supreme Soviet declares independence from the Soviet Union; Estonia declares independence through a transition period, and an independent Communist Party of Estonia is created
March 1990	Gorbachev elected first president of the USSR (indirectly by the USSR Congress of People's Deputies)
March 1990	USSR Constitution amended to remove the clause that confirmed the guiding role of the Communist Party
April 1990	Law adopted: "On the Procedure for Solving the Question of the Union Republics Secession from the USSR"
May 1990	Yeltsin elected chairman of the RSFSR Supreme Soviet
May 1990	Latvia establishes transition period to independence
June 1990	The RSFSR (Russian) Congress of People's Deputies votes for sovereignty
July 1990	The Supreme Soviets of Ukraine and Belarus declare sovereignty
December 1990	USSR Foreign Minister Edward Shevardnadze resigns and warns of an impending dictatorship; Gennady Yanayev appointed vice president
January 1991	In attempting to take control of radio and TV stations in Vilnius, Soviet troops kill some Lithuanians
February 1991	Lithuania holds a referendum on independence
March 1991	Gorbachev sponsors an All-Union referendum on preserving the Soviet Union
June 1991	Yeltsin elected president of the RSFSR by direct popular vote
August 1991	Planned signing by Russia, Belarus, Kazakhstan, Tajikistan, and Uzbekistan of the new Union Treaty
August 1991	Coup attempt in Moscow
September 6, 1991	Soviet Union recognizes Lithuania's, Latvia's, and Estonia's independence
September 1991	Lithuania's Declaration of Independence is recognized by the world community
October 25, 1992	Lithuania adopts a new constitution

the international arena. Lithuania's independence received full international recognition when the country joined the United Nations on September 17, 1991. The full dissolution of the Soviet Union occurred in December 1991.

THE DYNAMICS OF A SUCCESSFUL INDEPENDENCE MOVEMENT

The independence of Lithuania represents both a lengthy historical process and a confluence of critical events that came together in the late 1980s. From the early days of their rule, the Bolsheviks realized that to control the peripheral regions of the country, they would have to grant concessions to the national minority populations. During Lenin's leadership, the union republics were allowed extensive linguistic and cultural autonomy. With the signing of the **Union Treaty** of 1922 (and its eventual inclusion in the Soviet Constitution of 1924), national minorities were formally granted the right to self-determination, including the right to secede from the Soviet Union. In reality, however, the authority of the republics was restricted by the lack of independent taxing power, by subordination to an All-Union budget and joint union-republic ministries, and by the oversight of the CPSU. The December 1991 breakup of the Soviet Union was the culmination of a long-running debate over the appropriate division of power between Moscow and the republics.

The demise of the Soviet Union resulted in part from CPSU General Secretary Gorbachev's policies of perestroika and glasnost. Determined calls from the non-Russian nationality groups for the transfer of decision-making authority to republic-level governments, and the Kremlin's relatively benign response, contributed to a perception that Moscow would not use force—would not employ its formidable coercive tools—to smash the rising challenges to Soviet authority. With the lack of a punitive response from the Kremlin, nationalist leaders found it easy to convince followers that the open expression of grievances was physically safe. Through repeated experience, a convention of participation in anti-state demonstrations began to develop. Gorbachev's glasnost initiative allowed for the newly open and relatively uncensored electronic and print mass media to become a critical factor in increasing participation in demonstrations against the Soviet state. Through the mass media, people living in Lithuania were given access to images of pro-independence nationalist success. Pictures of hundreds of thousands of people filling the streets, together with a lack of a violent response from the authorities, provided an incentive to participate—a desire to be a part of a great historical transformation. Public opinion polls published in the press provided evidence that alienation from the regime was widespread.

These behavioral changes and emotive forces, however, could not have coalesced into a successful movement without the emergence of national leadership and the development of organizational structures. Ironically, the organizational framework of the Communist Party provided structural support for the nationalist movements. Many communists either gave up their party membership or, simultaneously, became members of both the party and the popular fronts. In some cases, former Communist Party members became leaders of the national front movements. Nationalist movements in the Baltic republics were able to absorb elites from state and party structures, as well as to recruit members of the national intelligentsia who had been displaced through Russification policies. By providing positive examples and by making personal sacrifices in support of the cause, the leaders themselves contributed to the strength of the movements.

Church buildings, which had historically provided a base for resistance to Soviet domination, became convenient meeting places and sites for political discussions. Religion provided another common thread of group identity and solidarity, together with an institutional focus. The language issue also became a powerful symbol that supported the cause of national separatism. In January 1989, Lithuanian was declared the state language of the republic and the teaching of Russian to children in kindergarten and the early grades was discontinued (Misiuna 1990, 219).

Glasnost and perestroika provided the Baltic people with an opportunity to reassert their national distinctiveness. Language, religion, culture, and concerns over environmental degradation became unifying forces and provided symbols for mobilizing the people. A widespread concern existed in many republics about the ecological damage that had occurred with the rapid industrialization process, and nationalist leaders were readily inclined to tie the environmental destruction of their homelands to Russian hegemony. As the national front movements gained strength, the leaders could offer more specific incentives for support; for example, they could offer the possibility of land grants and voting rights to future citizens in exchange for an oath of support. The Baltic States could point to their recent, inter-war period of independence and argue that this period demonstrated their potential for self-sufficiency.

The 1989 collapse of communism in Eastern Europe was also a critical event because it contributed to the belief that freedom from Soviet domination was a real possibility. The proximity of the Baltic republics to the West contributed to Estonia's, Latvia's, and Lithuania's belief that they could readily enter the world trading system. Indeed, a prevalent belief among the Baltic people was that their underdevelopment, as compared to Western Europe's, was directly attributable to their involvement in the Soviet system. The legitimacy of rule by Moscow decreased with prolonged economic decline, failed social policies, corruption, and incompetence on the part of the central leaders.

The dilemma, which culminated in the August 1991 coup attempt, was that although perestroika and glasnost appeared necessary to revive the system, the policies also allowed for the open expression of national interests, an opportunity for assertions of regional autonomy, and eventually outright demands for independence. The following were all stages in a center-periphery power struggle that resulted in a fundamental restructuring of the political system:

- The extended negotiation and the presentation of a draft of the new All-Union Treaty by Gorbachev between February and July of 1991
- The attempted coup of August 1991 by hard-line communists who opposed the treaty
- Gorbachev's effort to salvage the arrangement between August and November of 1991
- The establishment by the presidents of the Russian Federation (RF), Ukraine, and Belarus of a Commonwealth of Independent States (CIS) in December 1991

Decentralization as devolution by definition entails a substantial expansion of peripheral authority, especially the authority to raise and expend revenues; but in a divided society, decentralization can intensify rather than diffuse the centrifugal tendencies inherent in the system. This is particularly true when decentralization provides a political base for radicalized counter-elites, as in the Baltic States.

When Lithuania finally did achieve independence in 1991, the country was well-positioned to establish statehood given its relatively recent independence between World War I and World War II, homogeneous population, and proximity to the European Union (EU). The new government moved quickly to apply for membership in Western European institutions, most notably the North Atlantic Treaty Organization (NATO) and the European Union. Russia withdrew the last of its military forces from the country in August 1993. Lithuania became a member of the Council of Europe in May 1993 and, in 1995, became an associate member of the EU. By 2001, Lithuania was a member of the World Trade Organization (WTO). In 2004, Lithuania became a member of the European Union and NATO. In spite of its European leanings, Lithuania's relations with Moscow have been good.

THE NATURE OF SOCIETY AND POLITICAL CULTURE

Lithuania is the largest of the Baltic countries, with a population of approximately 3.6 million. Russians comprise about 6 percent of the population (see Table 1.1, p. 3). Because Lithuania remained agricultural into the 1950s, it did not experience as high in-migration of Russians as did Latvia and Estonia. According to the last Soviet census in 1989, just 52 percent of Estonia's population were ethnic Estonians, and 61.5 percent of Latvia's population were ethnic Latvians. In contrast, Lithuanians accounted for 79.6 percent of their republic's population in 1989.

The most recent data (the 2001 census) describe Lithuania's population as follows: Lithuanians 83.4 percent, Polish 6.7 percent, Russians 6.3 percent, and other or unspecified 3.6 percent. After independence, only limited out-migration of ethnic Russians occurred, except for those associated with the military. Relations between Russians and Lithuanians are good in Lithuania, in part because of the inclusive nature of Lithuania's citizenship laws. Residents who were not ethnic Lithuanians have been allowed to become citizens with relatively few conditions. Because ethnic Lithuanians were a clear majority in the country, they granted all permanent residents of the republic the chance to gain citizenship in 1989, regardless of nationality.

Relations with Lithuania's Polish minority have been somewhat more tense. During the Soviet era, Poles in Lithuania had their own Polish schools, a newspaper, and Polish radio and TV programs. When language laws were changed in January 1989 to make Lithuanian the state language and to require its use in official business, education, and social spheres, the Polish began to organize in the face of what appeared to them to be extreme nationalism. As a result, the implementation of the 1989 language law was delayed until 1995 in those regions where non-Lithuanian speakers made up the majority of the population. Ultimately, the law was actually changed to permit equal use of minority languages in local administrations. The state provided funding to cultural organizations of ethnic minorities and guaranteed minorities the right to an education in their native languages.

The vast majority of ethnic Lithuanians follow the Roman Catholic religion, which has played a critical role in Lithuanian politics and society. The delayed entry of Lithuania into the Soviet Union constrained efforts of Soviet authorities to destroy religion. Once Lithuania did enter the union, the authorities closed churches and persecuted nuns and priests. Still, even during the height of repression, it is estimated that at least half of Lithuanians were practicing Catholics, with 50 percent of the children baptized (Carrère d'Encausse 1979, 224).

According to a countrywide survey conducted in 1997, 80 percent of the Lithuanian population identified themselves as believers. Among women, 88 percent were believers; among men, 73 percent were believers. Among these believers, 87 percent—men and women combined—were Roman Catholic (5 percent Russian Orthodox).[*] A March 2003 survey demonstrated the consistency in these affiliations over time.[†] According to that poll, 79 percent of Lithuanians identified themselves as Roman Catholic, 3 percent as Orthodox believers, and less than 1 percent as Protestant. Only 11 percent said that they did not have a religious affiliation; the remaining portion had some other affiliation.

POLITICAL PARTIES AND POLITICAL PARTICIPATION

Political parties first emerged in Lithuania toward the end of the nineteenth century. The Lithuanian Social Democratic Party (LSDP) was founded in 1896, while

[*]The survey was conducted with funding from the National Science Foundation for research on political change in post-Soviet societies. Project directors were Arthur Miller, William Reisinger, and Vicki Hesli.
[†]This survey was conducted by Baltic Surveys, Ltd., under the direction of Rasa Alisauskiene.

the Christian Democrats were founded in 1902. After Lithuania declared independence from the Russian Empire in 1918, the political landscape from 1919 through 1926 was structured by political party competition between two major blocs: The right-wing was dominated by the Christian Democratic Coalition and the left-wing was dominated by the Peasant People's Party and the LSDP. This competition among political parties gradually ended after the 1926 coup d'état.

A major element of Lithuania's democratic transition during the late 1980s and early 1990s was the reemergence of political parties and a multiparty system. After 1991, Lithuania's political landscape was again dominated by two political blocs: the Social Democratic Coalition and the Homeland Union. The Social Democratic Coalition is headed by Algirda Brazauskas, who was reelected party chairman in May 2003. The Social Democrats were known previously as the Lithuanian Democratic Labour Party (LDLP)*, a restructured version of the former Communist Party of Lithuania.

The Homeland Union emerged originally from Sajudis under the leadership of Vytautas Landsbergis. When formed in November 1992 as a union of parliamentary factions supporting Landsbergis, the Concord for the Homeland included Sajudis, the Union of Lithuanian Political Prisoners, the Citizen's Charter, the Lithuanian Christian Democrat Party, the Democrat Party, the National Union, and the Independence Party. In February 1993, the name was changed to Union for the Rebirth of Homeland and changed again in May 1993 to Homeland Union/Lithuanian Conservatives or HU/LC. In May 2003, a congress of the party elected former Premier Andrius Kubilius as its new chairman and again changed the name to Homeland Union (Conservatives, Christian Democrats, and Freedom Fighters).

The Homeland Union cannot be easily classified as left or right. Party leadership clearly has been suspicious of the intentions of Russia and the CIS, and it has steadfastly supported land reform and privatization. The Homeland Union government, however, established a social welfare state by supporting workers, pensioners, and students. In addition, it continued subsidies to industry and to other organizations.

Prior to elections, individual parties regularly form coalitions. For the 2000 elections, the leftist parties formed a single slate around the Lithuanian Social Democratic Party of ex-President Brazauskas. Likewise the Lithuanian Conservatives coalesced around former President Landsbergis. Arguably the good showing of the Social–Democratic Coalition in 2000, as compared with the Homeland Union/Lithuanian Conservatives, had more to do with the greater popularity of Brazauskas at that time in comparison with Landsbergis than with any major policy differences between the two party blocs.

Lithuania does not have a stable political party system. The percentage of the population that is a member of any political party is very small—about 3

*During the post-Soviet period, Russians in Lithuania have tended to vote for the LDLP, which is seen as being the most sympathetic to their interests.

percent in 1996 (Krupavicius 1998, 485). The inability of Lithuania's political parties to establish strong membership bases has been demonstrated by volatility in their electoral support. New parties appear before each election and existing parties change their names and leadership. One factor that contributes to this phenomenon is that members of the **Seimas** (the Lithuanian parliament) are obligated to cast their votes as directed by the party faction. Thus, the only option a deputy has if he or she disagrees with the party position is to leave the party faction. At the same time, participation in local elections, and in the proportional representation (PR) portion of national elections, requires a party endorsement, so politicians launch new parties or join an existing party willing to change its name or accept new leadership.

THE MAIN CONSTITUTIONAL STRUCTURES AND GOVERNMENT PROCESSES

Lithuania's constitution was adopted by referendum on October 25, 1992, the same day as the first post-independence parliamentary election was held. Voters approved a constitution that represented a compromise between those who favored a strong presidency and those who favored a powerful parliament. The 1992 constitution replaced a constitution from 1938, which had been reinstated when Lithuania gained independence from the USSR.

According to the Constitution of the Republic of Lithuania, the powers of the state are exercised jointly by three branches of government: the President of the Republic and the Government (the executive branch), the Seimas (the legislative branch), and the Judiciary. In terms of the actual distribution of powers, Lithuania is a parliamentary republic with some presidential features.

Lithuania's Presidency

Lithuania's presidency is constitutionally weaker than the Russian presidency described in Chapter 6. The President of the Republic has the power to issue decrees, but these become valid only with the signature of the prime minister or another appropriate minister. According to Article 84 of the Lithuanian Constitution, the President of the Republic, as the head of state, also has the power to do the following:

- Sign and promulgate laws enacted by the Seimas or refer them back to the Seimas
- Appoint the prime minister to be approved by the Seimas
- Appoint or dismiss individual ministers on the recommendation of the prime minister

- Propose Supreme Court and Constitutional Court judge candidates to the Seimas, as well as candidates for State Controller and Chairperson of the Board of the Bank of Lithuania
- Settle basic foreign policy issues and, together with the government, implement foreign policy
- Sign international treaties and submit them to the Seimas for ratification
- Appoint or dismiss, on the approval of the Seimas, the Chief Commander of the Army and the Head of the Security Service
- Declare states of emergency and submit these decisions to the next sitting of the Seimas for approval

The president of Lithuania is elected by popular vote for a five-year term, and the same person cannot be elected president for more than two consecutive terms. A candidate for the position of president can be elected in a single round of voting if at least half of the eligible voters participate, and if the candidate receives more than half of the votes of all those who participate in the election. If less than half of the registered voters participate in the election, the candidate who receives the greatest number of votes, but no less than one-third of the votes of those who participated in the election, becomes president. If no candidate receives the required proportion of the votes in the first round, a runoff election is held between the two candidates who received the greatest number of votes. Whoever receives the most votes in the second-round election becomes president.

The first directly elected president, Algirdas Brazauskas, had served previously as First Secretary of the Lithuanian Communist Party (LCP). In December 1990, the LCP was reorganized into the Lithuanian Democratic Labour Party with Brazauskas as chairman. After the parliamentary elections of 1992, he became chairman of the Seimas. Upon being directly elected to the presidency by the people in February 1993, Brazauskas was obliged by the constitution to suspend his party membership, so the party's chairmanship was taken over by Adolfas Slezevicius. Valdemaras Katkus was elected to replace Brazauskas as Chairman of the Seimas at the end of February 1993, and Slezevicius was approved by the Seimas as prime minister in March 1993.

Brazauskas's opponent in the 1993 presidential race was Stasys Lozoraitis, who had served as Lithuania's ambassador to the United States. Only two candidates, Brazauskas and Lozoraitis, secured the 20,000 signatures needed to be listed on the ballot. Vytautas Landsbergis decided not to run and other candidates of the smaller parties withdrew in favor of Lozoraitis. Although Lozoraitis presented himself as an independent candidate, many people viewed him as being associated with Sajudis. Lozoraitis, because he had lived abroad for much of his life, was vulnerable to charges that he lacked an in-depth knowledge of Lithuanian affairs.

The main issues of this first presidential election were the economy and relations with Russia. Both candidates swore to develop Lithuania's full independence, both insisted on the removal of Russian troops stationed in the country, and both promised a free market economy. Brazauskas, however, prioritized relations with Russia and also promised a more moderate pace of reform than had been pursued by the Sajudis government before him. He promised to restore productive capacity and to hold down unemployment while staying within the guidelines set by the International Monetary Fund (IMF) and the World Bank for loans. In winning the February 15, 1993, election, Brazauskas received 60 percent of the national vote, gaining majorities in all of Lithuania's raions (districts), except for the Kaunas Raion. Turnout was 78 percent.[2]

A political realignment occurred when the next regularly scheduled parliamentary elections were held in 1996. The LDLP was defeated by Landsbergis's Homeland Union/Lithuanian Conservatives and President Brazauskas signaled that he would not run for a second term. In the run-up to Lithuania's presidential election of December 1997, Brazauskas endorsed former Prosecutor General Arturas Paulauskas. In the first round of the presidential election held on December 21, 1997, seven candidates were listed on the ballot. Paulauskas finished first with 45.3 percent of the vote, ahead of Valdas Adamkus with 27.9 percent. Vytautas Landsbergis finished in third place with 15.9 percent of the vote. At the time of the election, Landsbergis—former chairman of Sajudis and former president of Lithuania, elected by the Supreme Soviet in 1990—was serving as chairman of the Homeland Union/Lithuanian Conservatives (elected in 1993 and 1995) and as parliamentary speaker.

Because no candidate won the necessary 50 percent of the vote for a first-round victory, the two top candidates, Paulauskas and Adamkus, competed against each other in a second round of voting on January 4, 1998. In this runoff, the five candidates who were eliminated in the first round, including Landsbergis, switched their support to the eventual winner—Valdas Adamkus. He won the presidency with 50.4 percent of the votes in a narrow victory over Paulauskas, who received 49.6 percent of the votes. Turnout in the first round of voting (December 1997) was 71.5 percent, and it was 73.7 percent in the second round (January 1998).[3]

The media presented Paulauskas as a candidate of the old *nomenklatura*, and highlighted the fact that his father had been a colonel in the KGB. Adamkus, in contrast, had spent most of his life living in the United States, having emigrated there in 1949 to escape the Soviet occupation of Lithuania. After working for twenty-seven years for the U.S. Environmental Protection Agency in the Chicago area, he moved back in 1997. The victory of Adamkus in 1998 was interpreted as a statement by the Lithuanian people that they preferred a strongly pro-Western foreign policy.

For the 2002 presidential elections, seventeen candidates were listed on the ballot. Because none of them received a majority of the votes in the first round, a

TABLE 11.1 Results of First- and Second-Round Voting in Lithuania's 2002 and 2004 Presidential Elections

Candidate	Political Party	First Round December 22, 2002	Second Round January 5, 2003	First Round June 13, 2004	Second Round June 27, 2004
Valdas Adamkus (incumbent president)	Independent	35.53[a]	45.29	31.14	52.65
Kazimira Prunskiene (member of the Seimas)	Union of Peasants and New Democracy (VNDPS)	5.04		21.25	47.35
Rolandas Paksas (member of the Seimas)	Liberal Democratic Party (LDP)	19.66	54.71		
Petras Austrevicius	Independent			19.30	
Vilija Blinkeviciute	New Union (Social Liberals)			16.45	
Ceslovas Jursenas	Lithuanian Social Democratic Party (LSDP)			11.85	
Arturas Paulauskas (Chairman of the Seimas)	New Union (Social Liberals)	8.31			
Vytautas Serenas (producer of TV comedy program)	Independent	7.75			
Vytenis Andriukaitis (Vice Chairman of the Seimas)	Lithuanian Social Democratic Party	7.30			
Other candidates combined		16.46			
Turnout		**53.92%**	**52.65%**	**48.40%**	**52.46%**

Source: The data are from the Central Electoral Committee of the Republic of Lithuania at http://www.vrk.lt/2002/Prezidentas/rezultatai/reza.htm-14+2.htm; see also "Elections Around the World" at http://www.electionworld.org.

[a]All columns show the percentage of total number of votes cast.

second-round runoff election was held between incumbent President Adamkus and Rolandas Paksas on January 5, 2003 (see Table 11.1). Paksas, who had served twice as prime minister and twice as mayor of Vilnius (Lithuania's capital city), came in second in the first round of voting, but won the second round.

Analysts had predicted that incumbent President Adamkus would win a second term given the invitations that Lithuania had received to join the EU and NATO; the economy's growth between 2000 and 2002; and the backing that he had among the major political parties, including the Homeland Union. The victory of Paksas, therefore, must be explained by reference to other factors. Adamkus's age (seventy-six at the time of the election) was a significant factor that contributed to the victory of Paksas, who was relatively young (47 years old) when elected president in 2002. The low turnout also played a role in the outcome of the elections. Those who were supporters of Adamkus felt certain of his victory and many did not bother to come to the voting booth. Another factor that hurt Adamkus was that he had spent much of his life in the United States and could be portrayed as a foreigner.

The most significant factor in the electoral victory of Paksas, however, was his populist preelection campaign. He had sufficient funds to launch a high-profile campaign, with posters and media coverage throughout the country. Using the slogan "Vote for Change," Paksas presented himself as a political outsider and as a positive new force who could reverse lapses in the government's economic and social policies.[4] He assured the voters that the foreign policy of Lithuania would not change, referring particularly to Lithuania's anticipated ascension to membership in the European Union.

A pilot by training, Paksas's political career had taken off when he was elected mayor of Vilnius. His success in that job led to his appointment as prime minister. He stayed in that job for just a short period because he disagreed with the leadership of the ruling party—Homeland Union/Lithuanian Conservatives. After switching his party affiliation from the HU/LC to the Liberal Union, Paksas was elected to parliament in 2000. He became prime minister again, this time as the head of a **coalition government**. The coalition eventually collapsed, and Paksas not only lost his position in the government but also his position of leadership in the Liberal Union. He joined other members of parliament in forming a new political party called the Liberal Democratic Party.

Paksas entered the presidency with extremely limited support within parliament among Lithuania's main political parties. Indeed, he faced a devastating challenge from parliamentary leaders in the fall of 2003 when allegations of ties between the presidential staff and members of organized crime emerged. A special ad hoc commission was formed to investigate the potential threat to national security stemming from these alleged ties. In late November 2003, demonstrators gathered in Independence Square in Vilnius and called on President Paksas to resign. The main speakers at the rally were former Sajudis and Homeland Union Chairman Vytautas Landsbergis and Liberal and Centre Union chairman and Vilnius's mayor, Arturas Zuokas.[5]

In early December 2003, a special task force (consisting of one member from each of four parliament factions: the Social Democrats, the Social Liberals, the Liberal and Center Unionists, and the Conservatives) recommended that President Paksas be impeached under Article 74 of the Lithuanian Constitution. The relevant section of the constitution states the following: "For gross violation of the Constitution, breach of oath, or upon the disclosure of the commitment of felony, the Seimas may, by three-fifths majority vote of all the Seimas members, remove from office the President of the Republic." Through all of this, Paksas continued to maintain his innocence and declared that he had no intention of resigning.[6] Nonetheless, the Lithuanian parliament voted in April 2004 for **impeachment** of President Paksas and his removal from office. Speaker of the Parliament Arturas Paulauskas became acting president. New elections were held in June 2004, together with the scheduled elections to the European Parliament.

Former President Valdas Adamkus won the June 2004 presidential election. Thus, Lithuanians reinstated their previous (1998) president, who as an incumbent in January 2003 had lost the election to Paksas. Because Adamkus was not able to secure a full 50 percent of the votes in a first round with five candidates, a run-off election was held and Adamkus prevailed with 52 percent of the vote over Kazimira Prunskiene with 48 percent (see Table 11.1). Prunskiene had had a long history within the independence movement, having headed the first Cabinet of Ministers (serving as prime minister) after Lithuania declared independence in March 1990. Algirdas Brazauskas continued as prime minister, having served in the position since July 2001.

To summarize, each of Lithuania's presidential elections has led to a shift in leadership. Contrary to many other post-Soviet states, incumbents have not been successful in their reelection bids. Similar to other post-Soviet states, however, Lithuania has seen conflict between the position of prime minister and the position of president. In Lithuania, this led ultimately to an impeachment by the national parliament of a president. Lithuania represents the first time that a parliament within a post-Soviet state was successful in impeaching a president. As we saw in Russia, although the Duma pursued impeachment proceedings, these came to nothing. The November 2003 resignation of Georgian President Edward Shevardnadze represents another type of conflict, with a successful bid by a parliamentary opposition to unseat the president (see Chapter 13). The Orange Revolution in Ukraine (see Chapter 12) is also an example of conflict between the executive and legislative branches of government, which appears to be an unavoidable by-product of the establishment of new democratic institutions and jockeying for power among political elites.

Legislative Institutions

Article 55 of the constitution establishes the Seimas as the representative institution for the people. The Seimas is a **unicameral parliament** and membership is constitutionally set at 141 deputies. The Seimas is elected partly through single-member districts (SMD), 71 seats, and partly through a proportional representation party-list system, 70 seats, on an electoral cycle of every four years. Thus, voters cast two ballots—one for a representative from their district and one for a party on a national list. To gain any of the 70 PR seats, a party must win at least 5 percent of the vote nationally (coalitions of parties must win 7 percent).* Seats from the PR national list are allocated separately from the results of the SMD elections.

In July 2000, the Lithuanian Seimas passed changes to the election law, eliminating the need for second-round voting in single-mandate elections. Prior to the October 2000 parliamentary elections, a candidate had to win a majority in the constituency in the first round in order to win outright. If not, the two top vote-getters faced a runoff several weeks later. Starting with the 2000 elections, the seventy-one district seats are decided in only a single round, and winners need only a plurality of votes—much like the British and U.S. systems.

The following are the responsibilities of the Seimas as outlined in Article 67 of the constitution:

- Consider and enact amendments to the constitution
- Enact laws
- Approve or reject the candidate for prime minister proposed by the president
- Approve or reject the program of the government submitted by the prime minister
- Express no confidence in the prime minister or individual ministers
- Approve the state budget and supervise the implementation thereof
- Ratify or denounce international treaties and consider other issues of foreign policy
- Impose direct administration and martial law, declare states of emergency, announce mobilization, and adopt decisions to use the armed forces

Also, according to Article 74 of the constitution, by a three-fifths majority vote, the members of Seimas can remove the president from office through impeachment proceedings in cases in which the president has violated the constitution, breached the oath of office, or committed a felony.

Every year, the Seimas convenes for two regular sessions—one in the spring and one in the fall. Legislation (bills) can be proposed by Seimas

*Prior to June 1996, all parties needed 4 percent of the total votes to enter the Seimas, except political organizations representing minorities, which could enter with 2 percent. With the amendments to the electoral law of June 1996, the special threshold for minority ethnic parties was abolished.

members, by the president, and by members of the government. Ordinary citizens also have the **right of legislative initiative**—a draft law can be submitted to the Seimas for consideration if 50,000 citizens sign a petition in support of it.

Laws are adopted if a majority of those Seimas members who participate (vote) in favor of the legislation. Laws come into force after being signed by the president. The president has ten days to sign a law enacted by the Seimas, or the president must refer it back together with relevant reasons for reconsideration. If the president neither signs a law nor refers it back to the Seimas, it can become effective with the signature of the chair of the Seimas. Laws referred back to the Seimas, with amendments and supplements submitted by the president, are enacted when more than half of all the Seimas members vote in the affirmative. If it is a constitutional law, at least three-fifths of all the Seimas members must vote in the affirmative.

Preterm elections to the Seimas can be scheduled by the president if the Seimas fails to adopt a program of the government within thirty days of its presentation, or if the Seimas twice in succession disapproves of the program within sixty days of its initial presentation. Preterm elections can also be held if the Seimas expresses direct no confidence in the government. Seimas members can question the prime minister or a minister, and upon considering the response of the prime minister or minister, the Seimas may decide that the response is not satisfactory, and, by a majority vote of half of all the Seimas members, express no confidence in the prime minister or a minister.

Political party factions play an important role in the operation of the Seimas. Essentially all deputies join factions because these, along with committees, represent the center of legislative activity. Committee chairs (and deputy chairs) are divided up according to the size of the parliamentary factions. Even more significant, an Assembly of Spokespersons of Factions sets the parliamentary agenda and organizes the work of the Seimas. Factional representation on the Assembly of Spokespersons is set by a quota system whereby each faction gets one seat on the assembly for each ten members in the parliamentary faction (Krupavicius 1998, 476).

Legislative Elections

As a republic within the Soviet Union, Lithuania held elections to its Supreme Soviet in February 1990. Although political parties other than the Communist Party were only in the infant stages of development in 1990, the Lithuanian Movement for Perestroika (Sajudis) played a significant role in these elections.[7] The main issue in the 1990 election was Lithuania's bid for independence from the Soviet Union. All candidates associated with Sajudis and many candidates associated with the independent Communist Party of Lithuania supported independence.[8] Candidates supported by Sajudis won the lion's share of the seats in Lithuania's Supreme Soviet in the February elections.* On March 11, 1990, the newly elected Lithuanian Supreme Soviet voted in favor of reaffirming (no one voted against and only six abstained) the republic's 1918 Declaration of Independence.

By the summer of 1992, with the common goal of gaining independence having been achieved, differences among deputies and members of the pro-independence Sajudis led to the boycotting of legislative sessions. The most divisive issue was the attempt by parliamentary head Landsbergis to institute a strong presidency. When the parliament failed to approve his plan, he brought the question to the people in a May 1992 referendum, which failed to receive majority endorsement. After several attempts in parliament to remove the prime minister, Gediminas Vagnorius resigned in July 1992 and new parliamentary elections were scheduled for October.

The successor to the Lithuanian Communist Party, the Lithuanian Democratic Labour Party won the majority of the seats in this first post-independence (October 1992) parliamentary election. The LDLP won 73 of the 141 seats in the Seimas (formerly the Lithuanian Supreme Soviet) (see Table 11.2)[†] The significance of these elections was that the nationalist forces of Landsbergis suffered a crushing defeat, while the former communists, as experienced managers and adroit politicians led by Brazauskas, staged an amazing comeback. Support for the former communists did not represent a return to communism but rather disappointment in Sajudis and unfulfilled expectations. In the period immediately following independence, the popularity of Sajudis dropped as a result of political infighting, a severe economic crisis caused by the disruption of trade ties with the former Soviet republics, and worsening international relations with neighboring countries. Sajudis paid the price for the downward slide in the economy, their leadership had made some mistakes, and Brazauskas himself was very popular. Shortly after, in February 1993, Brazauskas won the presidency.

Within a few years, however, popular support for the LDLP government declined, in part because the government's attempt to pursue policies favored by the IMF contributed to economic difficulties for the general population. Allegations of widespread corruption and the alleged illegal privatization of many state enterprises raised doubts among the people about the LDLP's integrity.[9] Another factor that reduced popular support for the Liberal Democratic Labour Party was a 1995 amendment to the law on the restitution of church property; this was perceived as an attack on the traditionally popular Catholic Church. Also significant was the November/December 1995 banking crisis. The prime minister, as head of

---

*Noteworthy, in contrast, is the performance of the Communist Party in local elections in April 1990, where it won approximately 40 percent of votes and offices.
†Owing to a special concession to minorities, the Union of Poles, which received only 2.45 percent of the national vote, was awarded 2 of the 70 party-list seats.

TABLE 11.2 Voting Results for Lithuania's Parliamentary Elections Between 1992 and 2004

Political Party Names as of 2004	October 25, 1992[a]			October 20, 1996[b]			October 8, 2000			October 10, 2004		
	Party List	Single Member	Total	Party List	Single Member	Total	Party List	Single Member	Total	Party List	Single Member	Total
Labour Party (DP)										22	17	39
Working for Lithuania (LSDP-LS) (Brazauskas and Paulauskas coalition)—composed of Lithuanian Social Democratic Party (LSDP), 20 seats, and New Union (Social Liberals), 11 seats										16	15	31
Liberal Union–Central Union (LLC-LSC)										7	11	18
For Order and Justice (Paksas)—includes Liberal Democratic Party 10 seats, and Lithuanian's People's Union										9	2	11
Farmers' Party–New Democracy Party (LVP-NDP)										5	5	10

											See Working for Lithuania
Social-Democratic Coalition of Algirdas Brazauskas—composed of the Lithuanian Democratic Labour Party, the LSDP, the Union of Lithuanian Russians, and the Party of New Democracy; in 1992, it was just the Lithuanian Democratic Labour Party	36	37	73	10	2	12	28	23	51		*See Working for Lithuania*
Homeland Union/ Lithuanian Conservatives (HU/LC); in 2004, the Pro-Patria Union-Conservatives (TS-LK); in 1992, the Sajudis coalition was composed of the Lithuanian Movement Sajudis, Charter of Lithuanian Citizens, Union of Lithuanian Political Prisoners, and the Lithuanian Green Party	17	11	28	33	37	70	8	1	9	11	14	25

(Continued)

TABLE 11.2 Voting Results for Lithuania's Parliamentary Elections Between 1992 and 2004—cont'd

Political Party Names as of 2004	October 25, 1992[a]			October 20, 1996[b]			October 8, 2000			October 10, 2004		
	Party List	Single Member	Total	Party List	Single Member	Total	Party List	Single Member	Total	Party List	Single Member	Total
Lithuanian Christian Democratic Party (LKDP); in 1992, Joint List of LKDP, LPKTS, and the Lithuanian Democratic Party (LDP)	10	8	18	11	5	16	—	2	2	*See Homeland Union*		
Lithuanian Social Democratic Party	5	3	8	7	5	12	*See Social-Democratic Coalition*			*See Working for Lithuania*		
Lithuanian Centre Union (LCS)	0	2	2	9	4	13	0	2	2			
Electoral Action of Lithuania's Poles (LLRA)—Union of Lithuanian Poles	2	2	4	0	1	1	—	2	2	0	2	2
National Union; in 1992, it was the Lithuanian Nationalist Union (LTS) and Independence Party (NP); in 1996, it was the coalition of LTS and LDP	0	4	4	—	3	3	—	—	—	—	—	—

Lithuanian Liberty (Freedom) Union	0	0	0	0	—	1	1
Lithuanian Christian Democratic Union (LKDS)	—	0	1	1	0	1	1
Lithuania National Party "Young Lithuania" (LNPJL); in 2000, it was the Union of "Young Lithuania," New Nationalists, and Political Prisoners	—	0	1	1	—	1	1
Lithuania Women's Party	—	0	1	1	*See Social-Democratic Coalition*		
Lithuanian Liberal Union (LLS)	—	0	1	1	16	18	34
Lithuanian Peasants' Party (LVP)	—	0	1	1	0	4	4
Russian Union	—	0	0	0	*See Social-Democratic Coalition*		
Lithuania Union of Political Prisoners and Deportees (LPKTS)	1	1	0	1	*See Lithuania National Party*	*See Homeland Union*	
New Union (Social Liberals)	—	—	—	—	18	11	29
							See Working for Lithuania
Moderate Conservative Union	—	—	—	—	0	1	1

(Continued)

TABLE 11.2 Voting Results for Lithuania's Parliamentary Elections Between 1992 and 2004—cont'd

Political Party Names as of 2004	October 25, 1992[a]			October 20, 1996[b]			October 8, 2000			October 10, 2004		
	Party List	Single Member	Total	Party List	Single Member	Total	Party List	Single Member	Total	Party List	Single Member	Total
Others (Independents)	0	3	3	0	4	4	0	4	4	0	5	5
Total	70	71	141	70	67	137	70	71	141	70	71	141
Turnout	75.29% (first round) 64.76% (second round)			52.92% (first round) 38.16% (second round)			58.63%			46.1%		

Source: Richard Rose, Neil Munro, and David Mackie, 1998. *Elections in Central and Eastern Europe Since 1990*, Studies in Public Policy No. 300. Glasgow: University of Strathclyde; and Electoral Commission of Lithuania, "Elections to the Seimas of the Republic of Lithuania" at http://rc.lrs.lt/n/rinkimai/20001008/index_en.html, October 26, 2000. *See also* Elections in Lithuania, Centre for the Study of Public Policy, University of Strathclyde, at http://www.cspp.strath.ac.uk/index.html?litelec.html; and the official website of the Lithuanian Supreme Electoral Commission at http://www.lrs.lt/rinkimai/seim96/index.html.

[a]The runoff was held on November 15, 1992.
[b]The runoff was held on November 10, 1996.

the ruling party, was implicated in a scandal associated with the closing of two of Lithuania's main banks and was forced to resign; this contributed to a loss of support for the ruling party.

Thus, the LDLP majority was defeated in the 1996 parliamentary elections by the Homeland Union/Lithuanian Conservatives (see Table 11.2).* The HU/LC formed a center-right coalition government with the Christian Democratic Party and controlled the Seimas after 1996, with Gediminas Vagnorius of the HU/LC as prime minister.† He was replaced by Rolandas Paksas in May 1998 and was in turn replaced by Andrius Kubilius in November 1998.

The HU/LC conservative government of Prime Minister Kubilius experienced defeat in the October 2000 parliamentary voting. Prior to the 2000 elections, opponents of the Homeland Union–Christian Democratic coalition entered into two major electoral blocs. One of the blocs was a centrist group of the New Union (or Social Liberals), the Lithuanian Liberal Union (LLS), the Lithuanian Centre Union (LCS), and the Modern Christian Democratic Union (MCDS). The second bloc was the Social-Democratic Coalition made up of four parties— the Lithuanian Democratic Labour Party, Lithuanian Social Democratic Party, the New Democratic Party, and the Lithuanian Russian Union.

Ultimately, sixteen blocs/parties contested in the party-list section of the 2000 ballot (fewer than the twenty-five that competed in 1996). The Social-Democratic Coalition, led by former Communist Party leader and former Lithuanian President Algirdas Brazauskas, won the most seats in the 2000 parliamentary elections (see Table 11.2). The Liberal Union of Rolandas Paksas occupied second place, and the New Union third place. The only other group to receive PR seats was Homeland Union, which received eight such seats but won only one constituency.

The results of the 2000 parliamentary election represented a shift to the left. Popular discontent with the country's continued economic hardship was again a major factor in the electoral shift. Among other difficulties, the Russian economic collapse of 1998 hit Lithuania hard. The election occurred before Lithuania had achieved membership in the EU and the NATO alliance.[10]

The most successful individual party in the October 10, 2004, parliamentary elections was Labour with 29 percent of the vote (see Table 11.2). Placing next in the number of votes received were Working for Lithuania (composed of the Social Democrats and the Social Liberals) with 21 percent, Homeland Union/ Lithuanian Conservatives with 15 percent, For Order and Justice (Liberal Democrats and Lithuanian's People's Union) with 11.4 percent, the Liberal and Centre Union with 9 percent, and the Union of Peasants (Farmers) and New Democracy with 7 percent.‡ The coalition For Order and Justice was created by

---

*In 1996, 36 percent of the vote went to parties that failed to be allocated seats according to the PR formula because a party needs 5 percent of the vote to win seats.
†Vagnorius had previously served as prime minister under Landsbergis in 1991.
‡In 2003, the Liberal and Centre Union emerged from a merger of the Liberal Union, the Center Union, and the Modern Christian Democratic Union.

the then recently impeached president of Lithuania, Rolandas Paksas, while the Union of Peasants (Farmers) and New Democracy was led by Kazimiera Prunskiene.

The Labour Party (DP) was new to the Lithuanian political landscape. It was created as a leftist populist party by Viktor Ouspaskitch, a Russian-born millionaire member of parliament. The DP was able to win votes beyond the Russian-speaking minority, especially among poorer Lithuanians. Labour focused its campaign on small towns and semirural areas where living standards were the worst hit by the economic transition.

As Labour Party leader, Ouspaskitch was careful to clarify that he was committed to the established Lithuanian foreign policy, stating that "the European Union and NATO will remain our natural priorities." Born in 1959 in Russia's Siberia, Ouspaskitch first came to Lithuania in 1985 to build a gas pipeline. He returned again in 1987 and stayed, obtaining Lithuanian nationality once the republic gained independence in 1990. Ouspaskitch set up his first company in 1990 and was elected to parliament as an independent in 1996.

The coalition We Are Working for Lithuania, composed of Brazauskas's Social Democratic Party and its partner the Social Liberals, campaigned on its strong record as the governing coalition. Its electoral program promised to increase average salaries and retirement pensions, lower the unemployment rate of the working population, and increase the Lithuanian GDP so that it would be closer to the European average. The Pro-Patria Union-Conservatives (TS-LK), formerly the Homeland Union, led by Andrius Kubilius, focused its 2004 election campaign on the need for a strong state to protect Lithuania from any possible threat on the part of Russia. The TS-LK program promised "the return to Lithuanian, family, and Christian values." The Conservatives were able to increase their representation in the Seimas by playing on fears that if Ouspaskich's Labour Party won the 2004 election, Russian interference in the country would increase.

In the aftermath of the 2004 election, a ruling coalition was formed from the Labour Party, the Lithuanian Social Democratic Party, the New Union (Social Liberals), and the Union of Peasants and New Democrats. The opposition, composed of the Homeland Union and the Liberal and Centre Union, also formed a coordinating coalition under the leadership of Homeland Union party leader Andrius Kubilius. With Kubilius as opposition leader, the Liberal Centre faction leader Algis Caplikas assumed the post of deputy parliamentary chairman.

To summarize, each of Lithuania's parliamentary elections has resulted in dramatic votes against the incumbent government. In 1992, the LDLP triumphed as voters protested the reform efforts of the ruling Sajudis coalition. The 1996 elections witnessed a conservative landslide victory as the Homeland Union defeated the Lithuanian Democratic Labour Party. In 2000, the Brazauskas coalition won the most votes and the Homeland Union coalition took its second turn in suffering a backlash from the voters still suffering from economic reform. The strong showing of the Labour Party in 2004 once again shows reaction voting against those in power. In 2004, the governing alliance of Brazauskas and Paulauskas came in second to the entirely new Labour Party organized by a Russian immigrant to Lithuania.

The Prime Minister

According to Article 91 of Lithuania's Constitution, the Government of the Republic of Lithuania consists of the prime minister and ministers. The prime minister is appointed and dismissed by the president, with the approval of the Seimas. Ministers in turn are appointed by the president following nomination by the prime minister.

According to Article 94, the government of Lithuania has the authority to do the following:

- Administer the affairs of the country, protect the inviolability of the territory of the Republic of Lithuania, and ensure state security and public order
- Implement laws and resolutions of the Seimas as well as decrees of the president
- Prepare the draft budget of the state and submit it to the Seimas
- Execute the state budget and report on the fulfillment of the budget to the Seimas
- Draft bills and submit them to the Seimas for consideration
- Establish diplomatic relations and maintain relations with foreign countries and international organizations

Lithuanian governments, for the most part, have been formed from coalitions of political parties. For example, in July 2001, former President Algirdas Brazauskas, as head of the Social Democrats,* became prime minister when he formed a coalition government with the New Union (Social Liberals). Brazauskas was reappointed prime minister by Rolandas Paksas in the aftermath of the second round of the presidential elections in January 2003.

Local Government

Below the national government are local administrative units (ten counties), each with its own council. Councils elect their chairs (mayors), deputy chairs, and other officials. Local councils have limited power and limited financial resources. They are dependent on the central government, which collects nearly all taxes and determines their use and allocation.

---

*Brazauskas was chairman of the LSDP, which was formed in January 2001 from the merger of the LDLP and the Social Democratic Party.

Voting for the membership of the local councils is by lists submitted by parties or coalitions of parties. Only formal political organizations can field candidates in local elections, and to win a local council seat, a party must win at least 4 percent of the vote. The size of the council depends on the population of the city or the **raion**. The largest cities, Vilnius and Kaunas, have 51 and 41 deputies on their councils, respectively. Raion councils and smaller cities have between 21 and 17 members in their councils.

Because members of the councils are elected for two-year terms, midterm local elections for councils serve as bellwethers for coming parliamentary elections. For example, the March 1995 local elections brought defeat to the ruling Lithuanian Democratic Labour Party and victory to the Homeland Union/Lithuanian Conservatives.[11] As can be seen in Table 11.2, the LDLP had won a majority in the 1992 parliamentary elections, but the Homeland Union won the 1996 elections.

For the 2002 local elections, held simultaneously with the first round of the presidential election in December, about 10,000 candidates competed for 1,560 council member seats throughout the country. The most successful parties in the local elections were, respectively, the Social Democratic Party, the Lithuanian Farmers Party, the Homeland Union/Lithuanian Conservatives, the Lithuanian Liberal Union, the Lithuanian Centre Union, the New Union (Social Liberals), and the Liberal Democrats Party.

The Judicial Branch

The judicial branch in Lithuania is composed of the Constitutional Court, the Supreme Court, and the Court of Appeal. The court system also includes district courts and local courts with magistrates appointed by the president. The Procurator's Office is under the authority of the Procurator-General, who is appointed and dismissed by parliament.

The Constitutional Court is charged with the responsibility of deciding whether the laws adopted by the Seimas and the legal acts adopted by the president are in conformity with the constitution. This court, established in 1993, consists of nine judges appointed by parliament on a proposal from the president. The Constitutional Court played a very visible role during the impeachment process of President Paksas. Thus, the judiciary has demonstrated its independence from the executive branch.

The main problem affecting the process of justice in Lithuania is the fact that the courts take so long to deliver judgments. This is because of a shortage of qualified judges, the structure of the system, and an overload of work within the Procurator's Office. Prisons and detention centers are overcrowded, and credible reports of police abuse of suspects and detainees have surfaced. To combat corruption, Lithuania is cooperating with the UN in conducting comprehensive studies and in implementing educational programs (European Commission's Regular Report 1999).

POLITICAL PARTICIPATION

Lithuania is a parliamentary democracy that has earned the ranking of "Free" by Freedom House.* The results of the parliamentary and presidential elections demonstrate that Lithuanians can change their government democratically. The government generally respects freedom of speech and of the press, and there are a variety of privately owned newspapers and TV channels.

Disillusionment with politics, however, is indicated by a low level of citizen involvement. Political participation in parliamentary elections declined significantly from the early 1990s to the early 2000s. **Turnout** in the 1992 elections was 76 percent (in the first round), declined to only 53 percent in 1996 (in the first round), increased to 57 percent in 2000, but declined again to 46 percent in 2004. A special election in June 2003 for four vacant seats in the 141-member Lithuanian parliament failed due to low voter turnout. Parliament, therefore, operated with only 137 members until the elections in the fall of 2004.[12]

There also has been a precipitous decline in the turnout for presidential elections. Although more than 70 percent of the electorate participated in the 1993 and 1997 presidential elections, in 2002 only 54 percent voted in the first round of the presidential election (held in December 2002) and 53 percent in the second round (held in January 2003). For the 2004 presidential elections, 48 percent of the electorate participated in the first round and 52 percent participated in the second round. Turnout in local elections has tended to be even lower.

How can this decline in electoral turnout be explained? In part, it may be simply a reflection of the artificially high levels of protest political participation associated with the independence period. The victory of Sajudis candidates in 1990 and the victory of former communists in the 1992 elections can both reasonably be interpreted as protest votes. Thus, the more recent voter turnout figures represent a more normal pattern of participation. Continuing economic troubles at the individual level can also contribute to a sense of disenfranchisement, while corruption scandals at the national level create a degree of alienation. An overall disillusionment with politics has combined with a normal degree of citizen apathy to create a decline in participation levels.

Using post-election survey data, we can identify the people who are voting in Lithuania's elections as compared to those who stay home on election day. In looking at those who did vote in both the first and the second round of the 2002–2003 presidential elections, we find that men and women turned out in roughly equal proportions.[†] On all other sociodemographic dimensions, however, participation in the presidential elections has tended to reflect underlying

---

*Freedom House, is a nonprofit, nonpartisan organization working to advance worldwide political and economic freedom. According to its survey, 89 countries, out of the 192 surveyed, are "Free." For more information, see http://www.freedomhouse.org/ratings/index.htm.
[†]This survey was conducted by Baltic Surveys, Ltd., under the direction of Rasa Alisauskiene.

social cleavages. As has been demonstrated in other countries, older citizens are more likely to vote than are younger people. Better-educated Lithuanians are significantly more likely to vote than their less educated counterparts. Wealthier people are also more likely to vote than poorer people. Ethnic Lithuanians were more likely to vote in the 2002–2003 presidential elections than were ethnic Russians, but ethnic Poles were even more likely to vote than ethnic Lithuanians. Roman Catholics were more likely to vote than Orthodox believers or those without a religion.

Women hold very few leadership positions in Lithuania's national politics. The proportion of female members in the Seimas increased from 7.1 percent (of 141 members) in 1993 to 18 percent in 1996 and decreased to 11 percent in 2000.* In October 2004, however, twenty-nine women won seats in parliament, constituting 20.6 percent of the membership.[13] This places Lithuania above the world average (see Table 6.1, p. 136) for female representation in national parliaments. Women serve in similar proportions on the councils of Lithuania's municipalities. As of 2001, 18 percent of the members of municipal councils were women. In January 2002, 52 percent of judges, 42 percent of prosecutors, and 37 percent of lawyers were women.

THE MAIN PUBLIC POLICY QUESTIONS

Economic Development

According to Article 46 of its constitution, Lithuania's economy is based on the right to private ownership and on freedom of individual economic activity and initiative. The state is held constitutionally responsible for the regulation of economic activity so as to serve the general welfare of the people. Monopolization of production and the market is prohibited by the constitution.

In line with these constitutional mandates, privatization occurred rapidly between 1992 and 1994 through auctions, sales of shares, and sales for hard currency. The Law on the Initial Privatization of State Property of the Republic of Lithuania, passed in 1991 and amended several times in 1993 (primarily with regard to land sales), served as the principal basis for undertaking privatization. To start the process, vouchers were issued to all citizens, which could be used to buy apartments, shares in enterprises, shares in investment firms, and land. Most eligible housing property was privatized by the end of 1993. The vast majority (75 to 80 percent) of enterprises have since been privatized.

The privatization of land was particularly difficult. Lithuanian agriculture was relatively efficient (compared with other parts of the Soviet Union) despite collectivization. All collective and state farms were abolished in 1991. By the end of 1993, new agricultural associations were formed to replace the collective

---

*In 2000, only 18 percent of candidates for a seat in parliament were women.

farms and more than 100,000 individuals were granted rights to land. When land was made available for private ownership, the number of claimants was high. As a result, the size of land-holdings among the private farmers averaged only 8.8 hectares.[14] Many of the small holdings were not economically viable and often were not even farmed. Thus, agricultural production dropped in the early 1990s.

Overall, as Lithuania privatized its economy, the country suffered severe hardships. The economic difficulties began even earlier when industrial production dropped in 1990 because of Gorbachev's economic blockade. The price of Russian oil, coal, and natural gas dramatically increased during 1992. Lithuania's large factories that had been part of the Soviet military–industrial complex experienced a lack of access to raw materials and supplies.

During the 1990s, Lithuania's economy showed features common to other post-Soviet countries that undertook reform in the aftermath of the breakup of the Soviet Union. These features included hyperinflation (1,162.5 percent in 1992),[15] a significant reduction in GDP,* an increasing budget deficit, corruption in the privatization process, and legal problems associated with economic regulation. The loss of markets for goods in former Soviet republics, together with continued dependence on Russia for oil and gas, disrupted Lithuania's economy and contributed to major declines in agricultural and industrial production and in standards of living.

The depth and the severity of the economic downturn was aptly demonstrated when the Lithuanian Statistics Department announced in January 1993 that the volume of industrial production in 1992 had decreased by 51.6 percent from the level of the previous year. A breakthrough occurred in 1995 when the first positive growth rates were registered since gaining independence. Despite the fact that Lithuania's growth rates held at 3 to 8 percent between 1995 and 1998, the GDP in 1998 accounted for only 68.5 percent of the 1990 GDP (Geralavicius 1999, 88). For the entire decade (from 1990 to 2000), Lithuania registered a negative average annual growth rate (in GDP) of -3.1 percent. Although the 1998 Russian financial crisis had a harmful impact on the economy and the country's GDP declined in 1999, Lithuania's GDP growth rates returned to positive figures between 2000 and 2003 (see Table 11.3). Strong positive growth rates were also registered in 2004, driven primarily by private consumption, exports, and domestic construction.

Lithuania has a trade imbalance because the cost of imports exceeds the value of its exports. In 2004, Lithuania received most of its imports from Russia (23 percent) and Germany (18 percent), as noted in the CIA's figures. This represents a significant reduction in its dependence on Russia from 1992, when

*GDP is the sum of gross value added by all resident producers in the economy plus any product taxes and minus any subsidies not included in the value of the products. When industrial production fell off by 46 percent in 1993, the country's industries were working at only half of their capacity. Unemployment, however, did not increase precipitously because enterprises retained their workers but cut hours and forced them to take leaves.

TABLE 11.3 The World Bank's 1998 to 2003 Economic Development Indicators for Lithuania

	1998	1999	2000	2001	2002	2003
Agriculture, value added (% of GDP)	—	8.62	8.01	7.21	7.09	7.27
Exports of goods and services (% of GDP)	46.57	39.1	44.89	49.99	53.09	53.91
Foreign Direct Investment, net flows (BoP, US$)	926,000,000	487,000,000	379,000,000	446,000,000	713,000,000	—
GDP (US$)	10,900,000,000	10,800,000,000	11,400,000,000	12,100,000,000	14,100,000,000	18,200,000,000
GDP growth (annual %)	7.31	-1.7	3.92	6.38	6.76	6.51
GNI per capita, Atlas method (US$)	2,700	2,910	3,170	3,400	3,730	4,490
GNI, Atlas method (US$)	—	10,265,879,552	11,096,322,048	11,828,737,024	12,952,727,552	15,509,301,248
Illiteracy rate, adult total (% of people age 15 and above)	—	99.54	99.56	99.65	—	—
Imports of goods and services (% of GDP)	58.3	49.24	51.25	55.37	58.67	59.87
Industry, value added (% of GDP)	32.93	31.57	30.86	31.96	31.19	33.77
Inflation, GDP deflator (annual %)	5.37	-0.61	1.04	-0.1	-0.03	1.35
Life expectancy at birth, total (in years)	71.57	72.11	72.62	—	72.68	72.68

Military expenditures, dollar figure[a]	—	—	—	230,800,000	—	—
Military expenditures (% of GDP)	—	—	—	1.91	—	—
Population growth (annual %)	-0.68	-0.68	-0.74	-0.66	-0.37	-0.17
Population, total	3,555,000	3,531,000	3,505,000	3,482,000	3,469,000	3,476,000
Services, etc., value added (% of GDP)	56.63	59.81	61.13	60.82	61.72	58.02
Trade in goods (% of GDP)	88.44	73.52	82.93	92.1	96.39	—

[a]Figures for the two military expenditures rows are from the CIA's *World Factbook*, "Rank Order–Military expenditures—dollar figure," at http://www.odci.gov/cia/publications/factbook/rankorder/2067rank.txt.

Source: Unless otherwise noted, all figures for the table are from the World Bank at http://devdata.worldbank.org/data-query/.

approximately 60 percent of Lithuania's imports came from Russia; in 1994, 45 percent came from Russia. Imports consist primarily of mineral products, machinery and equipment (including transportation equipment), chemicals, textiles, and clothing.

During the Soviet era, all three Baltic republics depended heavily on Russian energy resources for heating, electricity, and transportation. Russia was able to use this dependency to pressure the countries in the early post-independence period. Remarkably, Lithuania, Estonia, and Latvia generally followed their own policy preferences regardless of Moscow's demands. They endured Russia's economic pressure by tolerating more winter cold and by driving less. Their survival was made easier because the energy demands of local industries declined as production stalled.[16] Lithuania's reliance on nuclear power also lessened its dependence on Russia; its Ignalina nuclear power plant generates nearly 80 percent of the country's electricity.*

A partial dependence on Russia for oil and natural gas is not necessarily dangerous. Other EU states are also net importers of energy and get significant oil and gas supplies from Russia. Russians need to be able to use Baltic ports, which gives these states their own source of leverage vis-à-vis Moscow. Lithuania also processes Russian crude oil for export, thereby providing a critical link in oil trade and transit services.† Moscow needs to use Baltic export terminals to service Western Europe.[17] Another issue linking Lithuania to Russia is Kaliningrad, an oblast of the Russian Federation that is physically separated from Russia by Lithuanian and Polish territory.

As of 2004, Lithuania's exports went primarily to Switzerland (11 percent), Russia (8 percent), Germany (9.5 percent), Latvia (10 percent), France (7.5 percent), the United States (5 percent), and the United Kingdom (5 percent).‡ This represents a significant shift to the West: In 1997, exports to former Soviet states were 45 percent of total Lithuanian exports. By 2004, exports to former Soviet states accounted for less than 20 percent of the total, while exports to EU states were more than 70 percent of the total. Thus, the European Union has become Lithuania's dominant trading partner. The figures for 2001 showed that exports consisted primarily of mineral products (23 percent), textiles and clothing (16 percent), and machinery and equipment (11 percent).

---

*The Ignalina nuclear power plant has a design similar to that of Chernobyl. EU accession negotiations resulted in a decision to shut down the plant by 2009. A serious and continuing challenge facing the economy of Lithuania is the environmental pollution, a legacy of Soviet rule. At military bases and around factories, Lithuania's soil and groundwater have been contaminated with petroleum products and chemicals. Currently the primary sources of pollutant emissions are the transportation, industrial, and energy sectors.
†Since 2002, the Russian oil corporation Yukos has held a majority interest in Lithuania's oil refinery, Mazeiku Nafta. Russia's Gazprom owns shares in the republic's largest gas utility.
‡This represents a change from 1992, when Russia, Ukraine, and Germany (in that order) received the greatest proportion of Lithuania's exports.

Overall, the structure of Lithuania's economy changed substantially over the decade from 1990 to 2000. Growth in the service sector was noteworthy during the 1990s, bringing the size of Lithuania's service sector into line with European Union countries. Its agricultural sector changed from 24 percent of GDP in 1992 to 6 percent for 2004. Even with this change, Lithuania's agricultural sector is large compared to the EU average; 20 percent of the country's labor force is employed there.

Despite impressive recovery figures, Lithuania's budget deficit stood at 4.8 percent of GDP in 2002 and problems with corruption have not been solved. Per capita income remains low by European standards and unemployment remains a problem. Average living standards in Lithuania in 2003 were just under 40 percent of the EU average. The 2004 unemployment rate was 8 percent.

European Union Participation

The primary focus of all of Lithuania's post-independence leaders has been on restructuring the economy for full integration into Western European institutions. Official relations and cooperation between Lithuania and the European Community began in August 27, 1991, when the European Community recognized Lithuania's independence. In May 1992, Lithuania and the EU signed the Agreement on Trade and Commercial and Economic Cooperation, and in July 1994, they signed a Free Trade Agreement. Lithuania's government submitted an official membership application to the European Union in December 1995. Lithuania was then required to draw up and adopt a National Programme for the Adoption of the Acquis (NPAA), which specified its plan to meet the regulations and conditions required for integration into the European Union. With the approval of the European Council, Lithuania began negotiations for EU membership in February 2000. A revised version of the National Programme, presented in 2001, became Lithuania's European Union Accession Programme. During this period, Lithuania received funding from the EU to help it institute required reforms, including assistance for nuclear decommissioning.

In preparation of Lithuania's entry into the European Union, the Seimas had to pass several laws in order to comply with EU regulations. For example, in October 2002, the Seimas voted to adopt the euro as a currency equal to the Lithuanian litas.* In January 2004, the parliament approved a valued-added tax (VAT) to comply with EU regulations. Entry into the EU also required the holding of a nationwide referendum. Thus, the citizens of Lithuania voted in May 2003 in a referendum to approve membership in the EU. Results showed that 91 percent of those who voted backed entry and turnout was more than 60 percent. In September 2003, Lithuania's parliament ratified the European Union

---

*Lithuania introduced its own national currency, the litas, in June 1993.

TABLE 11.4 Lithuania's June 2004 European Parliament Election Results

Party	Total
Labour Party (DP, *Darbo Partija*)	5
Lithuanian Social Democratic Party (LSDP, *Lietuvos Socialdemokratu Partija*)	2
Pro-Patria Union-Conservatives (*Tévynés Sajungos-Lietuvos Konservatoriai*)	2
Liberal Union—Centre Union (*Liberalu ir Centro Sajunga*)	2
Union of Peasants and New Democracy (VNDPS, *Valstieciu ir Naujosios Demokratijos Partiju Sajunga*)	1
Liberal Democratic Party (LDP, *Liberalu Demokratu Partija*)	1
New Union (*Naujosios Sajunga*) (Social Liberals, *Socialliberalai*)	0
Lietuvos Krikšonys Demokratai	0
Total Seats	13
Electorate	2,638,886

Source: From the BBC News at http://news.bbc.co.uk/1/shared/ bsp/hi/vote2004/euro/html/15.stm

Accession Treaty.* In May 2004, Lithuania was admitted into the European Union along with Cyprus, the Czech Republic, Estonia, Hungary, Latvia, Malta, Poland, Slovakia, and Slovenia.

The country's first-ever elections to the European Parliament occurred in June 2004. Lithuanian voters elected thirteen deputies to that parliament in a multiple-mandate district covering the whole country (see Table 11.4). All registered political parties had the right to present lists of between five and twenty-six candidates no later than sixty-five days prior to the election. A party needed to receive a minimum of 5 percent of the vote to win representation. Labour won 5 of the 13 seats in these elections. Although pro-EU, the Labour Party promised to campaign aggressively in the European Parliament for better conditions for the Baltic States, accusing the government of not being tough enough in EU membership negotiations.

Foreign Affairs and the Military

Lithuania is a member of the United Nations, the Organization for Security and Cooperation in Europe, and the World Trade Organization. Once Lithuania was accepted into NATO in March 2004, the country's international security was guaranteed by the alliance partners. Just as the majority of Lithuania's population supported entry to the European Union, a majority also supported

*The treaty goes into effect after it is ratified by the parliaments of the fifteen EU members and ten EU candidate countries.

membership in NATO. Lithuania was among the first to join NATO's Partnership for Peace Program in January 1994. The country's focus on the West rather than on Russia as its source of security results in part from the historical memory of forced incorporation into the Russian-dominated Soviet Union, but also reflects a reaction against Russia's more current aggressive orientation toward the Near Abroad. Independent Lithuania has consistently shown its aversion to joining any alliance with former Soviet states.

To win the North Atlantic Treaty Organization invitation, Lithuania had to make its armed forces compatible with NATO standards and had to establish a track record of military cooperation with alliance members. In November 2002, U.S. President George W. Bush flew to Vilnius following a meeting in St. Petersburg with President Putin. Bush held talks with Lithuanian President Valdas Adamkus, Prime Minister Algirdas Brazauskas, Parliament Chairman Arturas Paulauskas, and Foreign Minister Antanas Valionis. Bush congratulated Lithuania on its NATO invitation, declaring: "Our alliance has made a solemn pledge of protection, and anyone who would choose Lithuania as an enemy has also made an enemy of the United States of America."[18] In February 2004, Lithuania's defense minister visited Washington, D.C., and met with U.S. Secretary of Defense Donald Rumsfeld, who also welcomed Lithuania's membership in NATO.[19]

The Baltic countries are small and do not have the recruits to field large armies. In 1995, Lithuania was the only country among the Baltic States to have planes with fighter capabilities, but these were very few in number. In June 2003, the parliament approved a bill on the structure of the Lithuanian armed forces that called for a reduction in the number of soldiers in the armed forces and active reserves (including the army, navy, air force, border guard, and home guard) from the existing 22,000 to 17,000 by 2008. However, the number of senior officers was to increase in order to have adequate personnel to delegate suitably ranked representatives to work on NATO staffs.[20] With its security guaranteed through NATO, Lithuania is creating a military that focuses more on contributing to international operations than on territorial defense.

All post-Soviet states face the problem of limited funds available for food, uniforms, weapons, salaries, and housing for their troops. In fiscal year 2001, Lithuania devoted $230.8 million (in US$) to military expenditures. This represented 1.9 percent of its GDP. The lack of funds negatively affects morale and limits training possibilities. In addition, the hazing of new recruits contributes to widespread evasion of military conscription. Yet, a Lithuanian army is necessary to protect the borders against drug trafficking and smuggling, to deal with organized crime, to participate in international peacekeeping forces, to provide a mechanism for political socialization, and to maintain national unity and independence.[21]

Demographic Issues

Lithuania faces two demographic problems. First is the declining number of people, and second is the declining health of these people. The country has been concerned about its population for decades. Indeed, the Lithuanian Constitution explicitly promises help to families with children. Article 39 of the Constitution of the Republic of Lithuania states: "The State shall take care of families bringing up children at home, and shall render them support in the manner established by law. The law shall provide for paid maternity leave before and after childbirth, as well as for favourable working conditions and other privileges."

Although the total fertility rate is positive in Lithuania at 1.19 children born per woman, out-migration of the population has led to a negative population growth rate of –0.3 percent. Life expectancy at birth is 69 years for males and 79 years for females.*

Health-Care Access

Health care in Lithuania is nationally funded and available to all citizens. Private (nonstate) clinics are being established, but state-run facilities still provide most care for most people. Consultations with private physicians are relatively rare across the board, but when contact with a private physician does occur, it is primarily in an urban setting.

Lithuanian survey data confirm that health services are assumed to be free and the people are accustomed to this. People do pay extra for medications and for some needed supplies, such as syringes and dressings, but fees for examination or treatment are rare. The practice of giving gifts or "extra" payments for medical services, however, is fairly common. Thus, even though free services are taken for granted, the idea of extra payments, whether in the form of a gift or a monetary exchange, is not unusual in Lithuania or in other post-Soviet settings.

In general, the medical and health-care systems are not highly regarded in Lithuania. An overall perception exists that physicians do not care or that they are unqualified. Shortages of medical supplies are not a major reason for dissatisfaction with medical care, even though the media tends to give more attention to shortages than to standards of medical training or to doctor–patient relationships.

Violence

As in many post-Soviet societies, crime increased dramatically in Lithuania during the early 1990s. Both violent crimes and crimes against property were more extensive than during Soviet times. Organized crime became a serious problem when it became involved in trafficking humans, drugs, radioactive materials, and weapons.[22]

Comparatively, however, homicide rates in Lithuania are low for the region. The rate of homicides in Russia in 2002 was twice as high as in Lithuania for

---

*The numbers in this paragraph are from the 2005 CIA estimates.

2001 (Interpol International Crime Statistics 2003).* Homicide rates were, however, twice as high in Lithuania in 2001 as in the United States for the same year. In contrast, when evaluating all kinds of theft, the rates are much lower in Lithuania than in the United States; the theft rate is lower still in Russia.

Men perpetrate all forms of crime more frequently than women. Of persons charged with crimes in 2001 in Lithuania, 91 percent were men. Men were also more likely to be victims of violent crime than women; this includes murder and murder attempts and serious bodily injuries. The only exception was that women were more frequently victims of rape and rape attempts. The prison population in Lithuania in 2001 was 96 percent male.

CONCLUSION AND OVERVIEW

Public opinion within Lithuania is split as to whether the country's post-Soviet transition should be evaluated positively or negatively. In the March 2003 countrywide survey referred to earlier, people were asked to tell their general and overall impression about whether things were going in the right or the wrong direction. Just over half of the population responded that the country was moving in the right direction (54 percent), while just under half reported that the country was moving in the wrong direction (46 percent). The people were also asked to react specifically to the **democratization** reforms. When asked to register their level of satisfaction (or dissatisfaction) with the way that democracy is working in Lithuania, public opinion was again almost equally split—49 percent were satisfied, while 51 percent were dissatisfied. This is an amazingly equal divide in the population.

Despite the division in evaluations of democratization and the transition process, a majority does support market reform. When asked whether the introduction of a market economy free from state control is the right or wrong thing for Lithuania's future, 68 percent answered in the affirmative. This is a solid majority, although it is noteworthy that a sizable minority (32 percent) state that a market economy is wrong for Lithuania. Part of the problem here resides in the fact that even though the aggregate economic indicators show positive growth in Lithuania's productivity starting with 2000, at the individual level, many people are still suffering from the negative effects of the transition.

When asked to compare their households' current economic situation with their economic situation of a year ago, a full 31 percent reported that their situation had gotten worse, 50 percent said that their situation had stayed the same, and 19 percent said their situation had improved somewhat. It is understandable that some among the 31 percent whose financial situation was worse might blame the market reforms for their current economic woes. The relationship

---

*Comparing these figures across countries, however, is problematic given differences in reporting rates and in definitions of crimes.

between the financial situation in the household and support for market reform can be statistically checked; it is displayed graphically in Figure 11.1. As the economic situation of the household declines, so does support for a free market economy.

Until government and individual efforts are able to improve the lot of more people, support for both a market economy and democratic reforms will remain divided. Governments are judged by both their responsiveness and their performance. In terms of economic performance, Lithuania's national economy has turned the corner, but the trickle-down effects of this improved situation have not yet been felt by many of the people. With time, however, and with Lithuania's accession to the European Union, the population will likely experience more widespread well-being.

Adapting an argument presented by Algis Krupavicius (1998), we can summarize Lithuania's transition by reference to the following five stages.

- First was the Pre-Transitional Crisis Stage (1985–1988). During this stage, the Soviet regime under Gorbachev began to show its vulnerability. Would-be reformers began to believe that the Soviet system could indeed be changed.

- Second was the Confrontation Stage (1988–1990) when leaders from both within the Communist Party and outside it began to organize in opposition to Soviet rule. This was a stage when antisystem political organizations became fully mobilized.

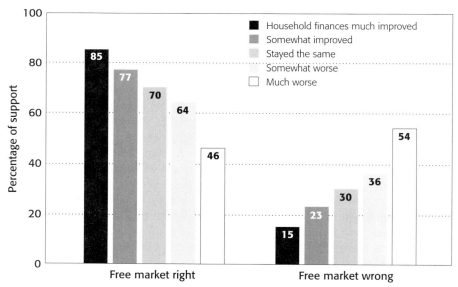

FIGURE 11.1 Lithuanians' 2003 Opinion with Regard to Support for a Market Economy, Based on Household Financial Situation

- Third was the Negotiated Revolution Stage (1990–1992), when Lithuania declared and obtained independence.

- Fourth was the Consolidation Stage (1992–1999), which began with the adoption of a new constitution in 1992. The democratization of electoral procedures represents the stage's real achievement. The problem with this stage, however, was that the ordinary people did not see much improvement in their economic and social situation. In part because of a lack of confidence in government, people began to withdraw from politics.

- Fifth should be a Stability Stage, when the number of political parties begins to show constancy and the articulation and aggregation of interests become routinized. During this stage, the new political structures and institutions acquire relative permanence and the system achieves a relatively stable level of electoral participation. The assumption here is that politics, although always competitive, follows the consensual rules of the game.

Accession to membership in the European Union was a major achievement of the fifth stage. The impeachment of Lithuania's president in early 2004, however, represented an important challenge to the stability of Lithuania's political system. The resolution of this crisis—within a set of consensual rules of the game—signifies a victory for Lithuania's institutions. Although the president was removed, constitutional rules were respected.

Government institutions (not government personnel) appear to be gaining legitimacy and therefore permanence. Other political structures, most notably political parties, however, continue to evidence a lack of stability. The 2004 strong showing of the newly created Labour Party indicates that individual leaders continue to create and dismantle parties at will. Thus, the political party system has not yet reached the stage of stability, even though the performance of the national economy and the government can now be rated as positive and effective.

Since the demise of the Soviet Union, the people of Lithuania have taken great strides in establishing a modern democratic state. New treaties and entrance into NATO and the EU have established Lithuania's place in the world order. Nonetheless, shifts from authoritarianism take time and are subject to both internal and external forces. Externally, Lithuania must maintain a balance between the East and the West. Internally, corruption and the misuse of power remain potential threats, although genuine respect for the rule of law is visibly growing.

Key Terms

Baltic republics
Coalition government
Decentralization
Democratization

Dissident activity
Impeachment
Political party factions
Popular front

Raion	Sovietization
Right of legislative initiative	Turnout
Sajudis	Unicameral parliament
Samizdat	Union Treaty
Seimas	USSR Congress of People's Deputies
Soviet–German Non-Aggression Pact	

Critical Thinking Questions

1. Using the example of the demand for independence from the Soviet Union made by the people of Lithuania, identify a set of factors that are important for a successful independence (separatist) movement.

2. What part does the former Communist Party (now the Lithuanian Social Democratic Party) play in Lithuania's current government? Does this represent a change from Soviet rule?

3. Why is there not a higher level of stability in the voting shares of the political parties in Lithuania? What has this meant for the political process?

4. Which factors contributed to the victory of Rolandas Paksas in Lithuania's 2002–2003 presidential elections?

5. How might the decline in electoral participation in Lithuania's national elections be explained? Which types of people are the most likely to vote in presidential elections? How might the differential participation affect the politics in the country?

6. What are some of the major economic problems that Lithuania faced during the post-independence transition? To what degree has each of these problems been overcome?

7. Discuss some of the pros and cons of Lithuania's membership in NATO. Consider them both from Lithuania's perspective and from Russia's perspective.

8. What still needs to be done for Lithuania to achieve "stability" in the fifth stage of its transition process?

Suggested Reading

Lane, Thomas. *Lithuania: Stepping Westward (Postcommunist States and Nations).* New York: Routledge, 2002.

Lieven, Anatol. *The Baltic Revolution: Estonia, Latvia, Lithuania and the Path to Independence,* 4th ed. New Haven, Conn.: Yale University Press, 1994.

Miller, Arthur H., William R. Reisinger, and Vicki L. Hesli. "Institutional Support in the Russian, Ukrainian and Lithuanian Republics." *Journal of Soviet Nationalities* 1(4): (Winter 1990–1991).

Misiunas, Romuald, and Rein Taagepera. *The Baltic States: Years of Dependence 1940–1990.* Berkeley: University of California Press, 1993.

Smith, David J., Artis Pabriks, Aldis Purs, and Thomas Lane. *The Baltic States: Estonia, Latvia and Lithuania (Postcommunist States and Nations).* New York: Routledge, 2002.

Snyder, Timothy. *The Reconstruction of Nations: Poland, Ukraine, Lithuania, Belarus, 1569–1999*. New Haven, Conn.: Yale University Press, 2003.

Vardys, V. Stanley. "Lithuanians." In *The Nationalities' Question in the Soviet Union*, edited by Graham Smith. New York: Longman, 1990.

Vardys, V. Stanley, and Judith B. Sedaitis. *Lithuania: The Rebel Nation*. Boulder: Westview Press, 1997.

Websites of Interest

General information about Lithuania:
http://www2.omnitel.net/ramunas/Lietuva/

Statistics published by the Department of Statistics for the Government of the Republic of Lithuania:
http://www.std.lt/web/main.php

Information about Lithuanian politics:
http://www.vaitasassociates.com/politics.htm

Journal articles on Lithuanian politics:
http://www.ce-review.org/thematicarchives/lithuania/ta_lithuaniapolitics.html

CHAPTER 12

Ukraine

WITH A POPULATION OF 51.4 MILLION, Ukraine was the second largest republic in the USSR in 1989; its population size has since declined to 47.4 million. Geographically, Ukraine is the largest country in Europe (excluding Russia), sharing borders with the Russian Federation, Belarus, Moldova, Romania, Hungary, Slovakia, and Poland. Historically, Ukraine was called the "breadbasket of Europe," serving as a principal producer of wheat and sugar at the end of the nineteenth century. In 1987, Ukraine contributed 22.3 percent of the Soviet Union's total agricultural output. Abundant natural resources and an excellent geographic position, coupled with Tsarist and Bolshevik investments during the nineteenth and twentieth centuries, allowed Ukraine to become an industrial powerhouse within the Soviet Union with machine- and ship-building, metallurgy, and huge chemical and military complexes. Ukrainian Black Sea ports were used during Soviet times for handling trade between countries of Asia and Africa and the Soviet Union.

Today, Ukraine plays an important role as a provider of transit services because it is situated between Western Europe and resource-rich Russia and the other countries of the Commonwealth of Independent States (CIS). The country also serves as a tourist destination because of its churches and palaces, as well as the recreational areas of Crimea, the Carpathian Mountains, and the Black and Azov Seas. Although Ukraine has had enormous growth potential since becoming independent in December 1991, it has been difficult to reestablish production levels equal to those realized during the Soviet era.

The Ukrainian state, with its current territorial boundaries, is a relatively recent historical creation. The country's international borders represent divisions of territory and authority made in the immediate aftermath of World War II. Thus, before the 1940s, not all the people of Ukraine were part of the same state. As a result, very different ideas about politics and state authority exist in different regions of the country.

This chapter presents an overview of important events in Ukraine's political history and examines the executive and legislative branches of government. The positions of Ukraine's main political parties on the primary issues that divide its society are also discussed. In this context, we explore the voting behavior of Ukrainian citizens as well as other modes of political participation. Toward the end of the chapter, we review Ukraine's economic reform process and its major foreign policy positions.

THE POLITICAL HISTORY OF UKRAINE

The princes of Kiev established a state known as Kievan Rus in the ninth century, Mongol Tatars occupied the region in the thirteenth century, and Poles and Lithuanians invaded in the fourteenth and fifteenth centuries. By the eighteenth century, the lands that comprise present-day Ukraine were part of either the Russian Empire or the Austrian Empire. After the 1917 Bolshevik Revolution, an independent Ukrainian People's Republic was proclaimed in Kiev on January 22, 1918. Western Ukrainians in turn proclaimed an independent Western Ukrainian People's Republic on November 1, 1918. The Western Ukrainian People's Republic united with the Ukrainian People's Republic in January 1919. Soon after, Ukrainian lands became the scene of a fierce civil war. Within a few years, the Bolsheviks took control of Eastern Ukraine and established the Ukrainian Soviet Socialist Republic (SSR). Most of Western Ukraine came under Polish control, although at different times smaller areas that are currently part of Ukraine were occupied by Romania, Hungary, and Czechoslovakia.

In the Ukrainian SSR, Stalin's collectivization campaigns together with forced requisitions of grain and livestock caused severe famine between 1931 and 1933. The famine resulted in the death of 7 to 10 million Ukrainians.[1] Bolshevik rule also took a heavy toll on Ukrainian cultural heritage. Churches were destroyed or converted to civilian use, and Ukrainian writers were limited in what they were allowed to publish.

With the signing of the Soviet–German Non-Aggression Pact in 1939, Western Ukraine, through the secret protocol, came under the Russian sphere of influence. When Germany invaded the Soviet Union in 1941, it sent a million Ukrainians to work in Germany's war industries and countless others to concentration camps. The territory of Ukraine became a main battlefield of World War II. All large cities and towns were bombed, plants and factories where evacuated to Central Asia, and the economy was devastated. By 1943, the Germans were pushed back westward, and Ukraine was reoccupied by Soviet troops.

With the end of World War II, most of Western Ukraine was incorporated into the Ukrainian SSR, although fierce, armed, underground resistance to Soviet control continued in Western Ukraine through to the mid-1950s. In 1954, the territory of the Crimean Peninsula came under Ukrainian jurisdiction, thus establishing the current borders of modern Ukraine.

Ukraine's incorporation into the Soviet Union can be interpreted historically as one of many stages in a legacy of invasion and foreign rule. Although by the 1980s, many Ukrainians had assimilated to the Russian language and identity, the policies of the Soviet leadership—notably collectivization, which led to severe famine, and the exploitation of natural resources, which resulted in cata-strophic environmental degradation—provided the foundation for considerable grievances. When the center of Soviet power began to weaken in 1990 and 1991, Ukrainian leaders demanded and ultimately achieved independent statehood.

Particularly significant in building support for the independence movement was an explosion that occurred in 1986 at a nuclear power plant in Chernobyl, Ukraine. Moscow did not promptly inform the public about the disaster and local officials, who became aware of the spreading contamination around the nuclear power plant, did not evacuate all vulnerable residents. The death rate from radiation exposure could have been lower if officials had acted differently. This led to widespread criticism of Soviet rule.

When people's anger over the handling of the Chernobyl accident joined with the long-standing desire to protect Ukrainian culture and language, it provided a catalyst for widespread anti-Soviet nationalism and ultimately a pro-independence movement. Ukraine, however, was not a leader among republics in the Soviet Union in pushing for sovereignty and independence in the late 1980s and early 1990s. Between 1988 and mid-1991, Ukrainian nationalists were far less vocal about the desire for independence than were nationalists in the Baltic States. Ukrainian nationalists spoke primarily about sovereignty within a reconstituted union of socialist republics. This difference in the degree and kind of nationalism in Ukraine as compared with the Baltic republics is related to a variety of factors.

The first of these factors was the integration of high-level Ukrainians into the Soviet system and the corresponding integration of Russians living in Ukraine into Ukrainian society. Russian and Ukrainian territories, long joined together, shared similar Slavic languages. Also important in forestalling the rise of seces-sionist demands in Ukraine was the tight control exercised by a very conservative Ukrainian Communist Party First Secretary, Volodymyr Shcherbitsky. Stalin's assertions of Ukrainian collaboration with the Germans had provided a rationale for the ruthless elimination of Ukrainian nationalists in the 1940s and 1950s.

Although Ukraine provided the home of a lively dissident movement in the 1960s and 1970s, open opposition to Soviet rule was confined to a small sector of the population. The most outspoken leaders of Ukrainian nationalism were repressed in the late 1960s and early 1970s.* In addition, even during the

---

*In 1972, Moscow attacked so-called "national deviations" in Ukraine, launching a wave of arrests of Ukrainian dissidents. Ukrainian Communist Party First Secretary Petro Shelest was ousted in May of that year and replaced by Volodymyr Shcherbitsky, who promoted an identity for the "Soviet people" and implemented policies of Russification. Shcherbitsky remained First Secretary of the Communist Party in Ukraine until 1989, when he was removed by Mikhail Gorbachev.[2]

heyday of the national independence movement (August 1991 to December 1991), the level of Ukrainian national consciousness was uneven. Ukrainians were ambivalent and divided about separation from the Soviet Union even after the failure of the Moscow coup of August 1991. Nonetheless, on August 24, 1991, the republic's Communist Party leaders joined Ukrainian nationalists in declaring Ukraine's independence.* The Ukrainian parliament ratified the declaration of independence and scheduled a nationwide referendum, to give public support to the declaration.

When a new transitional State Council was convened in Moscow on October 22, 1991, Ukraine, along with Georgia and Armenia, sent no delegates. Rather, on the same day, Ukraine's parliament took the extremely assertive step, arguably an aggressive step, of authorizing the creation of a Ukrainian army, contingent on the affirmation of the republic's declaration of independence on December 1. The parliament also pledged to turn the republic into a nuclear-free zone by removing or dismantling all Soviet-era nuclear weapons on its soil. When seven (Russia, Belarus, and the Central Asian republics) republican leaders met to consider a new Union Treaty on November 25, 1991, Ukraine again refused to participate.

When the day arrived, December 1, 1991, for the scheduled nationwide referendum on Ukraine's proclamation of independence, the vote provided popular legitimization for the country's independence from the Soviet Union. More than 80 percent of eligible voters participated, and 90 percent voted yes to the simple question: "Do you support the declaration of independence of Ukraine?"† Once the referendum legitimated Ukraine's declaration of independence, the Soviet Union could not be saved from disintegration. It was on December 8, just one week after Ukraine's referendum, that the leaders of Russia (Yeltsin), Ukraine (Kravchuk), and Belarus (Shushkevich) declared the formation of a **Commonwealth of Independent States (CIS).** In forming CIS, the parties agreed to coordinate internal and external economic relations, while affirming the integrity and independence of all the signing parties.

In ratifying the commonwealth agreement on December 10, 1991, Ukraine's parliament made some important modifications, asserting Ukraine's right to restrict migration (from other CIS states) and to have its own army and its own currency. Ukraine agreed only to "consult" on foreign policy, rather than to be bound by CIS decisions. On December 21, 1991, the commonwealth membership expanded to include the five Central Asian republics, and on December 25, 1991, Mikhail Gorbachev announced his resignation as president of the USSR. At that point, Ukraine and the other union-level republics of the former

---

*The sovereignty of Ukrainian laws over those emanating from Moscow had already been proclaimed in July 1990.
†A December 2002 poll by the Kiev International Institute for Sociology (KMIS) revealed that 77 percent of Ukrainians still supported independence. This corresponds to the same high levels that existed in the December 1991 referendum.

Soviet Union received international (diplomatic) recognition as independent countries.

The euphoria over independence, however, soon faded in the face of mounting problems. Above all else, the economy was the most pressing concern. The collapse of the Soviet Union accelerated the decline of an already seriously faltering economy. Among the factors that contributed to the economic difficulties was the demand by Russia that Ukraine pay market prices for oil and gas. In addition, the breakup of the Soviet Union disrupted supply and distribution links. President Kravchuk was slow in launching market-oriented reforms, and a continuing confrontation between the opposing political parties in the legislature further complicated the situation. As a result, Ukraine's immediate post-independence period was marked by uncertainty and severe economic hardship for many.

POLITICAL CULTURE AND REGIONAL DIFFERENCES

To understand government process and economic reform in Ukraine, it is best to have a brief background on the nature of the social cleavages within the society. Particularly important for understanding politics in Ukraine is a geographical divide that manifests itself in dramatically different voting behavior in different regions. Because the western part of Ukraine wasn't incorporated into the Soviet Union until World War II, and because Ukraine's ethnic Russian population lives primarily in the eastern and southern regions, different parts of the country exhibit dramatically dissimilar political orientations. As can be seen in Table 1.1 (see p. 3), more than 17 percent of Ukraine's population is ethnic Russian.* Many people, especially in Eastern and Southern Ukraine, speak Russian rather than Ukrainian during their daily work and at home. In Western Ukraine, most people use Ukrainian in their daily discourse. Since independence, public opinion polls have established that regions of Western Ukraine are more pro-Europe while regions of Eastern Ukraine are more pro-Russian in their orientations.

Historical analysts also emphasize a religious partition between the western part of Ukraine and the central and eastern regions. The major religions in Ukraine are Orthodoxy, the Ukrainian Greek Catholic Church (also referred to as the Uniate Catholics), and, for some, atheism or nonbeliever status. The diverse religious terrain also includes various Protestant and Muslim denominations and sects, but these are represented in small numbers. The Orthodox Church, historically identified with Tsarism, served as a vehicle of Russification during the Soviet period and, accordingly, stood in opposition to Ukrainian national consciousness (Armstrong 1963, 209–10). Today, the Ukrainian

---

*At the end of the Soviet era, Russians comprised 51 percent of the population of the entire USSR, and Ukrainians comprised 18 percent, making Ukrainians the second largest nationality group in the Soviet Union.

Orthodox Church under the Kievan Patriarchate (UOC-KP) sees itself as the head of Ukraine's national religious community. The Ukrainian Greek Catholic Church, liquidated between 1946 and 1949, maintains itself in the limited territory of Western Ukraine.

Based on survey data collected in 2005, the major religious groupings in Ukraine are: Ukrainian Orthodox–Kievan Patriarchate (consisting of 29 percent of the population), Ukrainian Orthodox–Moscow Patriarchate (24 percent of the population), Greek Catholic (8 percent), nonbeliever or atheist (12 percent), other or no organized religion (27 percent). Orthodox believers all together constitute about half of the population. The fact that significantly more people categorized themselves as religious believers in 2005 (81 percent) as compared with 1995 (41 percent) represents an important and consequential change for the population.

GOVERNMENT INSTITUTIONS AND STRUCTURES

Ukraine was the last of the former republics to adopt a new constitution. The country's constitution was not determined until June 1996 in large measure because of the inability of Ukrainian leaders to reach an agreement on the appropriate division of decision-making authority between the central government and regional or provincial (**oblast**) governments. Another controversy that contributed to the significant delay in building majority support for the wording of a new constitution was whether Russian should be included along with Ukrainian as a state language. In the end, the constitution preserved Ukrainian as the sole state language.

The lack of constitutional consensus also reflected disagreement on a power-sharing arrangement between the national legislature and the institution of the presidency. Ukraine's parliament did not want to relinquish law-making authority to the president; however, in the end, the president not only won the right of legislative initiative but also won the right to issue law-binding decrees without legislative approval. The question of how and whether to protect, in the constitution, the right of private ownership of enterprises and business, and, more seriously, private ownership of land was also extremely controversial.

The 1996 Constitution maintains Ukraine as a **unitary state**. Regional and local governments are subordinate to the central government in virtually every respect. There are three tiers of government: central government, regional government (including oblasts, Crimea, and Kiev), and local government (which includes cities, districts, raions, villages, and rural settlements.

Executive authority in oblasts and raions rests with appointed state administrations. The president of Ukraine has the power to appoint and to dismiss oblast governors; thus, the regional leaders hold their positions according to the will of the president. Decisions of lower-level entities can be overturned by superior entities. The unitary state is also reflected in Ukraine's budget structure, which mirrors the governmental structure. The budgets of lower-level governments are essentially "nested" within the budgets of their corresponding higher-level governments. Intergovernmental fiscal relations are marked by a high degree of revenue dependency, thus retaining the centralization of fiscal management that characterized the Soviet system.[3]

The President

The main institutions of Ukraine's government structure include the president, prime minister, Cabinet of Ministers, and Verkhovna Rada (Supreme Council or Parliament). The position of president was created through constitutional amendment in 1991 while Ukraine was still a constituent republic within the Soviet Union. Leonid Kravchuk, elected as Chairman of the Ukrainian Supreme Soviet in July 1990, became Ukraine's first directly elected president when he received 61.5 percent of the popular vote on December 1, 1991. In the first post-Soviet presidential election, held in 1994, Kravchuk's former prime minister, Leonid Kuchma, defeated Kravchuk, as the incumbent, in a second-round election (Kuchma won 52 percent of the vote to Kravchuk's 45 percent). Kuchma, who served as prime minister from November 1992 to September 1993, had worked as the director of a huge missile factory in Dnepropetrovsk, Ukraine, in Soviet times.

The central issues in the 1994 presidential campaign were the economic performance of the country and the question of what should be the proper relationship between Ukraine and Russia. Visible signs of economic deterioration were abundant. For example, people stood out on the streets trying to sell their own belongings in order to survive unemployment. Factory workers would sell materials from their factories because they did not receive wages. Kravchuk's rule was also fraught with hyperinflation, which caused the loss of lifetime savings for many Ukrainians. In sum, Kuchma defeated Kravchuk in the 1994 election because Kuchma enjoyed support of the former Communist elite, and because he built his campaign on promises of future prosperity, criticism of the incumbent president, and promises of improved relations with Russia.

During Kuchma's first year in office, he repeatedly complained that parliament was blocking his reform initiatives. After threatening in 1995 to hold a nationwide referendum on confidence in the president and in the parliament, parliament capitulated. A new constitution, giving the president broad powers, was ratified in June 1996.

The constitution defines the president as the head of state. The Cabinet of Ministers, as the highest executive body, is responsible to the president. The president appoints the prime minister and the members of the Cabinet of Ministers, to be approved by parliament. The president enjoys the right of legislative initiative along with deputies, the Cabinet of Ministers, and the National Bank. Although legislative authority resides with the parliament, the president has the right to issue decrees. It takes a two-thirds majority vote for parliament to override a presidential veto, although parliament can hold a vote of no confidence in the Cabinet of Ministers by a simple majority (Kuzio 2000, 130–34).

The president's powers are quite broad. Given that Ukraine is a unitary system rather than a federal system, the president also appoints the heads of local state administrations, on recommendation of the Cabinet of Ministers. Through the cabinet, the president indirectly controls oblast and raion state administrative activities. In addition, and similar to the Russian system, the president sets targets and spending priorities for the government and can change ministers, even dismiss the prime minister, without major political repercussions.

The president of Ukraine is elected for a five-year term by direct popular vote. According to a law on presidential elections adopted by the Verkhovna Rada in March 2004, presidential election campaigns may run for 120 days. A candidate must register 500,000 supporting signatures to get his or her name on the ballot. Presidential elections are held in October, and in the event that none of the candidates wins 50 percent plus one vote in the first round, a runoff between the two top candidates is held three weeks later.

Over the course of his first term (1994–1999), President Kuchma became unpopular because of the continuing deterioration in the life of many Ukrainians, corruption scandals, the rise of oligarchs to economic and political dominance, and increasingly authoritarian tendencies in politics. Kuchma's main opposition in the 1999 presidential election came from the leader of the Communist Party, Petro Symonenko. Symonenko became First Secretary of the Central Committee of the Communist Party of Ukraine in 1993 and was elected to the national parliament in 1994. His official platform promised to give the Russian language official status and explicitly called for state planning (state regulation) and a halt to privatization. The platform rejected North Atlantic Treaty Organization (NATO) membership and called rather for closer relations with Russia and Belarus, including the creation of a single economic space. Symonenko argued that reforms pushed by the International Monetary Fund (IMF) and the World Bank were creating a "national catastrophe" for Ukraine.

The first round of the Ukrainian presidential election (October 31, 1999) did not yield a victor as no one candidate received more than 50 percent of the vote. In the second round redundant (with only the top two candidates from the first round on the November 14, 1999 ballot), Kuchma prevailed with 56.3 percent of the vote over Symonenko with 37.8 percent.

In spite of the economic woes associated with the previous five years, the corruption, and an inability to attract foreign investment, Kuchma was reelected to the presidency of Ukraine in 1999. Believing that a protest vote against the president would be ineffective, some who had doubts about Kuchma voted for him anyway. Throughout the campaign, the mass media was heavily biased in favor of incumbent President Kuchma. When Kuchma refused to participate in debates with the other candidates, this was interpreted by the media not as a sign of weakness but as sign of superiority.

The overall campaign was marked by the heavy use of **administrative resources** in nearly all regions of Ukraine. The many forms of administrative resources included encouraging army personnel, police personnel, students, prisoners, workers in state enterprises, and peasants to vote for Kuchma; and using insinuation of possible repercussions should they not do so (loss of jobs, expulsion from the university; and refusing to distribute vital goods and services such as electricity, gas, and agricultural machines to villages). Another application of administrative resources is the participation of local state employees in direct campaigning for the incumbent. This can occur subtly when university administrators or professors, officers in military schools, or teachers in regular schools promote a vote for the president. As the most dramatic application of administrative resources, Kuchma dismissed, before the second round of the presidential elections, governors of regions of Ukraine where an opposition candidate had claimed victory in the first round. Governors of the regions are, in accordance with the Ukrainian constitution, not elected but appointed to their positions by the president. In general, it is easier to apply administrative resources in Eastern Ukraine, where a larger share of the population remains directly or indirectly dependent on the state, than in the less industrial Western Ukraine, where fewer people work in enterprises tied to the state.

The way in which Kuchma's campaign was conducted during the second round of the 1999 election resembled the electoral campaign of Boris Yeltsin during presidential elections in Russia in 1996 when Yeltsin also faced a Communist Party candidate. In the media throughout Ukraine, Kuchma was portrayed as a centrist and conservative reformer who was fighting against a hardcore Communist who would, if elected, return the country to Soviet practices. Rumors were spread about a possible civil war in the event of a Communist victory and about economic chaos and isolation from Europe and the Western world. A Communist victory was presented as a first step in reuniting Ukraine with Russia. Another rumor, intended to influence the parents of would-be conscripts, was that with a Communist victory, young men would be sent to fight in Chechnya.

Kuchma was prohibited by the constitution from seeking a third term as Ukraine's president. The two main contenders in the 2004 presidential race were Viktor Yanukovych, the prime minister at the time, and Viktor Yushchenko, a former prime minister. President Kuchma had elevated Yanukovych from his governorship of the Donetsk region to serve as prime minister in November 2002. Although Ukraine's economy registered impressive growth under Yanukovych, two criminal convictions from Soviet times colored his impressive career.[4]

Yushchenko had served as Ukraine's prime minister (December 1999–April 2001), having previously headed the National Bank of Ukraine (1993–1999). Although the economy performed well under Yushchenko, his government was defeated in a no-confidence vote in April 2001. Thereafter, Yushchenko went into opposition, and, in January 2002, united several pro-reform and nationalist parties to create the electoral bloc Our Ukraine and stood as its candidate.

Altogether twenty-four names were approved for the 2004 presidential ballot, but only two other candidates were serious contenders: Oleksander Moroz, a former speaker of parliament, Socialist Party leader, and a presidential candidate in 1994 and 1999; and Petro Symonenko, head of the Communist Party of Ukraine, who won nearly 38 percent of the vote in the 1999 presidential election.

Because both Yanukovych and Yushchenko had positive economic records and supported removing Ukraine's troops from Iraq, the electoral campaign revolved around other issues. Yanukovych vowed to maintain Kuchma's political course to ensure stability. In foreign policy, he opposed the European Union (EU) and NATO membership. Although not rejecting the West, he advocated strengthening economic and political ties with Moscow. He supported dual citizenship and Russian as a second state language, thereby appealing to Ukraine's ethnic Russian population. Yanukovych had the support of business leaders in the eastern Donbas industrial region and was backed by officials in the presidential administration. Yushchenko, by contrast, pledged to work for Ukraine's entry into the EU and, possibly, NATO. He pledged to take Ukraine further toward democracy, and promised to create a law-based state and religious freedom. In response to the Russian-speaking electorate's concerns, Yushchenko promised to uphold the Russian-language qualification for local official posts.

The first round of the election was held on October 31, 2004. The results reported by Ukraine's Central Election Commission (CEC) indicated an extremely close contest (see Table 12.1). Although Yushchenko had a slim lead over Yanukovych, neither candidate achieved a majority, so a second round was scheduled for November 21.

TABLE 12.1 First-Round Results for the Ukrainian 2004 Presidential Election

Name of Candidate	Party	First Round October 31, 2004
Viktor Yushchenko	Our Ukraine	39.9%
Viktor Yanukovych	Ukrainian Party of Regions	39.3
Oleksander Moroz	Socialist Party of Ukraine	5.8
Petro Symonenko	Communist Party of Ukraine	5.0
Nataliya Vitrenko	Progressive Party of Ukraine	1.5
Anatoliy Kinakh	Party of Industrialists and Entrepreneurs of Ukraine	.9
Other candidates (24 total)		8.5
Against all		2.0

Source: Central Election Commission of Ukraine at http://www.cvk.gov.ua/elect/wp0011.

The International Election Observation Mission (IEOM) concluded that the first round campaign did not meet a number of Organization for Security and Cooperation in Europe (OSCE), Council of Europe, and other European standards for democratic elections. During the last eight weeks of campaigning, Yanukovych received 64 percent of the airtime, 99 percent of which was considered to be positive or neutral, whereas Yushchenko received 21 percent of the airtime, 54 percent of which was considered to be negative. Other candidates had very limited coverage.[5] In addition, IEOM reported interference by the state administration in favor of Yanukovych, including:

- Disruption or obstruction of opposition campaign events by state authorities
- Failure to respect freedom of assembly
- Dissemination of inflammatory campaign material of unclear origin
- Significant problems with voter lists
- Insufficient number of polling stations
- Lack of transparency during tabulation
- Inadequacies in the CEC's handling of complaints

Even so, the high turnout (74.5 percent of eligible voters) was considered positive. Representatives of other international organizations, such as the European Network of Election Monitoring Organizations (ENEMO), also expressed disappointment with the campaign and the election process.

The runoff election was held on November 21, 2004. The CEC declared Yanukovych the victor with 49.5 percent of the vote compared with Yushchenko's 46.6 percent. Given that during the first round Yushchenko had won more votes than Yanukovych and that the third-place candidate from the first round (Moroz) explicitly endorsed Yushchenko for the second round, these results were hard to believe. Another first-round candidate, Anatoliy Kinakh, also threw his support behind Yushchenko. As a former prime minister and chairman of the powerful Ukrainian Union of Industrialists and Entrepreneurs, Kinakh brought Yushchenko's campaign support from Ukraine's business elite.

In reaction to the implausible results and the violations reported by election observers, hundreds of thousands of protesters filled the streets of Kiev, blockading the cabinet building and the headquarters of the presidential administration. Yushchenko's supporters also staged demonstrations in other large cities, including cities in Yanukovych-supporting regions. As the protest rallies continued, Yushchenko's support expanded to include many government employees and journalists. The ruling councils in Kiev, Ternopil, Vinnystsia, and Ivan-Frankivsk refused to recognize the second-round results. The opposition forces demanded the annulment of the November 21 election, the resignation of Yanukovych's government, and the dismissal of officials responsible for the most egregious violations. Given that Yushchenko had adopted orange as his campaign color, these events came to be known as the Orange Revolution.

Reacting to a claim submitted on Yushchenko's behalf, the Supreme Court of Ukraine agreed to hear arguments concerning election fraud. On the same day, Ukraine's parliament voted to declare the election results invalid, but lacked the constitutional authority to call new elections. Also, during the court's deliberations, the European Parliament passed a resolution calling for a re-run of the elections, while Russian President Putin spoke against repeating the November 21 vote. Numerous other leaders of foreign countries and international organizations published their opinions about the election (Penketh 2004; Maksymiuk 2004).

The Supreme Court issued its decision on December 3, invalidating the November 21 results and annulling both the election and the Central Election Commission's announcement of the results. The court cited massive errors by the government: the CEC's failure to consider allegations of violations by territorial election commissions, citizens who were entered numerous times on the electoral roll, disenfranchised voters added to lists, absentee ballots not controlled by the CEC, and failure of the mass media to adhere to equal conditions (Leovin 2004). The court ruled that the Central Election Commission was to conduct a new runoff election between Yanukovych and Yushchenko, which was scheduled for December 26, 2004.

Kuchma accepted the Supreme Court decision, changed the CEC's membership, and signed legislation changing the electoral law to disallow absentee ballots. In addition, those most directly associated with the electoral fraud left their posts and the officials remaining were no longer as willing to bend the rules. Some senior figures switched their support from Yanukovych to Yushchenko. Moreover, the world was watching more closely; indeed, the December 26 vote took place under the scrutiny of an unprecedented number of international observers. The "tent city" in central Kiev maintained its frontline opposition position through the December vote. By this point, the Orange Revolution was receiving worldwide media attention.

On December 26, 2004, Ukraine's electors turned out for the third time to elect their president. On January 20, 2005, the official results were finally published, with Yushchenko the winner. Table 12.2 shows the results as reported by the CEC for all three stages of the elections (the third stage was officially a re-run of the second round, which the Supreme Court declared invalid). The administrative units of Ukraine (oblasts) are grouped by region. A number of observations can be made on the basis of information in the table. First, Yanukovitch was unable to increase his vote share in any region of Ukraine between the second and third rounds. Although a good portion of the increased support for Yushchenko can be attributed to changes in the conduct of the elections, public support did swing toward Yushchenko. The media also presented Yushchenko more positively, and many members of the government shifted their loyalty, anticipating a Yushchenko victory in December.

The results shown in Table 12.2 reveal a pattern. In regions that were strongholds of support for Yanukovitch (East, Southeast, South, and Crimea), the

TABLE 12.2 Results for Three Rounds of the Ukrainian 2004 Presidential Election by Region

Region (Oblasts)	First Round (October 31)			Second Round (November 21)			Re-Run of Second Round (December 26)			Electorate Weight of Region (% of total)
	Percentage of Vote for Yushchenko	Percentage of Vote for Yanukovych	Voter Turnout	Percentage of Vote for Yushchenko	Percentage of Vote for Yanukovych	Voter Turnout	Percentage of Vote for Yushchenko	Percentage of Vote for Yanukovych	Voter Turnout	
Kiev	62.4	14.6	75.8	74.7	19.9	78.6	78.4	17.5	79.2	5.7
North Zhytomyrska, Kyivska, Chernihivska, Sumska	50.8	23.4	78.2	68.7	27.2	79.6	75.8	20.2	76.3	11.9
Central Poltavska, Vinnytska, Khmelnytska, Cherkaska, Kirovogradska	52.4	21.8	77.5	66.7	29.1	80.5	75.5	20.6	76.6	15.1
West Lvivska, Volynska, Ivano-Frankivska, Rivnenska, Ternopilska	83.5	7.8	82.9	89.3	8.9	84.7	92.7	5.5	86.4	14.8

East Donetska, Luganska	3.5	84.5	75.0	2.9	95.1	94.3	4.9	92.8	82.5	15.4
Southeast Kharkivska, Dnipropetrovska, Zaporizhska	17.1	53.8	69.8	26.4	67.5	76.9	28.3	65.7	72.3	17.8
Southwest Zakarpatska, Chernivetska	55.6	28.8	69.1	63.8	31.8	69.7	73.1	22.5	68.6	4.3
South Mykolaivska, Odesska, Khersonska	21.2	49.6	65.8	29.8	64.6	72.4	31.5	63.0	69.0	10.0
Crimea (including Sevastopol)	11.6	69.9	66.9	13.4	83.2	78.0	14.1	82.6	75.5	4.9
Total	39.9	39.3	74.5	46.6	49.5	80.4	52.0	44.2	77.2	100

Note: For full results by oblast, see IAC Election of the President of Ukraine at http://www.cvk.gov.ua/elect/wp0011.

Source: Central Election Commission of Ukraine.

officially reported results changed little between November 21 and December 26. In other regions, however, the reported vote percentage for Yushchenko was significantly greater in December than it was in November. In general, Yushchenko made his greatest gains between November and December in those regions where he already commanded majority support. Viktor Andriyovich Yushchenko became Ukraine's president on January 23, 2005, on taking an oath of office in the Verkhovna Rada.

Mass Media

Given the manipulation of the media that characterized these elections, we stop for a moment to consider how important to the functioning of politics the media is in many countries of the world. The mass media influences and helps shape public opinion. Under President Kravchuk, Ukraine's mass media was relatively free, but it came under heavy attack during the rule of Kuchma, who along with Russian President Putin was listed as one of the main enemies of free press in the world by the U.S.-based Committee to Protect Journalists (CPJ).[5] Television programming critical of the president was extremely rare under Kuchma; rather TV stations reported favorably on the president while discrediting the opposition.

The situation with newspapers was similar. Methods of controlling the media included not only troublesome and unwelcome audits but also more sinister means such as threats of violence and death against the journalists. The reluctance of police to investigate such threats and to search for perpetrators of violence left journalists essentially defenseless. As a result, journalism became the second most dangerous occupation in Ukraine after mining.

The courts were also used against independent newspapers. Courts would impose unreasonably large fines, or the work of the newspapers would be interrupted by police or tax inspections. Printing houses would refuse to provide their services to oppositional publications, and if they did, would charge exorbitant prices.

The most celebrated case of violence against a journalist in Ukraine was the Heorhiy Gongadze case in 2000. Gongadze had investigated the financial machinations of Ukraine's oligarchs and then published the information on the Internet. He repeatedly asked for police protection after he received threats. The protection was not provided. Gongadze disappeared in September 2000, and his decapitated body was found in a forest outside Kiev. Later, audiotapes surfaced of conversations between Kuchma, his chief of staff, the head of state security, and the interior minister complaining about Gongadze's criticism. The conversations included a discussion about how to get rid of Gongadze.[7] Investigations into the death of Gongadze were actively pursued with the ascension of Yushchenko to Ukraine's presidency in early 2005, and expectations are that the elaborate system of repression of free and unbiased media that emerged under Kuchma no longer exists.

The Legislative Branch

Turning from the executive branch to the legislative branch: Ukraine's national parliament is called the Verkhovna Rada. The right of legislative initiative for deputies is secured under the law, including compulsory examination of deputies' proposals and the opportunity for sponsors to address parliament concerning their initiatives. Referrals of legislative proposals and new bills are made to the appropriate "subject matter" committees. Once a bill reaches the floor, it must be voted on and approved twice before it can be enacted. These are referred to as votes taken on "first reading" and "second reading." If necessary, bills approved on first reading may be shelved or referred back to committee for revision. For the second reading, all bills are voted on the basis of an "article-by-article" vote, as well as on the bill as a whole. (If further revisions are appropriate, a "third reading" may be scheduled at this stage.) On enactment, the legislation is presented to the president, who has fifteen days within which either to sign the law or veto it. If vetoed, the bill returns to parliament, together with the president's remarks. Vetoed bills are subject to a two-thirds parliamentary override vote.[8] Even if the parliament overrides a presidential veto, however, no mechanism exists whereby a bill can be implemented without a presidential signature. Thus, such bills may simply rest in the president's office.

The Rada possesses oversight authority with respect to actions of the Cabinet of Ministers. The Rada can dissolve the government via a vote of no confidence; however, new elections are not necessarily implied by such a vote. In the case of a no-confidence vote, the president has sixty days in which to appoint a new cabinet. The speaker, or chairman, of the Verkhovna Rada presides over and manages the work of parliament, supervises the parliamentary administration (staff bureaucracy), and represents parliament in its relations with the president and other governmental bodies.

Results of the 1994 Parliamentary Elections

Ukraine's first fully competitive parliamentary elections (to the Verkhovna Rada) were held in March and April of 1994, with repeat elections in July and August of 1995. Candidates were elected from 450 single-member electoral districts for four-year terms. Because of the high number of registered candidates (5,833 in the first round), because the electoral law required that more than half of registered voters in a constituency needed to cast a vote for the election to be valid, and because the winner needed to acquire more than half of the votes cast, only 338 districts successfully completed their elections by the end of the second round of voting. This meant that the elections had failed to produce a winner in 112 constituencies. Although the overall turnout for the first (74.78 percent) and second (nearly 67 percent) rounds of voting was high enough to validate the elections, it was difficult for candidates to secure the necessary

50 percent of the vote; thus, additional repeat elections were held in November and December of 1995 and February of 1996.

In the 1994 parliamentary elections, the majority of the candidates for the Rada ran as independents rather than as nominees of a political party. The majority of those elected were also independents. To understand why more than half of Ukraine's parliamentarians between 1994 and 1997 did not have a party affiliation, we look at the electoral law. Under the "Law of Ukraine on Elections of People's Deputies of Ukraine," signed by President Kravchuk on November 18, 1993, nomination by election blocs or parties required a significant amount of organization, whereas nomination by a voter group or labor collective was organizationally less complicated.[9] Thus, the electoral law was friendly toward independents and tough on organized parties by making the nomination hurdles greater for party representatives than for independents. The early Ukrainian law, therefore, could be classified as "antiparty."

In addition to the large number of independent deputies in Ukraine's parliament after the 1994–1995 elections, the Communist faction that did exist within the Ukrainian parliament was at odds with the president over just about everything, from the naming of a prime minister, to budget issues, to the constitutional bill on the separation of powers. The Communist Party was able to stall and, in some cases, prevent large-scale privatization, at least from 1994 to 1996 (Wilson 2000, 1304). Relations between the parliament and the president were regularly antagonistic.

In 1997, the Ukrainian parliament revised the electoral law and initiated a mixed electoral system. Thus, the 1998 and 2002 parliamentary elections in Ukraine were based on a mixed voting system: 225 deputies were elected from a single national constituency from party or party-bloc lists; the remaining 225 members were elected from single-mandate constituencies by a majority vote. In the single-member districts (SMD), elections were by plurality in one round. With no minimum for voter turnout, elections could be finished in one round. For a party to gain seats through the proportional representation (PR) system, it needed to garner at least 4 percent of the vote. The goal was to create larger party blocs in parliament, thus (hypothetically) allowing for more effective lawmaking.*

In 2004, the Verkhovna Rada adopted another election law postulating a fully proportional party-list system for parliamentary elections. This election law came into force in October 2005 and requires that the entire parliament be elected from party lists, with seats distributed on a proportional basis. This law is quite opposite to Ukraine's first election law, which was antiparty in nature. According to the 2004 law, only political parties and blocs can take part in elec-

---

*Robert Moser (1995), however, has made the argument that mixed electoral systems are contributing to the proliferation of parties because some parties do well in the SMD half of the election and others do well in the PR half.

tions. The threshold was set at 3 percent of the national vote for gaining seats in the parliament, instead of the previous 4 percent threshold.

Results of the 1998 Parliamentary Elections

For the 1998 parliamentary elections, thirty political parties were listed in the party-list section of the ballot. The main result of having so many parties on the ballot was that votes were spread out and no single party emerged with a majority. The Communist Party of Ukraine (CPU) did the best with 25 percent of the party-list vote. Its nearest competitor, Rukh, secured only 9 percent of the vote. The Electoral Bloc of Socialist and Peasant Parties came in third and the Greens fourth. The People's Democratic Party (PDP), Hromada, the Progressive Socialists, and the United Social Democrats also crossed the 4 percent threshold. In the single-member district voting, the independent candidates were the winners with 114 independents winning seats. Running as an independent, however, generally did not mean that the candidate was unaffiliated, because most independents joined legislative factions after their election victories.

The CPU is the main left oppositional political party in Ukraine. Although the Communist Party was banned from August 1991 to mid-1993, a new Communist Party of Ukraine was officially registered in October 1993. The Communist Party's program is classical in its leftist orientation, calling for a renationalization of key sectors of the economy and a halt to privatization. Bowing to the reality of the times, the CPU program also pledged to respect existing private businesses, freedom of worship, and multiparty democracy. The party program has also called for reunification with Russia and recognition of the Russian language as having equal status with Ukrainian as a state language.

The Socialist Party of Ukraine was formed in the fall of 1992 under the leadership of Oleksander Moroz, who was a presidential candidate in 1994, 1999, and 2004. The socialists formed an electoral bloc with the Peasant Party to compete in the 1998 elections, but contended in 2002 on their own. Although the "leftist" political parties do have their differences, generally they agree on three themes: (1) a condemnation of pro-capitalist policies that have contributed to a multitude of problems such as joblessness; (2) a negative attitude toward incorporation into the West, especially NATO; and (3) a positive orientation toward cooperation with Russia.

At the time of the 1998 elections, Rukh was the most experienced and developed political party in the center-right bloc and held the position of leader among the "national-democratic" parties. Rukh was founded in 1989 as a Popular Front. Party leaders are concerned about maintaining national independence against any remnants of Moscow's imperial policy and advocate a foreign policy orientation toward the West (including NATO membership). With regard to domestic policies, Rukh has taken a supportive stance toward a market economy and liberal democratic principles.

Far right parties, such as the Ukrainian National Assembly (UNA), also exist in Ukraine. They are militant, openly hostile toward Russia, and appeal to only a very small minority (Andreev 1996; Luhovyk 1998). The UNA's paramilitary arm, the Ukrainian People's Self-Defense Forces (UNSO), formed the core of the guerrilla fighters that resisted Soviet control in the late 1940s and early 1950s.

The Green Party (ZPU) was founded in 1990 as the political wing of the environmental organization Zlaney Svit, which in turn had been founded in 1987. In 1994, the Green Party joined the European Federation of Green Parties.

Another important contender in 1998 was Hromada, which emerged in September 1997 under the leadership of former Prime Minister Pavlo Lazarenko as a party in opposition to the Kuchma government. Lazarenko was prime minister from May 1996 to July 1997, when he was dismissed by Kuchma amid allegations of corruption and a lack of dedication to reforms. The party of power in 1998 was the People's Democratic Party (PDP). Incumbent president Leonid Kuchma was nominated by the PDP as its presidential candidate for the 1999 elections. The PDP supported market reforms and promoted improved relations with both Russia and Europe.

Regional patterns to the vote followed lines similar to the 1994–1995 election results. The Communists performed disproportionately well in the east and the south, while Rukh's electoral strength was disproportionately in the west. The Electoral Bloc of Socialist and Peasant Parties won the largest portion of its votes in the central oblasts, while Hromada was disproportionately strong in the southeast. Votes in favor of the PDP and the ZPU were more evenly distributed across regions.

Although the Communist Party members organized the largest faction in parliament after the 1998 election, they still did not have a majority. The lack of majority control of the parliament by any one faction or by a coalition of factions was plainly realized when the deputies attempted to elect a new speaker from among themselves. The parliament opened its first session on May 12, 1998, and immediately ran into difficulty. The PDP, Rukh, ZPU, and the United Social Democrats together were able to oppose the election of Communist Party leader Petro Symonenko to the post of speaker despite his backing by Oleksander Moroz, the previous speaker and the leader of the Electoral Bloc of Socialist and Peasant Parties. By the beginning of July, fifty different deputies had been nominated for the speaker position, yet the Rada did not have a speaker and the work of the parliament was stalled. Finally, on July 7, deputies voted in favor of Oleksandr Tkachenko (of the Electoral Bloc of Socialist and Peasant Parties) as the new speaker. Tkachenko had been deputy speaker in the previous parliament and minister of agriculture before the collapse of the Soviet Union.[10]

Results of the 2002 Parliamentary Elections

In March 2002, Ukraine elected its third post-Soviet parliament. Six parties gained enough votes to win representation through the party-list voting system. Counting seats won in the SMD races, the pro-presidential For a United

Ukraine (ZYU) could claim 119 deputies in the Verkhovna Rada, thus making it the largest faction in the 2003 parliament (see Table 12.3). The Viktor Yushchenko Bloc, Our Ukraine, claimed 113 deputies; the Communist Party of Ukraine, 66 deputies; the Yuliya Tymoshenko Bloc, 23 deputies; the Socialist Party of Ukraine, 23 deputies; and the Social-Democratic Party of Ukraine–United (SDPU-O), 17 deputies.

For a United Ukraine was created just four months prior to the March 2002 parliamentary elections as an alliance of the People's Democratic Party, the Agrarians, the Party of Industrialists and Entrepreneurs, the Party of Regions, and Labor Ukraine. The ZYU's leader, Volodymyr Lytvyn, was the head of the presidential administration. After the election, Lytvyn was installed as parliamentary speaker in May 2002. Prime Minister Anatoliy Kinakh was second on the list of top names of For a United Ukraine; it was the **party of power** as Kuchma's open favorite in the 2002 parliamentary elections.

TABLE 12.3   Results for the Ukrainian 2002 Parliamentary Election

Party (Bloc)	Percent of the Vote	Number of PR Seats	Total Seats (includes SDM seats)
Election Bloc of Political Parties—Viktor Yushchenko Bloc, Our Ukraine Leader: Viktor Yushchenko	23.57%	70	113
Communist Party of Ukraine Leader: Petro Symonenko	19.98	59	66
Election Bloc of Political Parties— For a United Ukraine Leader: Volodymyr Lytvyn	11.77	35	119
Election Bloc of Political Parties— Yuliya Tymoshenko Bloc Leader: Yuliya Tymoshenko	7.26	22	23
Socialist Party of Ukraine Leader: Yuri Moroz	6.87	20	23
Social-Democratic Party of Ukraine—United Leader: Viktor Medvedchuk	6.27	19	17
Other parties/Independents	21.73		89
Against all	2.55		
Total	100%	225	450

Note: There was a turnout of 69.3 percent of registered voters.
Source: Central Election Commission of Ukraine.

The SDPU-O was also aligned with President Kuchma as it had been in the 1998 election. That party is often referred to as the "party of the oligarchs" because it is headed by two businessmen, Hryhory Surkis and Viktor Medvedchuk. In May 2002, SDPU-O leader Medvedchuk was appointed head of the presidential administration. Medvedchuk spearheaded a drive to limit the power of the opposition and to consolidate control of state institutions by parties and personnel friendly to Kuchma.[11]

In juxtaposition to the two pro-presidential parties (the SDPU-O and the ZYU) were the left opposition and the right opposition. As the core of the left opposition, the Communist Party platform pledged to prevent the massive purchase of land by the nouveau riche and foreigners; to stop "the criminal grabatization [privatization]"; and "[to] get rid of the dictatorship and the services of the U.S. administration, the IMF, and other financial-political octopi."[12]

Leading the center-right opposition in 2002 was the Victor Yushchenko Bloc, Our Ukraine. After Yushchenko became president of Ukraine in January 2005, his political bloc could no longer be referred to as the opposition since it had become the governing party. For the 2002 election campaign period and through 2004, however, Our Ukraine was in the opposition with its support of radical economic and political reform and in its call for Ukraine's integration into European and trans-Atlantic structures.

The second major electoral bloc that was part of the center-right opposition under President Kuchma was the Yuliya Tymoshenko Bloc. President Yushchenko appointed Tymoshenko prime minister in early 2005; thus, she became part of the governing coalition. In September 2005, President Yushchenko dismissed Tymoshenko amid allegations that she had abused her office and replaced her with Yuriy Yekhanurov as prime minister. The Yuliya Tymoshenko Bloc once again became part of the opposition; it supports radical reform in Ukraine's political system.

The most critical result of the 2002 elections to the Verkhovna Rada was that Our Ukraine, the Yuliya Tymoshenko Bloc, the Socialist Party, and the Communist Party crystallized as an anti-Kuchma opposition. The CPU was no longer the largest faction in the Verkhovna Rada, but it formed the core of the leftist opposition along with the Socialist Party. Our Ukraine and the Yuliya Tymoshenko Bloc formed the core of the center-right opposition. The relatively poorer performance of the Communists in 2002 compared with 1994 and 1998 can be attributed in part to the decline of the older voting population of Ukraine and the fact that many of the votes of the "protest electorate" went to the electoral bloc of Victor Yushchenko in 2002.

President Leonid Kuchma's party of power, the ZYU, did well in the 2002 elections. According to most observers, however, this victory did not accurately represent the preferences of the people throughout Ukraine, considering the fact that the use of administrative resources, vote falsification, and ballot rigging was allegedly pervasive. The ZYU's high vote count in majoritarian districts indicates that this was where most of the irregularities took place. The ZYU's result was assisted by high vote counts from closed institutions (for example, hospitals and military bases). The electoral fortunes of the pro-presidential SDPU-O were not necessarily indicative of grassroots support. The SDPU-O had massive financial resources and controlled the 1+1 and Inter TV channels.[13]

In evaluating the March 2002 parliamentary elections, the National Democratic Institute, led by former U.S. Secretary of State Madeleine Albright, received "credible reports" of intimidation of journalists, candidates being denied access to the media, unbalanced news coverage, and illegal use of public funds and facilities. The Parliamentary Assembly of the Council of Europe (PACE) reported that the 2002 parliamentary election campaign was marred by fear, harassment, and intimidation.[14] The IEOM recorded violations including the use of administrative leverage in promoting the election bid of the pro-presidential For a United Ukraine bloc. In the words of a U.S. State Department spokesman, the use of "administrative resources by For a United Ukraine (ZYU) was brazen and open."[15]

Thus, the election contributed to an already-existing sense of distrust and alienation between the Ukrainian people and their governing officials. The 2002 election results were also arguably influenced by both Russian and U.S. meddling. Russian presidential administration chief Aleksandr Voloshin was quoted in the Ukrainian media as saying that ZPU, the SDPU-O, and the CPU were the best blocs for strengthening Russian-Ukrainian relations. Just days before the March 2002 election, the Russian Ambassador to Ukraine, Viktor Chernomyrdin, voiced support for those parties and election blocs that called for the development and deepening of relations between Russia and Ukraine. Chernomyrdin noted specifically that Victor Yushchenko's Our Ukraine was not such a party.[16]

The United States in turn provided support for several nongovernmental organizations operating in Ukraine, the activities of which likely helped the election chances of Yushchenko's Our Ukraine and other opposition parties. Progressive Socialist Party leader Nataliya Vitrenko said on March 25, 2002, that U.S. pressure on that year's election campaign in Ukraine was the strongest in the contemporary history of the country. She alleged an "unprecedented" scale of interference by Washington in Ukrainian affairs.[17]

VOTING BEHAVIOR IN UKRAINE

In Ukraine, the majority of eligible voters do participate in both presidential and parliamentary elections. For the 1999 presidential election, 74.9 percent of the eligible voters participated. For the 2004 presidential election, turnout was 74.5 percent in the first round, 80.4 percent in the second round, and 77.2 percent in the re-run of the second round. This represents almost exactly the same overall turnout rate as in the first round of the 1994 parliamentary elections, which was 74.8 percent. Turnout for the March 1998 parliamentary elections was 69.6 percent. For the 2002 elections, voter turnout held steady at 69.3 percent.

In Ukraine, across all elections, a clear regional pattern underlies the choice of candidates and political parties. How Ukrainian citizens will vote can be predicted best by looking at their region of residence. Divisions between regions are conspicuous. For example, in 2002, Yushchenko's Our Ukraine found more voter support in Western Ukraine than in Eastern Ukraine, while the pro-government For a United Ukraine and the Communists found substantial support primarily in eastern and southern regions. The ZYU's main base of support was in the Donbas region, the same as that of the CPU, while it was less popular in Western and Central Ukraine, including Kiev. For the 2004 presidential election, the southern and eastern regions of Ukraine voted overwhelmingly in support of Viktor Yanukovych (Kuchma's prime minister at the time), while the lion's share of citizens in Central and Western Ukraine voted for Yushchenko. Such a regionally divided electorate creates challenges for building a national consensus in support of both domestic and foreign policy initiatives.

A related, but independent, predictor of voters' choice is language use, with Ukrainian speakers being more likely to vote for center-right parties in parliamentary elections. Issues are also important to the Ukrainian electorate. In general, those who vote for the Communists in contrast to those who vote for the center-right prefer more pro-Russian policies and a planned economy, and are hesitant about European integration.

The political platforms and policy positions advocated by candidates were critical in determining the outcome of the 2004 presidential election. The result of the election was that those who strongly preferred reintegrating with Russia voted in larger numbers for Yanukovych while those who prioritized relations with Europe more uniformly voted in support of Yushchenko. Ukrainian voters, despite the fluctuating political institutions they confront, vote in ways predicted by both issue position motivations and according to a cleavage- or identity-based model. When political parties or candidates converge into the same issue space (that is, when they have similar political platforms), identity factors and campaign effects emerge as the primary predictors of party choice. Many prominent Ukrainian politicians do have their names on blocs of political parties, and the names of presidential candidates on party lists clearly do play an important role in parliamentary vote choices. Nonetheless, political parties in Ukraine are operating as expressions of public attitudes, not simply as organizational vehicles for the advancement of the careers of presidential hopefuls.

Voting is the primary mode of political participation in Ukraine; the vast majority of citizens report no other active involvement in political life beyond voting. This is similar to most other countries of the world. In 2000, this book's author conducted a public opinion poll throughout all regions of Ukraine.* The

---

*The surveys reported in this chapter were conducted by the author together with Professors Andriy Gorbachyk and Volodymyr Volovych of Taras Shevchenko National University in Kiev. The funding for the surveys was provided by the U.S. Department of State.

people were given a list of political activities and asked whether they had ever done any of them. Table 12.4 shows the proportion of the Ukrainian population that reported having engaged in each of a series of activities.

In another public opinion poll conducted in 2005, the numbers who reported taking part in these activities remained small. In 2005, 8 percent of Ukrainians reported that they had signed a petition, and another 8 percent reported that they had contacted a deputy or public official. Reported levels of participation in demonstrations, however, increased dramatically to 29 percent of the population in the aftermath of the Orange Revolution. Thus, nationwide surveys show that, as in other countries, the vast majority of the population engages in no other political activity beyond voting. Yet, if we take the figure that reports the proportion of the population that has participated in demonstration (29 percent) and multiply it by the population of Ukraine (approximately 47.4 million), the figure that results is more than 13 million. Thus, almost 14 million Ukrainians had participated in a demonstration as of 2005. This is not a small number.

When Viktor Yanukovych was declared the winner after the second round of the 2004 presidential election, many perceived this as an attempt by the authorities to steal the election. Hundreds of thousands of Ukrainians filled the streets and nearly two months of intensive political activity followed, engaging people in all parts of the country. This tremendous upsurge in political involvement became a decisive factor in political change. Thus, the events of November and December of 2004 rightly may be called a *revolution*. Ukrainians broke free from a history of repression; they had long been subject to suppression, Russification, and the denial of an independent national identity. A good portion of the population, although discontent, had not believed in the possibility of any real

TABLE 12.4 Political Participation Levels of Ukrainian Citizens

Activity	Percentage of Citizens Who Have Ever Done the Activity
Participate in a rally or a demonstration	14.5%
Contact deputies or other public officials	13.4
Sign petitions (letters)	12.0
Take part in any volunteer work on behalf of a candidate or party	10.2
Contact by letter or phone, a central newspaper, magazine, or TV station	6.9
Join a social organization or initiative group	5.9
Take part in a strike	4.9

Orange Revolution demonstration in Kiev, 2004.

benefits associated with challenging or protesting the government. The Orange Revolution gave the people an experience with success in confronting the authorities, paving the way for significant change in both the political system and in the orientation of the people.

THE POLITICAL ECONOMY OF DEMOCRATIC TRANSITION

As can be seen from Table 12.5, Ukraine is a poor country. Its gross national income (GNI) per capita is less than 3 percent of that of the United States. Even more striking is that Ukraine's GNI per capita is less than half of Russia's; plus the economy still shows distortions dating back to Soviet times. The leading export positions are held by metallurgical products (44 percent) and by mineral and chemical products (22 percent).[18] This export structure has significant drawbacks for Ukraine because the production associated with these exports requires substantial imports of energy resources from Russia. In addition, Ukraine's exports tend to represent products with low added value, which is not advantageous in an age of high technology. Limited state financing and foreign direct investments prevent modern production techniques from being implemented. Ukraine's international competitiveness is further

TABLE 12.5 Ukraine's Economic Performance Indicators

Economic Indicator	1998	1999	2000	2001	2002	2003
Agriculture, value added (% of GDP)	—	14.28	17.08	16.37	15.30	14.06
Exports of goods and services (% of GDP)	—	53.70	62.45	55.46	55.08	52.95
Foreign Direct Investment, net flows (BoP, US$)	—	496,000,000	595,000,000	792,000,000	693,000,000	—
GDP (US$)	41,900,000,000	31,600,000,000	31,300,000,000	38,000,000,000	41,400,000,000	49,536,552,960
GDP growth (annual %)	−1.94	−0.2	5.8	9.1	4.5	9.4
GNI per capita, Atlas method (US$)	850	760	690	720	770	970
GNI, Atlas method (US$)	42,500,000,000	37,852,680,192	34,349,780,992	35,353,673,728	38,217,011,200	46,738,624,512
Illiteracy rate, adult total (% of people age 15 and above)	—	0.41	0.39	0.38	0.36	—
Imports of goods and services (% of GDP)	44.16	48.25	57.95	53.86	54.23	48.27
Industry, value added (% of GDP)	—	38.51	36.32	34.70	38.20	40.3
Inflation, GDP deflator (annual %)	12.06	27.4	23.12	9.95	5.12	6.93
Life expectancy at birth, total (years)	—	68.22	68.20	—	68.17	—
Population growth (annual %)	−0.79	−0.81	−0.83	−0.77	−0.75	−0.74
Population, total	50,300,000	49,900,000	49,500,000	49,100,000	48,700,000	48,356,000
Services, etc., value added (% of GDP)	—	47.21	46.60	48.93	46.50	45.64
Trade in goods (% of GDP)	—	74.18	91.26	84.30	84.26	—
Military expenditures, dollar figure[a]	—	—	—	—	617,900,000	—
Military expenditures (% of GDP)	—	—	—	—	1.5	—

Source: Unless otherwise noted, all figures are from the World Bank at http://devdata.worldbank.org/data-query/.

[a]Figures for the two rows of military data are from the CIA's *World Factbook*—Rank Order—Military expenditures—dollar figures at http://www.odci.gov/cia/publications /factbook/rankorder/2067rank.txt.

undermined by a **brain drain** of scientists and other skilled professionals abroad. Thus, although potentially competitive because of its resources, size, and location, Ukraine is restricted by an obsolete and noncompetitive economy.

Two top sectors of Ukraine's economy, the military-industrial complex and shipbuilding, have experienced particularly difficult times. A large portion of the country's production had been geared toward weaponry, aircraft, and other military hardware. This output is less competitive on the world market than it was within the relatively closed market of the Soviet sphere of influence. The shipbuilding industry has also suffered from a lack of orders and strong competition from Japan and South Korea. Tourism and land transit services, however, provide a potential bright spot on the economic horizon.

Privatization is a critical component of Ukraine's economic reform agenda. Before the launch of privatization, only 2.9 percent of employees worked in the private sector in Ukraine, while state enterprises (at both the central and municipal level) absorbed 94 percent of the workforce (Kuzio 2000, 153). The Ukrainian government adopted its first plan for the privatization of state enterprises in October 1991, with enabling legislation in 1992. The legislation outlined different methods of privatization—buy-out of small privatization objects by associations of buyers, lease of state property with the option of a future buy-out, sales through commercial or noncommercial tenders, sale of state properties by auction, and creation of joint stock companies and sale of shares (corporatization of enterprises).

Hyperinflation, however, along with a political and social environment unfriendly to such reform, delayed the process. The magnitude of the inflation problem cannot be overstated. Ukraine has experienced some of the highest inflation rates in the world's history.

To reform the country's economy, new policies needed to be adopted and new institutions needed to be built to allow for currency stabilization, monetary reform, international trade integration, and credit regulation. Targets set for the privatization of small, medium, and large firms passed unmet. By 1994, for example, only 28.4 percent of the State Program of Privatization was completed (Kuzio 2000, 154–159).

In July 1995, the Cabinet of Ministers issued a resolution criticizing the slow pace of privatization, blaming it on poor organization by agencies, ministries, and other central and local executive authorities. In November 1997, the Verkhovna Rada suspended the privatization process amid reports of inefficiency and corruption. The legislative ban on privatization ended in mid-February 1998. A revised program submitted by President Kuchma allowed privatization of the energy and telecommunications sectors but forbid the sale of farmland.[19] The Verkhovna Rada adopted a Land Code, specifying rules for the sale of land, in October 2001.

During the privatization process, the purchase of industries and enterprises was basically closed to companies from Western countries, and revenues from the privatization process did not contribute significantly to state reserves. Of the businesses that were privatized, some suffered bankruptcies because of the inexperience of the owners or because the owners, rather than investing in their companies, sold valuable equipment and shut down factories. More recently, many of the older privatized companies have been restructured and have increased their output. Other new entrepreneurs have also been successful.

The reprivatization and renationalization of some of Ukraine's major enterprises, however, became highly likely with Yushchenko's ascendancy to the presidency. Yuliya Tymoshenko, appointed prime minister in February 2005, said within weeks of her appointment that the government, jointly with the prosecutor general's office, would challenge many of the privatizations that occurred under Kuchma. Tymoshenko stated: "We will return to the state what was illegally transferred into private, but dishonest, hands."[20]

Ukraine's economy was in decline from 1990 through 1999; in 2000, it finally began to register positive growth rates. In January 2005, the State Statistics Committee announced that industrial production had grown by 12.5 percent in 2004. The agricultural sector is also extremely important to the overall health of Ukraine's economy. In January 2002, an agriculture ministry official, Serhiy Ryzhuk, told journalists that Ukraine exported $1.8 billion worth of farm produce in 2001, a 34 percent rise compared to 2000. Ryzhuk added that farm produce accounted for 12 percent of Ukraine's total exports in 2001;[21] unfortunately, 2002 and 2003 were not as strong. Ukraine imported grain in 2003, including grain from Russia, to compensate for a poor harvest. Agricultural productivity recovered in 2004. The Ukrainian harvest of grain and leguminous crops (including maize) in 2004 was double the 2003 figure.[22]

FOREIGN POLICY AND NATIONAL SECURITY

Ukraine and Russia

True to the history of the region, the contest over Ukrainian geographical space has continued in Ukraine's post-independence period. Some members of the parliament of the Russian Federation demanded that the **Crimean Peninsula**, placed under Ukrainian jurisdiction by Khrushchev in 1954, be returned to Russia. The peninsula is important strategically because it serves as a primary base for the Russian and Ukrainian Black Sea fleets. The population of the peninsula has a majority of ethnic Russians. An active, vocal, pro-Russian separatist movement in Crimea added to the tensions in the early 1990s.

Competition between Moscow and Kiev remained pervasive through the mid-1990s. A Russian-Ukrainian Friendship Treaty was finally signed by President Yeltsin and President Kuchma on May 31, 1997.[23] The treaty allowed for the basing of the Russian Black Sea fleet on the Crimean Peninsula. The fleet itself was divided between Russia and Ukraine. Since then, relations between Russia and Ukraine have been both friendlier and more conciliatory.

Ukraine's most important international relationship is the one that it has with Russia. Despite the inequality in the relationship and concerns over Russian hegemony, the two countries remain closely intertwined and interdependent. Many within Ukraine would like to reestablish an integrated union with Russia.

Russia is Ukraine's most important trading partner. In 1994, no less than 39 percent of the country's exports went to Russia, and 59 percent of Ukraine's imports came from Russia, mostly in energy supplies.[24] As of 2004, Russia remained Ukraine's biggest trading partner: Ukraine sent 17 percent of its exports to Russia and received from Russia 32 percent of its imports.[25] Ukraine is making a concerted effort to lessen its trade dependence on Russia and turn more toward Europe, but it remains critically dependent on oil and gas from Russia. Ukraine and Russia often dispute the cost of fuel, the timing of deliveries, and the terms for payment of Ukrainian energy bills.

In spite of these challenges, Presidents Kuchma and Yushchenko have steadfastly worked to maintain good relations with Russia, while trying to keep their options open with regard to Europe and the United States. Kuchma frequently assured the country's ethnic Russians that there would never be any forced "Ukrainization" and that Russia would "long remain a leading partner of Ukraine."[26] At the same time, President Kuchma declared that "the direction of Ukraine was integration into the EU."[27]

Yushchenko's first trips abroad in January 2005 as Ukraine's new president highlighted the need to appease Russia, while attempting to move closer to Europe. The day after his inauguration Yushchenko flew to Moscow, his first official visit. The following day, January 25, he addressed a session of the Parliamentary Assembly of the Council of Europe in Strasbourg and vowed to bring Ukraine into the European Union.

Ukraine and Europe

Progress in solidifying Ukraine's integration into the European Union (EU) took a giant step forward with the Orange Revolution. Prior to Yushchenko's victory in the 2004 presidential election, the prospects for EU membership were not encouraging. In early 2005, however, Ukraine signed an "action plan" with the European Union to increase political and economic cooperation. The three-year plan aims to bring Ukrainian laws more into line with EU norms and is a major step toward eventual membership. Under the plan, the EU pledged to support Ukraine's bid to join the World Trade Organization; to increase cooperation in areas ranging from transport and energy to security and foreign policy; and to work to ease visa restrictions on Ukrainians seeking to work, study, or visit the EU countries. President Yushchenko declared repeatedly during his presidential campaign and during his first weeks in office that Ukraine's entry into the EU is his primary objective.[28]

Ukraine's goal in seeking membership in the EU is reasonable. Eight post-Communist countries joined the EU in May 2004—Czech Republic, Estonia, Hungary, Latvia, Lithuania, Poland, Slovakia, and Slovenia. At that time Ukraine was not offered membership. In February 2005, Yushchenko appointed Borys Tarasyuk as his foreign minister. Tarasyuk had served previously in that position, but resigned after his pro-EU and pro-NATO activities put him into conflict with Moscow. After winning election to the Rada in 2002, Tarasyuk served as chair of the parliamentary Committee for European Integration.

In a 2005 survey conducted throughout Ukraine, respondents were asked how they thought relations between their country and Europe should develop.* Possible answers were as follows:

1. Ukraine should become integrated with the European Union.
2. Ukraine should gradually increase ties with Europe.
3. Relations should stay the same.
4. Ukraine should decrease its ties with Europe.
5. Ukraine and Europe should go in different directions completely.

As can be seen in Figure 12.1, 37 percent wanted to gradually increase ties with Europe and another 33 percent wanted full integration with the European Union.

In a second question, respondents were asked how they thought relations between Ukraine and Russia should develop. Possible answers were as follows:

1. Ukraine and Russia should unify.
2. Ukraine and Russia should increase ties, but not unify.
3. Relations should stay the same.
4. Ukraine should decrease its ties with Russia.
5. Ukraine and Russia should develop themselves independently and differently.

As shown in Figure 12.2, an even greater majority of the population wanted to increase ties with Russia or to unify with Russia. Thus, the people of Ukraine want to increase ties with both Russia and Europe.

In a third question, respondents were asked to choose between the two. The question was stated as follows: "Should Ukraine unify with Russia, even at the expense of better ties with Europe?" Respondents were to place themselves on a scale from 1 to 7, where "1" meant that Ukraine and Russia should unify and "7" meant that Ukraine should become a member of the European Union. Sixteen percent chose unification with Russia, but the responses were distributed across all categories. Thus, a broad range of opinion on this question was exhibited by Ukraine's population. There was no consensus. No wonder Ukrainians are still "sitting on the fence" concerning relations with both Russia and Europe.

*This is one of the surveys discussed earlier; it was conducted by the author with Ukrainian colleagues Gorbachyk and Volovych.

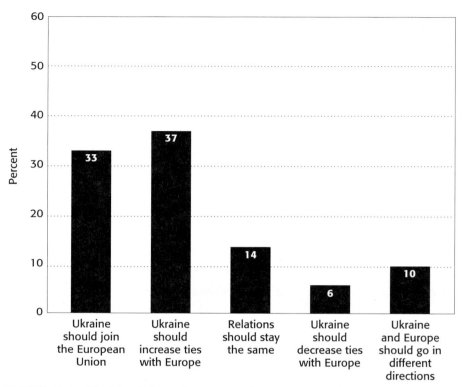

FIGURE 12.1 Ukrainians' Views About How Relations Between Their Country and Europe Should Develop (Data is from a representative sample of a countrywide public opinion poll conducted in 2005.)

Ukraine and the United States

With regard to relations with the United States, an impressive degree of cooperation has been manifested through the structure of the North Atlantic Treaty Organization. Since joining the organization's Partnership for Peace (PFP) in February 1994, Ukraine has been involved in a series of joint training exercises with NATO forces. NATO treats Ukraine's membership aspirations seriously, but challenges to full membership arise because of the organization's desire not to irritate Russia. Russian leaders openly oppose Ukraine's membership in NATO. Also related are concerns about corruption, human rights issues, Ukraine's arms exports, and the Russian-Ukrainian gas consortium. On becoming its new president, Viktor Yushchenko said that Ukraine was ready to join a NATO membership action plan; however, at the same time, he confirmed his country's strategic partnership with Russia, noting that Ukraine's Euro-Atlantic integration was not aimed against Russia or any other state.[29]

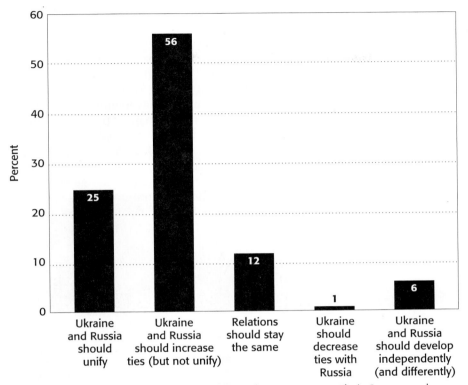

FIGURE 12.2 Ukrainians' Views About How Relations Between Their Country and Russia Should Develop (Data is from a representative sample of a countrywide public opinion poll conducted in 2005.)

Noteworthy is the fact that Ukraine was one of the few nations that sent military personnel to Iraq to assist the U.S.-sponsored overthrow of Saddam Hussein. Ukraine also opened its airspace to NATO for operations in Afghanistan and Iraq and then dispatched one of the largest peacekeeping units (the fourth largest after the United States, the United Kingdom, and Poland) to post-Saddam Iraq. With the exception of the United Kingdom, even the closest allies of the United States in NATO were unwilling to participate in bringing down Hussein. In the 2004 presidential campaign, however, both Yanukovych and Yushchenko promised to bring Ukraine's troops home from Iraq.

During the second half of the 1990s, Ukraine became the third largest recipient of U.S. assistance and the largest country with which the United Kingdom had a bilateral military relationship.[30] Nonetheless, the people of Ukraine are wary of NATO and of the United States. Public opinion polls conducted by the author confirmed that attitudes toward NATO and the United States are not very positive among the Ukrainian people.

In the 2005 survey conducted throughout Ukraine, respondents were asked to evaluate their feelings toward each of several countries and organizations according to a 10-degree "feeling thermometer." Ratings of "10" degrees meant that the respondent was extremely favorable toward the country or the organization. The more they liked a country (or organization), the higher was the degree that they chose. A "0" rating was the most negative, indicating that they did not like the country. In averaging scores for all respondents, it can be seen that Russia was rated the most positively with an average score of 7 (see Figure 12.3). NATO was rated the most negatively with an average score of 3. The United States was also evaluated significantly more negatively than the European Union or Germany. Nationalist organizations in Ukraine are now as likely to rally against the United States as against Russia. In March 2003, a new organization was formed to counteract "U.S. expansion into Ukraine" and to prevent "the transformation of Ukraine into an American ghetto."[31]

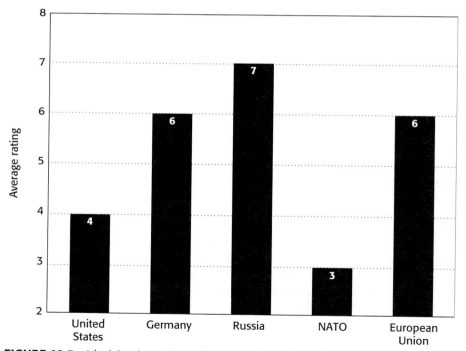

FIGURE 12.3 Ukrainians' Positive and Negative Evaluations of Other Countries and Organizations (Higher scores indicate more positive evaluations. Data is from a representative sample of a countrywide public opinion poll conducted in 2005.)

Ukraine's Military

Ukraine supports Europe's second-largest military force, after Germany. By 2003, the size of Ukraine's armed services had been reduced from the 780,000 inherited from the former USSR to 295,000. The Ukrainian military has been grossly underfunded, which has led to poor training and low standards, and these in turn have been blamed for a string of fatal accidents in recent years. In July 2003, Defense Minister Volodymyr Shkidchenko was fired for failure to initiate reforms to eliminate corruption and to modernize the country's army. Ukrainian Minister of Defense Anatoliy Hrytsenko under President Yushchenko is a staunch supporter of military reform and close cooperation with NATO. Hrytsenko, who speaks both Russian and English, served in the military for twenty-five years. Hrytsenko, however, has had limited resources with which to work. According to CIA figures, military expenditures were just 1.4 percent of GDP in 2002.

PROSPECTS FOR THE FUTURE

Ukraine has tremendous growth potential and recent indicators show positive signs of a strengthening in the economy. The country's potential may be even better under President Yushchenko because he has promised to improve economic freedoms such as the right of voluntary exchange, freedom to compete, and protection of person and property. Ukraine's weak economy in the 1990s had negative impacts on education, medicine, science, and other areas supported by government budget allocations. Low pay scales and the absence of a comprehensive system of social security contribute to worker malaise and poor work standards.

Likewise, Ukraine has lacked open competitiveness in the political sphere. Kuchma used administrative resources, control over the mass media, and intimidation of voters to ensure his continuing control over the levers of power. At the time of this writing, not long after Yushchenko's inauguration as Ukraine's new president in January 2005, it is too early to tell whether the country will be significantly different in the aftermath of the Orange Revolution.

The phenomenon of the Orange Revolution itself, however, is historical. After hundreds of thousands of people took to the streets in November and December 2004, Freedom House announced that democracy had triumphed in Ukraine. Particularly significant to Freedom House was the "peaceful character of this intensely waged political contest."[32] The European Network of Election Monitoring reported that the December election was "peaceful, better organized than previous rounds, and generally free of fraud."[33]

The 2004 presidential election does represent a turning point in the level of mass political involvement and activism in Ukraine. We are reminded of John Stuart Mill's contemplations on how to achieve the ideally best form of government: "The rights and interests of every or any person are only secure from being disregarded when the person interested is himself able, and habitually disposed, to stand up for them. . . . Nothing is more certain than that the improvement in human affairs is wholly the work of the [active] uncontented characters" (John Stuart Mill 1958, 14–15).

By this philosophy, Ukraine has taken a giant step toward better government. The respected Ukrainian political analyst Volodymyr Polokhalo concluded: "The main thing is the Orange Revolution. It reflects our citizens' active role in shaping their future. . . . It was the first event of its kind in the entire history of Ukraine."[34]

During his first weeks in power, Yushchenko built a new government that included representation from the diverse oppositional elements that together formed an alliance to defeat Yanukovych. Yuliya Tymoshenko, who supported Yushchenko's presidential bid and was a visible figure in the Orange Revolution, was designated Ukraine's new prime minister. Yushchenko also revitalized the country's regional leadership when he signed decrees that appointed new governors to Ukraine's oblasts.

Yushchenko's main challenge will be to live up to the high expectations of the activists that brought him to power and to heal the division in the country. The geographic distribution of the support for the two candidates plainly demonstrated the significant cultural, historical, and political divides still present in Ukraine. In the domain of foreign affairs, Ukraine still faces the delicate challenge of balancing relations between Russia and Europe. Yet, new opportunities are now opening up in Ukraine. All the attributes of full-fledged statehood have been successfully introduced, and Ukraine has institutionalized some democratic practices—for example, free and fair elections and a multiparty system. The Orange Revolution strengthened tendencies toward full democracy. Recent institutional changes and participatory experiences do help transform political cultures. It is now less likely that authoritarianism could reemerge in Ukraine.

Key Terms

Administrative resources
Brain drain
Commonwealth of Independent States (CIS)

Crimean Peninsula
Oblast
Party of power
Unitary state

Critical Thinking Questions

1. How does the regional divide in Ukraine influence the outcome of elections?

2. If there are differences in political orientations between Russians and Ukrainians (living in Ukraine), what might we expect the nature of these differences to be?

3. How does the fact that Ukraine is a unitary system rather than a federal system affect the power of the president?

4. How could an unpopular president (Kuchma) have won the presidential election of 1999?

5. What are "administrative resources"? Provide examples of their application.

6. What are the main political parties in Ukraine today? What are the main issues on which they are divided?

7. Why has Ukraine had trouble gaining membership in the EU and NATO?

8. What changes occurred in Ukraine as a result of the Orange Revolution?

Suggested Reading

D'Arnieri, Paul, Robert Kravchuk, and Taras Kuzio. *Politics and Society in Ukraine.* Boulder: Westview Press, 1999.

D'Arnieri, Paul, Robert Kravchuk, and Taras Kuzio. *State and Institution Building in Ukraine.* New York: St. Martin's Press, 1999.

Dyczok, Marta. *Ukraine: Movement Without Change, Change Without Movement.* New York: Routledge, 2000.

Kuzio, Taras. *Ukraine: Perestroika to Independence.* New York: Palgrave Macmillan. 2000.

Polokhalo, Volodymyr. *The Political Analysis of Postcommunism: Understanding Postcommunist Ukraine.* Austin: Texas A&M University Press, 1997.

Solchanyk, Roman. *Ukraine and Russia.* Lanham, Md.: Rowman & Littlefield, 2000.

Van Zon, Hans. *The Political Economy of Independent Ukraine.* New York: Palgrave Macmillan, 2001.

Websites of Interest

The oppositional Internet edition of "Ukrainian True":
http://www.pravda.com.ua

Information about Ukrainian politics, culture, and economy:
http://www.brama.com/

The Ukrainian Monitor—foreign and domestic policy of Ukraine:
http://foreignpolicy.org.ua/eng

Comprehensive guide to Ukraine, including politics:
http://ukraine-gateway.org.ua

An influential political newspaper:
http://www.mirror-weekly.com

Ukrainian news agency (photo section):
http://photo.unian.net/eng/

CHAPTER 13

The Republic of Georgia

THE REPUBLIC OF GEORGIA shares international borders with Russia, Azerbaijan, Armenia, and Turkey (see Map 13.1). The majority (70.1 percent) of its population of 5,126,000 is ethnic Georgian. The country also includes numerous ethnic minorities, the largest of which are Armenian (8.1 percent), Russian (6.3 percent), Azeri (5.7 percent), Ossetian (3 percent), and Abkhaz (1.8 percent).[1]

Although Georgia has been establishing a market economy and reforming its political system, the initial period of transition has failed to provide citizens with security. This chapter reviews Georgia's political history as well as its current political institutions and processes. It discusses the dramatic events of the Rose Revolution and evaluates reasons why settlements of the separatist conflicts in the regions of Abkhazia and Ossetia remain elusive.

HISTORICAL OVERVIEW

Historical evidence indicates that Georgia became a client state of the Roman Empire in 66 BC and became one of the first states to officially adopt Christianity in 317 AD. Although controlled through the years by Arabs, Mongols, Persians, and Turks, the Georgian Kingdom maintained its status as an identifiable political and cultural entity. In 1864, the Russian Empire overpowered the resistance of the native people and incorporated the **Transcaucasian region,** including Georgia, Azerbaijan, Armenia, and other small nations.

In the late nineteenth century, an emancipation movement against Tsarist Russia, together with reactions to the experiences of industrialization and the exposure of members of Georgia's elite to ideas of parliamentarianism, republicanism, and socialism when they traveled to Europe for their university educations, produced significant political mobilization within Georgia. The Marxist

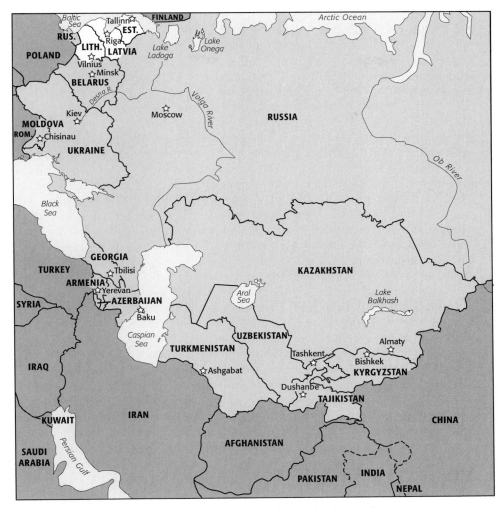

MAP 13.1 Countries of the Transcaucasian and Central Asian Regions

Social Democratic Party became the dominant political force and members of this organization occupied Georgia's seats in the Russian State Duma, which had been established after 1905. Stalin (Josef Vissarionovich Djugashvili) emerged among the Georgian revolutionaries and joined the Bolsheviks.

The Menshevik wing of the Marxist Social Democratic Party, with its broad base of support in Georgia, provided the popular base for Georgia's declaration of independence from Russia in May 1918. Major European powers gave official recognition to Georgia's independence in the same year. Multiparty elections to the Georgian Constituent Assembly, under a system of proportional representation, were held in February 1919; the Social Democratic Party won 109 of 130 seats (Jones and Parsons 1996, 293).

In 1921, the Bolshevik Red Army invaded the territory of Georgia and the short period of independent government ended. When the Union Treaty, which established the Soviet Union, was signed in 1922, Georgia was compelled to join as part of the Transcaucasian Socialist Federal Soviet Republic. Between 1921 and 1924, when the Bolsheviks were securing control of the region, as many as 30,000 Georgians were killed. Another 50,000 of Georgia's political leaders, intellectuals, workers, and peasants lost their lives during the industrialization and collectivization drives of 1928–1933 and the political purges of 1936–1938.

When a new constitution was written for the USSR in 1936, Georgia became a union republic—the Georgian Soviet Socialist Republic (SSR). This higher constitutional status, together with the death of Stalin and the adoption of Khrushchev's decentralizing reforms, increased opportunities for Georgian leaders to expand their political autonomy. Students could receive their education in the Georgian language, thereby allowing the nation to preserve its heritage.

Edward Shevardnadze was elevated to the position of Georgian Communist Party First Secretary in 1972, replacing the allegedly corrupt Vasily Mzhavanadze. Mikhail Gorbachev called Shevardnadze to Moscow in 1985 to serve as Foreign Minister of the USSR. Jumber Patiashvili replaced Shevardnadze as the First Secretary of Georgia's Communist Party. When Gorbachev introduced democratizing reforms, new political organizations emerged in Georgia, the most prominent of which by late 1989 was the Round Table Group under the leadership of Zviad Gamsakhurdia, a long-time Georgian nationalist and anti-Soviet dissident.

A turning point occurred when Soviet troops used force to break up a peaceful demonstration outside government buildings in Tbilisi, the capital of Georgia, in April 1989. The killing of twenty Georgian people during this attack radicalized the opposition to Communist rule, and opposition leaders began to demand openly Georgia's full independence from the Soviet Union. The first "competitive" elections took place in the Georgian SSR in October 1990 for a new republic-level Supreme Soviet. The Round Table Bloc won the elections and Gamsakhurdia, as the leader of the winning coalition, became head of the Supreme Soviet and Georgia's de facto head of state.[2] In a March 1991 referendum organized by Gamsakhurdia, 98.9 percent of the voters supported independence for Georgia from the Soviet Union. The Supreme Soviet formally declared the republic's independence from the USSR in April 1991. When Georgia held elections for its first president in May 1991, Gamsakhurdia won an overwhelming 86.5 percent of the vote by campaigning on an openly anti-Soviet platform.[3]

Gamsakhurdia's ensuing uncompromising tenure as president was a major factor that undermined emergent democracy in Georgia (Jones 1993). This tenure ended abruptly when, in the aftermath of the August 1991 coup attempt in Moscow, the majority of Georgia's National Guard followed its commander, Tengiz Kitovani, into opposition (Jones and Parsons 1996, 304). During

September and October, a number of opposition parties charged Gamsakhurdia with imposing an authoritarian style of leadership and staged a series of demonstrations demanding his resignation. Gamsakhurdia responded by ordering the arrest of opposition leaders and by declaring a state of emergency in Tbilisi. In December 1991, armed conflict broke out in the capital city and opposition forces besieged Gamsakhurdia at the government's headquarters. Gamsakhurdia fled Tbilisi in early January 1992, and the opposition declared him deposed. A Military Council established itself as the ruling authority and abolished Georgia's presidency.

Tbilisi still shows the battle scars of this uprising that occurred in the streets of the capital city. Throughout early 1992, two semimilitary groups vied for power—the National Guard under the leadership of Tengiz Kitovani and the Mkhedrioni Warriors under the leadership of Jaba Ioseliana. Fighting also continued in western territories that remained under the control of Gamsakhurdia's supporters and secessionist movements gained ground in the peripheral regions of the country (in South Ossetia and Abkhazia, two autonomous republics within Georgia).

Shevardnadze, having resigned as Mikhail Gorbachev's Foreign Minister of the Soviet Union in early 1991, returned to Georgia. In March 1992, Shevardnadze became head of the Military Council, which reorganized itself into a State Council. His government made progress in reducing violent conflict in South Ossetia, but the government's control over Abkhazia continued to weaken and the ethnic-territorial war there escalated in August 1992. After parliamentary elections were held in October 1992, Shevardnadze was elected Speaker of the Parliament and the State Council formally dissolved itself.

Although Shevardnadze commanded the central organs of power in the capital city, he did not exercise control throughout the full territory of the country. In late October 1993, separatist forces in Abkhazia drove out Georgian troops and most of the ethnic Georgian population. The government no longer had power over that secessionist region. In the same month, rebel forces led by Zviad Gamsakhurdia gained the advantage in the western regions of the country. With troops associated with Gamsakhurdia taking one town after another, Shevardnadze requested help from Russian forces to defeat the pro-Gamsakhurdia opposition. In return, Georgia agreed to enter the Commonwealth of Independent States (CIS). The government also agreed to give the Russians military bases in Georgia. After Georgian government troops received military aid from Russia, they were able to crush the pro-Gamsakhurdia opposition in western Georgia. Gamsakhurdia was killed on New Year's Eve of 1993. In early 1994, Georgia and Abkhazia signed a cease-fire agreement that included the stationing of peacekeeping forces under Russian command along the border between secessionist Abkhazia and Georgia.

Shevardnadze strengthened state institutions in the capital and curtailed the power of the militarized factions, but the civil and separatist wars had painful repercussions throughout society. By the end of 1993, 80 percent of Georgian industry was essentially idle and the harvest was about one-third that of 1985

(Urigashvili 1994, 21). The wars also created a major refugee problem. The looting, plundering, and reprisals against civil populations associated with warring political elites contributed to disillusionment and social nihilism among the citizenry.

Presidential and parliamentary elections were held simultaneously in November 1995. Shevardnadze won the presidential election with a reported 74.32 percent of the vote. Shevardnadze's major challenge came from Jumber Patiashvili, who had become Communist First Party Secretary when Shevardnadze left the post to go to Moscow to become the Soviet foreign minister. Patiashvili received 19.37 percent of the valid ballots.* Although Shevardnadze would likely have won the presidency in a free and fair election, allegations of biased media coverage and of **vote rigging** had solid foundations. The parliamentary elections resulted in a victory as well for Shevardnadze's political party—the Citizens' Union of Georgia (CUG).

Despite the economic hardships, which continued to be painful for most people; the widespread corruption; the failure to resolve Georgia's territorial disputes in Abkhazia and South Ossetia; and the failure to return some 250,000 refugees to their homes; when elections were held again for a new parliament in 1999, the CUG again won the majority of the seats. Observers questioned how the CUG could win 42 percent of the party-list vote given the continuing problems. One answer was the ability of the ruling party to control the election commissions, which register parties and candidates.† The successful campaigning of the president and his party was also crucial.‡ An equally important reason for the victory of the CUG was that while many Georgian voters were frustrated with the ruling party, which they did see as corrupt, voters saw the alternatives as being even worse. The main opposition party, the Revival of Georgia Bloc, suffered because of extremely damaging media coverage, which implied that a victory for the opposition would serve to secure Russia's military bases in Georgia for another twenty-five years. The outcome of the 1999 parliamentary elections, therefore, demonstrated both the power and the resources associated with incumbency, as well as the absence of a credible alternative.

Similar factors predetermined Shevardnadze's victory in the 2000 presidential race. Shevardnadze was reelected president in April 2000 with nearly

---

*All results from the 1995 elections come from the Central Electoral Commission of Georgia.

†In 1999, the opposition organization, the Revival [Rebirth] of Georgia Bloc, proposed amendments to the electoral law, some parts of which the parliament adopted in March 2000. Because of these amendments, opposition factions did receive additional representation in electoral commissions, including assignment to the position of deputy chairman of commissions.

‡Although all opposition parties claimed the campaign had been unfair and that the results had been falsified, the Organization for Security and Cooperation in Europe's (OSCE) observation mission gave the election a passing grade. The Office of Democratic Institutions and Human Rights (ODIHR) said the election represented a step toward compliance with OSCE commitments, although the election process failed to fully meet all commitments.[4]

79 percent of the vote. International observers seriously questioned the validity of these results, as did the Georgian people themselves. Election monitors reported numerous irregularities and violations such as a lack of **transparency** in vote tabulation, inflated turnout figures, and a strong pro-Shevardnadze bias in the media.[5] During the election campaign, and during the elections, international organizations alleged the mistreatment of opposition candidates, stuffing of ballot boxes, banishment of international observers from some polling stations, tampering with ballots, and police presence in polling stations. A report prepared by the Staff of the Commission on Security and Cooperation in Europe stated: "Considering the widespread cynicism and apathy among voters, the official results, especially turnout, strained credibility beyond the breaking point."[6]

In contrast to the officially reported 76 percent turnout and 79 percent vote for Shevardnadze, individual self-reports of voting behavior from an independent public opinion poll conducted shortly after the elections provided evidence of a turnout rate of 57 percent and a vote for Shevardnadze at 62 percent.* Steven Levitsky and Lucan Way (2002) have developed a useful rule of thumb for judging whether elections are free and fair. They say that if any candidate in any election receives more than 70 percent of the vote, it is reasonable to question the trustworthiness of the results.

Shevardnadze began to face increasing opposition within his government. The Speaker of Parliament, Zurab Zhvania, and the Minister of Justice, Mikhail Saakashvili, criticized the president for the corruption within his government and throughout the country. Parliamentary elections held in November 2003 also appeared to have been rigged by the government, with at least one district (Adjara) reporting more votes for the pro-Shevardnadze party than there were voters.[7] Within days of the 2003 parliamentary elections, opposition leaders called on the people of Tbilisi to take to the streets in protest. Claiming that his own party, the National Movement, had won the elections rather than Shevardnadze's party, For a Free Georgia, Mikhail Saakashvili called on the people to attend a mass rally and to demand the resignation of President Shevardnadze. The Speaker of Parliament, Nino Burdjanadze, joined the call for Shevardnadze's resignation and the demand for the annulment of the election results. Jumber Patiashvili also called for Shevardnadze's resignation. At first, Shevardnadze appealed to the population not to attend the rally and stressed that he would not step down as president; however, these appeals were short-lived.[8]

When it came time for the newly elected members of parliament to be sworn into office on November 22, 2003, opposition supporters stormed the parliament building. In the face of a chaotic situation, Shevardnadze fled the structure. Parliamentary Speaker Burdjanadze assumed the role of acting president.

*The public opinion poll involved a representative survey of Georgia's adult population conducted by the author with Merab Pachulia, director of the Georgian Institute of Public Opinion.

Although Shevardnadze declared a state of emergency in response, protests continued under the leadership of Mikhail Saakashvili. The next day, November 23, 2003, Georgia's Defense Minister David Tevzadze acknowledged that the president was not in control of the situation. Supporters of Shevardnadze began to switch sides when members of Georgia's National Guard pledged their loyalty to the opposition.[9]

When disturbances swelled and opposition politicians united, Shevardnadze resigned from his position as President of the Republic of Georgia. After he resigned, Shevardnadze said that he quit in order to avoid bloodshed.[10] When asked about the allegations that the parliamentary elections were rigged, Shevardnadze acknowledged that voter lists were falsified but would not cast blame.[11] Georgia's Supreme Court invalidated the November 2003 elections, leaving the previous parliament in place until new elections could be held in March 2004. (See Box 13.1 on Edward Shevardnadze.)

Mikhail Saakashvili, National Movement opposition leader, won the January 2004 elections for the presidency. When Saakashvili became presi-

---

BOX 13.1 EDWARD SHEVARDNADZE—PRESIDENT OF GEORGIA, 1992–2003

Shevardnadze was born in 1928 in Georgia. He worked most of his life within the Communist Party structures of the former Soviet Union (CPSU). The following are the main stages of his career path.

1957–1960	First Secretary of the Central Committee of the Georgian Komsomol
1961–1962	First Secretary of the Mtsketa Communist Party District Committee
1963–1964	First Secretary of the Tbilisi May 1 District Communist Party Committee
1964–1965	First Deputy-Minister of Social Order in Georgia
1965–1972	Minister of Home Affairs of Georgia
July–September 1972	First Secretary of Tbilisi City Communist Party Committee
September 1972–July 1985	First Secretary of the Central Committee of the Communist Party of Georgia (de facto leader of the Georgian SSR)
1985–1991	USSR Minister of Foreign Affairs and member of the Politburo of CPSU Central Committee
1991	Resigned from the Communist Party of the Soviet Union
March 1992	Returned to Georgia to head the State Council
October 1992	Elected chairman of the Georgian parliament, then the parliament elected him head of state
1993	Became chairman of the Citizens' Union of Georgia political party
November 1995	Elected President of Georgia by direct popular election
April 2002	Reelected President of Georgia
November 2003	Resigned the position of President of the Republic of Georgia

dent, he inherited a country with serious economic problems and separatist strongholds in Abkhazia and South Ossetia. Among Saakashvili's first acts as president was the release of many of Gamsakhurdia's supporters from prison and the arrest of several leading government officials on charges of corruption and embezzlement. Mikhail Saakashvili openly stated his desire for Georgia to be accepted for membership in the European Union and acknowledged the importance of his country's relationship with Russia.

When the interim parliament convened in February 2004, it adopted legislation to support Saakashvili's anticorruption drive and made constitutional changes, including the right of parliament to censure government (with a three-fifths majority) and the right of the president to dissolve parliament if it fails to approve the president's nomination for prime minister or to adopt the state budget after three separate votes. The parliament created a position of prime minister, which had not been included in the 1995 constitution. Zurab Zhvania became prime minister and held the position until his accidental death in February 2005.* Within days and following consultations with government officials and parliament, Saakashvili named a close associate of Zhvania's, Finance Minister Zurab Nogaideli, as successor to the late prime minister.

POLITICAL INSTITUTIONS AND PROCESSES

The rules for how the country is to be governed and how elections are to be conducted are set out in general form in the Constitution of the Republic of Georgia (adopted in 1995) and in more specific form in enabling legislation such as the "Law on Elections of the President of Georgia." The constitution established Georgia as a presidential republic and created a two-chamber parliament along with a Constitutional Court.

The Presidency and Presidential Elections

The 1995 constitution gives the president broad powers and gives significantly less scope to the legislative and judicial branches.[12] The President of Georgia, as the head of state, exercises executive power. He (or she) is the supreme commander in chief of the armed forces, concludes international agreements and treaties, and negotiates with foreign states. The president is responsible for appointing a government and has considerable power of nomination and appointment to the Supreme Court and to financial and monetary control institutions. The president has decree-making power separate from the legislature and is responsible for submitting a state budget to the parliament. The president can initiate a national referendum on the issues determined by the

---

*Zhvania had served as chairman of Georgia's parliament between 1995 and 2001.

constitution and law and sets the date for parliamentary elections. He can declare a state of emergency throughout the whole territory of the state or its parts but must submit it to parliament within forty-eight hours for approval.

Eligible voters elect Georgia's president directly for five-year terms. In the first round, voters select one candidate from those who have fulfilled the legal requirements for being listed on the presidential ballot.* If any one candidate receives more than 50 percent of the total vote in this first round, he or she becomes president (a 50 percent turnout is required for the election to be valid). If, however, no one candidate is able to garner more than 50 percent of the vote, the election goes into a second round, consisting of only those two candidates who received the highest number of votes in the first round. The election is valid if at least one-third of the electorate participates. The candidate who gets the most votes is elected.

Georgia's first popularly elected president was Zviad Gamsakhurdia, elected in May 1991 before the demise of the Soviet Union. After Gamsakhurdia's ouster, Edward Shevardnadze became the country's de facto leader in 1992. His victories in the 1995 and 2000 presidential elections were remarkably similar because he won both with a large majority in a single round. In 1995, Shevardnadze received 74 percent of the vote. In 2000, he won with 79 percent of the vote. In both elections, the next best vote-getter was Jumber Patiashvili. In 2000, Shevardnadze was nominated by Citizens' Union of Georgia while he was chairman of that political party. In contrast, Patiashvili ran as an independent candidate. At the time of his registration as a candidate for the 2000 election, Patiashvili, as leader of the parliament minority, was chair of the Union of Democratic Revival of Georgia party.

Among the candidates approved by the Central Electoral Commission for participation in the April 2000 presidential election was the chair of the Adjarian Supreme Soviet, Aslan Abashidze.† Although Abashidze was the strongest potential challenger to oppose Shevardnadze, the poor showing of his Revival of Georgia Bloc in the October 1999 parliamentary elections undermined his likelihood of success. Many Georgians also perceived him as more of a regional boss than a credible national leader. President Shevardnadze traveled to Batumi (the capital of the Adjara region) to meet with Abashidze just weeks before the election. Shortly after, Abashidze withdrew his candidacy for the presidential vote.

---

*Nominations for president are submitted by political parties and initiative citizen's groups. A candidate is registered with the Central Election Commission after he or she has submitted at least 50,000 supporting signatures. For independent candidates, their names are submitted by an "initiative group of voters."

†The Revival of Georgia Bloc had nominated Aslan Abashidze as its presidential candidate, but Abashidze withdrew from the contest. The Socialist Party from Revival of Georgia supported Jumber Patiashvili and Union of Traditionalists from the same bloc supported Abashidze.

When President Shevardnadze presented his electoral program (for the 2000 election), he promised to restore the territorial integrity of Georgia and to facilitate **repatriation**—the return of refugees to their homes.[13] Shevardnadze also noted that friendly countries, the United States especially, promised to assist Georgia in the settlement of conflicts and the rehabilitation of refugees. In addition, he stressed that Russia could play a positive role in the process of conflict resolution in South Ossetia and Abkhazia. With regard to economic development, Shevardnadze promised prosperity through the building of a socially oriented market economy.

Patiashvili declared the following priorities in his preelection campaign: restoration of territorial integrity of Georgia; elimination of poverty; establishment of a socially oriented, mixed economy; resolution of the problem of unemployment; development of small businesses; and increasing of pensions. He promised prosecution of those who had stolen from the people—those who had misappropriated state property during the privatization process.[14] Both candidates called for a war on corruption.

Shevardnadze's campaign for the presidency in 2000 benefited from international allies who contributed financial support and prestige to the incumbent president. During the period just prior to the election, Shevardnadze arranged for visits by heads of state and high-level dignitaries from neighboring countries. In contrast, the opposition revealed significant weaknesses. The public was aware of infighting between Abashidze and Patiashvili as to whose candidacy would best unite the opposition against Shevardnadze. Thus, during the period running up to the election, no one really questioned whether Shevardnadze would win; the only uncertainty was how large the margin of victory would be. The cloud of a boycott by several opposition parties overshadowed the presidential election held in Georgia on April 9, 2000.

Shevardnadze never reached the end of his second term as president. Massive political demonstrations—the Rose Revolution—in Tbilisi following the regularly scheduled November 2003 parliamentary elections led to Shevardnadze's resignation as President of the Republic of Georgia on November 23, 2003. Georgia's fourth presidential election, held on January 4, 2004, was called by acting President Burdjanadze. According to Georgia's constitution, new presidential elections are required within forty-five days of the previous president's resignation. The overwhelming winner was Mikhail Saakashvili. According to official results issued by Georgia's Central Election Commission, Saakashvili won 96.27 percent of the vote; the other candidates received less than 2 percent each.

When Saakashvili was sworn in as Georgia's president on January 25, 2004, he became the youngest president in Europe and the former USSR. His campaign promises included improving wages and pensions and cracking down on corruption. He is strongly pro-Western in his political orientation and seeks membership for Georgia in both the EU and NATO. (See Box 13.2 on Mikhail Saakashvili.)

BOX 13.2 MIKHAIL SAAKASHVILI—PRESIDENT OF GEORGIA, 2004

Saakashvili was born in 1967 in Tbilisi. His international education includes coursework, degrees, and certificates from Kiev University's Institute of International Relations in Ukraine, Columbia University in New York, George Washington University, and the Strasbourg Human Rights Institute in France.

In December 1995, as a candidate nominated by the Citizens' Union of Georgia (Shevardnadze's party), Saakashvili won a seat in parliament and was elected chairman of the Constitutional, Legal Issues and Legal Affairs Committee of the Parliament of Georgia.

In 1998, he was elected chairman of the Parliamentary Faction of the Citizens' Union (CUG).

In October 1999, he was elected a member of parliament from Vake District by the majoritarian system.

In October 2000, President Shevardnadze appointed him to the Minister of Justice position. He became involved in controversies with other members of government as he undertook reforms to reduce corruption in government.

In September 2001, Saakashvili resigned from his ministerial post, declaring that corruption had penetrated the heart of Shevardnadze's government.

In October 2001, he founded the United National Movement (UNM).

In June 2002, he was elected the chairman of the Tbilisi Assembly, in effect, the city's mayor.

In November 2003, after Georgia held parliamentary elections, Saakashvili claimed a landslide victory for his party, urged Georgians to demonstrate against Shevardnadze's government, demanded the ouster of Shevardnadze, and demanded new elections.

On January 4, 2004, by an overwhelming majority, Saaskashvili was elected President of Georgia.

Source: For more information, see Biography of Mikhail Saakashvili, the President of Georgia, at http://www.saakashvili.com/biography.html.

The Parliament, Parliamentary Elections, and Political Parties

The constitution formulates the parliament of Georgia as a two-chamber legislature, but because the upper house (the Senate) is supposed to represent all regions and republics, this body has not yet been constituted. The functioning house of the parliament is the Supreme Council (*Umaghiesi Sabcho*) with 235 seats. This body shares responsibility for some presidential appointments and can impeach the president if the courts confirm that he (or she) has violated the constitution. The parliament of Georgia exercises legislative power, determines the main directions of domestic and foreign policy, and exercises general control over the Cabinet of Ministers. The parliament elects a chair who leads its work. Committees prepare legislation issues and supervise government activities.

The right to initiate legislation is vested in the president, members of parliament, parliamentary factions, committees of parliament, the supreme representative bodies of Abkhazia and Adjara, and electors (if they present a petition signed by 30,000 voters). A bill is considered passed if supported by the majority of those present, if those present are not less than one-third of the total membership of parliament. A bill adopted by parliament is submitted to the president for his (or her) signature. If the president returns the bill to parliament with amendments, parliament can vote to adopt the amendments. If parliament votes against the amendments, the bill as originally passed is voted on again. The law is considered passed if supported by not less than three-fifths of the total number of deputies or by not less than two-thirds of the total number of deputies in the case of constitutional amendments. If the president refuses to sign, the law is signed and issued by the chair.

Supreme Council members are elected by popular vote to serve four-year terms; 85 members are elected directly by districts based on a plurality election system and 150 members are elected by party lists based on a proportional system, with a 7 percent threshold to gain parliamentary seats. At least 50 percent of registered electors must vote for the election to be valid; otherwise, the election is repeated. If no candidate obtains at least 33 percent of the vote within the plurality system, a runoff is held between the top two candidates. To participate in elections and be registered, a party either must collect 50,000 signatures or must already be represented in the parliament. A majority candidate must collect 1,000 signatures; an incumbent member does not need signatures.

Georgia held parliamentary elections in October 1990, October 1992, November 1995, October 1999, November 2003, and March 2004. The November 2003 elections were nullified after being marred by a number of irregularities and in response to demands for new elections. Thus, the results of the November 2003 elections did not stand and were replaced by the voting results from March 2004.

Those territories held by ethnic separatists have not participated in Georgia's elections; boycotts prevent voting in Abkhazia and South Ossetia. In the 1992 parliamentary elections, areas in West Georgia controlled by supporters of ousted President Gamsakhurdia also boycotted the elections. By the fall of 1993, an amorphous superfaction of about 125 deputies emerged within parliament in support of Shevardnadze. Within this majority, the parliamentary party, Citizens' Union of Georgia, was created in November 1993, with Shevardnadze as its chair. The general orientation of the parliament elected in 1992 was pro-independence and anti-Soviet.

When Georgia held parliamentary elections again in November 1995, the party-list portion of the ballot contained the names of 54 registered political parties. Based on the proportional system, only three parties overcame the minimum 5 percent threshold (raised from the previous 4 percent) to representation in parliament. The parties were the Citizens' Union of Georgia (with 23.71 percent of the vote, awarded 90 seats); the National Democratic Party (with 7.95

percent of the vote, awarded 31 seats); and the All Georgian Revival Union, later the Revival of Georgia Bloc (with 6.84 percent of the vote, awarded 25 seats).

Although the winning parties get the most attention and are the most important from the perspective of electoral outcomes, to better understand Georgian politics, some significant opposition political parties that did not receive representation in parliament also need to be mentioned. In the 1995 election, first among the losers were three Communist parties that, had they unified under a single name, would have broken the threshold for representation. The second set of significant losers was the nationalist parties associated with Zviad Gamsakhurdia. The most hardcore among these was the Round Table Bloc and its most ardent supporters refused to participate in the November 1995 voting. The nationalist blocs that did participate, if they had united under one banner, would also have had enough votes to have been awarded parliamentary seats on the basis of the party-list vote.

Parliamentary elections were also held on October 31, 1999 (first round) and November 14, 1999 (second round) according to the constitutionally mandated schedule. Thirty-three blocs and parties vied for proportional seats, and approximately 3,000 candidates contested the majoritarian races.[15] The three parties that passed the 7 percent threshold (raised from the previous 5 percent used in 1995) were the Citizens' Union of Georgia, the Revival of Georgia Bloc, and the Industry Will Save Georgia Bloc. Winning candidates from the eighty-five majoritarian races were Citizens' Union of Georgia, the Revival bloc, the Industry Will Save Georgia, the National Democratic Party, and the Labourist Party (see Table 13.1).*

As noted earlier, the Citizens' Union of Georgia (CUG), which secured a majority in the 1999 parliament, was founded in November 1993. The party was a mix of former communist-era intellectuals, regional apparatchiks, and business-people who united in support of Edward Shevardnadze's presidency. The CUG favored furthering the process of Western integration by applying for membership to NATO and accused the Revival of Georgia opposition bloc of favoring pro-Russian policies.[16] In its electoral program, the CUG specifically stated its support of free-market economics based on principles of private initiative and integration into European and world structures.

The Revival of Georgia Bloc (also referred to as the Batumi Alliance) was led by Aslan Abashidze, speaker of the Supreme Soviet of the Adjara Autonomous Republic (bordering Turkey); it came in second place in the 1999 election.

---

*The true size of the electorate in Georgia is one of the questions that has been under dispute. As of 1999, the official voting population (number of registered voters: 2,882,646) represented just 57 percent of the overall population (5,066,499 according to July 1999 estimates). Yet, the number of eligible voters reported by the CEC in November 2003 was 3,178,593. In January 2004, the number of eligible voters was reported as 2,130,000. This represents a 34 percent decrease in the size of the electorate over just three months. Since such a change could not be real, one of the two figures had to be wrong. For further information on this, see the International Foundation for Election Systems website, http://www.ifes.org.

TABLE 13.1 Results of Georgia's October 1999 Parliamentary Elections

| Party or Bloc | Proportional Results | | Seats Won by Majoritarian System |
	Percentage of Vote Received	Seats Allocated	
Citizens' Union of Georgia (CUG) Party Leader: President Edward Shevardnadze	41.75	85	46
Revival of Georgia Bloc, Aghordzineba—includes Democratic Revival Union, Socialist Party of Georgia, Union of Georgian Traditionalists, and Society of Konstantine Gamsakhurdia Leader: Alsan Abashidze	25.18	51	7
Industry Will Save Georgia Bloc—includes the Political Union—Industry Will Save Georgia, Union of Georgian Reformers and Agrarians, Political Union—Movement for Georgian State, and the Labor Party Leader: George Topadze	7.08	14	2
Labourist Party of Georgia Leader: Shalva Natelashvili	6.59		2
National Democratic Alliance-III WAY Bloc—includes the National Democrat Party, the Republican Party, and the Party of Producers Leader: Irina Sarishvili-Chanturia	4.45		2
People's Party, Didgori Bloc—includes the People's Party and the Party of Georgia Independence and Integrity Leader: Mamuka Giorgadze	4.11		0
United Communist Party of Georgia (UCP)	1.35		
Other parties—includes 10 members who have maintained their seats since 1992, until territorial disputes are resolved	9.49		16
Vacant seats[a]			12
Total	**100**	**150**	**85**

Note: Turnout—67.87 percent of the 3,143,851 registered voters cast votes.

Source: Data is from the International Foundation of Election Systems (IFES) at http://www.cnn.com/WORLD/election.watch/asiapcf/georgia.html.

[a]Some of which were filled in November 14, 1999, when a second round of elections was held in those constituencies where less than 50 percent of registered electors participated in the first round.

The bloc focused its campaign on combating corruption and improving living standards, especially the payment of salaries and pensions and job creation, while emphasizing the need for good relations with Russia. The platform of the Socialist Party of Georgia (a member of the Revival of Georgia Bloc) advocated moderate protectionism, state regulation of the market, and state support of industry. In foreign relations, it focused first on good relations with neighboring countries rather than on integration with Europe.[17]

The Industry Will Save Georgia Bloc came in third place with 7 percent of the party-list vote. The party, led by older-generation businesspeople, advocated liberalization of taxes and a hard-line position toward the International Monetary Fund (IMF).[18]

The Labourist Party did not break the 7 percent barrier to proportional list representation in 1999 but was important as a real opposition group to Shevardnadze's government. The Labourists were among the parties that boycotted the 2000 presidential election. The party takes a strong socialist stance in support of free health care, education, and social services. Labourists demand the nationalization of the strategically important facilities. More recently, party leader Shalva Natelashvili has advocated a pro-Western policy, particularly Georgia's integration into the Euro-Atlantic structures, but the party also presented itself in opposition to Mikhail Saakashvili's National Movement in the March 2004 elections.[19]

Also among the opposition in 1999 were the communists and the radical nationalist parties. The United Communist Party of Georgia (UCP), registered in November 1994, defines itself as the legitimate inheritor of the former Communist Party of the Soviet Union, and the successor of the Working People's Socialist Party of Georgia (created in February 1992 and renamed the Worker's Communist Party of Georgia in January 1994) and the Communist's Union of Georgia.* The party sets its programmatic goals as the reestablishment of Soviets, the abolition of the presidential system, and the joining with other former Soviet republics in a military union. The UCP gives priority to state property (but supports all types of ownership) and was sharply critical of President Shevardnadze.

Despite these oppositional perspectives, the Citizens' Union of Georgia functioned relatively unrestrained as the ruling, party of power during the decade from 1993 to 2003. For the November 2, 2003, elections, however, new parties and old parties with new names emerged on the political landscape. In the aftermath of the November 2003 and March 2004 parliamentary elections, the leading political party in Georgia became the National Movement–Democratic Front. This changeover to a new party of power was part of the Rose Revolution.

---

*The Communist Party of Georgia (CPG), officially founded in May 1995, also claims to be the successor to the Working People's Socialist Party of Georgia and the Worker's Communist Party of Georgia. The party defines its ideology as socialist enriched with national-patriotic ideals. Its declared positions included support for relations with the former USSR republics and an acceptance of Russian military bases as necessary.

The stage was set for the Rose Revolution when, in the aftermath of the 1999 election, support for the CUG eroded, primarily because of corruption within the upper echelons of the country's leadership. In addition, the lack of a resolution to the conflicts in Abkhazia and South Ossetia contributed to the weakening of its ruling power. As a result, the CUG broke into opposing factions in 2001. As the 2003 parliamentary elections approached, those members of the CUG who remained loyal to Shevardnadze joined with a few small parties and the National Democratic Party and the Socialist Party in an election bloc called For a New Georgia (registered in 2003). During its election campaign, For a New Georgia stressed Shevardnadze's role as a guarantor of the country's stability. The bloc publicly advocated a pro-Western stance; however, the opposition accused the bloc of being pro-Russian, especially after the entry of Russian energy giants Gazprom and United Energy Systems into Georgian markets.[20]

The main opposition party in the 2003 elections was the National Movement Bloc, led by Mikhail Saakashvili, who had started his political career as a member of the Citizens' Union and had organized the National Movement as a faction within it. Saakashvili's opposition to Shevardnadze became public when, in August of 2001, he resigned his Minister of Justice position. The formal spilt between the CUG and the National Movement was ratified in May 2002.

In the November 2003 election, the National Movement Bloc represented fundamental opposition to Shevardnadze's government. It united Saakashvili's National Movement, the Republican Party, and supporters of former President Zviad Gamsakhurdia in the Union of National Forces. Curbing corruption and "dismantling the Shevardnadze clan" were the key principles of the National Movement's election platform. The bloc advocated a law that would allow for the confiscation of assets illegally acquired by officials in high positions. It also advocated a strong pro-Western stance.[21]

Another opposition bloc, Democrats Alliance, was formed in August 2003 by Parliament Speaker Nino Burdjanadze and her predecessor, United Democrats' Chairman Zurab Zhvania (later the Traditionalists also joined the bloc). The bloc's objectives were to limit the power of the president, restore Georgia's territorial integrity, strengthen the armed forces, and improve social conditions by guaranteeing the payment of wages and pensions and by providing uninterrupted supplies of gas and electricity.[22]

Another alliance contesting the 2003 election was the New Rightist Bloc. When the CUG began to fragment in 2001, the first group of paliamentary deputies to leave the party and go into oppositon were those who formed the New Rightists Party. The party advocates a strong pro-Western stance. In domestic politics, the New Rightists promote liberalization of taxation and creation of a favorable investment climate. The Democratic Revival Union (Revival of Georgia Bloc from the 1999 election), the political power base of the then head of the Adjarian Autonomous Republic, Aslan Abashidze, also contested the 2003 elections.

The results released by the Georgian Central Electoral Commission for the November 2003 parliamentary election showed Saakashvili's National

Movement in a virtual tie for second place with Abashidze's Democratic Revival Union, both performing worse than Shevardnadze's For a New Georgia Bloc (see Table 13.2). Allegations of election fraud led to massive street demonstrations. These protests and the resignation of President Shevardnadze in the same month constituted the Rose Revolution. The Supreme Court of Georgia annulled the results of the November 2003 elections and new elections were set for March 28, 2004.

With the resignation of Shevardnadze, presidential elections were scheduled for January 2004. Mikhail Saakashvili won the presidential election before Georgia's parliamentary elections were held on March 28, 2004. In the months

TABLE 13.2 Results of Georgia's November 2, 2003, Parliamentary Elections[a]

Party	Proportional Results	
	Percentage of the Vote	Mandates (seats)
For a New Georgia Bloc (consisting of nine parties)[b] Leader: Shevardnadze	21.3	38
Democratic Revival Union Leader: Abashidze	18.8	33
National Movement Bloc (consisting of three parties) Leader: Saakashvili	18.1	32
Labourist Party of Georgia Leader: Shalva Natelashvili	12.0	20
Democrats Alliance Bloc (3 parties) Leader: Burdjanadze	8.8	15
New Rightists Bloc (2 parties) Leader: Gamkrelidze	7.4	12
Industry Will Save Georgia Bloc	6.2	
Other parties or blocs	6.4	
Total	**100**	**150**

Notes:

The turnout was 60.1 percent.

Registered voters: 3,178,593

Valid votes cast: 1,909,215 (3.4% of cast ballots were deemed invalid)

[a]As of November 25, 2003, the Georgian Supreme Court announced that the results in these parliamentary elections were invalid.

[b]For a complete list of the parties in each bloc, see the full results as reported by Hans Dieset, *Georgia: Parliamentary Elections November 2003,* published by the Norwegian Center for Human Rights; the NORDEM report is available online at http://www.humanrights.uio.no/forskning/publ/ publikas jonsliste.html.

immediately before the March elections, President Saakashvili's National Movement and the Democrats Alliance Bloc, jointly headed by Prime Minister Zurab Zhvania and Nino Burdjanadze, worked together to produce a combined list of candidates for the 150 parliament seats to be distributed under the proportional system.*

The reported results of the March 2004 elections showed that the National Movement–Democratic Front (NMD), the party supporting President Saakashvili, won with 68 percent of the PR vote (see Table 13.3).[†] It is noteworthy that fractionalization of the CUG led to the emergence of the National Movement–Democratic Front, as the replacement ruling party. The NMD was composed of President Mikhail Saakashvili's National Movement, Prime Minister Zurab Zhvania's United Democrats, Parliamentary Speaker Nino Burjanadze's Republican Party, and some of the supporters of the late President Zviad Gamsakhurdia.

The only other party to pass the 7 percent threshold for party-list representation in March 2004 was the Rightist Opposition. The two major parties in the Rightist alliance were the New Rightists and Industry Will Save Georgia (also called the Industrialists). Both the New Rightists and the Industrialists appealed mostly to voters involved in private enterprise, including some of the country's most successful businesspeople.

Prior to 2003, the strongest opposition to the ruling party had come from the Revival of Georgia Bloc, based in the autonomous republic of Adjara and led by Aslan Abashidze. Originally formed under the name All Georgian Revival Union (AGRU), the party was registered in February 1993 and reregistered in December 1994. The party used the name Democratic Revival Union when it contested the November 2003 parliamentary elections. It came in second place in those elections (as it had in 1999), but the November 2003 elections were annulled. In the 2004 elections, the Democratic Revival Union won less than 4 percent of the party-list vote.

Most political parties that were in opposition to Shevardnadze before his resignation in November 2003 criticized the government's failure to revive the econ-

*In the late 1980s, Zhvania founded Georgia's Green Party and in 1992 he was elected to Georgia's parliament. Within parliament, he was promoted by Shevardnadze to the position of chairman of the CUG. After the CUG won the majority of seats in the parliamentary elections in 1995, Zhvania became parliament chairman. Although it appeared that Shevardnadze was grooming Zhvania to succeed him as president, Zhvania became critical of Shevardnadze in the late 1990s. In May 2002, Zhvania formed the United Democrats parliament faction. Shevardnadze's forced resignation on November 23 paved the way for a division of power in which Saakashvili ran for, and won, the presidency, and then named Zhvania to the reintroduced post of prime minister and Burdjanadze as parliament speaker.[23]
[†]Only 150 of the 235 seats in parliament were contested during the election, as those elected from single-mandate districts maintained their mandates from the November 2003 election or were elected during the presidential election. Ten members elected in 1992 continue to hold their seats as representatives of Abkhazia in the Georgian parliament.

TABLE 13.3 Results of Georgia's March 28, 2004,[a] Parliamentary Elections

Party	Votes	Percentage of Valid Votes	Seats
National Movement–Democratic Front (NMD)	992,275	67.75	135
The Rightist Opposition–New Rightists and Industry Will Save Georgia	113,313	7.74	15
Labourist Party of Georgia	89,981	6.14	0
Freedom Movement–Konstantine Z. Gamsakhurdia	65,809	4.49	0
Democratic Revival Union	57,829	3.95	0
National Democratic Party–Union of Georgian Traditionalists	38,247	2.61	0
Unity Bloc (of Jumber Patiashvili)	37,054	2.53	0
Others	70,175	4.79	0

Notes:
Registered voters: 2,343,087
Votes cast: 1,498,012 (63.93 percent of registered voters)
Valid votes: 1,464,683 (97.78 percent of votes cast)
Invalid votes: 33,329 (2.22 percent of votes cast)
Source: International Foundation of Electoral Systems at http://www.ifes.org/eguide/resultsum/georgia_pres04.htm.
[a]In the March 2004 elections, only 150 seats within the 235-seat Supreme Council were being contested. This was due to a Supreme Court ruling that stipulated that the November 2003 elections were invalid and that a recount was necessary for 150 seats. The results for the remaining 85 seats, however, were deemed valid, hence allowing those members to retain their seats.

omy and to eradicate corruption. Most opposition parties were also strongly against the "Russia" policy adopted by Georgian President Shevardnadze and his ruling party. Opposition parties condemned the government for selling out its national interest to Russia with regard to rebellious provinces such as Abkhazia. They also warned against the danger of disintegration of Georgia due to the incessant demands for independence by the rebellious regions.

Thus, the two major issues on which candidates and political parties take positions in Georgia are the state of the economy and the question of Russian-Georgian relations. Many Georgians suspect individuals or interest groups in Moscow of doing everything in their power to undermine Georgian sovereignty and domestic political stability, and to prevent economic upswing. Many Russian observers, for their part, view with misgivings what they perceive as Georgia's unequivocal ambition to join NATO.[24]

Except for parties of power, the life cycle for most political parties is relatively short. New parties emerge to contest elections, but they do not survive.

A major obstacle to the survival of new political parties is the nature of the election rules. The 7 percent cutoff to proportional representation favors larger parties. Another factor that limits opposition parties and leaders from winning seats in parliament is the extralegal measures adopted by the ruling party to limit competition.[25] Many oppositional groups have simply opted not to take part in elections given the anticipated manipulation of the process by the government. These factors, combined with the heavily personalistic nature of Georgian political parties, accounts for their weak institutionalization and development in society.[26]

Political parties in Georgia simply cannot function in the ways that they do in Western liberal democracies because the environment within which they operate is so different. When Georgia abruptly became independent, the routines of daily life were thrown into disorder. A new system emerged wherein people often settled disputes violently and retreated deeper into their private worlds of patronage, family support, and informal, sometimes illegal, means of economic survival, such as stealing or evading taxes. So although many new political parties were formed, the basic preconditions for the effective **articulation** and **aggregation of interests**, such as authority structures, economic stability, protection of the law, and confidence in the state, were simply absent in Georgia.

Only after a period of relative economic stability, together with a free press and full rights of association, will political parties be able to play a role in shaping and framing issues and in providing for the representation of diverse viewpoints. Economic reforms have created new economic interest groups, and the influx of international organizations has provided money, information, and workshops for aspiring political activists, so the groundwork for a democratic society exists, but Georgia's transition has been halting.

Georgia's presidents themselves have been an obstacle to full democratic reform. Both Shevardnadze and Saakashvili are hostile to oppositional political parties. Rather than accepting proposals from the parties as legitimate representations of citizens' interests, they perceive such demands either as personal challenges or as evidence of disloyalty. In his February 2005 State of the Nation address to the parliament, Saakashvili ominously proposed that all political parties that do not support Georgia's unequivocally pro-Western foreign policy orientation should be banned.[27] Also working against the development of civil society has been the fact that most professional organizations remain dependent on the state for financial support.

The Judicial System

The judicial system of Georgia consists of the Supreme Court, the Constitutional Court, Supreme Courts of Autonomous Republics, Courts of Appeal, Circuit Courts, and Regional and City (district and town) Courts. The Constitutional Court of Georgia consists of nine judges. The president appoints three members of the court, three members are elected by the parliament, and the Supreme Court appoints three members. The tenure of the members of the Constitutional Court is ten years. The Constitutional Court decides the constitutionality of laws, presidential decrees, and acts of the supreme bodies of authority of Abkhazia and Adjara. It considers disputes about the jurisdiction of authority for state bodies and the constitutionality of referenda, elections, treaties, and international agreements.

Courts at lower levels, in regions and cities, consider both criminal and civil cases and are composed of at least two judges appointed by the Council of Justice. Overseeing the council is a chair (and deputy chairs) whom the president appoints for five-year terms. Judges in the autonomous republics are appointed by the legislature (council) of the republic with the approval of the president.

The Supreme Court of Georgia supervises the enforcement of justice in every other court in the country. The Supreme Court is the highest court for appeal. The chairman and judges of the Supreme Court, on nomination by the president, are elected for a period of not less than ten years by parliament. The president also approves the staff and the structure of the Supreme Court on the nomination of the Council of Justice.[28]

The procurator's office of Georgia is the institution of the judiciary that performs capital prosecution, supervises investigation, enforces sentences handed down by the courts, and prosecutes state indictments. The procurator's office is a single, centralized system. The president nominates the procurator general who is approved for a period of five years by parliament; the procurator general appoints subordinate procurators.

Article 84 of the Constitution of the Republic of Georgia guarantees that "a judge is independent in his activity and is subject only to the Constitution and law. Any interference in a judge's activities in order to influence his decision is prohibited and punished by law." In practice, pressure from the executive branch influences the courts. According to international human rights monitoring organizations, judges in Georgia do not operate autonomously from political authorities. The payment of bribes to judges is also common and networks of friendship, family, and village-based ties encourage the granting of personal favors.[29]

Those detained by the police may be subject to ill-treatment and prison conditions are extremely poor. Certain groups, such as religious and ethnic minorities, are sometimes subject to targeted identity checks and detention without specific charges. In September 2001 the Council of Europe condemned Georgia because of continued human rights violations: "Since its accession to the Council of Europe in April 1999, Georgia has made some progress, including ratification of the Council's cornerstone treaties and adoption of several laws and reforms, but is far from honoring all the commitments it made on joining the Organization."[30]

THE NATURE OF SOCIETY AND POLITICAL CULTURE

The emergence of the newly independent states at the end of 1991, as an outcome of the political crisis within the USSR, created problems of "national integration" throughout the region. As multiethnic entities, many of the former union republics have found it difficult to become cohesive nation-states. As one of these multiethnic entities, Georgia has, since the beginning of its bid for independence from the Soviet Union, experienced violent conflict because of ethnic and cultural divisions. Although the Georgians themselves have a developed sense of national identity with deep historical roots, rebellions against Georgian authority within autonomous regions inhabited by Ossetians and Abkhaz (along Georgia's borders with Russia) have substantially curtailed the process of state-building.

Georgia has faced some of the most serious ethnopolitical conflicts among former republics of the USSR. The regional concentrations of the ethnic groups along the international borders of the country have made it particularly difficult for Georgia to maintain its territorial integrity.[31] The only ethnic minority within Georgia that is not concentrated primarily in a single region are the Russians, who make up about 6 percent of the population of the country. Azeris who live within Georgia are located primarily along the border with Azerbaijan, and Armenians who live inside Georgia are concentrated in the regions bordering Armenia. The major conflicts, however, are not a result of hostilities with these two nationality groups. Georgia's problems have arisen rather from the inability of Georgian leaders to negotiate workable relations with the leaders of the Abkhazians, Ossetians, and Adjarians. (The Adjarian population, unlike the Ossetians and the Abkhaz populations, is similar to the Georgians in terms of language and racial background.)

The people who are not Georgian by nationality have challenged the right of the government in Tbilisi to rule particular regions within Georgia. Violent and destructive tactics used by Georgians, Abkhazians, South Ossetians, and other ethnic groups living in Georgia to secure control of the border regions have resulted in the expulsion of people from their homelands, forced assimilation, and repression. The full-scale warfare that has erupted is a powerful sign of the deep, internal divisions within Georgian society.

When it was part of the Soviet Union, the Georgian SSR contained within its borders three autonomous regions—the South Ossetian, the Abkhazian, and the Adjarian Autonomous Soviet Socialist Republics (ASSRs). As it became clear that Georgia was going to either become an independent country or gain increased sovereignty and autonomy within the structure of the USSR, the people in these regions argued that they also should have more autonomy and that they should be free from the authority of the Georgian people. Rather than responding positively to these demands, Georgian leaders adopted policies that lacked sensitivity to the diverse needs and values of the various populations. In fact, the Georgian government abolished the autonomy of the South Ossetian region in 1990. Rather than searching for solutions to the differences, politicians and public representatives attempted to suppress the conflicts. These efforts at suppression resulted in an escalation of the troubles.

The dominant religion within Georgia is Christianity. Soviet rule brought repression to religious leaders and churches were either destroyed or used as museums or for other purposes; however, under Gorbachev's reforming initiatives, churches were reopened and restored in the late 1980s. Although approximately 11 percent of the republic's population is Muslim, the divisions that exist in Georgia do not revolve primarily around religious differences.

The major unresolved problems of the Soviet era involve language and competing territorial claims. During the Soviet period, the Georgians fought hard to resist assimilation to Russian language and culture (Russification). Although Georgia's republic-level constitution designated Georgian as the state language, Russian was used in all official communication. When President Gamsakhurdia emphasized elevating Georgian language and culture to a higher status in the late 1980s, Georgia's minority populations perceived this as a threat to their rights. Rather than seeking compromise or modifying language laws, political elites in Tbilisi adopted dogmatic positions and applied military pressure. The missed opportunities for early conflict resolution led to an escalation of violence that further exacerbated political, ethnic, and social divisions within the country, resulting, ultimately, in civil war.

The Civil War that occurred in 1992–1993 and the armed conflict associated with the separatist movements led to the intercession of Russian military forces on Georgian soil. Russian intervention in these conflicts, however, further complicated the situation and, at least in the short run, resulted in conflict escalation rather than deescalation. From the perspective of many within Georgia, Russia used the ethnic conflicts as a tool to manipulate domestic Georgian politics and to ensure Russia's continued military and geopolitical influence in the region.

The conflict also created a seemingly insurmountable refugee problem. A return of refugees to their homes located within conflict zones appears impossible. In addition, people in the region live with the fear that any spark of violence could lead to wider military escalation. The continuing danger of violence creates an environment that is always insecure and tense. The political instability obstructs the development of participatory and democratic processes within Georgia and the secessionist regions. In order to understand these regions better, the next three sections are devoted to a more detailed study of the challenges posed by Ossetia, Abkhazia, and Adjara.

Separatism Within South Ossetia

A separatist movement first emerged in the autonomous region of South Ossetia in 1989, ostensibly over the issue of language rights.[32] The Ossetians, who are a Persian-related people who speak their own language, desired to form a union with their compatriots in the Autonomous Republic of North Ossetia, which is part of Russia. When the Georgian Supreme Soviet abolished the autonomous status of South Ossetia in 1990, the people of the region responded by declaring that they would no longer be part of Georgia, although they would remain in the Soviet Union. Open conflict erupted leading to the loss of 1,000 lives and creating 100,000 refugees. A cease-fire agreement, which included the introduction of a joint Russian-Georgian-Ossetian peacekeeping force, was reached in June 1992. The autonomous status of the region was reinstated, but it was not until 1995 that negotiations on a peace settlement were initiated. In 1996, talks under the auspices of the Organization for Security and Cooperation in Europe (OSCE) led to the May signing of a memorandum renouncing violence. Economic links between Tbilisi and the capital of South Ossetia, Tskhinvali, were also largely restored in 1996. In defiance of Georgian authority, however, Ossetians elected their own president and parliament.

In July 2003, mediation experts from the OSCE tried to assist delegations from Georgia, Russia, the Republic of North Ossetia, and the Republic of South Ossetia to settle on a power-sharing arrangement. Mutual suspicion and hostility between the Georgian and South Ossetian authorities, including South Ossetian President Edward Kokoity, however, remained high.[33]

When President Saakashvili came to power in January 2004, he offered to guarantee significant autonomy to South Ossetia if it would recognize Georgian authority, but the offer was rejected. Stanislaw Kochiev, president of Ossetia's parliament, affirmed the long-term commitment of the autonomous region to independence through association with North Ossetia (in the Russian Federation). In July 2004, Georgian Foreign Minister Salome Zourabichvili formally asked the OSCE Permanent Council in Vienna to increase the number of its observers and deploy them across the territory of South Ossetia, given continued problems with instability and poor security in the region. Russia disagreed and denounced the Georgian proposal to expand the OSCE mission's mandate.[34]

In January 2005, South Ossetian President Kokoity rejected another plan offering constitutionally guaranteed autonomy and Ossetian representation in Georgia's national government. He explained to journalists at a press conference in Moscow that South Ossetia's status was fixed by a referendum in 1992 during which 99.8 percent of the population voted to secede from Georgia, and that 95 percent of the population now have Russian passports and aspire to integration with the Russian Federation.[35] Thus, as of mid-2005, a settlement of the political status of the South Ossetian region had not been reached.

Abkhazia as a Sovereign Region

In contrast to the situation in South Ossetia, where Ossetians made up a majority of the population, Abkhazians constituted only a minority of the population in their autonomous republic. The demographic position of the Abkhazians was significantly less favorable than for the Ossetians because Abkhazians were just 18 percent of the population of the province according to the 1989 census, with Georgians constituting 44 percent, and the remainder consisting mostly of Russians and Armenians (Otyrba 1994, 283). (In the 1980s, Ossetians made up more than 60 percent of the population of South Ossetia.) During the Soviet era, Georgians migrated into Abkhazia, especially after the deportations of Abkhazians out of the region in the 1930s and 1940s.

Between 1921 and 1931, Abkhazia had the status of a soviet republic, so with the onset of perestroika, prominent Abkhazians demanded the restoration of Abkhazia's pre-1931 sovereign status (Otyrba 1994, 286). Some Abkhazians advocated a complete break from Georgia and the formation of a Confederation of Caucasian Peoples chiefly made up of the Muslim minorities in the Russian and Georgian Caucasian region. New Georgian language laws further threatened the maintenance of Abkhazian culture. The Abkhaz feared that Georgian (rather than Soviet or Russian) rule would destroy their distinct cultural identity. Conversely, the Georgians living in the region resented the disproportionate influence that ethnic Abkhaz had in the administrative affairs of the region.

Only months before the breakup of the USSR, Abkhaz leaders and the Georgian government worked out a compromise electoral law for a newly constituted parliament for the region (the Abkhazian Supreme Soviet). The law allocated a set number of parliamentary seats to each of the major ethnic groups in the region. However, the future status of Abkhazia remained uncertain. Tensions intensified in July 1992 when the Abkhazian Supreme Soviet voted to restore the constitution of 1925, which specified that Abkhazia was a separate Union Republic rather than a mere component of Georgia. In response, ethnic Georgians living in Abkhazia launched a campaign of noncompliance. The Georgian State Council in Tbilisi rejected the Abkhaz resolution and dispatched Georgian National Guard troops to the city of Sukhumi, the capital city of the region of Abkhazia. In the face of the Georgian attack, Abkhaz parliamentary deputies and other government officials withdrew to the majority-Abkhaz town of Gutauta in the north and called for armed resistance.*

The deployment of Georgian forces by Shevardnadze in August 1992 represented an attempt to suppress a separatist movement by force; an attempt to protect supply routes to Russia, which traversed the region; and an attempt to overpower pro-Gamsakhurdia rebels who were holding Georgian government officials hostage in the province. Large-scale violence in Abkhazia followed and by October 1992, Abkhaz forces were able to mount an offensive and seize control of the north. Georgian troops, being on the defensive, were forced to retreat from all Abkhazian territory north of the province's capital, Sukhumi, in November.

In addition to fighting against Abkhazians, Georgian troops were simultaneously fighting Zviadists rebels (supporters of the ousted Gamsakhurdia) in western Georgia. Some Russian military personnel and volunteers also fought on the side of the Abkhaz. In mid-September 1993, the Abkhazians launched a

---

*For an overview of the war in Abkhazia, see Gueorgui Otyrba (1994).

new offensive. Shevardnadze flew to Sukhumi personally to lead the defense, but within days the Abkhaz forces were victorious.

With its military victory, Abkhazia achieved de facto sovereignty. By October 1993, all Georgian forces were expelled from the province along with a large proportion of the ethnic Georgians who had lived in the region. An estimated 200,000 ethnic Georgians fled the region as it came under the control of Abkhazian forces.

Georgia signed a Friendship Treaty with Russia in February 1994 and, in return for his acquiescence to Russian interests, Russia provided Shevardnadze with badly needed military assistance. Abkhazian representatives and representatives of the Georgian government signed a United Nations and Russian-brokered cease-fire on May 14, 1994. In June 1994, Russian President Yeltsin deployed a CIS peacekeeping force (under UN auspices), composed principally of Russians, along the Ingur River to separate Georgian and Abkhaz troops. The presence of Russian troops in the country, together with a loss of control of territory that Georgians perceived to be theirs, represented a humiliating capitulation for the Georgian people.

In November 1994, the Abkhaz parliament approved a constitution, which declared the Republic of Abkhazia a sovereign state, and Vladislav Ardzinba was elected president of the Republic of Abkhazia. Throughout all of this, talks on territorial and constitutional arrangements between Abkhazia and Georgia continued, but intransigence on both sides and internal divisions within both the Abkhaz and Georgian leaderships have prevented compromise or settlement. Even with a Russian blockade in place, imposed on Abkhazia in an attempt to force the region to reach a political accord with Georgia, and despite international and Georgian criticism, Abkhazia underlined its quasi-independent status by holding regional parliamentary elections in November 1996.

Although the 1994 cease-fire has held, clashes do continue, and several thousand people have died. Talks sponsored by the UN and by the Russian government have not led to a resolution of the standoff. As of 2004, Abkhazia continued to regard itself as separate from Georgia. Residents of Abkhazia did not take part in the presidential or parliamentary elections held in the first months of 2004. Defying Georgian authority again, Abkhazia held its own presidential election, which Sergei Bagapsh won in January 2005 with more than 90 percent of the vote.[36] (Incumbent Abkhaz President Vladislav Ardzinba was barred by the constitution from seeking a third term.)* Bagapsh is head of the Abkhaz power company, ChernoMorEnergo, and, during Soviet days, was the Abkhaz Komsomol First Secretary.

Most neighboring states (including Russia) do not support Abkhazian independence from Georgia. In addition, no Western countries have acknowledged

---

*Bagapsh had (arguably) already won the election in October 2004, but in response to protests from Ardzinba's preferred candidate and former minister, Raul Khajimba, Abkhazia's Supreme Court ordered a recount of all ballots.

the de facto independence of Abkhazia.[37] In February 2004, Georgia's President Mikhail Saakashvili took the matter to the UN Security Council. He accused the leadership of the Republic of Abkhazia of pursuing a policy of deliberate ethnic cleansing.* Members of the UN Observer Mission in Georgia, however, reported that thousands of ethnic Georgians who had fled Abkhazia during the 1992–1993 war had returned and live permanently or semipermanently in their old homes. President Saakashvili argued that the UN Security Council should exert pressure on the Abkhaz leadership to accept a solution to the conflict that would bestow on Abkhazia "the highest degree of autonomy." Abkhaz leaders in turn argued that the republic's population had chosen independence. For that reason, the Abkhaz leaders have consistently refused to accept any documents that envisage Abkhazia as an integral part of Georgia.[38]

The Challenge from Adjara

Although not marked by armed conflict as in Ossetia and Abkhazia, a third region of Georgia has also refused to accept central authority. The Adjara Autonomous Republic borders the Black Sea and Turkey in the southwest corner of Georgia. The district contains the port of Batumi.

Adjara came under the control of Aslan Abashidze in 1991, and between 1991 and early 2004 he was able to maintain a semiautonomous fiefdom in the region. Instability in Georgia's capital inspired Abashidze to resist control by central authorities. He frequently condemned the Tbilisi government for failing to govern the country effectively and accused it of simply "doing its best to stay in power."[39]

Abashidze established himself as a credible opposition force when his electoral bloc, Revival of Georgia, garnered the second largest share of the parliamentary vote in 1999 after Shevardnadze's Citizens' Union party. In May 2003, Abashidze defied the central government by refusing to transfer taxes collected in Adjara to the Georgian central budget, keeping the revenues for local needs.[40] Abashidze went on record as opposing the closure of the Russian military base in the Adjar capital, Batumi; a closure which the Georgian leadership demanded.

After the ouster of Shevardnadze in November 2003, Abashidze, as chair of the Supreme Council of the Adjar Autonomous Republic, strongly opposed the holding of the presidential election in January 2004,† arguing that it was impossible to organize fair elections within such a short time span.[41] Escalating dif-

---

*In 2003, the International Criminal Court in The Hague rejected a demand by the Tbilisi-based Abkhaz government in exile to bring formal charges of genocide and ethnic cleansing against the Abkhaz authorities.
†Abashidze, along with Labor Party Chairman Shalva Natelashvili boycotted the January 2004 presidential ballot. The former KGB colonel and former State Security Minister, Igor Giorgadze, was refused registration as a candidate in the election.

ferences between the central government and the region led to a standoff on March 14, 2004, when Georgian President Saakashvili attempted to enter the Adjar region. Adjar troops, backed by armored personnel carriers, refused entry of Saakashvili's motorcade.

Saakashvili demanded that armed groups in the region turn in their weapons, and that Abashidze return to the central government control over customs, borders, communications, and finances in the region, as well as control over the port of Batumi. Saakashvili warned that if Abashidze failed to comply with his demands, the government would impose a total economic blockade on Adjara. Abashidze, for his part, said that Saakashvili was free to come to Adjara as long as he did not arrive with an armed entourage of several hundred.[42]

The two leaders did come together for talks in Batumi on March 18, 2004. In early May 2004, Saakashvili imposed presidential rule in the region and deployed Interior Ministry forces to Adjaria to maintain order. Almost immediately, most of Adjaria's police and border guards withdrew their support for Abashidze. He resigned on May 5, 2004, as Adjar Supreme Council Chairman and fled the country. Abashidze's departure represented a major victory for Saakashvili in asserting centralized control over one of Georgia's pro-self-rule regions.

ECONOMIC POLICY

Leaders have been attempting to transform Georgia's economy from the Soviet system of state ownership and central planning to one of mixed private and state ownership with more limited state regulation of the economy. The task of converting the old system is as difficult in Georgia as it has been in other post-Soviet states. Industrial managers from the Soviet days were determined to protect their interests and pushed for continued state subsidies as well as for a privatization process that would leave their control of resources intact. The state was subject to conflicting pressures: entrenched interests competed with pressures from reformers who wanted state funds directed elsewhere and with representatives of international organizations who demanded that the Georgian government adopt policies that would bring the country into line with the norms of the world financial community.

Although privatization and **reprivatization** processes are critical for improving state revenues (and reducing state subsidies), shortly after Mikhail Saakashvili took over the presidency of Georgia, Minister of the Economy Irakli Rekhviashvili announced that the country's privatization program would be "suspended" to allow for audits of all enterprises still wholly or partially owned by the state. Rekhviashvili explained that a new privatization policy would then be drafted based on the audits, taking into account the true worth of enterprises and prospects for their future restructuring. Prime Minister Zurab

Zhvania* offered assurances that, when privatization resumes, "the process will be transparent."[43]

Some major enterprises could be targets of *renationalization*. Examples are the Chiatura Ferrous Alloys plant, the Azot chemical plant in Rustavi, and the Poti seaport, which were sold to persons close to then-President Shevardnadze or to foreign interests at ridiculously low prices.[44] Saakashvili's government would like to bring such enterprises back under the control of the state.[45]

The International Monetary Fund is a key player in Georgia's economic transition. In July 2003, for example, the IMF issued a memorandum listing demands that the Georgian government was expected to fulfill, including cutting budget expenditures and increasing government revenues. To achieve these ends, the IMF said that electricity tariffs must be raised and a new tax code adopted. If Georgia did not comply with the demands, it risked losing IMF support and the possibility of rescheduling its foreign debt.[46] Clearly, such demands constrain if not determine the direction and the course that the government takes. Thus, a major issue within society revolves around the government's relationship with and Georgia's dependency on international organizations.

Georgia's economic development is tied not only to international organizations but also to regional economic interests. After much discussion and negotiation, a decision was made to build multibillion-dollar oil and gas pipelines through Georgia from Azerbaijan to Turkey. The oil pipeline connects the cities of Baku, Tbilisi, and Ceyhan; the gas pipeline connects Baku, Tbilisi, and Erzerum. The pipelines should provide new revenues and jobs for the country.

Georgia itself is dependent on external suppliers for meeting its energy needs. The government continues to suffer from inadequate revenues given the chronic failure to collect taxes and the overall weaknesses in the economy. A large percentage of Georgia's population is employed in the agricultural sector. Industry employs 20 percent, agriculture 40 percent, and services 40 percent. The main economic activities are the cultivation of products such as fruit, tea, hazelnuts, and grapes. Despite the severe damage to the economy caused by civil war and ethnic strife, Georgia has had positive gross domestic product (GDP) growth in the last several years. According to gross national income (GNI) per capita figures, Georgia is somewhat poorer than Ukraine (see Table 13.4 and Table 12.5, p. 333) and significantly poorer than Lithuania (see Table 11.3, pp. 296–97). Noteworthy as well is that foreign direct investment has been dramatically higher in Lithuania than in Georgia since 2000. Georgia's main trading partners are Russia and Turkey. Georgia also conducts a significant amount of trade with other former Soviet

---

*Zhvania, a key leader of the 2003 Rose Revolution that forced Shevardnadze out of power and brought Saakashvili into power, was accidentally killed by carbon monoxide gas poisoning in February 2005.

TABLE 13.4 Economic Indicators for Georgia

Economic Indicator	1998	1999	2000	2001	2002	2003
Agriculture, value added (% of GDP)	28.01	26.25	21.56	22.1	19.63	—
Exports of goods and services (% of GDP)	16.4	19.06	23.1	22.99	27.1	—
Foreign Direct Investment, net flows (BoP, current US$)	265,000,000	823,000,000	131,000,000	160,000,000	—	—
GDP (current US$)	3,620,000,000	2,800,000,000	3,040,000,000	3,200,000,000	3,320,000,000	3,937,488,000
GDP growth (annual %)	2.9	3	1.8	4.7	5.4	9
GNI per capita, Atlas method (current US$)	690	660	610	600	650	830
GNI, Atlas method (current US$)	3,640,000,000	3,470,000,000	3,190,000,000	3,130,000,000	3,350,000,000	3,779,818,000
Illiteracy rate, adult total (% of people ages 15 and above)	—	—	—	—	—	—
Imports of goods and services (% of GDP)	—	38.12	39.87	39.08	39.16	—
Industry, value added (% of GDP)	22.76	22.54	22.45	21.93	23.11	—
Inflation, GDP deflator (annual %)	5.6	9.13	4.29	5.3	4.41	4.66
Life expectancy at birth, total (years)	—	—	73.03	73.19	73.35	—
Military expenditures, dollar figure	—	—	—	—	—	23,000,000
Military expenditures, (% of GDP)	—	—	—	—	—	0.58
Population growth (annual %)	—	−0.34	−0.51	−0.72	−0.90	−0.99
Population, total	5,307,000	5,289,000	5,262,000	5,224,000	5,177,000	5,126,000
Services, etc., value added (% of GDP)[a]	49.23	51.21	55.99	55.98	57.27	—
Trade in goods (% of GDP)	24.45	29.96	32.44	32.82	—	—

Source: All figures for the table are from the World Bank unless otherwise noted, at http://devdata.worldbank.org/data-query. Figures for the last two rows of the table are from the CIA's *World Factbook*, "Rank Order—Military expenditures—dollar figure" at http://www.odci.gov/cia/publications/factbook/rankorder/2067rank.txt. The estimated unemployment rate for 2001 was 17 percent.

[a]Figures for the last two rows of the table are from the CIA's *World Factbook*, "Rank Order—Military expenditures—dollar figure" at http://www.odci.gov/cia/publications/factbook/rankorder/2067rank.txt. The estimated unemployment rate for 2001 was 17 percent.

states such as Azerbaijan, Turkmenistan, Armenia, and Ukraine. EU countries constitute a smaller, yet significant, set of Georgia's import and export partners.

FOREIGN POLICY AND INTERNATIONAL RELATIONS

Relations with Russia

Since the late 1980s, Russian-Georgian relations have been characterized by tension, threats, recriminations, and mutual suspicion. The war in Chechnya has caused considerable problems in relations between the two countries. Russia has accused Georgia of providing a safe haven within its borders for Chechen fighters. When Russia charged in 2002 that Chechen rebels were using an established base in Georgia's Pankisi Gorge region, and when Georgian authorities did not respond in a way acceptable to the Russians, the Russian military conducted bombing raids on Georgian territory. After vehemently protesting the Russian bombing raids, Tbilisi did send additional troops to the region in August 2002.

Russia continues to complain about Georgia's porous borders. In September 2004, former Russian General Leonid Ivashov said that several camps exist in Georgia's Pankisi Gorge that train terrorists for attacks on Russia. Georgia's Foreign Minister Salome Zourabichvili, however, countered that Georgian police and military are in full control of Pankisi and that terrorist bases no longer exist there.[47] The Pankisi Gorge region has had a reputation as a hideout for drug dealers, smugglers, and kidnappers. Thousands of refugees from the Chechen conflict have also settled there.

Georgia's friendly relations with the United States also cause tension between Russia and Georgia. Russian observers view with misgivings Georgia's unequivocal ambition to join the EU and NATO.[48] In November 1998, Russian and Georgian leaders reached a series of interrelated agreements intended to pave the way for a less confrontational relationship. The countries' officials signed a formal agreement whereby Georgia would gradually take over full responsibility for protecting its borders, currently guarded jointly by Russian and Georgian contingents.[49] In 2004, however, Saakashvili conceded that Georgia's borders with Russia can best be secured with joint Russian-Georgian patrols.

Russia still controls two military bases on Georgian soil, one in Batumi and the other in Alkhalkalaki. Saakashvili wants Russia to withdraw from the bases by 2007 and promised Moscow that U.S. or NATO forces would not use these same bases. Russia had agreed to withdraw its troops from Georgia (estimated at about 7,000); however, in January 2004, Russian Defense Minister Sergei Ivanov warned of the destabilizing implications of any hasty withdrawal of the forces. He said that Russia needs eleven years to complete the full withdrawal.[50]

Some Georgians also accused Moscow of encouraging the secessionist Abkhaz leadership to delay indefinitely any settlement of that conflict. These observers alleged that Russia's involvement in Abkhazia and in the Pankisi Gorge were part of a Russian effort to destabilize the Shevardnadze regime because of its overtly pro-Western policies.

Relations with the United States

Shevardnadze's presidency was shored up with large amounts of Western aid, making Georgia, by the mid 1990s, the third largest recipient of U.S. financial assistance per capita in the world. Shevardnadze reciprocated by faithfully supporting Washington's policies in the region. Georgia sent peacekeepers to Kosovo and has taken part in joint NATO training programs. In 1999, Georgia became an associate member of NATO's parliamentary assembly with the ultimate goal of joining the organization.

In October 2002, Georgia and NATO signed a memorandum of understanding on logistical cooperation to dispose of missile stockpiles and convert military sites.[51] Russia raised its objections to the Georgian-U.S. agreement on military cooperation, arguing that it could pose a threat to Russia's military security in the Caucasus. Particularly disconcerting to Russian leaders are provisions that grant privileges to U.S. service members in Georgia that do not also extend to Russian military personnel.

Georgia has allowed U.S. troops to use its bases as part of the war on terrorism.[52] Since 2001, Georgia has accepted hundreds of U.S. Special Operations Forces and U.S. military advisers help train Georgian soldiers to fight insurgents. The program has also provided Georgia with weapons, ammunition, uniforms, helicopters, and other equipment. Turkey has also helped rebuild Georgian airfields and other military facilities, while Germany has provided security assistance, including border patrol vessels.

Russian Duma Geopolitics Committee Chairman Aleksandr Shabanov told journalists in Moscow that the Georgian-U.S. agreement "seriously upsets the balance of forces in the region and poses a threat to international security."[53] Nonetheless, the United States and Georgia have continued their close military relationship. Georgia dispatched peacekeeping forces to Iraq in August 2003. In September 2003, however, the United States announced that it was cutting a major portion of its funding because of alleged violations of democratic norms by the Georgian government. The World Bank and the IMF also have threatened to discontinue loans until Georgia addresses its problems with corruption.[54]

The United States has strategic interests of its own in Georgia. The U.S. has worked to ensure the success of the Baku-Tbilisi-Ceyhan pipeline, the Caspian Pipeline Consortium Project, and the South Caucasus Gas Pipeline, creating new routes for the transit of oil from the Caspian Sea to the West.[55] The United States is hoping that Caspian oil resources will erode the power of OPEC to control the world's supply of oil and to maintain high oil prices.[56]

Relations with Europe

President Saakashvili has consistently stated that he wants Georgia to be integrated into the European Union. Saakashvili stated in a speech before the Foreign Affairs Committee of the European Parliament that Georgia is a country with a "European identity and culture." As preliminary steps, however, Georgia needs to fulfill previous commitments under the Partnership and Cooperation Agreement and new commitments under the EU's Neighborhood policy.[57]

In early 2004, the EU gave Georgia $11.94 million in food assistance and planned to add $4 million to support reforms of the judiciary and law-enforcement structures.[58] The European Union High Representative for Foreign and Security Policy, Javier Solana, announced that the EU was willing to deploy peacekeepers to Georgia to help resolve the Abkhaz and South Ossetian conflicts. Solana also praised the new Georgian leadership for its plans to tackle corruption.[59]

In October 2004, Solana reiterated his praise for the Georgian government since the Rose Revolution in November 2003, but he also emphasized that resolving the conflicts with Abkhazia and South Ossetia are decisive to Georgia's long-term success. EU's external relations commissioner, Chris Patten, observed the following:

> A good start has been made in addressing the structural problems facing Georgia, tackling, for example, endemic corruption, which has harmed every facet of life in Georgia. Georgia's state finances have been put on a more stable path to recovery. Revenue collection has increased, allowing the Georgian government to pay salaries on time. Reform of the law enforcement agencies has begun, and a new tax code has been presented to parliament.

However, Solana noted that the economic situation in Georgia remains bleak. In response, the EU doubled its financial aid to Georgia for the years 2004 to 2006.[60]

CONCLUSION

Although Georgia's citizens do participate in the election of their leaders, the unreasonably large margins of victories for the presidents cause concern about the fairness of the electoral process. The country also lacks mass media outlets that are free from harassment should they air or publish stories critical of the government. According to Freedom House's report on Georgia, the authorities do generally respect freedom of association, but corruption remains endemic throughout all levels of Georgian society. In its Corruption

Perceptions Index, Transparency International ranked Georgia number 85 out of 102 countries surveyed in 2002. In addition, ethnic conflicts have led to staggering refugee problems, which exacerbate weaknesses inherent in the economy. A large part of the population lives below the poverty line and as many as 300,000 displaced people from Georgia's various regional conflicts still await resettlement.

The question is the degree to which Georgia will change under the leadership of President Mikhail Saakashvili. It is reasonable to predict major reforms simply on the basis of the dramatic differences in career background, age, and general political orientation of Saakashvili when compared with Shevardnadze. The institutional structures, the economy, legacies of the past, and Georgia's geopolitical position, however, cannot be readily altered.

Georgia lacks a strong political party system that can provide the foundation for genuine political contestation. Oppositional political parties will likely not constitute a real counterweight to the power of the ruling party in Georgia in the immediate future. Part of the reason is the lack of experience with genuine opposition parties in a traditionally socialist state; another part is the repression and corruption. In addition, the ongoing ethnic conflict within Abkhazia contributes to the militarization of the society, which works against the seeking of negotiated settlements to conflict and compromise with political opponents. The lack of genuine competition in Georgian politics, therefore, remains a significant barrier to further democratization that should include an accountable and responsible government and political system. The limited nature of peaceful contestation and imperfect democratic accountability are common problems for many of the states of the former Soviet Union. Yet, Georgian society is changing, as a growing number of interest groups are now active, and they do have access to the parliament and to executive structures.

Both domestic instability and international problems, however, continue to plague the Georgian government. In 2004, the Cabinet of Ministers was reshuffled twice. The reorganizations, which occurred within six months of one another, involved the powerful ministries of the Interior, Defense, and State Security. Georgia faced an international setback by not being included in the latest round of candidates for NATO expansion. The uncontrolled territory around the Pankisi Gorge adversely affects both Russian-Georgian and U.S.-Georgian relations, as the United States has agreed with Russia that rebels remain in the region in spite of Georgia's repeated denials.

Georgia's future, because of its geopolitical location, will continue to depend on the nature of its relations with Russia. The presidents and other leaders in both countries will need to discover ways to find solutions to their bilateral differences. A commitment to the peaceful resolution of regional conflicts is key. Solving the problems in Abkhazia and South Ossetia will require Russian cooperation. It is apparent that, for Georgia's future, the challenges are formidable, as are the potentialities.

Key Terms

Aggregation of interests
Articulation of interests
Repatriation
Reprivatization

Transcaucasian region
Transparency
Vote rigging

Critical Thinking Questions

1. How has the Georgian post-independence experience been distinct from Russia's? What factors account for these differences?

2. In the aftermath of Soviet rule, how effective has the consolidation of democracy been in Georgia as compared to other post-Soviet states?

3. In the late 1990s and early 2000s, key opposition groups emerged in the Georgian parliament. What were their main critiques of the Shevardnadze government?

4. Why does Georgia's political party system remain weak so many years after the introduction of multiparty elections?

5. What was the Rose Revolution? Why did it happen?

6. Which regions have caused the most difficulty to providing a stable political system in Georgia? How have the conflicts been resolved in each of the separatist regions?

7. Which main policy questions divide the electorate in Georgia? Where do the elites stand concerning relations with Russia, the United States, and Europe?

Suggested Reading

Curtis, Glenn E. *Armenia, Azerbaijan, and Georgia: Country Studies*. Washington, D.C.: U.S. Government Printing Office, 1995.

Karumidze, Zurab, and James V. Wertsch, eds. *Enough!: The Rose Revolution in the Republic of Georgia 2003*. New York: Nova Science Publishers, 2005.

Suny, Ronald Grigor. *The Making of the Georgian Nation,* 2nd ed. Bloomington: Indiana University Press, 1994.

Wheatley, Jonathan. *Georgia from National Awakening to Rose Revolution: Delayed Transition in the Former Soviet Union*. Brookfield, Vt.: Ashgate Publishing Company, 2005.

Websites of Interest

Official site of the Parliament of Georgia:
http://www.parliament.ge/

The Constitution of the Republic of Georgia:
http://www.parliament.ge/LEGAL_ACTS/CONSTITUTION/consten.html

Complete reports on all of Georgia's elections, as compiled by the Organization for Security and Cooperation in Europe:
http://www.osce.org/odihr/index.php?page=elections &div=reports&country=ge

CHAPTER 14

Uzbekistan

U ZBEKISTAN IS ONE OF FIVE FORMER SOVIET republics located in Central Asia. This region came under the control of the Russian Empire in the nineteenth century. After the collapse of Tsarism in 1917, the people attempted to break free of Russian domination, but their resistance to the Bolshevik effort to reestablish control over the region was ultimately suppressed and a socialist government was installed in 1924. When the center of the Soviet Empire weakened in the late 1980s, Uzbekistan, like other union republics, asserted sovereignty in 1990 and ultimately seceded from the Soviet Union in 1991.

Geographically, Uzbekistan covers an area slightly larger than California. It shares borders with Afghanistan, Kazakhstan, Kyrgyzstan, Tajikistan, and Turkmenistan. It is located in the heart of Central Asia (see Map 13.1 on p. 345). During the Soviet era, intensive production of cotton left the land polluted and the Aral Sea partially dry. Since independence, an attempt has been made to diversify from cotton production and lessen dependence on agriculture while developing mineral and petroleum reserves.

The Republic of Uzbekistan, with its capital in Tashkent, is Central Asia's most populous country. Its estimated population was 26,851,195 as of July 2005. The Uzbeks are the largest group of Muslims living in an area of the former Soviet Union. The main religion in the country is Islam and the main languages are Uzbek and Russian. Uzbek is used as the primary language by about 74 percent of the population, Russian by about 14 percent, and Tajik by about 4 percent. Many Uzbeks are bilingual, speaking both their native language and either Russian or Tajik.

HISTORICAL OVERVIEW

Our overview of the history of Uzbekistan begins with the establishment of the Turkic Khaganate (Empire) in Central Asia in the middle of the sixth century.

The core of this empire comprised Turkic tribes ruled by a supreme ruler (emperor) known as a *Khagan*. The state was militarily administrated by tribes related to the emperor. Arabs took advantage of inter-tribal wars, invaded the Khaganate's territories, and by 715 AD occupied Central Asia completely. An Arabic Caliphate—a political entity centered on Islamic religious rule—was established in the region. Under the Arabs, Central Asia was Islamized. All natives were compelled to comply with Islamic regulations, and those who accepted Islam were released from different types of tax levies. Arabic became the official language.

Eventually local rebellions weakened the control of the Arab Caliphate. After it collapsed in the ninth century, various kingdoms emerged in the region. Khorezm was the strongest of these kingdoms, covering a vast territory from the Aral Sea, to the Caspian Sea, and into Iraq. But in 1219, the Mongols began their invasion, and Khorezm was conquered by 1231.

The Mongol invasion was devastating for the economy and culture of the area, and much of the population was killed. The Great Silk Road trade, which passed through China, India, Central Asia, Asia Minor, and stretched into Europe, was also destroyed. When the invaded territories were distributed among the sons of the great conqueror Genghis Khan, the territory of modern Uzbekistan came under the control of Chagatai. During the fourteenth century, the Chagatai Khanate adopted the religion of its subjects and became a Muslim state.

At the end of the fourteenth century, Emir Timour began a new empire in the region. Timour refused to serve the Mongols, took control of Samarkand (located in what is now Uzbekistan), and established his own army composed of soldiers from the Barlos tribe. One of the first areas added to his empire during the 1380s was the region of Khorezm. He nearly took control of Moscow in 1394 and overran the city of Delhi (in India) in 1399. Emir Timour marched troops into Beirut, Damascus, Baghdad, and Constantinople. He received letters of congratulations from the kings of France and England following his victory over the Ottoman Turks, whose expansion had posed a threat to Europe. In 1404, Timour set off to China with soldiers numbering at least 200,000, but on the way he died (in 1405), having lived for nearly seventy years.

The Great Emir Timour had succeeded in conquering a vast area that included parts of India, China, and the Persian Gulf. The lands under his control (the Timurid Empire) were given to his sons and the region was ruled by his heirs until the sixteenth century. From 1500 to 1601, Central Asia was ruled by an empire founded by Muhammad Shaybaniy Khan. After the Shaybaniy period, during the seventeenth to nineteenth centuries, three principal states emerged in Central Asia: the Emirate of Bukhara, the Khanate of Khiva, and the Khanate of Quqand (Kokand).

Beginning in the second half of the nineteenth century, Central Asia came under Russian control. To conquer the region, Russia launched large-scale military actions in 1860. Tashkent was in Russian hands by 1865 and Bukhara by

1866. In 1867, Russia established a military base in Tashkent, which also served as the capital for governance of the **Turkistan** region.* In 1873, Russia began a campaign against the Khanate of Khiva, and this state was also subdued. Rebel forces sprang up but were violently crushed. The lack of unity among the rebel forces, the relatively low level of economic development in the regions controlled by the Khanates, and their rejection of modern technology contributed to their subjugation by the Russians. Capital began to flow into the region for the purpose of creating an extraction system that would provide the Russian state with a continuous supply of cheap raw materials and other valuables.

A second phase of Russian rule over Central Asia began after the overthrow of the Tsarist regime in 1917. During the Civil War period that followed the Bolshevik Revolution, the center of the Russian Empire was weakened and leadership groups within Turkistan attempted to reassert their autonomy. Notable among those aspiring for freedom from Russian control was the **Jadids' movement**, made up of intellectuals who sought to interpret their Muslim heritage in light of the challenges facing their society as a result of Russian conquest. The Jadids formulated a harsh critique of turn-of-the-century Central Asian society and called for a rationalist interpretation of the scriptural texts and a mastery of "contemporary" or modern knowledge. Knowledge, it was claimed, made nations strong and wealthy and allowed them to embark on the path to progress.

Within the Bolshevik context, with religion considered to be a false consciousness, the Jadids' trajectory took them toward favoring a radical agenda of highly secularized social and cultural change.[1] The Jadids wanted a significant degree of autonomy for Turkistan or outright independence. The Bolsheviks, however, sought to prevent any form of independence from emerging in the Bukhara, Khiva, and Quqand regions. The Bolsheviks claimed that the local people were underdeveloped and chauvinistically argued that they needed the help of a developed nation. The Bolsheviks wanted the region to continue to supply needed raw materials, especially cotton. In fact, land used for other agricultural production was forcefully converted into cotton-growing farms. **Colonialism** thus inhibited the region from developing its economy in other directions.

In April 1918, the announcement was made that Turkistan was to be an autonomous soviet socialist republic within the Russian Soviet Federated Socialist Republic (RSFSR). In 1920, the Soviet republics of Bukhara and Khorezm were formed. In June 1924, the Politburo of the Russian Communist Party issued a resolution, "On the National Delimitation (Districting) of the Republics of Central Asia," which led to the creation of the Uzbek SSR and other Central Asian republics. The resolution was based on a redistricting plan that used the following criteria: irrigation district

*As the Tsarist government expanded into Central Asia, intense competition arose with the British Empire for regional influence.

management, economic specialization, suitability of urban areas for the management of agricultural areas, and distribution of ethnic groups (Bremner and Taras 1993, 336). In October 1924, the Turkistan, Bukhara, and Khorezm soviet republics were replaced with the newly formed Uzbek Soviet Socialist Republic (even then the Uzbek SSR was commonly known as Uzbekistan), Turkmen SSR, Tajik Autonomous SSR (part of Uzbek SSR until 1929), Kyrgyz province (within the RSFSR), and Karakalpak ASSR (originally part of the RSFSR [Kazakhstan] but moved to Uzbekistan in 1936).

These changes were duly approved by the first Congress of Soviets of Uzbekistan, and in May 1925 the congress recorded a vote in favor of joining the USSR. National structures coordinating industry and agriculture were brought into compliance with Soviet structures. From this point forward, until late in the 1980s, most of the major decisions affecting the Uzbek SSR were made by leaders in Moscow.

The second Congress of Soviets of Uzbekistan, held in 1927, approved the Uzbek SSR's first constitution, which formalized the republic's membership in the USSR.[2] A second constitution for Uzbekistan was approved in 1937, replacing the first and in line with the 1936 Constitution of the USSR. The official autonomy granted to Uzbekistan in the Soviet constitutions was limited in important respects. The most inhibiting was Lenin's principle of democratic centralism, which effectively subordinated all activity of the Communist Party to the leadership in Moscow. Although each Soviet republic had its own territory, its own administrative structures, and its own party organization, key positions were occupied by Russian-speaking officials. By the end of the 1920s, Stalin had abandoned Lenin's policy of **korenizatsya**, which had established programs to train local personnel to fill important posts within the government and party structures of the non-Russian union republics.

As Soviet power became stronger, Uzbekistan was transformed according to Moscow's directives. The Uzbek alphabet was twice changed. In 1929–1930, the Arabic script was replaced by the Latin script, and in 1940 the alphabet was changed to the Cyrillic script. An argument made for replacement of the Arabic script was that it would advance the spread of literacy. In fact, literacy did progress rapidly under Soviet rule, but the negative side effect was that the people of Uzbekistan lost easy access to much of their traditional written culture (Akiner 1996, 337).

In the 1930s, the Soviet people experienced a totalitarian system based on the bureaucratic apparatus of the Communist Party, the use of violence to repress opposition, and the deification of Stalin. The health and well-being of the agricultural workers took second place to the demand for the cotton products from the region. Those who protested, particularly the educated people, were expelled from the party, labeled as "enemies of the nation," and/or imprisoned. To ensure loyalty to Moscow, Stalin conducted a purge that killed many leaders of Uzbekistan. Between 1937 and 1939, 41,000 people were arrested, 37,000 of whom were sentenced to prison terms, and the rest were executed.[3] Famous writers and patriots of the Uzbek nation fell victim to the Stalinist repression.

On the eve of World War II, Uzbekistan was producing 60 percent of the cotton in the USSR. When the Soviet Union was invaded by the Germans in 1941, factories (heavy industry) were moved from Ukraine, Belarus, and Russia to Central Asia. Nearly a million people from other parts of the Soviet Union were resettled in Uzbekistan. Uzbek people joined the Soviet army and others labored to support the soldiers.[4]

When the war ended in 1945, much of Uzbekistan's industry was converted to producing machinery for agricultural and irrigation needs. The economy became even more dependent on a single export crop, cotton. The result was a shortage of food cultivation, soil pollution, and the shrinkage of the Aral Sea (because waters from the rivers flowing into the sea were diverted for cotton irrigation).

As in all parts of the Soviet Union, the Communist Party was the only legal party in Uzbekistan from the time that the Bolsheviks secured control over the region until 1990. Although the first secretary, or head, of the Communist Party of Uzbekistan—the republic's branch of the Communist Party of the Soviet Union (CPSU)—was consistently an ethnic Uzbek, ethnic Russians were sent to the region to work in managerial positions, and as party functionaries, to supervise compliance with Moscow's directives. The percentage of Uzbeks in the CPSU was significantly less than the percentage of Uzbeks in the population of the USSR.

After the death of Stalin in 1953, and with the ascension of Nikita Khrushchev and Leonid Brezhnev to the position of General Secretary of the CPSU, Uzbeks gained some degree of control over their own affairs, as did other titular nationality groups of the USSR. Republic authorities were allowed to make their own decisions about how to keep order and to fulfill the directives of the central planning agencies. In Uzbekistan, fulfilling the plan meant supplying cotton for both export and domestic consumption, while maintaining stability and peace in the region. Within this context, Sharaf Rashidov became the First Secretary of the Communist Party of Uzbekistan in 1959. Rashidov, who served as Uzbekistan's leader until 1983, developed the sciences, the arts, and culture, while acknowledging the authority of Moscow and producing cotton as directed by the central plans.

Following Rashidov's death in 1983, Moscow embarked on a massive purge of Uzbek leaders. A sweeping investigation was launched into allegations of corruption in Uzbekistan. Officials from the CPSU and from central Soviet governing bodies arrived in Uzbekistan to interrogate Uzbek personnel. Because Uzbeks felt that they had been singled out unfairly, the accusations of corruption led to the strengthening of Uzbek nationalism.

Inquisitions conducted in 1986 did reveal that republic officials, including those at the highest level, had falsified cotton production figures. Such practices as nepotism, bribery, and financial deception, however, were not exclusive to Uzbekistan; rather, they were omnipresent throughout the USSR.

Corruption was widespread during the Brezhnev era. In the mid-1980s the CPSU's national campaign to clean up corruption widely publicized the misdeeds of republic-level officials.

When Mikhail Gorbachev, as General Secretary of the CPSU, launched the perestroika initiative, Uzbek people raised doubts about the prospects of realizing social justice within the confines of the Soviet system. With a steadily worsening economic situation, an uncertain political climate, and a population in Uzbekistan marked by apathy and political cynicism, the ideology of communism was openly questioned. Noteworthy were increasing demonstrations of pride in Uzbek national identity. In October 1989, the Uzbek language was declared the official language of the Uzbek SSR.*

In the the late 1980s, intellectuals throughout the USSR formed political organizations to express their grievances. In Uzbekistan, the largest of these groups was Birlik (meaning *unity*). The Birlik leadership expressed its dissatisfaction with Soviet policies, called for a diversification of agriculture, and demanded that more attention be given to enhancing Uzbek language and culture. Although Birlik leaders were not able to make their appeal to broad segments of the population, the organization along with others, such as Erk (meaning *liberty* or *freedom*), did contribute to liberal thinking and did press for democratic development in Uzbekistan.

In 1990, the Constitution of Uzbekistan was amended to provide for a presidential government. Islam Karimov became Uzbekistan's first president, elected indirectly by the Supreme Soviet of the republic.† In June 1990, a Declaration of Sovereignty was adopted. In August 1990, new administrative positions were introduced, called *khokim* (analogous to a mayor or a governor), to help coordinate and implement presidential power in the regions of Uzbekistan.

On August 31, 1991, after the aborted coup attempt in Moscow, the Republic of Uzbekistan declared independence. On December 21, 1991, Uzbekistan's President Karimov joined the agreement to dissolve the Soviet Union and to form the Commonwealth of Independent States (CIS). When Uzbekistan held new presidential elections on December 29, 1991, Karimov was elected with an overwhelming majority, this time by direct popular vote. In a referendum held concurrently with the presidential vote, the country's declaration of independence was endorsed by more than 98 percent of the participating voters. Thus, Russia's official authority over the region came to an end. This authority had spanned two periods of fairly similar length: the period of dominance by Russian tsars (1867–1917) and the Soviet period of domination (1917–1991).

The world community recognized the independence of Uzbekistan, and in March 1992, it became a member of the United Nations. In December 1992,

*The issue of language remains problematic as several deadlines have been set and not met with regard to the transferral of the alphabet from Cyrillic script to Latin script.
†Karimov had been serving as the Communist Party's First Party Secretary of Uzbekistan since 1989.

a new constitution was approved. This constitution gave the president principal authority to make the major decisions in government. Features of democratic society were also confirmed, such as respect for human rights (including rights for minority groups), the rule of law, and public discourse based on the diversity of ideas. Five principles were accepted to guide the implementation of social, economic, political, and spiritual reforms in Uzbekistan: (1) the predominance of economics over politics (freedom from the ideological direction of the economy), (2) state responsibility for reform, (3) the predominance of law, (4) the need for a strong system of social protection, and (5) a gradual transfer to market relations.

POLITICAL INSTITUTIONS AND PROCESSES

With the breakup of the Soviet Union, Uzbekistan faced the daunting tasks of both state-building and nation-building. As in any society, history and culture shape the political institutions. In the context of Uzbekistan's history and culture, the primary function of a constitution is to legitimize state power. According to this conceptualization, all state bodies act in the name of the people and have a responsibility to govern according to their needs. In return, the acts adopted by the government bodies are compulsory for all citizens. In other words, it is understood that the government will fulfill its functions in administering the state and in providing for the welfare of the people. In return, the people are obligated to accept the decisions of the government as binding. In terms of the formality of the constitution, the government bodies of Uzbekistan are organized, and their functions are defined, on the basis of prevailing international norms—in particular, on the basis of the principle of separation of powers among legislative, executive, and judicial branches of government.

Citizens of the Republic of Uzbekistan elect the president, the Oliy Majlis (the national parliament), and Councils of People's Deputies at provincial, district, and city levels. Appointed state bodies, in contrast, are not elected directly by the people. For example, the khokims (administrative heads) of regions and the city of Tashkent are appointed and dismissed by the president with subsequent confirmation by the appropriate Councils of People's Deputies.[5]

According to constitutional and legal principles, elections in the Republic of Uzbekistan are carried out by universal and direct suffrage, and on the basis of multiparty competition through secret ballot. The constitution also states, in Article 9, that "major matters of public and state life shall be submitted for a nationwide discussion and put [to] a direct vote of the people [referendum]." Decisions adopted by referendum have the status of law and supreme legal validity. They can be canceled or changed only by another referendum.

The principles that were codified in the constitution of the Republic of Uzbekistan consist of people's sovereignty, social justice, democracy, humanism, and separation of powers. Other factors, including political culture, historical legacy, international influences, and decisions of major political actors, also influence the ways in which Uzbekistan's main political institutions operate. What this means is that even though the Constitution of Uzbekistan guarantees people's sovereignty and democracy, historical legacies, issues of security, and the desires of individual leaders to solidify their power do work against the realization of constitutional principles, in practice.

Uzbekistan's National Parliament—The Oliy Majlis (the Supreme Assembly)

According to Article 76 of the 1992 constitution, "the highest state representative body is the Oliy Majlis (the Supreme Assembly) of the Republic of Uzbekistan." Established as a unicameral parliament, a constitutional amendment in 2002 created a two-chamber parliament that began operating in January 2005. Thus, as of 2005, Uzbekistan's parliament consists of two chambers—the Legislative Chamber (lower chamber) and the Senate (upper chamber). The term of office for members of both chambers is five years. The joint powers of the Senate and the Legislative Chamber include the following:

- Adoption and amendment of the constitution
- Enactment and amendment of laws
- Determination of taxes
- Ratification of the state budget submitted by the Cabinet of Ministers
- Control over the execution of the budget
- Ratification of the decrees of the president on the formation and abolition of ministries, state committees, and other bodies of state administration
- Review and approval of nominations of prime minister, the first deputy, and deputies on the president's recommendation
- Ratification of the decrees of the president on proclaiming a state of war
- Ratification of international treaties and agreements.

The Legislative Chamber of the Oliy Majlis consists of 120 deputies elected on a multiparty basis from electoral districts. The speaker of the Legislative Chamber, elected by the membership, must, during his or her tenure, relinquish membership in a political party and forfeit participation in any political party faction or deputies' group. The speaker can, within the framework of his or her powers, issue decrees. The work of the chamber is arranged, activities of committees are coordinated, and preliminary drafts of bills are reviewed by the Council of the Legislative Chamber.[6] Committees of the chamber draft bills, prepare issues for discussion in the Legislative Chamber, and oversee the implementation of laws. Deputies of the chamber may establish factions and groups on political, professional, or another basis. The Legislative Chamber also has the authority to establish commissions to carry out specific activities.

Bills adopted by the chamber are sent to the Senate for consideration, which makes a decision on approval or refusal. If refused, the bill is returned to the Legislative Chamber.* If two-thirds of the deputies of the chamber approve the bill again, it is adopted and sent to the president for signature. The president must sign the bill or may refer the law, with his own amendments, back to the parliament for additional consideration.[7] For a bill returned by the president to the Legislative Chamber, one of the following decisions is made: (1) adopt the bill with the president's amendments, (2) halt consideration of the bill, or (3) confirm the bill on the basis of its previous structure. If the bill is reconfirmed by a two-thirds majority of all the deputies of the Legislative Chamber, it is sent again to the Senate for consideration.[8]

The Legislative Chamber can be dissolved by a decision of the president (if sanctioned by the Constitutional Court) if insurmountable differences arise within it that jeopardize its normal functioning, if it repeatedly makes decisions in opposition to the constitution, or if insurmountable differences arise between the Legislative Chamber and the Senate. In the event of the dissolution of the Legislative Chamber, elections are to be held within three months.

The law "On the Senate of the Oliy Majlis of the Republic of Uzbekistan" specifies that the Senate is the regional representative chamber.[9] Members of the Senate (Senators) are elected from the Supreme Council of the Karakalpakstan Republic and from among the members of the people's councils in the regions, districts, and cities. Six people are selected from each of the regions, from the Karakalpakstan Republic, and from the city of Tashkent. Sixteen members of the Senate are appointed by the president.

One of the distinctive features of the Senate is that it prohibits the creation of factions or groups based on regional affiliation or political orientation. The Senate participates in the legislative procedure as just outlined and has responsibility for the approval of the judges of the Constitutional Court, the Supreme Court, and the Supreme Arbitration Court on the nomination of the president. It is also responsible for the ratification of other presidential appointments such as the Prosecutor General and the chairman of the Board of the Central Bank. The chairman of the Senate is elected by the members on the nomination of the president. The Council of the Senate arranges the work of the Senate, coordinates the activities of committees, and reviews preliminary drafts of bills.

In actual practice, through 2005, the authority of Uzbekistan's unicameral parliament was primarily a formality. It met in full session only a few times a year and the expectation was that the Oliy Majlis would endorse the draft legislation presented to it. It remains to be seen whether the bicameral structure initiated in 2005 will provide the institutional foundation for more independent legislative authority. The representational structure of the Senate

---

*The Legislative Chamber and the Senate members may establish reconciliation commissions to avoid controversies arising from the Senate's refusal of a bill.

could provide regional leaders an opportunity to come together, to express their interests, and to press the government to respond to their needs.

Presidential Rule and Executive Authority

According to the 1992 Constitution of Uzbekistan, the president serves as both head of state and head of executive authority (head of the Cabinet of Ministers). The president holds extensive powers in Uzbekistan. As stated in the constitution, and subsequently amended, presidential powers include the following:

- Form the administration and lead it
- Set up and dissolve ministries, state committees, and other bodies of state administration
- Present nominees to the Senate for the leading posts in the court and banking systems
- Appoint and dismiss khokims (heads of administrations) of regions and the city of Tashkent with subsequent confirmation by the relevant Councils of People's Deputies
- Suspend and repeal any acts passed by the bodies of state administration or khokims
- Proclaim a state of emergency throughout the Republic of Uzbekistan or in a particular locality and submit the decision within three days to the Oliy Majlis' Chambers of the Republic of Uzbekistan for confirmation
- Form the National Security Service, appoint and dismiss its head, and submit decrees concerning these issues to the Senate of the Republic of Uzbekistan for confirmation

Islam Karimov was first elected president (indirectly) on March 24, 1990, by the Supreme Soviet of Uzbekistan. In the December 1991 presidential election, Karimov was proclaimed victorious with approximately 86 percent of the popular vote (just under 13 percent of the vote went to the challenger, Mohammed Salikh).[10] At the time, two political parties were officially registered and able to nominate candidates. These two parties were the Uzbekistan People's Democratic Party (UPDP), which nominated Karimov, and the political party Erk, which nominated Salikh.

According to the constitution, a person may not be elected to the office of the president of the Republic of Uzbekistan for more than two consecutive terms; originally the term was limited to five years. In February 1995, the parliament unanimously voted to hold a national referendum to approve an extension of the president's term. The turnout for the referendum was 99.6 percent of the eligible electorate, and 99.3 percent voted to extend President Karimov's term in office to 2000.

When presidential elections were held in January 2000, Karimov won another five-year term with 92 percent of the vote. Four percent of the vote was won by Abdulhasiz Dzjalalov (also spelled Jalalov), put forward by the Uzbekistan People's Democratic Party.[11] In 2002, following another nationwide referendum, the term of office of the president was extended to seven years. Thus, since 1990, Uzbekistan has had one president, Islam Karimov.

As discussed in previous chapters, when elections are won by incumbent presidents with such an overwhelming percentage of the vote, scholars and observers rightly question the degree to which such elections offered the voters meaningful choices among competing candidates. Such lopsided election results are generally indicative of a system of mobilized participation that represents not democracy but authoritarian control of society. Under authoritarianism, people would vote for Karimov because they believed it their duty to do so or because they were afraid to do otherwise. An alternative perspective is that Karimov was genuinely popular and that the people saw him as the best possible ruler during challenging times.

Cabinet of Ministers

The Cabinet of Ministers is composed of the prime minister of Uzbekistan, his or her deputies, ministers, and heads of government committees. The president nominates the prime minister and he (or she) is approved by both chambers of the parliament. The members of the Cabinet of Ministers are confirmed by the president on nomination by the prime minister.

Between independence and 2005, Uzbekistan had three prime ministers— Abdulhashim Mutalov, January 1992 to December 1995; Otkur Sultonov, December 1995 to December 2003; and Shavkat Mirziyayev (also spelled Mirziyoev), beginning in December 2003. Each of the prime ministers was President Karimov's choice, confirmed by parliament. The prime minister who came into office in December 2003, Shavkat Mirziyayev, had been governor of Karimov's native Samarkand Oblast since 2001. Karimov told the parliament that he had selected Mirziyayev because of his experience in the agricultural sector.[12]

The main functions of the Cabinet of Ministers are to provide guidance for economic, social, and cultural policy; to administer the laws and decisions of the Oliy Majlis; to execute the decrees of the President of the Republic of Uzbekistan; and to issue ordinances. In implementing the decisions of the chambers of the Oliy Majlis and the decrees of the president, the Cabinet of Ministers has the authority to issue its own orders and resolutions, which are binding on all legal entities and citizens.

Local (Regional) Government

Uzbekistan is organized administratively like Ukraine, with provinces, a special administrative region for the capital city, and an autonomous republic.

Uzbekistan has twelve provinces called *viloyatlar* (singular, *viloyat*), one autonomous republic (Karakalpakstan), and one special city (Tashkent). Below the provincial level are districts, cities, and towns.

The Republic of Karakalpakstan in western Uzbekistan was first recognized as an autonomous region in 1936. With the adoption of Uzbekistan's constitution, Karakalpakstan received republic status within independent Uzbekistan. Karakalpakstan is an agricultural region located where the Amu Darya River empties into the Aral Sea. The shrinking of the Aral Sea and the related pollution in the area have contributed to severe poverty in the region.

The executive and administrative head of each province, district, or city is the khokim. He (or she, in rare instances) has deputies who assist him in carrying out his duties and who direct various departments and divisions. The khokim also serves as head of an executive council, which has the authority to pass resolutions applicable to the respective administrative divisions.

The khokims of the provinces and the city of Tashkent are appointed and dismissed by the president with subsequent confirmation by the appropriate provincial council. The khokims of districts, cities, and towns are appointed and dismissed by the khokim at the next higher level of administration, with confirmation by the corresponding district or city council.[13]

Councils of People's Deputies are designated as the representative bodies of authority in the provinces, districts, cities and towns. Elections to the local councils are based more on actual multiparty competition than are elections at the national level. Nominations to these seats can come from political parties, local governmental bodies, and self-governing bodies of citizens. Thus, local government is based on both local representative bodies and local administrative bodies. The term of office for members of the councils and for khokims is five years. The khokims serve as heads of the councils and as executive authorities of their respective territories. Local khokims and councils are responsible for adherence to laws, maintenance of order, and security of citizens in their regions. Local authorities are also expected to direct economic, social, and cultural development within their territories; to implement the local budget; and to protect the environment.

Judicial Authority

Formally, judicial authority in Uzbekistan reflects the principles of "rule of law" and judicial independence from political influence. Judicial authorities are obligated to promote social justice and to protect human rights, freedoms, and legal interests as specified within the constitution. Judges, elected for a five-year period, are in principle independent and subject solely to the law. Judges cannot belong to any political parties or participate in political movements.

The judicial system is composed of the following courts: the Constitutional Court; the Supreme Court; the Supreme Arbitration Court; the Supreme Court of the Republic of Karakalpakstan; the Supreme Arbitration Court of the Republic of Karakalpakstan; regional and Tashkent city courts; interdistrict, district, city, and military courts; and arbitration courts.

The Constitutional Court of the Republic of Uzbekistan is empowered to judge the constitutionality of acts passed by the Chambers of the Oliy Majlis, decrees issued by the president, ordinances of local authorities, as well as obligations of the republic under interstate treaties and other documents. The Supreme Court is the highest judicial body of civil, criminal, and administrative law; its rulings are final and binding throughout Uzbekistan. The Supreme Court is also responsible for supervising the administration of justice by the provincial, city, town, and district courts and the military courts.

THE NATURE OF SOCIETY, POLITICAL CULTURE, AND POLITICAL OPPOSITION

Political systems respond to and reflect the political culture of the surrounding society. Political systems also reflect decisions about institutional design made by incumbent leaders at critical junctures in time. A political system may be reformed to accommodate demands for greater democracy. Likewise, the causal "arrow" may lead to movement in the opposite direction; that is, a political system may become more restrictive as a result of exogenous or external events or as a result of a desire of political elites to hold and maintain power in the face of political opposition. Either direction, toward more democracy or toward greater authoritarianism, will ultimately lead to changes in the ways that people think about politics and government.

In Uzbekistan, as the governing system evolved from socialism to a presidential republic, legacies of the former system endured. Yet, the government did adopt new approaches to policy and new issues emerged in society. Thus, Uzbekistan's current political culture has four primary sources: new political experiences, broadened foreign interactions, influences of the Soviet era, and restoration of traditional culture. A new political culture is reflected in the decisions made about Uzbekistan's developmental trajectory. For example, as religious practices increase, this affects both state policy and, reciprocally, the evolving political culture.

Uzbekistan is a multiethnic state (see Table 1.1, p. 3) with more than 120 nationalities in the country. According to 1996 estimates, the largest ethnic groups in the population are the Uzbeks (80 percent), Russians (5.5 percent), Tajiks (5 percent), Kazakhs (3 percent), Karakalpaks (2.5 percent), Tatars (1.5 percent), and others (2.5 percent). After gaining independence, a high priority of the government was to maintain peace among all nationalities with various religious affiliations.

Uzbekistan's ethnic diversity can be partially accounted for by the fact that the boundaries of the state, as drawn by the Bolsheviks, did not correspond to then-existing cultural and language divisions. Long-term inhabitants of ancestral lands found themselves to be a minority in a republic of a different titular nationality. For example, 24.4 percent of the total population of Tajikistan consists of ethnic Uzbeks. Uzbeks also comprise 13.8 percent of Kyrgyzstan's population, 9 percent of Turkmenistan's and 2.5 percent of Kazakhstan's.[14] Such population distributions have created problems in Central Asia. Examples include the ethnically motivated violence in the Ferghana Valley. The large Slavic populations in Central Asia represent migration by the colonizers during the Tsarist and Soviet periods.

Religious affiliations in Uzbekistan are also important politically. Although the Soviet regime unleashed a fierce anti-religious campaign in the late 1920s, most of the Uzbek population remains Sunni Muslim (approximately 88 percent in 2003). Under the Soviets, mosques were closed and Muslim schools and courts were suspended. Although a degree of toleration was characteristic of Soviet policy during and after World War II, in general, religion was repressed in Uzbekistan during the Soviet period on the basis of communist ideology.

Uzbekistan holds a special place in the Islamic world. In part, this is because of the outstanding Islamic scholars that historically had their roots in Uzbek lands. Since independence, religious expression is more open. New mosques have been erected, old ones refurbished, and religious facilities of all kinds expanded. The changed attitude toward Islam in Uzbekistan is also indicated by the designation of Ramadan and Qurban Khayit as holidays. Whereas only small numbers of people made religious pilgrimages to Mecca during the Soviet period, the number of **hajjes** (pilgrimages to Mecca made as an objective of the religious life of a Muslim) has increased to thousands per year. Nonetheless, Uzbekistan is a **secular country** where religion and state affairs are officially kept separate. The government has attempted to be tolerant and accepting of different religious professions—as long as these do not challenge the state.

About 8 percent of the population can be identified as Orthodox and most of the rest are Muslim. Religious differences between Muslims and Orthodox, however, have not been a source of conflict since independence. Sources of conflict, rather, are associated with divisions within the Muslim community and with demands placed on the secular state by Muslim groups. Although the vast majority of Uzbeks do consider themselves to be Muslims, this large group of people is heterogeneous and does not follow the same religious practices nor do they think alike. Most Uzbeks have a common Muslim identity, but they do not all observe common religious rituals.

Since Uzbekistan became independent, violent political conflict has periodically erupted among Islamic fundamentalists, more moderate Islamic organizations, and the secular state. Groups, such as Adolat and others, that emerged in Ferghana Valley require that people behave and dress like traditional Muslims. More militant groups, such as the Hizbutt Takhrir, Akramiys, Wakhabiys, and Nurchiys, have also formed.

Some groups within Uzbekistan are connected to global organizations. The Islamic Movement of Uzbekistan (IMU) was included by the U.S. government in its list of terrorist organizations.[15] Members of IMU allegedly fought alongside the Taliban during the Afghan conflict and some of its leaders were held by the U.S. government in Guantanamo Bay, Cuba. The goal of IMU is to establish an Islamic state throughout Central Asia. The idea and the organization, however, do not claim popular support throughout the country. Although the IMU has received support in regional enclaves, such as Ferghana Valley and the Namangan region (which have traditionally been very religious), other parts of Uzbekistan's population are not backers of such organizations.

The ideal among Muslims in Uzbekistan is generally one of tolerance, but the difficult living conditions provide fertile soil for support of any movement that promises to improve the situation. In this sense, the IMU and the purportedly nonviolent Hizbutt Takhrir, are a symptom of the Karimov regime's repression, and the groups are likely to retain a degree of support unless steps are taken to improve the quality of Uzbekistan's democracy and strengthen the economy. According to one scholar, Ahmed Rashid, "much of the religious extremism in Central Asia is fueled by the radicalization of politics rather than by political Islam."[16] He suggests that the only curative is for "local political systems to open up in order to prevent extremist Islamic groups from developing in Central Asia."[17] Such a policy will likely reduce support for the more radical groups by providing nonviolent democratic alternatives from which the public may choose.

In 1991, President Karimov visited the Namangan region, a stronghold of Uzbekistan's Islamic Warriors. His government was able to quell most violence and prevent bloodshed, but such groups came to be treated as anti-constitutional. Student disorders in 1992 also caused the government to adopt harsher reprisals against nationalistic and extremist organizations.[18]

Attacks by oppositional groups took place in February 1999 in Uzbekistan's capital city of Tashkent; explosions killed sixteen people. In March 2004, detonations by suicide bombers occurred again in the capital, at a main market and at the police checkpoint at an entrance to Tashkent. In July 2004, explosions happened within Tashkent at three locations: the U.S. embassy, the Israeli embassy, and the Prosecutor General's office building. Government authorities labeled this violence as the work of terrorists associated with Islamic militants and as efforts to overthrow the existing Uzbek government. In the attacks of March and July 2004, between twenty-five and fifty people were killed.[19] Journalists noted that the group under suspicion was the IMU and descibed it as follows:

> The group initially aimed to overthrow Karimov and replace his administration with a Muslim government, although in 2000 its objective changed to establishing a radical Islamist state across Central Asia. The group's leader Tahir Yuldashev is accused of orchestrating a series of deadly bomb attacks in Tashkent in 1999, one of which nearly killed Mr. Karimov.[20]

The assumption is that "terrorist" groups are attempting to overthrow the government of Uzbekistan and also have as their goal reducing the willingness of any country to participate in the George W. Bush administration's antiterrorist coalition. Other opinions have also been advanced; for example, an independent Uzbek journalist has argued that the people who detonate the bombs actually attempt to minimize casualties and that their statement is made by "blowing themselves up" not by killing others. He said that he believed the suicides were meant to protest "the lack of hope of ever being heard or understood by the authorities." If this opinion is correct, then the bomb blasts may be better labeled as suicide protests rather than as terrorist acts. A distinction can be made between "terrorism" and a "mass suicide act of protest," the latter action being an act of desperation and the former act being a political statement about rights and responsibilties. The journalist also argued that people who commit suicide in this way may not be extremist Islamic terrorists, but may rather be people who have lost all hope of conducting a meaningful dialogue with the authorities, and by killing themselves they are making the ultimate statement of discontent and disagreement with the authorities.[21]

Evidence confirms that Uzbekistan's government is hostile toward outspoken critics of the regime, to opposition political activists, and to suspected members of banned Islamic groups. The government uses repression to silence dissent. In June 2005, the European Parliament condemned the "excessive, brutal and indiscriminate use of force by the Uzbek security forces" when they ended demonstrations in the Uzbek city of Andijon.[22] Although accounts of the incident vary, Uzbek government forces did kill hundreds of people in Andijon on May 13, 2005. The Uzbek government described the events as a counterterrorism operation; it crushed an antigovernment rally prompted by an armed uprising and a prison break.

This type of repression has caused groups such as Human Rights Watch and Freedom House to label Uzbekistan's record on political liberties and freedoms as atrocious. An alternative perspective, however, argues that such heavy-handed tactics and strict control over society may be justified under certain circumstances. High levels of political participation, mobilization, and organizational activities may be problematic in societies with divided ethnic loyalties.

Thus, "democracy," as one among many possible forms of government, may not always be the best choice in deeply divided societies. The problem is that because most mobilization and political activity tends to be based on ethnic affiliations, this kind of participation is disruptive for the society and destabilizes the state. Too much organizational activity and free speech only exacerbate existing divisions without contributing to the development of a societal consensus. In such situations, some scholars have argued that a strong, effective, and stable government is more important for promoting economic growth and human development than is the type of government (democratic or authoritarian). Representative of this position is a quote from Esman: "Open competitive politics facilitate the politicization of ethnic communities and the consequent danger of ethnic extremism and violent destabilization of the political order" (1994, 41). According to this approach, we must not be overly judgmental of the "authoritarian" characteristics of Uzbekistan's government. The trade-off may well be that the limitations on freedom of speech and association have helped to prevent all-out civil war and have created a more stable and less violent society.

POLITICAL PARTIES AND PARLIAMENTARY ELECTIONS

Political parties first appeared in the territory of Uzbekistan at the end of the nineteenth century and the beginning of the twentieth century. Political movements mobilized people in support of autonomy within Tsarist Russia, with the further aim of marshaling support for national independence. Such political mobilization was repressed under the tsars and was also hindered by the growing influence of the Russian Social Democrats. Between 1917 and 1990, political parties other than the Communist Party were banned.

During the 1980s, it became possible for some political organizations to operate (somewhat) openly. Initially, the groups focused on Uzbekistan's environmental and economic issues, such as the shrinkage of the Aral Sea, the dominance of cotton growing, low salaries, and the misuse of natural resources. The long-standing resentment of the people toward the Soviet government became more evident when, in the late 1980s, many Uzbeks were implicated in the falsification of cotton production figures. These allegations were resented by the people as they led to a labeling of Uzbekistan as a particularly corrupt region of the country. The sense of injustice felt by the people was heightened by the discrimination that Uzbek recruits experienced in the Soviet Army. Identity issues, together with the political and economic grievances, provided the foundations for Uzbek nationalism. This revival of nationalistic ideas coincided with a revival of religious activity.

Birlik and the political party Erk emerged as autonomous organizational vehicles promoting reform within Uzbek society. Birlik, founded in May 1989, was registered as an organization formed to deal with "public issues" (not political issues), but soon the organization developed an overtly political agenda. The organization's leaders openly criticized the local administration. The focus on political and nationalistic demands led to a split among the movement's leaders and to the creation of the Erk Democratic Party of Uzbekistan.

In the 1991 presidential election, the leader of the Erk Democratic Party, Mukhammad Solikh, competed as a candidate against incumbent President Karimov. Although Erk proclaimed the goal of building a democratic society based on respect of human rights, activists associated with the party were portrayed in the state-controlled media as being "spontaneous" rather than "constructive." The conflict between the governing authorities and such "oppositional" organizations was intense and ultimately led to the denial of registration rights for both Erk and Birlik. The goal of creating a democratic system as put forward by Birlik and the Erk Democratic Party was interpreted by the government as a desire to overthrow the existing system. Birlik was barred from participation in the 1991 election and was refused registration as a political party in 1993. Erk was also denied registration in 1993 as a legal organization, meaning that both parties were officially banned from carrying out their mobilization activities within Uzbek society. The Islamic Renaissance Party (IRP) and other religious-based groups were also banned.[23] As of the mid-2000s, the leader of the national Birlik movement and the leader of the Erk Democratic Party lived outside the country as political refugees.

After being prohibited from activities deemed unconstitutional for ten years, the unregistered party Erk held a congress in Tashkent in June 2003. Some thirty members of the party's central committee participated in the congress, criticizing the authorities and resolving to be more active in Uzbek politics. Congress participants credited international pressure for making the gathering possible.[24] Members and supporters of the unregistered Erk Democratic Party also boldly picketed the Uzbek Prosecutor General's office in Tashkent on October 15, 2003. The picketers demanded that party property, which they said had been illegally confiscated, be returned; that police harassment of party members be ended; and that the party be allowed to hold another congress in October 2003.[25] Regardless of these developments, leaders and members of both Birlik and Erk remained subject to tight government surveillance, and neither party was allowed to contest the 2004–2005 elections.

Truly oppositional political parties are excluded from competing in Uzbekistan's presidential and parliamentary elections. Such parties promote an alternative conception of the state, either as significantly more open and free (democratic parties) or as ruled by religious law (Islamic organizations). Parties that accept and support the current regime, however, are allowed to compete in national elections and are encouraged to do so by President Karimov.

Although it may seem a contradiction, Uzbekistan represents multiparty authoritarianism. Competing parties are allowed to exist and they do have their own programs on issues pertaining to the development of the country and society. The 2004 parliamentary elections featured the participation of five political parties, but none was hostile or threatening to the position and course of the president. According to Freedom House's "Nations in Transit 2004" survey, Uzbek political parties "function more as interest groups than as genuine, competing political parties," and "they help create a false sense of political pluralism in the country."

The longest-operating party is the Uzbekistan People's Democratic Party (UPDP), the successor of the former Communist Party of Uzbekistan. At an assembly in May 1991, members unanimously voted to abolish the Communist Party of Uzbekistan and simultaneously founded the Uzbekistan People's Democratic Party. In the parliamentary elections of 1994 and 1999, this party won most of the seats. After the December 2004/January 2005 parliamentary election, the UPDP controlled twenty-eight of the elected seats in parliament (see Table 14.1). Despite the smaller number of seats, the UPDP maintained the largest official electoral infrastructure.[26]

In the 1991 presidential election, the UPDP nominated Karimov as its candidate and until June 1996 the president served as leader of the party. When new laws were adopted on the regulation of political parties, Karimov voluntarily resigned as party leader. In the 2000 presidential election, the Uzbekistan People's Democratic Party put forward an alternate candidate, professor of history Abdulhasiz Dzhalalov (also spelled Jalalov), but he received only a small portion of the vote (4 percent). Since 2003, Asliddin Rustamov has been the first secretary (party leader) of the UPDP.

Given that the UPDP officially controlled only a quarter of the seats in the Legislative Chamber after 2005, the system could be classified as *multiparty*. Yet, the other political parties represented in the chamber cannot be differentiated on the basis of significant programmatic variations between them. All legal parties are pro-Karimov, or at least sanctioned by him.

One such party, the Uzbekistan Liberal Democratic Party (ULDP), was organized in the fall of 2003. The party, led by Mahammadjon Ahmedjanov, has the stated objectives of protecting the interests of entrepreneurs and small- and medium-sized businesses, constructing market relations based on a democratic state, and encouraging democratic institutions. Noteworthy is the fact that the

TABLE 14.1 Results of Uzbekistan's 2004–2005[a] Oliy Majlis[b] (Parliamentary) Elections

Party	Number of Seats
Uzbekistan Liberal Democratic Party (ULDP) – Movement of Entrepreneurs and Businessmen of Uzbekistan	41
Uzbekistan People's Democratic Party (UPDP), formerly the Communist Party	28
Fidokorlor Party – Self-Sacrifice National Democratic Party	18
Millyi Tiklanish – Uzbekistan National Revival Democratic Party	11
Adolat – Justice Social Democratic Party	10
Initiative/Citizen groups	12
Total	120

Source: Data is from the Central Eurasia Project/IPU at http://www.ipu.org/parlinee/reports/2343_E.htm Version: 2/15/2005 15:22:45.

The turnout was 85.1 percent of eligible voters.

[a]The elections were held on December 26, 2004, and January 9, 2005.

[b]The Legislative Chamber of Uzbekistan, which is the successor of the Supreme Assembly.

party was created with the blessing of President Karimov; his hope was that the organization would provide a base of support among small businesspeople, whose help is needed to improve Uzbekistan's economic development.[27] The party experienced immediate electoral success in December 2004 and January 2005. Although the Uzbekistan Liberal Democratic Party is now the largest party in the Legislative Chamber, the sanctioning of the ULDP by President Karimov and the continuing strength of the Uzbekistan People's Democratic Party, suggest no real policy change resulting from the ULDP victory.

The third best performer in the 2004–2005 elections was the Fidokorlor Party (the Self-Sacrifice National Democratic Party). This party was established in 1998 under this slogan: "Reforms not for the sake of reforms but reforms for people's well-being"; its stated objectives are to construct a civic society, to raise living standards, and to make Uzbekistan one of the leading powers of the world. The current party head, Ahtam Tursunov, was also chair of the Defense and Security Committee in the 1999–2004 parliament.[28] In the 2000 presidential election, the Fidokorlor Party nominated incumbent President Karimov as its candidate; he won the election with 92 percent of the vote.

Another political party, the Adolat (Justice Social Democratic Party), held its first assembly and was registered at the Justice Ministry in February 1995. The party professes support for principles of social democracy and for the improved well-being of all nationalities living in Uzbekistan. Since 1996, Turgunpulat Daminov, president of the First Tashkent State Medical Institute, has been Adolat's party head.

The Milliy Tiklanish (Uzbekistan National Revival Democratic Party) was also formed in 1995. With a nationalist orientation expressed according to the overall goals of the Karimov regime, the program of the National Revival Democratic Party emphasizes the goal of building Uzbekistan into one of the leading states in the world community. Also known as the Democratic Party of Uzbekistan, Milliy Tiklanish runs a party newspaper of the same name and has been headed by journalist Hurshid Dostmuhammad.[29]

Elections held prior to 2004–2005, were for the unicameral, 250-member Oliy Majlis. The parliament elected in 1994 technically included only 69 candidates running for the Uzbekistan People's Democratic Party, but an estimated 120 more deputies were UPDP members nominated by local councils. Overall, the UPDP took 193 of the 250 seats and the rest were won by the candidates acceptable to the government. The 1999 elections for the Oliy Majlis (elected by popular vote to serve five-year terms) were also won by pro-government candidates and parties. As mentioned above, the largest vote-getter in the 1999 election was the Uzbekistan People's Democratic Party.

Four of the five parties that competed in the 2004–2005 parliamentary elections had also competed in 1999. The December 2004 elections required candidates to attain an absolute majority of the votes in the first round or elections went to a second round in January 2005. Changes to election laws required 30 percent of candidates put forth on party slates to be female, and some financial regulations were also modified.[30] While turnout was lower than in the previous parliamentary election (85.1 percent in 2004 compared to 93.5 percent in 1999), it was still well above the 33 percent threshold required by law for the elections to be deemed valid. Elections monitors from the Commonwealth of Independent States, however, raised some concerns that turnout numbers were inflated, and the Organization for Security and Cooperation in Europe (OSCE) stated that "the elections fell significantly short of commitments of the OSCE participating States to hold genuinely democratic elections in the broader context of respect for human rights and other international standards for democratic elections."[31] Given the classification of Uzbekistan's system as multiparty authoritarianism, it follows that political parties are weak organizations. Although the legal political parties do develop their own platforms, in practice all of them pursue policies in line with the president's views on the major issues. Parties in Uzbekistan are severely constrained as to what they can propose in terms of alternative ways of development for the state and society. Parties do, however, play a role in the nomination of candidates for public office. Parties can also provide an interest aggregation function by linking leaders and interest groups in society.

Nonetheless, a gap exists between political parties and the population. Most citizens do not even know the names of the different parties, let alone their programs or aims, plus they are skeptical of them. Parties, for their part, are limited in their ability to address critically the social problems in society and find it less risky and more expedient to promote the general goal of public development. The political parties that are allowed to operate legally were created from the top down, either under direct order or on the advice of the president and his government. The Council of the Federation of Trade Unions is also dependent on the state, and no real alternative union organizations exist.

The ability of parties to raise funds to support their activities is severely restricted. Regular membership fees are the primary source of funds for parties. Some income is also derived from publishing activities, but it is not sufficient to support party activities. The law on political parties prohibits direct or indirect financial support from public bodies, public organizations, foreign governments, international organizations, noncitizens, and religious organizations. Political parties are not allowed to open foreign bank accounts or have valuables in banks.

As mentioned earlier, organizations such as the Islamic Movement of Uzbekistan do advocate the violent overthrow of Uzbekistan's secular government and its replacement by an Islamic regime. Such groups do represent a real threat to the current government. Not every oppositional organization, however, calls for an overthrow of the existing regime. A constructive opposition can call for new leaders and new policies without challenging the fundamental institutions of the state.

A broad range of views exists on the compatibility of multiparty rule with Islam. The law on political parties that went into effect in January 1997 states that political parties in Uzbekistan cannot be formed on the basis of religious or ethnic affiliations (Melvin 2000, 34), yet such social cleavages are a natural basis for party formation in plural societies. The law does reflect public preferences—most Uzbeks are uncomfortable with ethnically or religiously based oppositional organizations. About one-fifth of citizens believe that religious parties should not be legalized, either because religion should not mix with politics or because it would make life more difficult for Muslims. Just under one-fifth believe that they should exist but be loyal to the government, while only about 2 percent think that there should be a religious party in opposition.[32]

In discussing the party system of Uzbekistan, we must also recognize that multiparty competition in and of itself is no panacea for government responsiveness and effectiveness. In addition, certain types of political parties that are appropriate for one group of countries (during particular historical periods) may be less useful or functional in different surroundings. Uzbekistan has had little experience with Western notions of liberal democracy (and multiparty competition) and the application of these ideas in the Central Asia setting must be considered to be an experiment, at best. It may be that other forms of government and interest aggregation will work better, notwithstanding the value of learning from international experience.

Just as we must recognize that no one form of government is appropriate for all states and for all people, we must also be accurate in our assessment of whether the human rights of people living within any given country are being respected and upheld. According to country ratings reported by Freedom House for 2005, Uzbekistan ranks among the least "free" countries in the world, with political rights and civil liberties on a par with China, Somalia, and Vietnam.* The Uzbek government restricts the activities of those opposition movements that it deems to be potentially "destructive" to the state and society. In the early 1990s, a series of demonstrations and the civil war in Tajikistan provided the government with its justification for the prohibition of opposition organizations. More recently, the government has rationalized the increased authoritarianism with reference to the threat of Islamic fundamentalism that could overthrow the secular state. Such repression leads to criticism from international human rights organizations.

*Freedom House measures freedom by assessing two broad categories: political rights and civil liberties. Political rights include the right to vote and compete for public office and to elect representatives who have a decisive vote on public policies. Civil liberties include the freedom to develop opinions, institutions, and personal autonomy without interference from the state. Freedom House assigns each country and territory a political rights and civil liberties rating, along with a corresponding status designation of Free, Partly Free, or Not Free. Uzbekistan's rating is Not Free. For more information, see http://www.freedomhouse.org/research/freeworld/2005/combined2005.pdf.

THE MAIN PUBLIC POLICY ISSUES

Uzbekistan's years since independence can be divided into three main periods:

- 1991–1994—The emergence of Uzbekistan as a member of the world community with a dramatic increase in international transactions and relations
- 1995–1997—An exploration of strategies for domestic and foreign policy, with an open orientation toward global issues
- 1997 to the present—The stabilization of domestic and foreign policy positions, together with continuing concerns about the threat of terrorism from Islamic militants

This section reviews the domestic and foreign policy developments that have emerged during these three periods.

The Economy

One might expect that the development of Uzbekistan's economy would reflect its history as a traditional hub for economic transactions, its position along the Great Silk Road, and its central location between Asia and Europe. In fact, however, the pattern of transactions established during the Tsarist and Soviet periods of colonization dramatically changed traditional trade relationships. Uzbekistan was a colony of the Russian and Soviet Empires with an export-oriented economy. In part as a result of this colonial heritage, current developments in Uzbekistan and Central Asia are strongly influenced by the interests of the major powers of the world.

Uzbekistan has considerable mineral resources. The export of these natural resources, particularly gold and energy products, contributes significantly to the budget of the country. Uzbekistan is fourth in the world in gold reserves and seventh in gold extracting; the country is tenth in the world in copper reserves and eleventh in copper mining; and the country is seventh in the world in uranium reserves and eighth in uranium mining. Uzbekistan has enormous energy resources in natural gas, coal, and oil.[33]

Despite its impressive mineral resources, agriculture has always been the core of Uzbekistan's economy and still is. Uzbekistan is a dry country, and agricultural production is concentrated in intensely cultivated, irrigated river valleys. More than 60 percent of the population lives in these densely populated rural communities. Uzbekistan served as the chief cotton supplier to the rest of the USSR and cotton production is still a central feature of the economy of Uzbekistan.[34] Uzbekistan is now the world's second-largest cotton exporter.*

*The information in this paragraph is from the CIA's *World Factbook*, http://www.cia .gov/cia/publications/factbook, and *Country Studies* (Federal Research Division, Library of Congress) at http://lcweb2.loc.gov.frd/cs/cshome.html.

Cotton is so valuable to the Uzbek economy that the government has been faced with a problem—the smuggling of cotton to neighboring countries. An October 2003 shooting incident on the Uzbek-Kyrgyz border reportedly involved a case of attempted cotton smuggling. In addition to harsh punishment for smuggling, the government has set a fine for failing to deliver cotton to government procurement points.[35] Related to this, which is a holdover from the Soviet period, is the practice that farmers still do not have the right to decide for themselves what to grow. President Karimov argues that because land is allotted to them by commissions headed by oblast governors, farmers should grow those crops specified in their contracts with the oblast administrations. Planting of other crops is considered a "grave violation" of a farmer's contract with legal consequences.[36] Cotton specialists at the Uzbek Academy of Sciences, however, have noted that the government monopoly on the export of cotton may deprive growers of incentives to produce.[37]

Since independence, investments in energy, mineral, automotive, and tobacco sectors of the economy have been increased. Improvements have been made in Uzbekistan's air transportation and telecommunications networks. Uzbekistan exports automobiles, primarily to other CIS countries, and is the only country in the region with an aircraft construction plant.

Overall, however, Uzbekistan's economy remains troubled. After 1991, Uzbekistan lost the trade and supply networks associated with the Soviet market, and its economy became subject to fluctuations in world commodity prices. In general, the 1990s were difficult years for Uzbekistan's economy, as they were for the other former Soviet republics. According to the World Bank's figures, Uzbekistan lost an average of 3.5 percent of its income per capita each year between 1990 and 1997.[38]

In 1994, the government introduced tighter monetary policies, expanded privatization, and slightly reduced the role of the state in the economy, but the changes were minor given the fact that the state continued to have extensive control of the economy. The Uzbek government has been reluctant to let go of the old Soviet-style system of control and slow to introduce and initiate structural change or build the institutions necessary to operate a market economy. The continuance of the Soviet-style system has caused Uzbekistan to be rated number 146 out of 154 countries in its relative level of "economic freedom."[39]

In the summer of 2003, the World Bank office in Tashkent published its first analysis of living standards in Uzbekistan. A sharp decline in foreign investment was reported to be a major factor contributing to increased poverty.*

---

*Foreign assistance to Uzbekistan has in the past been sizable, with money coming into the country from the United States, Russia, Turkey, South Korea, Japan, Germany, France, China, and others.

Picking cotton in Uzbekistan.
Photo by Vicki Hesli

According to World Bank experts, Uzbekistan had one of the lowest rates of foreign investment among members of the CIS.[40]

Tight government control over the economy and the lack of economic opportunity have contributed to demonstrations in several regions of the country. Rioting, involving thousands of protestors, occurred in November 2004 and led to the destruction of government property and acts of violence against police officers and tax collectors in the Ferghana and Kashkadarya provinces.[41] Protests also occurred in December 2004 in the Syrddarya and Sharkhrikhan provinces in response to government shutoffs of water, natural gas, and electricity.[42] Reports of sharp increases in suicide rates also indicate deep-seated hopelessness. Protests and reports of mass suicides support the assertion that much of the violence in Uzbekistan has domestic, not foreign, roots. Further economic liberalization appears to be the best possibility for reducing acts of political violence in the country.

Successful economic reform continues to remain at least partially dependent on considerable financial aid. If Uzbekistan can improve its investment climate by creating a legal framework more favorable to foreign investors, full convertibility of its currency, and a more vibrant private sector, it would have a better opportunity to benefit from such funds. Much of the economic aid, however, depends on developments in the political sector. The European Bank for Reconstruction and Development decided to reduce the level of its public-sector loans in 2004, expressing "serious concerns about the state of genuine multiparty democracy, respect for the rule of law, and human rights in Uzbekistan."[43] Despite continued reductions in direct foreign investment, growth in gross domestic product (GDP) has been positive since 1998 (see Table 14.2).

Foreign Policy

During the first years of Uzbekistan's independent statehood, the country became a participant in international organizations such as the International Monetary Fund (IMF), the International Bank for Reconstruction and Development (IBRD), the United Nations Educational, Scientific and Cultural Organization (UNESCO), the Organization for Security and Cooperation in Europe (OSCE), the European Bank for Reconstruction and Development (EBRD), and NATO's Partnership for Peace (PFP) program. Uzbekistan began cooperating with other countries through multilateral and bilateral agreements. Its first focus was on establishing agreements with neighboring countries for the purpose of enhancing regional stability. Tensions revolving around border issues and control over natural resources created significant challenges for the new regime. In addition, the country had to work out a positive way of interacting with Russia as the predominant power in the region.

Multilateral Foreign Relations   The Russian Federation remains the largest regional power in Central Asia. The Commonwealth of Independent States is an example of Russia's multilateral orientation to foreign policy in the region. Although hundreds of international documents have been approved within the structures of the CIS framework, few have been fully implemented or executed. For example, a collective security agreement was signed in Tashkent in March 1992, but it did not provide Uzbekistan the support it needed when the hostilities in Afghanistan and the rise of terrorism posed a threat to the national security of the country. Uzbekistan, therefore, has not had high expectations of assistance from CIS structures.

In 1993, Central Asian leaders agreed on the formation of a single economic space. The resulting organization, the Central Asian Cooperation Organization (CACO), includes Kyrgyzstan, Kazakhstan, Tajikistan, and Uzbekistan. Regional

TABLE 14.2 Uzbekistan's Economic and Social Indicators

Measure	1998	1999	2000	2001	2002	2003
Agriculture, value added (% of GDP)	—	33.52	34.36	34.01	34.73	35.18
Exports of goods and services (% of GDP)	—	18.15	24.59	28.08	30.81	36.74
Foreign Direct Investment, net flows (BoP, US$)	—	121,000,000	73,000,000	569,600,000	65,000,000	—
GDP (US$)	150,000,00,000	17,100,000,000	13,800,000,000	11,400,000,000	9,710,000,000	9,949,245,000
GDP growth (annual %)	4.3	4.3	3.8	4.2	4.2	4.4
GNI per capita, Atlas method (US$)	620	650	620	550	450	420
GNI, Atlas method (US$)	14,800,000,000	15,800,000,000	15,400,000,000	13,900,000,000	11,500,000,000	10,778,630,000
Illiteracy rate, adult total (% of people age 15 and above)	0.91	0.85	0.79	0.76	0.73	—
Imports of goods and services (% of GDP)	—	18.41	21.52	27.65	28.09	29.56
Industry, value added (% of GDP)	26.17	24.31	23.13	22.59	21.49	21.68
Inflation, GDP deflator (annual %)	39	44.12	47.34	45.19	45.54	24.25
Life expectancy at birth, total (years)	—	—	67.85	67.41	66.97	—

(Continued)

TABLE 14.2 Uzbekistan's Economic and Social Indicators—Cont'd

Measure	1998	1999	2000	2001	2002	2003
Military expenditures (US$)[a]	—	—	—	—	—	200,000,000
Military expenditures (% of GDP)	—	—	—	—	—	2.01
Population growth (annual %)	1.48	1.38	1.29	1.28	1.23	1.31
Population, total	24,000,000	24,400,000	24,700,000	25,100,000	25,400,000	25,604,000
Services, etc., value added (% of GDP)	42.52	42.17	42.51	43.36	45.63	43.14
Trade in goods (% of GDP)	—	73.20	79.49	82.93	79.98	—

Source: Unless otherwise noted, all figures for the table are from the World Bank at http://devdata.worldbank.org/data-query/.

[a] Figures for the two military expenditures rows are from the CIA's *World Factbook*, "Rank Order – Military expenditures – dollar figure" at http://www.odci.gov/cia/publications/factbook/rankorder/2067rank.txt.

economic integration, however, once again did not progress as far as the leaders had hoped; thus the government has learned not to place too much faith in the ability of a multinational organization to contribute to Uzbekistan's national interests.

Another regional grouping is the Shanghai Cooperation Organization (SCO), made up of Kazakhstan, Kyrgyzstan, Tajikistan, Uzbekistan, Russia, and China. Although a relatively weak structure functionally since its founding in 1996, the increased presence of the United States in Central Asia in the wake of the September 11, 2001, terrorist attacks has caused Russia and China to pitch the SCO as a regional security alternative to U.S. "unilateralism." Member states have approved a strategy for cooperation in fighting international terrorism, organized crime, drug and arms trafficking, religious extremism, and separatism. Both Russia and China prefer that Uzbekistan see the SCO as its primary source of security. Russian President Putin wants Uzbekistan to loosen its security ties to the United States and to bind itself more closely to Russia in political and economic affairs.[44]

Uzbekistan is also a member of the Economic Cooperation Organization (ECO); other states in the organization are Afghanistan, Azerbaijan, Iran, Kazakhstan, Kyrgyzstan, Pakistan, Turkey, Turkmenistan, and Tajikistan. Of particular consequence is an organizational provision that could provide member states with access to international ports in Pakistan, Iran, and Turkey; this is important because Central Asian states face a serious geopolitical challenge—none of them has direct access to international waterways. The achievement of such access is a top priority in the member states' foreign policies. Again, because of the lack of progress with this multilateral organization (because the ECO has not yet been able to ensure this access to member states), Uzbekistan has taken it upon itself to attempt to work out such arrangements bilaterally.

The European Union (EU) is also important to Uzbekistan as a multilateral international structure. According to a partnership agreement with the EU, the country is able to cooperate directly with major European states. Uzbekistan has also partnered with another European structure on the continent—the Organization for Security and Cooperation in Europe.

Although Uzbekistan is not a member of NATO, it has cooperated with North Atlantic Treaty Organization countries both on a multilateral and bilateral basis. Uzbekistan joined NATO's PFP program in 1995 and viewed the program as an opportunity to modernize its military and to improve the training of its military personnel. NATO member states have supported Uzbekistan's initiatives concerning Central Asian security, promotion of peace in Afghanistan, and a nuclear-free weapons policy for Central Asia.[45]

Bilateral Foreign Relations   During Uzbekistan's early days of independence, the country focused its foreign policy on the countries of the Middle East and tried to establish mutually beneficial bilateral relationships with Turkey,

Iran, India, and Saudi Arabia. Geographical proximity together with shared cultural and religious identities played crucial roles in the priority given to such relationships. With the exception of Turkey, whose secular model of state-building was selected as the preferred approach by Uzbek authorities, Uzbekistan's foreign policy since 1993 has been directed away from Middle Eastern states.

Bilateral relations with Russia are particularly crucial in Uzbek foreign policy. Uzbekistan understands the critical importance of Russia in its overall international position. Russia, however, has not always responded positively to Uzbekistan's strengthening foreign relations, given the historically dominant position of Russia in the region.

Uzbek-U.S. relations began to warm in 1995 during the Clinton administration and continued to develop positively during the early Bush administration. Particularly noteworthy was the increasing strategic (military) partnership between the United States and Uzbekistan, including the establishment of an official bilateral security relationship. A major factor in the deepening of cooperative agreements was the use of a military base in Uzbekistan by U.S. forces. The U.S. lost its use of Uzbekistan's Khanabad air base near the Afghanistan border, however, when the United States criticized the Karimov regime for the large-scale civilian casualties in Andijon in May 2005. Uzbek authorities justified their decision to evict U.S. forces from the base by citing changing circumstances and financial issues. The decision coincided with a request by the Shanghai Cooperation Organization that the United States withdraw its forces from bases in Central Asia and set up a timetable for U.S. withdrawal from Afghanistan.

Despite such setbacks, in general Uzbekistan's Western orientation has been welcomed by Europe and the United States. The negative side is the reactions among some Middle Eastern countries, Russia, and China. It was in part because of Uzbekistan's accommodation of U.S. forces, together with its insistence on remaining a secular rather than an Islamic state, that a few Middle Eastern countries helped to finance and supply some of the more radical Islamic groups that have attempted to penetrate Central Asia.

Uzbekistan is geopolitically located in the heart of the Central Asian and the Eurasian regions. Thus, even acknowledging the significance of its relationships with Western countries, its main issues and problems are regionally based. In addition to the question of the proper role of Islam within the governments and societies of the region, another main issue is the struggle for water resources. The problem is twofold: (1) an inadequate supply of water and (2) how to distribute and share this precious resource. The bulk of the water goes to agriculture, followed by industrial usage, and the rest is used for municipal purposes. Agreements between the countries of the region have been negotiated, interstate organizations have been established, and compacts have been made to manage the water supply problem.

Another major issue in the region concerns Uzbekistan's ethnic bonds, rather than its religious bonds, to its neighbors. In addition to the problems associated with the violent turmoil in Afghanistan, border disputes with the four neighboring former republics remain unsettled. Uzbeks, for example, constitute approximately 14 percent of Kyrgyzstan's population. Given that the international borders do not correspond to locations of ethnic populations, delimitation and demarcation of them remains a major issue. In addition, Kyrgyz people living in Uzbekistan have expressed dissatisfaction with their living conditions. Representatives of Kyrgyz communities in Uzbekistan have requested political and economic assistance, alleging that Kyrgyz schools are dilapidated and ignored by the Uzbek authorities, that members of the Kyrgyz minority cannot find jobs, and that there is pressure by Uzbek officials not to publicize the problems.[46]

Other top issues that drive the Uzbek-Kyrgyz relationship are water management and the supply of electric power. Some border districts of Uzbekistan receive electricity from Kyrgyzstan. In turn, Uzbekistan delivers gas to some Kyrgyz border districts. Problems have occurred with the delivery of these gas and electric power supplies.

The border with Tajikistan has also been a problem, exacerbated by Tajikistan's civil war that began right after independence. Uzbeks make up about 24 percent of the population of Tajikistan. Uzbekistan participated in a multinational CIS peacekeeping force that was sent to quell the civil war in Tajikistan. President Karimov has also been concerned about the spread of Islamic fundamentalism through Tajikistan.

Relations between Uzbekistan and Turkmenistan also face obstacles. Turkmenistan's refineries process not only domestic crude oil but also crude oil from Uzbekistan's Kokdumalok oil field. To access the Persian Gulf, Uzbekistan needs to pass through Turkmenistan. The two countries have very different views on regional security issues. Uzbekistan's relations with world powers have not been perceived positively by Turkmenistan's President Saparmurat Turkmenbashi, the Supreme Leader of All Turkmen.

Uzbekistan has been particularly challenged by developments in Afghanistan, with which it shares a border. Afghanistan is also home to a large Uzbek ethnic group. After the Taliban captured Kabul in 1996 and entered Mazar-I-Sharif (a town in Afghanistan very close to the Uzbek border), Uzbekistan called on the world community to take the Afghan problem seriously, emphasizing the destabilizing impact that the situation could have on Central Asia and on the whole world. Uzbekistan maintains bilateral relations with the Afghan government. Leaders of the U.S. military establishment and heads of the Russian General Staff have worked with Uzbek officials to fortify its international borders.

CONCLUSION

After gaining independence, President Karimov declared that his priorities were to establish stability in Uzbek society and in neighboring states, to unify the country through the strengthening of a common identity, and to dissolve the dependence of Uzbekistan on Russia. In attempting to realize these objectives, a system of centralized power was created based on the institution of the presidency and the person of Islam Karimov. The government has suppressed the development of destabilizing sources of opposition, particularly Islam, through tight control over the media and a near continuous surveillance of opposition leaders (Melvin 2000, 29).

Political reform in Uzbekistan has not led to the establishment of a liberal democracy based on Western norms. Since independence, the country has developed a political system with a number of authoritarian characteristics. Although the limitations that the Uzbek government has placed on the full participation of political parties in the political process may be viewed negatively, one may justifiably argue that political pluralism, which by definition involves conflict and competition between opposing ideas, cannot be realized without violence in Uzbekistan. Although all political opposition labeled as *destructive* by the government is prohibited, ethnic and religious diversity is tolerated. While the Uzbek language has acquired the status of official state language, national minorities have been provided opportunities for cultural expression and religious practices have become more open and free. Thus, the choice has been made to limit certain kinds of freedom for the sake of security, stability, and peace. Only the Uzbek people can decide for themselves whether this is the correct choice.

Economic reforms, likewise, have been limited. Uzbekistan has still not realized significant improvement in its overall productive capacity. Although the economy remains largely dependent on agriculture, in particular cotton, it has been at least partially diversified. Lack of progress may be related to the continued heavy involvement of the state in economic management, including retention of monopoly control over major sectors of the economy. Western analysts would surely argue that, in addition to reducing the role of the state in the economy, the extreme power of the executive branch of government should also be reduced. If a balance of power is established, a more efficient economy may emerge and Uzbekistan may become a more welcoming investment environment. Although the colonial legacy remains, Uzbekistan is no longer Moscow's captive supplier of raw materials; Uzbekistan's natural resources have become its national wealth.

With regard to foreign policy, Uzbekistan has established bilateral relationships with foreign countries and, through the framework of international organizations, has dealt with international terrorism, drug trade, environmental pollution, and many other important issues. Particularly impressive is the continuance of peaceful relationships with other countries in the region. Although Uzbekistan has adopted a cooperative foreign policy stance, it remains caught in a tug of war with the major powers in the region and around the globe. The interests of those powers, such as the United States, Russia, and China, shape and influence the prospects and potentialities for the enhancement of

Uzbekistan's national interests. Uzbekistan's leadership faces a major challenge in negotiating a workable balance between its own needs and the demands of the world's great powers.

Key Terms

Colonialism

Hajjes

Jadids' movement

Korenizatsya

Secular country

Turkistan (Turkestan)

Critical Thinking Questions

1. What are some of the important characteristics of the major periods in the history of Uzbekistan?

2. Thinking back to the previous chapter, would Georgia have been better off with greater presidential power to keep ethnic divisions in check?

3. How does its colonial legacy affect Uzbek society today?

4. What factors account for the establishment of the strong presidency in Uzbekistan?

5. What are the functions of political parties in Uzbekistan?

6. What is the role of Islam in Uzbek society? What is the relationship between economic well-being and sympathy among ordinary people for Islamic movements?

7. What are the main directions of Uzbekistan's foreign policy?

Suggested Reading

Cornell, S., and R. Spector. "Central Asia: More Than Islamic Extremists." *The Washington Quarterly* (2002): 193–206.

Gleason, Gregory. "Uzbekistan." In *Nations in Transit* 2003, edited by Adrian Karatnycky, Alexander J. Motyl, and Amanda Schnetzer. Lanham, Md.: Rowman and Littlefield, 2003, 631–48.

Kubicek, P. "Authoritarianism in Central Asia: Curse or Cure." *Third World Quarterly* 19(1) (1998): 29–43.

Luong, P. "After the Break-up: Institutional Design in Transitional States." *Comparative Political Studies* 33(5) (2000): 563–92.

Shafer, R., and E. Freedman. "Obstacles to the Professionalization of Mass Media in Post-Soviet Central Asia: A Case Study of Uzbekistan." *Journalism Studies* 4(1) (2003): 91–103.

Websites of Interest

Information about Uzbekistan from the press service of the President of the Republic of Uzbekistan:
http://www.press-service.uz/

Information about economic issues in Uzbekistan from the Center for Economic Research:
http://www.cer.uz/

Information about Uzbekistan from the Law Library of Congress:
http://www.loc.gov/law/guide/uzbekistan.html

U.S. State Department Report on Human Rights Practices in Uzbekistan:
http://www.state.gov/g/drl/rls/hrrpt/2002/18400.htm

EPILOGUE

Making Sense of Political Change

MOST COUNTRIES OF THE FORMER USSR have declared, and adopted within their constitutions, norms that characterize democratic regimes. But these systems generally come up short when measured along the dimensions by which consolidated democracies are distinguished. Legacies of the past, such as the one-party state, the repression of political opposition, and the centrally planned economy, are still significant in this part of the world and have undermined successful transitions to democracy. In addition, the decisions made by individual leaders to strengthen and secure their own power have further damaged prospects for democracy in the region.

Although all post-Soviet countries hold regularly scheduled elections, a necessary step in the implementation of democracy, key goals must also be realized in institutionalizing competition among political parties, freedom of speech and association, and the rule of law. According to Juan Linz and Alfred Stepan, democracy is consolidated when "[it] becomes routinized and deeply internalized in social, institutional and even psychological life" (1996: 5). A similarly well-accepted position in the field is that democracy becomes consolidated when major players accept the rules of the game; that is, when democracy becomes the "only game in town" (Guiseppe di Palma, as quoted in Linz and Stepan 1996, 5).

In every country that we have surveyed, with the sole exception of Lithuania, political opposition has been suppressed by pro-government forces. In Russia, Ukraine, Georgia, and Uzbekistan, elections are regularly held, but they are marked by manipulation of results and unequal playing fields. Administrative resources are employed for the purpose of keeping incumbent governments in power. Because many post-Soviet citizens are still directly dependent on the state for their wages, for utilities, and for other necessities of life, local officials can threaten to withhold wages or benefits should employees not vote in the preferred manner.

While Ukraine and Georgia have taken important steps away from authoritarianism, in Russia and Uzbekistan the pattern during the first half of the 2000 decade has been one of less freedom and greater restrictions on the rights of citizens over time. According to Freedom House, Uzbekistan is among the most repressive countries in the world. Russia is also rated as Not Free.* Russia's status fell from Partly Free to Not Free for several reasons, including the flawed nature of the country's parliamentary elections in December 2003 and presidential election in 2004, the further consolidation of state control of the media, and the imposition of official curbs on opposition political parties and groups.

In Georgia and Ukraine, popular demonstrations led to the annulment of flawed elections. People were unwilling to accept the extent and the degree of electoral fraud that came to characterize these systems. The Rose Revolution in Georgia and the Orange Revolution in Ukraine represent significant steps toward democracy given the direct involvement of citizens in the political process. Ukraine's rating with regard to civil liberties improved in the wake of pronounced civic activism, greater judicial independence, and widespread expansion of media freedoms following the 2004 presidential election. In Georgia, the January 2004 election of Mikhail Saakashvili as president, and a well-administered parliamentary election in March, improved the country's political rights score after international monitors deemed voting free and fair. The degree to which these revolutions will result in long-lasting reforms in the systems, however, is as yet uncertain.

Particularly problematic throughout the region are the restrictions on the media and the sanctions placed on political oppositional organizations. The authorities justify the use of repression with the argument that citizens themselves prefer stability, even if it means less democracy. In a region that has problems with securing its borders and controlling drug trafficking, smuggling, and other illegal forms of trade, governments argue that a strong hand is needed to survive. Likewise, in a region that has been marked by civil, ethnic, regional, and international warfare, governments can reasonably argue that limitations on the activities of oppositional organizations are necessary for the protection of the people and the state. If the alternative to authoritarianism is civil war, the costs of war or a breakdown of law and order must be weighed against the benefits associated with stability and economic growth.

Limitations on human rights should be questioned, but a narrow focus on political freedom has a distinctly Western bias. Evaluations of governments, instead, should be based on a variety of different performance indicators. The economies of all the countries surveyed in this book are now growing. Their leaders have attempted to diversify the economies and have allowed, although not necessarily encouraged, some degree of private enterprise. Most of the countries have become significantly more integrated into the world system.

*The status designation of Free, Partly Free, or Not Free, is determined by the combination of the political rights and civil liberties ratings; it indicates the general state of freedom in a country or territory.

With regard to economic growth, Ukraine's imbalance of trade associated with its need to import fuel is a major detriment to its economy. Russia, in contrast, earns money by exporting fossil fuels. Both Georgia and Ukraine, however, can benefit from their role as transit states given that major pipelines pass through their territories.

The breakup of the Soviet Union caused disruption in the economies of all the republics of the Soviet Union, but Uzbekistan and other Central Asian republics suffered more as colonies of the Russian Empire. Uzbekistan's economy became and remains extremely unbalanced because the region's agricultural structure had been almost exclusively geared toward the production of cotton. Conversion to other forms of agriculture and building of industrial and service sectors to supplement agricultural production requires heavy investment and the retraining of people. Uzbekistan's strapped economy simply has not had the funds for such a massive conversion process. In addition, vested interests have resisted full reform within the system. The early winners in the transition process have become a powerful conservative force that seeks to protect the status quo to the detriment of the majority of the people. Selfishness and greed are very real problems.

Lithuania and the other Baltic States provide a dramatic contrast to other post-Soviet republics because they are now members of the European Union. EU membership and the pre-membership process have brought infusions of capital, reform programs, and open access to European markets. Nonetheless, Lithuania remains dependent on external suppliers for its fuel, and it lacks the abundance of natural resources characteristic of Russia and, to a lesser extent, Ukraine and Uzbekistan. President Yushchenko of Ukraine is attempting to make the necessary reforms to meet the EU entry requirements, but external factors, such as Russia's role in the region, may keep this from happening.

In the social sphere, the poor health of the people, problems with alcohol abuse, and other unhealthy lifestyle behaviors, such as smoking and eschewing exercise, together with inadequate nutrition, poor sanitation, and inadequate health care are contributing to declining populations in Russia and Ukraine. The low birth rates, because people are unwilling to have more than one child, and the out-migration of many of the skilled and educated have had a negative impact on the human resources in these countries. The negative economic effects associated with labor shortages and unhealthy workers are significant. Uzbekistan is the only country among those studied in this book that is experiencing growth in its population.

In addition to disparity in levels of political and economic transformation in the region, post-Soviet states have also revealed significant differences in levels of ethnic harmony. Although Ukraine is marked by an historical geographical divide that is reinforced by nationality, language, and religious differences, the incongruity between Eastern and Western Ukraine has never been openly conflictual. The same can be said of Lithuania. The Russian minority living in Lithuania functions well within that society.

The peaceful management of nationality differences in Ukraine and Lithuania as compared with Russia and Georgia is striking. The likelihood of discord in interethnic relations is, perhaps, greater when a "Christian" government confronts a "Muslim" separatist region, as in the case with Chechnya (in Russia) and Abkhazia (in Georgia). The underlying problem, however, may be primarily socioeconomic—for example, the lower level of economic well-being that is characteristic of life for Chechens as compared with Russians. Another reason for interethnic conflict is intransigent leaders. Efforts to negotiate solutions to the Abkhaz and Chechen conflicts have been less than sincere. In addition, the goals of the Chechens and Abkhaz to establish their own authority over what they perceive to be their territory are long-standing and have been passed from generation to generation. Russian rule has never been regarded as legitimate by the Chechens, just as Georgian rule has never been accepted by the Abkhaz.

Nonetheless, it is unlikely that Chechnya or Abkhazia will win independence. Despite the violence and the history of subjugation and repression of the Chechen people at the hands of both Soviet authorities and the tsars before them, the major players in the international community have not come forward in support of these independence bids. The international community is reluctant, actually unwilling, to support nationalist goals in this part of the world for fear that the redrawing of territorial boundaries could lead to an infinite regression into smaller and smaller states, with little hope of economic viability in the competitive world system. The current Russian leadership is determined to keep Chechnya within the Russian Federation and is willing to use the full power of its military force for that purpose. The Russian military, although very weak in the mid-1990s, has been strengthened under President Putin and as a result of participation in the international antiterrorist coalition.

The factors that have contributed to violence in the Chechen and Abkhaz conflicts are those related to historical grievances and stereotypes, relative balances of power, and decisions made by leaders to use force rather than to negotiate. The religious differences between the central governments and the periphery do not adequately account for the intractable nature of these conflicts. Likewise, it is important to be careful not to exaggerate the role of radical Islam in conflicts that have occurred in Central Asia. Islam does represent an integral part of the culture of the people, but only recently and only among limited segments of the population has religion become a radical ideology and a consolidating force for those dissatisfied with the absence of a free press, an independent judicial system, and a responsive government. Most people in Uzbekistan identify themselves as Muslims, but for most, this identity does not have strong political ramifications. The violence that has occurred in Central Asia can be explained as easily by reference to economic discontent and feelings of relative deprivation as it can by reference to fundamentalist religious ideologies.

Thus, political, economic, and social developments are intertwined, and progress in each area is weighted down by a lack of improvement in the other parts.

GLOSSARY

Administrative resources: The ability to pressure citizens to vote for pro-government candidates and political parties through a carrot-and-stick allocation of government subsidies, programs, and regulations.

Aggregation of interests: Collection and compilation of policy desires, grievances, and concerns; one role that political parties play in a democracy.

Alienation: A feeling of removal or withdrawal from the existing political system; often stems from political inefficacy and cynicism.

All-Union Party Congress: The Congress of the Communist Party of the Soviet Union was the gathering of the delegates of the CPSU that generally occurred every five years; theoretically, the congress was the supreme ruling body of the entire party.

Anarchists: Those who promote an ideology of anarchism: that all forms of government are oppressive and should be abolished.

Articulation of interests: Expression of policy desires, grievances, and concerns; one role that political parties play in a democracy.

August 1991 coup: An attempt by conservative leaders within the Communist Party of the Soviet Union to oust Mikhail Gorbachev.

Authoritarianism: A government type that demands unquestioning support from citizens and limits individual freedoms and organized opposition.

Autocracy: Government by a single person who has essentially unlimited power.

Autonomy: Self-government with respect to local or internal affairs for a nationality group within a larger state.

Baltic region: The geographical area bordering the Baltic Sea.

Baltic republics: That part of the Soviet Union that now encompasses the countries of Estonia, Latvia, and Lithuania.

The base and the superstructure: The *base* is the economic structure of society, and the *superstructure* consists of legal, political, and cultural institutions that correspond to and are determined by the base.

Basmachi Rebellion: A nationalist movement during which the indigenous population of Central Asia offered fierce resistance to the Soviet regime. It occurred after the Bolsheviks attacked the Muslim religion, intervened directly in native society and culture, and engaged in armed seizure of food.

Bolsheviks: Those members of the Russian Social Democratic Workers' Party who adopted Lenin's theses on party organization in 1903 and seized power in Russia in November 1917.

Bourgeoisie: The social group opposed to the proletariat in the class struggle that occurs under capitalism.

Brain drain: The loss of scientists and other well-educated people who migrate to other countries in search of better wages.

Brezhnev Doctrine: The position that the USSR could intervene in the domestic affairs of any Soviet bloc nation if communist rule was threatened.

Capitalist encirclement: The idea that the Soviet Union was surrounded by hostile capitalist countries.

Central Asian republics: The part of the former Soviet Union that now contains the five countries of Kazakhstan, Turkmenistan, Kyrgyzstan, Uzbekistan, and Tajikistan.

Central Committee: In theory, the Central Committee of the CPSU directed all party and government activities between congresses, but the power of the Central Committee was limited by its infrequent meetings and large membership. This committee functioned more as a rubberstamp that legitimized decisions made by the Politburo.

Civil society: That part of a society made up of organizations and associations that are separate from state structures and free from direct government control.

Class struggle: The idea that conflict between the bourgeoisie and the proletariat is inevitable and will result in the triumph of socialism over capitalism.

Coalition government: An alliance of distinct parties for the purpose of building a majority in parliament in support of a particular prime minister and cabinet.

Collectivism: A theoretical or practical emphasis on the group, as opposed to the individual. The idea that what is good for the group is more important than what is good for the individual.

Collectivization: The process of establishing collective farms, which are agricultural production units organized under state control that include a potentially large number of farm households or villages working together.

Colonialism: Control by a country over foreign dependencies; usually colonies are governed by a representative of the colonial power and they provide raw materials and cheap labor to the colonial state.

Comintern: An international organization established to coordinate the action of communist parties around the world for the purpose of uniting workers in support of a worldwide revolution.

Command economy: An economy in which production quotas are dictated by the government.

Commonwealth of Independent States (CIS): Established as an organization of cooperation and policy coordination among successor states of the Soviet Union (excluding the Baltic States).

Communism: A revolutionary ideology that calls for societal transformation through the elimination of private property.

Conventional–legal participation: A category of political participation, more active than voting, which involves actions that seek to influence the direction of public officials; includes contacting public officials, signing petitions, or participating in legal demonstrations.

Corruption: Dishonest dealings associated with government administration; the abuse of power by political leaders for their private gain. The many forms of corruption range from vote-buying to the sale of political appointments to the exploitation of state resources.

Crimean Peninsula: A region of southern Ukraine on the Black Sea and the Sea of Azov. The area was annexed by Russia in 1783; it became an autonomous Russian republic in 1921 and a Ukrainian oblast in 1954.

Cult of personality: A code phrase for criticizing the excesses of one individual's personalistic rule.

Decentralization: The delegation of certain functions of the central government to branches or local administrative bodies.

Democracy: A government selected by the citizens through free and fair elections.

Democratic centralism: A method of governance through the Communist Party whereby members of the party were free to discuss and debate matters of policy and direction; however, once a decision was made, all members were expected to follow that decision unquestioningly.

Demokratizatsiia (democratization): The process of changing governing institutions to allow for increasing opportunities for citizens to participate in the selection of leaders and to influence policy decisions.

Détente: A French word used to refer to a relaxation of tensions among the world's superpowers during the era of the Cold War.

Dictatorship: A government in which a single leader or party exercises unrestricted control over all citizens.

Dictatorship of the proletariat: In the first stages of socialism, the state serves as an institution of force for the rule of the proletariat over the other classes.

Disproportionality: Describes the situation when the share of seats a political party is awarded in parliament does not accurately reflect the proportion of votes received during the election.

Dissident activity: Activity during the Soviet era that rejected Soviet domination and control.

Dual accountability: The idea that a given part of a government, often a ministry, is accountable to two different heads; in the former USSR, certain ministries were accountable both to the central government in Moscow and to the republic leaders.

Dual executive: A constitutional form of government in which powers are shared by both the prime minister and the president.

Double burden: The idea that women in the workplace have the burden of job responsibilities and also most of household chores.

Duma: The State Duma is the lower house of the Russian national parliament, consisting of 450 elected members.

Economic determinism: The view that all social relations are determined by the economic organization (the production relations) of society.

Electoral system: The basic rules that guide the selection of elected officials; often divided into four types: plurality, majority, proportional, and mixed systems.

Emancipation of the Serfs: In 1861, Tsar Alexander II abolished serfdom; although peasants were given land, they were obligated to pay for it with money or labor.

Ethnicity: Refers to a group of people within a larger society that are considered as distinct from others because of common traits or culture (language, religion, race, a common sense of ancestry, or a shared history) within the group.

Ethnocentrism: An attitude that one's own country, nation, or culture is superior to others.

Euro-Communism: The communism of certain Western European communist parties that supported democratic political procedures and claimed to be independent from the Soviet government.

Faction: An organizational group of like-mined deputies (or a party) within a parliament.

Federal Assembly: The bicameral national parliament of the Russian Federation consisting of the Federation Council and the State Duma.

Federation Council: The upper house of the Russian national parliament, consisting of members appointed by regional governors and councils.

General Secretary of the Communist Party: The Soviet Union's Communist Party general secretary (sometimes called the First Secretary) was the leader of the Secretariat; the title was synonymous with leader of the Soviet Union.

Glasnost: A declared policy of the Soviet Union to encourage greater openness and frankness in public statements, including the publication of news reflecting adversely on the government and political system; greater freedom of speech and information arising from this policy.

Gosplan: The State Planning Commission established in 1921 with the goal of obtaining an accurate view of the economy and setting tentative goals.

Government: The institutions responsible for making collective decisions for society.

Great Patriotic War: In the West, known as World War II.

Great Purges: A series of arrests, trials, imprisonments, and executions during the 1930s by which most veteran communist leaders were removed.

Hajjes: Pilgrimages to Mecca made as an objective of the religious life of a Muslim.

Historical stages: These include primitive communism characterized by hunting and gathering, a slave-based agricultural society, feudalism, capitalism, socialism, and communism. Each stage of history has its own ruling class, which uses the state to maintain its control. Under feudalism the ruling class is the nobility, under capitalism it is the capitalists, and under socialism it is the proletariat. Primitive communism and communism are classless.

Ideology: An individual's political values; often conceptualized as ranging from liberal (left) to conservative (right).

Impeachment: The proceedings associated with being charged with a crime or a violation of principle that may lead to the removal from elected office.

Incremental model: A model in which policy is remade in a series of minor adjustments rather than as a result of a single comprehensive plan.

Incumbent: The person currently holding a given political office; in politics, incumbents are often at a great advantage when running for reelection.

Insider parties: Parties formed by former members of the government, such as by a former prime minister.

Intelligentsia: People engaged in intellectual activities; the class of society regarded as possessing culture and political initiative.

Interest groups and pressure groups: Organizations that represent specific sectors of the community and that strive to influence the political process in ways favorable to that sector.

Jadids' movement: A movement that strived for changes in the society by bringing knowledge and developing culture aimed at "awakening" the general population and by struggling for reform.

Kievan Rus: A state composed of Slavic people located in the northern part of Eastern Europe beginning in the ninth century AD.

Korenizatsya: A policy that established programs to train local personnel to fill important posts within the Soviet government and Communist Party structures of the non-Russian union republics.

Kulaks: Russian peasants who had risen to relative prosperity.

Law of dialectics: Associated with the philosopher Hegel, it is the process of arriving at the truth by stating a thesis, developing a contradictory antithesis, and combining and resolving them into a coherent synthesis.

Left Opposition: Led by Trotsky, this political bloc called for an end to the NEP policy, a speeding up of "socialist construction," and an increased effort to promote world revolution.

Left–right ideological continuum: Used to characterize a general ideological position in politics as represented by different attitudes toward the causes of economic inequality and the extent of state involvement in the economy.

Legitimacy: Popular acceptance and support given to a government when it is perceived as acting in accordance with law or principle.

Majority electoral system: Candidates must win a certain percentage of the vote (often 50 percent) to be elected; if this percentage is not reached in the first round of an election, a second round may be held.

Marxism: A political philosophy based on the writings of Karl Marx and Friedrich Engels.

Mensheviks: Those members of the Russian Social Democratic Workers' Party that were in opposition to Lenin and the Bolsheviks.

Mixed electoral system: A form of electoral system that combines elements from both plurality and proportional representation (PR) systems; Russia is an example of this type of system

Mujahideen: Muslim "holy warriors," an example of which were the opposition groups that fought against the Soviet invasion of Afghanistan.

Multinational state: A state composed of more than one nationality group.

Muscovy: A princely state located in the region that is now Moscow.

Multiparty system: A political system that consists of more than two parties, with each party targeting its own segment of the population and designing an appeal to this group.

Multipolarity: An international system consisting of more than two opposed or competing alliances.

Narodniki: Russian populists influenced by the writings of Aleksandr Herzen, who envisaged a society in which sovereignty would rest with small self-governing economic units resembling the traditional Russian village commune and held together in a loose voluntary confederation replacing the state.

Nation: A people with a shared sense of identity based on history, language, religion, or ethnic origin.

Near Abroad: A term used in the Russian Federation to refer to other countries of the former Soviet Union.

New Economic Policy (NEP): The economic reconstruction phase from 1921 to 1928, marked by a return to limited capitalism. Forced requisition of grain was replaced by a tax in kind, small-scale private enterprise was allowed, and compulsory labor service was abolished. Large industry and financial institutions remained under state control.

Nomenklatura: In the former Soviet Union and other communist countries, a list of the most important positions in the government, the economy, the military, the media, and the sciences that required party approval whenever a personnel change was made. The term also refers to the people having the status of being included on the *nomenklatura* list.

Novoe myshlenie (new thinking): Mikhail Gorbachev's foreign policy position wherein a premise of equality among superpowers led to a call for collective security, demilitarization, and an increased role for the United Nations in settling world conflicts.

Nuclear disaster at Chernobyl: In April 1986, the world's worst nuclear power accident occurred at Chernobyl in the former USSR (now Ukraine). During testing of a reactor at the nuclear power plant located eighty miles north of Kiev, a chain reaction in the reactor created explosions that blew off the reactor's lid. Radioactive fallout spread throughout Europe. In addition to death from radiation, various cancers and birth defects occur at measurably higher rates in the region. Initially people in the path of the fallout were not warned, but once the extent of contamination was understood, all the inhabitants of the region were relocated.

Oblast: A political subdivision or region used in the Russian Federation and many Eastern European and post-Soviet countries, similar to a state in the United States.

October Manifesto: Issued by Tsar Nicholas II in 1905, it granted civil liberties and established an elected representative assembly.

Okrugs: The name for one of the levels of the administrative regions (districts) within the Russian federal structure.

Oligarchs: A small number of rich businesspeople who have been able to influence government decisions through financial leverage and close connections to government leaders.

Outsider parties: Parties formed by politicians who have never controlled government either through appointment or election; generally, they are considered to form the core of the political opposition.

Parliamentary system: A constitutional form of government in which the executive—the prime minister—is elected by the legislature and can be brought down by a no-confidence vote. Great Britain is an example of a parliamentary system.

Partiinost: A policy that required writings in the social sciences and philosophy to correspond to the Communist party's perception of reality; otherwise such writings were denounced as idealist or subjective.

Party identification: Also called partisanship; an enduring attachment to a political party that often determines the voter's choices.

Party-list electoral system: A form of the proportional representation electoral system; political parties provide a list of their candidates and voters cast their votes for the party list.

Party of power: The political party that is favored by and that supports the president.

Patriarchal system: A form of social organization that recognizes males as dominant, as heads of the family and the household, and as leaders in government.

Peaceful coexistence: A doctrine based on the avoidance of nuclear war while continuing the uncompromising ideological and economic competition between communist and capitalist states.

Perestroika: The "restructuring" or reform of the Soviet economic and political system actively promoted under the leadership of Mikhail Gorbachev.

Plurality electoral system: Also known as the first-past-the-post or winner-take-all type of system; the candidate who receives the most votes in the electoral district wins the seat for that district.

Pogrom: An organized and often officially encouraged massacre or persecution of a minority group, especially as conducted against Jews.

Policy discourse: The way in which an issue is framed, defined, and discussed.

Political apathy: A lack of political interest or concern; often stems from political inefficacy and cynicism.

Political efficacy: A sense of power to produce a desired effect; the belief an individual holds that what he or she does influences decision makers to take a desired position.

Political opposition: An organization or a person that does not share the basic positions (for example, values, policies, or strategies) of the decision maker(s) currently in control of the government.

Political participation: The behavioral expression of political interest, which can be categorized into voting, legal (conventional) participation, and violent participation.

Political party factions: Groups of deputies within a parliament with the same political party affiliation who vote and work together to pass their preferred legislation.

Politics: Those activities by which groups, whose opinions and interests are different, reach binding collective decisions.

Politburo: Known also as the Presidium between 1952 and 1966, the Politburo functioned as the central executive policymaking and governing body of the Communist Party of the Soviet Union.

Popular fronts: Movements organized in the Soviet Union in the late 1980s for the purpose of mobilizing broad participation in the reform efforts.

Presidential system: A constitutional form of government in which the president serves as chief executive and political head of state; the president is elected by the people independent of the legislature for a fixed term.

Pressure groups: See *Interest groups and pressure groups*.

Price liberalization: The removal by a government of restrictions placed on the import of goods, the movement of capital, and the cost of goods.

Primary party organization (PPO): The lowest level in the Communist party's organizational hierarchy. The PPO performed various tasks such as admitting new members to the party, organizing agitation and propaganda sessions, stimulating productivity in enterprises, and disciplining party members.

Privatization: The process by which property owned or controlled by a state is transferred to ownership by individuals or corporations.

Procurators: Those who work in the *procuracy*—the agency charged with investigating crimes and preparing and prosecuting cases. A procurator's responsibilities are like a prosecutor's in the United States, but much wider because he (or she) instigates investigations and responds to complaints of corruption, rights abuse, and abuses of power.

Proletariat: The industrial workers.

Proportional representation (PR) electoral system: A system of parliamentary representation based on numerical (rather than regional) divisions of the electorate. The most common form of PR is the party-list system, in which parties make lists of candidates to be elected, voters elect political parties, and seats in parliament get allocated in proportion to the number of votes the party receives.

Raion (rayon): A territorial administrative unit used in the Russian Federation and post-Communist states, smaller than an oblast; similar to a district or county.

Rational model: A model in which policy is made through a systematic search for the most efficient means of achieving defined goals.

Red Army: An army organized under the leadership of a Communist Party.

Referendum: A process by which legislative matters are referred to the voters for approval or rejection.

Repatriation: The returning of refugees and displaced persons to their home settlements.

Reprivatization: In former communist states, the process by which businesses that had been privatized are returned to government ownership in order fight corruption charges and/or boost the economy.

Revisionists: Around the end of the nineteenth century Edward Bernstein argued that it was possible for communists to win power peacefully by winning elections. The term came to have a more general meaning and has been applied to people who were accused of not being revolutionary enough.

Right of legislative initiative: The right to submit laws to the legislative body for consideration.

Russification: Enforcing and encouraging the use of the Russian language and adopting characteristics of Russian culture; used during the Soviet and Tsarist eras in the hopes of uniting the various nationalities of the region.

Russo-centric: Based on the word *ethnocentrism*, which means a belief in the superiority of one's own ethnic group. The term refers to policies or beliefs that place higher value on the culture or the characteristics of Russians than on other ethnic groups.

Sajudis: The popular front organization in Lithuania; also called the Lithuanian Movement for Perestroika.

Samizdat: Underground newspapers that were published during the Soviet era.

Second-round runoff: An election that is held after a first round of voting in which no candidate received the required percentage of the votes for a victory.

Secretariat of the Communist Party: The body within the Communist Party of the Soviet Union that was responsible for the central administration of the party as opposed to drafting government policy, which was usually handled by the Politburo. The Secretariat selected and placed party cadres and forwarded directives and orders to the local party committees.

Secular country: A country where religion and state affairs are officially kept separate.

Seimas: The Lithuanian Parliament.

Self-determination: Freedom of the people of a given territory to determine their own political directions.

Separation of powers: A division of power in the government among the executive, legislative, and judicial branches.

Shock therapy: An economic policy that abruptly eliminates price controls on most goods and services.

Single-member district (SMD) electoral system: A system of voting whereby each member of a parliament is elected from a district and only one member is elected per district. Voters in a given district cast one vote for their favorite candidate, and the candidate receiving the most votes is elected.

Single-party system: A type of party system in which one political party controls the government and where opposition parties are repressed. Often the Constitution designates a party as the only legal one in the country.

Socialism: An economic system in which the production and distribution of goods is controlled primarily by the government rather than by private owners, and in which cooperation rather than competition guides economic activity.

Soviet-German Non-Aggression Pact: A pact between the Soviet Union and Germany signed by USSR Foreign Minister Molotov and German Minister of Foreign Affairs Ribbentrop in 1939.

Sovereignty: A status where the laws of a political entity (such as a country) take precedence over and cannot be overruled by laws emanating from outside the entity.

Sovietization: Conversion to a Soviet system of government by bringing an existing system into conformity with Soviet, communist, and Marxist principles.

Soviets: Representative legislative assemblies.

Sovnarkom: An abbreviated name for the the Council of People's Commissars—the administrative arm of the early Soviet government; it could issue decrees carrying the full force of law when the Congress of the Soviets was not in session. In 1946, it was renamed the Council of Ministers.

The state: The institutions and the means by which the ruling class forcibly maintains its authority over the other classes.

Superpresidentialism: A presidential system of government characterized by a constitution that gives the president extremely broad powers.

Surplus value: The difference between what products sell for and what workers are paid. This surplus value is appropriated by the capitalist. The tendency to pay the workers bare survival wages in order to increase profits for capitalists leads to the increased suffering of the proletariat.

Territorial integrity: The status of keeping existing international borders the same (intact).

Threshold: In a proportional representation system, the minimum percentage of votes a party must receive in order to win seats in parliament.

Titular nationality: The term refers to the nationality group for which the republic or the administrative territory is named.

Titular republic: A republic whose name was derived from the name of the area's largest indigenous ethnic group.

Totalitarianism: A government system that exercises absolute and centralized control over all aspects of life: all opposing political ideas are suppressed.

Transcaucasian region: A transitional region between Europe and Asia that is between the Black and Caspian Seas; it consists of the countries of Georgia, Armenia, and Azerbaijan.

Transparency: With regard to voting, the degree to which the tabulation of the ballots is open to outside monitors and opposition groups; considered a necessary condition for free and fair elections.

Tsarism: A form of government found in Russia prior to 1917, with all official ruling authority resting with a single hereditary monarch.

Turkistan (Turkestan): An historic region of Central Asia that now includes the nations of Turkmenistan, Uzbekistan, Tajikistan, and Kyrgyzstan and the southern portion of Kazakhstan.

Turnout: The proportion of the total eligible electorate who vote in an election.

Two-party system: A political system that consists of only two major parties, with each party appealing to broad sections of the population.

Unicameral parliament: A parliament consisting of one legislative chamber.

Union Treaty: The treaty that established the Soviet Union in 1922.

Unitary state: A system of government in which lower-level administrative units are fully subordinate to central authorities; in contrast to a federal state, in which lower-level administrative units have jurisdictional authority in specified policy areas and have independent sources of revenue.

Unlimited presidential executive: Political system in which the president holds considerable power and the legislature acts as a mere rubber-stamp institution.

USSR Congress of People's Deputies: A representative body of the members of the congresses and soviets in the republics of the former USSR.

Violent participation: A category of political participation in which action is taken that challenges authority through potentially illegal and violent actions.

Vote rigging: The unlawful manipulation of election results; a concern in many transitionary states and in countries that are not democracies.

Voting: A category of political participation that is a major element of democratic governance; it serves to legitimize the system and is a mechanism for the expression of the electorate's preferences.

War Communism: The period from 1918 to 1921 characterized by the nationalization of industry, forced requisition of agricultural production, and strict labor control. The Bolsheviks placed Russia on a military footing in order to defeat the White armies during the Civil War.

Warsaw Pact: A Cold War alliance of Eastern European countries constructed to counter NATO.

ENDNOTES

Chapter 2

1. Sylvain Marechal, Manifesto of Equals, April 1796, http://www.kat.gr/kat/history/Mod/Leaders/Babeuf.htm.

2. Lenin's speech "For Bread and Peace" delivered in Petrograd on December 14, 1917, and published in Lenin's *Collected Works*, Progress Publishers, Moscow, Volume 26, 1972, pp. 386–387. See http://www.marxists.org/archive/lenin/works/1917/dec/14a.htm.

3. Simon Hartfree, "Leninism versus Stalinism," *Modern History Review* 8(2), http://www.angloeuropean.essex.sch.uk/History/IB_Notes/lenin.htm.

4. William Hayter, "The Meaning of Coexistence," *Survey* 50 (January 1994): 24.

5. Nikita S. Khrushchev as quoted in *Soviet World Outlook*, Department of State Publication no. 6836 (July 1959).

6. Khrushchev report delivered at the Twenty-First Party Congress, "On Peaceful Coexistence," reciting the "control figures for the economic development of the USSR," 1959, p. 43.

7. *Khrushchev and the Shifting Balance of World Forces*, Legislative Reference Service, Senate Document 86 (September 1959): 4.

8. Philip Mosely, "The Meaning of Coexistence," *Foreign Affairs* 41 (October 1962): 40.

9. Captain Richard J. Erickson, "Development of the Strategy of Peaceful Coexisting During the Khrushchev Era," *Air University Review* (January-February 1973), http://www.airpower.airuniv.edu/airchronicles/aureview/1973/jan-feb/erickson.html.

10. *MIA: Encyclopedia of Marxism*, Glossary of Terms: "Eurocommunism" at http://www.marxists.org/glossary/terms/e/u.html.

11. For more information, see Amos Yoder, *Communist Systems and Challenges* (New York: Taylor and Francis, 1990), 218–20.

Chapter 3

1. For more details on World War I, see "The Eastern Front: A World War One Summary" at http://www.richthofen.com/ww1sum2/. Copyright © 1996–2003 by *The War Times Journal*.

2. Andy Blunden, *Stalinism: Its Origins and Future*, Volume 1 at http://home.mira.net/~andy/slbs1-2htm, 1993.

Chapter 4

1. This information is taken from the All-Russia Population Census of October 9–16, 2002; for more details, see http://www.eastview.com/all_russian_population_census.asp.

2. *KPSS v. Resolyutsiyakh I Resheniyakh*, Part 1, Moscow: 1953, p. 40.

3. Pavel Isaev, *EastWest Institute's Russian Regional Report,* Vol. 8, No. 4, March 14, 2003.

4. See *Russian Regional Report,* Vol. 8, No. 18, September 20, 2003; see also Pavel Isaev, *Russian Regional Report,* Vol. 8, No. 4, March 14, 2003, and *Radio Free Europe/Radio Liberty* (hereafter *RFE/RL*) *Newsline,* Vol. 8, No. 95, Part I, May 20, 2004.

5. Igor Rabinovich, *Russian Regional Report*—Special Edition, Vol. 8, No. 13, July 23. 2003.

6. Bruno De Cordier, "The Republic of Sakha (Yakutia): Between Turkestan and North Asia"; available at http://www.turkiye.net/sota/yakut.html.

7. Lilia Troshina, "Regions Continue to Depend on Federal Budget for Key Support," *EastWest Institute Russian Regional Report,* Vol. 7, No. 3, January 23, 2002.

8. See *Report on the Tatarstan Referendum on Sovereignty,* prepared by the staff of the U.S. Commission on Security and Cooperation in Europe, April 14, 1992.

9. See *RFE/RL Security and Foreign Policy in Russia and the Postcommunist Region,* Vol. 4, No. 20, May 20, 2003.

10. See *RFE/RL Newsline,* Vol. 7, No. 43, Part I, March 6, 2003; *RFE/RL Newsline,* Vol. 6, No. 160, Part I, August 26, 2002; and "Tatar Muslim Women Win Lawsuit Over Headscarves Ban," Catherine Fitzpatrick, *RFE/RL Newsline,* Vol. 7, No. 100, May 29, 2003.

11. Midkhat Faroukshin, *Russian Regional Report* Vol. 5, No. 39, October 23, 2000.

12. Census 2002—see endnote 1.

13. Nabi Abdullaev, "Moscow Pays High Price for Dagestan's Stability,"*Russian Regional Report,* Vol. 7, No. 3, January 23, 2002.

14. See *RFE/RL,* Vol. 7, No. 175, Part I, September 15, 2003.

15. Sergei Markedonov, "Chechnya in the Context of Russian Federalism," *Russian Regional Report,* Vol. 8, No. 7, May 7, 2003.

16. "Chechen War," *RFE/RL Security and Foreign Policy in Russia and the Postcommunist Region,* Vol. 4, No. 27, July 8, 2003.

17. Liz Fuller, "Has Putin's Chechen Window of Opportunity Closed?" *RFE/RL Caucasus Report,* Vol. 6, No. 18, May 16, 2003.

18. See *RFE/RL Newsline,* Vol. 7, No. 190, Part I, October 6, 2003.

19. See *RFE/RL Newsline,* Vol. 7, No. 191, Part I, October 7, 2003.

20. See *RFE/RL Newsline,* Vol. 6, No. 186, Part I, October 2, 2002.

21. See *RFE/RL Newsline,* Vol. 8, No. 53, Part I, March 19, 2004.

22. See *RFE/RL Caucasus Report,* Vol. 7, No. 24, June 17, 2004.

23. See *RFE/RL Newsline,* June 18, 2003.

24. See *RFE/RL Newsline,* Vol. 8, No. 95, Part I, May 20, 2004.

25. See *RFE/RL,* June 17, 2004, op. cit.

26. Robert Bruce Ware, "Can Moscow Engineer a Political Solution in Chechnya?" *RFE/RL Newsline,* Vol. 8, No. 107, Part I, June 8, 2004.

27. See *RFE/RL Newsline,* Vol. 7, October 3, 2003.

28. Liz Fuller, *RFE/RL Caucasus Report,* Vol. 7, No. 28, July 15, 2004; and *RFE/RL Newsline,* February 26, 2003.

29. See *RFE/RL Newsline,* Vol. 8, No. 101, Part I, May 28, 2004.

Chapter 5

1. See *RFE/RL Newsline,* Vol. 4, No. 181, Part I, September 19, 2000.

2. "Putin Looks to Historians for National Ideas,"*RFE/RL Security Watch,* Vol. 3, No. 3, January 24, 2002.

3. *RFE/RL Security Watch,* Vol. 4, No. 24, June 18, 2003.

Chapter 6

1. See EastWest Institute's *Russian Regional Report*, Vol. 6, No. 43, December 5, 2001.
2. Danielle Lussier, "Putin Continues Extending Vertical of Power," *Russian Regional Report*, Vol. 8, No. 2, February 3, 2003.
3. See *RFE/RL Newsline*, Vol. 7, No. 75, Part I, April 18, 2003.
4. See The Levada Center at http://www.levada.ru.
5. See Julie Corwin and Victor Yasmann, "International, Domestic Monitors Criticize Presidential Election," March 16, 2004, at http://www.rferl.org/specials/russianelection/article/2004/3/E2392720-FC14-4D42-AB4E-F1CCE0F42CC0.html.
6. Information for this biographic study comes from http://www.nns.ru/e-elects/e-persons/eltzin.html and http://www.guardian.co.uk/yeltsin/Story/0,2763,194968,00.html; *Wilson Current Biography 2004;* and *Who's Who in the World, 1996.*
7. Donald N. Jensen, "How Russia Is Ruled – 1998" at http://www.rferl.org/nca/special/ruwhorules/institutions-4.html.
8. See *RFE/RL Newsline*, Vol. 7, No. 117, Part I, June 23, 2003.
9. See *RFE/RL Newsline*, Vol. 7, No. 115, Part I, June 19, 2003.
10. See "Russia," in *Library of Congress Country Studies* at http://lcweb2.loc.gov/cgi-bin/query/r?frd/cstdy:@field(DOCID+ru0214.

Chapter 7

1. "Communist Party Congress on Collision Course with Putin," *RFE/RL Newsline*, Vol. 6, No. 13, Part I, January 22, 2002; see also *RFE/RL Security Watch*, Vol. 3, No. 3, January 24, 2002.
2. See *RFE/RL Newsline*, July 7, 2003.
3. See *RFE/RL Newsline*, Vol. 7, No. 231, Part I, December 10, 2003.
4. See http://www.russiavotes.org.
5. Organization for Security and Cooperation in Europe, Office for Democratic Institutions and Human Rights, "Press Release," December 8, 2003, at http://www.osce.org/news/show_news.php?id=3757; see also *Pravda*, December 8, 2003, at http://english.pravda.ru/main/18/88/353/11481_.html.
6. Laura Belin, "Unified Russia's Winning Non-Message," *RFE/RL, The Russian Federation Votes: 2003–2004*, December 8, 2003.
7. Robert Orttung, "District Elections: Governors' Machines Dominate Vote," *Russian Regional Report*, Vol. 8, No. 24, December 10, 2003.
8. See *RFE/RL Newsline*, Vol. 7, No. 159, Part 1, August 21, 2003; see also http://www.wciom.ru.
9. See *RFE/RL Newsline*, Vol. 7, No. 227, Part I, December 4, 2003.
10. See *RFE/RL Newsline*, Vol. 7, No. 230, Part I, December 9, 2003.
11. The rest of this paragraph and part of the next come directly from Arkadii Lyubarev, "Russia Finishes Latest Round of Modifying Electoral Legislation," *Russian Regional Report*, Vol. 8, No. 2, February 3, 2003.
12. Danielle Lussier, "Putin Continues Extending Vertical of Power," *Russian Regional Report*, Vol. 8, No. 2, February 3, 2003.
13. Sergei Markedonov, "Chechnya in the Context of Russian Federalism," *Russian Regional Report*, Vol. 8, No. 7, May 7, 2003.
14. Julie A. Corwin, "Russia Bids Farewell to Regional Elections," *RFE/RL Newsline*, Vol. 9, No. 2, Part I, January 5, 2005.

15. Robert Coalson, "Putin Takes Control of the Status Quo Through Gubernatorial Appointments," *RFE/RL Newsline*, Vol. 9, No. 109, Part I, June 9, 2005.

16. Ibid.

17. *The Moscow Times*, June 6, 2005.

18. Coalson, op. cit.

Chapter 8

1. See *Moscow News*, MN-Files, at http://www.mosnews.com/mn-files/yabloko.shtml.

2. David White, "Russia's Nemtsov Comes A-Courting, and Yabloko Keeps Its Distance," *RFE/RL Newsline*, Vol. 7, No. 48, Part I, March 13, 2003.

3. See *RFE/RL Newsline*, Vol. 7, No. 180, Part I, September 22, 2003.

4. From http://www.mosnews.com/mn-files/unitedrussia.shtml.

5. See *RFE/RL Newsline*, Vol. 7, No. 175, Part I, September 15, 2003.

6. See *RFE/RL Newsline*, Vol. 6, No. 27, Part I, February 11, 2002.

7. See *RFE/RL Newsline*, Vol. 7, No. 236, Part I, December 17, 2003.

8. Ibid, see interview with Yuri Levada.

9. From *The Russia Journal* at http://www.russiajournal.com/news/cnews-article.shtml?nd=41980 and http://www.russiajournal.com/news/cnews-article.shtml?nd=41998.

10. Nick Paton Walsh, "Observers Condemn Russian Elections," *The Guardian*, December 9, 2003.

Chapter 9

1. For more on interest articulation in the Soviet system, see Barghorn (1973) and Rigby and Harasymiw (1983).

2. "Soviet Union: A Country Study," Library of Congress Country Studies at http://memory.loc.gov/frd/cs/sutoc.html.

3. See *RFE/RL Newsline*, Vol. 8, No. 97, May 24, 2004.

4. Sergei Khrushchev, "Russia After Yeltsin: A Duel of Oligarchs," *Mediterranean Quarterly* 11(3) (2000): 22–23.

5. "Russian Media Mogul Dismissed Yeltsin's Bid to Sack Him," *Izvestia*, March 5, 1999.

6. "Russian Tycoon Arrested in London," *RFE/RL Newsline*, July 18, 2000, and March 25, 2003.

7. See *RFE/RL Newsline*, Vol. 7, No. 193, Part I, October 9, 2003.

8. See *RFE/RL Newsline*, Vol. 8, No. 182, Part I, September 23, 2004.

9. "2003 List of the World's Wealthiest People," *Forbes*, Special Report: The World's Richest People, February 27, 2003, at http://www.forbes.com/lists/2003/02/26/billionaireland.html.

10. George Melloan, "In Russia, the Score Is Siloviki 6, Oligarchs 0," *Global View*, November 4, 2003.

11. See *RFE/RL Business Watch*, Vol. 3, No. 37, October 8, 2003.

12. Ibid.

13. See *RFE/RL Newsline*, Vol. 7, No. 129, Part I, July 10, 2003; and Vol. 7, No. 131, Part I, July 14, 2003.

14. See *RFE/RL Newsline*, July 9, 2004.

15. "Security and Foreign Policy in Russia and the Postcommunist Region," *RFE/RL Prague, Czech Republic,* Vol. 4, No. 10, March 11, 2003.

16. See *Nezavisimaya Gazeta,* August 15, 2002.

17. "Russian Paper Unimpressed by Defense Minister's Two Years in Office," *RFE/RL Newsline,* January 31, 2003.

18. See *RFE/RL Newsline,* Vol. 8, No. 137, Part I, July 21, 2004.

19. "Russian Court Acquits Officer in Journalist Murder Case," *Tavernise,* June 26, 2002.

20. See *RFE/RL Newsline,* Vol. 7, No. 117, Part I, June 23, 2003.

21. See *RFE/RL Newsline* Vol. 8, No. 137, Part I, July 21, 2004.

22. See ITAR-TASS, December 10, 1993, in FBIS-SOV-93-237, December 12, 1993, p. 30.

23. See *RFE/RL Newsline,* Vol. 2, No. 224, Part I, November 19, 1998.

24. See FBIS-SOV-94-007, January 11, 1994, p. 51.

25. "Soviet Union: A Country Study," *Library of Congress Country Studies* at http://memory.loc.gov/frd/cs/sutoc.html.

Chapter 10

1. See *RFE/RL Newsline,* Vol. 7, No. 135, Part I, July 18, 2003.

2. See *RFE/RL Newsline,* Vol. 7, No. 158, Part I, August 20, 2003.

3. See *RFE/RL Security and Foreign Policy in Russia and the Post-Communist Region,* Vol. 4, No. 40, October 7, 2003.

4. See *RFE/RL Business Watch,* Vol. 3, No. 26, July 15, 2003.

5. *The Economist* at http://www.economist.com/countries/Russia/profile.cfm?folder=Profile-Economic%20Data.

6. World Economic Forum at http://www.weforum.org/site/knowledgenavigator.nsf/Content/Russia+KN+sessions.

7. See *RFE/RL Newsline,* Vol. 7, No. 177, Part I, September 17, 2003.

8. See *RFE/RL,* July 18, 2003, op. cit.

9. Economic Research Service, U.S. Department of Agriculture at http://www.ers.usda.gov/.

10. Ibid.

11. See *RFE/RL Newsline,* Vol. 7, No. 89, Part I, May 13, 2003.

12. See *Russian Regional Report,* Vol. 9, No. 23, December 8, 2004.

13. See *Jane's Intelligence Digest,* March 7, 2003.

14. See *RFE/RL,* October 7, 2003, op. cit.

15. See *RFE/RL Security Watch,* Vol. 1, No. 12, October 9, 2000.

16. See *RFE/RL Security and Foreign Policy in Russia and the Post-Communist Region,* Vol. 4, No. 10, March 11, 2003.

17. See *RFE/RL Newsline,* Vol. 8, No. 229, Part I, December 8, 2004.

18. See *Gazeta.ru,* November 25, 2001.

19. See *RFE/RL,* October 7, 2003, op. cit.

20. Ibid.

21. Ibid.

22. See *RFE/RL Security and Foreign Policy in Russia and the Post-Communist Region,* Vol. 4, No. 20, May 20, 2003.

23. See *RFE/RL Newsline,* Vol. 7, No. 130, Part I, July 11, 2003.

24. See *RFE/RL Newsline,* Vol. 7, No. 138, Part I, July 23, 2003.

25. *Nezavisimaya Gazeta,* February 11, 2003.

26. See *RFE/RL Newsline,* Vol. 7, No. 115, Part I, June 19, 2003.

27. See *RFE/RL,* October 8, 2003, op. cit.

28. Ibid.
29. See *RFE/RL Security Watch,* Vol. 2, No. 44, November 21, 2001.
30. "Russia: Foreign Arms Sales" at http://www.russiansabroad.com/russian_history_345.html.
31. See *RFE/RL Security Watch,* Vol. 2, No. 33, August 30, 2001.
32. See *RFE/RL,* June 19, 2003, op. cit.
33. See *RFE/RL Business Watch,* Vol. 1, No. 24, December 27, 2001.
34. See http://www.mosnews.com/money/2004/11/04/armsexport.shtml.
35. See *RFE/RL Security Watch,* Vol. 1, No. 16, November 6, 2000.
36. Francis C. Notzon et al. "Causes of Declining Life Expectancy in Russia," *JAMA* 279 (1998): 793–800.
37. Irina Titova, "Russian Life Expectancy on Downward Trend," *St. Petersburg Times,* January 17, 2003.
38. See *RFE/RL Business Watch,* Vol. 2, No. 30, July 30, 2002.
39. See *RFE/RL Newsline,* Vol. 7, No. 127, Part I, July 8, 2003.
40. *Izvestiya,* March 10, 2002.
41. See *RFE/RL,* March 11, 2003, op. cit.
42. See *RFE/RL,* December 8, 2004, op. cit.
43. See http://www.idrc.ca/tobacco/Russia.htm.
44. For more details, see the 1999 Hesli study.
45. See *RFE/RL,* March 11, 2003, op. cit.
46. For more details, see http://www.nationmaster.com/country/rs/Crime&b_define=1.

Chapter 11

1. *Pravda,* July 30, 1986.
2. Saulius Girnius, "A Weary Lithuania Elects Brazauskas," *RFE/RL Research Report,* Vol.2, No. 10, March 5, 1993, p. 19.
3. Rose, Munro, and Mackie, *Elections in Central and Eastern Europe Since 1990,* Studies in Public Policy No. 300. Glasgow: University of Strathclyde, 1998; and "Elections in Lithuania," University of Strathclyde Centre for the Study of Public Policy at http://www.cspp.strath.ac.uk/index.html?litelec.html.
4. Valentinas Mite, "Lithuania: Former Prime Minister Scores Surprise Victory in Presidential Elections," *RFE/RL* (http://www.rferl.org).
5. *Kauno diena,* December 1, 2003.
6. See *RFE/RL Newsline,* Vol. 7, No. 236, Part II, December 17, 2003; Vol. 8, No. 7, Part II, January 13, 2004; and Vol. 7, No. 227, Part II, December 4, 2003.
7. Results of the February 24, 1990, elections to the Supreme Council of the Republic of Lithuania can be found in *Tiesa,* March 1, 1990, pp. 1–4; results of the March 7, 8, and 10, 1990, elections can be found in *Tiesa* 60(14279), March 13, 1990.
8. Dzintra Bungs, "Elections and Restoring Democracy in the Baltic States," *RFE/RL Research Report,* Vol. 2, No. 38, September 24, 1993, p. 13.
9. Saulius Girnius, "Leaning Toward the Right, for Now," *Transition,* July 14, 1995, p. 53.
10. Breffni O'Rourke, "Lithuania: Vote Results Unlikely to Alter EU, NATO Course," *RFE/RL,* October 10, 2000, at http://www.rferl.org/nca/features/2000/10/10102000193326.asp.
11. Girnius, "Leaning . . . ," op. cit.
12. See *RFE/RL Newsline,* Vol. 7, No. 112, Part II, June 16, 2003.

13. Data compiled by the Inter-Parliamentary Union at http://www.ipu.org/wmn-e/classif.htm.

14. Saulius Girnius, "The Economies of the Baltic States in 1993," *RFE/RL Research Report*, Vol. 3, No. 20, May 20, 1994, p. 5.

15. "EIU Country Profile 1993/1994 Baltic Republics" (London: The Economist Intelligence Unit).

16. Walter C. Clemens, Jr., "The Baltic Republics, Russia, and Energy: From Dependency to Interdependence." *SAIS Review* 19(1) (1990): 190–208.

17. Andrew C. Winner, "The Baltic States: Heading West," *The Washington Quarterly* 25(1) (2002): 207–19.

18. See *RFE/RL Newsline*, Vol. 6, No. 221, Part II, November 25, 2002.

19. See *RFE/RL Newsline*, Vol. 8, No. 23, Part II, February 5, 2004.

20. See *RFE/RL Newsline*, Vol. 7, No. 114, Part II, June 18, 2003.

21. Saulius Girnius, "Tiny Armed Forces Need Allies Aid," *Transition*, December 1, 1995.

22. "Lithuania: Crime and Law Enforcement," *Library of Congress Country Studies* (January 1995) at http://lcweb2.loc.gov/cgi-bin/query/D?cstdy:1:./temp/~frd_8tfh.

Chapter 12

1. "Ukraine," prepared by the Washington Office of the Ukrainian National Association, Inc. (400 North Capitol Street, NW, Suite 859, Washington, D.C. 20001).

2. See *The Ukrainian Weekly* LXIV(5), February 4, 1996.

3. The previous two paragraphs are paraphrased from D'Anieri, Kravchuk, and Kuzio (1999, 102–3).

4. See *inter alia* at http://www.theukrainian.com/contents/2-2004/article:Yanukovych; Kuzio (2004).

5. As reported by the OSCE Office for Democratic Institutions and Human Rights (ODIHR), International Election Observation Mission (IEOM), October 31, 2004 (p. 11) and November 1, 2004.

6. See http://www.cpj.org/enemies/enemies_01.html.

7. Adrian Karatnycky, "Meltdown in Ukraine," *Foreign Affairs* 80 (May/June, 2002): 73.

8. This description of the legislative process is taken from D'Anieri, Kravchuk, and Kuzio (1999, 118–19).

9. See "Law of Ukraine on Elections of People's Deputies of Ukraine," signed by President Kuchma on November 18, 1993; available from the International Republican Institute, Washington, D.C.

10. See *RFE/RL Newsline*, July 8, 1998.

11. Taras Kuzio, "Ukrainian President Orchestrates Oligarchic Takeover," *RFE/RL Newsline*, Vol. 6, No. 233, Part II, December 13, 2002.

12. See *RFE/RL Newsline*, Vol. 6, No. 31, Part II, February 15, 2002.

13. See *RFE/RL Newsline*, Vol. 6, No. 60, Part II, March 29, 2002.

14. See *RFE/RL Newsline*, Vol. 6, No. 41, Part II, March 4, 2002.

15. Taras Kuzio, "The OSCE and the CIS: Strange Election Bedfellows?" *RFE/RL Newsline*, Vol. 6, No. 66, Part II, April 9, 2002.

16. See *RFE/RL Newsline*, Vol. 6, No. 54, Part II, March 21, 2002.

17. See *RFE/RL Newsline*, Vol. 6, No. 57, Part II, March 26, 2002.

18. BBC Monitoring International Reports: Newspaper Analyses of Ukraine's Position on World Markets at http://ukraine-today.com/business/industry/a/industry2.shtm.

19. See *RFE/RL Newsline*, February 16, 1998.

20. See *RFE/RL Newsline*, Vol. 9, No. 32, Part II, February 17, 2005.

21. See *RFE/RL Newsline*, Vol. 6, No. 16, Part II, January 25, 2002.

22. State Statistics Committee's data as reported by the Interfax-Ukraine news agency in Kiev (in Russian), January 11, 2005; and the U.K.'s BBC Monitoring Service (in English), January 11, 2005.

23. For details on the treaty, see *RFE/RL Newsline*, Vol. 1, No. 43, Part 2, June 2, 1997.

24. Ustina Markus in the *OMRI Daily Digest*, March 1, 1995, February 28, 1995, February 13, 1995, and February 9, 1995.

25. Data are from the State Statistics Committee of Ukraine, the State Treasury of Ukraine, Ukraine, Ministry of Economy, and the Ministry of Finance.

26. See *RFE/RL Newsline*, November 5, 1997.

27. See *RFE/RL Newsline*, March 4, 1998.

28. See *RFE/RL Newsline*, Vol. 9, No. 36, Part II, February 24, 2005.

29. "Ukrainian President Yushchenko Says NATO Integration Not Aimed Against Russia," TV 5 Kanal, Kiev (UK's BBC Monitoring Service), February 22, 2005.

30. Taras Kuzio, "Op Ed," *Kyiv Post*, July 3, 2003.

31. See *RFE/RL Newsline*, Vol. 6, No. 58, Part II, March 27, 2002.

32. See http://freedomhouse.org/media/pressrel/122704.htm.

33. ENEMO's full statements are available at http://www.enemo.org.ua.

34. See "Yushchenko Takes Presidential Oath" at http://edition.cnn.com/2005/WORLD/europe/01/23/ukraine/index.html.

Chapter 13

1. These are July 2004 estimates from the CIA's *World Factbook*.

2. Election results by district were reported in *Akhali Sak'art'velo*, November 16, 1990, p. 3; and in *Zari Vostoka*, November 9 and 14, 1990.

3. *Foreign Broadcast Information Service Daily Report: Soviet Union*, 91–159, p. 148.

4. See *Georgia's Parliamentary Election, October 1999*; and *Report on the Presidential Elections in Georgia, April 9, 2000*, Commission on Security and Cooperation in Europe, Washington, D.C. (http://csce@mail.house.gov and http://www.house.gov/csce/).

5. "Country Report of Georgia," Freedom House.

6. See *Report on the Presidential . . .* , op. cit.

7. Charles H. Fairbanks Jr. "Georgia's Rose Revolution," *Journal of Democracy* 15(2) (2004): 110–24.

8. See *RFE/RL Newsline*, Vol. 7, No. 216, Part I, November 14, 2003.

9. "Top Stories," CNN.com International, November 25, 2003.

10. Ibid.

11. Ibid.

12. Fairbanks, 114.

13. *Black Sea Press*, Issue 3, March 24, 2000 (http://bspress@access.sanet.ge).

14. *Black Sea Press*, Issue 1, March 17, 2000 (http://bspress@access.sanet.ge).

15. See http://www.eurasianet.org/departments/election/georgia/geoverview.html.

16. For more information on political parties in Georgia, see http://www.civil.ge/eng and http://www.eurasianet.org/resource/georgia/index.shtml.

17. See http://www.eurasianet.org/departments/election/georgia/gparties.html.

18. See http://www.civil.ge/part_3.html.

19. See http://www.civil.ge/part_4.html.

20. Hans Dieset, *Georgia: Parliamentary Elections November 2003,* published by the Norwegian Center for Human Rights; the NORDEM Report is available online at http://www.humanrights.uio.no/forskning/publ/publikasjonsliste.html.

21. Dieset, 3–4.

22. See *RFE/RL Newsline,* Vol. 7, No. 160, Part I, August 22, 2003.

23. Liz Fuller, *RFE/RL Caucasus Report,* Vol. 8, No. 5, February 4, 2005.

24. Liz Fuller, "Sea Change in Georgian-Russian Relations?" *RFE/RL Caucasus Report,* Vol. 3, No. 5, Part I, January 8, 1999.

25. Liz Fuller, "Georgian Election Controversy Continues," *RFE/RL Caucasus Report,* Vol. 2, No. 120, Part I, June 24, 1998.

26. Ghia Nodia, "Georgia's Identity Crisis." *Journal of Democracy* 6(1) (1995): 112: and Fairbanks, op. cit., 114.

27. See *RFE/RL Newsline,* Vol. 9, No. 29, Part I, February 11, 2005.

28. See "The Court System of Georgia" at http://www.parliament.ge/gov/jud_sys/court_sys.html.

29. See "Country Report of Georgia," Freedom House.

30. "Human Rights in the Republic of Georgia (CIS)," International Society for Human Rights, 2001, at http://www.ishr.org/activities/countries/georgia/hrgeorgia 2001.htm.

31. See *Library of Congress Country Studies* at http://lcweb2.loc.gov/frd/cs/georgia/ge03_03a.pdf.

32. *RFE/RL Daily Reports,* No. 46, March 9, 1993.

33. Liz Fuller, *RFE/RL Newsline,* Vol. 7, No. 135, Part I, July 18, 2003.

34. *RFE/RL Caucasus Report,* Vol. 7, No. 31, August 5, 2004.

35. Liz Fuller, *RFE/RL Caucasus Report,* Vol. 8, No. 4, January 28, 2005.

36. See *RFE/RL Newsline,* January 13, 2005.

37. See *RFE/RL Newsline,* July 17, 2003.

38. See *RFE/RL Newsline,* Vol. 8, No. 38, Part I, February 27, 2004; see also *RFE/RL Caucasus Report,* December 3, 1999.

39. See *RFE/RL Newsline,* Vol. 7, No. 133, Part I, July 16, 2003.

40. See *RFE/RL Caucasus Report,* September 13, 2002; and *RFE/RL Newsline,* Vol. 7, No. 93, Part I, May 19, 2003.

41. See *RFE/RL Newsline,* Vol. 7, No. 227, Part I, December 4, 2003; and *Jane's Intelligence Digest,* March 7, 2003.

42. Liz Fuller, *RFE/RL Caucasus Report,* Vol. 7, No. 12, March 19, 2004.

43. Liz Fuller, *RFE/RL Caucasus Report,* Vol. 7, No. 11, March 12, 2004.

44. See *RFE/RL Newsline,* August 3, 2003.

45. Fuller, *RFE/RL,* March 12, 2004, op. cit.

46. See *RFE/RL Newsline,* Vol. 7, No. 127, Part I, July 8, 2003.

47. See *RFE/RL Newsline,* Vol. 8, No. 169, Part I, September 3, 2004.

48. Fuller, "Sea Change . . . ," January 8, 1999.

49. Ibid.

50. "Republic of Georgia," *RFE/RL Newsline,* February 27, 2004, op. cit.

51. *Jane's Intelligence Digest,* March 7, 2003.

52. See British Helsinki Human Rights Group, at http://www.bhhrg.org/CountryReport.asp?ChapterID=656&CountryID=10&ReportID=207&keyword=.

53. Liz Fuller, *RFE/RL Newsline,* Vol. 7, No. 73, Part I, April 16, 2003.

54. British Helsinki Human Rights Group, op. cit.

55. "The Republic of Georgia Moves Toward Stability and Security," The Jewish Institute for National Security Affairs at http://www.jinsa.org/articles/articles.html/function/view/categoryid/171/documentid/2809/history/3,2360,656,171,2809.

56. Emmanuel Karagiannis, *The Caspian Oil Market After Regime Change in Iraq*, November 2002, Perihelion of the European Rim Policy and Investment Council.
57. Ahto Lobjakas, *RFE/RL Caucasus Report*, Vol. 7, No. 15, April 1, 2004.
58. Ibid.
59. "Republic of Georgia," *RFE/RL Newsline*, Vol. 8, No. 10, Part I, January 16, 2004.
60. Ahto Lobjakas, *RFE/RL Caucasus Report*, Vol. 7, No. 40, October 22, 2004.

Chapter 14

1. Adeeb Khalid, "Reform and Contention in Central Asian Islam: A Historical Perspective," *Eurasia Insight*, March 8, 2000 at http://www.eurasianet.org.
2. According to 1926 figures, the Uzbek SSR had a population of 5,272,800; see *The Soviet Union: Facts, Descriptions, Statistics*, The Soviet Union Information Bureau, Washington D.C., 1929, found at http://www.marxists.org/history/ussr/government/1928/sufds/ch01.htm.
3. *Encyclopedia of the Republic of Uzbekistan:* Tashkent, 1997.
4. Ibid.
5. As stated in Article 102 of the Constitution of the Republic of Uzbekistan.
6. Constitution of the Republic of Uzbekistan, "On the Legislative Chamber of Oliy Majlis of the Republic of Uzbekistan," December 12, 2002.
7. Ibid., Article 32.
8. Ibid., Article 33.
9. Ibid., Article 1.
10. S. Juraev, *Civil Society: Theory and Practice*, Tashkent, 2003.
11. NRC-Handelsblad, Electionworld.org, "Elections Around the World" at http://www.electionworld.org/election/uzbekistan.htm, December 29, 2003.
12. *RFE/RL Newsline*, Vol. 7, No. 233, Part I, December 12, 2003.
13. See Articles 99, 101, and 102, Constitution . . . , op. cit.
14. I. Karimov, *Uzbekistan on the Threshold of the 21st Century*, Tashkent, 1996.
15. U.S. Department of State. "Foreign Terrorist Organizations," May 23, 2003, at http://www.state.gov/s/ct/rls/fs/2003/12389.htm.
16. EurasiaNet Partner Post from *RFE/RL*, "Central Asia: Is the IMU Still a Threat to Regional Security?" January 24, 2004.
17. Ibid.
18. A. Juska, "Ethno-political Transformation in the States of the Former USSR," *Ethnic and Racial Studies* 22(3) (1999): 526.
19. See "Official Statement on Terrorist Acts in Uzbekistan," March 29, 2004, at http://www.uzreport.com; see also Eurasianet.org.
20. "Militants Killed in Uzbek Siege," March 30, 2004, at http://news.bbc.co.uk/1/hi/world/asia-pacific/3581341.stm.
21. Bruce Pannier, "Human Rights: Uzbekistan: One Week Later, Many Questions Still Unanswered About Recent Violence," April 8, 2004, a EurasiaNet Partner Post from *RFE/RL* at http://www.eurasianet.org/departments/rights/articles/pp040804.shtml.
22. The resolution is published on the European Parliament's website at http://www.europarl.eu.int.
23. See "Uzbekistan," *Country and Territory Reports*, Freedom House, 2003.
24. See *RFE/RL Newsline*, Vol. 7, No. 112, Part I, June 16, 2003.
25. See *RFE/RL Newsline*, Vol. 7, No. 198, Part I, October 17, 2003.

26. See *Uzbekistan Information Directory,* current as of December 2004, at http://www.uzland.uz/fact/parties.htm.

27. See *RFE/RL Newsline,* Vol. 7, No. 193, Part I, October 9, 2003.

28. Ibid.

29. Ibid.

30. Central Eurasia Project/IPU at http://www.ipu.org/parline-e/reports/2343_E.htm.

31. Ibid.

32. "Is Radical Islam Inevitable in Central Asia? Priorities for Engagement." *ICG Asia Report* 72(December 22, 2003): 10.

33. *Republic of Uzbekistan: Encyclopedia,* Tashkent, 1997.

34. M. Spechler, "Uzbekistan: The Silk Road to Nowhere?" *Contemporary Economic Policy* 18(3) (2000): 297.

35. See *RFE/RL Newsline,* Vol. 7, No. 198, Part I, October 17, 2003.

36. See *RFE/RL Newsline,* Vol. 7, No. 206, Part I, October 30, 2003.

37. See *RFE/RL Newsline,* Vol. 7, No. 223, Part I, November 26, 2003.

38. Spechler, 297.

39. Spechler, 295.

40. See *RFE/RL Newsline,* Vol. 7, No. 129, Part I, July 10, 2003.

41. Esmer Islamov and Samariddin Sharipov, "Signs Show Uzbek Stability Buckling Under Economic Stress," November 16, 2004, at http://www.eurasianet.org.

42. "Eurasia Insight: A Power Struggle Brews in Uzbekistan," January 5, 2005, at http://www.eurasianet.org.

43. UN Office for the Coordination of Humanitarian Affairs, "Uzbekistan: Government Regrets EBRD Decision to Curb Loans," *IRINnews,* April 7, 2004, at http://www.IRINnews.org.

44. Adam Albion, "Uzbekistan's New Balancing Act After the SCO Summit," *RFE/RL Newsline,* Vol. 7, No. 176, Part I, September 16, 2003.

45. See *RFE/RL Newsline,* Vol. 8, No. 38, Part I, February 27, 2004.

46. See *RFE/RL Newsline,* Vol. 6, No. 144, Part I, August 2, 2002.

REFERENCES

Akiner, S. "Uzbekistan and the Uzbeks." In Graham Smith, ed. *The Nationalities Question in the Post-Soviet States*. London: Longman, 1996.

Almond, Gabriel, G. B. Powell, and R. Mundt. *Comparative Politics: A Theoretical. Framework*, 2nd ed. New York: HarperCollins, 1996.

Almond, Gabriel A., et al., *Comparative Politics: A Theoretical Framework*. New York: Longman, 2004.

Anderson, Benedict. *Imagined Communities*, Revised ed. New York: Verso, 1991.

Andreev, Vasily. "Ukrainian Nationalism: Ambitions and Reality." *The Jamestown Foundation PRISM*, Vol. 2, Part 1, August 1996.

Armstrong, J. *Ukrainian Nationalism*, 2nd ed. New York: Columbia University Press, 1963.

Attwood, Lynne. *The New Soviet Man and Woman: Sex Role Socialization in the USSR*. Bloomington: Indiana University Press, 1991.

Attwood, Lynne. "The Post-Soviet Woman in the Move to the Market: A Return to Domesticity and Dependence?" In Rosalind Marsh, ed., *Women in Russia and Ukraine*. Cambridge, U.K.: Cambridge University Press, 1996. 255–68.

Azamova, Asal. "The Military Is in Control of Drug Trafficking in Tajikistan." *Moscow News*. May 30, 2001.

Ball, Alan R., and B. Guy Peters. *Modern Politics and Government*. New York: Seven Bridges Press, LLC, 2000.

Barghorn, Frederick. *Politics in the USSR*. Boston: Little, Brown, 1973.

Barinov, Leonid. "More Than Just Crime." *Nezavisimaya Gazeta*. September 7, 2001.

Bird, R., and C. Wallich. *Fiscal Decentralization and Intergovernmental Relations in Transition Economies: Toward a Systemic Framework of Analysis*, Papers 1122, World Bank—Country Economics Department, 1993.

Blustain, Rachel. "The Yeast of Russia." *Russian Life* (April 1997): 4–6.

Bodansky, Yossef. "Where Is Terrorism Going?" *Defense & Foreign Affairs Strategic Policy* (October 9, 2000).

Boycko, Maxim, Andrei Sheifer, and Robert W. Vishny. "Privatizing Russia." *Brookings Papers on Economic Activity: 2*. Washington, D.C.: The Brookings Institution, 1993. 139–92.

Brady, Henry E., Sidney Verba, and Kay Lehman Scholzman. "Beyond SES: A Resource Model of Political Participation." *American Political Science Review* 89, no. 2 (1995): 271–94.

Braham, Denis C., and Howard E. Sachs. "The Unfinished Exodus—Russian Jewry Faces Old Challenges Anew." *New Jersey Jewish News* (April 1999): 28.

Bransten, Jeremy. "Chechnya: Barayev Death Highlights Russian Military Corruption." http://www.RFERL.org, June 26, 2001.

Bremner, Ian, and Ray Taras. *Nations and Politics in the Soviet Successor State*. New York: Cambridge University Press, 1993.

Brody, Richard A., and Paul M. Sniderman. "From Life Space to Polling Place." *British Journal of Political Science* 7 (1977): 337–60.

Brown, Archie, ed. *Contemporary Russian Politics: A Reader*. Oxford, U.K.: Oxford University Press, 2001.

Browning, Genia K. *Women and Politics in the USSR*. New York: St. Martin's Press, 1989.

Brym, Robert J., and Andrei Degtyarev. "Anti-Semitism in Moscow: Results of an October 1992 Survey." *Slavic Review* 52, no. 1 (1993): 1–12.

Buckley, M., ed. *Perestroika and Soviet Women*. New York: Cambridge University Press, 1992.

Carrère d'Encausse, Hélène. *Decline of an Empire: The Soviet Socialist Republics in Revolt*. New York: John Wiley, 1979.

Cassileth, B. R., Vlassov, V. V., and Chapman, C. C. "Health Care, Medical Practice, and Medical Ethics in Russia Today." *Journal of the American Medical Association* 273, no. 20 (1995): 1569–73.

Chuprov, Vladimir, and Julia Zubok. "An Education System in Crisis: Meeting the Demands of the Market." In Christopher Williams, Vladimir Chuprov, and Vladimir Staroverov, eds., *Russian Society in Transition*. Aldershot, U.K.: Dartmouth Publishing, 1996.

Clark, William A. "The 1999 Parliamentary Election in Russia." *Electoral Studies* 21 (2002): 101–54.

Cockburn, Patrick. "Corrupt Russian Officers Profit in Heroin Trade." *The Independent*. July 12, 2001.

Coxall, W. N. *Political Realities: Parties and Pressure Groups*, 2nd ed. New York: Longman, 1986.

Colton, Timothy. "Parties, Leaders, and Voters in the Parliamentary Election." In Vicki L. Hesli and William M. Reisinger, eds., *The 1999–2000 Elections in Russia: Their Impact and Legacy*. New York: Cambridge University Press, 2003.

Crawford, B., and A. Lijphart, eds. *Liberalization and Leninist Legacies*. Berkeley: University of California Press, 1997.

Curtis, Michael, ed. *Western European Government and Politics*. New York: Longman, 1997.

Dalton, Russell. "Democratic Political Culture and Participation in Europe." In Gabriel Almond, Russell Dalton, and G. Bingham Powell, eds., *European Politics Today*. New York: Longman, 1998. 28–50.

Dalton, R. J., and M. P. Wattenberg. *Parties Without Partisans: Political Change in Advanced Industrial Societies*. Oxford, U.K.: Oxford University Press, 2000.

Damrel, David. "The Religious Roots of Conflict: Russia and Chechnya, An Essay." *Religious Studies News* 10, no. 3 (September 1999): 10.

Daniels, Robert V. "Putting Putin to the Test." *The New Leader* (September/October 2000): 11–13.

Diller, Daniel C. *Russia and the Independent States*. Washington, D.C.: Congressional Quarterly, Inc., 1993.

Di Palma, G. *To Craft Democracies: An Essay on Democratic Transitions*. Berkeley: University of California Press, 1990.

Duverger, Maurice. *Political Parties*. New York: Science Edition, 1963.

Esman, M. *Ethnic Politics*. Ithaca, N.Y.: Cornell University Press, 1994.

Ettinger, Samuel. "The Jewish Question in the USSR." *Soviet Jewish Affairs* 15 (1985): 11–16.

European Commission's Regular Report 1999 on Lithuania's Progress Toward Assession, http://europa.eu.int/documents/comm/index_en.htm.

Fainsod, Merle. *How Russia Is Ruled*, revised ed. Cambridge, Mass.: Harvard University Press, 1967.

Fish, Steven M. "The Impact of the Elections on Political Party Development." In Vicki L. Hesli and William M. Reisinger, eds., *The 1999–2000 Elections in Russia: Their Impact and Legacy*. New York: Cambridge University Press, 2003.

Galbraith, John Kenneth. *The New Industrial State*, Rev. ed. Boston: Houghton Mifflin, 1971.

Geralavicius, Vaidievutis. "Lithuanian Economy: Present and Short-Term Prospects." In *Lithuania: From Transition to Convergence*, Conference Papers published by the Economic Research Center. Vilnius: Eugrimas, 1999.

Ginsborg, P. "Explaining Italy's Crisis." In S. Gundle and S. Parker, eds., *The New Italian Republic: From the Fall of the Berlin Wall to Berlusconi*. London: Routledge, 1996. 19–39.

Gitelman, Zvi. "The Decline of Leninism and the Jews of the USSR." *Soviet Jewish Affairs* 21, no. 1 (1991): 105–17.

Glickman, Rose L. *Russian Factory Women: Workplace and Society 1880–1914*. Berkeley: University of California Press, 1984.

Goldman, Minton F. *Russia, The Eurasian Republics, and Central/Eastern Europe*. Guilford, Conn.: Dushkin Publishing, 1994. 51–54, 74, 92–100.

Golosov, Grigorii V. "Party Support or Personal Resources? Factors of Success in the Plurality Portion of the 1999 National Legislative Elections in Russia." *Communist and Post-Communist Studies* 35 (2002): 23–38.

Hague, Rod, Martin Harrop, and Shaun Breslin. *Political Science: A Comparative Introduction*, 2nd ed. New York: Worth, 1998.

Hammer, Darrell. *Russian Nationalism and Soviet Politics*. Boulder, Colo.: Westview Press, 1989.

Hancock, M. Donald, ed. *Politics in Western Europe*. Chatham, N.J.: Chatham House Publishers, 1998.

Hanson, Stephen. "Instrumental Democracy: The End of Ideology and the Decline of Russian Political Parties." In Vicki L. Hesli and William M. Reisinger, eds., *The 1999–2000 Elections in Russia: Their Impact and Legacy*. New York: Cambridge University Press, 2003.

Herspring, Dale R. "The Russian Military: Three Years On." *Communist and Post-Communist Studies* 28, no. 2 (1995): 163–82.

Hesli, Vicki, Ebru Erdem, William Reisinger, and Arthur Miller. "Religion and Political Choice in Russia," *Demokratizatsiya* 7, no. 1 (1999): 42–72.

Hirszowicz, Lukasz. "Soviet Government Policy Toward the Extraterritorial National Minorities: Comparison Between the Jews and the Germans." In Yaacov Ro' and Avi Beker, eds., *Jewish Culture and Identity in the Soviet Union*. New York: New York University Press, 1991.

Horowitz, Donald. *Ethnic Groups in Conflict*. Berkeley: University of California Press, 1985.

Inglehart, Ronald. "Post-Materialism in an Environment of Insecurity." *American Political Science Review* 75, no. 4 (December 1981): 880–900.

Jones, Stephen. "Georgia: A Failed Democratic Transition." In I. Bremmer and R. Taras, eds., *Nation and Politics in the Soviet Successor States*. Cambridge, U.K.: Cambridge University Press, 1993.

Jones, Stephen F., and Robert Parsons. "Georgia and the Georgians." In G. Smith, ed., *The Nationalities Question in the Post-Soviet States.* New York: Longman, 1996.

Jowitt, Ken. "The Leninist Legacy." In Ivo Banac, ed., *Eastern Europe in Revolution.* Ithaca, N.Y.: Cornell University Press, 1992. 207–24.

Kasfir, Nelson, ed. *Civil Society and Democracy in Africa: Critical Perspectives.* Portland: Frank Cass, 1998.

Kernell, S. "Presidential Popularity and Negative Voting: An Alternative Explanantion of the Mid-term Congressional Decline of the President's Party." *American Political Science Review* 71 (1977): 44–66.

Kim, Chong Lim. *Political Participation in Korea.* Santa Barbara, Calif.: Clio Press, 1980.

King, A. "Political Parties in Western Democracies." In L. J. Cantor, ed., *Comparative Political Systems.* Boston: Holbrook Press, 1974.

Kopecky, Petr. "Developing Party Organizations in East-Central Europe: What Type of Party Is Likely to Emerge?" *Party Politics* 1 (1995): 515–44.

Krupavicius, Algis. "The Post-Communist Transition and Institutionalization of Lithuania's Parties." *Political Studies* 46, no. 3 (1998): 465–92.

Kuzio, T. "Yanukovych Tries to Clean Up His Image." *Eurasia Daily Monitor* 1(21) (June 1, 2004), Jamestown Foundation, http://www.jamestown.org/print_friendly.php?volume_idZ401&issue_idZ2970&article_idZ236789.

Lempert, David. "Where the Moose Have Now Blood: In Yakutsk, Siberia, the Myths Are Falling, Though Slowly." *Cultural Survival Quarterly* 16, no.1 (2002): 53–57.

Lenin, V. I. *State and Revolution.* New York: International Publishers, 1943.

Leovin, Antony. "The Orange Revolution." *Ukrayinska Pravda.* 22:22. November 11, 2004, http://www2.pravda.com.ua/en/archive/2004/november/7/1.shtml.

Levitsky, Steven, and Lucan A. Way, "Elections Without Democracy: The Rise of Competitive Authoritarianism." *Journal of Democracy* 13, no. 2 (2002).

Lewis, Paul G. *Political Parties in Post-Communist Eastern Europe.* New York: Routledge, 2000.

Lewis-Beck, Michael S., and Brad Lockerbie. "Economics, Votes, Protests: Western European Cases." *Comparative Political Studies* 22 (1989): 155–77.

Lieven, Anatol. *The Baltic Revolution: Estonia, Latvia, Lithuania and the Path to Independence.* New Haven, Conn.: Yale University Press, 1994.

Lijphart, A. *Electoral Systems and Party Systems.* Oxford, U.K.: Oxford University Press, 1994.

Lijphart, Arend, and Carlos H. Waisman. "Institutional Design and Democratization." In Arend Lijphart and Carlos H. Waisman, eds., *Institutional Design in New Democracies. Eastern Europe and Latin America.* Boulder Colo.: Westview Press, 1996. 1–13.

Lindblom, Charles. "The Science of Muddling Through." *Public Administration* 19 (1959): 78–88.

Linz, Juan. "The Perils of Presidentialism." *Journal of Democracy* 1 (1990): 51–70.

Linz, Juan. "Some Thoughts on Presidentialism in Postcommunist Europe." In Ray Taras, ed., *Postcommunist Presidents.* Cambridge, U.K.: Cambridge University Press, 1997. 1–14.

Linz, Juan, and Alfred Stepan. *Problems of Democratic Transition and Consolidation: Southern Europe, South America, and Post-Communist Europe.* Baltimore: Johns Hopkins University Press, 1997.

Lipset, Seymour M. *Political Man: The Social Bases for Politics.* Baltimore: Johns Hopkins University Press, 1981.

Lipset, Seymour M., and Stein Rokkan. *Party Systems and Voter Alignments.* New York: Free Press, 1967.

Lipsky, Michael. "Protest as a Political Resource." *American Political Science Review* 62 (1968): 1144–58.

Lissyutkina, Larissa. "Soviet Women at the Crossroads of Perestroika." In Nanette Funk and Magda Mueller, eds. *Gender Politics and Post-Communism.* New York: Routledge, 1993. 274–86.

Luhovyk, Viktor. "A Campaign Turned Upside Down in Lviv," *Kiev Post,* March 10, 1998.

Lussier, Danielle. "Putin Continues Extending Vertical of Power," *Russian Regional Report,* Vol. 8, No. 2, February 3, 2003.

Maksymiuk, Jan. "Analysis: Ukraine's Compromised Choice." Radio Free Europe/ Radio Liberty, November 19, 2004. http://www.rferl.org/featuresarticle/2004/ 11/b71b5c3f-80da-4292-acc4-e1c1ce0a2f37.html.

McAllister, Ian, and Stephen White. "To Vote or Not to Vote: Election Turnout in Post-Communist Russia." In Matthew Wyman, Stephen White, and Sarah Oates, eds., *Elections and Voters in Post-Communist Russia.* Cheltenham, U.K.: Edward Elgar, 1998. 15–40.

McCormick, John. *Comparative Politics in Transition,* 4th ed. Belmont, Calif: Wadsworth, 2004.

McFaul, Michael. "State Power, Institutional Change, and the Politics of Privatization in Russia." *World Politics* (The Johns Hopkins University Press, 1995) 47, no. 3: 210–43.

Medish, Vadim. *The Soviet Union.* Rev. 4th ed. Englewood Cliffs, N. J.: Prentice Hall, 1991.

Melvin, Neil J. *Uzbekistan: Transition to Authoritarianism on the Silk Road (Postcommunist States and Nations).* New York: Routledge, 2000.

Milbrath, Lester. *Political Participation. How and Why Do People Get Involved in Politics?* Chicago: Rand McNally, 1965.

Mill, John Stuart. *Considerations on Representative Government.* New York: Liberal Arts Press, 1958.

Millar, James. "Can Putin Jump-Start Russia's Stalled Economy." *Current History* 99, no. 639 (October 2000): 329–33.

Miller, Arthur M., Vicki L. Hesli, and William M. Reisinger. "Conceptions of Democracy Among Mass and Elite in Post-Soviet Societies." *British Journal of Politics Science* 27 (1997): 157–90.

Moro, David A. "The National Rebirth of Russia—A US Strategy for Lifting the Soviet Siege." *Policy Review,* http://www.mpr.co.uk/scripts/sweb.dll/li_archive_item? method=GET&object=POLR_1988_43_WINTER.

Moser, Robert G. "The Impact of the Electoral System on Post-Communist Party Development: The Case of the 1993 Russian Parliamentary Elections." *Electoral Studies* 14, no. 4 (1995): 377–98.

Nechemias, Carol. "Democratization and Women's Access to Legislative Seats: The Soviet Case 1989–1991." *Women and Politics* 14, no. 3 (1994): 1–18.

Otyrba, Gueorgui. "War in Abkkhazia." In Roman Szporluk, ed., *National Identity and Ethnicity in Russia and the New States of Eurasia.* London: Sharpe, 1994. 281–309.

Orttung, Robert. "*Sovetskaya Rossiya* (November 11, 1995) Predicts Poor Showing for Women of Russia." *Russian Duma Report No. 6* (November 14, 1995), Russian Duma Elections Special Report, Open Media Research Institute.

Parry, Geraint, George Moyser, and Neil Day. *Political Participation and Democracy in Britain.* Cambridge, U.K.: Cambridge University Press, 1992.

Pavlychko, Solomea. "Between Feminism and Nationalism: New Women's Groups in the Ukraine." In Mary Buckley, ed., *Perestroika and Soviet Women*. New York: Cambridge University Press, 1992. 82–96.

Penketh, Anne. "Havel Backs Opposition Leader's Stance." *The Independent*, November 24, 2004.

Plasser, Fritz, Peter A. Ulman, and Harald Waldrauch. *Democratic Consolidation in East-Central Europe*. New York: St. Martin's Press, 1998.

Powell, G. Bingham. *Contemporary Democracies: Participation, Stability, and Violence*. Cambridge, Mass.: Harvard University Press, 1982.

Przeworski, Adam. *Democracy and the Market*. Cambridge, U.K: Cambridge University Press, 1981.

Racanska, Luba. "The Yeltsin Presidency, Economic Reform, and Women." In Wilma Rule and Norma Noonan, eds. *Russian Women in Politics and Society*. Westport, Conn.: Greenwood Press, 1996. 120–31.

Racioppi, Linda, and Katherine O'Sullivan See. "Organizing Women Before and After the Fall: Women's Politics in the Soviet Union and Post-Soviet Russia." *Signs: Journal of Women in Culture and Society* 20, no. 4 (1995): 818–50.

Reisinger, William M. "Establishing and Strengthening Democracy." In Robert D. Grey, ed. *Democratic Theory and Post-Communist Change*. New York: Prentice-Hall, 1987. 52–78.

Reisinger, William M., Arthur H. Miller, Vicki L. Hesli, and Kristen Hill Maher. "Political Values in Russia, Ukraine and Lithuania: Sources and Implications for Democracy." *British Journal of Political Science* 21 (1994): 183–223.

Remington, Thomas. "Democratization and the New Political Order in Russia." In Karen Dawisha and Bruce Parrott, eds. *Democratic Changes and Authoritarian Reactions in Russia, Ukraine, Belarus, and Moldova*. Cambridge, U.K.: Cambridge University Press, 1997.

Remington, Thomas F. *Politics in Russia*, 2nd ed. New York: Longman, 2002.

Reshetar, John S., Jr. *The Soviet Polity*. New York: Harper and Row, 1989.

Richter, James. "Promoting Civil Society? Democracy Assistance and Russian Women's Organizations." *Problems of Post-Communism* 49, no. 1 (2002): 30–41.

Rigby, T. H., and Bohdan Harasymiw. *Leadership Selection and Patron-Client Relations in the USSR and Yugoslavia*. Boston: Unwin Hyman, 1983.

Rosenberg, Chanie. *Women and Perestroika: Past, Present and Future for Women in Russia*. Chicago: Bookmarks, 1989.

Rosenstone, Steven J. "Economic Adversity and Voter Turnout." *American Journal of Political Science* 26 (1982): 25–46.

Sakwa, Richard. *Russian Politics and Society*. London: Routledge, 1996.

Sartori, Giovanni. *Comparative Constitutional Engineering*. New York: New York University Press, 1994.

Scarrow, Susan. "Party Decline in the Parties State?" In Paul Webb, David Farrell, and Ian Holliday, eds., *Political Parties in Advanced Industrial Democracies*. Oxford, U.K.: Oxford University Press, 2002. 77–106.

Schlozman, Kay, and Sydney Verba. *Injury to Insult*. Cambridge, Mass.: Harvard University Press, 1979.

Shelley, Louise I. "The Challenge of Crime and Corruption" In Stephen K. Wegren, ed. *Russia's Policy Challenges: Security and Stability and Development*. Armonk, N. Y.: M. E. Sharpe, 2003.

Shields, Todd G., and Robert K. Goidel. "Participation Rates, Socioeconomic Class Biases and Congressional Elections: A Crossvalidation." *American Journal of Political Science* 41, no. 2 (1997): 683–91.

Shugart, Matthew Soberg. "The Inverse Relationship Between Party Strength and Executive Strength: A Theory of Politicians' Constitutional Choices." *British Journal of Political Science* 28 (1998): 1–29.

Shugart, Matthew Soberg, and John M. Carey. *Presidents and Assemblies: Constitutional Design and Electoral Dynamics*. New York: Cambridge University Press, 1992.

Shvetsova, Olga. "Resolving the Problem of Pre-Election Coordination: The Parliamentary Election as an Elite Presidential 'Primary.'" In Vicki L. Hesli and William M. Reisinger, eds. *The 1999–2000 Elections in Russia: Their Impact and Legacy*. New York: Cambridge University Press, 2003.

Simon, Herbert. *Models of Bounded Rationality*. Cambridge, Mass: MIT Press, 1982.

Slater, Wendy. "Female Representation in Russian Politics." *RFE/RL Research Report*, Vol. 3, No. 22, June 3, 1994, pp. 27–33.

Spechler, Dina. *Permitted Dissent in the USSR: Novyi Mir and the Soviet Regime*. New York: Praeger Publishers, 1982.

Strate, J. M., C. J. Parrish, C. D. Elder, and C. Ford III. "Life Span Civic Development and Voting Participation." *American Political Science Review* 83 (1989): 443.

Tilly, Charles. "Revolutions and Collective Violence." In F. Greenstein and N. Polsby, eds. *Handbook of Political Science*, Vol. 3. Reading, Mass.: Addison-Wesley, 1975.

Tishkov, Valery. "Ethnic Conflicts in the Former USSR: The Use and Misuse of Typologies and Data." *Journal of Peace Research* 36, no. 5 (1999): 571–91.

Treisman, Daniel. "Russia Renewed?" *Foreign Affairs* 81, no. 2 (November/December 2002): 58–60.

Tucker, Robert C., ed. *The Marx–Engels Reader*. New York: W. W. Norton, 1972.

Tucker, R. *Political Culture and Leadership in Soviet Russia: From Lenin to Gorbachev*. New York: W. W. Norton, 1987.

Urigashvili, Besik. "The Transcaucasus: Blood Ties." *Bulletin of the Atomic Scientists* 50, no. 1 (January/February 1994): 18–23.

Verba, Sidney, and Norman Nie. *Participation in America: Political Democracy and Social Equality*. Chicago: University of Chicago Press, 1972.

Verba, Sydney, Norman H. Nie, and Jae-On Kim. *Participation and Political Equality: A Seven-Nation Comparison*. New York: Cambridge University Press, 1978.

Verba, Sidney, Kay Lehman Scholzman, and Henry E. Brady. *Voice and Equality: Civic Voluntarism in American Politics*. Cambridge, Mass.: Harvard University Press, 1995.

Voronina, Olga. "Soviet Women and Politics: On the Brink of Change," in Barbara J. Nelson and Najma Chowdhury, eds., *Women and Politics Worldwide*. New Haven, Conn.: Yale University Press, 1994. 721–36.

Walker, Jack L. *Mobilizing Interest Groups in America: Patrons, Professions, and Social Movements*. Ann Arbor: University of Michigan Press, 1991.

Webb, Paul. "Introduction: Political Parties in Advanced Industrial Democracies." In Paul Webb, David Farrell, and Ian Holiday, eds. *Political Parties in Advanced Industrial Democracies*. New York: Oxford University Press, 2002. 1–15.

Weiner, Myron. "Political Participation: Crisis of the Political Process." In Leonard Binder, James S. Coleman, et al. eds. *Crisis and Sequences in Political Development.* Princeton, N. J.: Princeton University Press. 1971.

Williams, Brian Glyn, "Commemorating 'The Deportation' in Post-Soviet Chechnya. The Role of Memorialization and Collective Memory in the 1994–1996 and 1999–2000 Russo-Chechen Wars." *History and Memory* 12, no. 1 (Spring/Summer 2000).

Wilson, Andrew. *The Ukrainians' Unexpected Nation.* New Haven, Conn.: Yale University Press, 2000.

Wilson, James Q. *Political Organizations.* Princeton, N.J.: Princeton University Press, 1995.

Wolfinger, Raymond, and Steven Rosenstone. *Who Votes?* New Haven, Conn.: Yale University Press, 1980.

Yevgenyev, Ilya. "Women of Russia in the Center of the Political Spectrum." *Russian Parliamentary Bulletin, RIA Novosti,* no. 15 (1994): 11–12.

INDEX

Abashidze, Aslan, 352, 352*n*, 356, 357*t*, 359, 360*t*, 361, 370–71, 370*n*
Abkhaz Autonomous Soviet Socialist Republic (ASSR), 81, 365
Abkhazia, 347, 348, 355, 365–66, 367–70, 375, 377, 416
Abkhazian Supreme Soviet, 368
ABM Protocol Treaty, 246
Abramov, Sergei, 105
absolute rulers, under tsarism, 44. *See also* authoritarianism; totalitarianism
access channels, for interest groups, 209
Act of Emancipation, 43*t*
Adamkus, Valdas, 277, 278*t*, 279, 280, 301
Adiatulina, Almira, 96*n*
Adjaria Autonomous Soviet Socialist Republic (ASSR), 81, 356, 361, 365, 370–71
Adjarians, in Georgia, 365
administrative resources
defined, 417
use of, in Ukraine, 316, 329
Adolat (Justice Social Democratic Party), 393, 397*t*, 398
Adrzinba, Vladislav, 369
Afghanistan, 262, 339
Soviet invasion of, 247
U.S. military operation in, 251–52
Uzbekistan and, 408, 409
Africa, arms exports to, 255
"Against-all" voting, in regional elections, 180
age
political participation and, 160
voting behavior and, 157–58, 163
aggregation of interests
defined, 417
in Georgia, 363
Agrarian Party, 174*t*, 176, 327
agrarian proletariat, 21
Agrarian Reform of 1906, 47
Agreement on Trade and Commercial and Economic Cooperation, 299

agricultural associations, in Lithuania, 294–95
agriculture
in Brezhnev era, 62
collectivization, 56, 93–94, 233
economy, 242–43
following World War I, 52
in Lithuania, 294–95, 299
under Russian Empire, 45
transition process, 415
types of farms, 243
in Ukraine, 308, 335
in Uzbekistan, 383, 384, 395, 401–2, 403*f*, 410
Agro-Industrialists, 173, 200
Ahmedjanov, Mahammadjon, 398
AIDS, in Russian Federation, 257
Air Defense Agreement, 250
Albania, 245
Albright, Madeleine, 329
alcohol consumption, 415
in Brezhnev era, 62
in Russian Federation, 256, 257–58
Alexander I, 41, 42*t*, 44, 78
Alexander II, 19, 43*t*, 46
Alexander III, 46
Algeria, 255
alienation
defined, 417
voting behavior and, 163
Alkhanov, Alu, 104
Allende, Salvador, 35*n*
All Georgia Revival Union (AGRU), 356, 361
All-Russia Center for the Study of Public Opinion (VCIOM), 117, 145–46, 176
All-Russian Congress of Soviets, 43*t*
Second, 50, 51
All-Russian Society for the Preservation of Historical and Cultural Monuments (VOOPIK), 109
All-Russian Socio-Political Movement of Women, 225

All-Union Central Council of Trade
Unions (ACCTU), 212
All-Union Leninist Communist Youth
League (Komsomol), 210, 211
All-Union ministries, 126
All-Union Party Congress, 188
defined, 417
functions of, 186
Second, 80
American Jewish Committee, 121–22
anarchism, 19, 417
Andriukaitis, Vytenis, 278*t*
Andropov, Yuri, 63, 128*t*, 219–20
Angola, 246
Anna Karenina (Tolstoy), 45*n*
Anti-Ballistic Missile Treaty, 34, 254
anti-Semitism, 109, 119–22
in Russian Empire, 119–20
by Stalin, 120–21
Anti-Terrorism Centre, 250
AO (Autonomous Oblasts), 81
AOK (Autonomous Okrugs), 81
April Thesis (Lenin), 49
Arabic Caliphate, 380
Arabic languages, in Central Asian
republics, 380, 382
Arabic script, 382
armed forces. *See* military services
Armenia, 65, 80, 81, 250
ethnic Russians in, 83*t*
Armenians, in Georgia, 365
arms control treaties, 246–47
arms exports, 255–56
Articles of Confederation, U.S., 87
articulation of interests
defined, 417
in Georgia, 363
arts
Russian Empire, 45
Stalin and, 57
Assembly of Spokespersons of Factions,
282
assimilation, forced, 86
associational groups. *See also* interest
groups
in democracies, 208–10
environmental organizations, 229
future of, 229
in Gorbachev era, 211–12
human rights organizations, 229
labor organizations, 212–13
legislation allowing, 212
Russian Federation, 208–30

in Soviet Union, 210–11
types of, 208–10
women's organizations, 223–27
Association of Business Women of Russia,
224
Association of Russian Banks, 213
ASSRs. *See* Autonomous Soviet Socialist
Republics (ASSRs)
atheism, 16*n*
atomic bomb, Soviet development of, 59.
See also nuclear weapons
August 1991 coup, 67–68, 67*t*, 127, 143, 271
defined, 417
military and, 221
Austrevicius, Petras, 278*t*
authoritarianism. *See also* totalitarianism
alternatives to, 414
defined, 6, 417
in Georgia, 347
in Lithuania, 266–67
political culture and, 112
in Russia, 414
under tsars, 112
in Ukraine, 316
in Uzbekistan, 396, 414
autocracy, 44, 417
Autonomous Oblasts (AO), 81
Autonomous Okrugs (AOK), 81
Autonomous Republic of North Ossetia,
366
Autonomous Soviet Socialist Republics
(ASSRs), 81, 88. *See also specific
ASSRs*
autonomy, 78, 85, 97, 417
Ayatskov, Dmitrii, 91
Azerbaijan, 65, 80, 250
ethnic Russians in, 83*t*

Babeuf, François Noel, 14
Baburin, Sergei, 199
"backwardness"
political culture and, 112
Stalin's attack on, 55–57
Bakhimov, Mutaza, 180
Bakunin, Mikhail, 19
Baltic region, 2
defined, 417
territorial expansion into, 78
Baltic republics, 81, 265
defined, 417
democratization of, 415
deportation of residents from, 109
military services, 301

banking
    crisis, in Lithuania, 283, 289
    privatization of, 238
Basaev, Shamil, 99, 101, 104, 105, 222
base, of society
    defined, 417
    economic determinism and, 16
Bashkortostan, 95
Basmachi Rebellion, 80, 417
Batumi Alliance, 356. *See also* Revival of
        Georgia Bloc
Bauer, Otto, 85
Belarus, 68, 81, 240, 250, 253, 311
    ethnic Russians in, 83t
    Russian Federation agreements with,
        79
Belarusian Soviet Socialist Republic, 79
Berezovskii, Boris, 214–15, 218
Beria, Lavrentii, 60, 219
Berlin Blockade, 245
Berlin Wall, 248
Betin, Oleg, 180
bilateral agreements, 250
Birlik (unity) group, Uzbekistan, 384,
        395–96
Black Repartition *(Chernyi Peredel)*, 19–20
Blanqui, Louis Auguste, 22
Blinkeviciute, Vilija, 278t
Bloody Sunday, 43t, 47
Boldyrev, Yuri, 195
Bolshevik Central Committee, 50
Bolsheviks
    Central Asian republics and, 381
    defined, 418
    establishment of, 21, 185, 189
    execution of, by Stalin, 30
    factors affecting success of, 53
    in Georgia, 346
    ideology of, 13
    name change, to Communist Party, 24
    overthrow of Provisional Government
        by, 50
    popularity of, 23, 51
    repression of opposition by, 52–53,
        79–80
    revolutionary activities, 47
    revolutionary goals, 50–51, 244
    Stalin and, 54
Boone, Peter, 238
bourgeoisie
    class struggle and, 17
    defined, 16, 418
    under Russian Empire, 46

Boyars, 40
Braham, Denis C., 121
brain drain
    defined, 418
    from Ukraine, 334
Brandt, Willy, 246
Brazauskas, Algirdas, 267, 268, 274,
        276–80, 283, 289, 290, 291, 301
Brazil, 75
    economic indicators, 241t
    ethnic groups, 76t–77t
Breslin, Shaun, 243
Brest-Litovsk, Treaty of, 51–52
Brezhnev, Leonid, 60, 65, 109, 247f
    détente and, 33, 34
    economic policy, 234, 242
    foreign policy under, 246–47
    invasion of Afghanistan by, 247
    leadership of, 61–63, 125
    1977 constitution and, 123–24
    philosophical views of, 31, 33–34
    Politburo and, 186
    political culture and, 113
    security functions under, 219
    Uzbekistan and, 383
Brezhnev Doctrine, 33–34, 418
Bryzlov, Boris, 130, 177t, 202
Bukhara, 80, 381, 382
Bukharin, Nikolai, 27
Bulganin, Nikolay, 60
Bulgaria, 245, 253
Burdjanadze, Nino, 349, 353, 354, 359,
        360t, 361
Buryats, 93
Bush, George H. W., 248, 252
Bush, George W., 301, 394
business organizations, in Russian
        Federation, 213

Cabinet of Ministers, Georgia, 377
Cabinet of Ministers, Ukraine, 323,
        334
Cabinet of Ministers, Uzbekistan, 389
Canada, economic indicators, 241t
Capital (Marx and Engels), 15, 17n
capitalism
    as doomed by class struggle, 17
    imperialism and, 23
    nationalism and, 85
    as a necessary step toward socialism,
        17, 20
    "permanent revolution" and, 20n
    revolution and, 27

capitalist encirclement, 245
declared ended by Khrushchev, 32
defined, 27, 418
Stalin's views of, 28*t*
capital punishment. *See* death penalty
Caplikas, Algis, 290
Carey, John M., 147
Carter, Jimmy, 247
Cassileth, B. R., 259
Castro, Fidel, 35, 246*n*
Catherine II (the Great), 40–41, 42, 42*t*, 78
Catholic Church
Lithuania, 267, 273, 283
Ukrainian Greek, 312–13
censorship
Brezhnev and, 62
under Russian Empire, 46
Stalin and, 57
Central Asian Cooperation Organization
(CACO), 404, 407
Central Asian republics, 2, 4, 70, 379. *See
also specific countries*
defined, 418
deportation of non-Russian nationality
groups to, 109
Islam and, 380, 416
Russia and, 80, 380–81
territorial expansion into, 78
Central Committee of the Communist
League, 18
Central Committee of the Communist
Party of the Soviet Union (CPSU), 55,
66, 80
defined, 418
democratization program, 126
female representation in, 224
functions of, 186
Stalin's purge of, 58
Central Election Commission (CEC), 200
Georgia, 352, 352*n*
Ukraine, 317, 318, 319
Central Election Committee, Russian
Federation, 179
central government
limited control by, 88
territorial administration systems, 87
central planning agencies, 232
Charles XII, king of Sweden, 40
chauvinism, Russian, 80, 109
Chechen-Ingush ASSR, 81
division into Chechnya and Ingushetya,
98
establishment of, 98

Chechens
background, 92
deportation to Siberia, 98
refugees, 102
Chechnya, 170
amnesty offered to, 101
casualties, 100–101
conflict in, 70, 72, 92–93, 97–105, 170,
198, 222, 249, 416
constitution, 100, 101
elections, 101–2, 140
hostage-taking at Moscow theater,
104–5
military corruption in, 222–23
Muslims, 70, 98, 99, 101
natural resources, 98, 101, 102, 104
population, 98
public opinion and, 141
Putin's policy on, 100, 104, 179
refugee problems, 102
terrorism and, 99–105, 170
Yabloko criticism of war in, 196
Yeltsin and, 144
Cheka (Russian secret police), 52, 219
Chernenko, Konstantin, 63
Chernobyl nuclear disaster, 310, 422
Chernomyrdin, Victor, 148, 237
Chiang Kai-shek, 35
China, People's Republic of, 34, 35, 240,
245, 255
arms exports to, 255–56
economic indicators, 241*t*
ethnic diversity, 74, 76*t*–77*t*
Russian Federation and, 249
Soviet relations, 246, 248
Stalin and, 60*n*
Chornovil, Viacheslav, 61
Christian Democratic Coalition,
Lithuania, 274
Christian Democratic parties, 191
Chubais, Anatolii, 176, 197, 213, 236, 237
Churchill, Winston, 59, 245
Circuit Courts, Georgia, 363
Citizens' Union of Georgia (CUG), 348,
352, 354*t*, 355, 356, 357*t*, 358, 359,
361, 361*n*, 370
Civic Forum, 214
civilian service, as alternative to military
service, 254
civil liberties
reduction of, following Russian
Revolution, 52
in Ukraine, 414

in Uzbekistan, 400*n*
Yeltsin and, 72
civil society
absence of, 119, 192
defined, 418
establishment of, in Russia, 211–12
civil wars
Georgia, 366
Russia, 30, 44*t*, 52, 233, 381
Ukraine, 309
Clark, William A., 173
class, defined, 16
class struggle
defined, 16, 418
Lenin's views on, 25*t*
Marxist theory of, 16–19
coalition government
defined, 418
in Lithuania, 279
Cold War
foreign policy legacy of, 244–47
nuclear weapons and, 59
USSR/U.S. relations during, 1, 244–47
collectivism
defined, 418
market economy and, 114
political culture and, 113, 119
collectivization, defined, 418
collectivized agriculture, 233
effects on Sakha Republic (Yakutia),
93–94
in Lithuania, 294–95
Stalin's program for, 56
in Ukraine, 309, 310
Colombia, 260
colonialism
in Central Asian republics, 381
defined, 418
Marx's view of, 17*n*
World War I and, 23
combination (mixed) voting systems,
172
Comintern (Third International), 44*t*
defined, 418
dissolution of, 28
establishment of, 24, 244
goals of, 24
command economy, 233, 418
Commissariat of State Security (NKGB),
219
Committee for State Security (KGB).
See KGB (Committee for State
Security)

Committee of Soviet Women, 224
Committee to Protect Journalists (CPJ),
322
Commonwealth of Independent States
(CIS)
Collective Security Organization (CIS
CSO), 250
defined, 418
economic corruption in, 242
establishment of, 68, 249, 311
Free Trade Zone (CIS FTZ), 250
Georgia and, 347
leadership of, 214
Russian Federation and, 249–51
Uzbekistan and, 384, 399, 404
weaknesses of, 69–70
Commonwealth of Lithuania and Poland,
265–66
communal life, defined, 13
communism
defined, 13, 418
discrediting of, 114
in Eastern Europe, 34–35
ideological functions of, 36–37
methods of establishment of, 35–36
as natural evolution of socialism, 17
negative image of, 29
origins of, 21
personal fulfillment under, 18
political culture and, 112
use of force and, 35–36
in the world system, 34–36
Communist League, 15
Communist Manifesto (Marx and Engels),
15, 18, 20*n*, 43*t*
communist parties
hierarchical organization of, 24
in Western Europe, 191
Communist Party Congresses
Seventeenth, 58
Tenth, 30, 54
Twelfth, 55
Twentieth, 31–32, 60, 113, 186
Twenty-First, 32
Twenty-Second, 23
Communist Party for the Russian Soviet
Federated Socialist Republic
(RSFSR), 111
Communist Party of Georgia, 356
Communist Party of Russia
dissolution of, 68
establishment of, 24
repression of opposition by, 53

Communist Party of the Russian
  Federation (CPRF), 174*t*, 192, 193*t*,
  194, 197
  electoral performance of, 200, 201,
    201*t*, 202
  history and influence of, 195
  name changes, 186*n*
  organization, 194
  parliamentary elections and, 172–77
  party identification with, 204
  political support for, 163
  presidential elections and, 138
  relationship with other political parties,
    200
  role of, 170
  United Russia and, 202–3
  women's organizations and, 226
Communist Party of the Soviet Union
  (CPSU)
  activities banned, 143
  armed forces and, 220–21
  associational groups and, 210–11
  banned, 195
  Central Committee, 54, 58, 66, 80, 126,
    186, 418
  constitutional change in status of, 127
  economic reforms and, 236
  election procedures, 124–25
  general secretary, 125, 186, 420
  government control by, 188
  hierarchical organization of, 186, 187*n*
  historical role of, 184
  membership, 187, 188
  name changes, 186*n*
  1930s purges, 29, 30, 57–58
  one-party system and, 184–88
  Politburo, 54, 128*t*, 186, 424
  primary party organization (PPO),
    187–88
  reregistered, 195
  role of, Article 6 of Soviet Constitution
    and, 188, 210
  Secretariat, 186, 425
  as sole legal political party, 186
  suppression of opposition to, 30, 36
  totalitarianism and, 29
  Uzbekistan and, 383
Communist Party of Ukraine (CPU), 315,
  317, 317*t*, 324, 325, 326, 327, 327*t*,
  328, 329
Communist Party of Uzbekistan, 383, 397
Communist's Union of Georgia, 358
communist takeovers, 35–36

comparative analysis, 4–7
  components of, 4–5
  contextual characteristics, 5
  economic focus, 6
  geographic focus, 6
  political characteristics, 4–6
  systematic, 5
Confederation of Caucasian Peoples, 368
Confederation of German States, 87
confederations, administration of, 87
Congo, 246
Congress of People's Deputies, 64, 126,
  127–28, 147–48, 268, 427
  creation of position of president by, 137
  Declaration of Sovereignty, 143
  dissolution of, 68, 69, 143
Congress of Soviets of Uzbekistan, 382
conservative parties, 191
consolidated systems, 6
  democracy, 115, 413
Constituent Assembly, 49
  dissolution of, 51
  elections to, 51
constitution, Abkhazia, 369
constitution, Chechnya, 100, 101
constitution, Georgia, 351, 352, 355, 364
constitution, Lithuania, 266, 275, 302
constitution, Russia
  demand for, under Russian Empire, 44,
    46
  post-Soviet, 69
  reforms, under Russian Empire, 47
  Russian Federation, 128, 141
constitution, Soviet Union, 80, 123–27,
  346
  Article 6 on Communist Party role, 210
  political parties and, 191
  removal of Article 6 on Communist
    Party role, 188
constitution, Ukraine, 313, 314, 316
constitution, Uzbekistan, 382, 384, 385–86
Constitutional Court, Russian Federation
  Communist Party reregistered by, 195
  regional elections and, 180
  role of, 150–51
Constitutional Court, Georgia, 351, 363,
  364
Constitutional Court, Lithuania, 292
Constitutional Court, Uzbekistan, 387,
  391
Constitutional Democrats (Kadets), 185
constitutions, regional, 91–92
consumer goods, quality of, 234

containment, 245
contextual characteristics, 5
continuity argument, of totalitarianism
    under Stalin, 29–31
*Contribution to the Critique of
    Political Economy, A* (Marx and
    Engels), 15
controlled interest group systems, 210
conventional-legal participation, 160–61
    defined, 154, 160, 419
    nonvoting forms of, 160–61, 161t, 162t
    purposes of, 182
correctional task, 260
corruption
    defined, 419
    in economic system, 242
    in Georgia, 348, 353, 376–77
    in government, 262–63
    in Lithuania, 283, 292
    in military service, 222–23
    oligarchs, 213–18
    privatization and, 238–39
    in Ukraine, 334
    in Uzbekistan, 383–84, 395
Corruption Perceptions Index,
    Transparency International, 376–77
cotton production, in Uzbekistan, 383,
    395, 401–2, 403f
Council for the Struggle Against
    Corruption, 217
Council of Europe
    Georgia and, 364
    Lithuania and, 272
Council of Justice, Georgia, 364
Council of Ministers, 125, 146, 186
Council of Nationalities, 126
Council of People's Commissars, 51
Council of the Duma, 130
Council of the Federation of Trade
    Unions, Uzbekistan, 399
Council of the Union, 126
Councils of People's Deputies,
    Uzbekistan, 386, 390
Court of Appeal, Georgia, 363
Court of Appeals, Lithuania, 292
crime
    in Lithuania, 302–3
    organized, 262
    punishment for, 260
    in Russian Federation, 260–62
    statistics, 261t, 262
Crime and Punishment (Dostoevsky), 45n
Crimean Peninsula, 335, 419

Crimean War, 41
Cuba, Republic of, 34, 35, 246, 255
Cuban Missile Crisis, 245–46
cult of personality, 31, 57, 419
cultural change, 108
cultural diversity
    in ethnic republics, 75
    in Russian Empire, 75, 78
    in Russian Federation, 75, 76, 88–106
    Russian Social Democratic Labor Party
        (RSDLP) policy on, 78–79
    Soviet Union, 75, 78
cultural-pluralist approach, to ethnic
    conflict, 85–86
culture
    under Russian Empire, 45
    Stalin and, 57
Cyrillic alphabet, 96, 382, 384n
Czechoslovakia, 33, 245
Czech Republic, 252, 337

Dagestan, Republic of, 99, 99n
Daminov, Turgunpulat, 398
Daniels, Robert, 145
Dead Souls (Gogol), 45n
death penalty, 52, 58, 260
Decembrist Revolt (1825), 44
decentralization
    defined, 419
    in Lithuania, 267, 272
decision, in policymaking, 243
Declaration of Sovereignty, RSFSR
        Congress of People's Deputies, 143
decrees, by Presidium, 125
Defense Ministry, Russia, 141
democracy
    associational groups in, 208–10
    consolidated, 115, 413
    defined, 7, 419
    electoral competition in, 115
    following Russian Revolution, 51–54
    goals of, 7
    leadership in, 116
    minority rights in, 116
    political culture and, 114–16
    political parties and, 202–6
    public opinion and, 117–19
    transition to, 7–9, 72, 413–16
    transition to, in Georgia, 363
    transition to, in Ukraine, 332–35
    transition to, political parties and,
        202–6
Democratic Alliance Bloc, Georgia, 360t

democratic centralism, 188
  defined, 24, 419
  totalitarianism and, 29–30
  in Uzbekistan, 382
Democratic Centralists, 30
democratic interest group systems,
    209–10
Democratic Party of Uzbekistan, 398
Democratic Revival Union, Georgia, 359,
    360*t*, 361, 362*t*
democratic systems, 5
democratic values, in Russian society,
    116, 118*t*
Democrats Alliance Bloc, Georgia, 359,
    360*t*, 361
demokratizatsiia (democratization),
    64, 68
  defined, 419
  elections and, 7–8
  legacies of the past and, 7
  in Lithuania, 303, 415
  theories of, 7–9
denationalization of industry, 236
Denmark, parliamentary seats held by
    women, 131
dependency theory, 7
détente
  Brezhnev and, 33, 34
  defined, 245, 419
dialectics, law of, 17, 421
dictatorship, 5, 419
dictatorship of the proletariat, 22–23, 419
discontinuity argument, of totalitarianism
    under Stalin, 29–31
Discourse on the Origins of Inequality, The
    (Rousseau), 13
discrimination, against Jewish people,
    119–22
disproportionality, 419
dissident activity
  defined, 419
  in Lithuania, 266
  in Ukraine, 310–11
Donskoy, Dmitry, 39
Dostoevsky, Fyodor, 45, 45*n*
double burden, 224, 419
drug trafficking, by armed forces, 223
drug use, in Russian Federation, 262
dual accountability, 126, 419
dual executive, 140, 146–48, 419
Dudayev, Dzhokher, 98–99
Duma, defined, 420

Duma, Russian Federation
  assassination of members of, 136
  Communist Party control of, 195
  court system and, 150
  criticism of elections to, 175
  elections, 172–78, 185
  executive and, 203
  function of, 130, 147
  membership, 128
  1993 elections, 200
  1995 elections, 200
  1999 elections, 200, 201*t*, 202
  no-confidence votes, 147
  party alignment, 177*t*
  political factions, 173
  political parties, 200–202
  presidential authority and, 141
  regional governments and, 90–91
  2003 elections to, 173–75, 174*t*, 201–2,
      203
  United Russia and, 202–3
  women in, 225
Duma, Soviet Union
  elections, 47
  establishment of, 47
  First, 43*t*, 185
  Fourth, 48, 185
  Second, 43*t*, 185
  Third, 43*t*, 185
Duverger, Maurice, 189
Dzjalalov (Jalalov), Abdulhasiz, 389, 397

Eastern Europe
  communist states of, 34–35
  Lithuanian independence movement
      and, 271
  Soviet establishment of communist
      governments in, 245
  territorial expansion into, 78
Eastern Slavic people, 39
East Germany, 245
Economic Cooperation Organization
    (ECO), 407
economic councils, 60, 234
economic determinism, 16, 420
economic indicators, 239
  Lithuania, 296*t*–297*t*
  for select countries, 241*t*
  Ukraine, 333*t*
  Uzbekistan, 405*t*–406*t*
economic inequalities, in Russian
    Federation, 239

economic motivators, for voting behavior, 155, 159

economic policy. *See also* market economy
  agriculture, 242–43
  centralized, 234
  decentralization, 234
  following Russian Revolution, 52
  in Georgia, 371–74, 375*t*
  under Gorbachev, 236
  in Lithuania, 303–5
  market reform, 236–43
  market system economy, 235
  oil exports and, 240
  planning, Soviet Union, 233–35
  public policy decision making and, 232
  in Russian Federation, 236–43
  "second economy," 234–35
  shock therapy, 237
  socialist economy, 235
  under Stalin, 233, 236
  under Yeltsin, 236–38

economy
  Brezhnev and, 61–62
  downturns, 236, 239–42
  in Georgia, 415
  Gorbachev and, 64
  growth of, 414–15
  Khrushchev and, 60
  in Lithuania, 294–99
  in Russian Empire, 48
  in Ukraine, 308, 315, 332–35, 333*t*, 415
  in Uzbekistan, 382–83, 401–4, 410, 415
  Yeltsin and, 71

Edinstvo, 420

education
  political participation and, 160
  voting behavior and, 158, 163

election irregularities
  bias, 139–40, 175
  in Georgia, 348–50
  in post-Soviet states, 413
  rule of thumb for judging, 349
  in Ukraine, 318–19, 329
  in Uzbekistan, 399
  vote rigging, 348, 427

elections. *See also* voter turnout; voting; *specific presidential elections*
  democratization and, 7–8
  first multicandidate, 126, 137
  freedom and fairness of, 349
  future of, 181–82
  to parliament, 172–78
  presidential, 137–40
  reelection of incumbents, 136–37
  regional, 180–81
  transition to democracy and, 413
  voting, 155–59

Electoral Action of Lithuania's Poles (LLRA)-Union of Lithuanian Poles, 286*t*

Electoral Bloc of Socialist and Peasant Parties, Ukraine, 325, 326

electoral blocs, 177

electoral systems
  comparative analysis of, 171–72
  competition, in democracy, 115
  defined, 171, 420

elitist political culture, 113

Ellenstein, Jean, 33–34

Emancipation of Labor, 20

Emancipation of the Serfs, 45, 46, 420

employment
  government responsibility for, 118, 119*t*, 169
  political participation and, 161
  under Soviet system, 113
  by state, 234
  of women, 223–24

energy resources
  in Georgia, 372
  Lithuania and, 298
  in Uzbekistan, 401, 409

Engels, Friedrich, 13, 15, 17–19, 43*t*

environmental organizations, 229

environmental pollution, 263, 298*n*

Equatorial Guinea, 246

Erk Democratic Party of Uzbekistan, 384, 395–96

Esman, M., 395

Estonia, 65, 75, 81, 253, 265, 271, 337
  comparative study of, 4
  ethnic Russians in, 83*t*
  independence of, 68, 268, 298

Ethiopia, 246

ethnic Armenians, in Georgia, 365

ethnic cleansing, in Abkhazia, 370

ethnic conflict
  cultural-pluralist approach to, 85–86
  democratic transition and, 415–16
  in Georgia, 365–68, 377
  Marxist view of, 85
  Russification and, 86
  socioeconomic differences and, 416

ethnic Georgians, 344
   in Abkhazia, 370
ethnic groups
   case studies, 93–105
   conflict and, 85–86
   country comparisons, 3t
   functions of, 86
   in Georgia, 344
   identity, 85
   modernization process and, 85
   rights of minorities, 88
   in Russian Federation, 74–75
   in Ukraine, 312–13
   in USSR, rights of, 26–27
   in Uzbekistan, 391–92
ethnicity
   defined, 84–85, 420
   variation in, 86
ethnic Lithuanians
   in Lithuania, 272–73
   voting behavior, 294
ethnic republics
   cultural diversity, 75
   surrounded by Russian territory, 93,
      105
ethnic Russians
   in Georgia, 365
   grievances of, 110
   intolerance of others, 78
   in Lithuania, 272–73
   in newly independent states, 83t
   population, 110–11
   as proportion of Russian population,
      74–75, 76t–77t
   proportion of Soviet population, 81
   reimmigration to Russia, 257
   significant concentrations of (map), 82f
   in Ukraine, 312, 336
   voting behavior of, 158–59
ethnic Ukrainians, in Russian Federation,
      74, 75
ethnocentrism, 4, 420
Euro-Communism, 33–34, 420
Europe. See also Eastern Europe
   party ideology in, 191
   Russian integration into, 165–68
European Bank for Reconstruction and
      Development, 242, 404
European Federation of Green Parties,
      326
European Network of Election Monitoring
      Organizations (ENEMO), 318, 341

European Union (EU), 4
   Georgia and, 374, 376
   Lithuania and, 272, 279, 298, 299–300,
      305, 415
   Ukraine and, 317, 336–38
   Uzbekistan and, 407
European Union Accession Treaty,
      Lithuania, 299–300
evaluation, in policymaking, 243
Evenk AOK, 81
Evenks, 93
Evens, 93
exploitation of labor, Marxist theory and,
      14, 17
exports
   arms, to Africa, 255
   arms, to China, 255–56
   arms, to Iran, 255–56
   Lithuania, 298
   oil, 63, 240

factions, 195
   ban on, 30, 53, 54
   defined, 420
   in women's organizations, 225
Fainsod, Merle, 124
famine
   collectivized agriculture and, 56
   in Ukraine, 56, 309
Farmers' Party-New Democracy
      Party (LVP-NDP), 284t
Fatherland-All Russia (OVR) alliance, 173,
      175, 192, 193t, 198, 225
   electoral performance of, 200, 201t
   history and politics of, 197
   Primakov and, 200
   Putin and, 202
Federal Agency of Governmental
      Communications and Information
      (FAPSI), 220
Federal Assembly, 69, 128
   comparative analysis of, 131–37
   defined, 420
   function of, 129–31
   presidential authority and, 141
Federal Border Guard Service (FSP), 220
federal cities, 88
federalism
   administration of federal systems,
      87
   Russian Federation, 87, 88–92
   USSR, 87

Federal Law on the Election of the President of the Russian Federation, 178

Federal Security Service (FSB), 100, 141, 170
- functions of, 220
- oligarchs and, 217

Federal Tax Police Service (FSNP), 220

Federation Council, 88, 130–31
- defined, 420
- professional backgrounds of members, 131
- women members, 131

Federation of Independent Trade Unions of Russia (FNPR), 212–13, 217

Fedulova, Alevtina, 224, 225

feminism, 226. *See also* women

feudalism, 17

Fidokorlor Party, 397*t*, 398

Finland, 131

First International (International Working Men's Association), 15, 43*t*

first-past-the-post electoral systems, 171

First World, 6

Fish, Steven, 205

five-year plans, 233

For a Free Georgia, 349

For a New Georgia, 359, 360, 360*t*

For a United Ukraine (ZYU), 327, 329

forced labor camps. *See* labor camps

foreign-controlled companies, in Russian Federation, 242

Foreign Intelligence Service (SVR), 220*n*

Foreign Ministry, 141

foreign policy, 232, 244–56
- Cold War legacy, 244–47
- economic relations, Brezhnev and, 62–63
- Georgia, 374–76
- Lithuania, 300–301
- New Thinking, 248
- Russian Federation, 248–56
- Russian public opinion on, 117–18
- Ukraine, 335–41
- Uzbekistan, 404–9, 410–11
- voting behavior and, 168

foreign trade
- Lithuania, 295, 298
- Russian Federation, 240–41
- Russian treatment of Jews and, 121*n*
- Ukraine, 335

formulation, in policymaking, 243

For Order and Justice coalition, 284*t*, 289–90

Fourth International, 27

Fradkov, Mikhail, 147, 148

France
- arms trade, 255
- dual executive system in, 140
- interest groups in, 209
- life expectancy, 256
- Muslim headscarf restrictions, 96

Frederick the Great, of Prussia, 40

freedom
- Freedom House ratings, 293*t*, 376, 400*n*, 414
- Heritage Foundation ratings, 240, 242
- of the press, 218
- religious, 121
- of serfs, 43*t*
- in Uzbekistan, 410

Freedom House, 293*n*, 341, 376, 400*n*, 414
- Uzbekistan and, 394, 396, 400

Freedom Movement party, Georgia, 362*t*

free market economy. *See* market economy

French Worker's Party, 20

Gaidar, Yegor, 192, 197, 198, 236, 237

Galbraith, John Kenneth, 235

Gamsakhurdia, Konstantine, 357*t*, 362*t*

Gamsakhurdia, Zviad, 346–47, 351, 352, 355, 359, 361, 366, 368

Gargarin, Yuri, 61

Gavrilova, Tamara, 218

gender. *See also* women
- roles, 224, 227, 228*t*
- voting behavior and, 157–58

General Secretary, Communist Party, 186, 420

Genghis Khan, 39, 380

George, Bruce, 203

Georgia, 79, 81, 250, 344–77
- Abkhazia and, 367–70
- Adjara and, 370–71
- comparative study of, 3*t*, 4
- economy, 371–74, 373*t*, 415
- ethnic Russians in, 83*t*
- European Union and, 374, 376
- foreign policy, 374–76
- future of, 376–77
- government institutions, 351–64
- gross national income, 2
- historical overview, 344–51

Georgia (*Continued*)
    independence of, 346, 363
    judicial system, 364–65
    map, 345*f*
    natural resources, 372
    parliamentary elections, 354–63
    political culture, 364–71
    political parties, 354–63
    population, 344
    presidential elections, 351–53, 413
    resistance to RSFSR by, 80
    Rose Revolution, 353, 358–60, 372*n*,
        376, 414
    Russian Federation and, 374–75
    South Ossetia and, 366–67
    sovereignty declared by, 65
    transition to democracy, 363
    United States and, 375
Georgian Communist Party, 346
Georgian Constituent Assembly, 345
Georgian Social Democratic Party, 346
Georgian Soviet Socialist Republic (SSR),
    346
German Social Democratic Party
    (Worker's Party), 20
German-Soviet Non-Aggression Pact.
    See Soviet-German Non-Aggression
    Pact
Germany
    distrust of political parties in, 204
    economic indicators, 241*t*
    ethnic composition, 74–75, 76*t*–77*t*
    exports to Russia, 240
    interest groups, 210
    life expectancy, 256
    Ostpolitik, 246
    radical socialism in, 23
    unification of, 15*n*
Giorgadze, Mamuka, 357*t*
Giorgadze, Igor, 370*n*
glasnost
    associational groups and, 211–12
    August 1991 coup and, 68
    defined, 64, 420
    dissolution of Soviet Union and, 270
    non-Russian national groups and, 84
    Russian nationalism and, 109–10
    Yakuts and, 94
Glazyev, Sergei, 139, 139*t*, 176*n*, 177*t*, 199,
    199*n*
Gogol, Nikolay, 45, 45*n*
Going to the People movement, 19
Gongadze, Heorhiy, 322

Goodman, William, 14
Gorbachev, Mikhail, 4, 31, 55, 63, 81, 143,
    265, 269*t*, 310*n*, 346, 347
    associational groups and, 211–12
    attempted coup against, 67–68, 67*t*, 84,
        127, 143, 221, 271, 417
    biography, 128*t*
    demokratizatsia and, 64
    election of, 67*t*, 127
    foreign policy, 252
    glasnost and, 64
    government structure changes under,
        126–27
    institutional changes made by, 123
    leadership of, 63–65
    Lithuania and, 267–68, 269*t*
    media under, 218
    military service under, 221
    nuclear weapons concerns, 247–48
    perestroika and, 64
    popular front organizations and, 191
    reforms under, 64–65, 114–15
    resignation of, 311
    social policy, 257
    Uzbekistan and, 384
    Yeltsin's criticism of, 66
Gorbachyk, Andriy, 330*n*, 337*n*
Gosplan (State Planning Commission),
    233, 420
government. *See also* state
    comparative approach to, 4–7
    defined, 420
    regulation, Stalin and, 57
    repression by, under Russian Empire,
        46, 185
government institutions, 123–52. *See also*
        judicial systems; parliamentary
        systems; presidential systems
    comparative study of, 5
    dual executive, 146–48
    in Georgia, 351–64
    judicial branch, 148–52
    legislative function, 129–31
    legislative structure, 127–29
    legitimacy of, 7
    members of parliament, 131–37
    parliamentary systems, 140
    presidential approaches, 142–46
    presidential system, 137–42
    in Soviet era, 123–27
    in Ukraine, 313–29
    in Uzbekistan, 385–91
Grachev, Pavel, 222*n*

grain purchases, from U.S., by Soviet Union, 242, 247
Great Britain, oligarchs and, 215
Great Patriotic War, 420. *See also* World War II
Great Purges, 57–58, 420
"Great Russian Chauvinism," 80
Great Silk Road trade, 380, 401
Greece, 255
Green Party (ZPU), Ukraine, 326, 361n
Gromov, Boris, 180
Gromyko, Andrei, 128t
gross domestic product (GDP)
    Lithuania, 295
    Russian Federation, 239, 240t
gross national income (GNI)
    country comparisons, 2
    Georgia, 372, 373t
    Ukraine, 332, 333t
gross national product (GNP), Georgia, 373t
Growth Competitiveness Index, World Economic Forum, 240, 242
Grozny, 99, 103n
Gryzlov, Boris, 199
Guinea, 246
Guinea-Bissau, 246
Gusinsky, Vladimir, 214, 218

Hague, Rod, 243
hajjes (pilgrimages to Mecca), 392, 420
hard-liners, 68
Harrop, Martin, 243
headscarves, worn by Muslim women, 96
health-care policy
    issues, 415
    in Lithuania, 302
    mandatory health insurance, 259
    physicians and, 259
    reforms, 259
    Russian Federation, 256–60
heart disease, in Russian Federation, 257
Hegel, Georg Wilhelm Friedrich, 15–16, 17
Helsinki Accords, 34
Heritage Foundation, Index of World Economic Freedom, 240, 242
Herzen, Alexander, 19
historical-cultural analysis, 9–10
historical materialism, 16
historical stage, 17, 420
Hitler, Adolf, 55n, 58
Hizbutt Takhrir, 393
Ho Chi Minh, 35

Homeland Union/Lithuanian Conservatives (HU/LC) party, 274, 277, 279, 285t, 289, 290–91, 292
homicide, in Lithuania, 302–3
hooliganism, 260
housing quality, 234
Hromada, Ukraine, 326
Hrytsenko, Anatoliy, 341
human rights
    evaluation of, 414
    in Georgia, 364
    organizations, 229
    U.S. and, 247
    in Uzbekistan, 385
Human Rights Watch, 394
Hungarian uprising (1956), 33, 60, 245
Hungary, 245, 252, 337
    radical socialism in, 23
    Soviet invasion of, 33, 60
Hussein, Saddam, 252, 339
hyperinflation
    in Lithuania, 295
    in Russian Federation, 237
    in Ukraine, 314, 334

identity effects, voting behavior and, 155, 158
ideology
    of Bolsheviks, 13
    defined, 421
    party, 191
    of political parties, 195
Ignalina nuclear power plant, 298n
Ilyukhin, Vitkor, 223
imagined communities, nations as, 86
Imaledino, Viktor, 222
impeachment
    attempted, of Yeltsin, 128, 144
    defined, 421
    in Georgia, 354
    of Paksas, 280, 292, 305
imperialism, Lenin's views on, 23
implementation, in policymaking, 243
incremental model, 232–33, 421
incumbents
    defined, 421
    in Lithuanian elections, 280, 290
    reelection success of, 136–37
    in regional elections, 180, 181
    in Ukrainian elections, 316
independence, defined, 85
Independent Miners' Union (NPG), 212

independents, political party participation by, 176
Independent Trade Union of Workers in Coal-Mining Industry (NPRUP), 212
Index of World Economic Freedom, Heritage Foundation, 240, 242
India, 255
    economic indicators, 241*t*
individualism, 113, 114
Individual Labor Activity, Law on, 64
Indochina, 246
Industrialists (Industry Will Save Georgia), 361
industrial workers. *See* labor
industriels, les, 14
industry
    denationalization of, 236
    following World War I, 52–53
    Marxism and, 14
    nationalization of, 17, 52
    privatization of, 237–39
    Stalin's program for, 55–56, 233, 236
    in Ukraine, 308, 334
    Uzbekistan, 383
Industry Will Save Georgia Bloc, 356, 357*t*, 358, 360*t*, 361, 362*t*
infant mortality rates, in Russia, 256
inflation. *See also* hyperinflation
    Russian Federation, 237, 240*t*
Information-Telegraph Agency of Russia–Telegraph Agency of the Soviet Union (ITAR–TASS), 218
Ingushetya, 98
initiation, in policymaking, 243
insider parties, 192, 421
intelligentsia
    defined, 421
    in Lithuania, 267
    under Russian Empire, 46
interest groups
    controlled systems, 210
    defined, 421
    in democracies, 208–10
    effectiveness of, 209
    future of, 229
    influence by, 209
    limited pluralistic system, 229
    media and, 218
    pluralistic systems, 209
    promotional, 208
    sectional, 208
Interior Ministry of the Russian Federation, 141, 220

Intermediate Nuclear Forces (INF) treaty, 65, 248
International Bank for Reconstruction and Development (IBRD), 404
international debt, Russian Federation, 237
International Election Observation Mission (IEOM), 175, 318
International Monetary Fund (IMF), 237, 375
    Georgia and, 358, 372, 375
    Ukraine and, 317
    Uzbekistan and, 404
International Working Men's Association (First International), 15
interpersonal trust, in democracy, 116
investments, 242
Ioseliana, Jaba, 347
Iran, arms exports to, 255–56
Iraq War, 251, 252
    Ukraine and, 339
Iron Curtain, 245
Iron Law of Wages, The (Ricardo), 14
Ishaev, Viktor, 181
Islam. *See also* Muslims
    Central Asian conflicts and, 380, 416
    militant, in Uzbekistan, 393–95, 399–401
Islamic Movement of Uzbekistan (IMU), 393–94, 399
Islamic Renaissance Party (IRP), 396
issue-voting model, 165
Italian Communist Party, 33
Italy, 240
Ivan III (the Great), 39, 40*n*, 42, 42*t*
Ivan IV (the Terrible), 40, 42, 42*t*
Ivanov, Igor, 248, 252, 374
Ivanov, Sergei, 141, 221–22, 253, 254
Ivashov, Leonid, 374

Jackson-Vanik amendment, 121*n*
Jadids' movement, 381
Japan, 241*t*
Jewish Autonomous Oblast (AO), 81, 121
Jewish people. *See also* anti-Semitism
    blamed for problems, 119, 121
    discrimination against, 119–22
    dissident movements, 121
    relaxation of emigration restrictions, 248
    Russian attitudes toward, 78
John Paul II, pope, 248
Johnson, Lyndon, 246

journalists, violence against, 322
judges, role of, 149–50
judicial reforms, 46, 150
judicial systems, 148–52
  Georgia, 363–64
  Lithuania, 292
  preliminary investigations, 149–50
  procurators, 149–50
  under Russian Empire, 46
  Ukraine, 322
  Uzbekistan, 390–91
"July Days" uprising, 44*t*
Jursenas, Ceslovas, 278*t*
Justice Social Democratic Party, 397*t*, 398

Kadets (Constitutional Democrats), 185
Kadyrov, Akhmed-hadji, 100, 101–2, 103,
  104
Kaledin, Alexei, 51
Kalingrad, 298
Kamenev, Lev, 50, 55, 57
Kampuchea, People's Republic of, 34
Karakalpak ASSR, 81, 382
Karakalpakstan Republic, 387, 390
Karimov, Islam, 384, 384*n*, 388–89,
  393–94, 396, 397, 398, 402, 409–10
Kasyanov, Mikhail, 147, 148, 196, 217,
  239*n*
Katkus, Valdemaras, 276
Kazakhstan, 65, 80, 81, 250, 392
  ethnic Russians in, 83*t*
Kennedy, John F., 246
Kerensky, Alexander, 44*t*, 50, 51, 185
KGB (Committee for State Security), 219
  Brezhnev and, 61–62
  Putin and, 145, 179
Khagan, 380
Khakamada, Irina Mutsuovna, 139*t*, 176
Kharitonov, Nikolai, 138, 139*t*
Khasbulatov, Ruslan, 66*n*, 69, 151
Khodorkovskii, Mikhail, 215, 217
khokim (administrative head),
  Uzbekistan, 386, 390
Kholodov, Dmitry, 223
Khorezm, 80, 381, 382
Khrushchev, Nikita, 7, 55, 335
  communism and, 36
  denunciation of Stalin by, 31–33, 60,
    113, 186
  economic policy, 234
  Georgia and, 346
  leadership of, 59–61, 125
  philosophy of, 31–33

Politburo and, 186
political culture and, 113
removed from office, 61
Secret Speech, 60, 113
space program and, 60–61
Uzbekistan and, 383
Kiev, 39
Kievan Patriarchate (UOC-KP), 313
Kievan Rus (Russia), 39–40, 42*t*, 309, 421
Kinakh, Anatoliy, 317*t*, 318, 327
Kiriyenko, Sergei, 97, 142, 197, 200, 213
Kitovani, Tengiz, 347
Klimov, Igor, 223
Kocherian, Robert, 250
Kochiev, Stanislaw, 367
Kokoity, Edward, 367
Kolakowski, Leszek, 29
Komsomol (All-Union Leninist
  Communist Youth League), 210, 211
Korean War, 245
korenizatsya policy, 382, 421
Kornilov, Lavr, 51
Kosovo, 253, 375
Kosygin, Aleksey, 61, 125
Kozyrev, Andrei, 69, 248
krais, 88
Kravchuk, Leonid, 68, 311, 312, 314, 322,
  324
Kremlin, 214*f*
Krupavicius, Algis, 303
Kubilius, Andrius, 274, 289, 290
Kucher, Stanislav, 254
Kuchma, Leonid, 250*n*, 314, 315–16, 317,
  319, 322, 326, 327, 328, 334, 335, 341
kulaks (peasants), 54, 142, 421
Kuwait, 255
Kyrgyz people, in Uzbekistan, 409
Kyrgyz province, 382
Kyrgyzstan, 80, 81, 250, 392, 409
  ethnic Russians in, 83*t*

labor. *See also* industry; proletariat; working class
  Bolsheviks and, 53
  distribution of proceeds from, 18
  exploitation of, 14, 16–17
  Marxist theory and, 16
  under Russian Empire, 46, 47
  as voluntary, under communism, 18
  workers' collectives, 30*n*
labor camps, 30, 58, 60, 219
labor organizations, 212–13, 227
labor protests, in Soviet Union, 212

Labor Ukraine, 327
labor (trade) unions
    Comintern and, 24
    ineffectiveness of, 212–13
    in Soviet Union, 210–11
Labourist Party of Georgia, 356, 357*t*, 358,
    360*t*, 362*t*
Labour Party (DP), Lithuania, 284*t*, 290,
    291
Lakhova, Yekaterina, 224, 225
land, privatization of, in Lithuania,
    294–95
Land Code, Ukraine, 334
land decree, following Russian
    Revolution, 50
Landsbergis, Vytautas, 267, 268, 274,
    276–79, 283
languages
    country comparisons, 3*t*
    Georgia, 346, 366
    Lithuania, 271, 273
    RSDLP policy on, 78
    South Ossetia separatist movement
        and, 366–67
    Tatars, 96
    Ukraine, 312, 313, 317, 330
    Uzbekistan, 379, 382, 384*n*
Laos, People's Democratic Republic of,
    34
Latin alphabet, 96, 384*n*
Latvia, 65, 75, 81, 253, 265, 271, 337
    comparative study of, 4
    ethnic Russians in, 83*t*
    independence of, 68, 268, 298
Lavrov, Sergei, 141, 248
law enforcement agencies, 262–63
lawmaking
    in Georgia, 354, 355
    in Lithuania, 281–82
    Russian Federation, 129–31
    in Ukraine, 323, 324–25
    in Uzbekistan, 386–87
Law of Dialectics, 17, 421
Law of Ukraine on Elections of People's
    Deputies of Ukraine, 324
Law on Elections of the President of
    Georgia, 351
Law on Freedom of Conscience and
    Religion, 121
Law on Individual Labor Activity, 64
Law on Religion, 248
Law on State Enterprise Cooperatives, 64

Law on the Initial Privatization of State
    Property of the Republic of
    Lithuania, 294
Law on the Press and Other Media, 218
Lazarenko, Pavlo, 326
leadership
    Brezhnev era issues, 63
    in democracy, 115
    Lithuanian independence movement,
        270–71
    of non-Russian nationality groups, 84
    personalization of, 116
    public opinion on, 116–17, 179*n*
    Russian (1990–2004), 149*t*
    Soviet Union administrative positions,
        125
League of Nations, 244
Lebed, Alexander, 137
Lebedev, Igor, 177*t*
Lebedev, Platon, 215
Left Communists, 30
Leftist Socialist Revolutionaries (Left SRs),
    50–52
Left Opposition, 55, 421
left-right ideological continuum, 421
legacies of the past, 7, 9
Legislative Chamber, Uzbekistan, 386–87
legislative institutions, Georgia, 354–63
    election results, 357*t*
    elections, 354–63
legislative institutions, Lithuania, 280–91
    election results, 284*t*–288*t*
    elections, 282–91
    legislative functions, 281–82
legislative institutions, Russian
    Federation
    comparative analysis, 131–37
    role and function of, 129–31
    structure of, 127–29
legislative institutions, Ukraine, 323–29
legitimacy
    defined, 7, 421
    of rule by Moscow, in Lithuania, 271
Lenin, Vladimir Ilyich, 7, 22*f*, 43*t*, 46, 51,
    53
    April Thesis, 49
    assassination attempts against, 52
    concessions to non-Russian peoples,
        80
    criticism of Stalin by, 31, 55
    cultural diversity policy, 78–79
    death of, 54

dictatorship of the proletariat and, 22–23
fear of opposition by, 55
function of communism for, 36
government structure and, 51
illustrative quotations from, 25*t*
incorporation of autonomous republics and, 80
influence of Marx on, 20–21
leadership of, 50
Lithuanian independence and, 266
military service and, 220
national self-determination policy, 79
political culture and, 112
premier position and, 125
revolution advocated by, 21–22
Russian nationalism and, 110
totalitarianism and, 29–31
union republics under, 270
Uzbekistan and, 382
Leningrad, 110
"Leningrad Group," oligarchs and, 217
Leninism
development of, 20–25
Marxism and, 24
origins of, 21
revolution advocated by, 21–22
Stalinism and, 29–31
Levada Center, Moscow, 117
Levitsky, Steven, 349
Lewis-Beck, Michael S., 159
Liberal Democratic Party (LDP), Lithuania, 278*t*, 279
Liberal Democratic Party of Russia (LDPR), 121, 174*t*, 175, 193*t*, 194
electoral performance of, 200, 202–3
history and politics of, 196–97
party identification with, 204
Zhirinovskii bloc, 201, 201*t*, 202
liberal party ideology, 191
Liberal Russia Party, 136
Liberal Union-Central Union party (LLC-LSC), 284*t*
life expectancy
in Lithuania, 302
in Russian Federation, 256
Ligachev, Yegor, 66, 268
Lijphart, Arend, 147
limited pluralistic interest group system, 229
Lindblom, Charles, 232
Linz, Juan, 115, 147, 413

Lisitsyn, Anatolii, 180, 181
Lithuania, 81, 253, 265–305, 337
agriculture, 299
banking crisis, 283, 289
budget deficit, 299
coalition government in, 279
comparative study of, 3*t*, 4
constitution, 266, 275, 302
crime, 302–3
currency, 299
democratization in, 303, 415
demographics, 301–2
dissident activity in, 266
economy, 294–99, 296*t*–297*t*
ethnic populations, 272–73
ethnic Russians in, 83*t*
European Union and, 279, 298, 299–300, 305, 415
exports, 298
foreign affairs, 300–301
future of, 303–5
geography, 265
government institutions, 275–93
gross national income, 2
health care, 302
history, 265–70
independence, 68, 266
independence declared (1918), 266
independence declared (1990), 65, 67*t*
independence movement (1988–1991), 270–72, 283
judicial branch, 292
language issues, 271, 273
legislative institutions, 280–91
life expectancy, 302
local government, 291–92
military services, 300–301
political culture, 272–73
political decentralization in, 272
political participation, 273–75, 293–94
political parties, 273–75, 305
population, 272–73
presidency, 275–80
prime minister, 291
religions in, 267, 271, 273
Russian energy resources and, 298
Russification of, 266
service sector, 299
social culture, 272–73
Soviet repression in, 266
trade balance, 295, 298
Lithuania, Grand Duchy of, 40, 265–66

Lithuania National Party "Young Lithuania" (LNPJL), 287*t*
Lithuania Union of Political Prisoners and Deportees (LPKTS), 287*t*
Lithuanian Centre Union (LCS), 286*t*, 289
Lithuanian Christian Democratic Party (LKDP), 286*t*
Lithuanian Christian Democratic Union (LKDS), 287*t*
Lithuanian Communist Party (LCP), 267, 268, 270–71, 276, 283
Lithuanian Homeland Union/ Conservative Party, 277, 279
Lithuanian Democratic Labour Party (LDLP), 276, 277, 283, 289
Lithuanian Liberal Union (LLS), 287*t*, 289
Lithuanian Liberty (Freedom) Union, 287*t*
Lithuanian Movement for Perestroika (Sajudis), 267, 268, 274, 276, 279, 282–83, 425
Lithuanian Peasants' Party (LVP), 287*t*
Lithuanian Russian Union, 289
Lithuanian Social Democratic Party (LSDP), 273–74, 278*t*, 286*t*, 289, 290
Lithuanian Supreme Soviet, 268
Lithuanian Women's Party, 287*t*
local government
    employees used in election campaigns, Ukraine, 317–18
    in Lithuania, 291–92
    in Uzbekistan, 390
Lockerbie, Brad, 159
lower-level government, territorial administration systems and, 87
Lozoraitis, Stasys, 276
Lukin, Vladimir, 196
Lussier, Danielle, 130–31
Luzhkov, Yuri, 180, 197, 198
Lvov, Georgii, 185
Lvov, Prince, 43*t*, 44*t*
Lytvyn, Volodymyr, 327, 327*t*
Lyubarev, Arkadii, 177

macroeconomic growth, in Russian Federation, 239–40
majority electoral systems, 171, 177, 421
Malaysia, 255
Malenkov, George, 60
Malyshkin, Oleg, 139*t*
Manchu dynasty, 43*t*
Manifesto of Equals (Marechal), 14
Mao Zedong, 35, 59, 60*n*, 246

Marechal, Sylvain, 14
market economy. *See also* economic policy
    characteristics of, 235
    five stages of transition to, 304–5
    in Lithuania, 303–5
    outcomes of market reform, 239–43
    public attitudes toward, 168, 304*f*
    Russian transition to, 236–39
Marx, Karl, 13, 43*t*
    biographical information, 15
    on class struggle, 17–19
    dictatorship of the proletariat and, 22
    influence on Lenin, 20–21
Marxism, 13, 14–19
    basic principles of, 15–19
    defined, 13, 14, 421
    growth in popularity of, 18–19
    industrialization and, 14
    Leninism and, 24
    militant, 18–19
    nationalities and, 85
    revisionists, 19
    Stalin's modifications of, 27–28
Marxism and the National Question (Stalin), 26
Marxist-Leninism, 24
    ideological functions of, 36–37
    Stalin and, 25, 26
Marxist Social Democratic Party, 344–45, 346
Maskhadov, Aslan, 99, 100, 100*n*, 101, 102*n*, 103–5
mass media. *See* media
Matvienko, Valentina, 181
media
    Lithuanian independence movement and, 270
    newspapers, 218, 322
    oligarch control of, 218
    regulation of, 218, 414
media coverage, of elections
    bias in, 139–40, 175, 180
    political parties and, 184
    regulations on, 179
    in Ukraine, 318, 319, 322
    United Russia and, 202
Medved, 198. *See also* Unity Party (*Yedinstvo*)
Medvedchuk, Viktor, 327*t*, 328
Mensheviks
    defined, 421
    establishment of, 21, 185, 189

Georgia and, 345
  revolutionary activities, 47
  Russian Revolution and, 50
Merkushkin, Nikolai, 202
Mikhail, Grand Duke, 43*t*
militant Marxists, 18–19
military-industrial complex, in Ukraine, 334
Military Revolutionary Committee of the Petrograd Soviet, 50
military services
  civilian service alternative, 254
  corruption in, 222–23
  drug trafficking by, 223
  Lithuania, 300–301
  necessity of, in class struggle, 18
  reform of, 254–55
  Russian Federation, 220–23, 227
  Soviet Union, 220–21
  Ukraine, 341
Miliukov, Paul, 185
Mill, John Stuart, 341–42
Miller, Arthur, 116
Milliy Tiklanish (Uzbekistan National Revival Democratic Party), 398
Ministry of Defense, 220
Ministry of Internal Affairs (MVD), 219, 220
minority groups. *See* ethnic groups
minority rights, 88, 115, 122
Mironov, Sergei, 128–29, 139*t*
Mirziyayev (Mirziyoev), Shavkat, 389
mixed electoral systems, 422
Mkhedrioni Warriors, 347
Moderate Conservative Union, Lithuania, 287*t*
moderate Marxists (revisionists), 19
Modern Christian Democratic Union (MCDS), 289
modernization. *See also* industry
  ethnic identity and, 85
Moldova, 70, 250, 253
  ethnic Russians in, 83*t*
Molotov, Vyacheslav, 60
Molotov-Ribbentrop nonaggression treaty, 58, 244, 266
Mongolian People's Republic, 34
Mongol invasion, of Central Asian republics, 380
Moroz, Oleksander, 317, 318, 325, 326
Moroz, Yuri, 329*t*
Moscow, 40, 239*n*

Moscow Center for the Study of the Problem of Disarmament, 255
Moscow Patriarchate, Ukrainian Orthodox, 313
Moser, Robert, 324*n*
Motherland National-Patriotic Union (Rodina), 139, 174*t*, 175, 176, 176*n*, 193*t*
  Communist Party and, 202
  electoral performance of, 203
  history and politics of, 199
Mozambique, 246
mujahideen, 103, 422
multilateral organizations, 250
multinational state
  defined, 422
  Russia as, 74–75
multiparty authoritarianism, in Uzbekistan, 396–97, 399–400
multiparty systems, 189
  defined, 422
  ideology and, 191
  in Uzbekistan, 396–97, 399–400
multipolarity, 248–49, 422
murder, 260
Muscovy, 39–40, 42*t*, 78, 422
Muslims, 61, 81. *See also* Islam
  in Abkhazia, 368
  in Chechnya, 70, 98, 99, 101
  in Dagestan, 99
  in Georgia, 366
  militants, in Uzbekistan, 393–95, 399–401
  Russian attitudes toward, 78, 95–96, 98–99
  socioeconomic conflict and, 416
  Tatars, 95–96
  in Uzbekistan, 379, 392–95, 399–401
Mutalov, Abdulhashim, 389
Mzhavanadze, Vasily, 346

Nagorno-Karabakh AO, 65, 81
Nakhichevan ASSR, 81
Napoleon, 41
Narodniki movement, 19–20, 20*n*, 422
Natelashvili, Shalva, 357*t*, 358, 360*t*, 370*n*
nation, defined, 422
national bank, Lenin's call for, 49
national character, 85
National Democratic Institute, 329
National Democratic Party, Georgia, 355–56, 357*t*, 359, 362*t*

"national deviations," in Ukraine, 310*n*
national front movements. *See also* popular front organizations
  in Lithuania, 270–71
nationalism
  anti-Russian, 81, 83
  breakup of Soviet Union and, 81–86
  defined, 85
  modernization process and, 85
  in Ukraine, 310–11
nationalist parties, Russia, 195
Nationalist Party, Soviet Union, 185
nationality groups
  defined, 85
  Marxist theory of, 85
  non-Russian, 26–27, 84, 109
  voting behavior and, 158–59
nationalization
  of industry, 17
  of land, 49
  renationalization, 218, 335, 372
National Movement (EM) Bloc, 349–50, 358, 359, 360, 360*t*
National Movement–Democratic Front (NMD), 358, 361, 362*t*
National Programme for the Adoption of the Acquis (NPAA), 299
national self-determination. *See* self-determination
National Union party, Lithuania, 286*t*
nations
  future of, Stalin's views on, 28*t*
  as imagined communities, 86
Near Abroad, 249–51, 422
Nemtsov, Boris, 176, 197
neo-institutional tradition, 7
Netherlands, 131, 240
New Democratic Party, Lithuania, 289
New Economic Policy (NEP), 24, 30
  Bolshevik concessions on, 80
  defined, 422
  goals of, 54
  Stalin's rejection of, 55
New Force, 197
New Rightist Bloc, Georgia, 359, 360*t*, 361, 362*t*
newspapers. *See also* media
  election coverage by, in Ukraine, 322
  oligarch-owned, 218
New Thinking, 248
New Union (Social Liberals) party, Lithuania, 278*t*, 287*t*, 289, 290, 291

Nicaragua, 246
Nicholas I, 42*t*, 44
Nicholas II, 43*t*, 46–47, 79, 185
  abdication of, 48–49
Nigeria, 75
  economic indicators, 241*t*
  ethnic groups, 76*t*–77*t*
Nikolayev, Mikhail, 94
Nixon, Richard M., 34, 246, 247*f*
no-confidence votes, Duma, 147
Nogaideli, Zurab, 351
nomenklatura system, 62, 188, 227
  associational groups and, 210
  defined, 422
  in Lithuania, 277
  oligarchs and, 213
  political culture and, 113
non-Russian nationality groups
  growth of, 84
  Stalin's oppression of, 109
  in USSR, rights of, 26–27
North Atlantic Treaty Organization (NATO)
  establishment of, 245
  Georgia and, 356, 362, 374, 375
  Lithuania and, 272, 300–301
  NATO-Russia Permanent Joint Council, 253
  Partnership for Peace (PFP) program, 404
  Russian Federation and, 252–54
  Soviet Union and, 252
  Ukraine and, 315, 317, 338–39, 341
  Uzbekistan and, 407
North Korea, 245
Norway, 131
novoe myshlenie (new thinking), 64, 422
NTV, 218
Nuclear Nonproliferation Treaty, 34
nuclear power
  Chernobyl disaster, 310, 422
  in Lithuania, 298
nuclear war, peaceful coexistence and, 32
nuclear weapons
  agreements, 65, 246–47, 253–54, 255
  Gorbachev's concerns about, 247–48
Nurgaliev, Rashid, 141

oblasts, 75
  defined, 81, 423
  Russian federalism and, 88
  in Ukraine, 313

occupational status, voting behavior and, 158

October Manifesto, 43*t*, 47, 423

Octobrists, 185

Office of Democratic Institutions and Human Rights (ODIHR), 348*n*

oil resources
in Brezhnev era, 63
economic growth and, 240
Lithuania and, 298
pipeline, Georgia, 372, 375

Okhrana (tsar's secret police), 48

okrugs
central government powers over, 90–91
defined, 423
listing and data on, 90*t*
procurators in, 91
Russian federalism and, 88

oligarchic empires, 244

oligarchs
defined, 423
influence of, 227
media and, 218
privatization and, 213–18, 238
prosecution of, 214–15
public opinion on, 215, 216*f*
Putin's repression of, 8, 217–18
in Ukraine, 315, 328

Oliy Majlis (Uzbekistan parliament), 386–88, 389, 391
elections, 395–401

"one-and-a-half-party" system, 203

opposition parties. *See also* political opposition
in Georgia, 359–62
in Uzbekistan, 396, 400, 410

Orange Revolution, 4, 280, 318, 319, 331–32, 341, 342, 414

Organization for Security and Cooperation in Europe (OSCE), 203, 318, 348*n*, 349, 367, 399, 404

Organization of Petroleum Exporting Countries (OPEC), 249

organized crime
in Lithuania, 302
in Russia, 262

Orthodox Church. *See also* Russian Orthodox Church
in Ukraine, 312–13
in Uzbekistan, 393

Ossetians, 365, 366–67

Ostpolitik, Germany, 246

Our Home is Russia (NDR), 193*t*, 200, 201*t*

Our Ukraine party, 313*t*, 316, 327, 328, 329, 330

Ouspaskitch, Viktor, 290

outsider parties, 192, 194, 423

Pachulia, Merab, 349*n*

Paksas, Rolandas, 289, 290, 291, 292
election of, 278*t*, 279
impeachment of, 280, 292, 305

Pamfilova, Ella, 225

Pamyat, 109

Pankisi Gorge region, 374, 375, 377

Parliamentary Assembly of the Council of Europe (PACE), 329

Parliamentary Faction of the Citizens' Union (CUG), 354

parliamentary systems
comparative analysis, 131–37
defined, 140, 423
Georgia, 351, 354–63
political parties and, 172–78
presidential systems compared to, 140
reelection of incumbents, 136–37
reelection rates, 136–37
Russian Federation, 127–37
Ukraine, 313–14
Uzbekistan, 395–401
women in, 132*t*–136*t*

participation. *See* political participation

partiinost (party mindedness), 23, 423

Partnership for Peace (PFP), 338

party identification
defined, 423
limited applicability of, 204

party-list voting systems, 171, 197, 200
defined, 423
in Georgia, 348, 356
in Lithuania, 292
in Ukraine, 324, 326
women's seats, 225

Party of Industrialists and Entrepreneurs of Ukraine, 317*t*, 327

Party of National Rebirth, 199

party of power, 423

Party of Regions, Ukraine, 327

Party of Russian Regions, 199, 200, 201

party unity resolution, 53

Pasha, Enver, 80

Patiashvili, Jumber, 346, 348, 352, 352*n*, 353, 362*t*

patriarchal system, 224, 227, 423
Patrushev, Nikolai, 141, 220
Patten, Chris, 376
Paulauskas, Arturas, 277, 280, 301
Pavlychko, Solomea, 226
peace decree, Russian Revolution, 50
peaceful coexistence doctrine, 245
    defined, 423
    Khrushchev and, 32–33
Peasant Party, Ukraine, 325
Peasant People's Party, Lithuania, 274
peasants
    communes (*mir*), 45, 48
    land ownership by, 48
    under Russian Empire, 45, 46
    uprisings, repression of, 53
People's Commission for Internal Affairs
    (NKVD), 219
People's Democratic Party (PDP),
    Ukraine, 325, 326, 327
People's Deputy Group, 173, 200, 201
People's Party, Didgori Bloc, Georgia, 357t
People's Party of the Russian Federation
    (NPRF), 174t, 176n, 193t
People's Will party (*Narodina Volya*),
    19, 199
perestroika, 64, 66, 68, 128t
    Abkhazia and, 368
    defined, 423
    dissolution of Soviet Union and, 270
    economic growth and, 236
    Jews and, 121
    Lithuania and, 267
    nostalgia for Soviet system prior to, 116
    popular front organizations and,
        191–92
    Russian nationalism and, 109
    Uzbekistan and, 384
"permanent revolution," 20n
personal characteristics, voting behavior
    and, 155–58
personalization of political leadership,
    116
Peter I, 42, 42t
Peter III, 40
Peter the Great, 40, 78, 110
Petrograd, street demonstration, 49f
Petrograd Military Revolutionary
    Committee, 52
Petrograd Soviet of Peoples' Deputies, 49
Petrov, Nikolai, 181
physicians, 259

Plato, 13
Plekhanov, Georgi V., 20, 43t
pluralistic interest group systems, 209
plurality electoral systems, 171, 177, 423
Pochinok, Aleksandr, 254
Podgorny, Nikolay, 61
pogroms
    defined, 423
    against Jews, 120, 121
Poland, 245, 252, 337
    Lithuania and, 266
police, 219, 260
policy discourse, 233, 423
policymaking process, 232–33
    analytical stages of, 243–44
    incremental model of, 232–33
    rational model of, 232
Polish minority, in Lithuania, 273
Politburo, Communist Party, 54, 128t, 381
    defined, 424
    functions of, 186
political activism
    belief in efficacy of, 229
    measurement of, 162t
political apathy, 423
Political Bureau, Central Committee,
    of Bolshevik Party. *See* Politburo,
    Communist Party
political change, 413–16
political culture
    anti-Semitism and, 119–22
    authoritarianism and, 112
    Brezhnev and, 113
    communism and, 114
    defined, 112
    democracy and, 115–16
    elitist, 113
    in Georgia, 364–71
    historical factors affecting, 112–14
    Khrushchev and, 113
    proletarian, 112
    Russian and Soviet, 112–14
    Russian nationalism and, 108–11
    Russian themes, 116–19
    socialism and, 114
    in Ukraine, 312–13, 334–35
    in Uzbekistan, 391–95
political efficacy
    defined, 423
    in democracy, 116
    political activism and, 229
    voting behavior and, 159, 163, 174–75

political knowledge, political participation and, 160–61, 162*t*
political opposition, 163–71
  defined, 163, 424
  in Georgia, 358–62
  suppression of, 413, 414
  in Uzbekistan, 396, 400, 410
political participation
  conventional-legal participation, 154, 160–61, 182, 419
  defined, 154, 160, 424
  electoral systems, 171–72
  forms of, 154
  government-legal, 160–61
  in Lithuania, 293–94
  parliamentary elections, 172–78
  political opposition, 163–71
  presidential elections, 178–79
  regional elections, 180–81
  Russian public opinion on, 116–17
  in Ukraine, 330–32
  violent, 154, 427
  voting, 154–59
  of women, 224–26
political parties, 184–206. *See also* factions
  categorization of, 188–89, 192, 194–95
  coalitions, in Lithuania, 274
  comparative study of, 5
  defined, 184
  direct power of, 190
  distrust of, 204
  election rules and, 363
  electoral performance of, 199–202
  emergence of, in Russia, 191–92
  European ideologies, 191
  factions, 424
  functions of, 184, 190, 204–5
  future of, 205–6
  in Georgia, 354–63
  goals of, 189–90
  ideological orientation of, 191, 194–95
  independents, participation in, 176
  indirect power of, 190
  insider, 192, 421
  legality of, 188
  legislation strengthening, 205
  in Lithuania, 273–80, 282–91, 305
  major Russian parties, 192–99
  multiparty systems, 189
  nationalist, 195
  one-party system, in USSR, 184–88
  opposition parties, in Georgia, 359–62

outsider, 192, 194, 423
  in parliamentary elections, 172–78
  party identification issues, 204
  in proportional representation voting systems, 171–72
  repression of, during Russian Empire, 185
  single-party systems, 188–89
  superpresidentialism and, 205
  transition to democracy and, 202–6
  two-party systems, 189
  in Ukraine, 324–30
  in Uzbekistan, 395–401
  as vehicles for individual office seekers, 194, 195
  Yeltsin's restrictions on, 69
political policy, country comparisons, 2
political trust, in democracy, 116
political values, voting behavior and, 155, 159
politics, defined, 424
Polokhalo, Volodymyr, 342
popular front organizations, 67*t*
  defined, 424
  in Lithuania, 267, 270–71
  role of, 191–92
population
  Chechnya, 98
  country comparisons, 3*t*
  declines, 415
  ethnic Russians, 74–75, 76*t*–77*t*, 81, 110
  Georgia, 344
  growth, under Russian Empire, 47
  Lithuania, 272–73
  Russian Federation, 257, 260
  Soviet Union, 81
  Ukraine, 308, 312–13
  urban areas, under Russian Empire, 47
post-Soviet transition
  to democracy, 7–9, 72
  democratization and, 7–9
  elections and, 413
  ethnic conflict and, 415–16
  in Georgia, 363
  market economy, 236–39, 304–5
  political parties and, 202–6
  in Russian Federation, 69–72
  transitional regimes, 6
  in Ukraine, 332–35
poverty
  among women, 224
  in Uzbekistan, 402–3

Powell, Colin, 252
premier, Soviet Union, 125
president, Georgia, 351–53
president, Lithuania, 275–80
  powers of, 275–76, 283
  prime minister and, 280
president, Russian Federation, 137–48
  administration staff, 142
  creation of, 64–65, 66, 137
  Duma and, 203
  envoys, 142
  ministries, 141–42
  policymaking model, 243–44
  powers of, 127, 140–42, 205
  prime minister and, 140, 146
  public opinion and, 141
president, Ukraine
  elections, 314, 315–22
  powers of, 314–15
president, Uzbekistan, 388–89
  election of, 388–89
  powers of, 388
presidential elections, Georgia, 351–53
  nominations, 352n
presidential elections, Lithuania,
    276–80
  turnout, 276, 279, 293
presidential elections, Russian
    Federation, 178–79
  campaign funding, 179
  constitutional requirements, 178
  1991 elections, 137, 178
  1996 elections, 137, 138, 178
  2000 elections, 137–38, 138t, 155–59,
    157t, 163–70
  2004 elections, 138–40, 139t
presidential elections, Ukraine, 315–22,
    341–42
  election violations, 319
  fairness monitoring, 318
  results, 317t, 320t–321t
presidential systems
  authority of, 140–42
  country comparisons, 2
  defined, 140, 424
  democratic accountability and, 9
  efficiency of, 147
  fundamental deficiencies in, 147
  parliamentary systems compared
    to, 140
  superpresidentialism, 141
  unlimited presidential executive, 141

Presidium, Soviet Union
  leadership of, 127
  powers of, 125
pressure groups. *See also* associational
    groups; interest groups
  defined, 421
  in democracies, 208–9
preterm elections, in Lithuania, 282
price controls, 236–37
price liberalization, 424
Primakov, Yevgenii, 178n, 192, 197,
    198, 200, 220n, 248
primary party organization (PPO),
    187–88, 424
prime minister, Lithuania, 280, 291
prime minister, Russian Federation
  decisionmaking by, 244
  in dual executive system, 140
  function of, 146–48
prime minister, Soviet Union, 125
Principles of Leninism (Stalin), 26
prison camps. *See* labor camps
private property, aggrandizement of, 14
privatization
  corruption and, 238–39, 283, 334
  defined, 424
  economic policy, 236
  in Georgia, 353, 372
  in Lithuania, 283, 294–95
  oligarchs and, 213–18
  reasons for, 237
  redistribution of wealth and, 199
  in Ukraine, 324, 334–35
  vouchers, 237–38
  Yeltsin and, 71
Procurator General, 150
procurators, 91, 149–50, 424
procurator's office, Georgia, 364
procurator's office, Lithuania, 292
professional revolutionaries, 21, 25t
profits, as surplus value, 17
Progressists, 185
Progressive Party of Ukraine, 317t
Progressive Socialists, Ukraine, 325
proletariat. *See also* working class
  agrarian, 21
  defined, 16, 424
  dictatorship of, 22–23
  expected overthrow of capitalism by, 17
  political culture and, 112
promotional interest groups, 208
Pronin, Vladimir, 136

propaganda
  in one-party systems, 188–89
  by political parties, 190
Pro-Patria Union-Conservatives (TS-LK),
    290
property crimes, 260
proportional representation (PR) voting
    systems, 171–72, 173, 177, 189, 197,
    200
  defined, 424
  in Georgia, 345–46, 355
  in Lithuania, 281
  in Ukraine, 324
  women's seats, 225
protest activities
  by interest groups, 209
  samizdat (underground publications),
    267
  in Uzbekistan, 403–4
Provisional Government, 48–50, 185
Prunskiene, Kazimira, 278t, 280, 290
Prussia, 15n
public opinion
  on democratic values, 116–18, 119t,
    179t
  on foreign relations, 118–19
  on leadership, 117–18
  on oligarchs, 215, 216f
  on participation, 117–18
  presidential authority and, 141
  on Russian Federation, 117–19
  on security, 118, 120t
  on territorial integrity, 118–19
  on Yeltsin, 118–19
Public Russian Television (ORT), 218
purges
  Great Purges, 57–58, 420
  Stalin and, 29, 30
  in Uzbekistan, 382–83
Pushkin, Aleksandr, 45
Putin, Vladimir, 8f, 9, 99, 123, 129, 138t,
    139t, 175, 301, 322, 416
  accomplishments of, 72
  anti-oligarch campaign, 215, 217
  ascension of, 70–72
  biography, 71, 144–45
  Chechnya and, 100, 104, 179
  election of, 137–40, 149t, 163–70, 178,
    179, 214
  envoys to federal districts, 90
  foreign policy, 248–49, 253
  KGB experience, 145, 179, 219

leadership skills, 145
legislative activity and, 130–31
Liberal Democratic Party of Russia
    (LDPR) and, 194
media and, 218
military service and, 221–22, 254–55
policymaking issues, 232, 244
political parties and, 205
presidency of, 144–46
presidential system and, 141
public approval of, 117, 139, 145–46,
    146t, 148, 179, 215
regional appointments by, 181
regional autonomy issues, 97
regional consolidation legislation,
    91
regional elections and, 180
Russian federalism under, 87, 88, 90,
    105
security functions under, 220
State Council created by, 142
support for ethnic Russians by, 257
support for rights of Jews by, 122
2003 Duma elections and, 177
United Russia and, 190, 198, 199, 201,
    202, 203
Unity party and, 198, 200
U.S. relations and, 251–52
Uzbekistan and, 407
women's organizations and, 225
Yabloko and, 196

Questions on Leninism (Stalin), 26

raion (rayon)
  courts, 151
  defined, 424
  in Lithuania, 292
Rashidov, Sharaf, 383
rational model, 232, 425
Reagan, Ronald, 248
Red Army, 3, 52, 55, 220–21, 346
  defined, 425
  Lithuania and, 266
Reds (Bolsheviks), 44t
referendum, 425
reformers (democrats), following breakup
    of Soviet Union, 68
refugees
  Chechen, 102
  Georgia, 348, 367
regional and city courts, Georgia, 364

regional elections, 180–81
central control of, 180
control of outcomes of, 203–4
disqualifications of candidates, 180
incumbents in, 180, 181
replaced by appointment system, 180–81
regional governors, 203–4
Reisinger, William, 116
Rekhviashvili, Irakli, 371
religion. *See also* Jewish people; Muslims
country comparisons, 3*t*
in Georgia, 366
in Lithuania, 267, 271, 273, 283
Roman Catholic Church, 267, 273, 283
in Ukraine, 312–13
in Uzbekistan, 392–93
religious discrimination. *See also* anti-Semitism
against Jewish people, 119–22
against Muslims, 95–96
religious freedom, 121
religious lands (*vakuf*), 80
religious schools (*medresse* and *mektebe*), 80
Remington, Thomas, 194, 212–13
renationalization
in Georgia, 372
repression of oligarchs and, 217–18
in Ukraine, 335
repatriation, 425
repression
by Bolsheviks, 52–53, 79–80
by Communist Party of Russia, 53
in Georgia, 346
in Lithuania, 266
of oligarchs, 8, 217–18
in one-party systems, 189
of peasants, 53
of political parties, 185
in Russian Empire, 46
by Stalin, 55, 57–58
reprivatization
in Georgia, 371
in Ukraine, 335
Republican Party, Georgia, 359, 361
revisionists, 425
revivalists, Russian nationalism, 110
Revival of Georgia Bloc, 348, 348*n*, 352, 352*n*, 356, 357*t*, 358, 361

revolution
agrarian, 21
establishment of communism through, 35–36
Lenin's advocacy of, 21, 25*t*
moderate and radical approach to, 23–24
professional leadership of, 21, 25*t*
"socialism in one country" and, 27
worldwide, advocacy of, 23–24, 27, 51
revolutionaries, elite party of, 21, 25*t*
RIA-Novosti, 218
Ricardo, David, 14
Rightist Opposition Bloc, Georgia, 361, 362*t*
right of legislative initiative
defined, 425
in Lithuania, 282
Rodina (Motherland) Party. *See* Motherland National-Patriotic Union (Rodina)
Rodionov, Denis, 238
Rogozin, Dmitri, 176*n*, 199
Roman Catholic Church, in Lithuania, 267, 273, 283
Romania, 245, 253
Romanov, Mikhail, 40, 42*t*
Romanov dynasty, 42*t*
Roosevelt, Franklin D., 59, 245
Rose Revolution, 353, 358–59, 360, 372*n*, 376, 414
Round Table Bloc, Georgia, 346, 356
Rousseau, Jean-Jacques, 13–14
RSFSR Congress of People's Deputies. *See* Congress of People's Deputies
RTR (Russian Television and Radio), 218
RTV, 238
Rukh party, Ukraine, 327
Russian American Company, 41
Russian Armed Forces, 221
Russian Congress of People's Deputies, 127–28, 147–48
Russian Constitutional Court, 90, 91–92
Chechnya constitution and, 100
Russian Empire
annexation of Lithuania by, 266
anti-Semitism in, 119–20
collapse of, 48
cultural diversity, 75, 78
establishment of, 40
Georgia and, 344
historical background, 39–44

intolerance of diverse cultures, 78
Napoleon's invasion of, 41
origins of, 39–40
repression of political parties under, 185
Russian Revolution (1905) and, 46–48
Russian Revolution (1917) and, 48–50
territorial expansion under, 40–41, 44, 75, 78
Tsarism, 44–46
Russian Federation (RF)
  administrative divisions (map), 89*f*
  alcohol abuse, 256, 257–58
  alcohol consumption, 62, 256, 257–58
  arms exports, 255–56
  associational groups, 208–30
  business organizations, 213
  characteristics of, 108–9
  Chechnya and, 93, 97–105
  China relations, 249
  Commonwealth of Independent States and, 249–51
  comparative study of, 3*t*
  constitution, 128
  court system, 150
  crime, 260–62
  cultural diversity, 75, 76
  democratic experience, 8
  distrust of political parties in, 204
  drug use, 262
  economic indicators, 241*t*
  economic policy, 236–43
  ethnic conflicts and, 366
  ethnic groups, 74–75, 76*t*–77*t*
  European community and, 165–68
  Federal Districts (okrugs), 90*t*
  federal system, 75, 87
  foreign policy, 244–56
  Georgia and, 374–75
  government structure, 129*f*
  gross domestic product, 239, 240*t*
  gross national income, 2
  health care, 256–60
  heterogeneity of, 74
  inflation, 240*t*
  international debt, 237
  labor organizations, 212–13
  military services, 220–23, 254–55
  as multinational state, 74
  NATO and, 252–54
  oligarchs, 213–18
  parliamentary elections, 155–59, 156*t*, 172–78, 199–202
  parliamentary system, 127–37

political parties, 184–206
population, 257, 260
post-Soviet transition, 69–72
presidential system, 137–48
privatization laws, 236
regional consolidation, 91
Russian public opinion on, 116–19
security agencies, 219–20
socialist movement origins in, 19–20
South Ossetia and, 367–68
Tatarstan and, 95–97
tobacco use, 257
Ukraine and, 314, 315, 316, 329, 335–36, 338
United States and, 251–52
Uzbekistan and, 404, 408
Western aid to, 237, 251
women's roles in, 224–27
world image of, voting and, 165
Yakuts and, 93–95
Russian Federation Treaty, 95–97
Russian-Georgian Friendship Treaty, 369
Russian Health Ministry, 260
Russian identity
  nationalism and, 110–11
  Putin and, 122
  in Soviet Union period, 109
Russian nationalism, 108
  grievances of, 110
  perestroika and, 109
  Russian identity and, 110–11
  types of, 110–11
  Yeltsin and, 110
Russian Orthodox Church, 44, 110*f*
  in Lithuania, 273
  political culture and, 119
  under Russian Empire, 45
  Russian Revolution and, 50–51
Russian Party of Pensioners and Party of Social Justice, 174*t*
Russian political culture, 108–22
  anti-Semitism, 119–22
  democratic ideas and, 114–16
  history of, 111–14
  nationalism, 108–11
  themes, 116–19
Russian Revolution (1905), 46–48
Russian Revolution (1917), 43*t*–44*t*, 48–50
  cultural change and, 108
  democratic failures following, 51–54
  government restructuring after, 50–51
  Russian nationalism and, 110
  totalitarianism and, 31

Russian Social Democratic Labor Party
(RSDLP or Worker's Party), 24, 55,
185, 395
cultural diversity policy, 78–79
division of, 21, 185, 189
First Party Congress, 20
name change to Communist Party,
186*n*
Second Congress, 21
Russian socialist ideology, 13–37
Russian Soviet Federated Socialist
Republic (RSFSR), 66, 381
administrative status of, 81
Communist Party, 110
creation of position of president by, 137
treaties with conquered territories, 79
Russian State Corporation for Export and
Import of Armaments
(Rosoboronexport), 255
Russian Television and Radio (RTR), 218
Russian-Ukrainian Friendship Treaty, 335
Russian Union of Industrialists and
Entrepreneurs (RUIE), 213, 217
Russian Union party, Lithuania, 287*t*
Russia's Democratic Choice, 194, 197
Russification, 78
defined, 425
ethnic conflict and, 86
in Georgia, 366
of Lithuania, 266
Orthodox Church and, 312
in Ukraine, 312, 333
Russo-centric, 79, 425
Russo-Japanese War, 41, 43*t*
Rustamov, Asliddin, 397
Rybkyn, Ivan, 130
Ryzhkov, Nikolai, 137
Ryzhkov, Vladimir, 181
Ryzhuk, Serhiy, 335

Saakashvili, Mikhail, 358, 360*t*, 414
Abkhazian separatist movement
and, 370
Adjara and, 371
economic policy, 372
European Union and, 376
hostility to opposition parties, 363
as president, 350–51, 360–61
Rose Revolution and, 349–50, 359–60
Russia and, 374
South Ossetia and, 367
timeline, 354*t*

Saint-Simon, Henri de, 14
Sajudis (Lithuanian Movement for
Perestroika), 267, 268, 274, 276, 279,
282–83, 293
defined, 425
Sakha Republic (Yakutia), 93–95
collectivization effects, 93–94
economic issues, 92, 94
geography of, 93
glasnost and, 94
relations with Russia, 93–95
Sakharov, Andrei, 61, 64
Sakwa, Richard, 110, 204
Salikh, Mohammed, 388
SALT (Strategic Arms Limitation Treaties),
34, 246, 247
Sambo (Self-Defense Without Weapons),
145*n*
samizdat (underground publications),
267, 425
samogon (home-brewed liquor), 257
Sarishvili-Chanturia, Irina, 357*t*
Sarkozy, Nicolas, 96
Sartori, Giovanni, 147
Saudi Arabia, 249
Sberbank, 238
scientific socialism, 15, 16*n*
secession rights, for USSR union
republics, 80
Second All-Russian Congress of Soviets,
50, 51
Second All-Union Party Congress, 80
"second economy," 234–35
Second International (Socialist
International), 15, 24
second-round runoff elections, 425
Second World, 6
Secretariat of the Communist Party, 186,
425
secret police, 30
Cheka (Russian), 52, 219
KGB, 61–62, 145, 179, 219–20
tsar's (Okhrana), 48
sectional interest groups, 208
secular country
defined, 425
Uzbekistan as, 393
security
Brezhnev and, 219
public opinion on, 118, 119*t*
Putin and, 220
Russian Federation agencies, 219–20

Russian public opinion on, 118, 119*t*
under Soviet system, 113
Security Council, 142
Seimas (Lithuanian parliament), 275, 276, 280–91
defined, 425
elections, 282–91, 300*t*
European Union and, 299
lawmaking process, 281–82
powers of, 281
Seleznev, Gennadii, 130, 203
Self-Defense Without Weapons (Sambo), 145*n*
self-determination
Bolsheviks and, 50, 53, 79
defined, 425
for minority nationalities, 270
for oppressed nationalities, 50, 53
RSDLP policy on, 78
as step toward socialist unity, 79
Self-Sacrifice National Democratic Party, 397*t*, 398
Senate, Georgia, 354
Senate, Uzbekistan, 386–87
separation of church and state, 50–51
separation of powers, 150, 425
separatist movements, goals of, 86
September 11, 2001, terrorist attacks, 1, 253
Serenas, Vytautas, 278*t*
serfs, freedom of, 43*t*, 45, 46
Sergeev, Igor, 222
service sector, Lithuania, 299
sex-role stratification, 224, 227, 228*t*
Shabanov, Aleksandr, 375
Shaimiev, Mintimer, 192, 198
Shaimiev, Sharipovich, 97, 181
Shanghai Cooperation Organization (SCO), 407
Shanghai Group, 249
Shaybaniy Khan, Muhammad, 380
Shcherbitsky, Volodymyr, 310, 310*n*
Shelest, Petro, 310*n*
Shevardnadze, Edward, 4, 269*t*, 347, 348, 354*t*, 357*t*, 360*t*, 370, 377
Abkhazian separatist movement and, 368, 369
campaign for reelection (2000), 353
as de-facto leader of Georgia, 347, 352
elected president, 348, 352
as foreign minister of USSR, 209*t*, 346
as Georgian Communist First Party Secretary, 346

hostility to opposition parties, 363
opposition to, 349–50, 358, 361–62
reelection, 348–49, 352
resignation, 280
Rose Revolution and, 349–50, 353, 360
timeline, 350*t*
U.S. and, 375
shipbuilding industry, in Ukraine, 334
Shkidchenko, Volodymyr, 341
shock therapy, 237, 425
Shoigu, Sergei, 142, 192, 198, 199
show trials, 30
Shtyrov, Vyacheslav A., 94
Shugart, Matthew Soberg, 147
Shushkevich, Stanislau, 68, 311
Siberia
deportation to, 98, 109
territorial expansion into, 78
single-member district (SMD) voting systems, 126, 171, 172–75, 189, 200
defined, 426
in Lithuania, 281
in Ukraine, 324, 325
women's seats, 225
single-party systems
defined, 188–89, 426
in Soviet Union, 184–88
Sino-Soviet relations, 246, 248
Slavic, defined, 39*n*
Slavic republics, 81
Slavophiles, political culture and, 114
Slezevicius, Adolfas, 276
Slovakia, 253, 337
Slovenia, 253, 337
small businesses, in Russian Federation, 239
Smith, Adam, 14
Smith, Graham, 86
Social Democratic Coalition, Lithuania, 274, 285*t*, 289, 291
Social Democratic party ideology, 191
Social-Democratic Party of Ukraine-United (SDPU-O), 327, 327*t*, 328, 329
socialism, 13–37
defined, 13, 426
economy, characteristics of, 235
failure to achieve goals of, 114
Marxism, 13, 14–19
in one country, 27
origins of, 13–14, 19–20
in Russia, 19–20
Socialist International, 15

Socialist Party of Georgia, 352*n*, 358, 359
Socialist Party of Ukraine, 317*t*, 325, 327*t*, 328, 329
"socialist realism," 57
Socialist Revolutionary Party (SR), 20*n*, 50, 51, 185
Socialist Unified Party of Russia, 199
social policy, 232
societal transformation, Stalin's program for, 57
socioeconomic status
  political participation and, 161
  voting behavior and, 157, 158
Solana, Javier, 376
Solikh, Mukhammad, 395–96
Solzhenitsyn, Alexander, 61
Somalia, 246
South Africa, 260
South Korea, 245
South Ossetia, 347, 348, 355, 366–67, 377
  separatism movement, 366–67
sovereignty, defined, 426
Soviet-German Non-Aggression Pact, 58, 244, 266, 309, 426
Sovietization
  defined, 426
  in Lithuania, 266
Soviet Military Revolutionary Committee, 55
Soviet of Workers' Deputies, 47
soviets (government councils)
  defined, 47, 51, 426
  establishment of, 47
  female representation in, 224
Soviet Socialist Republics (SSRs), 80–81
Soviet Union
  associational groups in, 210–11
  capitalist encirclement of, 27
  China and, 246, 248
  Cold War and, 1, 59, 244–47
  constitutions, 80, 123–27
  cultural diversity, 75, 78
  Czechoslovakia and, 33
  dissolution of, 67*t*, 68, 81–86, 110, 127, 143, 270, 415
  Eastern Europe and, 245
  economic planning in, 233–35
  establishment of, 26–27, 50–51, 80, 346
  federalism under, 80–81
  as federal system of government, 87
  Georgia and, 346
  government structures and functions, 123–27

Hungary and, 33, 60
labor unions, 212
Lithuania and, 266
military service, 220–21
nationalism and, 81–86
NATO and, 252
nostalgia for, 116, 117*t*
oil resources, 298
one-party system in, 184–88
political culture, 111–14
population diversity, 81
right of secession of union republics, 80
security under, 113
"socialism in one country" doctrine and, 27
Supreme Soviet elections, 124–25
territorial expansion of, 41–42
totalitarian legacy of, 192
trade unions in, 210–11
U.S. grain purchases by, 242, 247
wars of national liberation and, 32
women's roles in, 224–25, 226
sovnarkhozy (Economic Councils), 60
Sovnarkom (Council of People's Commissars), 50, 54
  defined, 426
space program, 60–61
SSRs (Soviet Socialist Republics), 80–81
Stalin, Joseph, 6, 26–28, 54–58
  attack on "backwardness" by, 55–57
  autonomous republics and, 80
  biography, 26, 54
  Commissariat of State Security (NKGB) under, 219
  cult of personality, 31, 57
  deportation of Chechens to Siberia by, 98
  Eastern Europe and, 245
  economic policy, 233, 236
  Georgia and, 346
  illustrative quotations, 28*t*
  KGB under, 219
  Khrushchev's denunciation of, 31–32, 60, 113
  Lenin's criticism of, 31, 54
  modification of doctrine by, 27–28
  nostalgia for, 116, 117*t*
  opposition to, 55
  oppression of non-Russian nationality groups by, 109, 382–83
  persecution of Jews by, 120–21
  personal responsibility for totalitarianism, 29–31

political culture and, 112–13
power held by, 54, 55
purges, 29, 30, 57–58, 382–83
repression of opposition by, 55, 57–58
Ukraine and, 309, 310
Uzbekistan and, 382–83
World War II settlements, 59, 245
Stalinism
development of, 26–28
Leninism and, 29–31
START treaties, 65, 254
starvation, collectivized agriculture and, 56, 309
state. *See also* government
defined, 426
dependence on, 118, 119*t*, 169, 413
as instrument of ruling class, 18, 23
responsibility for caring for citizens, 113, 114, 118, 119*t*, 169
withering away of, 18, 23, 24, 27
State and Revolution (Lenin), 29
state-builders, Russian nationalism, 110
State Committee on Drug Trafficking, 220
State Council, 68, 142
State Enterprise Cooperatives, Law on, 64
State Planning Commission (Gosplan), 233
Stepan, Alfred, 115, 413
Stockholm International Peace Research Institute (SIPRI), 255
Stolypin, Peter, 47, 47*n*, 185
St. Petersburg, 40, 110
Strategic Arms Limitation Treaties (SALT), 34, 246, 247
Strategic Offensive Reduction Treaty, 252
strikes, Bolshevik repression of, 53
structural theories of democracy, 7
suicide rates, 260
in Russian Federation, 257
in Uzbekistan, 403–4
suicide terrorists, in Uzbekistan, 394
Sunni Muslims. *See also* Muslims
Tatars, 95–96
in Uzbekistan, 392–93
Superior Court of Arbitration, 151–52
superpresidentialism, 141, 205, 426
superstructure, of society
defined, 417
economic determinism and, 16
Supreme Arbitration Court, Uzbekistan, 387, 391
Supreme Assembly, Uzbekistan, 386–88
Supreme Council, Georgia, 354, 355

Supreme Council, United Russia party, 199, 202
Supreme Court, Georgia, 360, 363, 364
Supreme Court, Lithuania, 292
Supreme Court, Ukraine, 319
Supreme Court, Uzbekistan, 387, 391
Supreme Courts of Autonomous Republics, Georgia, 363
Supreme Soviet, Lithuania, 282–83
Supreme Soviet, RSFSR, 66, 69
Supreme Soviet, Russian Federation, 151
Supreme Soviet, Soviet Union, 64, 65
court system and, 148
dissolution of, 143
elections to, 124–25, 126–27
policymaking role, 127
role of, 124
union republic Supreme Soviets and, 125–26
Surikov, Anton, 223
Surkis, Hryhory, 328
surplus value, 17, 426
Sweden, 131
Switzerland, 87
Symonenko, Petro, 317, 317*t*, 326, 327*t*
Syria, 255
systematic comparative analysis, 4–7

tactical flexibility, 24
Tajik SSR, 382
Tajikistan, 80, 81, 250, 392, 400
drug trafficking in, 223
ethnic Russians in, 83*t*
Uzbekistan and, 409
Tanzania, 246
Tarasyuk, Borys, 337
Tashkent, 390, 393
Tatar ASSR, 81, 95–97
Tatars, 92
case study, 95–97
Islamic faith of, 95–96
languages, 96
Tatarstan, Republic of, 95–97
economic autonomy of, 92–93
legislative authority, 96–97
natural resources, 96–97
power-sharing agreement with Russia, 97
Russian exploitation of resources in, 92
taxation, federal administration and, 87
Taymyr AOK, 81
Temirov, Isa, 100*n*
term limits, 181

territorial administration systems, 87
territorial integrity, 75
    defined, 426
    Russian public opinion on, 117–18
terrorism
    Chechnya conflict and, 99–105, 170
    CIS response to, 250
    by interest groups, 209
    Islamic militants, Uzbekistan, 393–95,
        399–401
    Lenin's acceptance of, 24, 30
    regional elections and, 181
    as threat to integrity of Russian
        Federation, 251
    U.S.-Russian cooperation on, 251
Testament, The (Lenin), 31
Tevzadze, David, 350
Theories of Surplus Value (Marx and
    Engels), 15
Third International (Comintern).
        See Comintern (Third International)
Third World, 6
threshold, 172, 426
Threshold Test Ban Treaty, 246
Tikhonov, Vladimir, 91
Time of Troubles, 40
Timour, Emir, 380
Tito, 35
Titov, Konstantin, 197
titular nationality, 88, 426
titular republic, 426
Tkachenko, Oleksandr, 326
tobacco use, in Russian Federation, 257
Tolstoy, Leo, 45, 45n
Topadze, George, 357t
totalitarianism. *See also* authoritarianism
    continuity argument, 29–31
    defined, 28, 426
    discontinuity argument, 29–31
    elimination of, 68
    legacy of, 192
    political culture and, 112
    Stalin's personal responsibility for,
        29–31, 57–58
trade. *See* foreign trade
trade unions. *See* labor (trade) unions
Trade Unions and Industrialists of Russia
    party, 212
traditional values, Stalin and, 57
Transcaucasia, 2, 70, 250, 344, 427
Transcaucasian Socialist Federal
    Republic, 79, 346

transitional regimes, 6
transparency, 426
Transparency International, Corruption
    Perceptions Index, 376–77
Treaty on Conventional Forces in Europe
    (CFE), 252
Triple Alliance, 43t
Trotsky, Leon, 20n, 27, 43t, 44n, 49, 50, 51,
    55, 58n, 120n
Truman Document, 245
Tsarism
    absolute authority and, 112
    collapse of, 48
    defined, 427
    legacies of, 44–46
    origins of, 40n
    totalitarianism and, 31
Tuleev, Aman, 138t
Turgenev, Ivan, 45
Turkey, 255, 408
Turkic Khaganate (Empire), 379–80
Turkistan (Turkestan), 381, 382
    defined, 427
    ethnic Russians in, 83t
Turkmenistan, 80, 81, 392
    Uzbekistan and, 409
Turkmen SSR, 382
Tursunov, Ahtam, 398
two-party systems, 189, 427
Tymoshenko, Yuliya, 327t, 328, 335, 342
Tymoshenko Bloc, 327t, 328

Ukraine, 68, 69, 70, 81, 172, 240, 250–51,
    253, 308–42
    agriculture, 308
    assistance to, 340
    civil war, 309
    collectivized agriculture in, 56
    comparative study of, 3t, 4
    dissident movement in, 310–11
    economy, 308, 312, 316, 415
    ethnic Russians in, 83t
    European Union and, 336–37
    foreign policy, 335–40
    future of, 341–42
    government institutions, 313–31
    gross national income, 2
    incorporation into Soviet Union,
        309–10
    independence of, 84, 310–11
    industrial development, 308
    legislative branch, 323–31

mass media, 318, 322
military services, 341
Orange Revolution, 4, 280, 318, 319, 331–32, 341, 342, 414
political culture of, 312–13
political economy, 332–35
political history of, 309–12
political parties, 324–31
population, 308, 312–13
presidential elections, 315–22, 413
regional differences, 312–13, 330
relationships with other countries, 340
resistance to RSFSR by, 80, 84
Russian Federation and, 79–80, 315, 316, 335–36, 337, 338
United States and, 338–39
voting behavior, 329–32
World War II and, 309
Ukrainian Communist Party, 310
Ukrainian Greek Catholic Church, 312–13
Ukrainian National Assembly (UNA), 326
Ukrainian Orthodox Church, 312–13
Ukrainian Orthodox-Kievan Patriarchate, 312–13
Ukrainian Orthodox-Moscow Patriarchate, 313
Ukrainian Party of Regions, 313t
Ukrainian People's Republic, 309
Ukrainian People's Self-Defense Forces (UNSO), 326
Ukrainian Soviet Socialist Republic (Ukrainian SSR), 75, 125
Ukrainian Sovnarkom, 79
Ukrainian Supreme Soviet, 315–16
Ukrainian Union of Industrialists and Entrepreneurs, 318
Ulyanov, Alexander, 46
Ulyanov, Vladimir Ilyich. See Lenin, Vladimir Ilyich
Uniate Catholics, 312–13
unicameral parliament
defined, 427
in Lithuania, 280–81
Union of Democratic Revival of Georgia party, 352
Union of Lubin (1569), 265
Union of National Forces, Georgia, 359
Union of Peasants and New Democracy (VNDPS), 278t, 289–90
Union of Petroleum Industrialists, 213

Union of Right Forces (SPS), 174t, 176, 192, 193t, 194
electoral performance of, 200, 201t, 202
history and politics of, 197–98
Kirienko and, 200
Union of Traditionalists, Georgia, 352n
Union of Women in the Navy, 224
Union of Women of Russia, 224, 225
union-republic ministries, 126
union-republic Supreme Soviets, 125–26
Union Treaty (1922), 270, 346, 427
Union Treaty (1924), 26–27
Union Treaty (planned, 1991), 143, 269t
unitary state, 87
defined, 427
Ukraine, 313, 315
United Arab Emirates, 255
United Communist Party of Georgia (UCP), 357t, 358
United Democrats, Georgia, 359, 361n
united fronts, 244
United Kingdom
arms trade, 255
economic indicators, 241t
interest groups in, 209
parliamentary system, 140
United National Movement (UNM), 354t
United Nations, Abkhazia and, 369–70
United Nations Educational, Scientific and Cultural Organization (UNESCO), 404
United Russia, 174t, 175, 176, 181–82, 190, 192, 193t
electoral performance of, 201–2
history and politics of, 198–99
as majority party, 202–3
media coverage of, 202
Supreme Council, 199, 202
United Social Democrats, Ukraine, 326
United States
arms trade, 255
crime statistics, 261t
economic indicators, 241t
ethnic groups, 76t–77t
Georgia and, 353, 375
grain sales to Soviet Union, 242, 247
life expectancy, 256
pluralistic interest group system, 209
Russian Federation and, 251–52
Russian treatment of Jews and, 121n
Soviet human rights violations and, 247
Soviet relations with, 1, 244–47

United States (*Continued*)
  tobacco companies, 258
  trade with Russian Federation, 240
  Ukraine and, 329, 338–40
  Uzbekistan and, 407
  women in Congress, 131, 225
Unity Bloc, Georgia, 362*t*
Unity movement, 173, 175
Unity Party (Yedinstvo), 193*t*, 200
  electoral performance of, 200, 201*t*
  history and politics of, 198
  Putin and, 200, 202
unlimited presidential executive, 141, 427
urban areas, 47
USSR. *See* Soviet Union
utility prices, 237*n*
Uzbekistan, 69, 80, 81, 379–411
  agriculture, 383, 384, 395, 401–2, 403*f*,
    410
  aid to, 402*n*, 404
  comparative study of, 3*t*, 4
  corruption in, 383–84, 395
  dependence on Russia, 7
  economy, 383–84, 401–4, 405*t*–406*t*,
    410, 415
  ethnic diversity issues, 391–92, 408
  ethnic Russians in, 83*t*
  foreign investment in, 402–3
  foreign policy, 404–9, 410–11
  freedom ratings, 400, 402, 410
  future of, 409–11
  geography of, 379, 408
  gross national income, 2
  historical overview, 379–85
  independence of, 379, 384–85
  Islamic militants in, 393–95
  living standards, 402–3
  mineral resources, 401
  Muslims in, 379, 392–95, 399–401
  national identity, 382, 384
  parliamentary elections, 395–401, 413
  political culture, 391–95
  political institutions, 385–91
  political parties, 395–401
  Russian Federation and, 404, 408
  water resources, 408
Uzbekistan alphabet, 382
Uzbekistan Liberal Democratic Party
  (ULDP), 397*t*, 398
Uzbekistan National Revival Democratic
  Party, 398
Uzbekistan People's Democratic Party
  (UPDP), 388, 397, 397*t*, 398

Uzbekistan's Islamic Warriors, 393
Uzbek Soviet Socialist Republic (SSR),
  381, 382

Vagnorius, Gediminas, 283, 289, 289*n*
Valionis, Antanas, 301
Verkhovna Rada (Supreme Council),
  Ukraine, 314, 315, 323–29
  1994 elections, 323–25
  1998 elections, 325–26
  2002 elections, 326–29
VESTI, 238
Vietnam, Socialist Republic of, 34, 35, 255
Vietnam War, 246
viloyatlar (provinces), Uzbekistan, 390
violent participation, 154, 427. *See
  also* terrorism
Virgin Lands Campaign, 60
Vitrenko, Nataliya, 329
Vladimir, prince of Kievan Rus, 39*n*
Vneshtorgbank, 238
Voice of Russia, 197
Voloshin, Aleksandr, 242
Volovych, Volodymyr, 330*n*, 337*n*
VOOPIK (All-Russian Society for
  Preservation of Historical and
  Cultural Monuments), 109
vote rigging
  defined, 427
  in Georgia, 348
voter turnout. *See also* elections; voting
  in Georgia presidential elections, 352
  in Lithuanian presidential elections,
    276, 279, 293
  in 1999 parliamentary elections, 155
  in Ukrainian presidential elections,
    318, 329
  in Uzbekistan, 399
voting. *See also* election irregularities;
  elections; voter turnout
  comparative analysis of, 171–72
  defined, 427
  factors predicting, 155–59
  in Georgia, 355
  in Lithuania, 293–94
  people most likely not to vote, 159
  public participation through, 154–59
  in Ukraine, 325, 330–32

wage controls, 236–37
War Communism period, 52
  defined, 427
  economy during, 233

Warsaw Pact, 245, 252, 427
wars of national liberation, 32, 246, 247
water resources, Uzbekistan, 408
Way, Lucan A., 349
wealth
  of oligarchs, 213
  redistribution of, 14, 199
We Are Working for Lithuania, 290
Weiner, Myron, 160
Western Europe, party ideology in, 191
Western Ukrainian People's Republic, 309
What Is to Be Done? (Lenin), 21
White Army, 52
Whites (anti-Bolsheviks), 44*t*
William I, emperor of Germany, 15*n*
winner-take-all electoral systems, 171
Winter Palace, 50
women
  blamed for societal problems, 226
  crime rates, in Lithuania, 303
  employment of, 223–24
  home *vs.* career choices, 224, 226–27,
    228*t*
  in parliaments, 131, 132*t*–136*t*
  political participation by, 224–26
  social status of, 224–25
  voting behavior of, 158
Women of Russia, 224–26
women's organizations, 223–27
  decline in strength of, 225–26
  factionalism in, 225
workers. *See* labor
workers' collectives, 30*n*
Worker's Communist Party of Georgia,
  358, 358*n*
Workers' Opposition, 30
working class. *See also* labor; proletariat
  expansion of, under Russian Empire,
    48
  exploitation of, 14
  impoverishment of, 14
  legislation supporting, 48
  Lenin's views on leadership of, 21
  nationalism and, 85
working conditions, Russian Empire, 48
Working for Lithuania (LSDP-LS), 284*t*,
  289
Working People's Socialist Party of
  Georgia, 358, 358*n*
World Bank, 237, 315, 375
World Economic Forum, Growth
  Competitiveness Index, 240, 242
World Health Organization (WHO), 260

World Trade Organization (WTO), 250
  Lithuania and, 272
  Ukraine and, 336
World War I, 43*t*, 58–59
  devastation of Russia by, 48
  Lenin's views on, 23, 49
  response of socialism to, 23–24
  Russian pull-out of, 41, 51
  Russian territorial losses, 51
World War II, 420
  Russian identity and, 109
  Russian territorial expansion in, 41–42
  Soviet casualties, 58–59
  territorial settlements following, 59
  Uzbekistan and, 383
worldwide revolution. *See also* revolution
  advocacy of, 23–24, 27
  failure of, 51

xenophobia, 109

Yabloko Russian Democratic Party, 174*t*,
    176, 177, 193*t*, 197, 202
  electoral performance of, 200, 201, 201*t*
  history and politics of, 195–96
  party identification with, 204
Yakut (ASSR), 93
Yakutia. *See* Sakha Republic (Yakutia)
Yakuts, 92
  case study, 93–95
  Declaration of Sovereignty, 94
  economic issues, 94
  relations with Russia, 93–95
Yalta agreement (1945), 245
Yanayev, Gennady, 143, 269*t*
Yandarbiev, Zelimkhan, 100*n*
Yanukovych, Viktor, 316–22, 320*t*–321*t*,
    330, 331, 339, 342
Yates, Julian Peel, 139
Yavlinsky, Grigorii, 138*t*, 139, 147, 178, 195
Yekhanurov, Yuriy, 328
Yeltsin, Boris, 9, 65, 123, 130, 145, 197,
    200, 269*t*, 311, 316, 335, 369
  accomplishments of, 71
  biography, 142–43
  breakup of Soviet Union and, 68, 69
  Chechnya conflict and, 144
  Communist Party opposition to, 190
  Constitutional Court and, 151
  criticism of, 143–44, 148
  criticism of Gorbachev by, 66
  election of, 66–67, 67*t*, 137, 149*t*, 178
  health of, 144

Yeltsin, Boris (*Continued*)
 impeachment attempt, 128, 144
 leadership of, 65–68
 military service under, 221
 oligarchs and, 217
 perestroika and, 66
 policymaking issues, 232
 political parties and, 205
 presidency of, 142–44
 privatization and, 213–14
 public opinion of, 117–18, 138, 143–44,
  144*f*
 as a reformer, 143
 resignation of, 71, 137, 144
 RSFSR restructuring and, 84
 Russian federalism under, 88
 Russian nationalism and, 110
 second term of office, 70–72
 Unity party and, 198
Young Russia, 197
youth
 crime committed by, 262
 death rates, 257
 smoking rates, 258
 suicide by, 257
Yugoslav Communist Party, 35

Yugoslavia, 35, 245, 253
Yuldashev, Tahir, 394
Yurgens, Igor, 217
Yushchenko, Viktor, 316–22, 320*t*–321*t*,
  327*t*, 328–29, 330, 335, 336–37, 338,
  341, 415
Yushenkov, Sergei, 136

Zhdanov, Andrei, 109
zhdanovshchina, 109
Zhirinovsky bloc, Liberal Democratic
  Party of Russia, 202
 electoral performance of, 200, 201, 201*t*
Zhirinovsky, Vladimir, 121, 137, 138*t*, 178,
  196*f*, 200, 202
Zhvania, Zurab, 349, 351, 351*n*, 359, 361,
  361*n*, 372, 372*n*
Zinoviev, Grigorii, 43*t*, 50, 55, 57
Zionism, 121
Zlaney Svit, 326
Zorkin, Valerii, 151
Zourabichvili, Salome, 367, 374
Zuokas, Arturas, 279
Zyuganov, Gennadii, 137, 138–39, 147,
  177*t*, 178, 202
 political support for, 163–70, 164*t*